Composing Gender

Composing Gender

Edited by

RACHAEL GRONER
JOHN O'HARA

for the First-Year Writing Program
at Temple University

BEDFORD/ST. MARTIN'S
Boston ◆ New York

Manufactured in the United States of America.

2 3 4 5 6   11 10 09

For information, write: Bedford/St. Martin's, 75 Arlington Street, Boston, MA 02116   (617-399-4000)

ISBN-10: 0-312-38805-5
ISBN-13: 978-0-312-38805-8

Acknowledgments
    Lila Abu-Lughod, "Is There a Muslim Sexuality?: Changing Constructions of Sexuality in Egyptian Bedouin Weddings" in *Gender in Cross-Cultural Perspective*, 4th Edition by eds. Caroline B. Brettell and Carolyn F. Sargent, pp. 247–56. Copyright © 2005 by Pearson Education, Inc., Upper Saddle River, NJ. Reprinted with permission of the publisher.
    Beth Berila and Devika Dibya Choudhuri, "Metrosexuality the Middle Class Way: Exploring Race, Class, and Gender in *Queer Eye for the Straight Guy*" from *Genders Journal* 40. Copyright © 2005 Genders Journal. Reprinted with permission.

Acknowledgments and copyrights are continued at the back of the book on pages 553–55, which constitutes an extension of the copyright page.

Contents

Thematic Contents

Body Practices ●
○

Economics/Work/Class ●
○

Politics ●
○

Family ●
○

Media/Representation ●
○

Technology

Global and Transnational Contexts

Sexuality ●
○

Gender Rituals ●
○

Beauty

Masculinity

Composing Gender

JOHN O'HARA, Ph.D., AND RACHAEL GRONER, Ph.D.

Introduction

At first glance, differences between men and women seem significant and hard-wired. When we look around us, there are noticeable differences in how men and women look, dress, sit, move, and speak; differences in the rituals they perform, the activities they engage in, the work they do; differences in their desires, interests, and emotions, and even apparently in their physical and intellectual strengths and weaknesses. Such differences seem to substantiate the idea that men and women are two distinct types of human beings, created by nature to occupy and perform different roles in life.

However, most scholars disagree that gender behavior roles and identities are, in fact, natural or stable. While scientists continue to search for the bedrock determinants of social behavior in biology—with some arguing that aspects of gender may emerge from biological origins—the fact is that society and culture powerfully influence the ways masculinity and femininity take shape. Sociologists, psychologists, anthropologists, political scientists, historians, arts and media scholars, among others, have shown the flexibility of gender according to distinct and changing social codes and cultural norms. In American society and throughout the world, many elaborate cultural systems exist which produce a variety of "men" and "women." Gender thus has come to be seen not as a permanent set of natural instincts emerging from two inherently different biological groups, but as a cultural practice and an individual performance, each unhinged from the body in significant ways.

So where do we learn to "practice" or "perform" gender roles? Of what consequence is gender to our individual sense of self, our personal happiness, our familial and romantic relationships? In what ways are life opportunities made possible and limited by gender assumptions, pressures, and expectations? What power relationships are structured according to gender? How is gender intertwined with education, law, media, technology, globalization?

These are just some of the questions addressed in the readings that follow. Gender touches us all, is relevant to every field of study, and to every personal and social activity in which we engage. Therefore, not only is gender worthwhile to analyze for the sake of our own growth and self-awareness, but it is also a crucial site of social and political engagement. This is why gender is the focus of this book and the theme of this course. We hope the following selections offer intriguing and fruitful inroads for response, analysis, and critique.

LILA ABU-LUGHOD

Is There a Muslim Sexuality?: Changing Constructions of Sexuality in Egyptian Bedouin Weddings

Lila Abu-Lughod is Professor of Anthropology at Columbia University. Her research focuses on culture and media in the Middle East, and she is currently working on a project about the Palestinian experience.

The project of defining the nature of Muslim Arab sexuality—what it is or what it should be—has engaged many people with different stakes and interests. Western discourses have tended to contrast the negative sexuality of "the East" with the positive sexuality of the West. French colonial settlers in Algeria depicted Algerian women in pornographic postcards that suggested a fantastic Oriental world of perverse and excessive sexuality (Alloula 1986). Western feminists concerned with global issues dwell on veiling and other practices like clitoridectomy found in the Muslim Arab world as signs of the repressive control over or exploitation of women's sexuality (e.g., Daly 1978).

From the Muslim world itself come other discourses on Arab Muslim sexuality. These include religious and legal texts and pronouncements, but also more recently, some critical studies by intellectuals and scholars. How different the understandings can be is clear from two important books. One, by a Tunisian scholar with a background in psychoanalytic thought, argues that the misogynist practices of sexuality in the Muslim world are corruptions of the ideals of the Quran and other religious texts (Bouhdiba 1985). The second, by a Moroccan sociologist, argues from a feminist perspective that the legal and sacred texts themselves, like the erotic texts that flourished in the medieval period, carry negative messages about and perpetuate certain consistent attitudes toward the bodies and behavior of Muslim women (Sabbah 1984).

What these various discourses on Arab Muslim sexuality, by outsiders and insiders, defenders and critics, share is the presumption that there is such a thing as "Muslim sexuality." An anthropologist like myself, familiar with the tremendous variety of communities to be found in the regions composing the Muslim Arab world, would have to question this presumption. Neither Islam nor sexuality should be essentialized—taken as things with intrinsic and trans-historical meanings. Rather, both the meaning of Islam and the constructions of sexuality must be understood in their specific historical and local contexts.[1]

3

To show why I argue this, I will analyze wedding rituals in a community of Awlad 'Ali Bedouin in Egypt's Western Desert — a community I worked in over a period of twelve years. Weddings are the highlight of social life, awaited with anticipation and participated in with enthusiasm. Each wedding is different. And each wedding is a personal affair of great moment for the bride and groom, even if only one dramatic event in what will be their marriage, lasting for years. Yet public rituals in face-to-face societies are also arenas where people play out their social and political relations. There are other discourses and practices related to sexuality in this Bedouin community but none so powerfully seek to produce, and are now transforming, people's experiences of sexuality and gender relations as weddings do. Without pretending that a symbolic analysis exhausts the meaning of weddings for the individuals involved, I would still insist that such an analysis of Awlad 'Ali weddings is useful: It reveals both how sexuality is constructed by the symbols and practices of members of particular communities and how these symbols and practices themselves are open to change and political contestation. Islam, it will be seen, figures not so much as a blueprint for sexuality as a weapon in changing relations of power.

SEXUALITY AND CULTURAL IDENTITY

In the twelve years between 1978 and 1990 that I had been regularly returning to this community of Arab Muslim sedentarized herders in Egypt, the same questions had been asked of me, sometimes even by the same people, as were asked in the first month of my stay. Usually in the context of a gathering of older women, one old woman would lean toward me and ask if I were married. After a short discussion of the fact that I was not, she or another older woman would ask me the next intense question: "Where you come from, does the bridegroom do it with the finger or with 'it'?" The first time they asked me this, I did not know what they meant by "it" and they had a good laugh. The question that followed inevitably in such conversations was, "And do they do it during the daytime or at night?" They were asking about weddings and particularly about the defloration of the virgin bride, which is for them the central moment of a wedding.[2]

In the obsessive concern with whether they do it with the finger or "it," at night or during the daytime, is a clue to one of the things the discourse on this aspect of sexuality has become as the Awlad 'Ali Bedouins have greater contact and interaction with outsiders, primarily their Egyptian peasant and urban neighbors. Whatever its former or current meaning within the community, meanings I will analyze in the following section, the central rite of weddings has now also become a marker of cultural identity — essential to the Awlad 'Ali's self-defining discourse on what makes them distinctive.

Individuals vary in how they evaluate their differences from their compatriots. When I met the Bedouin representative to the Egyptian Parliament, a sophisticated man in sunglasses whose long contact with other Egyptians showed in his dialect, he assured me that there were a few Bedouin practices that were wrong: One was that they used the finger in the daytime. But he defended the practice by saying that it reminded girls to be careful. Another respected man of the community explained to me that "entering" with the finger was wrong. "We're the only ones who do it this way," he noted. Then he added, "Nothing in our religion says you should." By way of excuse, though, he said, "But the faster the groom does it, the better—the more admired he is because it means he wasn't timid or cowardly." Even women occasionally complained that is was stupid how the female wedding guests waited and waited, just to see that drop of blood. But they too defended the ceremony, saying that the defloration had to take place in the afternoon so that everyone could see and there would be no doubts about the reputation of the girl. Their horror at the idea that the groom would use "it" came from their fear that it would be more painful for the bride.

Besides asking whether they do it with the finger or "it," day or night, the women I knew often asked whether, where I came from, there was anyone with the bride to hold her down. They were surprised to hear that she needed no one and marveled that she wasn't afraid to be alone with the man. Among themselves, they almost always had a few older women, usually aunts or close neighbors of the groom and bride, in the room with the bride when the groom came to her. There in theory to hold the bride, these women also end up giving advice to the groom and making sure he knew what to do so that everything—the display of the blood on the cloth—would turn out right.

For their part, somewhat like most Europeans and Americans, non-Bedouin Egyptians and assimilated Awlad 'Ali from the agricultural areas find Bedouin weddings scandalous and distasteful. Bedouin women are not un-aware of these views and the men discussed previously were probably react-ing defensively to them. These outsiders may laugh at some customs but they are embarrassed by others. After one wedding in the community in which I was living, the bride's aunt, who had spent most of her life in a non-Bedouin provincial town, talked about the wedding and some of the customs she had witnessed that made her laugh "until her stomach hurt." She obviously con-sidered her new in-laws backward.[3]

What seemed to disturb her most was the nature of what she felt should be private. She thought it humiliating, for example, that at night, the young men from the community (peers of the bridegroom) hung around the room, listening, shining a flashlight under the door and through the window, and generally being disruptive. More horrible to her was the public display of the blood-stained cloth. "It was incredible," she exclaimed. "After the defloration didn't you hear my son saying to his aunt when she went to hang the cloth on the tent ropes, 'It's shameful, my aunt, it's shameful to put the cloth out for people to see.'" Like other urban and rural Egyptians, she thought that the bride and groom should be brought together at night and left alone.

Although other Egyptians and Americans might feel that such privacy is more civilized, the Awlad 'Ali women I knew did not see it that way. Bedouin women were scandalized by the secrecy of night deflorations, the immediate and explicit link such weddings make between marriage and sexual intercourse, and what they view as either the total vulnerability of the poor bride forced to be alone with a man or, even worse, the bride's immodest desire for a man. They knew that instead of struggling, the Egyptian bride has her photo taken with her husband-to-be, she sits with him at weddings where the sexes mix, and she dresses in make-up and fancy clothes for all to see. Because poorer Bedouin men sometimes marry young women from peasant areas, whether they are of Egyptian stock or long-sedentarized Bedouin involved in agriculture, the Bedouin women also knew that unmarried sisters accompanied the bride. They interpreted this practice as a shameful attempt to display and "sell" marriageable daughters. They also knew that such brides sometimes arrived bringing a cooked duck or goose to feed a new husband; they took this as a sign of the bride's unseemly eagerness to please the groom.

Egyptian weddings, much like American ones, construct the couple as a separate unit, distinct from families or ties to members of the same gender group. At their center is a sexual joining that is private and intimate. For the Awlad 'Ali, this is a strange thing. The secrecy of private sex, in the dark, behind closed doors, and preferably in the foreign or anonymous setting (for the honeymoon) produces sexuality as something personal, intensely individual, apparently separate from society and social power. It produces sexuality as something belonging in an inviolable private sphere — the bedroom — a sphere in which others cannot interfere with whatever pleasure or violence and coercion accompanies it. One of the consequences of this construction of sexuality is that we, and perhaps Egyptians, come to think there is a part of oneself that is not social or affected by the prevailing power relations in society.[4]

The three crucial elements in Bedouin discourse on differences between their wedding and those of other groups are (1) whether the defloration is public and participatory, (2) whether it involves sexual intercourse, and (3) whether it is seen as a contest, especially between the bride and groom. These elements also had meaning within the local context. In Bedouin weddings the ways in which sexuality is related to power relations and the social order were clear. Marriages have been the occasion for people to collectively enact and reproduce this social order and the individual's place in it. And the individual's place was, until recently, very much a part of the group — whether the kin group or the group defined by gender.

Weddings as Public Rites: The Power of Kinship and Gender

The participants in Awlad 'Ali Bedouin weddings instantiate, by means of a bride and groom, the relations between families or kin groups on the one hand, and the relations between men and women on the other. A symbolic analysis of the central rite, the defloration, enacted in a homologous fashion on the bodies of the bride and groom and on the collective bodies of the gathered kin and friends, reveals that it produces an understanding of sexuality as something public and focused on crossing thresholds, opening passages, and moving in and out. There are no strong messages of mingling or joining or even interchange in a private sexual act. The emphasis is on opening the bride's vagina by breaking the hymen and bringing out or making visible what was in there. And although people say that deflorations should be done during the daytime so everyone can see the cloth, the fact that in the rhythm of daily life morning and daytime generally are times of opening and going out from home or camp, while evening is a time of returning inward, cannot but reinforce the auspiciousness of this time for opening and taking outward.[5]

That this opening is a prelude to the insemination which should eventuate in childbirth is suggested by some practices associated with the bloodstained virginity cloth. It is taken out of the room by the groom and thrown to the women gathered just outside. It is said that if the cloth is then brought back into the room without the bride having exited first—if, as they say, the cloth enters upon her—it will block her from conceiving.[6] Young women are told to save their virginity cloths; if they have trouble conceiving, they must bathe in water in which they have soaked the cloth.

Everything in the rites and the songs that accompany them suggests that the individuals engaged in this opening and being opened, taking out and showing, and having something taken out and shown, embody both their kin groups and their gender groups. The connection to kin, and control by the kin group, is clear in the key role they have in arranging and negotiating marriages and is reflected in the songs the groom's female relatives sing as they go to fetch the bride from her father's household. It is also reinforced in the songs the bride's female kin sing to greet these people. Most of the songs compliment the social standing of the families of the bride and groom.

Even the practices and movements of the wedding itself perpetuate the identifications with kin groups. Most brides, even today, are brought from their fathers' households completely covered by a white woolen woven cloak (*jard*) that is the essential item of men's dress. The cloak must belong to the girl's father or some other male kinsman. So, protected and hidden by her father's cloak, she is brought out of her father's protected domain and carried to her husband's kin group's domain. There she is rushed, still hidden, into the room (or in the past, the tent) which she will share with her husband. Although nowadays the woven cloak is usually removed once she enters the room, in the past the bride remained under her father's cloak and was not revealed even to the women gathered around her until after the defloration.

The virginity of the bride is also constructed as something inseparable from her family's honor. Although one unmarried girl explained the importance of the blood-stained cloth in terms of her own reputation, she stressed the effect it would have on others.

> For us Bedouins, this is the most important moment in a girl's life. No matter what anyone says afterward, no one will pay attention as long as there was blood on the cloth. They are suspicious of her before. People talk. "She went here, she went there." "She looked at So-and-so." "She said hello to So-and-so." "She went to the orchard." But when they see this blood the talk is cut off. . . . When they see the cloth, she can come and go as she pleases. They love her and everything is fine.

The best way to get a sense of who has a stake in the girl's virginity and why is to listen to the conventional songs sung wildly outside the door of the bride's room as the defloration is underway. Unmarried girls and some young married women clap and sing rhyming songs that refer to the effect of the proof of the bride's virginity on various members of her family and community.

> Make her dear Mom happy, Lord
> Hanging up her cloth on the tent ropes
> O Saint 'Awwaam on high
> Don't let anyone among us be shamed

Older women sing more serious songs that take up similar themes:

> When the people have gathered
> O Generous One favor us with a happy ending . . .
> Behind us are important men
> who ask about what we are doing . . .

Relatives of the bride show their support and faith in the bride in songs like this:

> I'm confident in the loved one
> you'll find in there intact . . .

Even the groom's behavior during the defloration reflects on his relatives. One song a relative of his might sing as he arrives or is inside with the bride is the following:

> Son, be like your menfolk
> strong willed and unafraid . . .

After the virginity cloth is brought out by the groom and thrown to the women, a different set of songs is sung. These praise the cloth and the honor of the girl who had remained a virgin. The songs reflect on who is affected by her purity and who is proud. At one wedding a female relative of the bride sang to a nephew nearby:

> Go tell your father, Said
> the banner of her honor is flying high . . .

About the bride a woman might sing:

> Bravo! She was excellent
> she who didn't force down her father's eyelashes . . .

Given this group investment in the bride's virginity, the central rite of the wedding becomes a drama of suspense and relief that must powerfully shape people's experiences of sexuality as something that belongs to the many, and especially to one's family. The wedding is also, importantly, an occasion when families find themselves in some rivalry, the honor of each at stake. This was more apparent in the past when the young men celebrated all night on the eve of the wedding and expressed the rivalry through singing contests that sometimes broke out into actual fights between lineages.

Kinship is not the only power-laden aspect of social life that finds itself reflected and reinforced in the wedding. The second set of power relations weddings play with are those of gender. The bride and groom in the wedding rite enact the charged relations between men and women as distinct genders in a kind of battle of the sexes. Although most activities in the community are informally segregated by gender, at weddings—in part because there are non-family members present—the sexual segregation is more obvious and fixed, women and men forming highly separate collectivities for nearly all events.

Given this separation of the sexes, the defloration, taking place in the middle of the day when all are gathered in their distinct places, becomes a ritualized and extreme form of encounter between both the bride and groom and the women and men who surround each of them. The movements of the groom and his age-mates as they penetrate the crowd of women surrounding the bride mirror the groom's penetration of his bride, who forms a unit with the women in the room with her. The young men stand just outside the door, sometimes dancing and singing, ready to fire off guns in celebration when the groom emerges. They rush him back away from the women. This mirroring is expressed in the ambiguity of the term used for both moments of this event: the entrance (*khashsha*) refers both to the entry with the finger and the whole defloration process when the groom enters the bride's room, which can be thought of as his kin group's womb.

The encounter between male and female takes the form of a contest. The groom is encouraged to be fearless. He is expected to finish the deed in as short a time as possible. The bride is expected to try valiantly to fight him off. Taking the virginity she has been so careful to guard and thus opening the way for his progeny is the groom's victory; the bride doesn't give it up without a struggle. Calling this, as the literature often does, a virginity test is a misnomer in that it misses this combative dimension of the ritualized act. The way people describe what happens even on the wedding night suggests again that the groom and bride are involved in a contest. The rowdy young men who listen outside the marital chamber want to know "who won." They know this, some adolescent girls informed me, not just by whether the groom succeeds in having intercourse with his bride (a rare event), but by whether the groom succeeds in making his bride talk to him and answer his questions. This is, perhaps, another kind of opening up.

There is other evidence that weddings provoke a heightened attention to issues of gender and sexual mixing. One of the most revealing and intriguing is the spontaneous cross-dressing that sometimes happens at weddings. At several weddings I attended one woman in our community actually put on men's clothes, a fake mustache and beard, and covered her head in a man's headcloth. Amidst much hilarity she came out to dance in front of the bride. Others expressed some disapproval and called this woman a bit mad. But they laughed riotously anyway. One woman who thought it excessive described someone else who she thought was quite funny: All she did was dance in front of the bride with a shawl bunched up in front like male genitalia. Sometimes it was reported that the unmarried men and young boys had celebrated the night before the wedding by dressing up a boy with women's bracelets and a veil and dancing in front of him as if he were a bride.

SEXUAL TRANSFORMATIONS

Many Awlad 'Ali claim that their rituals are changing. In this final section, I want to explore how in these changed wedding practices we can begin to track changes in the nature of power and social relations. This is further support for my initial argument that constructions of sexuality cannot be understood apart from understandings of particular forms of social power. Most people talked about changes in weddings over the last twenty years or so in terms of what had been lost. Many said weddings were not fun any more. As far as I could determine, the main element that seems to have been lost is the celebration the night before the wedding (saamir). Not only do the young men no longer sing back and forth, but no longer is it even thinkable that a young woman from the community would come out to dance in front of them. This is what used to happen and the change is crucial for Bedouin gender relations.

What happened in the past was that an unmarried sister or cousin of the groom would be brought out from among the women by a young boy. She would dance amidst a semi-circle of young men. Her face veiled and her waist girded with a man's white woven cloak, like the one the bride would come covered in the following day, she danced with a stick or baton in her hands. According to one man who described this to me, the young men tried to "beg" the stick from her, sometimes using subterfuges like pretending to be ill;

she would often bestow the stick, he said, on someone she fancied. But according to the women I spoke with, the young men would sometimes try to grab the stick from her and she would, if they were too aggressive, get angry with them and leave. The young men took turns singing songs that welcomed the dancer and then described her every feature in flattering terms. The standard parts praised in such songs were her braids, her eyes, her eyebrows, her cheeks, her lips, her tattoos, her neck, her breasts, her arms, her hands, and her waist—most of which, it should be remembered, because of the way she was dressed were not actually visible. Thus in a sense the dancer was, through men's songs, made into the ideal woman, attractive object of men's desires.

The dancer must be seen as the bride's double or stand-in, in an interpretation supported by the other occasion on which a young woman danced in front of men. In the days before cars, brides were carried from their fathers' households to their husbands' on camel-back, completely cloaked and sitting hidden inside a woven litter (*karmuud*) covered in red woven blankets. Another woman always preceded her on foot, dancing as young men sang to her and shot off guns near her.

In both cases, the dancer as bride and as ideal womanhood went out before men who complimented and sought her. What is crucial to notice is how the women described the dancer. They attributed to her a special bravery and described her actions as a challenge to the young men. One wedding in which a young woman was accidentally wounded by a poorly aimed gun was legendary. The wedding went on, the story went, as a second dancer who had been near her merely wiped the blood from her forehead and continued to dance. More telling is the ritualized struggle over the stick, which one anthropologist who worked with a group in Libya has argued is associated with virginity (Mason 1975). A woman explained to me, "If the dancer is sharp they can't take the stick from her. They'll be coming at her from all sides but she keeps it."

But perhaps some of the short songs traditionally exchanged between the women (gathered in a tent some distance away from the young men standing in a line near the dancer) and the young men, make clearest the ways in which a challenge between the sexes was central to weddings. One especially memorable competitive exchange was the following. As her sister danced a woman sang of her:

A bird in the hot winds glides
and no rifle scope can capture it . . .

A man responded with the song:

The heart would be no hunter
if it didn't play in their feathers . . .

In the loss and delegitimation of this whole section of the wedding ritual, an important piece of the construction of Bedouin sexual relations has disappeared. Today, all that is left in a ritual that was a highly charged and evenly matched challenge between the sexes is the enactment of the men's hunt. The groom is the hunter, the bride his prey. Decked out in her make-up and white satin dress, she is brought from her father's house and her "virginity" taken by her groom in a bloody display.

Wedding songs, only sung by women now, reinforce this construction of the bride as vulnerable prey. They liken the bride to a gazelle. This is a compliment to her beauty but also suggests her innocence and defenselessness. Other songs liken the groom to a falcon or hunter. This is no longer balanced by women's former powers to create desire but elude capture.

The disappearance of the female dancer can thus be seen to have shifted the balance such that women's capacities to successfully challenge men have been de-emphasized. Although the sexes are still pitted against each other, the contest is no longer represented as even.

There is a second important point to be made about the dancer that relates to some transformations in constructions of power and sexuality. For it is not completely true that women no longer dance in front of men at Awlad 'Ali weddings. It has become unacceptable for respectable young kinswomen to dance, but there are now some professional dancers. They accompany musical troupes hired to entertain at weddings of the Bedouin nouveau riche. These women may or may not be prostitutes but they are certainly not considered respectable.[7] In that sense, and in the fact that ordinary women go nowhere near the areas where these musicians and dancers perform, one cannot any longer claim that the dancer represents Woman or enacts women's challenge of men. The opposite may be true. This new kind of wedding may be introducing a new view of women, one quite familiar to us in the United States but quite strange to the Awlad 'Ali: women as sexual commodities stripped of their embeddedness in their kin groups or the homosocial world of women.

The professionalization of weddings as entertainment and spectacle (if spectacles that retain vestiges of the participatory in that young men seize the microphone to sing songs) may also be signaling a fundamental shift in the relationship of the construction of sexuality and the construction of the social order. What seems to be disappearing is the participation of the whole community in the responsibility of ritually reproducing the fundamental social and political dynamics of the community. Does this indicate the emergence of a new kind of power? One that works differently? One whose nexus is perhaps the individual rather than the kin group or gender group? This new form of wedding is not being adopted universally in the Bedouin region since the poor cannot afford it and the respectable condemn it as undignified and inappropriate for pious Muslims. Nevertheless, as a public discourse it must enter and shape the field of sexuality for all.

The third and final historical shift I will discuss comes out in the comments women made about what had happened to weddings. One old woman reminisced about weddings of the past. She shook her head and laughed, "No, the things they did before you can't do anymore. Nowadays weddings are small, like a shrunken old man. People used to really celebrate, staying up all night, for days! But they have become like the Muslim Brothers now." The younger woman she was talking to had explained for me. "They say it is wrong. Now everything is forbidden. People before didn't know. They were ignorant." She used a term with connotations of the pre-Islamic era.

These women's invocations of Islam and the proper behavior of the pious in the contexts of weddings mark some significant changes in power relations. It has always been important to the Awlad 'Ali that they are Muslims and that they are good Muslims. And these two women themselves were devout. They prayed regularly and the old one had been on the pilgrimage to Mecca. Yet when they and other women brought up the religious wrongness of their traditional wedding practices, it was with some ambivalence since they were also nostalgic for the richer days of the past. After one wedding there was a hint of disapproval in women's gossip about one aunt in the community. Someone with a good voice who usually sang at weddings, she had just returned from the pilgrimage to Mecca and had refused this time. "It is wrong," she told them. They though she was being self-righteous—and selfish.

What is really at stake comes out clearly from women's discussions of a happy wedding that had taken place in my absence. I was told that, as usual, for days before the wedding the women and girls had been celebrating by themselves every evening, drumming and singing. The older men of the community wanted them to stop and instructed them that at least once the guests (non-relatives) had begun to arrive, they would have to stop. It was shameful to sing in front of people, the men insisted. On the eve of the wedding as the women and girls gathered and began to sing and dance in celebration, the groom's father came in to greet his visiting female relatives. He also wanted to try to silence the group of women. When he entered the tent, he saw his own older sister, a dignified woman in her sixties, dancing. "Hey, what's this?" he said. "Rottenest of days, even you, Hajja?" He called her by the respectful title reserved for those who have performed the pilgrimage to Mecca. "That's right," she answered definitely, "even me!" Everyone laughed then and each time they retold the story.

Women still refuse to be stopped from celebrating weddings. But the older men, armed with religious righteousness, are clearly trying to assert authority over them in domains that were previously inviolable. Weddings, like the discontinued sheep-shearing festivities to which they are often likened, were always before classified as occasions where young men and young women could express desires. Elder men were not to interfere. At sheep-shearing festivities young men used to sing with impunity oblique sexual songs to flirt with the women present. The songs often insulted the patriarch whose herds the young men were shearing. Similarly, at weddings young men sang to women, not just the dancer. Even more important, women sang back—songs of love and desire. Older men made sure they were not in the vicinity.[8]

Now, not only have the exchanges between young men and women stopped but older men seem to be trying to assert control over the separate women's festivities. Their motives for this intervention are irrelevant. They may genuinely believe they are encouraging their families to live up to an interpretation of Islam that denounces such frivolity as impious. The effect, however, on women and young men, is that by means of this discourse of Islamic propriety wielded by older men, they are being displaced as the prime actors in the rites that produced and reproduced Bedouin constructions of sexuality and desire.

If, as I have tried to show, in a small Bedouin community in Egypt, sexuality can come to be a crucial marker of cultural identity, and if the construction of sexuality is so closely tied to the organization of kinship and gender and changes as the community is transformed by such broad processes as its incorporation into the wider Egyptian nation and economy, then it seems impossible to assert the existence of a Muslim sexuality that can be read off texts or shared across communities with very different histories and ways of life. Instead, we need to think about specific constructions of sexuality and, in the case of the Muslim Arab world, about the variable role discourses on religion can play in those constructions.

AUTHOR'S NOTE

Most of the research in Egypt on which this article is based was supported by an NEH Fellowship for College Teachers and a Fulbright Award under the Islamic Civilization Program. I am grateful to Samia Mehrez for inviting me to present an early version at Cornell University. I am more grateful to the women and men in the Awlad 'Ali community who shared their lives, including their weddings, with me.

NOTES

1. The literature, especially the feminist literature, on sexuality has become vast in the last decade or two. A helpful early text is Vance (1984). Anthropologists have recently begun to pay more attention to constructions of sexuality and their cross-cultural perspective should contribute to our understanding of the way that sexuality is constructed. For a good introduction to some of that work, see Caplan (1987).

2. For this reason the weddings of divorcees or widows are not celebrated with as much enthusiasm and are considered somewhat ordinary affairs.

3. For example, she described what is known as the *dayra* (the circling). On the evening of the wedding day, they had seated the bride and groom on a pillow, back to back. A neighbor carrying a lamb on his back, holding one foreleg in each

of his hands, had walked around and around them—seven times. She mimicked the audience counting: "Hey, did you count that one? One, two, three, four." "Thank God," she said at one point, "there were no outsiders (non-relatives) from back home with us. How embarrassing it would have been."

4. The theorist who has most developed this notion of the effects on subjectivity and sense of individuality of the Western discourses on sexuality is Michel Foucault (1978, 1985).

5. For an analysis of similar kinds of symbolic constructions of gender and sexuality, see Bourdieu's (1977) work on Algerian Kabyles. My analysis of the meaning of this rite differs significantly from that of Combs-Schilling (1989), who worked in Morocco.

6. For more on rituals related to fertility and infertility, see my *Writing Women's Worlds* (1993). Boddy (1989) has analyzed for Muslim Sudanese villagers the extraordinary symbolic stress on women's fertility over their sexuality.

7. As Van Nieuwkerk (1995) has documented, this is generally true about professional dancers in Egypt.

8. Peters (1990) describes a similar avoidance by elders of wedding celebrations among the Bedouin of Cyrenaica in the 1950s.

REFERENCES

Abu-Lughod, Lila 1993. *Writing Women's Worlds: Bedouin Stories.* Berkeley and Los Angeles: University of California Press.

Alloula, Malek. 1986. *The Colonial Harem.* Myran and Wlad Godzich, trans. Minneapolis: University of Minnesota Press.

Boddy, Janice. 1989. *Wombs and Alien Spirits: Women, Men, and the Zar Cult in Northern Sudan.* Madison, WI: University of Wisconsin Press.

Bouhdiba, Abdelwahab. 1985. *Sexuality in Islam.* London and Boston: Routledge & Kegan Paul.

Bourdieu, Pierre. 1977. *Outline of a Theory of Practice.* Cambridge: Cambridge University Press.

Caplan, Patricia, ed. 1987. *The Cultural Construction of Sexuality.* London and New York: Tavistock Publications.

Combs-Schilling, M.E. 1989. *Sacred Performances: Islam, Sexuality and Sacrifice.* New York: Columbia University Press.

Daly, Mary. 1978. *Gyn/ecology, the Metaethics of Radical Feminism.* Boston: Beacon Press.

Foucault, Michel. 1978. *The History of Sexuality: Volume 1: An Introduction.* New York: Random House.

————. 1985. *The Use of Pleasure.* Vol. 2 of *The History of Sexuality.* New York: Pantheon.

Mason, John. 1975. "Sex and Symbol in the Treatment of Women: The Wedding Rite in a Libyan Oasis Community." *American Ethnologist* 2: 649–61.

Peters, Emrys. 1990. *The Bedouin of Cyrenaica*. Edited by Jack Goody and Emanuel Marx. Cambridge: Cambridge University Press.

Sabbah, Fatna A. 1984. *Woman in the Muslim Unconscious*. New York and Oxford: Pergamon Press.

Vance, Carole. 1984. *Pleasure and Danger: Exploring Female Sexuality*. Boston and London: Routledge & Kegan Paul.

Van Nieuwkerk, Karin. 1995. *"A Trade Like Any Other": Female Singers and Dancers in Egypt*. Austin, TX: University of Texas Press.

BETH BERILA AND DEVIKA DIBYA CHOUDHURI

Metrosexuality the Middle-Class Way: Exploring Race, Class, and Gender in Queer Eye for the Straight Guy

Beth Berila is Director of Women's Studies at St. Cloud State University, Minnesota. Her interests include popular cultural representations of gender, race, class, and sexuality. Devika Dibya Choudhuri is a professor in the Graduate Counseling Program at Eastern Michigan University.

> Each week their mission is to transform a style-deficient and culture-deprived straight man from drab to fab in each of their respective categories: fashion, food and wine, interior design, grooming, and culture.
> — *Queer Eye for the Straight Guy,* Bravo Web site blurb

The recent popularity of Bravo's *Queer Eye for the Straight Guy* has been heralded as evidence of increased tolerance of queerness and a model of friendly interactions between gay and straight men (Hart, 241). (The show has been so warmly received in some circles as a positive sign for gay rights that it won a GLAAD award in the reality TV category in 2004 ["GLAAD Honors *Queer Eye*"]). While the show's popularity does, on some level, reflect a kind of cultural fusion that could potentially herald a more equitable and less violent form of interaction between gay and straight cultures, it also reproduces economic, racial, and sexual power inequalities at a time when gay rights and the rights of communities of color are under assault by the U.S. nation state. (As this article was being written, the Bush administration was advocating a constitutional amendment to define marriage as between a man and a woman, thus denying same sex marriages, at the same time that it was proposing heterosexual marriage as a way to get individuals off welfare, a policy that disproportionately affects poor women of color. Moreover, communities of color, both gay and straight, have been targeted by racial profiling and other assaults to civil liberties in the aftermath of the tragedy at the World Trade Center on September 11, 2001). It is not accidental that this show in particular has come to represent gayness in dominant popular culture at this historical moment, when Lesbian, Gay, Bisexual, and Transgender communities are gaining more prominence in public issues and debates.

Queer Eye is the inheritor of a long list of specifically male depictions of queerness in the media, such as *Will and Grace, My Best Friend's Wedding,* and *Sex in the City,* that represent such men as the heterosexual woman's best friend

17

(Creekmur and Doty). This immaculate intimacy consists of being able to gossip, complain about their male lovers, and get advice on fashion. *Queer Eye* simply takes this concept to rarified levels, where the straight woman gets a five in one package to help "straighten out" her man, who will still be unthreateningly hers at the end of the process. Indeed, the show follows the standard makeover narrative that promises an individual's ability to be transformed through the right advice and the right products.

The show features five gay men who enter the home of a straight man, detect, interrogate, and mock the faults of the home décor and the man's style, and then proceed to revamp the space and the man into a more stylish metrosexual. The Fab 5 consist of Kyan, the "Grooming Guru," Jai, the "Culture Vulture," Ted, the "Food and Wine Connoisseur," Thom, the "Design Doctor," and Carson, the "Fashion Savant." After throwing out much of the straight man's unfashionable possessions, each member of the Fab 5 take him to the appropriate places to learn new techniques, labeled as culture and grooming, and pick out new furniture, clothes, and food. They then return him to his redesigned home, and turn him loose to cook a meal for his girlfriend, wife, or family, who gush at the successful makeover while the Fab 5 watch on a TV screen from afar.

The surprising success of the show's concept begs attention. *Queer Eye* has enjoyed its extreme popularity precisely because it both commodifies gayness and reinscribes the heterosexual imperative, thus reinforcing hegemonic power dynamics while seeming to transgress them (Rogers). As the show becomes the "face of queerness" in mainstream popular culture, it raises critical questions about what form of queerness it represents and what parts of queer communities it renders invisible. Though the show reveals some potentially valuable contradictions, ultimately *Queer Eye* sets up a racialized and class-based binary that keeps lesbians off stage and invisible, heterosexual men dumbed down, heterosexual women present only in the context of their relationships with men, and people of color buying into a consumerist lifestyle that reifies white middle class normativity just touched up by appropriate color. The portrayals on the show contain numerous contradictions, some of which contribute to gay visibility. However, ultimately, the show contains gayness by reducing it to a commodity that services heteronormativity. Given the recent decision by the U.S. Supreme Court overturning the Hardwick vs. Bowers case (Lawrence and Garner vs. Texas), and the growing international debate over same-sex marriage, these portrayals serve to depoliticize queerness.

Much work in feminist visual culture has explored the gendered power relations in the gaze that is constructed by filmic representation, while critical race theorists have analyzed the colonizing nature of that gaze and queer critics have discussed the commodification of the "gay" hip look. This article brings together these bodies of work in order to suggest that the cultural function of *Queer Eye* does more than perpetuate problematic stereotypes. Specifically, this article analyzes the interrelated links between the commodification of gayness, the reinscription of the heterosexual imperative, and the problematic racial and class-based constructs of masculinity perpetuated by the show in order to argue that *Queer Eye* ultimately serves to dramatically limit radical queer resistance.

COOPTING QUEERNESS

The surprising popularity of *Queer Eye* amongst a variety of audiences suggests that it is worth noting some of its contradictions. One of the most potentially progressive elements of the show is that it troubles false binaries of gay and straight space. The show brings queerness into mainstream television space and into the homes of both straight and queer viewers, creating a kind of contact zone that potentially disrupts heteronormative assumptions by revealing that gay and straight masculinities are deeply connected. They're defined in relation to each other. Lauren Berlant and Michael Warner define heteronormativity as the ways in which social institutions have prescribed heterosexuality as normative. The show creates creative and often humorous interventions into spatial divisions, as gay men literally enter the homes of select heterosexual men, including their kitchens, their bedrooms, and, yes, their closets. In a parallel process, gay men come into our homes via our television sets. The show thus reveals that heteronormative space is not impenetrable and in fact highlights the fact that queer communities have regularly shaped what is often assumed to be gay-free mainstream space. We know, for instance, that gay men had major influences on the Hollywood musical and that Madonna's Vogueing came from drag clubs, to name just a few random examples. As the Fab 5 revamp their subjects' styles, they frequent various public consumer spaces, such as stores, salons, museums, and restaurants (not to mention television). More importantly, they do so authoritatively: they know the terrain and they play the role of experts to explain it to the straight men on the show. They thus unsettle the heteronormative presumption that mainstream space is not inhabited or influenced by gay presence.

This disruption of spatial and sexual boundaries is potentially productive, as is the suggestion of radical politics implicit in the title *Queer Eye for the Straight Guy*. The choice of the word "queer" in the title could be read as a more radical statement than some of the other options (it could, for instance, have been called "Gay Eye for the Straight Guy," which would be a more accurate name) (Meyer and Kelley). On some level, the show takes a word that has historically been used to do violence to members of the Lesbian, Gay, Bisexual, Transgender community and makes visible to the broader public the ways that LGBT communities have reclaimed the word. Queer, in its more radical political sense, refers to identity categories that are constantly shifting, hard to pin down, and which trouble normative categories of gender, race, and sexuality (thought it can also erase racial differences in problematic ways)

(Muñoz; Ferguson). Initially, *Queer Eye* seems to fulfill that radical potential, since it is at times difficult to distinguish who is gay and who is straight on the show. One episode, for instance, cuts from a scene in a bar during a heavy metal concert in which a crowd of presumably straight men are cheering the singer, to a nearly indistinguishable performance of the Fab 5 shouting "girls, girls, girls" (Episode 117 "Radio Ralph"). This juxtaposition draws clear parallels between how the men on the show, whether gay or straight, perform masculinity. *Queer Eye* often features similar moments that blur common assumptions of what gay and straight performances look like. The show also troubles interpretations of both masculinity and sexuality as the Fab 5 make campy jokes or, in the episode just mentioned, are horrified by the sexually explicit heterosexual dancing occurring at the bar. In another episode, much is made of the straight man's involvement in musicals as a question mark of his transgression of gay territory (Episode 119 "Compose Yourself"). These moments call viewers' attention to how we are reading the links between masculinity and sexuality, revealing the inability to neatly interpret gender performance and sexual identity, and thus becoming potentially "queer."

However, while the show "queers" certain stereotypes about sexuality, it nonetheless falls far short of "queering" gender or sexuality and ultimately reaffirms the gay/straight binary. The show never offers any options other then being gay or straight, nor does it fundamentally blur the boundaries of even those categories. Indeed, the entire purpose of the show is to uphold the heteronormative imperative, which is the primary way in which gayness is allowed to be embraced in hegemonic popular culture. Most of the heterosexual guests on the show are nominated by women in their lives—either their girlfriends, their wives, or their mothers who want to help their sons get girlfriends or wives. The Fab 5 then come on the scene and show the straight guests how to be more sensitive and stylish straight men. In doing so, they create the epitome of the metrosexual, the sensitive straight man who is confident enough to demonstrate some "gay elements" (whatever that means) and, not accidentally, coopt those "gay" elements to work in the service of heteronormativity. Critic Sasha Torres suggests that this constant need for gay men to help incompetent straight men perform "normal" domestic tasks reflects a "crisis in the reproduction of heterosexuality," and that the show indicates that "heterosexuality constitutes its own undoing"(96). This potential crisis is yet another of the show's contradictions: it troubles heteronormativity on one level while reinscribing it through the commodification of gayness on the other. The show ultimately contains queerness, robbing queer identity of any meaning other than aesthetics that work in the service of heteronormativity. Queer no longer means a sexual identity, an understanding of gender bending, or a history of oppression and resistance. Instead, as an article *Queer Eye* in *The Advocate* puts it:

> Simply by being themselves—openly gay men who are commanding, funny, whip-smart, and disarmingly personable—they are shedding light on the subject of gayness for the nation to see (And what a flattering light it is

too!). Just knowing them makes it that much more difficult to dismiss gay people as threatening the American way of life. After all, their entire mission is to make straight America feel better about itself when it looks in the mirror. (Vary, "Pride, Patriotism, Queer Eye")

Thus, queer presence on the show shores up middle America heterosexual whiteness, rather than troubling the elements of that citizenship that render LGBT communities second-class citizens. It is notable, after all, that the issue of *The Advocate* in which that story appeared featured the Fab 5 on the cover in front of an American flag, and that *Queer Eye* debuted soon after the events at the World Trade Center while President George W. Bush was encouraging U.S. citizens to show their patriotism by continuing to spend money. The makeover narrative has always played a role in constructing proper citizens of the U.S. nation. *Queer Eye* simply renders more visible the role of heteronormativity in the production of the proper subject. The ultimate measure of success on *Queer Eye* is often the degree to which the straight guest can pull off the Fab 5's tips and the degree of pleasure the woman in question demonstrates at her new metrosexual man. The show, then, invites "nice" friendly gay men into the homes of straight men not because of any radical understanding of queerness, but because the gay men become tools through which heteronormativity is reinforced.

Interestingly enough, the longer the show remains on the air, the more the fissures in the relations between the straight men and the Fab 5 are revealed. While the heterosexual men on the show always express their profound thanks to the Fab 5 at the end of the show, often saying that their time spent with gay men "opened their eyes" to the "normalcy" of gay men, this response rings hollow in some episodes. For instance, in one episode, the straight guest resists cooking a meal for his party, saying it would be too time consuming, but Ted bluntly says he doesn't have a choice (it is probably part of the contract the straight man agrees to when he comes on the show) (Episode 22, "Help a Soldier Begin Again"). In another episode with the Red Sox, one player runs onto the field during the fashion show doing a "girly" dance with his hands that in any other context would be read as a homophobic statement (Episode 204 "Championship Make-Better"). Given that this performance is in front of a stadium of baseball fans, arguably a bastion of masculinist heteronormativity, the Fab 5's disruption of that space is mitigated by the player's display.

This affirmation of hegemonic American masculinity and heteronormativity is evident in numerous ways throughout the show, particularly since the identities of the gay men are constructed exclusively through their service to the straight men. We know nothing about their histories, their communities, or their politics, and instead only know them through stereotypically gay realms of consumption. Their mission in every episode is to make the guest a better straight man, usually by assigning some task that ensures his success with his wife or girlfriend. For example, in more than one episode, the man proposes marriage and is accepted (such as John B., in Episode 107, "He's a Little Bit Country," or Kevin D. in Episode 118, "Stand up and Deliver"), in other episodes he introduces his parents to his fiancées parents (Alan C. in Episode 111, "Meet the Folks"). Sometimes, he helps with an engagement party, sometimes along with making a scrapbook for his girlfriend with images of the two of them in their relationship. In doing so, they perform what Anna McCarthy calls a queer pedagogy. According to McCarthy, by "[t]eaching domesticity and care of the self to facilitate heterosexual coupling," the Fab 5 "construct templates for citizenship that compliment the privatization of public life, the collapse of the welfare state, and, most importantly, the discourse of individual choice and personal responsibility" (qtd. in McCarthy 98). Thus, while *Queer Eye* is not the first to feature gay men as connoisseurs who work in the service of heterosexual masculinity, this makeover narrative once again reproduces heteronormativity and proper citizenship by suggesting that learning a few self-care tricks is all that's needed. Indeed, like many contemporary reality makeover shows, *Queer Eye* promotes a cultural citizenship in which individual self-care choices are constructed as "redemptive narratives that overcome social positioning" based on gender, racial, or class differences (Wood and Skeggs 206). For instance, the Fab 5 might help prepare the straight guests to do a sports broadcast or go on a corporate job interview. As always, the show is full of contradictions, so the Fab 5 also help the guests show their photography, prepare for a concert or informal musical performance, or an opening night for a musical (Warren L. in Episode 119, "Compose Yourself"), all activities that do not as clearly or inevitably conform to hegemonic masculinity. But the markers of heteronormativity are consistently and invariably upheld, particularly when the "truest" markers of the guest's success are his wife or girlfriend's approval and the Fab 5's assessment of how successfully he performed his revised straight masculinity.

Even the spin off from *Queer Eye*, *Queer Eye for the Straight Girl*, applies the same makeover narrative to straight women in a way that embeds queerness neatly within heteronormativity. It's telling that the "Gal Pals," the show's equivalent of the Fab 5, include one woman and four men, as though the help and advice of gay men is essential to a successful makeover. And while the lesbian on the show, Honey Labrador, makes visible the presence of feminine lesbians, her gender performance continues a long line of media portrayals of lesbians, including *Queer as Folk* and *The L Word*, that erase the presence of gender bending within the queer community. Honey is entitled "The Lady," a generalist with a hand in the areas of each of the other three men who are specifically assigned, Life, Locale, and Look. Moreover, Honey spends an excessive amount of time helping the straight women with their makeup and giving them sex advice for how to please their men in bed (a level of advice that even the Fab 5 don't engage in). In fact, the Gal Pals spend an inordinate amount of time talking about the breast size and other sexualized features of the straight women on the show. The heteronormative gender binary is thus squarely upheld. While the Web site touts Honey as "the first lesbian Queer Eye" her sexual orientation is oddly muted and she rarely engages in the flirtatious banter with the straight girl that the Fab 5 engage in with the men they groom.

THE RACIALIZATION OF GAY PRESENCE

The term queer refers to the inability of heteronormativity to fully establish stable definitions of sexuality because identities are often "overdetermined by other issues and conflicts . . . [such as] race or national identity" (Hennessey 1998). On *Queer Eye*, white gay masculinity is established through the exploitation of men of color, both gay and straight. The show privileges particular forms of both heterosexual and gay masculinities, so that it is often hard to tell which forms of masculinity are "gay" and which are "straight." In doing so, it not only perpetuates forms of masculinity, it also *constructs* them. That is, after all, the entire purpose of the show—to turn straight guys from "drab to fab" by teaching them how to perform masculinity "properly." While producing more stylish and sensitive men may seem on the surface to be a desirable endeavor, the show establishes hierarchies of masculinity by invoking problematic long-standing racialized and class-based ideologies. The representational practices on the show, then, uphold patterns of racialization for both gay and straight men of color that have historically been used to enact violence on them.

Queer Eye treats gay men of color on the show notably different then it portrays heterosexual men of color, revealing yet another contradiction embedded in the show. The show disproportionately eroticizes Jai Rodriguez, a member of the Fab 5 who identifies as Puerto Rican and Italian. Jai is frequently depicted in far more intimate positions with the heterosexual guest than are the white gay members of the Fab 5. For instance, in one episode, Jai is posed lying in bed with the heterosexual guest as they talk about romance (Episode 115, "Mr. Clean Comes Clean"). This scene does, on some level, trouble homophobic assumptions, since Jai is not hitting on the straight guest but is instead giving him advice about how to be more romantic with his wife. But Jai's position on the bed is far more intimate then are most of the scenes that feature other members of the Fab 5, and it participates in a problematic pattern of portrayal. Probably the clearest example of the pattern involves the making of the *Queer Eye* video, in which Jai dances in a sexually suggestive manner with another dancer, in what Jai describes as a "gay Justin Timberlake" routine. Given that Jai is a dancer and a performer, this number is on some level a rather normalized reflection of artistic expression. Jai's portrayals can be seen as a performance of gay male femininity that reworks dominant white straight femininity in interesting ways, revealing that both gender constructions need to be understood in the plural: masculinities and femininities.

Given the range of gender performance that exists in queer communities, this portrayal is politically useful. But its progressiveness is mitigated by the racial hierarchies the show upholds. It is notable that Jai is so regularly eroticized while the white members of the Fab 5 are not sexualized themselves, though they do make numerous sexual innuendos about the straight guests on the show. In other words, the white members of the Fab 5 sexualize the heterosexual guests, but they themselves are not eroticized in the way that Jai is. The difference in the portrayals, then, needs to be read in the context of feminizing gay men of color and, by extension, eroticizing them through racialized constructs (Meyers and Kelley). For instance, Carson and Kyan, the two most dominant of the Fab 5, and not coincidentally, as the couture and grooming experts, the ones who most physically transgress the straight guest's boundaries, use a very dominant form of teasing with their guests. Jai, on the other hand, is often supplicant, affectionate, and depicted as sentimental. Moreover, this representation of Jai is not an anomaly. One of the Fab 5's earlier members, Blair Boone, was a man of color who also played the "culture guy," but was quickly discarded. Interestingly, visually he fit much the same physical model that Jai does of being small built and not physically assertive. He appeared in a few episodes and was quickly dropped. Given that the Fab 5 are supposed to be a team, the uncommented substitution of one man of color for another invites the notion that they are interchangeable.

It is also telling that Jai is in charge of "Culture" on the show. "Culture," as presented as one of the five categories on the show, is a problematic and enigmatic construct. In this context, it appears to be a range from teaching the straight guy to say "I love you" in his girlfriend's language even if he can say nothing else, picking up some Hatha Yoga to sweat out toxicities, visiting an art gallery, or learning to salsa. Culture therefore is a rarified version of popular culture and is characterized by a global appropriation. The implication, then, is that "culture" is the purview of men of color, at the same time that the concept is robbed of any specific cultural context, heritage, or tradition. Even the term "Culture Vulture" that appears on screen and on the Web site to introduce Jai marks him as one who exploits culture; vultures, after all, circle dead prey. Jai performs what Judith Butler refers to as the "merely cultural" and José Esteban Muñoz refers to as "inane culture mavens," in which racial difference is erased and queers of color become merely window dressing, while the white gay men perform the "real" makeover work (Butler qtd. in Muñoz 101–102). Culture on the show is gesture and packaging, but contains no substance. As in the blurb on the successful Fab 5 book states, culture is "all the things to do on the date to impress your companion" (Allen et al.). In one episode, Jai tells a straight guy to think of making charming gestures such as warming a bath towel for his spouse by throwing it in the dryer. Once again, the way to a woman's heart is through her comfort by upholding consumer culture. Moreover, while the Fab 5 supposedly train the straight man to help out around the house, it is still only an occasional thing, thus continuing the long-standing narrative that men's domestic activity is an anomaly (Bordo; Miller). *Queer Eye* moves culture from a worldview, set of values, or living generational history of a people to an easily available set of do's and don'ts that allow for smoother schmoozing. In another shift, the term culture-deprivation is used to mock the straight man's lack of knowledge of these little tips, a twist given the original assignation of the term as one applied in the 1960's Moynihan report to African American families (Moynihan).

This portrayal has serious implications for feminist, anti-racist, and queer politics, because as the show marginalizes and erases queer of color, it once again renders as white the "face of queerness," which *Queer Eye* has come to represent in hegemonic popular culture. Moreover, it achieves its supposed "tolerance" and "openness" about gayness at the expense of queers of color. It is long past time to heed the cautions of activists such as June Jordan, Audre Lorde, Gloria Anzaldúa, and numerous others, that we cannot eradicate oppression and achieve liberation on the backs of other marginalized groups, nor can we afford to see racial, economic, gendered, or sexual oppression as unconnected systems. They are deeply interdependent and many people experience systems of oppression simultaneously. *Queer Eye* is popular *precisely* because it overlooks this complexity and pits one set of oppression — white gay middle class masculinity — against that experienced by other marginalized gay masculinities of color.

This narrow portrayal becomes particularly clear in the show's use of camp humor. As a style of taste, aesthetics, and humor, camp is a part of a long tradition of LGBT politics and resistance (Sontag). At times, the show's campy humor comes close to parodying normative constructs of masculinity. The Fab 5 regularly crack jokes that reflect a knowledge of gay culture and that can, at times, serve as a form of insider recognition for its queer viewers. Carson, for example, will look at an article of clothing that he thinks lacks style and ask the heterosexual male guest if he was "a lesbian in a former life." (Presumably he is not referencing the Honey Labrador sort of lesbian but rather the stereotype of the man-hating lumberjack). Of course, the gendered and anti-lesbian stereotype in this comment needs to be noted, as it reflects the privileging of gay masculinity over other forms of queer identity. It also participates in the pattern of disparaging women — both gay and straight — that is all too common on the show. In another scene, Carson asks a heterosexual guest what "you people" do with fly fishing paraphernalia, commenting that "my people would use it to decorate shoes or perhaps as a festive tiara" (Episode 113, "Neither Rain Nor Sleet Nor Length of Hair"). The campy jokes and the subversion of "my people" and "your people" invoke campy humor to invert language often used to stereotype LGBT communities and instead reclaim it in a way that troubles the assumptions underlying those statements. The show's use of camp humor is one key reference to a history of cultural resistance through the production of "insider" humor. But the limitations of this strategy become quickly clear when the comments become racialized. In the same fly fishing store, Carson tells the straight guest to pretend they are "hungry Indians hunting squirrels" (Episode 113, "Neither Rain Nor Sleet Nor Length of Hair"). Carson is also depicted in the *Queer Eye* book wearing a T-shirt that reads "Gay is the New Black." These types of comments and portrayals — which are all too common on the show — turn this type of camp into racism, and reveal that problematic racial formations provide the foundation for the gay presence the show creates.

The frequent racialized comments also highlight the paucity of heterosexual men of color featured on the show. When heterosexual men of color do become guests on the show, the racialized hierarchies of representation become even more visible. For instance, one episode featured Rob M. (Episode 120. "Meeting Mildred"), a Black man who identified himself as part Jamaican. In this episode, "camp" quickly became racism, as virtually every comment out of Carson's mouth is deeply racially problematic, including references to Rob's "cocoa colored skin." The other members of the Fab 5 also enact problematic racialized behaviors. In the opening scenes in which the Fab 5 usually tears apart the guest's abode, Kyan draped himself in Rob's shower curtain, which had a vibrant pattern on it. He then made a comment about how "unstylish" the look was, implying that Kyan considered the shower curtain on a par with Rob's wardrobe, which included many dashikis. Significantly, Rob resisted this construction by arguing that he didn't wear his shower curtain, while his body language indicated that he both recognized and was uncomfortable with the racism and the ethnocentrism in Kyan's behavior.

This episode is worth discussing at length because of its complexity. The show contains several levels of problematic racializations, some of which Rob resists and some of which he is complicit with. One of the most blatant elements to note in the episode is the hypersexualization of Rob in a way that echoes a long-standing pattern of doing violence to heterosexual Black men in U.S. culture. Whereas Jai is eroticized by representational practices that mark his "feminine" performances, which results from a combination of racializing Puerto Rican gay men and portraying them as effeminate, Rob is constructed as a hyper-masculine and highly sexualized Black man. This portrayal participates in a long history in the U.S. of hypersexualizing black men and marking them as threats to white femininity through the myth of the Black male rapist (Davis). One scene in a fashion boutique, for instance, depicts Carson flirting with Rob and referring to him as "daddy." In this scene, Rob is seated on a sofa while Kyan and Carson lie touching him on either side, but Carson is literally curling up next to him in a kind of lover pose that clearly makes Rob uncomfortable. Kyan assures Rob that he will protect him from Carson if Rob simply says the code word "zucchini," an all too obvious phallic reference.

We cannot underestimate the racial dynamics of the ways that Carson sexualizes Rob. In one of the next scenes, Carson follows Rob into the dressing room, and while the camera shoots Rob in a tank top and boxer shorts,

Carson exclaims with admiration that Rob is "bursting out" of his shorts. These moments clearly hypersexualize Rob in a way that cannot be read as simply gay male camp, but must be read in a history of violence, sexuality, and race around Black men that includes the lynching of black men, the myth of the Black male rapist, racial profiling, and the fact that Black men in the U.S. are far more likely to be prosecuted for charges of rape then are white men as a result of institutionalized racism. In this context, *Queer Eye* cannot be read as evidence that gay and straight men can now "get along," but instead must be read as a tool through which acceptance of white middle class gay presence is bought through constructs of violence around Black men and an erasure of queers of color.

At the same time that the show eroticizes and hypersexualizes men of color, it also renders diverse ethnic traditions as interchangeable. The few times that *Queer Eye* has featured men of color as guests on the show, it has treated ethnic traditions as another product and technique of style. During the show that featured Rob for instance, Thom's interior design strategy was to advise Rob to "diversify" his ethnic decors so that he was not limited by any one tradition. To that end, Thom took Rob to a store that featured furniture from all over the world, encouraging him to choose a table from Africa, chairs and lights from the Philippines, and so on. Ethnic, then, becomes removed from the particular context of its meaning and personal significance, and instead becomes an interchangeable commodity. Having ethnic items in one's home then reflects only where one shops rather than any deeply personal roots. A clear example of this erasure of substantive ethnic traditions involves Rob's fashion segment, in which Carson, like Thom, suggests that he diversify his wardrobe to combine dashikis with more casual "everyday" clothing (again an ethnocentric assumption). Carson's solution is to purchase Rob the Donna Karan collection and hot glue small segments of African cloth to a jacket or belt buckle, so that it becomes an accessory to more "mainstream" fashion. Given the way that the show has framed the issue, there was no way that Carson could have fully integrated the various styles, because to do so would require troubling the cultural context and racial formations that the show explicitly works to reinforce. Manthia Diawara's observations for understanding the implications of Rob's portrayal. Diawara writes that:

> dominant cinema situates Black characters primarily for the pleasure of white spectators (male or female). To illustrate this point, one may note how Black male characters in contemporary Hollywood films are made less threatening to Whites either by White domestication of Black customs and culture—a process of deracination and isolation—or by the stories in which Blacks are depicted by playing by the rules of White society and losing. (215)

Though Diawara is discussing film not television, the analysis of deracination is clearly relevant here.

In a subsequent show, Kyan encourages James M. (Episode 123, "Training Day"), one of the few Asian American men to be featured on the show, to learn how to do a Thai massage in order to better connect with his girlfriend. While the idea of a massage is certainly a potentially romantic one, the segment clearly participates in stereotypes around Asian American masculinity. It is also one of the only episodes where the girlfriend, Taebee, an Asian woman, is thoroughly criticized and portrayed as a spoilt princess who doesn't deserve her man because she doesn't appreciate the show the Fab 5 facilitate from the meal to the massage. As the episode synopsis comments, "Would it have killed her to be a better sport about it?" (*Queer Eye* Web site). Thus, *Queer Eye* does more than participate in making ethnic "trendy," a pattern that is evident as suburban whites purchase African masks or decorative Buddha statues without being fully aware of the meaning of those objects in various cultural contexts. More problematically, *Queer Eye* robs ethnic traditions of their cultural specificity and suggest that their only purpose is to look stylish, at the same time that it tends to "go ethnic" mostly when men of color are involved.

The racial formations that are perpetuated on the show are integral to the forms of masculinity that are constructed on the show. Let us return for a moment to the episode mentioned above which features Rob M. sandwiched between Carson and Kyan on the couch. This scene involves complex layers of masculinity that also pit Kyan's more "metrosexual" gay masculinity with Carson's more stereotypical display of gay masculinity by racializing and hypersexualizing Rob's masculinity. The phallic symbol of the code word "zucchini" is obvious, of course, but even more significant are the complex layers of power and masculinity that are played out in the scene. Kyan is depicted as the one in control *precisely* because he performs a form of white middle class gay masculinity that is hard to distinguish from white middle class heterosexual masculinity. For instance, in a scene with Ross M., a former Marine (Episode 114, "Create an Officer and a Gentleman"), Kyan outperforms him in push-ups, asserting his fitness. Kyan then is the one who can "protect" Rob from Carson's stereotypically gay performance of masculinity, though not before Rob has already been sexually objectified. Rob's masculinity thus becomes the conduit through which the hierarchies of Kyan's masculinity and Carson's masculinity are established.

Indeed, the show sets up a clear power dynamic between Jai, the feminized gay man of color, Ted and Thom, who perform fairly nice and gentle metrosexual forms of masculinity, and Kyan and Carson, who, though they perform very different types of gay masculinity, nevertheless have the most visible power on the show. Interestingly, the opening promo of the show, depicts Kyan, Ted, and Thom holding tools of their trade that are clear phallic symbols (a hair dryer, a whisk, and a paintbrush, respectively), while Carson and Jai are shown holding objects that are not phallic: shopping bags and an art pad. However, the pattern on the show is to establish a rather different binary. While Thom, and Ted are much warmer, less controversial, and physically further away in many of the shots, it's Carson and Kyan who hold the prominent positions on the show. Though Carson's performance of masculinity is most stereotypically "gay," he holds disproportionate power in the show an in the media representation. He is the first of the pack, so to speak, in the opening credits, gazing directly into the camera—a powerful gaze that is not at all campy and that, not accidentally, suggests that he is the most definitive "Queer Eye" on the show. Along with Kyan, he transgresses the most and he tends to take the humor to its sharpest edge. This division between the forms of masculinity does not go unnoted as the show is received by popular audiences. The December 1, 2003 issue of *People* magazine, for instance, names Kyan Douglas as one of the sexiest men alive, and his photograph bears no significant difference from the images of all the other, presumably heterosexual "sexy" men in the issue. On one level, this blurring of the lines between gay and straight masculinity points out that it is not so easy to "read" different masculinities along the lines of sexuality, and it illustrates that not all members of the queer community enact stereotypical forms of gender performance. As such, this display has the potential to be radically productive as it troubles assumptions about sexuality, but its radical potential is drastically mitigated by the power hierarchies the show establishes between the different forms of masculinity.

COMMODIFYING MASCULINITY

The constructions of masculinity that are represented on the show, then, are deeply racialized, but they are also deeply class-based. In the end, *Queer Eye* reifies a commodified masculinity: being a sensitive and stylish man means consuming products. As the website states, "With help from family and friends, the Fab 5 treat each new guy as a head-to-toe project. Soon, the straight man is educated on everything from hair products to Prada and Feng Shui to foreign films. At the end of every fashion-packed, fun-filled lifestyle makeover, a freshly scrubbed, newly enlightened guy emerges—complete with that 'new man' smell!" (*Queer Eye*).

In essence, the straight man himself becomes a commodity, constructed through the judicious application of the right products. And should viewers miss the actual names of the products used on each show, the *Queer Eye* website gives detailed accounting of brand names and product availability. When the straight male guest knows how to dress more fashionably, has a well-decorated house, applies lots of hair and skin care products, knows a few tidbits about "high" culture, cooks food in a trendy way and serves it on the right dishes and with the right wine, he is deemed a "success." This commodified masculinity reflects an important shift, as it involves daily maintenance rituals. Feminist scholars such as Susan Bordo and Sandra Lee Bartky have long pointed out the constant maintenance required to produce "proper" femininity, a routine that also regulates women's behaviors in conformity with power structures. According to *Queer Eye*, masculinity now requires similar expenditures of time and energy in order to produce docile bodies. Men on the show spend a great deal of time in from of mirrors, and in salons, malls, and kitchens. Being a "successful" or "attractive" man, in other words, means policing one's body through daily rituals that require participating in conspicuous consumption, so that one has the right accessories and accoutrements to "produce" and maintain this sensitive masculinity. The show highlights this maintenance with regular shots of men in front of mirrors applying skin care products and in stores trying on clothes. So the show does indeed tell us that "proper men" must exert labor to produce the image they want (something women have always known about femininity). It is presented as "you owe it to yourself," a message that smacks of self-pampering, and which transfers to men the makeover narrative so often applied to women (such as in the Loreal "I'm worth it" campaign). Thus, whereas the personal transformation narrative has historically always informed the production of gendered subjects in the U.S. nation through the "land of opportunity" and "pull yourself up by your bootstraps" ideologies, this new version has men enacting the kinds of labor that are often attached to femininity. So while *Queer Eye* continues the long standing production of the bourgeois heterosexual masculine subject as the sophisticated connoisseur, it now requires additional daily rituals of self-care (Breazeale). This shift thus helps produce the metrosexual while linking that production to the stereotypical "gay" realms of fashion, cuisine, grooming, interior design, and certain elements of culture.

But, significantly, the show conveniently obscures other forms of labor. *Queer Eye* predicates gay visibility on the condition of a participation in the consumer logic of late capitalism, constructing both gay and heterosexual masculinity as dependent upon consumer spending and the erasure of class differences as well as on the exploitative division of labor that makes possible the makeovers on the show. This form of masculinity, then, perpetuates international divisions of labor while simultaneously rendering them invisible.

The show obscures the labor that makes possible the "makeovers"—the crews that redecorate the houses and often exploited labor that produce the goods that the men purchase. The interior design segments are probably the best example of this. Though Thom is arguably the member of the Fab 5 who does the most "work" on *Queer Eye*—he revamps entire rooms and apartments, while other members make one dinner—the show usually doesn't film the labor required to do so (Gallagher). We don't see the crews paint whole houses, move furniture in and out, polish wood floors and install wood paneling. Instead, we see the before shots, we see the Fab 5 harshly critiquing the place, often with humor, and we see them make a few small decorating changes. The fiction presented is that Thom does it all between lunch and the main event. *Queer Eye* obscures the hours of labor that obviously go into redesigning some of the spaces, much of which is not dome by the Fab 5. Like

Martha Stewart, they have a staff. As Rosemary Hennessey suggests about queer visibility,

> Redressing gay invisibility by promoting images of a seamlessly middle-class gay consumer or by inviting us to see queer identities only in terms of style, textuality, or performative play helps produce imaginary gay/queer subjects that keep invisible the divisions of wealth and labor that these images and knowledges depend on. (148)

The makeovers on the show, then, render invisible the economic privileges and inequalities that make them possible. For instance, we also don't see other important labor. The show often goes to stores like Crate and Barrel, Ralph Lauren, and other upscale places to buy their products, some of which are produced overseas by exploited labor through the globalization of capitalism.

The show privileges an upscale model of masculinity that requires consumption and is therefore unattainable for working class and even lower-middle class men. The Fab 5 rarely take their guests to Wal-Mart or JCPenney (both of which would also perpetuate international divisions of labor), and rarely do they shop at local farmer's markets or community-based stores. Instead, they take them to upscale salons, furniture stores such as Pottery Barn, and to couture fashion boutiques. In fact, *Queer Eye* has arguably done for men's fashion what *Sex and the City* did for women's fashion. The latter has been credited with bringing high couture fashion, such as Prada and Dolce and Gabana, into the homes of mainstream America (or, more precisely into the living rooms of those who can afford cable). *Sex and the City* is also credited with popularizing eclectic fashion combinations, so that women no longer have to wear an entire expensive outfit but can instead pair one high-end piece with other lower priced clothing (which of course makes the style more accessible to middle class women) (Sasvari). Similarly, Carson, *Queer Eye*'s fashion expert, regularly uses the word couture and takes the guests to Ralph Lauren, where, not accidentally, Carson worked at one time. In one show, he even tells viewers—with a clear disdain—that the proper pronunciation is Ralph Lau*ren*, not Ralph Lau*ren*.

Of course, other shows, such as *Seinfeld* and *Friends*, have also popularized high-end fashion names for their predominantly white middle class audiences. But what's important about *Queer Eye*'s use of upscale products is the way it suggests that the regular use of these products is precisely how one *becomes* an attractive and successful heterosexual man and, by extension, a proper subject of the U.S. nation. Indeed, the Fab 5 regularly scoff at the guests who lack this upscale sense. Carson shrieks at fake Mohair and jean shorts, Kyan is put out by disposable razors, Ted is deeply offended by paper cups and frozen hamburgers, and Thom groans at 70s style mass-produced furniture. Their "tasteful tips" make it clear that this form of masculinity can only be properly achieved by middle to upper class men—it is unavailable to people who cannot afford it.

This consumerism runs rampant through the show, starting with General Motors logo on the SUV the Fab 5 drive all over (though they never fill up with gas). Virtually every other scene involves a close-up on a storefront, a label, or a smartly designed tube of styling gel. Apparently, companies are lining up to have similar product placement in the show, a move welcomed by the show's producers since it generates additional revenue. It is ironic, given that the Fab 5 are supposed to be making recommendations based on their own stylistic expertise rather than brand name, that their recommendations are frequently brand names. Paradoxically, on the *Queer Eye* Website where biographies of the Fab 5 give more information about them for the chronically curious, two of the Fab 5 respond that the worst faux pas a person could commit was "trying too hard to be something they are not" (Jai) or "not being yourself" (Carson).

Each of the products works in the service of the Fab 5's area of specialty: grooming, interior design, food, fashion, and culture. The show therefore commodifies gayness, reducing it to a series of products and other accoutrements rather than an identity, community, or politics. In effect, it reduces identity to a product that can be bought and constructed. Since no one on the Fab 5 is a plastic surgeon, we are perhaps lucky that the makeovers do not involve the straight guests going under the knife as is increasingly done to women in shows such as *The Swan* and *Extreme Makeover*. Nevertheless, aside from *Queer Eye*'s campy humor (which, as we have noted, is also problematic at times), gayness gets constructed in terms of stereotypical elements of fashion and grooming, while other elements of queer culture, such as social issues, relationships, or queer resistance, remain absent. Indeed, the Fab 5 have themselves become celebrities, and the show's websites even assigns UPC labels to the photos of each member of the Fab 5. However, they are neatly removed from any real discussion of queer sexuality, as they contain their queerness and shore up heterosexual coupling. This is just the latest version Hennessey's point that gayness can only be tolerated in public visibility when it can be commodified and marketed to heteronormative audiences. The result is a "safe" reduction of gayness, a way to contain it at a time when gay rights are once again under assault by the state, (and the debate over gay marriage is just the most recent of many assaults). And yet this reduction is only "safe" for those few members of LGBT communities who are made visible by the show.

Indeed, if we follow Foucault's notion that the resistance is ever-present but will always be coopted by dominant power structures, we can see *Queer Eye* as a way to limit more progressive advances made by LGBT communities. That is, as LGBT communities make political progress, we need to be contained by reductive portrayals. As we become more public, we are allowed to be visible in mainstream media only as long as the representations reproduce stereotypes and work in the service of conspicuous consumption and racialized hierarchies. Indeed, one of the most disturbing implications of the show is the way it is being touted as the bastion of gay tolerance even as it buys that acceptance at the expense of queers of color, heterosexual men of color, and the working class (categories which are not mutually exclusive). Racism, ethnocentrism, and classism thus become tools through which public gay visibility of certain groups are bought, giving a surface nod toward "tolerance" while merely shoring up the hierarchies already deeply entrenched in the U.S. nation.

When *Queer Eye* gets marked as a progressive representation of queerness, it not only reduces queerness to a narrow and class-based subset, it also puts a public face on some forms of gayness at the expense of other marginalized groups, particularly queers of color. Feminist, anti-racist, and queer cultural critics and activists need to take careful note of this strategy, not only for its import for cultural studies scholarship, but also because we should be cautious of any strategy that on the surface benefits one marginalized group while further scapegoating others. This form of gay visibility, while generating a few laughs, ultimately serves as a decoy to obscure the way gayness is used here to maintain constructs of the white heteronormative U.S. nation state.

WORKS CITED

Allen, Ted, Kyan Douglas, Thom Filicia, Carson Kressley, and Jai Rodriguez. *Queer Eye for the Straight Guy: The Fab 5's Guide to Looking Better, Cooking Better, Dressing Better, Behaving Better, and Living Better.* 1st ed. NY: Clarkson Potter, 2004.

Bartky, Sandra Lee. "Foucault, Femininity, and the Modernization of Patriarchal Power." In *Feminist Social Thought.* Diana Tiejens Meyer, ed. NY: Routledge, 1997. 93–111.

Berlant, Lauren and Michael Warner. "Sex in Public." *Critical Inquiry* 24:2 (Winter 1998): 547–66

Bordo, Susan. *Unbearable Weight: Feminism, Western Culture and the Body.* 10th ed. Berkeley: University of California Press, 2004.

Breazeale, Kenon. "In Spite of Women: Esquire Magazine and the Construction of the Male Consumer." *Signs* 20:1 (1994): 1–22

Butler, Judith. "Merely Cultural." *Social Text* 52–53 (1997): 265–77.

Creekmur, Corey K. and Alexander Doty, eds. *Out in Culture: Gay, Lesbian, and Queer Essays on Popular Culture.* Durham, NC: Duke University Press, 1995.

Davis, Angela. *Women, Race, and Class.* NY: Vintage Books, 1983.

Diawara, Manthia. "Black Spectatorship." In *Black American Cinema.* Ed. Manthia Diawara. NY: Routledge, 1993.

Ferguson, Roderick A. *Aberrations in Black: Toward a Queer of Color Critique.* Minneapolis, MN: University of Minnesota Press, 2004.

Gallagher, Mark. "Queer Eye for the Heterosexual Couple." *Feminist Media Studies* 4:2 (2004): 223–26.

"GLAAD Honors Queer Eye, Sex and the City, and I Am My Own Wife." *The Advocate.* 15 Apr. 2004. http://www.advocate/com/

Hart, Kylo-Patrick R. "We're Here, We're Queer—and We're Better Than You: The Representational Superiority of Gay Men to Heterosexuals on *Queer Eye for the Straight Guy*." *Journal of Men's Studies* 12:3 (Spring 2004): 241+

Hennessey, Rosemary. "Queer Visibility in Commodity Culture." In *Contemporary Feminist Theory: A Text/Reader*. Ed. Mary F. Rogers. NY: McGraw Hill, 1998. 140–52.

Meyer, Michaela D.E. and Jennifer M. Kelley. "Queering the Eye? The Politics of Gay White Men and Gender (In)visibility." *Feminist Media Studies*. 4:2 (2004) 214–17.

Miller, Toby. "A Metrosexual Eye on Queer Guy." In Queer TV Style." Eds. Chris Straayer and Tom Waugh. *GLQ* 11:1 (2005) 112–16.

Moynihan, D.P. *The Negro Family: The Case for National Action*. U.S. Department of Labor. 1965. Retreived Oct. 17, 2002 from http://www.dol.gov/asp/programs/history/webid-moynihan.htm

Muñoz, José Esteban. "Queer Minstrels for the Straight Eye: Race as Surplus in Gay TV." In "Queer TV Style." Eds Chris Straayer and Tom Waugh. *GLQ* 11:1 (2005) 100–2.

Queer Eye for the Straight Guy. Bravo. 26 April 2004 <http://www.bravotv.com/Queer_Eye_for_the_Straight_Guy/>

Rogers, Steve. "Bravo to Air 'Queer Eye for the Straight Girl' Spin-off Series." 12 April 2002. <http://www.realitytvworld.com/index/articles/story.php?s=2467>

Sontag, Susan. "Notes on 'Camp.' " In *Come Out Fighting: A Century of Essential Writing on Gay and Lesbian Liberation*. Ed. Chris Bull. NY: Nation Books, 2001. 52–66.

Torres, Sasha. "Why Can't Johnny Shave?" in "Queer TV Style" edited by Chris Straayer and Tom Waugh. *GLQ* 11:1 (2005): 95–96.

Sasvari, Joanne. "The Longest Runway on TV: *Sex and the City* Changed the Way We Dress." *Calgary Herald* 3 February 2004, Final edition: D1 Front.

Vary, Adam B. "Pride, Patriotism, and *Queer Eye*." The Advocate, 08 June 2004, http://www.advocate.com/

Wood, Helen and Beverly Skeggs. "Notes on Ethical Scenarios of Self on British Reality TV." In *Feminist Media Studies* 4:2 (2004): 205–8.

AMY BEST

From Prom Night:
Youth, Schools and Popular Culture

Amy Best is Professor of Sociology at George Mason University. Her research focuses on youth culture as it intersects with race, class, gender, sexuality, and nationality. The following selection is drawn from her book, Prom Night: Youth, Schools and Popular Culture *(2000), which won the Critics' Choice Award from the American Educational Studies Association in 2002.*

> Before the twentieth century, girls simply did not organize their thinking about themselves around their bodies. Today, many young girls worry about the contours of their bodies—especially shape, size, and muscle tone—because they believe the body is the ultimate expression of the self. The body is a consuming project for contemporary girls because it provides an important means of self-definition, a way to visibly announce who you are to the world. From a historical perspective, this particular form of adolescent expression is a relatively recent phenomenon.
> —Joan Jacobs Brumberg, *The Body Project*

The popular 1999 teen prom films *She's All That* and *Never Been Kissed* are Cinderella-inspired tales of transformation. As the narratives unfold, the central female characters, both wallflowers, submit to a series of changes culminating in their emergence as beauty queens at the prom. Each wins the adulation of her peers, and best of all, each gets the man of her dreams. In these Hollywood productions, the process of getting ready for the prom is a privileged space in which bodies are magically reworked and identities completely refashioned.

Predictably, the popular construction of the prom as a moment in which to reinvent the self is a gendered one; this narrative is almost always told through the voice of a girl and the transformation that occurs is mapped fundamentally through her body. This is because the prom belongs to "the feminine." The prom is a feminine space, conventionally thought to be the domain of girls. Constructed as such, it is a site where girls are expected to be heavily invested because they can use this space to solidify and display their feminine identities. Such expectations are inscribed in both popular culture forms and everyday talk. Girls are repeatedly told that going to the prom is a fundamentally important part to their being and becoming feminine. In prom magazines, "making a statement" is the very promise of the prom: "the prom is

35

your night to shine." "Dare To Stand Out" and "Be The Babe of the Ball" these magazines tell their readers. One magazine article asks, "On your special night will you steal the social scene?" The message is that a carefully fashioned feminine self is the key to an unforgettable prom. The packaging of the prom in this way virtually ensures girls' participation in the consumption of goods and in feminine body work. And why wouldn't girls want to make a dramatic statement about themselves at the prom? There is tremendous pleasure in the project of self-change.

Yet while girls are expected to take up the work of becoming feminine at the prom, they are also confronted with the inherent contradiction in doing this kind of work. The very practices that girls are expected to invest in and to find pleasurable are also dismissed as trivial. "When I was a freshman I couldn't wait to go. I worked at the postprom party at my school but by the time senior year came around it all seemed so irrelevant an unimportant to the future," one young woman wrote. The basic paradox lies in the following: the project of becoming feminine is defined as frivolous, and that which is frivolous is also feminine.[1]

So profound is this contradiction for girls that many young women I talked to expressed an initial ambivalence about going to the prom. One white young woman wrote,

> I wasn't originally going to attend my prom simply because I was broke and didn't want to get dressed up for one night. But somehow my best friend convinced me to go. So then I went home and told my mom that I was going and she didn't believe me until two weeks later when I shelled out $50 for two tickets.

Elise, a biracial, bisexual student at Woodrow, originally rejected the prom because she felt it reflects a space ordered by a set of gendered practices that privilege consumption and heterosexuality. "At first I was like, screw the prom, you know. It's kind of cheesy. Everyone's going parading around, this is my dress, and who's he bringing?" But she also said later in the interview, "You know, I'm kinda getting into it." Elise did end up going, as did many young women who originally thought they might not. Most girls found themselves—for some reason or another—mysteriously "caught up" in the preparations for the prom despite their initial resistance. Only a few girls in this study decided they were not going to attend their proms. One young white woman discussed her decision to not go:

> I choose not to attend my junior or senior prom because it was not impor-
> tant to me. I had opportunities my sophomore, junior, and senior years to
> attend and I worked on the prom committee to organize the event. I think
> that the prom is blown completely out of proportion. I came from a small
> town and there were some people who became obsessed with the prom.
> This was the case with one of my friends. She got mad at me because I
> didn't want to go. I think my mom was a little hurt by this too because we
> didn't go dress shopping, etc.

Even the marketers of the prom magazines realize the weight of this contradiction. Consider one article from a 1997 special prom edition of *YM*, which began, "In your opinion, the prom is so, well, not hip. So though you're majorly excited for the big night, you're saying 'See ya!' to flowing ball gowns and stretch limos—you've got to make a statement girl!"[2]

The contradictions among delighting in the work of getting ready for the prom, of wanting to be seen, and of feeling that the prom is an event having little true social value point to an ongoing tension (significantly beyond that of the prom) that many girls experience when taking up a position of femininity in a culture organized around consumption in which men and the practices authorized by masculine ideologies are privileged. Leslie Roman and Linda Christian-Smith, in their book *Becoming Feminine*, elaborate the connections between the contradictory nature of popular cultural forms and the struggles girls face in becoming feminine. As they explain, "At stake in the struggles and contestations over these meanings are not only textural representations of femininity and gender relations in particular cultural commodities, but also their place and significance in the lives of actual women and men who consume, use and make sense of them in the context of their daily practices and social relations. The struggle for girls and women, then (whether they are feminist or not), over gendered meanings, representations and ideologies in popular cultural forms is nothing less than a struggle to understand and hopefully transform the historical contradictions of becoming feminine within the context of conflicting sets of power relations."[3] This struggle, a struggle fundamentally formed in relation to the self, was narrated by girls as they prepared for and then attended their proms. While the prom highlights more general dilemmas about the continuing influence of dominant gender meanings on girls' lives and their bodies, it also emerges as a distinct site where context-specific forms of femininity—that surprisingly cut across race and class lines—arise. From hairstyles to dresses, these girls' narratives tell the story of the work and the lessons offered by the prom.

SEEING AND BEING SEEN: THE MAKING OF FEMININE BODIES

> I want something that makes my dad a little nervous . . . something
> pretty . . . maybe make him lose a little sleep. I want something that will
> make me the center of attention . . . I want something the other girls
> wish they could wear . . . something that makes everyone stop and stare.
> —Advertisement for Flirtations, *Your Prom*, 1996

Despite the tensions some girls initially felt about investing in an event that had been framed as silly and superficial, many young women looked forward to the prom as a place to be seen. As John Berger explains in his important book, *Ways of Seeing*, "A woman must continually watch herself. She is almost continually accompanied by her own image of herself. Whilst she is walking across a room or whilst she is weeping at the death of her father, she can scarcely avoid envisaging herself walking or weeping. From earliest childhood she has been taught and persuaded to survey herself continually."[4]

Proms are moments in which girls in particular are on display. The structuring of physical space at the four proms I attended ensured that the prom would be designated in this way: the entrances to the prom sites were situated so that girls could be looked at by others. "Even at the prom, people said it was the best looking dress, I remember," one young white woman offered. Many purposely delay their arrival to the prom so that they can make a grand entrance. As one African-American young woman wrote,

> When I stepped out of the limo I remember thinking that I was just the princess of the night. All lights were on me and this was my night. No one and nothing was going to spoil it for me. So we walked in about an hour late. When I made my entrance everyone's eyes were on me. I even remember one of my enemies sitting on the table that was right next to the door. And when she turned around and took a look at me her whole face fell. By the way she looked, it seems like she had just decided at the last minute she was going to the prom.

Though especially pronounced at the prom, being looked at is a normalized and naturalized dimension of life as a girl; as a result, its embeddedness within a gender and heterosexual order usually goes unnoticed.[5] One girl related,

> I'm looking forward to seeing everyone in a different dress. Everybody keeps telling everybody else what their dress looks like and you can get an idea but you can't *really* get an idea until you actually see it. You can get rolls and rolls of film and take lots of pictures.

As this young woman suggests, seeing carries as much significance as being seen in this cultural scene. While suggestive of the agency girls can claim in the space of the prom (being able to look rather than just being looked upon), this agency continues to be lodged in an organization of gender; the practice of seeing chiefly centers on girls' bodies, and in this way offers little room for girls to reject fully their participation in the project of becoming feminine.

Getting Ready

> Your 30-Day Beauty countdown. Don't let prom put you in a panic!
> With one month to go, you've still got tons of time to get perfect skin,
> beautiful hair and a hot bod. Just follow our head-to-toe guide to getting
> gorgeous.
> —"Your 30-Day Beauty Countdown," article in *YM*, 1997

Because of the importance of being seen in this context, preparations of the body are extensive. Many girls spent considerable time during interviews and in their written narratives providing detailed descriptions of their dresses and hair, how they came to select their dresses, and their efforts to coordinate what they wore with what their date wore. Sally, a white student from Woodrow, had originally bought two dresses, the first of which she returned once her friend found her a new dress.

> AB: So what made you choose this dress over the first dress?
> SB: The first dress was like, I would have to buy jewelry too. Like, dress it up and get, like, different shoes. It was very plain. It was, like, something you would wear out to a nice restaurant.
> AB: How did you find your first dress?
> SB: I was so lazy. I was like, I went to the prom last year. I don't feel like shopping again so I was like, I'll just look through catalogues. And I looked through a *Victoria's Secret* catalogue and I just picked out the first dress that I saw.
> AB: That was the short dress?
> SB: Yeah, so that's my big mistake. I didn't go looking around at stores or anything.

Sally, while initially ambivalent about the work required to experience the prom in a feminine way, ultimately acquiesces. Her self-critique for not initially engaging in the work that is in many ways for girls the very foundation of the prom points to the ongoing pressure many girls experience in fashioning themselves to be seen.

For a number of girls, how they worked and "disciplined" their bodies directly related to their having a successful prom. "When the day started off I thought it would be the best day. I had the perfect dress (no one had anything else like it) and my hair was done beautifully," one African-American young woman wrote. Success for her not only centers on but is bound to the body.

The process of preparing for the prom for many of these girls was as important as the end product, if not more so. Many girls declared that getting ready for the prom was an entire day's commitment (though preparations began months in advance). Hair, nails, and face were thoroughly worked over; many girls attended tanning salons, while others reported that they dieted to lose weight before the prom:

> All I can remember was that the prom wore me out. From half a day at school, to a morning appointment to get my hair done to an afternoon appointment for my friend to do her hair I was literally exhausted. I also remember fasting so that I could fit into my prom dress.

Another girl wrote,

> We all went shopping for dresses. This didn't take just one trip to the mall. We looked at dresses at every mall in the area and even traveled to malls where there is more selection. Some of my friends even had their dresses made by professional seamstresses. We all had our "dream dress" in mind and it was all a matter of finding it. Then, of course, we had to look perfect in

those dresses, so a bunch of my friends and I joined the gym. We exercised three months before.

Social class emerges to organize these feminine practices in a range of ways. One girl, discovering on the day of the prom that her dress was too small, went out and bought another. Sally was able to buy two dresses, though she planned to return one. Clearly the availability of disposable income made this possible. For these girls, class status often means whether or not their parents are able to "support" their prom by covering the significant expense.

The availability of unlimited money enabled some girls to organize the activities in ways that directly hooked them into the spheres of consumption. Several young women enlisted the help of beauty professionals. One girl reported that she and her friends had rented a limousine to take them from the hair salon to lunch at a local café, while another girl and her friends hired a cosmetics representative to come to her home and do their makeup. One white middle-class girl wrote,

> I remember the preparation for my senior prom being really formal. I remember going to NYC to pick the dress, which took two days, starting to get ready at 10:30 in the morning. That day a group of six friends including myself made a day out of it: hair, nails, pedicures, facials, lunch—the works. Even though we all rode in the limo during the day while getting ready and going from place to place, we all took separate limos to the prom.

Most girls, constrained by limited money but also wanting to participate in this beauty work, compromised by getting just their hair, nails, or face done. Tracey, a young African-American woman, explains,

> I know it's like I have to get my hair done and then I have to get my nails done and that costs a lot of money. My dress was expensive, you know, my dress was $275. So it's like I'm broke. I have no money, you know, so if like somebody loans you jewelry or something, you know, that's a lot cheaper than going out and buying it.

Several girls deciding that this beauty work should be done by professionals, sought jobs to pay for these added expenses; some even started separate bank accounts to save for the cost of the prom.

As many of these young women suggest, these preparations for the prom, while fundamentally being about setting oneself apart, were often a collective process. For many of these girls, talk started about how they intended to prepare for the prom months before the actual event. Some girls reported that these conversations transformed their initial ambivalence about the prom into excitement about the prospects of working on their bodies for the upcoming event.

The process of getting ready came to represent for many a space of shared experience. It was not uncommon for female family members, friends, and more experienced promgoers to assemble at one girl's house to get ready together. Consider my fieldnotes from observing as one young white woman, helped by two others, got ready for the prom:

> *Susie came in from having taken a shower in a panic, wrapped in robe and towel. Her day, she said, had been a succession of preparations: getting the camp-site ready for after the prom, having her nails done. She had had a French mani-cure. Susie left to put some clothes on after calling a friend to remind her to bring the boutonnieres. We, the three helpers, sat on the floor in the middle of the room, talking casually about last year's prom, which one of the girls, Lori, had attended. Lori told us a story about sticking her head out the sunroof of the limo they had rented and messing up the big curls she had so carefully put in her hair. Lori was supposed to put those same big curls in Susie's hair. Before they began working on Susie's hair, Lori and her friend Donna decided to go have a smoke, on the roof, while Susie began drying her short bobbed hair. After a few minutes Lori came through the window "refreshed" and began working on Susie's hair. As Lori styled Susie's hair around the curling iron, the three girls chatted about the prom, how Susie had found her dress, their skipping school to lay out in the sun that day and the boys outside playing basketball in the driveway across the street. The conversation jumped from one topic to another quickly. From the pace of their talk it was easy to tell these three girls were good friends and that their lives were bound up with one another. What I realized after being there for just an hour was that while these girls came together ostensibly to help Susie prepare for her prom, the social significance of this space was more meaningful. More than just getting ready, this was a space to "rehash" aspects of their daily lives with other girls who shared in it. (May 1996)*

The pleasure many of these girls expressed as they spoke about this collective process was difficult to miss. Consider the following three narratives written by young African-American women:

> The house is going to be filled with people coming to help me. My mom and her friends they're gonna come help me get ready and stuff and do my make-up. I'll already have my hair and nails done and then my friends are gonna come help me get dressed. They're gonna be taking pictures and videotaping. One of my friends, she's a year younger and then her sister's a year older. She graduated last year and I went last year and helped her get ready and get her stuff together. Her and her mom are gonna come help me. My grandmother will probably come over. My brother, his girlfriend and my niece, they're gonna come over and take pictures and watch when I leave.

> I woke up out of bed about 9:00 a.m. that morning because I had a million things to do. I called my cousin and we went shopping. We picked up my dress, accessories and shoes. After doing that I spent another 10 hours get-ting my hair and nails done. I didn't get home until about 6:15 and the limo was scheduled to pick me up at 6:30. So thanks to my mother and cousin I was able to get ready in about 25–30 minutes.

I have to go get my nails done. I don't want my hair to fall. How do I do this? How do I do that? I have to make sure I do the make-up, this that. Well, I don't wear make-up, but this is just what we were all talking about, just the girl-type of stuff. Like, "Oh make sure you bring an extra pair of pantyhose, make sure your shoes are this, that everything matches, you don't put on too much make-up because the light looks this way on your face." All that type of stuff.

Pictures were often taken to record the elaborate work that goes into getting ready.

The Burdens of Beauty

Beauty Make Me Over: From Toned-down to Terrific, From Low-key to Luminous; From Sweet to Sophisticated.
—Beauty article in *Your Prom*, 1996

Some girls, while enjoying the process of getting ready for the prom, were also aware of the extent to which these preparations are distinctly feminine. One white middle-class girl wrote:

This elaborate process of preparation was done by most of the people attending the prom (well, girls). It was ridiculous when you think of all the time and money that went into one night. But it was fun.

Another young white woman wrote,

This whole procedure for preparing for the prom was pretty hectic. That's because, I mean, I don't mean to create more stereotypes for my gender but, girls who do go to the prom have the tendency to over-exaggerate things. Speaking for most of my friends, we worried too much. There were many questions that ran through my mind as the prom night got closer and closer: what type of dress should I wear? Should I wear long or short? What color dress should I wear? How should I get my hair done? Who should do my hair? Should I do my nails? What type of jewelry should I wear with my dress? What type of shoes? While on the other hand guys have one major question: Should I rent or buy?

Like these two girls above, most took it for granted that boys and girls engaged in a different set of practices as they prepared for the prom. These young women are drawing from a set of social assumptions about what it means to be a "man" or a "woman." Treating gender as simply a matter of social difference and not social power not only works to naturalize a gendered division of labor, it also obscures how this very talk produces and maintains a social organization of gender. Mary and Sarah, two white students from Woodrow, related,

MD: I don't think they [boys] really care quite as much as the girls do. I mean, like, what they care about is what they're doing before and what they're doing after and with who.

SJ: They don't really have a lot to get ready.

MD: "My tux is a double-breasted gray." [she laughs]

SJ: The girls are—the girls have to do a lot more planning with their dress and their . . .

MD: Yeah, go through their hair and their nails, their dress.

While many girls were willing to acknowledge that the work required of them was entirely different from the work required of boys to get ready for the prom, few referred to these preparations as burdensome. Exceptions to the rule, two white young women described their experiences as follows:

I'm all through with dress shopping. I'm done. It's tiring. You go from store to store trying on dresses, taking off clothes and putting it on, oh no. It's very tiring shopping for a dress. I'm glad that part is over with.

Shopping for all the prom stuff was a hassle. I went through four dresses and two pair of shoes until I was set on the perfect outfit. The night before the prom I ended up puking my brains out all night and was running a high fever. My mother dragged me to the beauty parlor drugged up, while I had my nails, hair, and makeup done. They had to put extra makeup on me because I was so pale from being sick.

As this last young woman suggests, mothers are central players in the prom, often as invested as these girls in the project of becoming feminine. One young woman laughingly reported to her friends in the bathroom at the prom that her mother had "attacked" her with mascara. In these last two scenes, it is the mothers who enlist their daughters to do the work of looking feminine for the prom. One girl is "dragged" by her mother, while the second had been "attacked." Though clearly expressed in jest, both provide compelling imagery of the ways the practices of femininity are passed from mother to daughter.

While at the prom, a lot of girls talked openly among themselves about the labor-intensive work they do on their bodies to achieve an idealized feminine image. Most common were girls' tales of struggles to find the right dress and their efforts toward having the "perfect" hairstyle. Stories of this kind were exchanged and compared at the prom in the girl's bathroom, a space at the prom reserved exclusively for girls. After observing four proms, I realized that these bathroom discussions about their bodies, dresses, and preparations were not only a source of pleasure, but were also an integral part of the actual prom. In my fieldnotes from Hudson's prom this is most evident:

I watched girls come and go and check themselves out in the mirror as they passed. Three girls came in the bathroom and I started to talk with them as they primped. One girl was wearing a green dress, with a green sheer shawl and a full tulle skirt and I told her how pretty it was. She twirled around for me. I asked her if she'd had it made and she said she had. She told me she wanted it to be fuller on the bottom so that she would get more attention. She also told me that her jewelry came from the makeup artist who did her makeup. She was heavily *made up in green eye shadow with her hair pulled up into large ringlets. Her friend, who had also had her dress made to look like a traditional ball gown, with a purse to match, said her sister had done her makeup. The girl in the green dress told me she had only had hers done by a professional because she didn't know how to do it herself. I asked her if she normally wore makeup and she said no. The three of them talked among themselves about their lipstick, comparing prices, mostly. One girl had bought hers for $2.00, while the other had gone and gotten her lipstick from Lancôme for close to $15.00. Another girl walked by showing off her gold shoes and said, "These are toe crackers." Soon after another girl came by whose dress was bursting at the sides. She and her friends were in search of a pin of some sort. They had done a botched job to repair the dress by the bathroom stalls. This led to the three girls' discussion of the mistakes about their own dresses. The girls in the green dress pointed to some gapping around the neckline, while the other pointed to her uneven hemline. (June 1997)*

While in many ways this kind of "body talk" represents an articulation of feminine identity and mastery, it also undermines the idealization of feminine display because it exposes it as work that requires money, time, and body alteration. Contrary to the idea that femininity is something girls simply possess, their talk helps to define femininity as something one actively undertakes.[6] I overheard one girl as she rushed up to greet her friend in the beginning of Rudolph's prom, pointing to the top of her head, exclaiming, "Three hours, it took three hours to get my hair to look like this!"

More than just a set of frivolous practices of primping, these are fertile sites of identity negotiation and construction, where girls are making sense of what it means to be women in a culture that treats the surface of the body as the consummate canvas on which to express the feminine self. There is also a clear sense that many of these girls enjoyed the attention they received after such significant transformations—their labors were not in vain. Indeed, this is the very promise of the prom, highlighted in girls' talk, and telegraphed in prom films and magazines. The pleasure in being seen in "a new light" helps to gain girls' consent to consume, to ensure their participation in beauty culture and the ongoing creation of gender.

THE POLITICS OF PLEASURE

The achievement of femininity for the prom depends on an endless consumption of products; makeup, clothing, hair accessories, shoes, lingerie, handbags, and jewelry are all products readily available in a commodity market and heavily marketed as tools for feminine display and self-reinvention at the prom. These are tools that require time, patience, and skill to master. Susan Bordo elaborates on the more lasting effects this kind of exacting and intensive work has on women and how they experience life in their bodies, explaining,

"Through the pursuit of an ever-changing, homogenizing, elusive ideal of femininity—a pursuit without a terminus, requiring that women constantly attend to minute and often whimsical changes in fashion—female bodies become docile bodies—bodies whose forces and energies are habituated to external regulation, subjection, transformation, 'improvement'."[7] But this kind of body work is not just about producing disciplined bodies for consumption; there is more here. The meanings girls themselves attach to this work is significant for understanding why they engage in such practices in the first place.[8]

Engaging in the work of becoming "beautiful" for the prom represents a struggle to stake a claim to one's identity. For many of these girls, participating in beauty work enables them to occupy a position within a public space, a significant fact when considering women's historical relegation to the private sphere. As consumers of beauty culture, these young women are able to possess a sense of power and visibility by claiming public space that often is not experienced in their everyday lives in school, with family, or in their relationships with young men. They occupy hair salons, nail salons, and dress shops in a way similar to that of middle-class women in the 1920s who, just after winning the right to vote, proudly (and paradoxically) announced their new freedom by wearing shorter skirts, bobbing their hair, and smoking cigarettes in public.

Not only are these girls able to demonstrate a public commitment to feminine practices, they are also able to express their competence as beauty practitioners. The desire to do so is so significant that girls who were either unable (or sometimes unwilling) to indulge in the extravagances of the beauty/hair salon performed this work in private spaces, most often their homes. These girls created a situation resembling, in remarkable ways, the experience of going to a salon. Friends and female family members were enlisted to perform the beauty work provided to other girls by service workers. Though done in the private setting of home, getting ready signified a public act.

While young women arguably do beauty work for the prom to express their heterosexual desirability, they also do this work to experience a self-pleasure by making themselves feel special.[9] For many of these girls, the prom presents itself as an opportunity to indulge themselves in ways that many of them are simply unable to in their day-to-day school lives. Part of what makes this body work around the prom worth undertaking stems directly from how they experience everyday life as young women.

Teenage girls are often denied control over their bodies, their desire, and their self-definition. Engaging in this elaborate consumption-oriented body work enables them to craft a space of self-control, self-definition, and self-pleasure that is experienced immediately. Many girls perceive adult women as possessing greater control over their lives than they as girls can. Transforming themselves to look more like adult women through these beauty practices allows many of them to feel more like adult women, to possibly experience adult freedoms and liberties, even if momentarily, and to negotiate those everyday constraints they experience because of their age and consequent position in society. Of course, the result is that the pleasure of excess conceals the ideological workings of the prom; proms structure girls' investments in both gender and heterosexuality, exacerbate their anxieties about the body, and focus their attention toward the all-consuming project of the body.

NOTES

1. Griggers, 1997.
2. "Discover Your Perfect Prom Look," *YM* special prom edition, 1997: 37.
3. Roman and Christian-Smith, 1988: 4.
4. Berger, 1977: 46.
5. McRobbie, 1991; Montgomery, 1998.
6. See West and Zimmerman, 1987, for a discussion on how gender is actively constructed and reconstructed through day-to-day relations.
7. Bordo, 1993: 166.
8. Carrington, 1989; Craik, 1989; Clark, 1987; Fiske, 1989a; McRobbie and Garber, 1981; Radner, 1995, 1989; Radway, 1984; Roman and Christian-Smith, 1988.
9. Hillary Radner (1989) suggests in her work on femininity and consumption that women find pleasure in the consumption of beauty culture because it provides a space in which women can be the agents of their own desire. Radner develops a compelling analysis of how feminine pleasure in the production of appearance is tied to beauty and culture industries. In the 1980s, she argues, these industries recognized the influence of women's struggle to articulate an autonomous self-identity on women's patterns of consumption. In so doing, the market repositioned beauty work within a discourse of self-pleasure; the focus shifted from making oneself over for others to doing it simply for oneself. Beauty work at this particular historical moment not only is rooted in the discourses of heterosexual desirability, but in a discourse of feminine desire (e.g., "I'm beautiful and I'm worth it").

REFERENCES

Berger, John. 1977. *Ways of Seeing*. London: Penguin.

Bordo, Susan. 1993. *Unbearable Weight: Feminism, Western Culture and the Body*. Berkeley and Los Angeles: University of California Press.

Carrington, Kerry. 1989. "Girls and Graffiti." *Cultural Studies* 3 (89–100).

Clark, Ann K. 1987. "The Girl: A Rhetoric of Desire." *Cultural Studies* 1 (195–203).

Craik, Jennifer. 1989. "'I Must Put My Face On': Making Up the Body and Marking Out the Feminine." *Cultural Studies* 3 (1–14).

Fiske, John. 1989. *Understanding Popular Culture*. Boston: Unwin Hyman.

Griggers, Camilla. 1997. *Becoming Woman*. Minneapolis: University of Minnesota Press.

McRobbie, Angela, ed. 1991. *Feminism and Youth Culture: From Jackie to Just Seventeen*. Boston: Unwin Hyman.

McRobbie, Angela and Jennifer Garber. 1981. "Girls and Subcultures." *Feminism and Youth Culture: From Jackie to Just Seventeen*, ed. Angela McRobbie. Boston: Unwin Hyman

Montgomery, Maureen E. 1998. *Displaying Women: Spectacles of Leisure in Edith Wharton's New York*. New York: Routledge.

Radner, Hilary. 1995. *Shopping Around: Feminine Culture and the Pursuit of Pleasure*. New York: Routledge.

———. 1989. " 'This Time's For Me': Making Up and Feminine Practice." *Cultural Studies* 3 (301–21).

Radway, Janice. 1984. *Reading the Romance: Women, Patriarchy and Popular Literature*. Chapel Hill: University of North Carolina Press.

Roman, Leslie, G. and Linda Christian-Smith, eds. 1988. *Becoming Feminine: The Politics of Popular Culture*. London: The Falmer Press.

West, Candice and Don Zimmerman. 1987. "Doing Gender." *Gender and Society* 1 (125–51).

SHARON R. BIRD

Welcome to the Men's Club: Homosociality and the Maintenance of Hegemonic Masculinity

Sharon R. Bird is a Professor in the Department of Sociology at Iowa State University who studies gender, race, class, work, and inequality.

To understand gender inequality, one must do more than study relations *between* genders. The nature of gender relations is such that asymmetries exist between men and women and among men and among women (Connell 1987, 1992). Recognition of masculinity as a social construct began only a couple of decades ago, and recognition of a power dynamic differentiating "normative" from "non-normative" masculinities began only a few years ago (Kimmel 1990). Investigation of the many possible types of masculinity conceptualizations has been rare (Connell 1987; Kimmel 1990). Connell's (1992) research on homosexual masculinities and their subordination to heterosexual masculinities is a notable exception. As Connell's work demonstrates, delineation of relations among masculinities is important because it facilitates a better understanding of how the structural order of gender is maintained. Hegemonic masculinity, or "the maintenance of practices that institutionalize men's dominance over women" and is "constructed in relation to women and to subordinate masculinities" (Connell 1987, 185–86), shapes the overall framework of gender relations. By problematizing masculinity, Connell challenges typically undisputed meanings associated with male dominance.

In this study, I focus on how meanings that correspond to hegemonic masculinity are maintained and how meanings that do not correspond to hegemonic masculinity are suppressed. Within the existing gender order, meanings associated with behaviors that challenge hegemonic masculinity are denied legitimation as *masculine*; such meanings are marginalized, if not suppressed entirely. Contradictions to hegemonic masculinity posed by male homosexuality, for example, are suppressed when homosexual masculinity is consistently rendered "effeminate" (Connell 1992).

The maintenance of hegemonic masculinity is explored here through investigation of male homosocial interactions. *Homosociality* refers specifically to the nonsexual attractions held by men (or women) for members of their own sex (Lipman–Blumen 1976). Homosociality, according to Lipman–Blumen, promotes clear distinctions between women and men through segregation in social institutions. I add, further, that homosociality promotes clear distinctions between hegemonic masculinities and nonhegemonic masculinities by the segregation of social groups. *Heterosociality*, a concept left untheorized by Lipman-Blumen, refers to nonsexual attractions held by men (or women) for members of the other sex.

Also critical to this analysis is an investigation of the relationship between sociality and the self-conceptualization of masculinity. As I argue here, homosocial interaction, among heterosexual men, contributes to the maintenance of hegemonic masculinity norms by supporting meanings associated with identities that fit hegemonic ideals while suppressing meanings associated with nonhegemonic masculinity identities. I focus specifically on the connection between individual masculinity and gender norms in small group interactions to capture subtle mechanisms of control. When personal conflicts with ideal masculinity are suppressed both in the homosocial group and by individual men, the cultural imposition of hegemonic masculinity goes uncontested (see Kaufman 1994).

The following meanings are crucial to our understanding of how homosociality contributes to the perpetuation of hegemonic masculinity: (1) *emotional detachment*, a meaning constructed through relationships within families whereby young men detach themselves from mothers and develop gender identities in relation to that which they are not (Chodorow 1978); (2) *competitiveness*, a meaning constructed and maintained through relationships with other men whereby simple individuality becomes competitive individuality (Gilligan 1982); and (3) *sexual objectification of women*, a meaning constructed and maintained through relationships with other men whereby male individuality is conceptualized not only as *different from* female but as *better than* female (Johnson 1988).

CONCEPTUALIZING MASCULINITIES

Gender identity is distinguished from the heavily criticized concept of gender *role* in that the latter is used to refer to behavioral expectations associated with more or less static social positions, whereas the former refers to a continual *process* whereby meanings are attributed by and to individuals through social interaction. Gender, in other words, is relational. Gender identity originates in early interactions, becoming more stable through the accumulation of meanings attributed by and to the self over time (see Burke 1980; Burke and Reitzes 1981). Information received through interactions may be used either to reinforce existing self-notions of gender meanings or to weaken them. That is, mere socialization does not sufficiently explain how individuals conceptualize identity. Socialization provides the terms of social interaction but does not determine how individuals incorporate interactional meanings into their own conceptualizations of gender (Connell 1987).

The unique experiences of men, embedded within particular social institutions and subject to varying historical contexts, facilitate conceptualizations of masculinities that may differ considerably. Each male incorporates a variety of meanings into his gender identity, some of which are consistent with hegemonic masculinity and others of which are not (e.g., Connell 1992; Messner 1992b). The social ideal for masculinity, which in itself is a nonstatic notion, may be internalized (i.e., central to one's core self [see Chodorow 1980]) or simply interiorized (i.e., acknowledged by the self), enabling individuals to understand the gender norms to which they are held accountable. In either case, each male comes to understand both socially shared meanings of masculinity and the idiosyncratic meanings that comprise his unique gender identity. Internalization of hegemonic meanings provides a base of shared meanings for social interaction but also quells the expression of nonhegemonic meanings. The presumption that hegemonic masculinity meanings are the only mutually accepted and legitimate masculinity meanings helps to reify hegemonic norms while suppressing meanings that might otherwise create a foundation for the subversion of the existing hegemony. This presumption is especially prevalent in male homosocial interactions, which are critical to both the conceptualization of masculinity identity and the maintenance of gender norms.

MALE HOMOSOCIAL INTERACTIONS: EMOTIONAL DETACHMENT, COMPETITIVENESS, AND SEXUAL OBJECTIFICATION OF WOMEN

Three of the shared meanings that are perpetuated via male homosociality are emotional detachment, competition, and the sexual objectification of women. These meanings characterize hegemonic masculinity but are not always internalized as central to individual identity. First, emotional detachment (i.e., withholding expressions of intimacy) maintains both clear individual identity boundaries (Chodorow 1978) and the norms of hegemonic masculinity. To express feelings is to reveal vulnerabilities and weaknesses; to withhold such expressions is to maintain control (Cancian 1987). Second, competition in the male homosocial group supports an identity that depends not on likeness and cooperation but on separation and distinction (Gilligan 1982). Competition facilitates hierarchy in relationships, whereas cooperation suggests symmetry of relationships (Messner 1992a). Finally, the sexual objectification of women facilitates self-conceptualization as positively male by distancing the self from all that is associated with being female. The objectification of women provides a base on which male superiority is maintained (Johnson 1988), whereas identification with women (and what it means to be female) helps remove the symbolic distance that enables men to depersonalize the oppression of women.

Individual conceptualizations vary in the extent to which these meanings characterize one's masculinity. Masculinities that differ from the norm of hegemonic masculinity, however, are generally experienced as "private dissatisfactions" rather than foundations for questioning the social construction of gender (Thomas 1990; see also Kaufman 1994). Hegemonic masculinity persists, therefore, despite individual departures from the hegemonic form.

METHOD

The data collected for this study were gathered through personal interviews and field observations. Eight in-depth interviews were conducted in the fall of 1992 in a small northwestern city in the United States. Later, additional follow-up interviews were conducted with four new respondents to clarify how male homosocial and heterosexual interactions facilitate the perpetuation of hegemonic masculinity, on the one hand, but suppress nonhegemonic masculinity, on the other.

The men who participated in the interviews for this study were all selected from within the academic community of the city in which the study took place. Responses to questions, therefore, may reflect a level of education higher than that of the general population. The findings of this study, however, are consistent with findings of previous studies regarding the meanings associated with masculinity (e.g., Lehn 1992; Messner 1992a, 1992b; Phillips 1986). The men's educational level ranged from three years of undergraduate study to graduate level and post-Ph.D. The men ranged in age from 23 to 50 years. All but one of the interviewees were native-born Americans from various geographical regions of the country. The other male, a native of East Africa, had maintained residence in the United States for approximately two years before the time of the interview. Although the data received through the interview with this respondent were consistent with accounts offered by the respondents from the United States, this information was excluded from the analysis because of cultural differences that could contribute to misleading conclusions. Most of the men reported middle-class family origins, although three reported working-class backgrounds. Two of the men interviewed were Black, and the other nine were white. All of the men were raised primarily by female caretakers, and all were heterosexual.

The primary focus of the interviews was on the development of perceived consensual masculinity and the corresponding relationship between self-conceptualizations and hegemonic masculinity. Respondents were first asked questions about childhood. Each was asked to describe childhood memories of time spent with playmates, with siblings, and with parents. Responses to these questions provided general information from which more specific inquiries could be made regarding the meanings associated both with masculinity personally (i.e., identity) and with masculinity more generally (i.e., the beliefs, attitudes, and expectations of the group and of society).

To establish the parameters for the discussion during the interviews, each man was asked to consider the kinds of relationships he would find most desirable given non-work-related situations.[1] Each was then prompted to elaborate on his experiences within groups, especially those experiences within the male homosocial group. Although the men varied in how much they desired male homosocial group interaction, each explained that such groups have had a significant impact on their beliefs, attitudes, and behaviors. The men were asked to elaborate on what exactly would be considered appropriate or inappropriate, desirable or undesirable, for conversation among men and what interests were commonly or not commonly shared within their homosocial groups. The topics of sports, women, business, politics, and drinking were most commonly specified as desirable for conversation, while the topics of feelings and gossip were most frequently mentioned as undesirable. Each man was then asked to explain his views on the degree to which his personal interests corresponded to interests more generally shared by the group. I also made inquiries about why certain interests and topics are so prevalent among men in homosocial groups and whether they had experienced any repercussions when norms for male homosocial interaction were disregarded.

Additional data were collected during the fall of 1992 through field observations of male homosocial interactions in small-group contexts. Observations and interviews were conducted within the same academic community, but the men *observed* were not the same as the men *interviewed*. Approximately 25 hours of observations were conducted. The majority of the observations were made at a single location: a deli/bar frequented by men associated with the university but also visited regularly by men not associated with academia. Remaining observations were conducted at two coffee shops and three taverns, all located in the same academic community. The focus of the observations was on the interactions among male customers, including their conversations. Field notes were taken in one- to two-hour time periods at various times of the day and/or night and on various days of the week. Because the locations in which observations were made are consistently patronized by students and university faculty, the recording of observations went unnoticed. A running description was kept of interactions that transpired between men seated within hearing distance of the researcher (usually only a few feet away). Observations were made of groups ranging in size from two to eight men. Observations were also made of groups that were initially all male but were temporarily interrupted by a woman. Most of the conversations were recorded verbatim. Gestures, facial expressions, and the physical location of each group member were also noted.

The meanings described in the interviews and that emerged from the observations have been organized under the following subtopics: (1) emotional detachment, (2) competition, and (3) sexual objectification of women. The remainder of this article focuses on the processes through which these meanings are sustained and the processes through which alternative meanings are suppressed in male homosocial interaction.

EMOTIONAL DETACHMENT: "WE WERE MASCULINE LITTLE KIDS!"

The rules that apply to homosocial friendships and to masculinity are so familiar that they are typically taken for granted by men and women alike. Rarely does anyone (other than the social scientist) seriously question the expectations associated with gender identity or gender norms. Instead, it is assumed that "boys will be boys" and will just naturally do "boy things." By the same token, "men will be men" and will continue to do "men things." Doing men things or "doing masculinity" is simply the commonplace activity of men's daily lives, recreated over and again, maintaining the norms of social behavior (West and Zimmerman 1987).

The men interviewed and those observed explained that being "one of the boys" is a key principle of symbolic and, in some cases, physical separation of "the boys" from "the girls." One man, for example, explained how, as a youngster, he and his pals "were rough and rugged . . . masculine little kids." He said,

> When you're a little boy, you hang out with other little boys and you do little boy things. You know, you burn ants and things like that. You just don't hang out with females because you don't want to be a wuss, you don't play with dolls, you don't whine, you don't cry . . . you do boy things, you know, guy stuff.

Being masculine, in other words, means being not-female. The masculinity ideal involves detachment and independence. The men interviewed indicated that emotions and behaviors typically associated with women were inappropriate within the male homosocial group. Among the emotions and behaviors considered most inappropriate, and most highly stigmatized, were those associated with feminine expressions of intimacy (e.g., talking "feelings"). As one of the men interviewed explained, "I usually talk about 'things' rather than getting into your head and asking, you know, that real intimate stuff."

This suppression of feminine emotions is more than merely a means of establishing individual masculinity. Emotional detachment is one way in which gender hierarchies are maintained. Expressing emotions signifies weakness and is devalued, whereas emotional detachment signifies strength and is valued (Cancian 1987).

In their discussions of feelings, the men hesitated; none of them made consistent use of the word *feelings*. Instead of feelings, they referred to "personal stuff," "those things," and "those matters," and when asked, many indicated that "ultimately you're doing it alone." The expectation is that "because you're going to be in situations where you're away from any support system . . . you're going to have to handle your stuff alone."

What these men explained was that within the male homosocial group, emotional detachment is viewed not only as desirable but as imperative. Those who do express their intimate emotions are excluded. On this point, the interviewees were quite clear: "If I was having a beer with a friend and they started crying, I would suspect that that person, if it were a male . . . I'd suspect that that person didn't have a very good definition of the social situation." If a guy did start crying, this interviewee was asked, where would that put him in relation to other guys? "Hmm, well, since . . . actually that would put him on the outs." The repercussion for violating the hegemonic meaning of emotional detachment, in other words, is to be "put on the outs," that is, to be ostracized from one's male homosocial group. Interviewees explained that violations of the norm of emotional detachment do not result in an alteration of the norm but instead result in the exclusion of the violator (see Schur 1984).

Data collected through observations clearly supported the pattern described by the men interviewed. Emotional detachment was exercised in even the most sensitive of topics. Two men observed, for example, appeared rather matter-of-face as they discussed the marital problems that one of the men was experiencing: "Think of it this way, ya got a toothache . . . You've got to have it taken out of you're gonna live with the bitch. Unless you bite the bullet and get the goddamn thing pulled out, you're gonna live with the pain." Feelings, as discussed by these two men, were something to "get over," not to experience — much less express. One man, when questioned about the possible repercussions for expressing feelings in the context of the male homosocial group, explained that feelings are "something for us all to joke about" because

> you certainly don't want to take things too seriously and have to deal with the heavy side, the emotional side to it. . . . Tears are a very extreme thing in these male circles, partly because its messy. . . . It has a lot to do with not looking soft and weak because if you do . . . it makes it difficult for men to have relationships with each other.

He explained that "developing emotional types of relationships with each other" is something men stereotypically do not do. Hegemonic masculinity is not expressed and maintained through excessive emotionality. This distinction separates the boys from the girls as well as the men who fit the hegemonic norm from those who do not. Through emotional detachment, the meanings formed in regard to masculinity are exaggerated so as to distinguish clearly that which all men are not, that is, female. The burden for demonstrating difference is on those trying to avoid the default meanings. Difference becomes an aspect of self in which men have a valued investment.

Departures from the norm of emotional detachment, however, do exist. Individual departures reflect an understanding of the dominant meanings but not necessarily an incorporation of them into one's self-concept. One man explained that although most men "do what the culture says and hide it" (i.e., hide their feelings), he had hoped to be able to express his feelings with other men: "A couple of times when I was hurting, uhm, I did kind of see out a couple of male friends and I was really disappointed. . . . It was like they were embarrassed, you know, to talk about that shit, and so, uh, fuck it!" Five of the men who participated in the in-depth interviews and three of the four who participated in the follow-up interviews expressed discrepancies between hegemonic masculinity and their own masculinity. Each explained that although they knew they were *supposed* to separate themselves from things considered feminine, they did not assess their own identities to be as polarized as the hegemonic form would suggest.

> It was really unfortunate. As I grew older, I really wished that I wasn't so detached from my mom. I'm not that way now, though. After a while, I stopped caring about what everybody else thought. I mean, the intimate side got pushed aside for so long because that's not what "real" men are supposed to do. I got over it, though. . . . I guess I'm not what "real" men are supposed to be.

The degree to which the masculinity meanings individuals hold for themselves correspond to the meanings of hegemonic masculinity may vary over time and from person to person. The point, however, is that although individual conceptualizations of masculinity depart from the hegemonic norm, nonhegemonic meanings are suppressed due to perceptions of "appropriate" masculinity. Even in a community where notions of the "new man" are common and where antisexist attitudes are often expected, hegemonic patterns of masculinity prevail. One whose masculinity conceptualization is nonhegemonic still understands himself as "not what 'real' mean are *supposed* to be" (emphasis added).

The men who made the distinction between self-masculinity and hegemonic masculinity made three things clear. First, they explained that hegemonic masculinity was the form that prevailed in their interactions with other men throughout childhood and adolescence. Second, they asserted that when they found themselves in homosocial situations in the present, the expectation of emotional detachment continued to prevail. Third, they described themselves in the present as more heterosocially than homosocially oriented. These men explained that they did not *prefer* exclusively male social interaction groups. In sum, homosocial and heterosocial masculinity meanings are clearly differentiated. For these men, homosocial masculinity was characterized by emotional detachment, whereas heterosocial masculinity downplayed these factors.

COMPETITION:
"IT'S A PECKING ORDER BETWEEN MALES"

Competition with other men provides a stage for establishing self both as an individual and as appropriately masculine. Competition also contributes to the perpetuation of male dominance. When asked to explain what competition meant to him, one interviewee replied,

> By nature I'm terribly competitive. I suppose one's ego gets wrapped around the things that you do. It's pretty important for me to win because I do have my ego wrapped up in that [games] and so, uhm, you know when I play a game at a party or whatever I kind of expect to win and play pretty fiercely.

To establish self as not female, young men seek out other men with whom to display "non-femaleness" (Johnson 1988). Homosocial group inter-actions provide feedback and support for masculinity self-conceptualization. In this sense, masculinity conceptualization is itself a form of competition. Four men described competition as a critical part of their self-conceptualizations and stressed that the competitions they preferred were those with men. Men, they believed, could understand the intensity and importance of competition, whereas women seemed less accepting and less understanding. When asked about participating in athletics with women, one interviewee responded that "women start getting angry at you and it gets ugly" when "you start getting really intense." Another added that "women typically don't want to play [bas-ketball] or sort of want to but feel they'll be intimidated or whatever."

The men who described themselves as less competitive (or noncompeti-tive), on the other hand, explained that they considered the intensity with which other men engaged in competitions (especially sports) as relatively unimportant for themselves. At the same time, however, these men recognized the *expectations* of masculinity to be competitive. One man explained,

> Guys don't know what it means not to be competitive. Even those men who tell you that competition is silly know they have to [compete]. It's like oth-erwise you're gonna get walked on. Nobody appreciates that. I'm not as aggressive as most guys, but I can sure act it.

Again, the norms and expectations of hegemonic masculinity and individual conceptualizations do not necessarily fit; further, among the less competitive men, nonhegemonic masculinity and hegemonic masculinity meanings differ by sociality. Men whose conceptualizations of masculinity were nonhege-monic specified their lack of preference for homosocial interactions in both sporting and nonsporting activities. Men whose conceptualizations of mas-culinity were consistent with the hegemonic form specified a clear preference for homosocial interactions in sports. Homosociality corresponded with a focus on competitiveness, whereas heterosociality deemphasized competition. Homosocial and heterosocial meanings were clearly differentiated. In male homosocial groups, a man risks loss of status and self-esteem unless he competes. The meaning of competition is assumed under male homosocial circumstances, and violators of this norm are disadvantaged.

SEXUAL OBJECTIFICATION:
"YOU KNOW, WOMEN WERE 'OTHERED' EARLY"

The competitions that support hegemonic masculinity continue throughout life in a variety of forms. Among the forms of competitions in which men engage are those that involve the objectification of women. Men often compete with one another in efforts to gain the attention and affections of women and in boasting about their sexual exploits. Observations revealed numerous stories about sexual objectification of women. In male homosocial conversations, references were made to women as "them," as clearly "other," as the nonthreatening "girl," and/or as objects to be used for sexual pleasure. While the use of these terms may or may not imply a conscious effort on the part of the speaker to objectify, they promote meanings that support hegemonic masculinity nonetheless.

The men not only explicated the objectification of women, they also explained and demonstrated the competition for objectified women. These competitions illustrate the interconnectedness of the meanings of emotional detachment, competition, and objectification. Conversations overheard at the deli/lounge, for example, shifted frequently from "shop talk" to competitive sex talk. Bantering sessions, in which one-upsmanship on stories of sexual exploits was the name of the game, were frequently overheard. For example, one man began,

> I've run across those kind. . . . I'll tell 'em, "I'll buy ya a beer." [And the hypothetical woman replies,] "Na, I'll buy you a beer." Then I'm thinkin' she's ready to get outa there with me. I just want one I can step out with, shoot up her, and get back in the bar in 5 or 10 minutes.

Another man then added his own story:

> Aw, shit, I had one down near Vegas. . . . Well, to make a long story short, when it was time to hit the rack we went back to her room. . . . We found a bucket of ice and a bottle of liquor at the door with a note from some other guy attached to it. . . . I just went ahead and drank the stuff and screwed her!

Not to be outdone, the remaining participant in the discussion followed with an account of his own:

> Yeah, one night I had a couple of beers, then went out to that country and western bar. . . . She was a bartender there. I'm tellin' ya, she was hanging all over me so much that the other bartender had to get on to her. Then later,

she came knockin' on my trailer door. I thought, "What the hell, Judy won't find out, let's hop to it." She was a wicked thing.

Such conversations, according to the men interviewed, occur frequently but are less likely to be carried out with verbal explicitness when a woman or women actually join the interaction. In this case, the conversation will likely shift; but, as my interviewees explained, the competition will continue. The questions, "What happens if a woman enters the scene where you are engaging in a conversation with another man or men?" prompted the following response: "Weird. Weird setup . . . because everybody is checking everybody else out . . . it's uncomfortable for everybody. You know, people are checking each other out. We'd see her as an issue of conquest." The men interviewed explained that men in homosocial groups both objectify and compete for women. When asked to describe the nature of interactions between men when an "available" woman is present among the group, one man explained, "It's competitive, you see, and it's a pecking order between men. If you do not peck, you get pecked. And so, one of the things over which there is a great deal of pecking is women."

To be "pecked" is an undesirable experience — one to be avoided if a man wishes to maintain status within the male homosocial group. Objectification of women and men's competitiveness over objectified women constitute the very essence of what hegemonic masculinity means in this society (Connell 1992). Not all men view themselves in accordance with hegemonic masculinity, however, when it comes to objectifying women. Even so, men often go along with hegemonic norms to avoid being pecked. All of the men interviewed, when asked how an individual man avoids being pecked by other members of the group, explained that, on the one hand, they knew what the rules of the game were because

> there's always an assessment going on in the group. Always. . . . Some guys will go along but wouldn't make a degrading comment about women themselves. But when some guy says something, because you want to be a member of the group, it becomes, "Yeah." You follow the lead.

Some men argued, however, that these hegemonic rules did not fit their own identities:

> That stuff [sexual objectification of women] doesn't interest me terribly much because for the most part I don't really talk about those things and I don't hang out with men who do. It's a very nasty type of chat, and the goal seems to be to hurt somebody anyway.

Although the rules of hegemonic masculinity included sexual objectification, some individual conceptualizations minimized and/or disregarded its importance. Even among those men who rejected hegemonic masculinity for themselves, however, the hegemonic norm for sexual objectification prevailed in male homosocial groups. In fact, none of the men in the study, for example, mentioned ever verbally rejecting these hegemonic meanings in their all-male groups. The meanings of emotional detachment, competitiveness, and sexual objectification all were understood and behaviorally followed. Hegemonic masculinity was maintained despite individual departures from the norm, as individual departures were suppressed in homosocial settings. Nonhegemonic masculinity was subordinated through relegation to heterosocial settings. Emotional detachment, competitiveness, and the sexual objectification of women remained as the criteria to which men are held accountable, especially in all-male interactions.

CONCLUSIONS: HEGEMONIC MASCULINITY AND THE GENDER ORDER

Hegemonic masculinity is consistently and continually recreated despite individual conceptualizations that contradict hegemonic meanings. Violations of the norms of hegemonic masculinity typically fail to produce alterations in the gender order; instead, they result in penalties to violators. With particular attention to the meanings that help sustain a pecking order among men, I have outlined some of the processes that pose barriers to gender equality in the United States, that is, the devaluation of meanings considered feminine, the suppression of these meanings in male heterosexual homosocial settings, and the relegation of nonhegemonic masculinity to heterosocial settings. Hegemonic masculinity, as demonstrated here, prevailed even in an academic community where ideals of gender equality are generally promoted. Reification of existing gender arrangements continues despite individual conflicts with hegemonic masculinity. The contradictions that nonhegemonic masculinity meanings (e.g., expression of intimate emotions, cooperation, and identification with women) potentially pose to dominant masculinity patterns are suppressed in male homosocial heterosexual interactions, inhibiting change. When individual departures from dominant masculinity are experienced as private dissatisfactions rather than as reason for contesting the social construction of masculinity, hegemonic patterns persist.

Because the barriers that distinguish appropriate from inappropriate masculinity generally are not accomplished through reconceptualization of individual masculinity alone, recasting the gender order in more favorable terms must also involve changes instigated at levels of social organization beyond that of social interaction. Subversion of widely accepted gender beliefs, attitudes, and expectations requires special attention to the processes that facilitate their *institutionalization*. That which must be continually challenged and ultimately eradicated in terms of masculinity, therefore, is the taken-for-granted assumption that being male means being emotionally detached, competitive, and supportive of the sexual objectification of women as well as the assumption that men whose identities do not embody these meanings are not true men. These changes must take place not only within heterosocial contexts but also within homosocial contexts and throughout all social institutions. In even broader terms, the goal yet to be accomplished is the *degenderization* of meanings. In other words, emotional detachment, competitiveness, and the sexual objectification of women must cease to exist as criteria by which being a man is measured. Indeed, the beliefs, attitudes, and expectations that decree the valuation and/or devaluation of distinctive masculine and feminine meanings in the first place must be deconstructed.

NOTE

1. Leisure situations, rather than work-related situations, were focused on to specifically highlight social interaction preferences.

REFERENCES

Burke, Peter J. 1980 The self: Measurement requirements from an interactionist perspective. *Social Psychology Quarterly* 43:18–29.

Burke, Peter J., and Donald C. Reitzes. 1981. The link between identity and role performance. *Social Psychology Quarterly* 44:83–92.

Cancian, Francesca M. 1987. *Love in America: Gender and self-development.* Cambridge, UK: Cambridge University Press.

Chodorow, Nancy. 1978. *The reproduction of mothering.* Berkeley: University of California Press.

———. 1980. Gender, relation, and difference in psychoanalytic perspective. In *The future of difference*, edited by Hester Eisenstein and Alice Jardine. Boston: G. K. Hall.

Connell, R. W. 1987. *Gender and power: Society, the person, and sexual politics.* Stanford, CA: Stanford University Press.

———. 1992. A very straight gay: Masculinity, homosexual experience, and the dynamics of gender. *American Sociological Review* 57:735–51.

Gilligan, Carol. 1982. *In a different voice: Psychological theory and women's development.* Cambridge, MA: Harvard University Press.

Johnson, Miriam. 1988. *Strong mothers, weak wives.* Berkeley: University of California Press.

Kaufman, Michael. 1994. Men, feminism, and the men's contradictory experiences of power. In *Theorizing masculinities*, edited by Harry Brod and Michael Kaufman. Thousand Oaks, CA: Sage.

Kimmel, Michael S. 1990. After fifteen years: The impact of the sociology of masculinity on the masculinity of sociology. In *Men, masculinities, and social theory*, edited by Jeff Hearn and David Morgan. London: Unwin Hyman.

Lehn, Gregory K. 1992. Homophobia among men: Supporting and defining the male role. In *Men's lives*, edited by Michael S. Kimmel and Michael A. Messner. New York: Macmillan.

Lipman-Bluman, Jean. 1976. Toward a homosocial theory of sex roles: An explanation of the sex segregation of social institutions. *Signs: Journal of Women and Culture and Society* 1:15–31.

Messner, Michael A. 1992a. Boyhood, organized sports, and the construction of masculinity. In *Men's lives*, edited by Michael S. Kimmel and Michael A. Messner. New York: Macmillan.

———. 1992b. *Power at play: Sports and the problem of masculinity.* Boston: Beacon.

Phillips, Gerald M. 1986. Men talking to men about their relationships. *American Behavioral Scientist* 29:321–41.

Schur, Edwin M. 1984. *Labeling women deviant: Gender, stigma, and social control.* New York: Random House.

Thomas, Alison. 1990. The significance of gender politics in men's accounts of their "gender identity." In *Men, masculinities, and social theory*, edited by Jeff Hearn and David Morgan. London: Unwin Hyman.

West, Candace, and Don H. Zimmerman. 1987. Doing gender. *Gender & Society* 1:125–51.

●
○

SUSAN BORDO
Reading the Slender Body

Susan Bordo is Professor of English and Gender and Women's Studies at the University of Kentucky. She has written several best-selling and highly esteemed books, including Unbearable Weight: Feminism, Western Culture and the Body *(1993) and* The Male Body: A New Look at Men in Public and Private *(1999). This selection is taken from a collection of essays titled* Body/Politics: Women and the Discourses of Science *(1989).*

In the late-Victorian era, arguably for the first time in the West, those who could afford to eat well began systematically to deny themselves food in pursuit of an aesthetic ideal.[1] Certainly, other cultures had "dieted." Aristocratic Greek culture made a science of the regulation of food intake, in the service of the attainment of self-mastery and moderation.[2] Fasting, aimed at spiritual purification and domination of the flesh, was an important part of the repertoire of Christian practice in the Middle Ages.[3] These forms of "diet" can clearly be viewed as instruments for the development of a "self"—whether an "inner" self, for the Christians, or a public self, for the Greeks—constructed as an arena in which the deepest possibilities for human excellence might be realized. Rituals of fasting and asceticism were therefore reserved for the select few, aristocratic or priestly in caste, deemed capable of achieving such excellence of spirit. In the late nineteenth century, by contrast, the practices of body management begin to be middle-class preoccupations, and concern with diet becomes attached to the pursuit of an idealized physical weight or shape; it becomes a project in service of "body" rather than "soul." Fat, not appetite or desire, is the declared enemy, and people begin to measure their dietary achievements by the numbers on the scale rather than the level of their mastery of impulse and excess. The bourgeois "tyranny of slenderness" (as Kim Chernin has called it[4]) had begun its ascendancy (particularly over women), and with it the development of numerous technologies—diet, exercise, and, later on, chemicals and surgery—aimed at a purely physical transformation.

Today, we have become acutely aware of the massive and multifaceted nature of such technologies and the industries built around them. To the degree that a popular critical consciousness exists, however, it has been focused largely (and not surprisingly) on what has been viewed as pathological or extreme—on the unfortunate minority who become "obsessed," or go "too far." Television talk shows features tales of disasters caused by stomach stapling, gastric bubbles, gastrointestinal bypass operations, liquid diets, compulsive exercising. Magazines warn of the dangers of fat-reduction surgery and lipo-suction. Books and articles about bulimia and anorexia nervosa proliferate. The portrayal of eating disorders by the popular media is often lurid and sen-sational; audiences gasp at pictures of skeletal bodies or at item-by-item descriptions of the volumes of food eaten during an average binge. Such pre-sentations of the volumes of food eaten during an average binge. Such presen-tations encourage a "side show" experience of the relationship between the ("normal") audience and those on view ("the freaks"). To the degree that the audience may nonetheless recognize themselves in the behavior or reported experiences of those on stage, they confront themselves as "pathological" or outside the norm.

Of course, many of these behaviors *are* outside the norm, if only be-cause of the financial resources they require. But preoccupation with fat, diet, and slenderness are not.[5] Indeed, such preoccupation may function as one of the most powerful "normalizing" strategies of our century, ensuring the production of self-monitoring and self-disciplining "docile bodies," sensitive to any departure from social norms, and habituated to self-improvement and transformation in the service of those norms.[6] Seen in this light, the focus on "pathology," disorder, accident, unexpected disaster, and bizarre behavior obscures the normalizing function of the technologies of diet and body man-agement. For women, who are subject to such controls more profoundly and, historically, more ubiquitously than men, the focus on "pathology" (unless embedded in a political analysis) diverts recognition from a central means of the reproduction of gender.

This paper is part of a larger analysis of the contemporary preoccupation with slenderness as it functions within a modern, "normalizing" machinery of power in general, and, in particular, as it functions to reproduce gender-relations. For the purposes of this larger analysis, I make use of Foucault's distinction between two arenas of the social construction of the modern body—the "intelligible body" and the "useful body": (1) the representational, and (2) the practical, direct locus of social control, through which culture is converted into automatic, habitual bodily activity. The "intelligible body" includes scientific, philosophic, and aesthetic representations of the body, norms of beauty, models of health, and so forth. These representations, how-ever, may also be seen as legislating a set of *practical* rules and regulations (some explicit, some implicit), through which the living body is "trained, shaped, obeys, and responds . . . ;" becomes, in short, a socially adapted and "useful body."[7] So, for example, the seventeenth-century philosophic conception of body-as-machine arguably both mirrored and provided a metaphysical and technical model for an increasingly automated productive machinery of labor.

Understanding the "political anatomy" (as Foucault would call it) of the slender body requires the interrogation of both "useful" and "intelligible" arenas—interrogation of the practices or "disciplines" of diet and exercise which structure the organization of time, space, and the experience of embodiment for subjects; and, in our image-bedazzled culture, interrogation of the popular representations through which meaning is crystallized, symbolized, metaphorically encoded, and transmitted. My overall argument emphasizes the primacy of practice for evaluating the role of bodies in the nexus of power relations. In this light, we should certainly be "politically" disturbed by recent statistics on the number of young girls (80% of the nine-year-olds surveyed in one study[8]) who are making dedicated dieting the organizing principle of their days. This particular paper, however, will approach the normalizing role of diet and exercise via an examination of the representational body—the cultural imagery of ideal slenderness—which now reigns, increasingly across racial and ethnic boundaries, as the dominant body-standard of our culture.[9] More specifically, I wish to pursue here Mary Douglas's insight that images of the "microcosm"—the physical body—may symbolically reproduce central vulnerabilities and anxieties of the macrocosm—the "social body."[10] I will explore this insight by "reading" (as the text or surface on which culture is symbolically "written") some dominant meanings that are connected, in our time, to the pursuit of slenderness.[11]

Decoding cultural images is a complex business—particularly when one considers the wide variety of ethnic, racial, and class differences that intersect with, resist, and give distinctive meaning to dominant, normalizing imagery. Even on the level of homogenizing imagery (my focus in this paper), contemporary slenderness admits of many variants and has multiple and often mutually "deconstructing" meanings. To give just one example, an examination of the photographs and copy of current fashion advertisements suggests that today's boyish body ideals, as in the 1920s, symbolize a new freedom, a casting off of the encumbrance of domestic, reproductive femininity. But when the same slender body is depicted in poses that set it off against the resurgent muscularity and bulk of the current male body-ideal, other meanings emerge. In these gender/oppositional poses, the degree to which slenderness carries connotations of fragility, defenselessness, and lack of power over against a decisive male occupation of social space is dramatically represented.

Since it is impossible for any cultural analyst to do a full reading of the text of slenderness in the space of a single article, I will instead attempt to construct an argument about some elements of the cultural context that has conditioned the flourishing of eating disorders—anorexia, bulimia, and obesity—in our time. The first step in that argument is a decoding of the contemporary slenderness ideal so as to reveal the psychic anxieties and moral valuations contained within it—valuations concerning the correct and incorrect management of impulse and desire. In the process, I will be describing a key contrast between two different symbolic functions of body shape and size: (1) the designation of social position, e.g., marking class status or gender role; and (2) the outer indication of the state of the "soul." Next, aided by the significant work of Robert Crawford, I will turn to the "macro-body" of consumer culture, in order to demonstrate how the "correct" management of desire in that culture, requiring as it does a contradictory "double-bind" construction of personality, inevitably produces an unstable bulimic personality-type as its norm, along with the contrasting extremes of obesity and self-starvation.[12] These symbolize, I will argue, the contradictions of the "social body"—contradictions that make self-management a continual and virtually impossible task in our culture. Finally, I will introduce gender into this symbolic framework, showing how additional resonances (concerning the cultural management of female desire, on the one hand, and female flight from a purely reproductive destiny on the other) have overdetermined slenderness as the current ideal for women.

SLENDERNESS AND CONTEMPORARY ANXIETY

In a recent edition of the magazine show *20/20*, several ten-year-old boys were shown some photos of fashion models. The models were pencil thin. Yet the pose was such that a small bulge of hip was forced, through the action of the body, into protuberance—as is natural, unavoidable on any but the most skeletal or the most tautly developed bodies. We bend over, we sit down, and the flesh coalesces in spots. These young boys, pointing to the hips, disgustedly pronounced the models to be "fat." Watching the show, I was appalled at the boys' reaction. Yet I couldn't deny that I had also been surprised at my own current perceptions while re-viewing female bodies in movies from the 1970s; what once appeared slender and fit now seemed loose and flabby. *Weight* was not the key element in these changed perceptions—my standards had not come to favor *thinner* bodies—but rather, I had come to expect a tighter, smoother, more "contained" body profile.

The self-criticisms of the anorectic, too, are usually focused on particular soft, protuberant areas of the body (most often the stomach) rather than on the body as a whole. Karen, in *Dying to Be Thin*, tries to dispel what she sees as the myth that the anorectic, even when emaciated, "misperceives" her body as fat:

> I hope I'm expressing myself properly here, because this is important. You have to understand. I don't see my whole body as fat. When I look in the mirror, I don't really see a fat person there. I see certain things about me that are really thin. Like my arms and legs. But I can tell the minute I eat certain things that my stomach blows up like a pig's. I know it gets distended. And it's disgusting. That's what I keep to myself—hug to myself.[13]

Or Barbara:

> Sometimes my body looks so bloated, I don't want to get dressed. I like the way it looks for exactly two days each month: usually, the eighth and ninth days after my period. Every other day, my breasts, my stomach—they're just

awful lumps, bumps, bulges. My body can turn on me at any moment; it is an out-of-control mass of flesh.[14]

Much has been made of such descriptions, from both psychoanalytic and feminist perspectives. But for now, I wish to pursue these images of unwanted bulges and erupting stomachs in another direction than that of gender symbolism. I want to consider them as a metaphor for anxiety about internal processes out of control—uncontained desire, unrestrained hunger, uncontrolled impulse. Images of bodily eruption frequently function symbolically in this way in contemporary horror movies—as in recent werewolf films (*The Howling, A Teen-Age Werewolf in London,*) and in David Cronenberg's remake of *The Fly*. The original *Fly* imagined a mechanical joining of fly parts and person parts, a variation on the standard "half-man, half-beast" image. In Cronenberg's *Fly*, as in the werewolf genre, a new, alien, libidinous, and uncontrollable self literally bursts through the seams of the victims' old flesh. (A related, frequently copied image occurs in *Alien*, where a parasite erupts from the chest of the human host.) While it is possible to view these new images as technically inspired by special-effects possibilities, I suggest that deeper psycho-cultural anxieties are being given form.

Every year, I present my metaphysics class with Delmore Schwartz's classic "The Heavy Bear" as an example of a dualist imagination of self, in which the body is constructed as an alien, unconscious, appetitive force, thwarting and befouling the projects of the soul. Beginning with an epigraph from Alfred North Whitehead, "The withness of the body," Schwartz's poem makes "the heavy bear who goes with [him]" into "A caricature, a swollen shadow,/A stupid clown of the spirit's motive." Last year, for the first time, quite a few students interpreted the poem as describing the predicament of an obese man. This may indicate the increasing literalism of my students. But it also is suggestive of the degree to which the specter of "fat" dominates their imaginations, and codes their generation's anxieties about the body's potential for excess and chaos. In advertisements, the construction of the body as an alien attacker, threatening to erupt in an unsightly display of bulging flesh, is a ubiquitous cultural image. Until the last decade, excess weight was the target of most ads for diet products; today, one is much more likely to find the enemy constructed as bulge, fat, or "flab." "Now" (a typical ad runs), "get rid of those embarrassing bumps, bulges, large stomach, flabby breasts and buttocks. Feel younger, and help prevent cellulite build-up. . . . Have a nice shape with no tummy." To achieve such results (often envisoned as the absolute eradication of body: e.g., "no tummy") a violent assault on the enemy is usually required; bulges must be "attacked" and "destroyed," fat "burned," and stomachs (or, more disgustedly, "guts") must be "busted" and "eliminated." The increasing popularity of liposuction, a far from totally safe technique developed specifically to suck out the unwanted bulges of people of normal weight (it is not recommended for the obese), suggests how far out disgust with bodily bulges has gone. The ideal here is of a body that is absolutely tight, contained, "bolted down," firm (in other words, body that is protected against eruption from within, whose internal processes are under control). Areas that are soft, loose, or "wiggly" are unacceptable, even on extremely thin bodies. Cellulite management, like liposuction, has nothing to do with weight loss, and everything to do with the quest for firm bodily margins.

This perspective helps illuminate an important continuity of meaning between compulsive dieting and bodybuilding in our culture, and reveals why it has been so easy for contemporary images of female attractiveness to oscillate back and forth between a spare "minimalist" look and a solid, muscular, athletic look. The coexistence of these seemingly disparate images does not indicate that a postmodern universe of empty, endlessly differentiating images now reigns. Rather, the two ideals, though superficially very different, are united in battle against a common platoon of enemies: the soft, the loose; unsolid, excess flesh. It is perfectly permissible in our culture (even for women) to have substantial weight and bulk—so long as it is tightly managed. On the other hand, to be slim is simply not enough—so long as the flesh jiggles. Here, we arrive at one source of insight into why it is that the image of ideal slenderness has grown thinner and thinner over the last decade, and why women with extremely slender bodies often still see themselves as "fat." Unless one goes the route of muscle building, it is virtually impossible to achieve a flabless, excess-less body unless one trims very near to the bone.

SLENDERNESS AND THE STATE OF THE SOUL

This "moral" (and, as we shall see, economic) coding of the fat/slender body in terms of its capacities for self-containment and the control of impulse and desire represents the culmination of a developing historical change in the social symbolism of body weight and size. Until the late nineteenth century, the central discriminations marked were those of class, race, and gender; the body indicated one's social identity and "place." So, for example, the bulging stomachs of successful mid-nineteenth-century businessmen and politicians were a symbol of bourgeois success, an outward manifestation of their accumulated wealth.[15] By contrast, the gracefully slender body announced aristocratic status; disdainful of the bourgeois need to display wealth and power ostentatiously, it commanded social space invisibly rather than aggressively, seemingly above the commerce in appetite or the need to eat. Subsequently, this ideal began to be appropriated by the status-seeking middle class, as slender wives became the showpieces of their husbands' success,[16] I will return to the gender symbolism of slenderness later.

Corpulence went out of middle-class vogue at the end of the century (even William Howard Taft, who had weighed over three hundred pounds while in office, went on a reducing diet); social power had come to be less dependent on the sheer accumulation of material wealth and more connected to the ability to control and manage the labor and resources of others. At the same time, excess body weight came to be seen as reflecting moral or personal inadequacy, or lack of will.[17] These associations are only possible in a culture of "overbundance" (that is, in a society in which those who control the production of "culture" have more than enough to eat). The moral requirement to diet depends upon the material preconditions that make the *choice* to "diet" an option and the possibility of personal "excess" a reality. Although slenderness has hitherto retained some of its traditional class-associations ("a woman can never be too rich or too thin"), the importance of this equation has eroded considerably over the last decade. Increasingly, the size and shape of the body has come to operate as a marker of personal, internal order (or disorder)—as a symbol for the state of the soul.

Consider one particularly clear example, that of changes in the meaning of the muscled body. Muscularity has had a variety of cultural meanings (until recently largely reserved for male bodies) which have prevented the well-developed body from playing too great a role in middle-class conceptions of attractiveness. Of course, muscles have symbolized masculine power. But at the same time, they have been associated with manual labor and chain gangs (and thus with lower-class and even criminal status), and suffused with racial meaning (via numerous film representations of sweating, glistening bodies belonging to black slaves and prizefighters). Given the racial and class biases of our culture, they were associated with the body as material, unconscious, or animalistic. Today, however, the well-muscled body has become a cultural icon; "working out" is a glamorized and sexualized yuppie activity. No longer signifying lower-class status (except when developed to extremes, at which point the old association of muscles with brute, unconscious materiality surfaces once more), the firm, developed body has become a symbol of correct *attitude*; it means that one "cares" about oneself and how one appears to others, suggesting willpower, energy, control over infantile impulse, the ability to "make something" of oneself. "You exercise, you diet," says Heather Locklear, promoting Bally Matrix Fitness Centre on television, "and you can do anything you want." Muscles express sexuality, but controlled, managed sexuality that is not about to erupt in unwanted and embarrassing display.[18]

To the degree that the question of class still operates in all this, it relates to the category of social mobility (or lack of it) rather than class *location*. So for example, when associations of fat and lower-class status exist, they are usually mediated by qualities of attitude or "soul"—fat being perceived as indicative of laziness, lack of discipline, unwillinginess to conform, and absence of all those "managerial" abilities that, according to the dominant ideology, confer upward mobility. Correspondingly, in popular teen movies such as *Flashdance* and *Vision Quest*, the ability of the (working-class) heroine and hero to pare; prune, tighten, and master the body operates as a clear symbol of successful upward aspiration, of the penetrability of class boundaries to those who have "the right stuff." These movies (as one title explicitly suggests) are contemporary "quest myths"; like their prototype, *Rocky*, they follow the struggle of an individual to attain a personal grail, against all odds, and through numerous trials. But unlike the film quests of a previous era (which sent Mr. Smith to Washington and Mr. Deeds to town to battle the respective social evils of corrupt government and big business), *Flashdance* and *Vision Quest* render the hero's and heroine's commitment, will, and spiritual integrity through the metaphors of weight loss, exercise, and tolerance of and ability to conquer physical pain and exhaustion. (In *Vision Quest*, for example, the audience is encouraged to admire the young wrestler's perseverance when he ignores the fainting spells and nosebleeds caused by his rigorous training and dieting.)

Not surprisingly, young people with eating disorders often thematize their own experience in similar terms, as in the following excerpt from an interview with a young woman runner:

> Well, I had the willpower. I could train for competition, and I could turn down food any time. I remember feeling like I was on a constant high. And the pain? Sure, there was pain. It was incredible. Between the hunger and the muscle pain from the constant workouts? I can't tell you how much I hurt.
>
> You may think I was crazy to put myself through constant, intense pain. But you have to remember. I was fighting a battle. And when you get hurt in a battle, you're proud of it. Sure, you may scream inside, but if you're brave and really good, then you take it quietly, because you know it's the price you pay for winning. And I needed to win. I really felt that if I didn't win, I would die . . . all these enemy troops were coming at me, and I had to outsmart them. If I could discipline myself enough—if I could keep myself lean and strong—then I could win. The pain was just a natural thing I had to deal with.[19]

As in *Vision Quest*, the external context is training for an athletic event. But here, too, that goal becomes subordinated to an internal one. The real battle, ultimately, is with the self. At this point, the limitations of the brief history that I presented in the opening paragraph of this paper are revealed. In that paragraph, the contemporary preoccupation with diet is contrasted to historical projects of body management suffused with moral meaning. In this section, however, I have suggested that examination of even the most "shallow" representations (teen movies) discloses a moral ideology—one, in fact, seemingly close to the aristocratic. Greek ideal described by Foucault in *The Use of Pleasure*. The central element of that ideal, as Foucault describes it, is "an agonistic relation with the self"—aimed, not at the extirpation of desire and hunger in the interest of "purity" (as in the Christian strain of dualism), but at a "virile" mastery of desire through constant "spiritual combat."[20]

For the Greeks, however, the "virile" mastery of desire operated within a culture that valorized moderation. The culture of contemporary body-management, struggling to manage desire within a system that is dedicated to the proliferation of desireable commodities, is very different. In cultural fantasies such as *Vision Quest* and *Flashdance*, self-mastery is presented as an attainable and stable state; but, as I will argue in the next section of this paper, the reality of the contemporary agonism of the self is another matter entirely.

SLENDERNESS AND THE SOCIAL BODY

Mary Douglas, looking on the body as a system of "natural symbols" that reproduce social categories and concerns, has argued that anxiety about the maintenance of rigid bodily boundaries (manifested, for example, in rituals and prohibitions concerning excreta, saliva, and the strict delineation of "inside" and "outside") is most evident and intense in societies whose external boundaries are under attack.[21] Let me hypothesize, similarly, that preoccupation with the "internal" management of the body (i.e., management of its desires) is produced by instabilities in the "macro-regulation" of desire within the system of the social body.

In advanced consumer capitalism, as Robert Crawford has elegantly argued, an unstable, agonistic construction of personality is produced by the contradictory structure of economic life.[22] On the one hand, as "producer-selves," we must be capable of sublimating, delaying, repressing desires for immediate gratification; we must cultivate the work ethic. On the other hand, as "consumer-selves" we serve the system through a boundless capacity to capitulate to desire and indulge in impulse; we must become creatures who hunger for constant and immediate satisfaction. The regulation of desire thus becomes an ongoing problem, as we find ourselves continually besieged by temptation, while socially condemned for overindulgence. (It goes without saying that those who cannot afford to indulge, teased and frustrated by the culture, face different problems.)

Food and diet are central arenas for the expression of these contradictions. On television and in popular magazines with a flip of the page or barely a pause between commercials, images of luscious foods and the rhetoric of craving and desire are replaced by advertisements for grapefruit diets, low-calorie recipes, and exercise equipment. Even more disquieting than these manifest oppositions, however, are the constant attempts by advertisers to mystify them, suggesting that the contradiction doesn't really exist—that one *can* "have it all." Diets and exercise programs accordingly present themselves via the imagery of instant gratification ("From Fat to Fabulous in 21 Days," "Size 22 to Size 10 in No Time Flat," "Six Minutes to an Olympic-Class Stomach") and effortlessness ("3,000 Sit-Ups Without Moving an Inch . . . Ten Miles of Jogging Lying Flat on Your Back," "85 pounds Without Dieting," and even, shamelessly, "Exercise Without Exercise"). In reality, however, the opposition is not so easily reconciled. Rather, it presents a classic "double-bind," in which the self is torn in two mutually incompatible directions. The contradiction is not an abstract one but stems from the specific historical construction of a "consuming passion" from which all inclinations toward balance, moderation, rationality, and foresight have been excluded.

Conditioned to lose control at the very sight of desirable products, we can only master our desires through rigid defenses against them. The slender body codes the tantalizing ideal of a well-managed self in which all is "in order" despite the contradictions of consumer culture. Thus, whether or not the struggle is played out in terms of food and diet, many of us may find our lives vacillating between a daytime rigidly ruled by the "performance principle" while our nights and weekends capitulate to unconscious "letting go" (food, shopping, liquor, television, and other addictive drugs). In this way, the central contradiction of the system inscribes itself on our bodies, and bulimia emerges as a characteristic modern personality construction, precisely and explicitly expressing the extreme development of the hunger for unrestrained consumption (exhibited in the bulimic's uncontrollable food-binges) existing in unstable tension alongside the requirement that we sober up, "clean up our act," get back in firm control on Monday morning (the necessity for purge — exhibited in the bulimic's vomiting, compulsive exercising, and laxative purges).

The same structural contradiction is also inscribed in what has been termed (incorrectly) the "paradox" that we have an "epidemic" of anorexia nervosa in this country "despite the fact that we have an overweight majority."[23] Far from paradoxical, the coexistence of anorexia and obesity reveals the instability of the contemporary personality construction, the difficulty of finding homeostasis between the "producer" and "consumer" aspects of the self. While bulimia embodies the unstable "double-bind" of consumer capitalism, anorexia and obesity embody an attempted "resolution" of that double-bind. Anorexia could therefore be seen as an extreme development of the capacity for self-denial and repression of desire (the work ethic in absolute "control"); obesity similarly points to an extreme capacity to capitulate to desire (consumerism in control). Both are rooted in the same consumer-culture construction of desire as overwhelming and overtaking the self. Given the construction, total submission or rigid defense become the only possible postures.[24]

Neither anorexia nor obesity is accepted by the culture as an appropriate response. The absolute conquest of hunger and desire (even in symbolic form) could never be tolerated by a consumer system — even if the Christian dualism of our culture also predisposes us to be dazzled by the anorectic's ability seemingly to transcend the flesh.[25] Anorectics are proud of this ability; but, as the disorder progresses, they usually feel the need to hide their skeletal bodies from those around them. If cultural attitudes toward the anorectic are ambivalent, however, reactions to the obese are not. As Marcia Millman documents in *Such a Pretty Face*, the obese elicit blinding rage and disgust in our culture, and are often viewed in terms that suggest an infant sucking hungrily, unconsciously at its mother's breasts — greedy, self-absorbed, lazy, without self-control or willpower.[26] People avoid sitting near the obese; comics feel no need to restrain their cruelty; socially, they are unacceptable at public functions (one man wrote to "Dear Abby," saying that he was planning to replace his brother and sister-in-law as honor attendants at his wedding, because "they are both quite overweight"). Significantly, the part of the obese anatomy most often targeted for vicious attack, and most despised by the obese themselves, is the stomach—symbol of consumption (in the case of the obese, unrestrained consumption taking over the organism; one of Marcia Millman's interviewees recalls how the husband of a friend called hers "an awful, cancerous-looking growth").[27]

SLENDERNESS, SELF-MANAGEMENT AND NORMALIZATION

Self-management in consumer culture, I have been arguing, becomes more elusive as it becomes more pressing. The attainment of an acceptable body is extremely difficult for those who do not come by it "naturally" (whether aided by genetics, metabolism, or high activity-level) and as the ideal becomes firmer and tauter it begins to exclude most people. Constant watchfulness over appetite and strenuous work on the body itself are required to conform to this ideal, while the most popular means of "correction"—dieting— often ensures its own failure, as the experience of deprivation leads to compensatory bingeing, with its attendant feelings of defeat, worthlessness, and loss of hope. Between the media images of self-containment and self-mastery and the reality of constant, everyday stress and anxiety about one's appearance lies the chasm which produces bodies habituated to self-monitoring and self-normalization.

Ultimately, the body (besides being evaluated for its success or failure at getting itself in order) is seen as demonstrating correct or incorrect attitudes toward the demands of normalization themselves. The obese and anorectic are therefore disturbing partly because they embody resistance to cultural norms. Bulimics, by contrast, typically strive for the conventionally attractive body shape dictated by their more "normative" pattern of managing desire. In the case of the obese, in particular, what is perceived as their defiant rebellion against normalization appears to be a source of the hostility they inspire. The anorectic at least pays homage to dominant cultural values, outdoing them in their own terms:

> I wanted people to look at me and see something special. I wanted to look in the face of a stranger and see admiration, so that I would know that I accomplished something that was just about impossible for most people, especially in our society. . . . From what I've seen, more people fail at losing weight than at any other single goal. I found out how to do what everyone else couldn't: I could lose as much or as little weight as I wanted. And that meant I was better than everyone else.[28]

The anorectic thus strives to stand above the crowd by excelling at its own rules; in so doing, however, she exposes the hidden penalties. But the obese—particularly those who claim to be happy although overweight—are perceived as not playing by the rules at all. While the rest of us struggle to be acceptable and "normal," they must not be allowed to get away with it; they must be put in their place, humiliated,and defeated.

A number of recent talk shows make this abundantly clear. On one, much of the audience reaction was given over to disbelief, and the attempt to prove to one obese woman that she was *not* happy: "I can't believe you don't want to be slim and beautiful, I just can't believe it," "I heard you talk a lot about how you feel good about yourself and you like yourself, but I really think you're kidding yourself," "It's hard for me to believe that Mary Jane is really happy . . . you don't fit into chairs, it's hard to get through the doorway. My God, on the subway, forget it." When Mary Jane persisted in her assertion that she was happy, she was warned, in a viciously self-righteous tone, that it wouldn't last: "Mary Jane, to be the way you are today, you had better start going on a diet soon, because if you don't you're going to get bigger and bigger and bigger. It's true."[29] On another show, in an effort to subdue an increasingly hostile and offensive audience, one of the doctor-guests kept trying to reassure them the "fat and happy" target of their attacks did not *really* mean that she didn't *want* to lose weight; rather, she was simply tired of trying and failing. This is the construction that allows people to give their sympathy to the obese, assuming as it does the obese person's acknowledgment that to be "normal" is the most desired goal, elusive only because of personal inadequacy. Those who are willing to present themselves as pitiable, in pain, and conscious of their own unattractiveness—often demonstrated, on these shows, by self-admissions about intimate physical difficulties, orgies of self-hate or descriptions of gross consumption of food, win the sympathy and concern of the audience.

SLENDERNESS AND GENDER

It has been amply documented that women in our culture are more tyrannized by the contemporary slenderness ideal than men, as they typically have been by beauty ideals in general. It is far more important to men than to women that their partners be slim.[30] Women are much more prone than men to perceive themselves as "too fat."[31] And, as is by now well known, girls and women are more likely to engage in crash dieting, laxative abuse, and compulsive exercising, and are far more vulnerable to eating disorders than males.[32] But eating disorders are not only "about" slenderness, any more than (as I have been arguing) *slenderness* is only—or even chiefly—about slenderness. My aim in this section, therefore, is not to "explain" facts about which so much has now been written from historical, psychological, and sociological points of view.

Rather, I want to remain with the image of the slender body, confronting it now both as a gendered body (the slender body as female body—the usual form in which the image is displayed) and as a body whose gender meaning is never neutral. This "layer" of gender-coded signification, suffusing other meanings, overdetermines slenderness as a contemporary ideal of specifically *female* attractiveness.

The exploration of contemporary slenderness as a metaphor for the correct management of desire becomes more adequate when we confront the fact that hunger has always been a potent cultural metaphor for female sexuality, power, and desire—from the blood-craving Kali, who in one representation is shown devouring her own entrails, to the language of insatiability and voraciousness that marks the fifteenth-century discourse on witches, to the "Man-Eater" of contemporary rock lyrics: "Oh, oh, here she comes, watch out boys, she'll chew you up." This is a message, too, as I have argued elsewhere, that eating-disordered women have often internalized when they experience their battle with hunger in the gendered terms of a struggle between male and female sides of the self (the former described as "spiritual" and disciplined, the latter as appetitive and dangerous). In the anorectic's lexicon, and throughout dominant Western religious and philosophical traditions, the "virile" capacity for self-management is decisively coded as male. By contrast, all those "bodily" spontaneities—hunger, sexuality, the emotions—seen as needful of containment and control have been culturally constructed and coded as female.[33]

The management of female desire becomes a particular problem in phallocentric cultures. Women's desires are "other," mysterious, threatening to erupt and challenge the patriarchal order. Some writers have argued that female hunger (as a code for female desire) is especially problematized during periods of disruption and change in established gender-relations and in the position of women. In such periods (of which our own is arguably one), nightmare images of what Bram Djikstra has called "the consuming woman" theme proliferate in art and literature (images representing female desire unleashed), while dominant constructions of the female body become more sylphlike—unlike the body of a fully-developed woman, more like that of an adolescent or boy (images that might be called female desire unborn). Djikstra argues such a case concerning the late nineteenth century, pointing to the devouring sphinxes and bloodsucking vampires of *fin-de-siècle* art, and the accompanying vogue for elongated, "sublimely emaciated" female bodies.[34] A commentator at the time vividly describes the emergence of a new body-style, not very unlike our own:

> Women can change the cut of their clothes at will, but how can they change the cut of their anatomies? And yet, they have done just this thing. Their shoulders have become narrow and slightly sloping, their throats more slender, their hips smaller and their arms and legs elongated to an extent that suggests that bed, upon which the robber, Procrustes, used to stretch his victims . . .[35]

The fact that our own era has witnessed a comparable shift (from the hourglass figure of the fifties to the lanky, "androgynous," increasingly elongated slender look that has developed over the past decade) cries out for interpretation. This shift, however, needs to be interpreted not only from the standpoint of male anxiety over women's desires (Djikstra's analysis, while crucial, is only half the story), but also from the standpoint of the women who embrace the "new look." For them, it may have a very different meaning; it may symbolize, not so much the containment of female desire, as its liberation from a domestic, reproductive destiny. The fact that the slender female body can carry both these (seemingly contradictory) meanings is one reason, I would suggest, for its compelling attraction in periods of gender-change.[36]

To elaborate this argument in more detail: earlier, I presented some quotations from interviews with eating-disordered women in which they describe their revulsion to breasts, stomachs, and all other bodily bulges. At that point, I subjected these quotations to a "gender-neutral" reading. While not rescinding that interpretation, I want to overlay it now with another reading, which I have developed at greater length elsewhere.[37] The characteristic anorexic revulsion toward hips, stomach, and breasts (often accompanied by a disgust at menstruation, and relief at amenorrhoea) might be viewed as expressing rebellion against maternal, domestic femininity—a femininity that represents both the suffocating control the anorectic experiences her own mother as having had over her, *and* the mother's actual lack of position and authority outside the domestic arena. Here we encounter another reason for anxiety over soft, protuberant body-parts. They evoke helpless infancy and symbolize maternal femininity as it has been constructed over the last hundred years in the West. That femininity, as Dorothy Dinnerstein has argued, is perceived as both frighteningly powerful and, as the child comes increasingly to recognize the hierarchical nature of the sexual division-of-labor, as utterly powerless.[38]

The most literal symbolic form of maternal femininity is represented by the nineteenth-century "hourglass" figure, emphasizing breasts and hips—the markers of reproductive femaleness—against a wasp waist.[39] At the same time, the sharp contrast between the female and male form, made possible by the use of corsets, bustles, and so forth, reproduced on the body the dualistic division of social and economic life into clearly defined "male" and "female" spheres. It is not until the post–World War II period, with its relocation of women from factory to home and its coercive bourgeois dualism of the happy-homemaker-mother and the responsible, "provider" father, that such clear bodily demarcation of "male" and "female" spheres surface again. The era of the cinch belt, the pushup bra, and Marilyn Monroe could be viewed, for the body, as an era of "resurgent Victorianism."[40] It was also the last coercively normalizing body-ideal to reign before the beginnings of the ascendancy of boyish slenderness, in the mid-1960s.

From this perspective, one might speculate that the boys who reacted with disgust or anxiety to fleshy female parts were reacting to evocations of maternal power, newly threatening in an age when women can bring their desires out of the confinements of the home and into the public, traditionally male arena.[41] The buxom Sophia Loren was a sex goddess in an era when women were trained to channel their energy and desire into home, husband, and family. Today, it is required of that energy, loose in the public world, to be stripped of its psychic resonances with maternal power, and normalized according to the professional "male" standards of the public arena. From the standpoint of male anxiety, the lean body of the professional businesswoman today may symbolize such a neutralization. With her body and her dress, she declares symbolic allegiance to the professional, white, male world, along with her lack of intention to subvert that arena with alternative "female values." At the same time, insofar as she is clearly "dressing up," *playing* "male" (almost always with a "softening" fashion touch to establish traditional feminine decorativeness), she represents no serious competition (symbolically, that is) to the "real men" of the workplace.

The cultural association of slenderness with reduced power and contracted social space is strikingly revealed, as I mentioned earlier, in fashion poses that juxtapose the slender female body against the currently quite solid and powerful male body ideal. But for many women, this "androgynous" ideal, far from symbolizing reduced power, may symbolize freedom (as it did in the 1890s and 1920s) from a reproductive destiny and a construction of femininity seen as constraining and suffocating. Correspondingly, taking on the accoutrements of the white, male world may be experienced as empowerment by women themselves, and as their chance to embody qualities—detachment, self-containment, self-mastery, control—that are highly valued in our culture.[42] The slender body, as I have argued earlier, symbolizes such qualities. "It was about power," says Kim Morgan, speaking of her obsession with slenderness, "that was the big thing . . . something I could throw in people's faces, and they would look at me and I'd only weigh this much, but I was strong and in control, and hey *you're* sloppy . . ."[43] The taking on of "male" power-as-self-mastery is another locus where shedding pounds and developing muscles, for all their surface dissimilarities, intersect. Appropriately, the new "Joy of Cooking" takes place in the gym, in one advertisement that shamelessly exploits the associations of female bodybuilding and liberation from a traditional, domestic destiny.

In the intersection of the gender-issues and more general cultural dilemmas concerning the management of desire, we see how the tightly managed body—whether demonstrated through sleek, minimalist lines or firmly developed muscles—has been overdetermined as a contemporary ideal of specifically female attractiveness. The axis of consumption/production is gender-overlaid, as I have argued, by the hierarchical dualism which constructs a dangerous, appetitive, bodily "female principle" in opposition to a masterful "male" will. We would thus expect that when the regulation of desire becomes especially problematic (as it is in advanced consumer cultures), women and their bodies will pay the greatest symbolic and material toll. When such a situation is compounded by anxiety about *women's* desires in periods when traditional forms of gender-organization are being challenged, this toll is multiplied. It would be wrong to suppose, however, that it is exacted through the simple *repression* of female hunger. Rather, here as elsewhere, power works also "from below," as women associate slenderness and self-management via the experience of newfound freedom (from a domestic destiny) and empowerment in the public arena. In this connection, we might note the difference between contemporary ideals of slenderness, coded in terms of self-mastery and expressed through traditionally "male" body symbolism, and mid-Victorian ideals of female slenderness, which symbolically emphasized reproductive femininity corseted under tight "external" constraints. But whether externally bound or internally managed, no body can escape either the imprint of culture or its gendered meanings.

NOTES

1. See Keith Walden. "The Road to Fat City: An Interpretation of the Development of Weight Consciousness in Western Society," *Historical Reflections* 12:3 (1985): 331–73.

2. See Michel Foucault, *The Use of Pleasure* (New York: Random House, 1986).

3. See Rudolph Bell, *Holy Anorexia* (Chicago: University of Chicago Press, 1985); and Carolyn Bynum, *Holy Feast and Holy Fast: The Religious Significance of Food to Medieval Women* (Berkeley: University of California Press, 1987), 31–48.

4. See Kim Chernin, *The Obsession: Reflections on the Tyranny of Slenderness* (New York: Harper and Row, 1981).

5. See Thomas Cash, Barbara Winstead, and Louis Janda, "The Great American Shape-up," *Psychology Today*, April 1986; "Dieting: The Losing Game," *Time*, 20 January 1986, among numerous other general reports. Concerning women's preoccupation in particular, see n. 41 below.

6. For Foucault on "docile bodies," see *Discipline and Punish* (New York: Vintage, 1979), 135–69. For an application of Foucault's ideas to the practices of diet and fitness, see Walden, "The Road to Fat City." For a Foucauldian analysis of the practices of femininity, see Sandra Bartky, "Foucault, Femininity, and the Modernization of Patriarchal Power," in *Feminism and Foucault*, ed. Irene Diamond and Lee Quinby (Boston: Northeastern University Press, 1988), 61–86.

7. Foucault (1979), 136.

8. "Fat or Not, 4th Grade Girls Diet Lest They Be Teased or Unloved," *Wall Street Journal*, 11 February 1986 (based on a University of California study.) A still more recent study–conducted at the University of Ottawa concluded that by age 7, a majority of young girls are anxious about their weight, and convinced they are much fatter than they are. ("Girls, at 7, Think Thin, Study Finds," *New York Times*, February 11, 1988).

9. On the "spreading" nature of eating disorders, see Paul Garfinkel and David Garner, *Anorexia Nervosa: A Multidimensional Perspective* (New York: Bruner Mazel, 1982), 102–3; and George Hsu, "Are Eating Disorders Becoming More Common in Blacks?" *The International Journal of Eating Disorders* 6:1 (January 1987): 113–24. Despite these trends, resistance to the slenderness ideal persists, and should not be overlooked as a source of insight into different cultural models of beauty and the conditions that promote them.

10. See Mary Douglas, *Natural Symbols* (New York: Pantheon, 1982); and *Purity and Danger* (London: Routledge and Kegan Paul, 1966).

11. This approach presupposes, of course, that popular cultural images *have* meaning, and are not merely arbitrary formations spawned by the whimsy of "fashion," the vicissitudes of Madison Avenue, or the "logic" of postindustrial capitalism, within which (as it has been argued, by Frederick and others) a producer or image's attraction derives solely from pure differentiation, from its cultural positioning, its suggestion of the novel or new. Within such a "postmodern" logic, Gail Faurschou argues, "Fashion has become the commodity 'par excellence.' It is fed by all of capitalism's incessant, frantic, reproductive passion and power. Fashion *is* the logic of planned obsolescence—not just the necessity for market survival, but the cycle of desire itself, the endless process through which the body is decoded and recoded, in order to define and inhabit the newest territorialized spaces of capital's expansion;" "Fashion and the Cultural Logic of Postmodernity," *Canadian Journal of Political and Social Theory* 11:1–2 (1987):72. While I don't disagree with Faurschou's general characterization of "fashion" here, the heralding of an absolute historical break, after which images have become completely empty of history, substance, and symbolic determination, seems *itself* an embodiment, rather than a de-mystifier, of the compulsively innovative logic of postmodernity. More important to the argument of this piece, a "postmodern logic" cannot explain the magnetic cultural hold of the slenderness ideal, long after any novel juxtaposition with more fleshy forms from the 1950s has worn off. Many times, in fact, the principle of the "new" has made tentative, but ultimately nominal, gestures toward the end of the reign of thinness, announcing a "softer," "curvier" look, and so forth. How many women have picked up magazines whose covers declared such a turn, only to find that the images within remain essentially continuous with prevailing norms? Large breasts may be making a comeback, but they are attached to extremely thin, often athletic bodies. Here, I would suggest, there are constraints on the pure logic of postmodernity—constraints that this paper tries to explore.

12. See Robert Crawford, "A Cultural Account of 'Health'—Self-Control, Release, and the Social Body," *Issues in the Political Economy of Health Care*, ed. John McKinlay (New York: Methuen, 1985), 60–103. I want to stress that my own analysis is not intended to "explain" eating disorders, which, as I have argued elsewhere, are a complex, multidetermined formation requiring analysis and interpretation on many levels.

13. Ira Sacker and Marc Zimmer, *Dying To Be Thin* (New York: Warner, 1987), 57.

14. Dalma Heyn, "Body Vision?" *Mademoiselle*, April 1987, 213.

15. See Lois Banner, *American Beauty* (Chicago: University of Chicago Press, 1983), 232.

16. Ibid., 53–55.

17. See Walden, *Historical Reflections* 12:3. 334–35, 353.

18. I thank Mario Moussa for this point, and for the Heather Locklear quotation.

19. Ira Sacker and Marc Zimmer, 149–50.

20. Foucault (1986), 64–70.

21. See Mary Douglas, *Purity and Danger*, 114–28.

22. See Robert Crawford, "A Cultural Account of 'Health.' "

23. John Farquhar, Stanford University Medical Center, quoted in "Dieting: The Losing Game," *Time*, 20 February 1986, 57.

24. I discuss the construction of hunger in eating disorders more fully in "Anorexia Nervosa: Psychopathology as the Crystallization of Culture," *The Philosophical Forum* 17:2 (Winter 1985), 33–103.

25. While there has been controversy over the appropriateness of describing medieval saints as "anorexic" (see, for example, Bell, *Holy Anorexia*, and Bynum, *Holy Feast and Holy Fast* for different views on the subject), no one, as far as I am aware, has noticed that a stronger case can be made for focusing on the "spiritual" aspects of the ascetism of modern-day anorectics. As I suggest in "Anorexia Nervosa: Psychopathology as the Crystallization of Culture," it is striking how often the imagery of anorectics includes Christian/ascetic themes, with a dualistic construction of mind/matter and spirit/appetite coded in terms of purity/contamination, and the ultimate goal of cleansing the soul of desire/hunger. Thus, certain foods are seen by the anorectic as tainted, contaminating, and dangerous, while the practice of self-denial and, at times, self-mortification, is seen as purifying. "Fasting," says Clement of Alexandria (d.ca. 215), "empties the soul of matter and makes it, with the body, clear and light for the reception of divine truth: (Bynum, p. 36). A similar war against matter, and the association of the de-materialized (i.e., thin) body with enhanced and purified vision, provides common images in the self-descriptions of anorectics, where comparisons with medieval ascetism are explicitly offered. Compare, for example, the words of "a certain Daniel" from the medieval *Sayings of the Fathers*: "As the body waxes fat, the soul grows thin; and as the body grows thin, the soul by so much waxes fat" (Bynum, p. 216) with those of a contemporary anorectic: "My soul seemed to grow as my body waned. I felt like one of those early Christian saints who starved themselves in the desert sun" (Bordo, "Anorexia Nervosa," p. 88).

26. See Marcia Millman, *Such a Pretty Face: Being Fat in America* (New York: Norton, 1980), esp. 65–79.

27. Ibid., 77.

28. Ira Sacker and Marc Zimmer, 32.

29. These quotations are taken from transcripts of the Phil Donahue show, provided by Multimedia Entertainment, Cincinnati, Ohio.

30. The discrepancy emerges very early, according to recent studies. "We don't expect boys to be that handsome," says a nine-year-old girl in the California study cited above. "But boys expect girls to be perfect and beautiful. And skinny." Her male classmate agrees: "Fat girls aren't like regular girls," he says. Many of my female

students have described in their journals the pressure their boyfriends place on them to stay or get slim. They have plenty of social support for such demands. Sylvester Stallone told Cornelia Guest that he liked his woman "anorexic"; she immediately lost 24 pounds (*Time*, 18 April, 1988, 89). But few men want their women to go that far; Actress Valerie Bertinelli reports (*Syracuse Post*) how her husband, Eddie Van Halen, "helps keep her in shape": "When I get too heavy, he says, 'Honey, lose weight.' Then when I get too thin, he says, "I don't like making love with you, you've got to gain some weight."

31. The most famous of such studies, by now replicated many times, appeared in *Glamour*, February 1984; a poll of 33,000 women revealed that 75 percent considered themselves "too fat," while only 25 percent of them were above Metropolitan Life Insurance standards, and 30 percent were *below*. ("Feeling Fat in a Thin Society," p. 86). See also Kevin Thompson, "Larger than Life," *Psychology Today*, April 1986; Dalma Heyn, "Why We're Never Satisfied With Our Bodies," *McCalls*, May 1982; Daniel Goleman, "Dislike of Own Body Found Common Among Women," *New York Times*, 19 March 1985.

32. 90 percent of all sufferers from eating disorders are female, a fact that has been explored from many clinical, historical, psychological, and cultural angles. Some of the most profound insights—insights that have become incorporated, often without adequate acknowledgement, into more recent clinical and scholarly literature—have come from Kim Chernin, *The Obsession, the Hungry Self* (New York: Harper and Row, 1981) and Susie Ohrbach, *Hunger Strike: he America's Struggle as a Metaphor for Our Age* (New York: Norton, 1986).

33. See Bordo, "Anorexia Nervosa." On female hunger as a metaphor for female sexuality in Victorian literature, see Helena Mitchie, *The Flesh Made Word* (New York: Oxford, 1987). On cultural associations of male/mind and female/matter, see, for instance, Dorothy Dinnerstein, *The Mermaid and the Minotaur* (New York: Harper and Row, 1977), Genevieve Lloyd, *The Man of Reason* (Minneapolis: University of Minnesota Press, 1984), and Luce Irigaray, *Speculum of the Other Woman* (Ithaca: Cornell University Press, 1985).

34. Bram Djikstra, *Idols of Perversity* (New York: Oxford University Press, 1986), 29.

35. "Mutable Beauty," *Saturday Night*, 1 February, 1902, 9.

36. Mary Jacobus and Sally Shuttleworth, pointing to the sometimes boyish figure of the "new Woman" of late-Victorian literature, have suggested to me the appropriateness of this interpretation for the late-Victorian era; I have, however, chosen to argue the point only with respect to the current context.

37. Bordo, "Anorexia Nervosa."

38. See Chernin, for an exploration of the connection between early infant experience and attitudes toward the fleshy, female body. For the impact on clinical literature of the feminist/cultural argument about anorexia, see Susan Wooley, "Intensive Treatment of Bulimia and Body-Image Disturbance," in *Handbook of Eating Disorders*, ed. Kelly D. Brownell and John P. Foreyt (New York: Basic Books, 1986), 476–502.

39. Historian LeeAnn Whites has pointed out to me how perverse this body-symbolism seems when we remember what a pregnant and nursing body is actually like. The

hourglass figure is really more correctly a symbolic "advertisement" to men of the woman's reproductive, domestic *sphere* than a representation of her reproductive *body*.

40. See Banner, 283–85.

41. It is no accident, I believe, that Dolly Parton, now down to 100 pounds and truly looking as though she might snap in two in a strong wind, opened her new show with a statement of its implicitly antifeminist premise: "I'll bust my butt to please you!" (Surely she already has?) Her television presence is now recessive, beseeching, desiring only to serve; clearly, her packages are exploiting the cultural resonances of her diminished physicality. Parton, of course, is no androgynous body-type. Rather, like *Wheel of Fortune's* Vanna White (who also lost a great deal of weight at one point in her career, and is obsessive about staying thin) she has tremendous appeal to those longing for a more "traditional" femininity in an era when women's public presence and power have greatly increased. Parton and White's large breasts evoke a nurturing, maternal sexuality. But after weight-reduction regimens set to anorexic standards, those breasts now adorn bodies that are vulnerably, breakably thin, with fragile, spindly arms and legs like those of young colts. Parton and White suggest the pleasures of nurturant female sexuality without any encounter with its powers and dangers.

42. See my essay, "The Body and the Reproduction of Femininity: A Feminist Appropriation of Foucault" in *Gender/Body/Knowledge: Feminist Reconstructions of Being and Knowing*, ed. Susan Bordo and Alison Jaggar (New Jersey: Rutgers University Press, 1989), for elaboration of these points.

43. "The Waist Land: Eating Disorders in America," 1985, Gannett Corporation, *MTI* Teleprograms. The analysis presented here becomes more complicated with bulimia, in which the hungering "female" self refuses to be annihilated, and feminine ideals are typically not rejected but embraced. See also Bordo, "How Television Teaches Women to Hate Their Hungers," *Mirror Images* (Newsletter of Anorexia/Bulimia Support, Syracuse, N.Y.), 4:1 (1986): 8–9.

R. W. CONNELL

Arms and the Man: The Question of Peace

R. W. Connell is a leading international scholar in sex and gender studies. He is Professor of Education at the University of Sydney, a Fellow of the Academy of Social Sciences in Australia, and a recipient of the American Sociological Association Award for distinguished contribution to his field. The following is from Connell's book, The Men and the Boys *(2000).*

> Arma virumque cano, Troiae qui primus ab oris Italiam fato profugus
> Lavinaque venit Litora . . .
>
> (I sing of arms and the man who came first from the shores of Troy,
> exiled by fate, to Italy and its Lavinian coast . . .)
> —Virgil, *Aeneid*, Book I

THE PROBLEM OF MEN AND VIOLENCE

It is not hard to show that there is some connection between gender and violence. This is obvious in the institutions which are dedicated to the techniques of violence, state agencies of force. The twenty million members of the world's armed forces today are overwhelmingly men. In many countries all soldiers, military sailors and aviators are men. Even in those countries which admit women to the military, women are a small minority, and commanders are almost exclusively men. Men also dominate other branches of enforcement, both in the public sector as police officers and prison guards, and in the private sector as police officers and prison guards, and in the private sector as security agents. Further, the targets of enforcement are mainly men. For instance, in 1999 no less than 94 per cent of the prisoners in Australian gaols were men; in the United States in 1996, 89 per cent of prison inmates were men.

In private life too, men are more likely to be armed and violent. In the United States, careful research by the criminologists Smith and Smith (1994) established that private gun ownership runs four times as high among men as among women, even after a campaign by the gun industry to persuade women to buy guns. In the same country, official statistics for 1996 show men accounting for 90 per cent of those arrested for aggravated assault and 90 per cent of those arrested for murder and manslaughter (U.S. Bureau of the Census 1998). In Australia in 1992–93 men were 90 per cent of those charged with homicide (Australian Institute of Criminology 1995). These figures are not exceptional.

There is a debate about the gender balance of violence within households, and it is clear that many women are capable of violence (e.g. in punishing children). The weight of evidence, however, indicates that major domestic violence is overwhelmingly by husbands towards wives, in wealthy countries at least (Dobash et al. 1992). Rape is overwhelmingly by men on women. Criminal rape shades into sexual intercourse under pressure. The national survey of sexual behaviour in the United States by Laumann et al. (1994) finds women six times as likely as men to have had an experience of forced sex, almost always being forced by a man.

Further, men predominate in warlike conduct in other spheres of life. Body-contact sports, such as boxing and football, involve ritualized combat and often physical injury. These sports are almost exclusively practised by men. Dangerous driving in increasingly recognized as a form of violence. It is mainly done by men. Young men die on the roads at a rate four times that of young women, and kill on the roads at an even higher ratio. Older men, as corporate executives, make the decisions that result in injury or death from the actions of their businesses — industrial injuries to their workers, pollution injury to neighbours and environmental destruction. Case studies of such decisions (e.g. Messerschmidt's [1997] study of the *Challenger* spacecraft explosion) show their connection to a masculinized management style emphasizing toughness, risk-taking, and ruthlessness about profit.

So men predominate across the spectrum of violence. A strategy for peace must concern itself with this fact, the reasons for it, and its implications for work to reduce violence.

There is a widespread belief that it is natural for men to be violent. Males are inherently more aggressive than women, the argument goes. "Boys will be boys" and cannot be trained otherwise; rape and combat — however regrettable — are part of the unchanging order of nature. There is often an appeal to biology, with testosterone in particular, the so-called "male hormone," as a catch-all explanation for men's aggression.

Careful examination of the evidence shows that this biological essentialism is not credible. Testosterone levels for instance, far from being a clearcut *source* of dominance and aggression in society, are as likely to be the *consequence* of social relations (Kemper 1990). Cross-cultural studies of masculinities (e.g. Cornwall & Lindisfarne 1994) reveal a diversity that as impossible to reconcile with a biologically fixed master pattern of masculinity.

When we speak statistically of "men" having higher rates of violence than women, we must not slide to the inference that therefore *all* men are violent. Almost all soldiers are men, but most men are not soldiers. Though most killers are men, most men never kill or even commit assault. Though an appalling number of men do rape, most men do not. It is a fact of great importance, both theoretically and practically, that there are many non-violent men in the world. This too needs explanation, and must be considered in a strategy for peace.

Further, when we note that most soldiers, sports professionals, or executives are men, we are not just talking about individuals. We are speaking of masculinized institutions. The organizational culture of armies, for instance, is heavily gendered. Social research inside armed forces in Germany (Seifert 1993), the United States (Barrett 1996) and Australia (Agostino 1998) reveals an energetic effort to produce a narrowly defined hegemonic masculinity.

Similarly, organized sport does not just reflect, but actively produces, particular versions of masculinity (Messner & Sabo 1994). Boys' schools too may display a vehement gender regime designed to produce a combative, dominating masculinity (Morrell 1994).

So it is in social masculinities rather than biological differences that we must seek the main causes of gendered violence, and the main answers to it.

IMPLICATIONS OF MASCULINITY RESEARCH

Multiple Masculinities

Different cultures and different periods of history construct gender differently. In multicultural societies there are likely to be multiple definitions of masculinity. Equally important, more than one kind of masculinity can be found within a given culture, even within a single institution such as a school or workplace.

Implications.   In any cultural setting, violent and aggressive masculinity will rarely be the only form of masculinity present. There is, then, usually some alternative for anti-violence programs to build on—a point strongly made by Denborough (1996) in his work with boys and male youth.

It is important that education and other anti-violence programs should recognize diversity in gender patterns, such as ethnic diversity. They must also recognize the tensions that develop around social difference; racism, of course, is a well-recognized source of violence. On the positive side, the research which documents multiple masculinities may itself be an asset. Peace education programs need concrete examples of more peaceable ways of living and acting.

Hierarchy and Hegemony

Different masculinities exist in definite relations with each other, often relations of hierarchy and exclusion. There is generally a hegemonic form of masculinity, the centre of the system of gendered power. The hegemonic form need not be the most common form of masculinity.

Implications.   The hierarchy of masculinities is itself a source of violence, since force is used in defining and maintaining the hierarchy. Bashings and murders of gay men reveal this, even in the language used by perpetrators; while the fear of being at the bottom of the hierarchy, being defined as a poofter or a sissy, is a familiar way of training boys and men to participate in combat and violent sports.

Large numbers of men and boys have a divided, tense, or oppositional relationship to hegemonic masculinity. This is an important fact of life though it is often concealed by the enormous attention focussed (e.g. in the media) on hegemonic masculinity. Clearcut alternatives, however, are often culturally discredited or despised. Men who practise them are likely to be abused as wimps, cowards, fags etc. The most powerful groups of men usually have few personal incentives for gender change. At the same time, however, the very hierarchy of masculinities may give other groups strong motives for change.

Collective Masculinities

Masculinities are sustained and enacted not only by individuals, but also by groups, institutions, and cultural forms like mass media. Multiple masculinities may be produced and sustained by the same institution.

Implications.   Violent masculinities are usually collectively defined and/or institutionally supported, whether in informal peer groups (youth "gangs"), formal armies, or groups somewhere in between (such as the murderous "militias" in East Timor). Most violence is not a matter of individual pathology.

Therefore the institutionalization of masculinity is a major problem for peace strategy. Building a culture of peace means changing the organizational culture of police forces, the military, the media etc. In practice, this means that corporations, workplaces, voluntary organizations, and the state are all important sites of action in producing or popularizing less violent forms of masculinity. The reshaping of institutions in as necessary as the reform of individual life.

Bodies As Arenas

Men's bodies do not fix patterns of masculinity, but they are still very important in the construction and expression of masculinities. This constantly involves bodily experience, bodily pleasures, and the vulnerabilities of bodies.

Implications.   Violence is, of course, a relationship between bodies; it is power exercised directly on the body. The bodily capacity to commit violence becomes, for many boys and young men, part of their sense of masculinity, and a willingness to put their bodies on the line in violence remains as a test of hegemonic masculinity.

If people's experience of masculinity to such a large extent involves their bodies, then bodies must be an important site of action for peace. It is a mistake if anti-violence work and peace education is all "in the head." Health, sport and sexuality are issues which must be addressed in changing masculinity. Part of the task is finding nonviolent forms of embodiment for men, and making these as satisfying as violent forms currently seem to be.

Active Construction

Masculinities do not exist prior to social interaction, but come into existence as people act. Masculinities are actively produced, using the resources available in a given milieu.

Implications.   The process of constructing masculinity, rather than the end state, is often the source of violence. We often see men involved in violence in order to prove their masculinity, or to defend their masculine honour, or to challenge others. We might pre-empt some of this violence by removing the occasions for these challenges or proofs.

This also means that no pattern of masculine violence is fixed, beyond all hope of social reform. This is ground for optimism. Unfortunately it also means that no reform is final. Gender reforms can be overthrown and more violent patterns of masculinity re-introduced. This seems to be the goal of some current neo-fascist groups, and it will be dangerous if this agenda gets wider support.

Internal Complexity and Contradiction

Masculinities are not homogeneous but are likely to be internally divided. Men's lives often embody tensions between contradictory desires or practices.

Implications.   Any pattern of masculinity has potential for change. Certainly some are less likely to change than others—especially where a certain pattern of masculinity is strongly buttressed by the surrounding institutions and culture— but in principle no pattern of masculinity is entirely proof against change.

It is also important to recognize that any given group of men is likely to have complex and conflicting interests. We cannot speak of "men" as a single bloc with exactly the same interests. Some have interests (e.g. in their relations with women and children) which will support change towards more peaceable gender patterns.

Dynamics

Masculinities are created in specific historical circumstances. They are liable to be contested, reconstructed or displaced. The forces producing change include contradictions within gender relations, as well as the interplay of gender with other social forces.

Implications.   Masculinities are always changing. Though many people deny this in principle, everyone is aware in practice that gender relations change, and the lives of men change too. This creates motives for learning, since boys and men have a need to understand what is happening to them.

However, as any agenda for change is likely to be against some groups' interests, controversy and conflict are to be expected. No reforms or changes in this area of life are likely to be smooth and trouble-free.

These conclusions can be put to work in practical ways, in programs to reduce violence and build peace. Anti-violence programs addressed to men have now accumulated a certain amount of experience. Much of it concerns violence against women, particularly domestic violence and rape, and some concerns violence against gay men and lesbians. However, broad crime-prevention measures are still usually gender-unaware.

. . .

PEACE STRATEGIES AND MASCULINITIES

There are many causes of violence, including dispossession, poverty, greed, nationalism, racism and other forms of inequality, bigotry and desire. Gender dynamics are by no means the whole story. Yet given the concentration of weapons and the practices of violence among men, gender patterns appear to be strategic. Masculinities are the forms in which many dynamics of violence take shape.

Evidently, then, strategy for peace must include a strategy of change in masculinities. This is the new dimension in peace work which studies of men suggest: contesting the hegemony of masculinities which emphasize violence, confrontation and domination, replacing them with patterns of masculinity more open to negotiation, cooperation and equality. . . .

A gender-informed strategy for peace must, therefore, be sophisticated about patterns of masculinity. It must also be designed to operate across a broad front, broader than most agendas of sex-role reform would suggest. The arenas for action to reduce masculine violence include:

- *development*—schooling, child rearing and adult-child relationships in families, classrooms, play groups etc. (including the issues commonly thought of as "sex-role modelling");

- *personal life*—marital relations and sexuality, family relationships, friendship (including the role of sexual and domestic violence in constructions of masculinity);

- *community life*—peer groups, neighbourhood life, leisure including sports (and youth subcultures as bearers of violent masculinities);

- *cultural institutions*—higher education, science and technology, mass media, the arts and popular entertainment (including exemplary masculinities in broadcast sports);

- *workplaces*—occupational cultures, industrial relations, corporations, unions and bureaucracies; the state and its enforcement apparatuses (armies, police etc.); and

- *markets*—the labour market and the effects of unemployment; capital and commodity markets both international and local; management practices and ideologies.

What principles might link action across this very broad spectrum? I do not think we should follow the model of gender reform that demands men adopt a new character and instantly become "the new man." Such hero-making agendas deny what we already know about the multiplicity and the internal complexity of masculinities.

Rather, strategy for peace needs to be embedded in a practicable strategy of change in gender relations. The goal should be to develop gender practices for men which shift gender relations in a democratic direction. Democratic gender relations are those that move towards equality, nonviolence, and manual respect between people of different genders, sexualities, ethnicities and generations.

A peace strategy concerned with masculinities, then, does not demand a complete rupture with patterns of conduct men are now familiar with. Some of the qualities in "traditional" definition of masculinity (e.g. courage, steadfastness, ambition) are certainly needed in the cause of peace. Active models of engagement are needed for boys and men, especially when peace is understood not just as the absence of violence but as a positive form of life.

The task is not to abolish gender but to reshape it; to disconnect (for instance) courage from violence, steadfastness from prejudice, ambition from exploitation. In the course of that reshaping, diversity will grow. Making boys and men aware of the diversity of masculinities that already exist in the world, beyond the narrow models they are commonly offered, is an important task for education.

Though the hierarchy of masculinities is part of the problem in gender relations, the fact that there are different masculinities is in itself an asset. At the lowest level, it establishes that masculinity is not a single fixed pattern. More positively, multiple masculinities represent complexity of interests and purposes, which open possibilities for change. Finally the plurality of gender prefigures the creativity of a democratic social order.

For men, the democratic remaking of gender practices requires persistent engagement with women, not the separatism-for-men which is strong in current masculinity politics. Educational and social action must be inclusive in another sense too, responding to the differing cultural meanings of gender and the different socio-economic circumstances in which students live. A program apt for suburban middle-class students may be very inappropriate for ethnically diverse inner-city children in poverty, or rural children living in villages.

No one with experience of struggles for peace, or of attempts at gender reform, will imagine these are easy tasks. Recognizing the interplay of masculinities with strategies for peace is not a magic key. In some ways, indeed, it makes familiar strategies seem more complex and difficult.

But it also, I believe, opens ways of moving past obstacles which both peace movements and the movement for gender democracy have encountered.

REFERENCES

Agostino, K. 1998, "The making of warriors: men, identity and military culture," *Journal of Interdisciplinary Gender Studies* vol. 3 no. 2, pp. 58–75

Australian Institute of Criminology 1995, *Homicides in Australia 1992–93*, AIC, Canberra

Barrett, F. J. 1996. "The organizational construction of hegemonic masculinity: The case of the U.S. Navy," *Gender, Work and Organization* vol. 3, no. 3, pp. 129–42

Cornwall, A. & Lindisfarne, N. (eds.) 1994, *Dislocating Masculinity: Comparative Ethnographics*. Routledge, London

Denborough, D. 1996, "Step by step: developing respectful ways of working with young men to reduce violence" in *Men's Ways of Being*, eds. C. McLean, M. Carey & C. White, Westview Press, Boulder

Dobash, R. P., Dobash, E. R. & Wilson, M. 1992, "The myth of sexual symmetry in marital violence," *Social Problems* vol. 39, pp. 71–91

Kemper, T. D. 1990, *Social Structure and Testosterone*, Rutgers University Press, New Brunswick

Laumann, E. O., Gagnon, J. H., Michael, R. T. & Michaels, S. 1994, *The Social Organization of Sexuality: Sexual Practices in the United States*, University of Chicago Press, Chicago

Messerschmidt, J. W. 1997, *Crime as Structured Action: Gender, Race, Class, and Crime in the Making*, Sage, Thousand Oaks

Messner, M. A. & Sabo, D. F. 1994, *Sex, Violence and Power in Sports: Rethinking Masculinity*, Crossing Press, Freedom, CA

Morrell, R. 1993–4, "Masculinity and the white boys' boarding schools of Natal, 1880–1930," *Perspectives in Education* vol. 15, pp. 27–52

Seifert, R. 1993, *Individualisierungsprozesse. Geschlechterverhältnisse und die soziale Konstruktion des Soldaten*, Socialwissenschaftliches Institut der Bundeswehr, München

Smith, T. W. & Smith, R. J. 1994, "Changes in firearm ownership among women, 1980–1994," Paper presented to the American Society of Criminology, Miami

United States Bureau of the Census 1998, *Statistical Abstract of the United States: 1998*, 118th edn, Washington, DC

STEPHANIE COONTZ

Leave it to Beaver *and* Ozzie and Harriet: *American Families in the 1950s*

Stephanie Coontz, Professor at Evergreen State University, works on gender, history, and family studies. Her books include Marriage, A History: From Obedience to Intimacy, or How Love Conquered Marriage *(2005) and* The Way We Really Are: Coming to Terms with America's Changing Families *(1997). The following selection is from her classic book,* The Way We Never Were: American Families and the Nostalgia Trap *(1992; 2000).*

Our most powerful visions of traditional families derive from images that are still delivered to our homes in countless reruns of 1950s television sit-coms. When liberals and conservatives debate family policy, for example, the issue is often framed in terms of how many "Ozzie and Harriet" families are left in America. Liberals compute the percentage of total households that contain a breadwinner father, a full-time homemaker mother, and dependent children, proclaiming that fewer than 10 percent of American families meet the "Ozzie and Harriet" or "Leave It to Beaver" model. Conservatives counter that more than half of all mothers with preschool children either are not employed or are employed only part-time. They cite polls showing that most working mothers would like to spend more time with their children and periodically announce that the Nelsons are "making a comeback," in popular opinion if not in real numbers.

Since everyone admits that nontraditional families are now a majority, why this obsessive concern to establish a higher or a lower figure? Liberals seem to think that unless they can prove the "Leave It to Beaver" family is on an irreversible slide toward extinction, they cannot justify introducing new family definitions and social policies. Conservatives believe that if they can demonstrate the traditional family is alive and well, although endangered by policies that reward two-earner families and single parents, they can pass measures to revive the seeming placidity and prosperity of the 1950s, associated in many people's minds with the relative stability of marriage, gender roles, and family life in that decade. If the 1950s family existed today, both sides seem to assume, we would not have the contemporary social dilemmas that cause such debate.

At first glance, the figures seem to justify this assumption. The 1950s was a pro-family period if there ever was one. Rates of divorce and illegitimacy were half what they are today; marriage was almost universally praised; the

90

family was everywhere hailed as the most basic institution in society; and a massive baby boom, among all classes and ethnic groups, made America a "child-centered" society. Births rose from a low of 18.4 per 1,000 women during the Depression to a high of 25.3 per 1,000 in 1957. "The birth rate for third children doubled between 1940 and 1960, and that for fourth children tripled."

In retrospect, the 1950s also seem a time of innocence and consensus: Gang warfare among youths did not lead to drive-by shootings; the crack epidemic had not yet hit; discipline problems in the schools were minor; no "secular humanist" movement opposed the 1954 addition of the words *under God* to the Pledge of Allegiance; and 90 percent of all school levies were approved by voters. Introduction of the polio vaccine in 1954 was the most dramatic of many medical advances that improved the quality of life for children.

The profamily features of this decade were bolstered by impressive economic improvements for vast numbers of Americans. Between 1945 and 1960, the gross national product grew by almost 250 percent and per capita income by 35 percent. Housing starts exploded after the war, peaking at 1.65 million in 1955 and remaining above 1.5 million a year for the rest of the decade; the increase in single-family homeownership between 1946 and 1956 outstripped the increase during the entire preceding century and a half. By 1960, 62 percent of American families owned their own homes, in contrast to 43 percent in 1940. Eighty-five percent of the new homes were built in the suburbs, where the nuclear family found new possibilities for privacy and togetherness. While middle-class Americans were the prime beneficiaries of the building boom, substantial numbers of white working-class Americans moved out of the cities into affordable developments, such as Levittown.

Many working-class families also moved into the middle class. The number of salaried workers increased by 61 percent between 1947 and 1957. By the mid-1950s, nearly 60 percent of the population had what was labeled a middle-class income level (between $3,000 and $10,000 in constant dollars), compared to only 31 percent in the "prosperous twenties," before the Great Depression. By 1960, thirty-one million of the nation's forty-four million families owned their own home, 87 percent had a television, and 75 percent possessed a car. The number of people with discretionary income doubled during the 1950s.

For most Americans, the most salient symbol and immediate beneficiary of their newfound prosperity was the nuclear family. The biggest boom in consumer spending. For example, was in household goods. Food spending rose by only 33 percent in the five years following the Second World War, and clothing expenditures rose by 20 percent, but purchases of household furnishings and appliances climbed 240 percent. "Nearly the entire increase in the gross national product in the mid-1950s was due to increased spending on consumer durables and residential construction," most of it oriented toward the nuclear family.

Putting their mouths where their money was, American consistently told pollsters that home and family were the wellsprings of their happiness and self-esteem. Cultural historian David Marc argues that prewar fantasies of sophisticated urban "elegance," epitomized by the high-rise penthouse apartment, gave way in the 1950s to a more modest vision of utopia: a single-family house and a car. The emotional dimensions of utopia, however, were unbounded. When respondents to a 1955 marriage study "were asked what they thought they had sacrificed by marrying and raising a family, an overwhelming majority of them replied, 'Nothing.'" Less than 10 percent of Americans believed that an unmarried person could be happy. As one popular advice book intoned. "The family is the center of your living. If it isn't, you've gone far astray."

THE NOVELTY OF THE 1950S FAMILY

In fact, the "traditional" family of the 1950s was a qualitatively new phenomenon. At the end of the 1940s, all the trends characterizing the rest of the twentieth century suddenly reversed themselves: For the first time in more than one hundred years, the age for marriage and motherhood fell, fertility increased, divorce rates declined, and women's degree of educational parity with men dropped sharply. In a period of less than ten years, the proportion of never-married persons declined by as much as it had during the entire previous half century.

At the time, most people understood the 1950s family to be a new invention. The Great Depression and the Second World War had reinforced extended family ties, but in ways that were experienced by most people as stultifying and oppressive. As one child of the Depression later put it, "The Waltons" television series of the 1960s did not show what family life in the 1930s was really like: "It wasn't a big family sitting around a table radio and everybody saying goodnight while Bing Crosby crooned 'Pennies from Heaven.'" On top of Depression-era family tensions had come the painful family separations and housing shortages of the war years: By 1947, six million American families were sharing housing, and postwar family counselors warned of a widespread marital crisis caused by conflicts between the generations. A 1948 *March of Time* film, "Marriage and Divorce," declared: "No home is big enough to house two families, particularly two of different generations, with opposite theories on child training."

During the 1950s, films and television plays, such as "Marty," showed people working through conflicts between marital loyalties and older kin, peer group, or community ties; regretfully but decisively, these conflicts were almost invariably "resolved in favor of the heterosexual couple rather than the claims of extended kinship networks. . . . homosociability and friendship." Talcott Parsons and other sociologists argued that modern industrial society required the family to jettison traditional productive functions and wider kin ties in order to specialize in emotional nurturance, childrearing, and production of a modern personality. Social workers "endorsed nuclear family separateness and looked suspiciously on active extended-family networks."

Popular commentators urged young families to adopt a "modern" stance and strike out on their own, and with the return of prosperity, most did. By the early 1950s, newlyweds not only were establishing single-family homes at an earlier age and a more rapid rate than ever before but also were increasingly moving to the suburbs, away from the close scrutiny of the elder generation.

For the first time in American history, moreover, such average trends did not disguise sharp variations by class, race, and ethnic group. People married at a younger age, bore their children earlier and closer together, completed their families by the time they were in their late twenties, and experienced a longer period living together as a couple after their children left home. The traditional range of acceptable family behaviors—even the range in the acceptable number and timing of children—narrowed substantially.

The values of 1950s families also were new. The emphasis on producing a whole world of satisfaction, amusement, and inventiveness within the nuclear family had no precedents. Historian Elaine Tyler May comments: "The legendary family of the 1950s . . . was not, as common wisdom tells us, the last gasp of 'traditional' family life with deep roots in the past. Rather, it was the first wholehearted effort to create a home that would fulfill virtually all its members' personal needs through an energized and expressive personal life."

Beneath a superficial revival of Victorian domesticity and gender distinctions, a novel rearrangement of family ideals and male-female relations was accomplished. For women, this involved a reduction in the moral aspect of domesticity and an expansion of its orientation toward personal service. Nineteenth-century middle-class women had cheerfully left housework to servants, yet 1950s women of all classes created make-work in their homes and felt guilty when they did not do everything for themselves. The amount of time women spent doing housework actually *increased* during the 1950s, despite the advent of convenience foods and new, labor-saving appliances; child care absorbed more than twice as much time as it had in the 1920s. By the mid-1950s, advertisers' surveys reported on a growing tendency among women to find "housework a medium of expression for . . . [their] femininity and individuality."

For the first time, men as well as women were encouraged to root their identity and self-image in familial and parental roles. The novelty of these family and gender values can be seen in the dramatic postwar transformation of movie themes. Historian Peter Biskind writes that almost every major male star who had played tough loners in the 1930s and 1940s "took the roles with which he was synonymous and transformed them, in the fifties, into neurotics or psychotics." In these films, "men belonged at home, not on the streets or out on the prairie . . . not alone or hanging out with other men." The women who got men to settle down had to promise enough sex to compete with "bad" women, but ultimately they provided it only in the marital bedroom and only in return for some help fixing up the house.

Public images of Hollywood stars were consciously reworked to show their commitment to marriage and stability. After 1947, for example, the Actors' Guild organized "a series of unprecedented speeches . . . to be given to civic groups around the country, emphasizing that the stars now embodied the rejuvenated family life unfolding in the suburbs." Ronald Reagan's defense of actors' family values was especially "stirring," noted one reporter, but female stars, unlike Reagan and other male stars, were obliged to *live* the new values as well as propagandize them. Joan Crawford, for example, one of the brash, tough, independent leading ladies of the prewar era, was now pictured as a devoted mother whose sex appeal and glamour did not prevent her from doing her own housework. She posed for pictures mopping floors and gave interviews about her childrearing philosophy.

The "good life" in the 1950s, historian Clifford Clark points out, made the family "the focus of fun and recreation." The ranch house, architectural embodiment of this new ideal, discarded the older privacy of the kitchen, den, and sewing room(representative of separate spheres for men and women) but introduced new privacy and luxury into the master bedroom. There was an unprecedented "glorification of self-indulgence" in family life. Formality was discarded in favor of "livability," "comfort," and "convenience." A contradiction in terms in earlier periods, "the sexually charged, child-centered family took its place at the center of the postwar American dream."

On television, David Marc comments, all the "normal" families moved to the suburbs during the 1950s. Popular culture turned such suburban families into capitalism's answer to the Communist threat. In his famous "kitchen debate" with Nikita Khrushchev in 1959, Richard Nixon asserted that the superiority of capitalism over communism was embodied not in ideology or military might but in the comforts of the suburban home, "designed to make things easier for our women."

Acceptance of domesticity was the mark of middle-class status and upward mobility. In sit-com families, a middle-class man's work was totally irrelevant to his identity; by the same token, the problems of working-class families did not lie in their economic situation but in their failure to create harmonious gender roles. Working-class and ethnic men on television had one defining characteristic: They were unable to control their wives. The families of middle-class men, by contrast, were generally well behaved.

Not only was the 1950s family a new invention, it was also a historical fluke, based on a unique and temporary conjuncture of economic, social, and political factors. During the war, Americans had saved at a rate more than three times higher than that in the decades before or since. Their buying power was further enhanced by America's extraordinary competitive advantage at the end of the war, when every other industrial power was devastated by the experience. This privileged economic position sustained both a tremendous expansion of middle-class management occupations and a new honeymoon between management and organized labor: During the 1950s, real wages increased by more than they had in the entire previous half century.

The impact of such prosperity on family formation and stability was magnified by the role of government, which could afford to be generous with education benefits, housing loans, highway and sewer construction, and job training. All this allowed most middle-class Americans, and a large number of working-class ones, to adopt family values and strategies that assumed the availability of cheap energy, low-interest home loans, expanding educational and occupational opportunities, and steady employment. These expectations encouraged early marriage, early childbearing, expansion of consumer debt, and residential patterns that required long commutes to work — all patterns that would become highly problematic by the 1970s.

A COMPLEX REALITY: 1950s POVERTY, DIVERSITY, AND SOCIAL CHANGE

Even aside from the exceptional and ephemeral nature of the conditions that supported them. 1950s family strategies and values offer no solution to the discontents that underlie contemporary romanticization of the "good old days." The reality of these families was far more painful and complex than the situation-comedy reruns or the expurgated memories of the nostalgic would suggest. Contrary to popular opinion, "Leave It to Beaver" was not a documentary.

In the first place, not all American families shared in the consumer expansion that provided Hotpoint appliances for June Cleaver's kitchen and a vacuum cleaner for Donna Stone. A full 25 percent of Americans, forty to fifty million people, were poor in the mid-1950s, and in the absence of food stamps and housing programs, this poverty was searing. Even at the end of the 1950s, a third of American children were poor. Sixty percent of Americans over sixty-five had incomes below $1,000 in 1958, considerably below the $3,000 to $10,000 level considered to represent middle-class status. A majority of elders also lacked medical insurance. Only half the population had savings in 1959; one-quarter of the population had no liquid assets at all. Even when we consider only native-born, white families, one-third could not get by on the income of the household head.

In the second place, real life was not so white as it was on television. Television, comments historian Ella Taylor, increasingly ignored cultural diversity, adopting "the motto 'least objectionable programming,' which gave rise to those least objectionable families, the Cleavers, the Nelsons and the Andersons." Such families were so completely white and Anglo-Saxon that even the

Hispanic gardener in "Father Knows Best" went by the name of Frank Smith. But contrary to the all-white lineup on the television networks and the streets of suburbia, the 1950s saw a major transformation in the ethnic composition of America. More Mexican immigrants entered the United States in the two decades after the Second World War than in the entire previous one hundred years. Prior to the war, most blacks and Mexican-Americans lived in rural areas, and three-fourths of blacks lived in the South. By 1960, a majority of blacks resided in the North, and 80 percent of both blacks and Mexican-Americans lived in cities. Postwar Puerto Rican immigration was so massive that by 1960 more Puerto Ricans lived in New York than in San Juan.

These minorities were almost entirely excluded from the gains and privileges according white middle-class families. The June Cleaver or Donna Stone homemaker role was not available to the more than 40 percent of black women with small children who worked outside the home. Twenty-five percent of these women headed their own households, but even minorities who conformed to the dominant family form faced conditions quite unlike those portrayed on television. The poverty rate of two-parent black families was more than 50 percent, approximately the same as that of one-parent black ones. Migrant workers suffered "near medieval" deprivations, while termination and relocation policies were employed against Native Americans to get them to give up treaty rights.

African Americans in the South faced systematic, legally sanctioned segregation and pervasive brutality, and those in the North were excluded by restrictive covenants and redlining from many benefits of the economic expansion that their labor helped sustain. Whites resisted, with harassment and violence, the attempts of labor helped sustain. Whites resisted, with harassment and violence, the attempts of blacks to participate in the American family dream. When Harvey Clark tried to move into Cicero, Illinois, in 1951, a mob of 4,000 whites spent four days tearing his apartment apart while police stood by and joked with them. In 1953, the first black family moved into Chicago's Trumbull Park public housing project; neighbors "hurled stones and tomatoes" and trashed stores that sold groceries to the new residents. In Detroit, *Life* magazine reported in 1957, "10,000 Negroes work at the Ford plant in nearby Dearborn, [but] not one Negro can live in Dearborn itself."

MORE COMPLEXITIES: REPRESSION, ANXIETY, UNHAPPINESS, AND CONFLICT

The happy, homogeneous families that we "remember" from the 1950s were thus partly a result of the media's denial of diversity. But even among sectors of the population where the "least objectionable" families did prevail, their values and behaviors were not entirely a spontaneous, joyful reaction to prosperity. If suburban ranch houses and family barbecues were the carrots offered to white middle-class families that adopted the new norms, there was also a stick.

Women's retreat to housewifery, for example, was in many cases not freely chosen. During the war, thousands of women had entered new jobs, gained new skills, joined unions, and fought against job discrimination. Although 95 percent of the new women employees had expected when they were first hired to quit work at the end of the war, by 1945 almost an equally overwhelming majority did not want to give up their independence, responsibility, and income, and expressed the desire to continue working.

After the war, however, writes one recent student of postwar reconstruction, "management went to extraordinary lengths to purge women workers from the auto plants," as well as from other high-paying and nontradtional jobs. As it turned out, in most cases women were not permanently expelled from the labor force but were merely downgraded to lower-paid, "female" jobs. Even at the end of the purge, there were more women working than before the war, and by 1952 there were two million more wives at work than at the peak of wartime production. The jobs available to these women, however, lacked the pay and the challenges that had made wartime work so satisfying, encouraging women to define themselves in terms of home and family even when they were working.

Vehement attacks were launched against women who did not accept such self-definitions. In the 1947 bestseller, *The Modern Woman: The Lost Sex*, Marynia Farnham and Ferdinand Lundberg described feminism as a "deep illness," called the notion of an independent woman a "contradiction in terms," and accused women who sought educational or employment equality of engaging in symbolic "castration" of men. As sociologist David Riesman noted, a woman's failure to bear children went from being "a social disadvantage and sometimes a personal tragedy" in the nineteenth century to being a "quasi-perversion" in the 1950s. The conflicting messages aimed at women seemed almost calculated to demoralize: At the same time as they labeled women "unnatural" if they did not seek fulfillment in motherhood, psychologists and popular writers insisted that most modern social ills could be traced to domineering mothers who invested too much energy and emotion in their children. Women were told that "no other experience in life . . . will provide the same sense of fulfillment, of happiness, of complete pervading contentment" as motherhood. But soon after delivery they were asked, "Which are you first of all, Wife or Mother?" and warned against the tendency to be "too much mother, too little wife."

Women who could not walk the fine line between nurturing motherhood and castrating "momism," or who had trouble adjusting to "creative homemaking," were labeled neurotic, perverted, or schizophrenic. A recent study of hospitalized "schizophrenic" women in the San Francisco Bay Area during the 1950s concludes that institutionalization and sometimes electric shock treatments were used to force women to accept their domestic roles and their husbands' dictates. Shock treatments also were recommended for women who sought abortions, on the assumption that failure to want a baby signified dangerous emotional disturbance.

All women, even seemingly docile ones, were deeply mistrusted. They were frequently denied the right to serve on juries, convey property, make contracts, take out credit cards in their own name, or establish residence. A 1954 article in *Esquire* called working wives a "menace"; a *Life* author termed married women's employment a "disease." Women were excluded from several professions, and some states even gave husbands total control over family finances. There were not many permissible alternatives to baking brownies, experimenting with new canned soups, and getting rid of stains around the collar.

Men were also pressured into acceptable family roles, since lack of a suitable wife could mean the loss of a job or promotion for a middle-class man. Bachelors were categorized as "immature," "infantile," "narcissistic," "deviant" or even "pathological." Family advice expert Paul Landis argued: "Except for the sick, the badly crippled, the deformed, the emotionally warped and the mentally defective, almost everyone has an opportunity [and, by clear implication, a duty] to marry."

Families in the 1950s were products of even more direct repression. Cold war anxieties merged with concerns about the expanded sexuality of family life and the commercial world to create what one authority calls the domestic version of George F. Kennan's containment policy toward the Soviet Union: A "normal" family and vigilant mother became the "front line" of defense against treason; anticommunists linked deviant family or sexual behavior to sedition. The FBI and other government agencies instituted unprecedented state intrusion into private life under the guise of investigating subversives. Gay baiting was almost as widespread and every bit as vicious as red baiting.

The Civil Service Commission fired 2,611 persons as "security risks" and reported that 4,315 others resigned under the pressure of investigations that asked leading questions of their neighbors and inquired into the books they read or the music to which they listened. In this atmosphere, movie producer Joel Schumacher recalls, "No one told the truth. . . . People pretended they weren't unfaithful. The pretended that they weren't homosexual. They pretended that they weren't horrible."

Even for people not directly coerced into conformity by racial, political, or personal repression, the turn toward families was in many cases more a defensive move than a purely affirmative act. Some men and women entered loveless marriages in order to forestall attacks about real or suspected homosexuality or lesbianism. Growing numbers of people saw the family, in the words of one husband, as the one "group that in spite of many disagreements internally always will face its external enemies together." Conservative families warned children to beware of communists who might masquerade as friendly neighbors; liberal children learned to confine their opinions to he family for fear that their father's job or reputation might be threatened.

Americans were far more ambivalent about the 1950s than later retrospectives, such as "Happy Days," suggest. Plays by Tennessee Williams, Eugene O'Neill, and Arthur Miller explored the underside of family life. Movies such as *Rebel Without a Cause* (1955) expressed fears about youths whose parents had failed them. There was an almost obsessive concern with the idea that the mass media had broken down parental control, thus provoking an outburst of "delinquency and youthful viciousness." In 1954, psychiatrist Fredric Wertham's *Seduction of the Innocents* warned: "The atmosphere of crime comic books is unparalleled in the history of children's literature of any time or any nation." In 1955, Congress discussed nearly 200 bills relating to delinquency. If some of these anxieties seem almost charmingly naïve to our more hardened age, they were no less real for all that.

Many families, of course, managed to hold such fears at bay — and it must be admitted that the suburbs and small towns of America were exceptionally good places for doing so. Shielded from the multiplying problems and growing diversity of the rest of society, residents of these areas could afford to be neighborly. Church attendance and membership in voluntary associations tended to be higher in the suburbs than in the cities, although contact with extended kin was less frequent. Children played in the neighborhoods and cul-de-sac with only cursory warnings about strangers.

In her autobiographical account of a 1950s adolescence, Susan Allen Toth remembers growing up "gradually" and "quietly" in a small town of the period: "We were not seared by fierce poverty, racial tensions, drug abuse, street crimes." Perhaps this innocence was "constricting," she admitted, but it also gave a child "shelter and space to grow." For Toth, insulation from external problems meant that growing up was a process of being "cosseted, gently warmed, transmuted by slow degress."

For many other children, however, growing up in 1950s families was not so much a matter of being protected from the harsh realities of the outside world as preventing the outside world from learning the harsh realities of family life. Few would have guessed that radiant Marilyn Van Derbur, crowned Miss America in 1958, had been sexually violated by her wealthy, respectable father from the time she was five until she was eighteen, when she moved away to college. While not all family secrets were quite so shocking, author Benita Eisler recalls a common middle-class experience:

> As college classmates became close friends, I heard sagas of life at home that were Gothic horror stories. Behind the hedges and driveways of upper-middle-class suburbia were tragedies of madness, suicide, and — most prevalent of all — chronic and severe alcoholism. . . .
>
> The real revelation for me was the role played by children in . . . keeping up appearances. Many of my new friends had been pressed into service

early as happy smiling fronts, emissaries of family normalcy, cheerful proof that "nothing was really wrong" at the Joneses.

Beneath the polished facades of many "ideal" families, suburban as well as urban, was violence, terror, or simply grinding misery that only occasionally came to light. Although Colorado researchers found 302 battered-child cases, including 33 deaths, in their state during one year alone, the major journal of American family sociology did not carry a single article on family violence between 1939 and 1969. Wife battering was not even considered a "real" crime by most people. Psychiatrists in the 1950s, following Helene Deutsch, "regarded the battered woman as a masochist who provoked her husband into beating her."

Historian Elizabeth Pleck describes how one Family Service Association translated this psychological approach into patient counseling during the 1950s. Mrs. K came to the Association because her husband was an alcoholic who repeatedly abused her, both physically and sexually. The agency felt, however, that it was simplistic to blame the couple's problems on his drinking. When counselors learned that Mrs. K refused her husband's demands for sex after he came home from working the night shift, they decided that they had found a deeper difficulty: Mrs. K needed therapy to "bring out some of her anxiety about sex activities."

We will probably never know how prevalent incest and sexual abuse were in the 1950s, but we do know that when girls or women reported incidents of such abuse to therapists, they were frequently told that they were "fantasizing" their unconscious oedipal desires. Although incest cases were common throughout the records of caseworkers from 1880 to 1960, according to historian Linda Gordon's study of these documents, the problem was increasingly redefined as one of female "sex delinquency." By 1960, despite overwhelming evidence to the contrary, experts described incest as a "one-in-a-million occurrence." Not until the 1970s, heartened by a supportive women's movement, were many women able to speak out about the sexual abuse they had suffered in silent agony during the 1950s; others, such as Marilyn Van Derbur, are only now coming forward.

Less dramatic but more widespread was the existence of significant marital unhappiness. Between one-quarter and one-third of the marriages contracted in the 1950s eventually ended in divorce; during that decade two million legally married people lived apart from each other. Many more couples simply toughed it out. Sociologist Mirra Komarovsky concluded that of the working-class couples she interviewed in the 1950s, "slightly less than one-third [were] happily or very happily married."

National polls found that 20 percent of all couples considered their marriages unhappy, and another 20 percent reported only "medium happiness." In the middle-class sample studied by Elaine Tyler May, two-thirds of the husbands and wives rated their marriages "decidedly happier than average," but an outside observer might well have scaled this back to a percentage much like Komarovsky's, for even the happiest couples reported many dissatisfactions and communication problems. "The idea of a 'working marriage' was one that often included constant day-to-day misery for one or both partners."

A successful 1950s family, moreover, was often achieved at enormous cost to the wife, who was expected to subordinate her own needs and aspirations to those of both her husband and her children. In consequence, no sooner was the ideal of the postwar family accepted than observers began to comment perplexedly on how discontented women seemed in the very roles they supposedly desired most. In 1949, *Life* magazine reported that "suddenly and for no plain reason" American women were "seized with an eerie restlessness." Under a "mask of placidity" and an outwardly feminine appearance, one physician wrote in 1953, there was often "an inwardly tense and emotionally unstable individual seething with hidden aggressiveness and resentment."

Some women took this resentment out on their families. Surely some of the bizarre behaviors that Joan Crawford exhibited toward her children, according to her daughter's bitter remembrance, *Mommie Dearest,* flowed from the frustration of being forced into a domestic role about which she was intensely ambivalent. Other women tried to dull the pain with alcohol or drugs. Tranquilizers were developed in the 1950s in response to a need that physicians explicitly saw as female: Virtually nonexistent in 1955, tranquilizer consumption reached 462,000 pounds in 1958 and soared to 1.15 million pounds merely a year later. Commentators noted a sharp increase in women's drinking during the decade, even though many middle-class housewives kept their liquor stash hidden and thought no one knew that they needed a couple of drinks to face an evening of family "togetherness."

But not even "the four *b's*," as the mother of a colleague of mine used to label her life in the 1950s—"booze, bowling, bridge, and boredom"—could entirely conceal the discontents. In 1956, the *Ladies' Home Journal* devoted an issue to "The Plight of the Young Mother." When *McCall's* ran an article entitled. "The Mother Who Ran Away" in the same year, the magazine set a new record for readership. A former editor commented: "We suddenly realized that all those women at home with their three and a half children were miserably unhappy." By 1960, almost every major news journal was using the word *trapped* to describe the feelings of the American housewife. When *Redbook's* editors asked readers to provide them with examples of "Why Young Mothers Feel Trapped," they received 24,000 replies.

Although Betty Friedan's bestseller *The Feminine Mystique* did not appear until 1963, it was a product of the 1950s, originating in the discontented responses Friedan received in 1957 when she surveyed fellow college classmates from the class of 1942. The heartfelt identification of other 1950s women with "the problem that has no name" is preserved in the letters

Friedan received after her book was published, letters now at the Schlesinger Library at Radcliffe.

Men tended to be more satisfied with marriage than were women, especially over time, but they, too, had their discontents. Even the most successful strivers after the American dream sometimes muttered about "mindless conformity." The titles of books such as *The Organization Man*, by William Whyte (1956), and *The Lonely Crowd*, by David Riesman (1958), summarized a widespread critique of 1950s culture. Male resentments against women were expressed in the only partly humorous diatribes of *Playboy* magazine (founded in 1953) against "money-hungry" gold diggers or lazy "parasites" trying to trap men into commitment.

CONTRADICTIONS OF THE 1950s FAMILY BOOM

Happy memories of 1950s family life are not all illusion, of course — there were good times for many families. But even the most positive aspects had another side. One reason that the 1950s family model was so fleeting was that it contained the seeds of its own destruction. It was during the 1950s, not the 1960s, that the youth market was first produced, then institutionalized into the youth culture. It was through such innocuous shows as "Howdy Doody" and "The Disney Hour" that advertisers first discovered the riches to be gained by bypassing parents and appealing directly to youth. It was also during this period that advertising and consumerism became saturated with sex.

In the 1950s, family life was financed by economic practices that were to have unanticipated consequences in the 1970s. Wives and mothers first started to work in great numbers during the 1950s in order to supplement their families' purchasing power; expansion of household comforts came "at the cost of an astronomical increase of indebtedness." The labor-management accord of the 1950s helped erode the union movement's ability to oppose the takebacks and runaway shops that destroyed the "family wage system" during the 1970s and 1980s.

Family and gender strategies also contained some time bombs. Women who "played dumb" to catch a man, as 40 percent of Barnard College women admitted to doing, sometimes despised their husbands for not living up to the fiction of male superiority they had worked so hard to promote. Commitment to improving the quality of family life by manipulating the timing and spacing of childbearing led to the social acceptability of family planning and the spread of birth-control techniques. Concentration of childbearing in early marriage meant that growing numbers of women had years to spare for paid work after the bulk of their child-care duties were finished. Finally, 1950s families fostered intense feelings and values that produced young people with a sharp eye for hypocrisy; many of the so-called rebels of the 1960s were simply acting on values that they had internalized in the bosom of their families.

TEEN PREGNANCY AND THE 1950S FAMILY

Whatever its other unexpected features, the 1950s family does appear, at least when compared to families in the last two decades, to be a bastion of "traditional" sexual morality. Many modern observers, accordingly, look back to the sexual values of this decade as a possible solution to what they see as the peculiarly modern "epidemic" of teen pregnancy. On closer examination, however, the issue of teen pregnancy is a classic example of both the novelty and the contradictions of the 1950s family.

Those who advocate that today's youth should be taught abstinence or deferred gratification rather than sex education will find no 1950s model for such restraint. "Heavy petting" became a norm of dating in this period, while the proportion of white brides who were pregnant at marriage more than doubled. Teen birth rates soared, reaching highs that have not been equaled since. In 1957, 97 out of every 1,000 girls aged fifteen to nineteen gave birth, compared to only 52 of every 1,000 in 1983. A surprising number of these births were illegitimate, although 1950s census codes made it impossible to identify an unmarried mother if she lived at home with her parents. The incidence of illegitimate, although 1950s census codes made it impossible to identify an unmarried mother if she lived at home with her parents. The incidence of illegitimacy was also disguised by the new emphasis on "rehabilitating" the white mother (though not the black) by putting her baby up for adoption and encouraging her to "start over"; there was an 80 percent increase in the number of out-of-wedlock babies placed for adoption between 1944 and 1955.

The main reason that teenage sexual behavior did not result in many more illegitimate births during this period was that the age of marriage dropped sharply. Young people were not taught how to "say no" — they were simply handed wedding rings. In fact, the growing willingness of parents to subsidize young married couples and the new prevalence of government educational stipends and home ownership loans for veterans undermined the former assumption that a man should be able to support a family before embarking on marriage. Among the middle class, it became common for young wives to work while their husbands finished school. Prior to the 1950s, as David Riesman wrote of his Depression-era classmates, it would not "have occurred to us to have our wives support us through graduate school."

Contemporary teenage motherhood in some ways represents a *continuation* of 1950s values in a new economic situation that makes early marriage less viable. Of course, modern teen pregnancy also reflects the rejection of some of those earlier values. The values that have broken down, however, have little to do with sexual restraint. What we now think of as 1950s sexual morality depended not so much on stricter sexual control as on intensification of the sexual double standard. Elaine Tyler May argues that sexual "repression" gave way to sexual "containment." The new practice of going steady "widened the boundaries of permissible sexual activity," creating a "sexual brinksmanship" in which women bore the burden of "drawing the line," but that line was constantly changing. Popular opinion admitted, as the *Ladies' Home Journal* put it in 1956, that "sex suggestiveness" was here to stay, but insisted that it was up to women to "put the brakes on."

This double standard led to a Byzantine code of sexual conduct: "Petting" was sanctioned so long as one didn't go "too far" (though this was an elastic and ambiguous prohibition); a woman could be touched on various parts of her body (how low depended on how serious the relationship was) but "nice girls" refused to fondle the comparable male parts in return; mutual stimulation to orgasm was compatible with maintaining a "good" reputation so long as penetration did not occur.

The success of sexual containment depended on sexual inequality. Men no longer bore the responsibility of "saving themselves for marriage"; this was now exclusively a woman's job. In sharp contrast to the nineteenth century, when "oversexed" or demanding men were considered to have serious problems, it was now considered "normal" or "natural" for men to be sexually aggressive. The "average man," advice writers for women commented indulgently, "will go as far as you let him go." When women succeeded in "holding out" (a phrase charged with moral ambiguity), they sometimes experienced problems "letting go," even after marriage; when they failed, they were often reproached later by their husbands for having "given in." The contradictions of this double standard could not long withstand the period's pressures for companionate romance: By 1959, a more liberal single standard had already gained ground among older teenagers across America.

THE PROBLEM OF WOMEN IN TRADITIONAL FAMILIES

People who romanticize the 1950s, or any model of the traditional family, are usually put in an uncomfortable position when they attempt to gain popular support. The legitimacy of women's rights is so widely accepted today that only a tiny minority of Americans seriously propose that women should go back to being full-time housewives or should be denied educational and job opportunities because of their family responsibility. Yet when commentators lament the collapse of traditional family commitments and values, they almost invariably mean the uniquely female duties associated with the doctrine of separate spheres for men and women.

Karl Zinsmeister of the American Enterprise Institute, for example, bemoans the fact that "workaholism and family dereliction have become equal-opportunity diseases, striking mothers as much as fathers." David Blankenhorn of the Institute for American Values expresses sympathy for the needs of working women but warns that "employed women do not a family make. The goals of women (and of men, too) in the workplace are primarily individualistic: social recognition, wages, opportunities for advancement, and self-fulfillment. But the family is about collective goals . . . building life's most important bonds of affection, nurturance, mutual support, and long-term commitment."

In both statements, a seemingly gender-neutral indictment of family irresponsibility ends up being directed most forcefully against women. For Blankenhorn, it is not surprising that *men's* goals should be individualistic; this is a parenthetical aside. For Zinsmeister, the problem with the disease of family dereliction is that it has spread to women. So long as it was confined to men, evidently, there was no urgency about finding a cure.

The crisis of commitment in America is usually seen as a problem associated with women's changing roles because women's family functions have historically mediated the worst effects of competition and individualism in the larger society. Most people who talk about balancing private advancement and individual rights with "nurturance, mutual support, and long-term commitment" do not envision any serious rethinking of the individualistic, antisocial tendencies in our society, nor any ways of broadening our sources of nurturance and mutual assistance. Instead, they seek ways—sometimes through repression, sometimes through reform—of rebuilding a family in which women can continue to compensate for, rather than challenge, the individualism in our larger economy and polity.

ROBBIE E. DAVIS-FLOYD

Gender and Ritual:
Giving Birth the American Way

Robbie E. Davis-Floyd has authored or co-authored eleven books on ritual, gender, and reproduction. She is a Research Fellow in the Department of Anthropology at the University of Texas, Austin, and lectures nationally and internationally. For additional information, visit www.davis-floyd.com.

Although the array of new technologies that radically alter the nature of human reproduction is exponentially increasing, childbirth is still an entirely gendered phenomenon. Because only women have babies, the way a society treats pregnancy and childbirth reveals a great deal about the way that society treats women. The experience of childbirth is unique for every woman, and yet in the United States childbirth is treated in a highly standardized way. No matter how long or short, how easy or hard their labors, the vast majority of American women are hooked up to an electronic fetal monitor and an IV (intravenously administered fluids and/or medication), are encouraged to use pain-relieving drugs, receive an episiotomy (a surgical incision in the vagina to widen the birth outlet in order to prevent tearing) at the moment of birth, and are separated from their babies shortly after birth. Most women also receive doses of the synthetic hormone pitocin to speed their labors, and they give birth flat on their backs. Nearly one-quarter of babies are delivered by Cesarean section.

Many Americans, including most of the doctors and nurses who attend birth, view these procedures as medical necessities. Yet anthropologists regularly describe other, less technological ways to give birth. For example, the Mayan Indians of Highland Chiapas hold onto a rope while squatting for birth, a position that is far more beneficial than the flat-on-your-back-with-your-feet-in-stirrups (lithotomy) position. Mothers in many low-technology cultures give birth sitting, squatting, semi-reclining in their hammocks, or on their hands and knees, and are nurtured through the pain of labor by experienced midwives and supportive female relatives. What then might explain the standardization and technical elaboration of the American birthing process?

One answer emerges from the field of symbolic anthropology. Early in this century, Arnold van Gennep noticed that in many societies around the world, major life transitions are ritualized. These cultural rites of passage make

106

it appear that society itself effects the transformation of the individual. Could this explain the standardization of American birth? I believe the answer is yes.

I came to this conclusion as a result of a study I conducted of American birth between 1983 and 1991. I interviewed over 100 mothers, as ell as many of the obstetricians, nurses, childbirth educators, and midwives who attended them.[1] While poring over my interviews, I began to understand that the forces shaping American hospital birth are invisible to us because they stem from the conceptual foundations of our society. I realized that American society's deepest beliefs center on science, technology, patriarchy, and the institutions that control and disseminate them, and that there could be no better transmitter of these core values and beliefs than the hospital procedures so salient in American birth. Through these procedures, American women are repeatedly told, in dozens of visible and invisible ways, that their bodies are defective machines incapable of giving birth without the assistance of these other, male-created, more perfect machines.

RITES OF PASSAGE

A *ritual* is a patterned, repetitive, and symbolic enactment of a cultural belief or value; its primary purpose is alignment of the belief system of the individual with that of society. A *rite of passage* is a series of rituals that move individuals from one social state or status to another as, for example, from girlhood to womanhood, boyhood to manhood, or from the womb to the world of culture. Rites of passage transform both society's perception of individuals and individuals' perceptions of themselves.

Rites of passage generally consist of three stages, originally outlined by van Gennep: (1) *separation* of the individuals from their preceding social state; (2) a period of *transition* in which they are neither one thing nor the other; and (3) an *integration* phase, in which, through various rites of incorporation, they are absorbed into their new social state. In the year-long pregnancy/childbirth rite of passage in American society, the separation phase begins with the woman's first awareness of pregnancy; the transition stage lasts until several days after the birth; and the integration phase ends gradually in the newborn's first few months of life, when the new mother begins to feel that, as one woman put it, she is "mainstreaming it again."

Victor Turner, an anthropologist famous for his writings on ritual, pointed out that the most important feature of all rites of passage is that they place their participants in a transitional realm that has few of the attributes of the past or coming state. Existing in such a non-ordinary realm, he argues, facilitates the gradual psychological opening of the initiates to profound interior change. In many initiation rites involving major transitions into new social roles (such as military basic training), ritualized physical and mental hardships serve to break down initiates' belief systems, leaving them open to new learning and the construction of new cognitive categories.

Birth is an ideal candidate for ritualization of this sort, and is, in fact, used in many societies as a model for structuring other rites of passage. By making the naturally transformative process of birth into a cultural rite of passage, a society can ensure that its basic values will be transmitted to the three new members born out of the birth process: the new baby, the woman reborn into the new social role of mother, and the man reborn as father. The new mother especially must be very clear about these values, as she is generally the one primarily responsible for teaching them to her children, who will be society's new members and the guarantors of its future.

THE CHARACTERISTICS OF RITUAL

Some primary characteristics of ritual are particularly relevant to understanding how the initiatory process of cognitive restructuring is accomplished in hospital birth. We will examine each of these characteristics in order to understand (1) how ritual works; (2) how the natural process of childbirth is transformed in the United States into a cultural rite of passage; and (3) how that transformation works to cement the patriarchal status quo.

Symbolism

Above all else, ritual is symbolic. Ritual works by sending messages in the form of symbols to those who perform and those who observe it. A *symbol* is an object, idea, or action that is loaded with cultural meaning. The left hemisphere of the human brain decodes and analyzes straightforward verbal messages, enabling the recipient to either accept or reject their content. Complex ritual symbols, on the other hand, are received by the right hemisphere of the brain, where they are interpreted holistically. Instead of being analyzed intellectually, a symbol's message will be *felt* through the body and the emotions. Thus, even though recipients may be unaware of incorporating the symbol's message, its ultimate effect may be extremely powerful.

Routine obstetric procedures are highly symbolic. For example, to be seated in a wheelchair upon entering the hospital, as many laboring women are, is to receive through their bodies the symbolic message that they are disabled; to then he be put to bed is to receive the symbolic message that they are sick. Although no one pronounces, "You are disabled; you are sick," such graphic demonstrations of disability and illness can be far more powerful than words. Suzanne Sampson told me:

> I can remember just almost being in tears by the way they would wheel you in. I would come into the hospital, on top of this, breathing, you know, all in control. And they slap you in a wheelchair! It made me suddenly feel like maybe I wasn't in control any more.

The intravenous drips commonly attached to the hands or arms of birthing women make a powerful symbolic statement: They are umbilical cords to the hospital. The cord connecting her body to the fluid-filled bottle places the woman in the same relation to the hospital as the baby in her womb is to her. By making her dependent on the institution for her life, the IV conveys to her one of the most profound messages of her initiation experience: In American society, we are all dependent on institutions for our lives. The message is even more compelling in her case, for *she* is the real giver of life. Society and its institutions cannot exist unless women give birth, yet the birthing woman in the hospital is shown, not that she gives life, but rather that the institution does.

A Cognitive Matrix

A *matrix* (from the Latin *mater*, mother), like a womb, is something from within which something else comes. Rituals are not arbitrary; they come from within the belief system of a group. Their primary purpose is to enact, and thereby, to transmit that belief system into the emotions, minds, and bodies of their participants. Thus, analysis of a culture's rituals can lead to a profound understanding of its belief system.

Analysis of the rituals of hospital birth reveals their cognitive matrix to be the *technocratic model* of reality which forms the philosophical basis of both Western biomedicine and American society. All cultures develop technologies. But most do not supervalue their technologies in the particular way that we do. This point is argued clearly by Peter C. Reynolds (1991) in his book *Stealing Fire: The Mythology of the Technocracy* (a *technocracy* is a hierarchical, bureaucratic society driven by an ideology of technological progress). There he discusses how we "improve upon" nature by controlling it through technology. The technocratic model is the paradigm that charters such behavior. Its early forms were originally developed in the 1600s by Descartes, Bacon, and Hobbes, among others. This model assumes that the universe is mechanistic, following predictable laws that the enlightened can discover through science and manipulate through technology, in order to decrease their dependence on nature. In this model, the human body is viewed as a machine that can be taken apart and put back together to ensure proper functioning. In the seventeenth century, the practical utility of this body-as-machine metaphor lay in its separation of body, mind, and soul. The soul could be left to religion, the mind to the philosophers, and the body could be opened up to scientific investigation.

The dominant religious belief systems of Western Europe at that time held that women were inferior to men—closer to nature and feebler both in body and intellect. Consequently, the men who developed the idea of the body-as-machine also firmly established the male body as the prototype of this machine. Insofar as it deviated from the male standard, the female body was regarded as abnormal, inherently defective, and dangerously under the influence of nature.

The metaphor of the body-as-machine and the related image of the female body as a defective machine eventually formed the philosophical foundations of modern obstetrics. Wide cultural acceptance of these metaphors accompanied the demise of the midwife and the rise of the male-attended, mechanically manipulated birth. Obstetrics was thus enjoined by its own conceptual origins to develop tools and technologies for the manipulation and improvement of the inherently defective, and therefore anomalous and dangerous, process of birth.

The rising science of obstetrics ultimately accomplished this goal by adopting the model of the assembly-line production of goods as its template for hospital birth. Accordingly, a woman's reproductive tract came to be treated like a birthing machine by skilled technicians working under semiflexible timetables to meet production and quality control demands. As one fourth-year resident observed:

> We shave 'em, we prep 'em, we hook 'em up to the IV and administer sedation. We deliver the baby, it goes to the nursery, and the mother goes to her room. There's no room for niceties around here. We just move 'em right on through. It's hard not to see it like an assembly line.

The hospital itself is a highly sophisticated technocratic factory; the more technology the hospital has to offer, the better it is considered to be. Because it is an institution, the hospital constitutes a more significant social unit than an individual or a family. Therefore it can require that the birth process conform more to institutional than personal needs. As one resident explained,

> There is a set, established routine for doing things, usually for the convenience of the doctors and the nurses, and the laboring woman is someone you work around, rather than with.

The most desirable end-product of the birth process is the new social member, the baby; the new mother is a secondary by-product. One obstetrician commented, "It was what we were all trained to always go after—the perfect body. That's what we were trained to produce. The quality of the mother's experience—we rarely thought about that."

Repetition and Redundancy

Ritual is marked by repetition and redundancy. For maximum effectiveness, a ritual concentrates on sending one basic set of messages, repeating it over and over again in different forms. Hospital birth takes place in a series of ritual procedures, many of which convey the same message in different forms. The open and exposing hospital gown, the ID bracelet, the intravenous fluid, the bed in which she is placed—all these convey to the laboring woman that she is dependent on the institution.

She is also reminded in myriad ways of the potential defectiveness of her birthing machine. These include periodic and sometimes continuous electronic monitoring of that machine, frequent manual examinations of her cervix to make sure that it is dilating on schedule, and, if it isn't, administration of the synthetic hormone pitocin to speed up labor so that birth can take place within the required 26 hours.[2] All three of these procedures convey the same messages over and over: *Time is important, you must produce on time, and you cannot do that without technological assistance because your machine is defective.* In the technocracy, we supervalue time. It is only fitting that messages about time's importance should be repeatedly conveyed during the births of new social members.

Cognitive Reduction

In any culture, the intellectual abilities of ritual participants are likely to differ, often markedly. It is not practical for society to design different rituals for persons of different levels of intellectual ability. So ritual utilizes specific techniques, such as rhythmic repetition, to reduce all participants to the same narrower level of cognitive functioning. This low level involves thinking in either/or patterns that do not allow for consideration of options or alternative views.

Four techniques are often employed by ritual to accomplish this end. One is the *repetition* already discussed above. A second is *hazing*, which is familiar to undergraduates who undergo fraternity initiation rites but is also part of rites of passage all over the world. A third is *strange-making*—making the commonplace appear strange by juxtaposing it with the unfamiliar. Fourth is *symbolic inversion*—metaphorically turning things upside-down and inside-out to generate, in a phrase coined by Roger Abrahams (1973), "The power attendant upon confusion."

For example, in the rite of passage of military basic training, the initiate's normal patterns of action and thought are turned topsy-turvy. He is made strange to himself: His head is shaved, so that he does not even recognize himself in the mirror. He must give up his clothes, those expressions of his past individual identity and personality, and put on a uniform identical to that of the other initiates. Constant and apparently meaningless hazing, such as orders to dig six ditches and then fill them in, further breaks down his cognitive structure. Then through repetitive and highly symbolic rituals, such as sleeping with his rifle, the basic values, beliefs, and practices of the Marines are incorporated into his body and his mind.

In medical school and again in residency, the same ritual techniques that transform a youth into a Marine are employed to transform college students into physicians. Reduced from the high status of graduate to the lowly status of first-year medical student, initiates are subjected to hazing techniques of rote memorization of endless facts and formulas, absurdly long hours of work, and intellectual and sensory overload. As one physician explained:

> You go through, in a six-week course, a thousand-page book. You have pop quizzes in two or three courses every day the first year. We'd get up around 6,

attend classes till 5, go home and eat, then head back to school and be in anatomy lab working with a cadaver, or something, until 1 or 2 in the morning, and then go home and get a couple of hours sleep, and then go out again.

Subjected to such a process, medical students often gradually lose any broadminded goals of "helping humanity" they had upon entering medical school. A successful rite of passage produces new professional values structured in accordance with the technocratic and scientific values of the dominant medical system. The emotional impact of this cognitive narrowing is aptly summarized by a former resident:

> Most of us went into medical school with pretty humanitarian ideals. I know I did. But the whole process of medical education makes you inhuman . . . you forget about the rest of life. By the time you get to residency, you end up not caring about anything beyond the latest techniques and most sophisticated tests.

Likewise, the birthing woman is socialized by ritual techniques of cognitive reduction. She is made strange to herself by being dressed in a hospital gown, tagged with an ID bracelet, and by the shaving or clipping of her pubic hair, which symbolically de-sexualizes the lower portion of her body, returning it to a conceptual state of childishness. (In many cultures, sexuality and hair are symbolically linked.) Labor itself is painful, and is often rendered more so by the hazing technique of frequent and very painful insertion of someone's fingers into her vagina to see how far her cervix has dilated. This technique also functions as a strange-making device. Since almost any nurse or resident in need of practice may check her cervix, the birthing woman's most private parts are symbolically inverted into institutional property. One respondent's obstetrician observed, "It's a wonder you didn't get an infection, with so many people sticking their hands inside of you."

Cognitive Stabilization

When humans are subjected to extremes of stress and pain, they may become unreasonable and out of touch with reality. Ritual assuages this condition by giving people a conceptual handle-hold to keep them from "falling apart" or "losing it." When the airplane starts to falter, even passengers who don't go to church are likely to pray! Ritual mediates between cognition and chaos by making reality appear to conform to accepted cognitive categories. In other words, to perform a ritual in the face of chaos is to restore order to the world.

Labor subjects most women to extremes of pain, which are often intensified by the alien and often unsupportive hospital environment. They look to hospital rituals to relieve the distress resulting from their pain and fear. They utilize breathing rituals taught in hospital-sponsored childbirth education classes for cognitive stabilization. They turn to drugs for pain relief, and to the reassuring presence of medical technology for relief from fear. LeAnn Kellog expressed it this way:

> I was terrified when my daughter was born. I just knew I was going to split open and bleed to death right there on the table, but she was coming so fast, they didn't have any time to do anything to me. . . . I like Cesarean sections, because you don't have to be afraid.

When you come from within a belief system, its rituals will comfort and calm you. Accordingly, those women in my study who were in basic agreement with the technocratic model of birth before going into the hospital (70%) expressed general satisfaction with their hospital births.

Order, Formality, and a Sense of Inevitability

Its exaggerated and precise order and formality set ritual apart from other modes of social interaction, enabling it to establish an atmosphere that feels both inevitable and inviolate. To perform a series of rituals is to feel oneself locking onto a set of "cosmic gears" that will safely crank the individual through danger to safety. For example, Trobriand sea fishermen described by anthropologist Bronislaw Malinowski (1954) regularly performed an elaborate series of rituals on the beach before embarking. The fishermen believed that these rituals, when carried out with precision, would obligate the gods of the sea to do their part to bring the fishermen safely home. Likewise, obstetricians, and many birthing women, feel that correct performance of standardized procedures ought to result in a healthy baby. Such rituals generate in humans a sense of confidence that makes it easier to face the challenge and caprice of nature.

When women who have placed their faith in the technocratic model are denied its rituals, they often react with fear and a feeling of being neglected:

> My husband and I got to the hospital, and we thought they would take care of everything. I kept sending my husband out to ask them to give me something for the pain, to check me, but they were short-staffed and they just ignored me until the shift changed in the morning.

Hospital rituals such as electronic monitoring work to give the laboring woman a sense that society is using the best it has to offer—the full force of its technology—to inevitably ensure that she will have a safe birth.

However, once those "cosmic gears" have been set into motion, there is often no stopping them. The very inevitability of hospital procedures makes them almost antithetical to the possibility of normal, natural birth. A "cascade of intervention" occurs when one obstetric procedure alters the natural birthing process, causing complications, and so inexorably "necessitates" the next procedure, and the next. Many of the women in my study experienced such a "cascade" when they received some form of pain relief, such as an epidural, which slowed their labor. Then pitocin was administered through the

IV to speed up the labor, but pitocin very suddenly induced longer and stronger contractions. Unprepared for the additional pain, the women asked for more pain relief, which ultimately necessitated more pitocin. Pitocin-induced contractions, together with the fact that the mother must lie flat on her back because of the electronic monitor belts strapped around her stomach, can cause the supply of blood and oxygen to he fetus to drop, affecting the fetal heart rate. In response to the "distress" registered on the fetal monitor, an emergency Cesarean is performed.

Acting, Stylization, Staging

Ritual's set-apartness is enhanced by the fact that it is usually highly stylized and self-consciously acted, like a part in a play. Most of us can easily accept this view of the careful performances of TV evangelists, but it may come as a surprise that those who perform the rituals of hospital birth are often aware of their dramatic elements. The physician becomes the protagonist. The woman's body is the stage upon which he performs, often for an appreciative audience of medical students, residents, and nurses. Here is how one obstetrician played to a student audience observing the delivery he was performing:

> In honest-to-God natural conditions babies were *sometimes* born without tearing the perineum and without an episiotomy, but without artificial things like anesthesia and episiotomy, the muscle is torn apart and if it is not cut, it is usually not repaired. Even today, if there is no episiotomy and repair, those women quite often develop a rectocoele and a relaxed vaginal floor. This is what I call the saggy, baggy bottom. [Laughter by the students. A student nurse asks if exercise doesn't help strengthen the perineum.] No, exercises may be for the birds, but they're not for bottoms. . . . When the woman is bearing down, the leveator muscles of the perineum contract too. This means the baby is caught between the diaphragm and the perineum. Consequently, anesthesia and episiotomy will reduce the pressure on the head, and hopefully, produce more Republicans. (More laughter from the students.) (Shaw 1974: 90)

Cognitive Transformation

The goal of most initiatory rites of passage is cognitive transformation. It occurs when the symbolic messages of ritual fuse with individual emotion and belief, and the individual's entire cognitive structure reorganizes around the newly internalized symbolic complex. The following quote from a practicing obstetrician presents the outcome for him of such transformative learning:

> I think my training was valuable. The philosophy was one of teaching one way to do it, and that was the right way. . . . I like the set hard way. I like the riverbanks that confine you in a direction. . . . You learn one thing real well, and that's the way.

For both nascent physicians and nascent mothers, cognitive transformation of the initiate occurs when reality as presented by the technocratic model, and reality as the initiate perceives it, become one and the same. This process is gradual. Routine obstetric procedures cumulatively map the technocratic model of birth onto he birthing woman's perceptions of her labor experience. They align her belief system with that of society.

Take the way many mothers come to think about the electronic fetal monitor, for example. The monitor is a machine that uses ultrasound to measure the strength of the mother's contractions and the rate of the baby's heartbeat through electrodes belted onto the mother's abdomen. This machine has become the symbol of high technology hospital birth. Observers and participants alike report that the monitor, once attached, becomes the focal point of the labor.[3] Nurses, physicians, husbands, and even the mother herself become visually and conceptually glued to the machine, which then shapes their perceptions and interpretations of the birth process. Diana Crosse described her experience this way:

> As soon as I got hooked up to he monitor, all everyone did was stare at it. The nurses didn't even look at me anymore when they came into the room—they went straight to the monitor. I got the weirdest feeling that *it* was having the baby, not me.

This statement illustrates the successful conceptual fusion between the woman's perceptions of her birth experience and the technocratic model. So thoroughly was this model mapped on to her psyche that she began to feel that the machine was having the baby, that she was a mere onlooker. Soon after the monitor was in place, she requested a Cesarean section, declaring that there was "no more point in trying."

Consider the visual and kinesthetic images that the laboring woman experiences—herself in bed, in a hospital gown, staring up at an IV pole, bag, and cord, and down at a steel bed and a huge belt encircling her waist. Her entire sensory field conveys one overwhelming message about our culture's deepest values and beliefs: Technology is supreme, and the individual is utterly dependent upon it.

Internalizing the technocratic model, women come to accept the notion that the female body is inherently defective. This notion then shapes their perceptions of the labor experience, as exemplified by Merry Simpson's story:

> It seemed as though my uterus had suddenly tired! When the nurses in attendance noted a contraction building on the recorder, they instructed me to begin pushing, not waiting for the urge to push, so that by the time the **urge** pervaded, I invariably had no strength remaining but was left gasping and dizzy. . . . I felt suddenly depressed by the fact that labor, which had progressed so uneventfully up to this point, had now become unproductive.

Note that she does not say "The nurses had me pushing too soon," but "My uterus had tired," and labor had "become unproductive." These responses reflect her internalization of the technocratic tenet that when something goes wrong, it is her body's fault.

Affectivity and Intensification

Rituals tend to intensify toward a climax. Behavioral psychologists have long understood that people are far more likely to remember, and to absorb lessons from, those events that carry an emotional charge. The order and stylization of ritual, combined with its rhythmic repetitiveness and the intensification of its messages, methodically create just the sort of highly charged emotional atmosphere that works to ensure long-term learning.

As the moment of birth approaches, the number of ritual procedures performed upon the woman will intensify toward the climax of birth, whether or not her condition warrants such intervention. For example, once the woman's cervix reaches full dilation (10 cm), the nursing staff immediately begins to exhort the woman to push with each contraction, whether or not she actually feels the urge to push. When delivery is imminent, the woman must be transported, often with a great deal of drama and haste, down the hall to the delivery room. Lest the baby be born *en route*, the laboring woman is then exhorted, with equal vigor, *not* to push. Such commands constitute a complete denial of the natural rhythms of the woman's body. They signal that her labor is a mechanical event and that she is subordinate to the institution's expectations and schedule. Similar high drama will pervade the rest of her birthing experience.

Preservation of the Status Quo

A major function of ritual is cultural preservation. Through explicit enactment of a culture's belief system, ritual works both to preserve and to transmit the culture. Preserving the culture includes perpetuating its power structure, so it is usually the case that those in positions of power will have unique control over ritual performance. They will utilize the effectiveness of ritual to reinforce both their own importance and the importance of the belief and value system that legitimizes their positions.

In spite of tremendous advances in equality for women, the United States is still a patriarchy. It is no cultural accident that 99 percent of American women give birth in hospitals, where only physicians, most of whom are male, have final authority over the performance of birth rituals—an authority that reinforces the cultural privileging of patriarchy for both mothers and their medical attendants.

Nowhere is this reality more visible than in the lithotomy position. Despite years of effort on the part of childbirth activists, including many obstetricians, the majority of American women still give birth lying flat on their backs. This position is physiologically dysfunctional. It compresses major blood vessels, lowering the mother's circulation and thus the baby's oxygen supply. It increases the need for forceps because it both narrows the pelvic outlet and ensures that the baby, who must follow the curve of the birth canal, quite literally will be born heading upward, against gravity. This lithotomy position completes the process of symbolic inversion that has been in motion ever since the woman was put into that "upside-down" hospital gown. Her normal bodily patterns are turned, quite literally, upside-down—her legs are in the air, her vagina totally exposed. As the ultimate symbolic inversion, it is ritually appropriate that this position be reserved for the peak tranformational moments of the initiation experience—the birth itself. The doctor—society's official representative—stands in control not at the mother's head nor at her side, but at her bottom, where the baby's head is beginning to emerge.

Structurally speaking, this puts the woman's vagina where her head should be. Such total inversion is perfectly appropriate from a social perspective, as the technocratic model promises us that eventually we will be able to grow babies in machines—that is, have them with our cultural heads instead of our natural bottoms. In our culture, "up" is good and "down" is bad, so the babies born of science and technology must be delivered "up" toward the positively valued cultural world, instead of down toward the negatively valued natural world. Interactionally, the obstetrician is "up" and the birthing woman is "down," an inversion that speaks eloquently to her of her powerlessness and of the power of society at the supreme moment of her own individual transformation.

The episiotomy performed by the obstetrician just before birth also powerfully enacts the status quo in American society. This procedure, performed on over 90 percent of first-time mothers as they give birth, expresses the value and importance of one of our technocratic society's most fundamental markers—the straight line. Through episiotomies, physicians can deconstruct the vagina (stretchy, flexible, part-circular and part-formless, feminine, creative, sexual, non-linear), then reconstruct it in accordance with our cultural belief and value system. Doctors are taught (incorrectly) that straight cuts heal faster than the small jagged tears that sometimes occur during birth. They learn that straight cuts will prevent such tears, but in fact, episiotomies often cause severe tearing that would not otherwise occur (Klein 1992; Shiono et al. 1990; Thorp and Bowes 1989; Wilcox et al. 1989[4]). These teachings dramatize our Western belief in the superiority of culture over nature. Because it virtually does not exist in nature, the line is most useful in aiding us in our constant conceptual efforts to separate ourselves from nature.

Moreover, since surgery constitutes the ultimate form of manipulation of the human body-machine, it is the most highly valued form of medicine. Routinizing the episiotomy, and increasingly, the Cesarean section, has served both to legitimize and to raise the status of obstetrics as a profession, by ensuring that childbirth will be not a natural but a surgical procedure.

Effecting Social Change

Paradoxically, ritual, with all of its insistence on continuity and order, can be an important factor not only in individual transformation but also in social change. New belief and value systems are most effectively spread through new rituals designed to enact and transmit them; entrenched belief and value systems are most effectively altered through alterations in the rituals that enact them.

Nine percent of my interviewees entered the hospital determined to avoid technocratic rituals in order to have "completely natural childbirth," yet ended up with highly technocratic births. These nine women experienced extreme cognitive dissonance between their previously held self-images and those internalized in the hospital. Most of them suffered severe emotional wounding and short-term post-partum depression as a result. But 15 percent did achieve their goal of natural childbirth, thereby avoiding conceptual fusion with the technocratic model. These women were personally empowered by their birth experiences. They tended to view technology as a resource that they could choose to utilize or ignore, and often consciously subverted their socialization process by replacing technocratic symbols with self-empowering alternatives. For example, they wore their own clothes and ate their own food, rejecting the hospital gown and the IV. They walked the halls instead of going to bed. They chose perineal massage instead of episiotomy, and gave birth like "primitives," sitting up, squatting, or on their hands and knees. One of them, confronted with the wheelchair, said "I don't need this," and used it as a luggage cart. This rejection of customary ritual elements is an exceptionally powerful way to induce change, as it takes advantage of an already charged and dramatic situation.

During the 1970s and early 1980s, the conceptual hegemony of the technocratic model in the hospital was severely challenged by the natural childbirth movement which these 24 women represent. Birth activists succeeded in getting hospitals to allow fathers into labor and delivery rooms, mothers to birth consciously (without being put to sleep), and mothers and babies to room together after birth. They fought for women to have the right to birth without drugs or interventions, to walk around or even be in water during labor (in some hospitals, Jacuzzis were installed). Prospects for change away from the technocratic model of birth by the 1990s seemed bright.

Changing a society's belief and value system by changing the rituals that enact it is possible, but not easy. To counter attempts at change, individuals in positions of authority often intensify the rituals that support the status quo. Thus a response to the threat posed by the natural childbirth movement was to intensify the use of high technology in hospital birth. During the 1980s, periodic electronic monitoring of nearly all women became standard procedure, the epidural rate shot up to 80 percent, and the Cesarean rate rose to nearly 25 percent. Part of the impetus for this technocratic intensification is the increase in malpractice suits against physicians. The threat of lawsuit forces doctors to practice conservatively—that is, in strict accordance with technocratic standards. As one of them explained,

> Certainly I've changed the way I practice since malpractice became an issue. I do more C-sections . . . and more and more tests to cover myself. More expensive stuff. We don't do risky things that women ask for—we're very conservative in our approach to everything. . . . In 1970 before all this came up, my C-section rate was around 4 percent. It has gradually climbed every year since then. In 1985 it was 16 percent, then in 1986 it was 23 percent.

The money goes where the values lie. From this macro-cultural perspective, the increase in malpractice suits emerges as society's effort to make sure that its representatives, the obstetricians, perpetuate our technocratic core value system by continuing through birth rituals to transmit that system. Its perpetuation seems imperative, for in our technology we see the promise of our eventual transcendence of bodily and earthly limitations—already we replace body parts with computerized devices, grow babies in test tubes, build space stations, and continue to pollute the environment in the expectation that someone will develop the technologies to clean it up!

We are all complicitors in our technocratic system, as we have so very much invested in it. Just as that system has given us increasing control over the natural environment, so it has also given not only doctors but also women increasing control over biology and birth. Contemporary middle-class women do have much greater say over what will be done to them during birth than their mothers, most of whom gave birth during the 1950s and 1960s under general anesthesia. When what they demand is in accord with technocratic values, they have a much greater chance of getting it than their sisters have of achieving natural childbirth. Even as hospital birth still perpetuates patriarchy by treating women's bodies as defective machines, it now also reflects women's greater autonomy by allowing them conceptual separation from those defective machines.

Epidural anesthesia is administered in about 80 percent of American hospital births. So common is its use that many childbirth educators are calling the 1990s the age of the "epidural epidemic." As the epidural numbs the birthing woman, eliminating the pain of childbirth, it also graphically demonstrates to her through lived experience the truth of the Cartesian maxim that mind and body are separate, that the biological realm can be completely cut off from the realm of the intellect and the emotions. The epidural is thus the perfect technocratic tool, serving the interests of the technocratic model by transmitting it, and of women choosing to give birth under that model, by enabling them to use it to divorce themselves from their biology:

> Ultimately the decision to have the epidural and the Cesarean while I was in labor was mine. I told the doctor I'd had enough of this labor business and I'd like to . . . get it over with. So he whisked me off to he delivery room and we did it. (Elaine)

For many women, the epidural provides a means by which they can actively witness birth while avoiding "dropping into biology." Explained Joanne, "I'm not real fond of things that remind me I'm a biological creature—I prefer to think and be an intellectual emotional person." Such women tended to define their bodies as tools, vehicles for their minds. They did not enjoy "giving in to biology" to be pregnant, and were happy to be liberated from biology during birth. And they welcomed advances in birth technologies as extensions of their own ability to control nature.

In dramatic contrast, six of my interviewees (6 percent), insisting that "I am my body," rejected the technocratic model altogether. They chose to give birth at home under an alternative paradigm, the *holistic model*. This model stresses the organicity and trustworthiness of the female body, the natural rhythmicity of labor, the integrity of the family, and self-responsibility. These homebirthers see the safety of the baby and the emotional needs of the mother as one. The safest birth for the baby will be the one that provides the most nurturing environment for the mothers.[5] Said Ryla,

> I got criticized for choosing a home birth, for not considering the safety of the baby. But that's exactly what I was considering! How could it possibly serve my baby for me to give birth in a place that causes my whole body to tense up in anxiety as soon as I walk in the door?

Although homebirthers constitute only about 2 percent of the American birthing population, their conceptual importance is tremendous, as through the alternative rituals of giving birth at home, they enact—and thus guarantee the existence of—a paradigm of pregnancy and birth based on the value of connection, just as the technocratic model is based on the principle of separation.

The technocratic and holistic models represent opposite ends of a spectrum of beliefs about birth and about cultural life. Their differences are mirrored on a wider scale by the ideological conflicts between biomedicine and holistic healing, and between industrialists and ecological activists. These groups are engaged in a core value struggle over the future—a struggle clearly visible in the profound differences in the rituals they daily enact.

CONCLUSION

Every society in the world has felt the need to thoroughly socialize its citizens into conformity with its norms, and citizens derive many benefits from such socialization. If a culture had to rely on policemen and make sure that everyone would obey its laws, it would disintegrate into chaos, as there would not be enough policemen to go around. It is much more practical for cultures to find ways to socialize their members from the *inside*, by making them *want* to conform to society's norms. Ritual is one major way through which such socialization can be achieved.

American obstetrical procedures can be understood as rituals that facilitate the internalization of cultural values. These procedures are patterned, repetitive, and profoundly symbolic, communicating messages concerning our culture's deepest beliefs about the necessity for cultural control of natural processes. They provide an ordered structure to the chaotic flow of the natural birth process. In so doing, they both enhance the natural affectivity of that process and create a sense of inevitability about their performance. Obstetric interventions are also transformative in intent. They attempt to contain and control the process of birth, and to transform the birthing woman into an American mother who has internalized the core values of this society. Such a mother believes in science, relies on technology, recognizes her biological inferiority (either consciously or unconsciously), and so at some level accepts the principles of patriarchy. She will tend to conform to society's dictates and meet the demands of its institutions, and will teach her children to do the same.

Yet it is important to note that human beings are not automatons. Human behavior varies widely even within the restraints imposed by particular cultures, including their rituals. As July Sanders sums it up:

> It's almost like programming you. You get to the hospital. They put you in this wheelchair. They whisk you off from your husband, and I mean just start in on you. Then they put you in another wheelchair, and send you home. And then they say, well, we need to give you something for the depression. [Laughs] Get away from me! That will help my depression!

Through hospital ritual procedures, obstetrics deconstructs birth, then inverts and reconstructs it as a technocratic process. But unlike most transformations effected by ritual, birth does *not* depend upon the performance of ritual to make it happen. The physiological process of labor itself transports the birthing woman into a naturally transitional situation that carries its own affectivity. Hospital procedures take advantage of that affectivity to transmit the core values of American society to birthing women. From society's perspective, the birth process will not be successful unless the woman and child are properly socialized during the experience, transformed as much by the rituals as by the physiology of birth. In the latter half of this century, women have made great strides in attaining equality with men on many cultural fronts. Yet, as I noted at the beginning, the cultural treatment of birth is one of the most revealing indicators about the status of women in a given society. In the United States, through their ritual transformation during birth, women learn profound lessons about the weakness and defectiveness of their bodies and the power of technology. In this way, every day in hospitals all over the country, women's status as subordinate is subtly reinforced, as is the patriarchal nature of the technocracy.

NOTES

1. The full results of this study appear in Davis-Floyd 1992.

2. In Holland, by way of contrast, most births are attended by midwives who recognize that individual labors have individual rhythms. They can stop and start; can take a few hours or several days. If labor slows, the midwives encourage the woman to eat to keep up her strength, and then to sleep until contractions pick up again (Beatriz Smulders, Personal Communication, 1994; Jordan 1993).

3. As is true for most of the procedures interpreted here as rituals, there is no scientific justification for the routine use of the electronic fetal monitor: Numerous large-scale studies have shown no improvement in outcome (Leveno et al. 1986; Prentice and Lind 1987; Sandmire 1990; Shy et al. 1990). What these studies do show is that a dramatic increase in the rate of Cesarean section accompanies routine electronic monitoring. Most commonly, this increase is due both to the occasional malfunctioning of the machine, which sometimes registers fetal distress when there is none, and to the tendency of hospital staff to overreact to fluctuations on the monitor strip.

4. See Goer 1995: 274–284 for summaries and interpretations of these studies and others concerning electronic fetal monitoring.

5. For summaries of studies that demonstrate the safety of planned, midwife-attended home birth relative to hospital birth, see Davis-Floyd 1992, Chapter 4, and Goer 1995.

REFERENCES

Abrahams, Roger D. 1973. "Ritual for Fun and Profit (or The Ends and Outs of Celebration)." Paper delivered at the Burg Wartenstein Symposium No. 59, on "Ritual Reconciliation in Change." New York: Wenner-Gren Foundation for Anthropological Research.

Davis-Floyd, Robbie E. 1992. *Birth as an American Rite of Passage*. Berkeley: University of California Press.

Goer, Henci. 1995. *Obstetric Myths Versus Research Realities: A Guide to the Medical Literature*. Westport, CT: Bergin and Garvey.

Jordan, Brigitte. 1993. *Birth in Four Cultures: A Cross-Cultural Investigation of Birth in Yucatan, Holland, Sweden and the United States* (4th edition revised). Prospect Heights: Waveland Press.

Klein, Michael et al. 1992. "Does Episiotomy Prevent Perineal Trauma and Pelvic Floor Relaxation?" *Online Journal of Current Clinical Trials* 1 (Document 10).

Leveno, K. J., F. G. Cunningham, S. Nelson, M. Roark, M. L. Williams, D. Guzick, S. Dowling, C. R. Rosenfeld, A. Buckley. 1986. "A Prospective Comparison of Selective and Universal Electronic Fetal Monitoring in 34,995 Pregnancies." *New England Journal of Medicine* 315 (10): 615–619.

Malinowski, Bronislaw. 1954. (orig. pub. 1925). "Magic, Science, and Religion." In *Magic, Science and Religion and Other Essays*, pp. 17–87. New York: Doubleday/Anchor.

Prentice, A. and T. Lind. 1987. "Fetal Heart Rate Monitoring During Labor—Too Frequent Intervention, Too Little Benefit." *Lancet* 2: 1375–1877.

Reynolds, Peter C. 1991. *Stealing Fire: The Mythology of the Technocracy*. Palo Alto, CA: Iconic Anthropology Press.

Sandmire, H. F. 1990. "Whither Electronic Fetal Monitoring?" *Obstetrics and Gynecology* 76 (6): 1130–1134.

Shaw, Nancy Stoller. 1974. *Forced Labor: Maternity Case in the United States*. New York: Pergamon Press.

Shiono, P. M. A. Klebanoff, and J. C. Carey. 1990. "Midline Episiotomies: More Harm Than Good?" *American Journal of Obstetrics and Gynecology* 75 (5): 765–770.

Shy, Kirkwood, David A. Luthy, Forrest C. Bennett, Michael Whitfield, Eric B. Larson, Gerald van Belle, James P. Hughes, Judith A. Wilson, Martin A. Stenchever. 1990. "Effects of Electronic Fetal Heart Rate Monitoring, as Compared with Periodic Auscultation, on the Neurologic Development of Premature Infants." *New England Journal of Medicine* 322 (9): 588–593.

Thorp, J. M. and W. A. Bowes. 1989. "Episiotomy: Can Its Routine Use Be Defended?" *American Journal of Obstetrics and Gynecology* 160 (5Pt1): 1027–1030.

Turner, Victor. 1979. (orig. pub. 1964). "Betwixt and Between: The Liminal Period in Rites de Passage." In W. Lessa and E. Z. Vogt (eds.). *Reader in Comparative Religion*, pp. 234–243. 4th edition. New York: Harper and Row.

van Gennep, Arnold. 1966. (orig. pub. 1908). *The Rites of Passage*. Chicago: University of Chicago Press.

Wilcox, L. S. et al. 1989. "Episiotomy and Its Role in the Incidence of Perineal Lacerations in a Maternity Center and a Tertiary Hospital Obstetric Service." *American Journal of Obstetrics and Gynecology* 160 (5Pt1): 1047–1052.

KIRSTEN DELLINGER AND CHRISTINE L. WILLIAMS

Makeup at Work: Negotiating Appearance Rules in the Workplace

Kirsten Dellinger is Professor of Sociology and Anthropology at the University of Mississippi and Christine Williams is Professor of Sociology at the University of Texas. They have co-authored several articles on gender in the workplace, including the following selection, which first appeared in the journal Gender & Society *in 1997.*

Why do women wear makeup to work? Countless books and articles in women's magazines insist that wearing makeup enhances a woman's career. Researchers have also found that conventionally attractive people are perceived as having greater occupational potential than are less attractive people (Jackson 1992, 97; see also Rubinstein 1995). On the other hand, Kanter (1977), Gutek (1985), and several others have argued that the tendency in organizations to define women in terms of their sexuality often has a negative impact on their careers. One study found that while women in high-status occupations view attractiveness as an asset in acquiring new job opportunities, many consider attractiveness a liability in terms of getting along with male colleagues and being taken seriously on the job (Kaslow and Schwartz 1978, cited in Jackson 1992). Since physical attractiveness appears to have both positive and negative consequences for women in the workplace, the question remains, Why do women wear makeup to work?

There is a substantial literature in feminist theory that addresses women's conformity with appearance standards. Recently, feminists have appropriated Foucault's (1979) *docile body thesis* to understand the obsessive practices of weight control, fashion, and cosmetic surgery (Bartky 1990; Bordo 1993). Foucault maintained that the body is a central location for the expression and reproduction of power relationships. Through self-surveillance and everyday disciplinary practices, individuals internalize and reproduce hierarchies of social status and power, transforming their own bodies into "carriers" or representatives of prevailing relations of domination and subordination. Bordo uses this approach to argue that contemporary disciplines of diet and exercise "train the female body in docility and obedience to cultural demands while at the same time [these practices often are] experienced [by women] in terms of power and control" (1993, 27). This thesis can help to explain why some women are drawn into and feel empowered by practices that reproduce male dominance and female subordination.

124

Interestingly, Foucault's theories have also been appropriated by feminists who emphasize women's resistance to oppressive beauty regimens. These theorists draw on Foucault's observation that domination is always met with resistance Thus, instead of examining how women are victimized by a patriarchal beauty culture, by subverting the meaning of oppressive cultural forms. Butler (1990), for example, argues that individuals may resist the very categories of sex and gender through a masquerade of practices of femininity; she suggests that drag may be one form of making such "gender trouble" with our bodies. This approach is useful in preserving a sense of women's cultural agency and asserting the possibility for change in oppressive social relations.

What is too often missing in the theoretical debates about femininity and the body is the complicated relationship between powerful hegemonic ideologies and women's agency reflected in their actual lived experiences. Deveaux warns that feminists should not overemphasize either the docile body thesis or the liberatory aspects of Foucault's work because doing so "blocks meaningful discussion of how women feel about their bodies, their appearances, and social norms. It obscures the complex ways that gender is constructed, and the fact that differences among women — age, race, culture, sexual orientation, and class — translate into myriad variations in response to ideals of femininity and their attendant practices" (1994, 227). The challenge for feminist researchers is to treat women as "active and knowledgeable agents" in the construction of social life while simultaneously acknowledging how women's activities are "limited through asymmetrical power structures" (Fisher and Davis (1993, 3). . . .

This article seeks to understand women's use of makeup in the workplace without treating women as cultural dopes of oppressive patriarchal regimes. Makeup is a topic that has been largely ignored by sociologists, including many feminists. Although many women spend a significant amount of time each day applying makeup, sustaining a multibillion-dollar industry (Chapkis 1986; Wolf 1991), women's concerns about their personal appearance often are trivialized and considered unworthy topics for sociological investigation. . . .

The few social researchers who have discussed makeup have viewed it as an imposition of patriarchal culture (Adkins 1995; Barthel 1988) or as an expression of women's pleasure in their identity as women (Beausoleil 1994; Rubinstein 1995). Both approaches suffer from the limitations discussed by Deveaux (1994). The former approach ignores women's agency and fails to explain the processes whereby oppressive patriarchal ideologies are translated into women's actual practices. The latter approach exaggerates the possibilities for women's self-expression and resistance to appearance norms by underplaying the significance of the specific social contexts that frame women's use of makeup.

In this article, we attempt to move beyond the depiction of women as either oppressed victims or freewheeling agents. By examining women's lived experiences with makeup within the context of their work settings, we explore how women express themselves and assert autonomy within the structural constraints imposed by social institutions. We examine the appearance rules that women confront at work and how these rules reproduce assumptions about sexuality and gender. We also explore several ways that women negotiate these rules and what wearing makeup means to them in their specific work contexts. We argue that wearing makeup does contribute to the reproduction of inequality at work, but we emphasize that women who wear makeup are seeking empowerment and pleasure. The institutionalized workplace norms about appearance effectively limit the possibilities for resistance.

METHODS

The goal of this study is to explore how norms of female attractiveness shape women's use of makeup in a variety of work settings and how a diverse group of women alter the meanings of these norms and determine their own makeup practices. A total of 20 women were selected for hourlong, in-depth interviews. The same includes 12 non-Hispanic Whites, 2 Mexican Americans, 2 African Americans, 1 Asian American, 1 Mexican, 1 Taiwanese, and 1 Venezuelan. Fifteen of the women identify as heterosexual, and 5 identify as lesbian. Their ages range from 20 to 64. Nine of the women identify themselves as married or partnered; 7 are single; 4 are divorced.

Of the women, 18 were employed full-time in the paid labor force at the time of the study; 1 was employed part-time (Jennifer); and 1 (Melissa) was not currently in the paid labor force but was working as a full-time homemaker. The women's occupations include both predominantly female and predominantly male jobs. Their workplaces range from professional downtown office buildings to church day care facilities to an at-home office for massage therapy. Respondents were selected to enable us to investigate the broadest possible range of work environments, including professional and service-sector settings.

The interviews were conducted by the first author. Respondents were asked about their current everyday experiences with and feelings about makeup, dress codes, or informal appearance requirements at work; coworkers' reactions to their appearance; their own feelings about wearing or not wearing makeup at work; and the consequences of not wearing makeup at work.

FINDINGS

When asked about their makeup practices, 14 women said they wear makeup everyday at work, 2 said they wear it most of the time, and 4 said they never or almost never wear makeup to work. Many of the women who wear makeup daily report that they do not consciously think about their use of cosmetics. They suggest that it becomes "a routine," "a habit," or "unconscious." Sarah, a 42-year-old Mexican American administrative assistant, wears makeup "everyday":

> Except Saturdays. I mean, of course, I get up early every morning and makeup is one of my routines. It's just a way of life, I mean. and it's probably rather silly when you think about it, but I'm so used to it. I mean, it's such a normal part of my life that I just do it.

None of the women interviewed recalled a specific written requirement for makeup use even when their workplace was regulated by a formal dress code policy. Women said that they themselves—as opposed to formal regulations—determine what constitutes an appropriately attractive appearance and whether they attempt to meet those standards. In other words, the women believed it was their personal choice whether or not to wear makeup. Nonetheless, many women experience or perceive they will experience negative consequences if their makeup is not properly applied. They expressed three major concerns: Respondents felt that women who do not wear makeup do not appear to be (1) healthy, (2) heterosexual, or (3) credible. We will discuss each of these issues, focusing on how women internalize the assessments of their coworkers, transforming institutionalized norms governing makeup use into their "personal choices." Subsequently, we will discuss how some women resisted or subverted the institutional norms of their workplaces.

INSTITUTIONALIZED NORMS

Looking Well-Rested and Healthy

Women who routinely wear makeup to work said that coworkers express concern about their health if they show up to work without any makeup. Magda, a 31-year-old Mexican American financial administrator, explains that Friday is "casual day" at her downtown office and that she takes a break from full makeup and only wears blush and lipstick. On these days, she notices that people ask her if she is feeling OK:

> During the week, I wear full makeup. I wear the base, I wear powder, I wear the whole thing. When I don't wear the whole thing [on Fridays], it looks like I've tired out by noon. And people will come and say, "Are you tired? You don't look good." . . . I've noticed that when they tell me that, my attitude starts going down.

Magda internalizes her coworkers' comments about her appearance with less makeup; she actually feels more productive while wearing full makeup.

Adrienne, 62-year-old white administrator, explains that she wears makeup to work everyday and never forgets to wear it. However, when she was working at a previous job, she did forget to wear her eye makeup one day, and she still remembers the reactions of her coworkers:

> I was there for a long time and I worked with the same people so they weren't shy at all. "Feel all right?" And people would really—and it was the eyeliner because my eyes look very bland and sunk back in my head and I have these heavy lids and everything. So if I forget to put on my eyeliner, people would really notice that. "Your eyes look so peaked."

Adrienne associates her coworkers' comments about her health with her lack of eyeliner.

Maria, a 28-year-old massage therapist originally from Venezuela, runs her business out of her home. She says she wears makeup to look "presentable" to clients:

> Right now, I feel like I need to wear it everyday so not to look like I just woke up because I have clients that come to the house, so I have to look presentable. So, if I go out somewhere around where my clients go or to the school, I need to look presentable. And so that's one thing they really emphasized in [massage] school—that you need to be aware of the way you look because you might run into clients or run into people who might become your clients and you want them to see you in a presentable way and they don't want to see you all looking bad.

Although Maria does not mention any instances when clients commented directly about her appearance, that is exactly what her training at massage school instructed her to avoid by wearing makeup on a daily basis. Maria wears makeup because she has internalized the idea that when she is not wearing it, she looks like she just woke up or is "looking bad."

When Janet, a 27-year-old white radio DJ, tells a story about forgetting to wear makeup one morning and feeling self-conscious, she also illustrates the degree to which appearance standards are internalized and self-imposed:

> I do remember one day when I went to work and I forgot to put on makeup. And I didn't even think about it, you know, I have my little thing that I go through every day and somehow I just skipped a step and it never went on. And I don't think I really noticed it because I work so early in the morning, so I think of myself as looking like crap anyway and I went into the bathroom or something and I remember looking at the mirror, going, "God, you know, you've really got some bags under your eyes." . . . And it wasn't 'til later, like a second trip into the bathroom or whatever, that I realized, "I don't have any makeup on." And then after that, I felt self-conscious about it because at least, even though you don't think you look good, you think at least if you have a little bit of makeup on that other people won't notice or they're not saying, "God what's the matter with her? Is she sick or something?"

Janet explains that one of the purposes of makeup is to avoid negative attention or comments from other people. According to Janet, makeup is not about thinking you look good; it is about preventing the embarrassing questions: "God, what's the matter with her? Is she sick or something?"

Thus, women who regularly wear makeup to work and do not wear it for some reason on a particular day receive comments expressing concern about their health and level of fatigue. On the other hand, women in the sample who did not regularly wear makeup to work received extremely positive comments about their appearance on occasions when they did wear it. When asked how she feels when she is wearing makeup, Jackie, a 32-year-old white parks and recreation leader, answers, "Well, I usually feel pretty good. I feel pretty confident . . . I think I look better probably or I feel like I look better and other people have commented, 'Hey, you look good today. What is it? Hey, you have makeup on.'" Mona, a 64-year-old African American day care worker, says that her coworkers are sure to notice when she paints her fingernails and puts on lipstick and a dress.

Janet's coworkers also comment favorably on her appearance: "Only good things . . . you know, nobody's going to come and say, 'You look like a slob' or anything." These positive comments can bolster a woman's self-confidence. When asked if she thought women should wear makeup today, Barbara, a 34-year-old Mexican legal assistant, replied immediately,

> Oh definitely—it brings a lot out of you. It gives you a lot of security. It's like when you're wearing a new dress, you feel very secure. . . . Let's say when you go to a party, you feel good, comfortable when you're wearing a new dress than if you were wearing one that you were wearing before. Nobody knows, but you know it, and it doesn't make you be yourself because you're kind of intimidated that you're not wearing a new dress even though you wanted it. So I think that makeup, in a way, makes you feel that way. At least, it makes me feel that.

In fact, many women say they wear makeup because it makes them feel confident about themselves. They explain that they feel "more polished" and "prepared to meet the public" (Helen) and "More attractive. More self-confident. Just more put together" (Kelly). Denise and Kathy explain that makeup is part of a "package" that allows them to feel powerful.

However, those who report feeling more confident wearing makeup to work also express a significant amount of ambivalence about the source of this confidence. In many cases, women talked about empowerment and self-consciousness in the same breath. For example, Adrienne says,

> I think you should come to work looking like you're here to be a professional person, and I think it says something about how you feel about yourself and how often—of course a lot of people will argue that that's all false. But I want to put my best foot forward. So I don't want to inflict my sloppiness or bumps and ugly complexion on anybody else [laughs].

When Adrienne is asked how she feels with makeup on, she replies,

> I feel better. Like at home, if I'm going to stay at home, I don't like to look
> at myself in the mirror when I don't have it on. But I don't see any sense in
> putting it on because I'm there by myself all day.

In Adrienne's case, confidence is about putting her best foot forward and hiding her "bumps and ugly complexion." She reports feeling better while wearing makeup but suggests that she does not like to look in the mirror when she does not wear it. Her confidence in her appearance with makeup is thus linked with a negative self-image without makeup.

Kelly, a 42-year-old white administrative associate, who said she felt more attractive, self-confident, and put together while wearing makeup, continued by saying,

> But also there's a little bit of facade in that I don't need it at home. I'm comfortable at home with my family, but I wouldn't be comfortable to come to work everyday without makeup on. So it's also just that . . . I don't know, not quite real . . . I feel more confident when I have my makeup on. I feel sort of self-conscious if I—there's I'm sure a few occasions where my husband will talk me into going to the store or something real quick without makeup on, but I'm real uncomfortable like that.

Kelly feels comfortable at home without makeup, presumably because she feels secure in her family relationships, yet she is uncomfortable in public places unless she is wearing makeup. By calling makeup "a little bit of facade," she seems to acknowledge that the confidence it brings hides her insecurity about her personal appearance. During the interview, she explained that she was jealous of women who did not care so much about their public appearance. But she concluded, "That's just the way I am."

A 30-year-old Taiwanese homemaker explains that she puts lipstick and eyeliner on when she goes out of the house so that she will look "more energetic." Melissa says she enjoys makeup because it makes her feel good about herself and because her Chinese friends often compliment her on the "wide-eyed" American look she achieves with mascara. Melissa expresses some ambivalence, however, about the way in which Caucasian eye shapes are considered more attractive than Asian features. She explains,

> Chinese people like American female eyes. They're just like a doll. I felt very confused about why we always got American-style dolls when we were younger. All of the dolls in Taiwan were like that. So from a very young age, I thought, in the future, I would look like that.

Melissa senses that the confidence she achieves by wearing makeup is linked to a devaluation of her Asian features.

In sum, many women in the sample indicate that wearing makeup to work gives them what is defined as a healthy and rested appearance, and thus enhances their self-confidence. Because their coworkers constantly monitor and evaluate their appearance, responding most favorably when women wear makeup, it is not surprising that some report feeling more confident and productive when they are wearing makeup. Current societal definitions of health, success, and beauty are intertwined: Cultural images of healthy, energetic, and successful working women are, for the most part, young, white or Anglo-featured, thin, and made-up. The ambivalence some women express about the connection between makeup and their self-confidence is fostered by the difficulty of meeting all of the requirements for a "healthy" look. Societal definitions of health and beauty are incorporated into institutional norms about makeup use and, in this way, shape women's personal choices about their appearances.

Heterosexuality

In addition to marking women as healthy and well rested, makeup also marks women as heterosexual. Recent studies suggest that normative constructions of sexuality are built into and reproduced by work organizations (Leidner 1993; Pringle 1988; Woods with Lucas 1993). The experiences of both straight and lesbian women in this sample illustrate how a system of compulsory heterosexuality (Rich 1980) is maintained through workplace appearance norms.

Suzanne, a 31-year-old white administrative assistant, works in a downtown real estate office. When referring to the prevalence of women who wear makeup in her building, she suggests that women who do not wear it are at a disadvantage: "You can't walk into this building and find anyone in any office on 22 floors who is not wearing makeup. . . . Women who don't wear makeup, I guess, are thought to be either tomboys, homebodies, or . . . it's not a professional picture." The threat of being labeled "tomboys, homebodies, or . . ." strongly implies the threat of being labeled a lesbian, or, more generally, someone not concerned with attracting men.

Thus, there is an assumption of heterosexuality built into professionalism. An implicit requirement for looking appropriately feminine is that women look "pleasing" to men. When asked what it meant to be beautiful, Magda, who is heterosexual, responded after a long pause—"Successful." She then added,

> I guess it's because in the work I do, being pleasant to look at helps a lot. In the financial business it really does, when there are a lot of men involved. They tend to work easier with someone who is easy to look at. And that's, that's terrible, you know, to say, but that's how men think.

Several times during the interview, Magda mentions that her husband "interacts better with women whose appearance pleasing to look at." She once asked him if he thought that women had to be pretty to be competent employees; she reported that he said, "Magda, it has nothing to do with beauty, it has to do with . . . just the effort they make to look good. . . . That effort means everything." When asked to explain the context of her husband's comments on this topic, Magda said:

> The reason I had asked him is because he had just hired a young lady who we took out to dinner the night before. And I told him she was fabulous. I said, "She's witty. She's intelligent and she could do those things you don't want to do." He goes, "Yeah, but she doesn't try to maintain herself." And I said, "What do you mean? Does she fight? Is she aggressive?" . . . He said, "Her appearance. Didn't you see how she was so—just so simple?" And I said, "But that was the good quality in her—she looked fine." . . . And then he went on to say, "I just don't want everybody on my staff to feel that she doesn't fit in or she's not performing because of her carelessness in her appearance."

While Magda focuses on the woman's competence for the job, her husband is more fixated on her "questionable appearance" as a significant liability to office morale. When he explains that the woman "didn't try to maintain herself," Magda's first thoughts are about potential disruptive conduct in the office, not her physical appearance.

This example suggests that for some men and women, caring about one's appearance signifies caring for or respecting men. Magda has incorporated the importance of looking pleasing to men into her definition of success, and her husband's reactions to the apparent "lack of effort" his future employee puts into her appearance supports Magda's decision to do this. Yet, her comments regarding the importance of women's appearance for their careers reflect significant ambivalence. While Magda feels more competent and successful when she wears makeup, she also expresses discomfort when her husband implies that women must be pretty (or at least try to be pretty) to be considered competent by men.

Except for Suzanne and Magda, none of the other heterosexual women in the sample discussed makeup in relation to norms regarding heterosexuality. In contrast, all of the lesbian women we interviewed noted a link between heterosexuality and makeup. Recent feminist theory has focused on the importance of analyzing the active construction of heterosexuality, and the pleasure and privilege associated with that identity from the viewpoint of heterosexual women (e.g., Kitzinger and Wilkinson 1993; Segal (1994). Although this agenda is extremely important to pursue, we found that the heterosexual women we interviewed did not talk about their appearance practices at work in connection with their own ideas about sexual attractiveness, pleasure, or desire. . . .

Joan, who is a 31-year-old white lesbian social worker and the only woman in the sample who never wears makeup at home or at work, offers several important insights about the link between heterosexuality and conventional workplace appearance standards, and about the costs of nonconformity. Although Joan says that at her current job as a social worker she can be "pretty comfortable" in terms of her appearance, she reports that she received many comments and suggestions about her appearance when she first began working there. When asked what her coworkers said, she explains that

> just sitting around and talking it would just come up and people would be like, "You need to wear a little bit of makeup" or "You need to get a perm" or "You need to get some better clothes." Not mean-like, but that's kind of the message that you get when you're sitting on the other end of it because they mean you would look better if you did this to yourself.

. . .

Rebecca, a 41-year-old white copywriter, actively uses makeup at work as a way to smooth workplace interactions with men and women. Because she is tall and a lesbian, she feels she may be intimidating to some people. She explains that she always wears makeup to mute what she calls her "difference":

> And I'm not doing it to be attractive, especially to [men]. . . . Mostly it's so that that's not what we're meeting about. So it's not like, "What does that [no makeup] mean?" And I am aware of that, especially with men in corporations. . . . There is sometimes . . . a natural edge with them. . . . I even try to take a little bit of that threat off, you know, by saying you don't have to worry about me being different as well as bigger than you.

The difference Rebecca is trying to tone down has to do with "appropriate" gender differentiation and sexual orientation. She indicates that makeup makes clients less likely to think about the fact that she is different because she is a lesbian and that it may neutralize the threat she may pose to men who are uncomfortable with a woman who is physically taller than they are.

Similarly, Denise, a 42-year-old white lesbian lawyer, reported that she pays close attention to how she dresses in the courtroom so that her appearance is not "a distraction." The first day of a trial she wears a traditional navy blue suit and a plain, white blouse and then mixes in brighter, more feminine clothes throughout the week. The juries she has worked with in the past have commented that they like these more feminine suits and, consequently, are less likely to think Denise is "too serious looking." Denise sums it up when she says, "I don't think that having [the jury] say they like something [I wear] sways them to your client's side, but it takes—kind of makes you into a non-issue."

Both Rebecca and Denise are clear that their use of makeup and dress has something to do with compliance to heterosexual norms of feminine appearance. While they adamantly insist that they are not dressing to be attractive to men, they have learned that not wearing makeup or dressing in a "masculine" style will cause problems in their workplace interactions with both men and women.

. . .

Expectations for wearing makeup do vary by occupation and organization, but in all the cases we encountered, makeup connoted heterosexual femininity. In occupations in which makeup use is normative, those who refuse to wear it are typically suspected of being lesbian. Suzanne's comment that women who do not wear makeup in her building "are thought to be tomboys, homebodies, or . . . it's not a professional picture" illustrates the conflation of gendered norms of appearance and compulsory heterosexuality. Magda's conclusion that success is partially dependent on "looking pleasing to men" and Rebecca and Denise's use of makeup to "smooth" workplace interactions also reinforce this link. Joan suggests that being single and not wearing makeup may mark her as different from her current (straight and mostly married) coworkers. Kit, who is "out" at work, also felt that her choice not to wear makeup at work was construed by her coworkers as connected to her lesbian identity. When individuals in this sample challenged the makeup norms at work, the consequences ranged from pressure to appear more "feminine" to outright discrimination, for example, Joan reported that she was denied jobs for which she was qualified because she did not look "feminine enough."

In sum, the experiences of the women in this sample suggest that wearing makeup is a form of "doing heterosexuality" as well as "doing gender" (Giuffre and Williams 1994; West and Fenstermaker 1995). In the workplace, individuals are often held accountable to heterosexual norms of appearance in interactions with others. Conforming to these norms reproduces heterosexuality and reinforces a dichotomous conception of gender difference.

Credibility

In addition to displaying gender difference and heterosexuality, some women wear makeup because they feel it makes them appear more competent. Diane, a 25-year-old heterosexual white woman, explains that as a hairdresser, looking good by wearing "attractive" makeup and a fashionable hairstyle is required. Her appearance directly reflects the degree to which her clients can trust her as an able "beauty consultant." When asked if she feels like her appearance is important when she goes to work, Diane answers straightforwardly, "Yeah. It is. It is real important in the industry that I'm in just because you can't look like crap and tell somebody how they should look and expect them to believe you if you look like shit."

Kathy, a 29-year-old lawyer in a highly male-dominated field, explains that makeup also enhances a woman's credibility in the courtroom. She says,

> It's one of the things you do to excel. To survive. . . . If you don't—I mean I've seen people—I've seen female attorneys go to court and looked washed out and people just do not react as positively as they could to someone who was more attractive. And I've seen male attorneys and judges react more favorably to someone they consider to be attractive, who's got the makeup and the hair and is dressed just so. It's part of competing.

For many women in the sample, makeup use at work is a significant "part of competing."

Kathy is one of two women in the sample who felt that wearing makeup was particularly important for enhancing their status as women of color in the workplace. Sarah, a heterosexual Mexican American woman, wears makeup because "I feel like a role model, you know, to my own daughter as well as, you know, to my nationality. I want to look nice." Kathy, who is a heterosexual African American woman, views her personal use of makeup as an effort to enhance her credibility in a racist society:

> I have always experienced racism in my life and I'm more attuned to iden-
> tify when someone is being racist and I let the sexism pass. It's more offen-
> sive to me for you to be racist than to be sexist. So I do find that because I'm
> an African American, there are certain things that I need to do because I'm
> African American, and one of those things is to look professional and all the
> other good things.

Kathy believes that she must "look professional" because she is an African American. For women, looking professional entails a degree of sexual objecti-fication. So when Kathy says she will "let the sexism pass," she seems to sug-gest that the difficult task of "fitting in" that women of color experience may require her to gain status at the expense of putting up with sexual objectifica-tion. Thus, racism is noted and resisted while sexism is not only tolerated but viewed as an unspoken, yet taken-for-granted condition for "looking profes-sional." Kathy suggests that maintaining a professional appearance can trans-form racial stereotypes:

> The appearance is not necessarily to prevent racism or do anything about
> racism but to educate people because there are so many non–African Amer-
> icans that are not exposed to African Americans that they have a tendency
> to stereotype African Americans and African American women, and they
> sometimes don't expect to see a professional African American woman with
> excellent credentials who dresses conservatively, who can be articulate, who
> can perform in the courtroom. So, it's beating the stereotypes and not giving
> them what they expect sometimes.

Both Sarah and Kelly feel that wearing makeup is a necessary part of being respected as women of color in a racist world. Looking professional for these women may have a different meaning than it does for many white women: Wearing the "right" makeup plays a part in gaining respect (perhaps gaining the status of white women) in the workplace, even though it entails sexual objectification.

Women's use of makeup in the workplace is also linked in a complex way to women's status in regard to age. Dominant cultural ideas about women's "need" to be concerned with youth are constantly perpetuated by the media (Barthel 1988). And while some women in the sample do express their plan to "fight age back any way you can with creams and makeup and the whole works" (Barbara), some express a desire to age with dignity and to "take it as it comes" even if it is uncomfortable sometimes (Rebecca). Helen joked that she bought "Turn-Around" cream from Clinique "some time when [she] was feeling old or something" but that nothing has "turned around" because the jar sits unopened in her bathroom closet. While women recognize that youthful standards of beauty predominate in the United States, they explain that status in the workplace is more complicated than matching an ideal image of beauty in a magazine.

So how are makeup use and age associated in the workplace? Is there a trade-off between a youthful appearance and the knowledge and competence that comes with more years of experience in a job? . . . Helen, who is 57, elaborates the former point:

> Teaching is not a place where you're going to be discarded because you look sort of middle-aged. I mean if you're a good teacher, they're going to pretty much value your services as long as you have your wits about you.

Denise, who is currently a lawyer and was previously in law enforcement, states that when she first began her career in both areas, she tried to make herself look older in order to be taken seriously:

> I've had clients who . . . have said things like, "I'm glad that you're a little bit older." And sometimes they don't realize how young I am. . . . I think that coming across as too young makes people—people aren't quite as trusting as you.

. . .

When it comes to youthful appearance and status, women must negotiate societal standards of beauty, the demands of their particular workplace and occupation, and the difficult task of trying not to look like they are trying to look too young. . . .

In sum, according to the interviews, women who wear makeup are seen as healthy, heterosexual, and competent. The women in this study appreciate the value that is associated with these qualities in the workplace and many consequently wear makeup so that they might be successful. A woman's personal choice to wear makeup cannot be understood outside the context of these institutionalized workplace appearance norms.

Thus far, our analysis has emphasized how workplace appearance norms are internalized. We have noted a significant degree of ambivalence in the women's comments about their makeup practices. Both women who wear makeup and those who do not struggle with the fact that their appearance is constantly being evaluated and that others' perception of their competence as employees is linked to wearing makeup.

. . .

CONCLUSION

Appropriate makeup use is strongly linked to assumptions of health, hetero-sexuality, and credibility in the workplace. In turn, these qualities are asso-ciated with professional success. Foucault's (1979) docile body thesis is compatible with the experiences of women in this sample, particularly with their descriptions of everyday makeup use and their self-imposed surveillance. Women also reported experiences in which their bodies were central locations for the expression and reproduction of power relationships. For example, the monitoring of appearance norms by coworkers not only reinforced assump-tions about heterosexuality but privileged this sexuality. Yet, as Bordo (1993) argues, women's bodies are trained into docility and obedience to cultural demands, while at the same time these practices are often experienced as sources of power and control. Thus, some women spoke of their use of makeup as necessary to gain credibility and as a way to bolster their confidence at work.

Yet, women do not wear makeup at work solely because of the pressures imposed by institutionalized appearance norms. Some pointed to the pleasure they received by talking about makeup with other women and getting compli-ments on their appearance. Others explained that they actively bent the rules in their compliance with appearance expectations for work.

We found very little evidence of outright resistance to appearance norms in the workplace. Those who refuse to wear makeup may suffer job sanctions in certain work contexts. Although some women may wear makeup to parody femininity or destabilize sex/gender categories (Butler 1990), our data suggest that such attempts at subversion can be easily co-opted to bolster gender dif-ferentiation and compulsory heterosexuality.

Deveaux (1994) suggests that feminists must work toward conceptual-izing women's relationship to their bodies both as a reflection of social con-struction and as their own response to (and mediation of) the cultural ideals of femininity. Similarly, Davis (1995) argues that we must recognize women as knowledgeable agents faced by asymmetrical power relationships if we are to move beyond the cultural dope model of understanding women's participa-tion in oppressive beauty practices. Our analysis of women's use of makeup at work illustrates how women act as knowledgeable agents within institutional constraints. By taking this approach, we avoid the dual pitfalls of characteriz-ing women as completely passive victims of beauty norms or as unsituated agents of resistance. Instead, we attend to the various ways that race, age, gen-der, and sexual orientation affect women's negotiation of ideals of femininity within the institutional constraints imposed by different workplace contexts.

While we do not argue that women wear makeup to work because they are sexist, homophobic, or racist, we do suggest that this cultural practice has consequences that reproduce inequality between men and women, and also between different groups of women. But resistance to workplace inequality through the body is problematic granted existing institutional constraints. We call for more research that contextualizes women's and men's appearance practices in specific institutional settings. By taking this approach, we do not abandon the search for agency and resistance, but we insist that researchers attend to the necessary task of analyzing how social institutions shape and limit individual choices.

REFERENCES

Adkins, Lisa. 1995. *Gendered work: Sexuality, family, and the labour market*. Buckingham, UK: Open University Press.

Barthel, Diane. 1988. *Putting on appearances: Gender and advertising*. Philadelphia: Temple University Press.

Bartky, Sandra Lee. 1990. *Femininity and domination: Studies in the phenomenology of oppression*. New York: Routledge.

Beausoleil, Natalie. 1994. Make-up in everyday life: An inquiry into the practices of urban American women of diverse backgrounds. In *Many mirrors: Body image and social relations*, edited by Nicole Sault. New Brunswick, NJ: Rutgers University Press.

Bordo, Susan. 1993. *Unbearable weight: Feminism, Western culture, and the body*. Berkeley: University of California Press.

Butler, Judith. 1990. *Gender trouble: Feminism and the subversion of identity*. New York: Routledge.

Chapkis, Wendy. 1986. *Beauty secrets: Women and the politics of appearances*. Boston: South End.

Davis, Kathy. 1995. *Reshaping the female body: The dilemma of cosmetic surgery*. New York: Routledge.

Deveaux, Monique. 1994. Feminism and empowerment: A critical reading of Foucault. *Feminist Studies* 20:223–47.

Fisher, Sue, and Kathy Davis. 1993. *Negotiating at the margins: The gendered discourses of power and resistance*. New Brunswick, NJ: Rutgers University Press.

Foucault, Michel. 1979. *Discipline and punish*. New York: Vintage.

Giuffre, Patti, and Christine Williams. 1994. Boundary lines: Labeling sexual harassment in restaurants. *Gender & Society* 8:378–401.

Gutek, Barbara. 1985. *Sex and the workplace*. San Francisco: Jossey-Bass.

Jackson, Linda A. 1992. *Physical appearance and gender: Sociobiological and sociocultural perspectives*. Albany: State University of New York Press.

Kanter, Rosabeth Moss. 1977. *Men and women of the corporation*. New York: Basic Books.

Kitzinger, Celia, and Sue Wilkinson. 1993. Theorizing heterosexuality. Editorial introduction. In *Heterosexuality: A feminism and psychology reader*, edited by Sue Wilkinson and Celia Kitzinger. London: Sage.

Leidner, Robin. 1993. *Fast food, fast talk: Service work and the routinization of everyday life.*
Berkeley: University of California Press.

Pringle, Rosemary. 1988. *Secretaries talk: Sexuality, power, and work.* Sydney: Allen and
Unwin.

Rich, Adrienne. 1980. Compulsory heterosexuality and lesbian existence. *Signs*
5:631–60.

Rubinstein, Ruth. 1995. *Dress codes: Meanings and messages in American culture.* Boulder,
CO: Westview.

Segal, Lynne. 1994. *Straight sex: Rethinking the politics of pleasure.* Berkeley: University of
California Press.

West, Candace, and Sarah Fenstermaker. 1995. Doing difference. *Gender & Society*
9:8–37.

Wolf, Naomi. 1991. *The beauty myth: How images of beauty are used against women.* New
York: William Morrow.

Woods, James D., with Jay Lucas. 1993. *The corporate closet: The professional lives of gay
men in America.* New York: Free Press.

AARON DEVOR

Becoming Members of Society: Learning the Social Meanings of Gender

Aaron Devor is an award-winning sociologist and author specializing in gender, sexuality, and transsexuality. He is Professor of Sociology at the University of Victoria, Canada. The following selection is from the book, Gender Blending: Confronting the Limits of Duality *(1998). For more, visit his homepage at http://web.uvic.ca/~ahdevor/.*

THE GENDERED SELF

The task of learning to be properly gendered members of society only begins with the establishment of gender identity. Gender identities act as cognitive filtering devices guiding people to attend to and learn gender role behaviors appropriate to their statuses. Learning to behave in accordance with one's gender identity is a lifelong process. As we move through our lives, society demands different gender performances from us and rewards, tolerates, or punishes us differently for conformity to, or digression from, social norms. As children, and later adults, learn the rules of membership in society, they come to see themselves in terms they have learned from the people around them.

Children begin to settle into a gender identity between the age of eighteen months and two years.[1] By the age of two, children usually understand that they are members of a gender grouping and can correctly identify other members of their gender.[2] By age three they have a fairly firm and consistent concept of gender. Generally, it is not until children are five to seven years old that they become convinced that they are permanent members of their gender grouping.[3]

Researchers test the establishment, depth, and tenacity of gender identity through the use of language and the concepts mediated by language. The language systems used in populations studied by most researchers in this field

---

[1]Much research has been devoted to determining when gender identity becomes solidified in the sense that a child knows itself to be unequivocally either male or female. John Money and his colleagues have proposed eighteen months of age because it is difficult or impossible to change a child's gender identity once it has been established around the age of eighteen months. Money and Ehrhardt, p. 243.

[2]Mary Driver Leinbach and Beverly I. Fagot, "Acquisition of Gender Labels: A Test for Toddlers," *Sex Roles* 15 (1986), pp. 655–66.

[3]Maccoby, pp. 225–29; Kohlberg and Ullian, p. 211.

conceptualize gender as binary and permanent. All persons are either male or female. All males are first boys and then men; all females are first girls and then women. People are believed to be unable to change genders without sex change surgery, and those who do change sex are considered to be both disturbed and exceedingly rare.

This is by no means the only way that gender is conceived in all cultures. Many aboriginal cultures have more than two gender categories and accept the idea that, under certain circumstances, gender may be changed without changes being made to biological sex characteristics. Many North and South American native peoples had a legitimate social category for persons who wished to live according to the gender role of another sex. Such people were sometimes revered, sometimes ignored, and occasionally scorned. Each culture had its own word to describe such persons, most commonly translated into English as "berdache." Similar institutions and linguistic concepts have also been recorded in early Siberian, Madagascan, and Polynesian societies, as well as in medieval Europe.[4]

Very young children learn their culture's social definitions of gender and gender identity at the same time that they learn what gender behaviors are appropriate for them. But they only gradually come to understand the meaning of gender in the same way as the adults of their society do. Very young children may learn the words which describe their gender and be able to apply them to themselves appropriately, but their comprehension of their meaning is often different from that used by adults. Five-year-olds, for example, may be able to accurately recognize their own gender and the genders of the people around them, but they will often make such ascriptions on the basis of role information, such as hair style, rather than physical attributes, such as genitals, even when physical cues are clearly known to them. One result of this level of understanding of gender is that children in this age group often believe that people may change their gender with a change in clothing, hair style, or activity.[5]

The characteristics most salient to young minds are the more culturally specific qualities which grow out of gender role prescriptions. In one study, young school age children, who were given dolls and asked to identify their gender, overwhelmingly identified the gender of the dolls on the basis of attributes such as hair length or clothing style, in spite of the fact that the dolls

[4]See Susan Baker, "Biological Influences on Human Sex and Gender," in *Women: Sex and Sexuality*, ed. Catherine R. Stimpson and Ethel S. Person (Chicago: University of Chicago Press, 1980), p. 186; Evelyn Blackwood, "Sexuality and Gender in Certain Native American Tribes: The Case of Cross-Gender Females," *Signs* 10 (1984), pp. 27–42; Vern L. Bullough, "Transvestites in the Middle Ages," *American Journal of Sociology* 79 (1974), 1381–89; J. Cl. DuBois, "Transsexualisme et Anthropologie Culturelle," *Gynecologie Pratique* 6 (1969), pp. 431–40; Donald C. Forgey, "The Institution of Berdache among the North American Plains Indians," *Journal of Sex Research* 11 (Feb. 1975), pp. 1–15; Walter L. Williams, *The Spirit and the Flesh: Sexual Diversity in American Indian Culture* (Boston: Beacon, 1986).

[5]Maccoby, p. 255.

were anatomically correct. Only 17 percent of the children identified the dolls on the basis of their primary or secondary sex characteristics.[6] Children five to seven years old understand gender as a function of role rather than as a function of anatomy. Their understanding is that gender (role) is supposed to be stable but that it is possible to alter it at will. This demonstrates that although the standard social definition of gender is based on genitalia, this is not the way that young children first learn to distinguish gender. The process of learning to think about gender in an adult fashion is one prerequisite to becoming a full member of society. Thus, as children grow older, they learn to think of themselves and others in terms more like those used by adults.

Children's developing concepts of themselves as individuals are necessarily bound up in their need to understand the expectations of the society of which they are a part. As they develop concepts of themselves as individuals, they do so while observing themselves as reflected in the eyes of others. Children start to understand themselves as individuals separate from others during the years that they first acquire gender identities and gender roles. As they do so, they begin to understand that others see them and respond to them as particular people. In this way they develop concepts of themselves as individuals, as an "I" (a proactive subject) simultaneously with self-images of themselves as individuals, as a "me" (a member of society, a subjective object). Children learn that they are both as they see themselves and as others see them.[7]

To some extent, children initially acquire the values of the society around them almost indiscriminately. To the degree that children absorb the generalized standards of society into their personal concept of what is correct behavior, they can be said to hold within themselves the attitude of the "generalized other."[8] This "generalized other" functions as a sort of monitoring or measuring device with which individuals may judge their own actions against those of their generalized conceptions of how members of society are expected to act. In this way members of society have available to them a guide, or an internalized observer, to turn the more private "I" into the object of public scrutiny, the "me." In this way, people can monitor their own behavioral impulses and censor actions which might earn them social disapproval or scorn. The tension created by the constant interplay of the personal "I" and the social "me" is the creature known as the "self."

But not all others are of equal significance in our lives, and therefore not all others are of equal impact on the development of the self. Any person is available to become part of one's "generalized other," but certain individuals, by virtue of the sheer volume of time spent in interaction with someone, or by virtue of the nature of particular interactions, become more significant in

---

[6]Ibid., p. 227.
[7]George Herbert Mead, "Self," in *The Social Psychology of George Herbert Mead,* ed. Anselm Strauss (Chicago: Phoenix Books, 1962, 1934), pp. 212–60.
[8]G. H. Mead.

the shaping of people's values. These "significant others" become prominent in the formation of one's self-image and one's ideals and goals. As such they carry disproportionate weight in one's personal "generalized other."[9] Thus, children's individualistic impulses are shaped into a socially acceptable form both by particular individuals and by a more generalized pressure to conformity exerted by innumerable faceless members of society. Gender identity is one of the most central portions of that developing sense of self. . . .

GENDER ROLE BEHAVIORS AND ATTITUDES

The clusters of social definitions used to identify persons by gender are collectively known as femininity and masculinity. Masculine characteristics are used to identify persons as males, while feminine ones are used as signifiers for femaleness. People use femininity or masculinity to claim and communicate their membership in their assigned, or chosen, sex or gender. Others recognize our sex or gender more on the basis of these characteristics than on the basis of sex characteristics, which are usually largely covered by clothing in daily life.

These two clusters of attributes are most commonly seen as mirror images of one another with masculinity usually characterized by dominance and aggression, and femininity by passivity and submission. A more even-handed description of the social qualities subsumed by femininity and masculinity might be to label masculinity as generally concerned with egoistic dominance and femininity as striving for cooperation or communion.[10] Characterizing femininity and masculinity in such a way does not portray the two clusters of characteristics as being in a hierarchical relationship to one another but rather as being two different approaches to the same question, that question being centrally concerned with the goals, means, and use of power. Such an alternative conception of gender roles captures the hierarchical and competitive masculine thirst for power, which can, but need not, lead to aggression, and the feminine quest for harmony and communal well-being, which can, but need not, result in passivity and dependence.

Many activities and modes of expression are recognized by most members of society as feminine. Any of these can be, and often are, displayed by persons of either gender. In some cases, cross gender behaviors are ignored by observers, and therefore do not compromise the integrity of a person's gender

---

[9]Hans Gerth and C. Wright Mills, *Character and Social Structure: The Psychology of Social Institutions* (New York: Harcourt, Brace and World, 1953), p. 96.

[10]Egoistic dominance is a striving for superior rewards for oneself or a competitive striving to reduce the rewards for one's competitors even if such action will not increase one's own rewards. Persons who are motivated by desires for egoistic dominance not only wish the best for themselves but also wish to diminish the advantages of others whom they may perceive as competing with them. See Maccoby, p. 217.

display. In other cases, they are labeled as inappropriate gender role behaviors. Although these behaviors are closely linked to sexual status in the minds and experiences of most people, research shows that dominant persons of either gender tend to use influence tactics and verbal styles usually associated with men and masculinity, while subordinate persons, of either gender, tend to use those considered to be the province of women.[11] Thus it seems likely that many aspects of masculinity and femininity are the result, rather than the cause, of status inequalities.

Popular conceptions of femininity and masculinity instead revolve around hierarchical appraisals of the "natural" roles of males and females. Members of both genders are believed to share many of the same human characteristics, although in different relative proportions; both males and females are popularly thought to be able to do many of the same things, but most activities are divided into suitable and unsuitable categories for each gender class. Persons who perform the activities considered appropriate for another gender will be expected to perform them poorly; if they succeed adequately, or even well, at their endeavors, they may be rewarded with ridicule or scorn for blurring the gender dividing line.

The patriarchal gender schema currently in use in mainstream North American society reserves highly valued attributes for males and actively supports the high evaluation of any characteristics which might inadvertently become associated with maleness. The ideology which the schema grows out of postulates that the cultural superiority of males is a natural outgrowth of the innate predisposition of males toward aggression and dominance, which is assumed to flow inevitably from evolutionary and biological sources. Female attributes are likewise postulated to find their source in innate predispositions acquired in the evolution of the species. Feminine characteristics are thought to be intrinsic to the female facility for childbirth and breastfeeding. Hence, it is popularly believed that the social position of females is biologically mandated to be intertwined with the care of children and a "natural" dependency on men for the maintenance of mother-child units. Thus the goals of femininity and, by implication, of all biological females are presumed to revolve around heterosexuality and maternity.[12]

Femininity, according to this traditional formulation, "would result in warm and continued relationships with men, a sense of maternity, interest in caring for children, and the capacity to work productively and continuously in female occupations."[13] This recipe translates into a vast number of proscrip-

---

[11]Judith Howard, Philip Blumstein, and Pepper Schwartz, "Sex, Power, and Influence Tactics in Intimate Relationships," *Journal of Personality and Social Psychology* 51 (1986), pp. 102–9; Peter Kollock, Philip Blumstein, and Pepper Schwartz, "Sex and Power in Interaction: Conversational Privileges and Duties," *American Sociological Review* 50 (1985), pp. 34–46.

[12]Chodorow, p. 134.

[13]Jon K. Meyer and John E. Hoopes, "The Gender Dysphoria Syndromes: A Position Statement on So-Called 'Transsexualism'," *Plastic and Reconstructive Surgery* 54 (Oct. 1974), pp. 444–51.

tions and prescriptions. Warm and continued relations with men and an interest in maternity require that females be heterosexually oriented. A heterosexual orientation requires women to dress, move, speak, and act in ways that men will find attractive. As patriarchy has reserved active expressions of power as a masculine attribute, femininity must be expressed through modes of dress, movement, speech, and action which communicate weakness, dependency, ineffectualness, availability for sexual or emotional service, and sensitivity to the needs of others.

Some, but not all, of these modes of interrelation also serve the demands of maternity and many female job ghettos. In many cases, though, femininity is not particularly useful in maternity or employment. Both mothers and workers often need to be strong, independent, and effectual in order to do their jobs well. Thus femininity, as a role, is best suited to satisfying a masculine vision of heterosexual attractiveness.

Body postures and demeanors which communicate subordinate status and vulnerability to trespass through a message of "no threat" make people appear to be feminine. They demonstrate subordination through a minimizing of spatial use: people appear feminine when they keep their arms closer to their bodies, their legs closer together, and their torsos and heads less vertical then do masculine-looking individuals. People also look feminine when they point their toes inward and use their hands in small or childlike gestures. Other people also tend to stand closer to people they see as feminine, often invading their personal space, while people who make frequent appeasement gestures, such as smiling, also give the appearance of femininity. Perhaps as an outgrowth of a subordinate status and the need to avoid conflict with more socially powerful people, women tend to excel over men at the ability to correctly interpret, and effectively display, nonverbal communication cues.[14]

Speech characterized by inflections, intonations, and phrases that convey nonaggression and subordinate status also make a speaker appear more feminine. Subordinate speakers who use more polite expressions and ask more questions in conversation seem more feminine. Speech characterized by sounds of higher frequencies are often interpreted by listeners as feminine, childlike, and ineffectual.[15] Feminine styles of dress likewise display subordinate status through greater restriction of the free movement of the body, greater exposure of the bare skin, and an emphasis on sexual characteristics. The more gender distinct the dress, the more this is the case.

---

[14]Erving Goffman, *Gender Advertisements* (New York: Harper Colophon Books, 1976); Judith A. Hall, *Non-Verbal Sex Differences: Communication Accuracy and Expressive Style* (Baltimore: Johns Hopkins University Press, 1984); Nancy M. Henley, *Body Politics: Power, Sex and Non-Verbal Communication* (Englewood Cliffs, New Jersey: Prentice Hall, 1979); Marianne Wex, *"Let's Take Back Our Space": "Female" and "Male" Body Language as a Result of Patriarchal Structures* (Berlin: Frauenliteraturverlag Hermine Fees, 1979).

[15]Karen L. Adams, "Sexism and the English Language: The Linguistic Implications of Being a Woman," in *Women: A Feminist Perspective*, 3rd edition, ed. Jo Freeman (Palo Alto, Calif.: Mayfield, 1984), pp. 478–91; Hall, pp. 37, 130–37.

Masculinity, like femininity, can be demonstrated through a wide variety of cues. Pleck has argued that it is commonly expressed in North American society through the attainment of some level of proficiency at some, or all, of the following four main attitudes of masculinity. Persons who display success and high status in their social group, who exhibit "a manly air of toughness, confidence, and self-reliance" and "the aura of aggression, violence, and daring," and who conscientiously avoid anything associated with femininity are seen as exuding masculinity.[16] These requirements reflect the patriarchal ideology that masculinity results from an excess of testosterone, the assumption being that androgens supply a natural impetus toward aggression, which in turn impels males toward achievement and success. This vision of masculinity also reflects the ideological stance that ideal maleness (masculinity) must remain untainted by female (feminine) pollutants.

Masculinity, then, requires of its actors that they organize themselves and their society in a hierarchical manner so as to be able to explicitly quantify the achievement of success. The achievement of high status in one's social group requires competitive and aggressive behavior from those who wish to obtain it. Competition which is motivated by a goal of individual achievement, or egoistic dominance, also requires of its participants a degree of emotional insensitivity to feelings of hurt and loss in defeated others, and a measure of emotional insularity to protect oneself from becoming vulnerable to manipulation by others. Such values lead those who subscribe to them to view feminine persons as "born losers" and to strive to eliminate any similarities to feminine people from their own personalities. In patriarchally organized societies, masculine values become the ideological structure of the society as a whole. Masculinity thus becomes "innately" valuable and femininity serves a contrapuntal function to delineate and magnify the hierarchical dominance of masculinity.

Body postures, speech patterns, and styles of dress which demonstrate and support the assumption of dominance and authority convey an impression of masculinity. Typical masculine body postures tend to be expansive and aggressive. People who hold their arms and hands in positions away from their bodies, and who stand, sit, or lie with their legs apart—thus maximizing the amount of space that they physically occupy—appear most physically masculine. Persons who communicate an air of authority or a readiness for aggression by standing erect and moving forcefully also tend to appear more masculine. Movements that are abrupt and stiff, communicating force and threat rather than flexibility and cooperation, make an actor look masculine. Masculinity can also be conveyed by stern or serious facial expressions that suggest minimal receptivity to the influence of others, a characteristic

---

[16]Elizabeth Hafkin Pleck, *Domestic Tyranny: The Making of Social Policy Against Family Violence from Colonial Times to the Present* (Cambridge: Oxford University Press, 1989), p. 139.

which is an important element in the attainment and maintenance of egoistic dominance.[17]

Speech and dress which likewise demonstrate or claim superior status are also seen as characteristically masculine behavior patterns. Masculine speech patterns display a tendency toward expansiveness similar to that found in masculine body postures. People who attempt to control the direction of conversations seem more masculine.[18] Those who tend to speak more loudly, use less polite and more assertive forms, and tend to interrupt the conversations of others more often also communicate masculinity to others. Styles of dress which emphasize the size of upper body musculature, allow freedom of movement, and encourage an illusion of physical power and a look of easy physicality all suggest masculinity. Such appearances of strength and readiness to action serve to create or enhance an aura of ag-gressiveness and intimidation central to an appearance of masculinity. Expansive postures and gestures combine with these qualities to insinuate that a position of secure dominance is a masculine one.

Gender role characteristics reflect the ideological contentions underlying the dominant gender schema in North American society. That schema leads us to believe that female and male behaviors are the result of socially directed hormonal instructions which specify that females will want to have children and will therefore find themselves relatively helpless and dependent on males for support and protection. The schema claims that males are innately aggressive and competitive and therefore will dominate over females. The social hegemony of this ideology ensures that we are all raised to practice gender roles which will confirm this vision of the nature of the sexes. Fortunately, our training to gender roles is neither complete nor uniform. As a result, it is possible to point to multitudinous exceptions to, and variations on, these themes. Biological evidence is equivocal about the source of gender roles; psychological androgyny is a widely accepted concept. It seems most likely that gender roles are the result of systematic power imbalances based on gender discrimination.[19]

---

[17]Goffman, *Gender Advertisements*; Hall; Henley; Wex.
[18]Adams; Hall, pp. 37, 130–37.
[19]Howard, Blumstein, and Schwartz; Kollock, Blumstein, and Schwartz.

●

○

CYNTHIA ENLOE
From Globalization and Militarism

Cynthia Enloe, a leading feminist scholar, is Professor of International Development, Community, and Environment and Director of Women's Studies at Clark University. Her research on gender revolutionized the field of international relations and she has published many influential books, including Bananas, Beaches and Bases: Making Feminist Sense of International Politics *(2000). This selection is from her most recent study,* Globalization and Militarism: Feminists Make the Link *(2007).*

CRAFTING A GLOBAL "FEMINIST CURIOSITY" TO MAKE SENSE OF GLOBALIZED MILITARISM: TALLYING IMPACTS, EXPOSING CAUSES

Developing a "curiosity" involves exploring, questioning—refusing to take something for granted. One is *not* curious about the things one takes for granted. For instance, most of us most of the time (unless we have a rotten cold or have started going to yoga classes) aren't very curious about breathing. Most of us most of the time (unless we read the science pages of our newspapers) also don't spend much time wondering about the melting arctic ice caps.

A major theme we will chart here is "feminist curiosity": How to develop it? What's distinctive about it? We will discover what it is that a feminist curiosity can reveal about the workings of globalization and militarization—and track the links *between* them—that we would otherwise miss. In other words, this is a very practical, down-to-earth enterprise.

Developing a new kind of curiosity is not just academic. It takes energy. It is political. It is cultural. It is personal. To insist upon posing questions about things that other people take for granted can be a political act.

A feminist curiosity is a crucial tool to use today in making sense of the links between two of the world's most potent trends: *globalization* and *militarization.*

Like any "ization" (e.g., industrialization, urbanization), globalization and militarization are actually many-layered processes of transformation. For instance, it turns out to be possible to track, step by step, strategic decision by strategic decision, precisely how the Nazi regime of 1930s Germany transformed the conscience of so many ordinary Germans. Advertising techniques and popular moviemaking played central roles (Koonz 2003). Thus you will need to watch each over time—a quick snapshot isn't going to reveal much—and you'll need to keep your eye on several layers at once, watching individuals change and at the same time paying attention to changes occurring in local communities, public institutions, companies, and whole societies. It's a tall order. Using a feminist curiosity should help you do it more realistically and with more reliable results.

Globalization is the step-by-step process by which anything—a movie industry, vegetable production, law enforcement, banking, the nursing profession, higher education, an individual's own sense of identity, human rights, environmental activism, or a women's movement—becomes more interdependent and coordinated across national borders. The rubber industry, for instance, has been globalized almost from its very start.

Rubber. The first time I wondered where the rubber for my car's tires came from was when I was a graduate student living for a year in Malaysia trying to understand the ethnic tensions inside this former British colony's complex education system. My little apartment, though, was in a new development just outside the capital on land carved out of a rubber plantation. So in addition to education politics, I began to ponder rubber. There were rubber trees just outside my back door. In the early morning I watched rubber tappers working, skillfully slicing crescent-shaped cuts into the dappled bark of the slender rubber trees, then placing underneath the new cuts small cups into which the rubber tree's treasure, white liquid latex, would drip. Standing there in the early morning tropical light, I thought about the tires on my VW Beetle. But I don't think I realized that I was watching globalization at work.

For it was British scientists a century ago who surreptitiously took rubber trees from Brazil to their famous Kew botanical gardens in England, developed a commercial strain of rubber trees, transplanted them in their then British-ruled colony of Malaya in Southeast Asia, and hired thousands of Indian migrant workers to tap the white fluid latex flowing from the slim rubber trees on their vast plantations. The result: Dunlop, a British company operating rubber plantations in Malaya, became an international powerhouse when the development of the auto industry made rubber tires essential to modern transportation worldwide. The American company Firestone similarly used Liberia and France's Michelin used Vietnam to develop their global tire and rubber businesses. And other iconic American companies such as Singer, maker of the famous Singer sewing machines, were consciously developing global marketing strategies by the early twentieth century (Domosh 2006). So globalizing trends—in science, political control, labor migration, product marketing—are not new. What is new is the scale and breadth of globalizing trends since the late twentieth century.

Often *globalization* is used as a shorthand label only for the worldwide sprawl of capitalist business organizations and flows of technology, labor, and capital designed to enhance the profits of those businesses. Likewise, then, *antiglobalization* is used to refer to the many-stranded social movement inspired by critiques of that capitalist globalizing trend. But it is more useful to understand that globalization can happen to anything, not just to profit-seeking companies and their products and employees. In fact, the antiglobalization movement, with its loose but often effective networks of environmental activists, antisweatshop activists, prodemocracy advocates, and local culture defenders, is itself a major result of globalizing trends: activists in Nigeria are now trading information and strategic lessons with people in Canada and India.

On the other hand, it is true that not everyone enters into globalization with equal access to the Internet; not everyone has scientific laboratories or banking credit at their fingertips, not everyone has equal access to English, the increasingly dominant "lingua franca" of globalized communication; not everyone gets to discuss their international issues privately over cocktails with a senator.

Militarization may be a less familiar concept. But it too is a transforming process that happens over time — sometimes rapidly, though often at a slow, hard-to-spot creep. And like the process of globalization, militarizing trends can simultaneously change the influence one person has on another, can alter how stories are interpreted, can turn meanings upside down. To become militarized is to adopt militaristic values (e.g., a belief in hierarchy, obedience, and the use of force) and priorities as one's own, to see military solutions as particularly effective, to see the world as a dangerous place best approached with militaristic attitudes. These changes may take generations to occur, or they may happen suddenly as the response to a particular trauma. Most of the people in the world who are militarized are not themselves in uniform. Most militarized people are civilians.

A husband and wife's marriage can become militarized if the husband decides to enlist in his country's military and that military operates on the assumption that a soldier's spouse will put the needs of the soldier in the family ahead of any other marital need. If a wife finishes her engineering degree and decides to accept a job offer to work for a large corporation that relies on defense contracts from governments and expects its engineers to accept a culture of secrecy, that can create deep pockets of silence within the couple's home life. Similarly, a town's elected officials can become militarized if they begin to think that getting and keeping a nearby military base enhances the town's economic health or if they believe a local weapons-producing corporation offers the best chance for sustaining decently paid jobs for their residents.

A government's international intelligence service can be militarized if intelligence gathering is done chiefly by the country's department of defense. Even if an independent intelligence agency exists on the government's organizational chart, intelligence gathering and, especially important, the interpreting of that intelligence, can become militarized if in daily reality it is the defense bureaucracy that possesses the greater budget and resources to conduct its own intelligence operations — and the country's elected representatives accept this as normal or even effective.

A country's international borders likewise can become militarized if a majority of voters and their representatives begin to think that danger lurks on the other side of those borders, dangers that must be addressed not through cultural understanding, diplomatic negotiations, immigration regulations, and ordinary policing, but instead through fortification, militarized policing, and even the deployment of soldiers. Such border transformations can spark intense public discussions and debates over whether militarization is the most useful process by which to address the movement of peoples from state to state in today's increasingly globalized world.

A civilian court judge can become militarized if that judge begins to believe that she or he must defer to a government lawyer's claims that, when a government agency is sued by a civilian plaintiff, the government's need to protect "national security" trumps all other claims before the court. Judicial deference in the face of executive branch claims of national security necessity is one of the most common modes of judges' militarization. That is, militarization can look less like conventional aggressiveness and more like deferential passivity.

Ordinary citizens can become militarized whenever they start to think that the world is so dangerous that the necessarily slow processes of legislative hearings, compromise, and open voting don't match the sense of speed and urgency — and maybe secrecy — they have come to think are needed to address those alleged dangers. This is the point at which officials in the executive wing of government — presidents, prime ministers, politically appointed officials, career civil servants — may think they have been given the green light to act behind the legislature's back, without public oversight, in the name of protecting the public from the perceived danger. If some members of the elected legislature also share this sense of danger and urgency and the resultant impatience with compromise and transparency, then that green light will shine all the more brightly. An elected legislator becomes militarized when she or he starts to demote civil liberties to second place behind purported military necessity. Any civilian voter assessing the legislators becomes militarized when she or he begins to see military solutions to international problems as more effective than the often painfully slow and complex diplomatic solutions.

A globalizing corporation becomes militarized insofar as its executives come to believe that its overseas factories will be more secure if the foreign government is willing to use military troops or militarized police to put down labor protests.

This book explores how these two potent contemporary trends — globalization and militarization — often feed each other. That is, as the example of the corporation that locates its factories in a country whose government is quick to wield military force against employees who demonstrate for better working conditions shows, *globalization can become militarized*. Globalization depends on militarization whenever militarized ideas about national security come to be seen as central to creating or sustaining certain international relationships.

Similarly, *militarization can be globalized.* Think of all the national and international sales of rifles, land mines, armored vehicles, submarines, fighter aircraft, radar systems, guided missiles, and unmanned surveillance aircraft. There are so many players — scientists, engineers, producers, sellers, middlemen, buyers, and users — involved that peace advocates have formed several independent, globally conscious groups (e.g., the Small Arms Survey, based in Geneva, Switzerland, and the Swedish Institute for Peace Research in Stockholm) just to track the complex flows of large and small arms, together worth billions of dollars.

For instance, just looking at the contracts won by the largest military defense corporations from the U.S. Department of Defense in fiscal year 2005, we see that Lockheed Martin tops the list with $19.45 billion worth (that amounts to 7.2 percent of the total Pentagon business), followed closely by Boeing with $18.32 billion. Third and fourth among the American defense manufacturing giants are Northrop Grumman and General Dynamics, respectively. Moving down the list, there is Raytheon in fifth place and Halliburton in sixth. Each of these corporations shapes the lives of thousands of employees — and the family members and local communities that depend on their wages. Number seven on the list caught some observers' eyes: It was not American. The British company BAE Systems was the only non-U.S. company in the "top ten" for 2005. It had benefited from the "special relationship" between the U.S. and British governments in foreign policy, which persuaded Pentagon officials that, while not American, BAE could be trusted with contracts for sensitive weaponry. BAE's executives said it was not really an anomaly but an indicator of more to come — namely, defense manufacturers headquartered in diverse countries seeking profitable weapons contracts from any government eager to buy (Wayne 2006).

While it is usually the large companies producing the large weapons systems that make the news, small weapons kill more people day in and day out around the world. Where do the guns and ammunition that are causing death and dislocation among thousands of civilians in the Darfur region of Sudan come from? How do they get from their manufacturers to Sudan? Who is profiting?

Consider the recent emergence of globally active private military contractors such as Blackwater USA. Unlike the more familiar defense manufacturers, private military contractors actually provide, for a substantial fee, the services formerly provided by government militaries and police forces — guarding embassies and mines, providing food for soldiers, running supply convoys. By 2006, in Iraq alone, nearly 50,000 private military and security personnel had been contracted by the U.S. government, private businesses (including newspapers and television companies), and the fledgling Iraqi government to provide various services (Holmquist 2005). In addition, there are scores of companies—some little known to the public, others as well known as Halliburton, AT&T, Pizza Hut, and Burger King—that may not deliver armed men overseas, but do make profits by providing goods and services to soldiers in war zones, including Iraq.

Or imagine a map of the world showing all the military bases—large and small—that just the U.S. government operates. Today, there are American military bases from Cuba to San Diego to Britain and Italy, from Qatar to North Carolina to Japan, from Bulgaria and Bosnia to Kazakhstan, Aruba, and Guam. Now, thirty years after the end of the brutal Vietnam-United States War, there are even negotiations going on between the U.S. and Vietnamese governments to allow the U.S. Navy to use Vietnam's port Da Nang. Every one of these American bases is the result of bargaining and pressure and formal agreements between the U.S. government and the officials of another country or territory. These bases and their immediate neighborhoods take the mundane forms of fences, tarmac, playgrounds, bowling alleys, bars, discos, grocery stores, clinics, tattoo parlors, tailors, mechanics shops, target ranges, file cabinets, memos, e-mails, love letters, sexually transmitted diseases, take-offs, landings, parades, and pornographic pin-ups. Together, however, these everyday base fixtures and operations and the negotiations that create and sustain them add up to a globalization of militarization.

Again, some of these globalizing militarization engines were fired up more than a century ago. The imperial governments of Britain, France, the Netherlands, Spain, Portugal, the United States, and Belgium deliberately exported their own models of militaries to the countries they colonized around the world. Britain sought to replicate the British army in India, Nigeria, Malaysia, Fiji, Australia, and Egypt, complete with its own homegrown presumptions about ethnic hierarchies and notions of "martial races"—that is, ethnic groups whose men were imagined by the colonizers to be "traditional warriors" (Barkawi 2006). Britain's imperial rivals did the same in Indonesia, Vietnam, Mozambique, the Philippines, Senegal, Algeria, Peru, and Mexico (Enloe 1980). Still today, the British military is seeking recruits into its own military from young men in its former colonies, especially Fiji and Nepal (for its famed Gurkha regiments) (Gillan 2005). When you next hear about Gurkhas serving in the British peacekeeping forces in Bosnia or Kosovo, think of the long-lasting gendered militarized legacies of imperialism, as well as the hopes of young men and their parents in impoverished former colonies.

So the globalization of militarizing processes is not new. What is new is (a) the global reach of these business, cultural, and military ideas and processes; (b) the capacity of promoters of globalizing militarism to wield lethal power; (c) the fact that so many private companies are now involved in this globalization of militarization; and (d) the intricacy of the international alliances among the players.

Asking feminist questions is a valuable means of understanding how and why *both* the globalization of militarization *and* the militarization of globalization happen. Posing feminist questions, furthermore, can help reveal the potential consequences of these processes for both women and men. Each of us probably has had the experience — with friends, with family, perhaps even with teachers — of insisting upon asking about things that others would much rather take for granted. They think you are a nuisance to be posing these questions:

> "Dad, how come on farms producing food for export it's usually the women who do the weeding?"
>
> "Well, because they always have. That's just the way it is! Anyway, what's the big deal about weeding?"

Of course, we might be the lazy ones. Other people might have to nudge us toward becoming curious. Perhaps we are the ones who don't want to be bothered asking new questions. It can be quite comfortable taking a lot of things for granted. That is why it takes so much effort by so many people to turn something most people take for granted — the fact that it is mainly women who weed, the fact that miners breathe in coal dust, the fact that many high school students join a military cadet corps, the fact that people become poorer as they grow older — into an *issue*.

Something becomes an "issue" only when a lot of people do two things: first, they start questioning it and stop taking it for granted, and second, they begin to believe it deserves public attention and public resolution. Persuading people to do both of these things is not easy. Since so many cultures and so many governments treat women's experiences as not worth exploring and create the impression that the condition of women is merely a private matter, converting any aspect of women's lives into an issue has taken — and still takes — enormous effort.

For instance, if a lot of people begin to be curious about why it is mainly women who weed, but they still stop short of calling for public responsibility for this situation, then the fact that it is mainly women who weed won't become an issue. However, even the emergence of just a popular curiosity about why women are designated as the weeders may, further down the road, provoke people to call for more public responsibility for the causes and consequences of that agricultural division of labor. They may start looking into the international politics of cotton, of strawberries, of coffee.

Creating a new curiosity is an important first step — and it's not so easy to take. But nothing can become an issue if the exercise of curiosity remains a private activity or if what you uncover is deemed unworthy of public response.

So it is tough to turn something into an issue. Issue making is a political activity. It requires developing a new curiosity plus spreading that curiosity among a lot of people in their roles as public citizens. Think of all the things that today are being treated nationally or internationally as issues, things that fifteen years ago were not considered "issues." When, for example, did male soldiers' use of women as prostitutes become an issue at least in a few countries? How about "stalking"? When did militaries' use of land mines become an issue? Becoming an issue is never automatic. Each issue's development has its own history. Each issue needs to be explained. Every issue has become an issue only because some people stopped taking it for granted, developed a new curiosity about it, and managed to persuade a lot of us who used to be complacent about it to become newly curious, too—and to start finding answers that made them think afresh about citizens' and governments' responsibilities for those dynamics that they had discovered.

Using a *feminist* curiosity is asking questions about the condition of women—and about relationships of women to each other and about relationships of women to men. It is also *not* taking for granted—thus it is insisting upon exploring—the relationships of women to families, to men, to companies, to movements, to institutions, to ideologies, to cultural expressions, to the state, and to globalizing trends.

Developing a *feminist* curiosity can be energizing. It motivates one to treat as puzzling the relationships of women to any aspect of social life and nature that other people take for granted. So many people in most societies usually say (and many of us said before we begin to cultivate our own feminist curiosity) that we do not need to ask about the condition of women or assumptions about women because they are "natural" or because they are "trivial."

"Mom, why do all these carmakers drape women models over their new automobiles?"

"Oh, dear, don't worry. Nobody takes that seriously."

Beware the adjective "natural." Beware "trivial." Both are boulders rolled up against a door you may want to open. Rolling away those boulders can take a lot of intellectual and social stamina. Using a feminist curiosity, one discovers that who weeds is not "natural"; it flows from who is assigned to weed, which child is pulled out of school because a life of weeding won't require the ability to read and write. Who is assigned to weed may determine who in the village is not trained to operate a tractor. Who weeds may turn out to have a lot to do with who is not legally permitted to inherit land. Following the bread crumbs of these questions reveals that "Who weeds and who doesn't?" is not a trivial question to pursue. It is a question whose exploration can shed a bright light on globalized agriculture, on who benefits from it, and on who stays mired in poverty because of it.

Developing and using a feminist curiosity does take a lot of energy. Many of you might have sat in a class and felt hesitant to raise your hand to ask a question, sensing people around you letting out an audible sigh, "Oh, there she goes again." It takes energy to go ahead and ask that question, to not let a misleading assumption about women or about men, about boys or about girls just slide by. Continuing to pose feminist questions even takes a kind of courage.

"Thinking about your lecture about international terrorism, Professor, shouldn't we ask 'Where are the women?'"

Or: "Excuse me, sir, but in your discussion about nuclear trade policy, do you think that it matters to ask about international contests over masculinity?"

Exercising a feminist curiosity, therefore, is not a passive endeavor. It is not a quiet intellectual pastime. It is intellectual, but it takes stamina. And, I have become convinced, exercising a feminist curiosity calls on us to develop a kind of politics that has to be nurtured and cultivated; it does not just grow by itself. And lot those who raise their eyebrows or utter an audible sigh or theatrically roll their eyes when a friend or colleague poses a feminist question—that raising of an eyebrow, letting out a sigh, or rolling one's eyes each is also a political act. Each of those gestures is meant to discredit, maybe even to silence, the feminist questioner. Each of those gestures is meant to keep the boulders firmly up against the door.

. . .

A "gender impact analysis" is a new tool in local and global policymaking. Gender impact analysis should be—but is rarely—completed before any final decision is made; decisions such as allowing a new foreign company to come into one's region or country to open a new copper mine, signing an alliance with another government that entails building a new air force base, permitting a foreign film distribution company to buy up most of the country's movie theaters, and legalizing a new anti-AIDS drug call for asking:

- How will this decision (in contrast to the other options on the table) affect men? Which men especially?

- How will this affect women? Will it affect certain women more than other women?

- How will this policy choice affect the relationships between women and men? Will it shrink the inequalities? Widen the disparities? Globally or locally or both?

Gender impact analyses are difficult to do. It takes skills and training. Some professional schools are still refusing to incorporate this training into their curriculum, depriving their students of the skills they will need. Today, however, those gender-analysis skills are being taught in new graduate programs and special training programs all over the world. Networks of feminist scholars, women engaged in local women's groups, and feminist-informed agency staff members are meeting, for instance, in Canada, Thailand, and Kenya to write new gender-analysis training manuals and to create new courses to increase the number of people who have the skills to perform gender investigations and assessments of policy proposals. These gatherings don't make headlines, CNN crews don't arrive there with their cameras, but nevertheless, the people who travel across time zones to take part in these meetings are helping to globalize a feminist curiosity. Among the most effective globalized feminist networks are

- *Women Living Under Muslim Laws (WLUMI)*, whose activists, themselves women from Muslim backgrounds, monitor and challenge nationalist discourses, religious intolerance, sexist laws, and sexist practices rationalized in the name of Islam and organize international campaigns to support local women subjected to patriarchal Islamist regimes;

- the *Women's International League for Peace and Freedom (WILPF)*, which was founded in The Hague in 1915, during World War I, by 1,300 women activists from Europe and North America who opposed this devastating war (one million men were killed or maimed in the stalemated muddy trench warfare in France in the five-month Battle of the Somme alone) and now has its headquarters in Geneva, with active branches in Sweden, Norway, Burundi, Sierra Leone, Canada, Russia, Japan, Australia, the United States, and other countries (Stiehm 2006);

- the *Women's Initiatives for Gender Justice*, a newer network of feminists pressuring the new International Criminal Court (established in 1999 as the first international war crimes court) to take explicit actions to ensure that systematic rape and sexual slavery in wartime are explicitly recognized and prosecuted as war crimes;

- *Women in Conflict Zones Network (WICZNET)*, which is coordinated from Canada and brings together women from the former Yugoslavia, Sri Lanka, Canada, and Britain who work in research institutions and international organizations, such as the International Committee of the Red Cross, UNICEF, and the UN High Commissioner for Refugees, as well as grassroots feminists, to shine light on the experiences and analyses of women living in war-torn regions (Giles, de Alwis, Klein, and Silva 2003);

- *Women Waging Peace*, which was first launched by a former U.S. ambassador who had seen firsthand both the impact of war on women in Bosnia during the early 1990s and local women's own courage and organizing skills, and has become a network designed to support and build bridges between often isolated local women's peace groups, among them groups in the Congo, Bosnia, Georgia, and Sierra Leone; and

- *Women in Black*, a network of women in countries around the world—in Israel, Serbia, Spain, Italy, Japan, the United States, Britain—who oppose militarism and its roots in patriarchy and nationalism and who hold silent vigils open to all women, standing prominently every week in their own city's busy intersections (Women in Black 2005; Cockburn 2007).

· · ·

All six of these globalizing feminist networks have made the exposing of, and the rolling back of, local and international militarist policies, ideas, and practices central to their work. Members of all six also have become convinced that, given the ways in which hydra-headed militarization works, the most effective actions are those that not only are sensitive to local cultures, politics, and priorities but also embrace international alliances in which to share ideas and information and to coordinate actions. Members of all six of these groups, furthermore, have become convinced that women have special roles to play in exposing and challenging militarization, *not* because women are somehow innately, biologically wired for peacefulness, but because women are so often outside the inner circles where militarizing decisions are being made yet are likely to be called upon to support, and even work on behalf of, militarizing agendas. . . .

Yet many international and national decision makers prefer to leave these new feminist analytical tools to rust in the basement. If the policy elites did use the gener analysis tools, they might have to change their agendas. For example, if they commissioned gender impact analyses and then acted on their findings, officials in natural disaster relief agencies might have to significantly reallocate their resources. When planning for future tsunami, earthquake, or hurricane relief, many people (though not all, and not necessarily those with authority) have learned the hard way that it is always important to ask ahead of time about the likely impacts both on women and on men—of every economic class, of every ethnic group. Why? Because, of all the thousands of people who died in the giant waves set off by the December 2004 Indian Ocean tsunami, a majority turned out to be women and their dependent children. Likewise, in the chaotic aftermath of Hurricane Katrina, which devastated the Gulf Coast of the southern United States in September 2005, it was African American women and their dependent children who were especially endangered by the lack of government preparedness and the resultant overcrowding of unsanitary emergency shelters. . . .

Impacts matter. Wielding a feminist curiosity about impacts is a valuable analytical activity. When that feminist curiosity is not used there are real-life consequences.

· · ·

TRACKING THE MILITARIZED GLOBAL SNEAKER

Let's start testing this feminist causal explanatory tool by looking at the international politics of factory work. If we consciously use a feminist curiosity, we can see how the promoters of globalizing factory work rely on manipulations of ideas about "femininity" and the "dutiful daughter." Their goal to cheapen the cost of the labor needed to produce those globalized goods for export and company profit.

Those efforts to make—and keep—that labor cheap often become dependent on militarism. In other words, many of the sneakers that look white or blue or neon pink on the surface may turn out to be threaded with khaki on the inside.

"Cheap labor" is the work of some employees who are paid relatively little for their effort. The challenge for us is to question this commonly accepted (i.e., unquestioned) notion of "cheap labor" by using a feminist curiosity. This won't be easy because "cheap labor" is so commonly used to explain the increasingly globalized world we live in. The concept of "cheap labor" is offered to listeners and leaders every day in media debates, in legislatures, and sometimes even in antiglobalization movements to explain why some regions or countries are more attractive to business investors than others.

"Oh, Company X is moving its factories to Asia because they're attracted by its cheap labor."

Or: "Sure, the Mexican government is going to win out over the Canadian government in attracting foreign investment because the Mexicans can offer companies cheap labor."

Women's labor is especially likely to be thought of as cheap. While men's labor—particularly the labor of men from ethnically and racially marginalized groups—can be thought of as cheap (think about the history of gold mining and the building of railroads), in the past 150 years it has been women's labor that has most often been imagined as allegedly "cheap," or worthy only of low pay. In globally competitive industries such as the textile industry, the garment industry, the shoe industry, the processed food industry, the electronics industry, and the toy industry, therefore, it has been women who have been deliberately hired to produce goods cheaply. Think "Barbie," ask about women's cheap labor; think computer chips, ask about women's cheap labor; think blue jeans, ask about women's cheap labor.

Staying uncurious while employing this easy phrase "cheap labor" depends on making the assumption that labor of women inevitably is cheap. It depends on making the deeper assumption that women's labor is "naturally" cheap, that women's labor is automatically cheap, that women's labor is cheap in a way that requires no policy decisions, no pressure, no manipulation. If we take for granted that women's labor is cheap labor, then we (students, civil servants, legislators, economists, activists, corporate executives) can comfortably move right ahead to build our corporate strategy or our international development plan on this unexplored assumption.

Now let's look at a radically different analytical possibility. Using a feminist curiosity, let's not accept an assumption, let's ask a question: is women's labor *made* cheap? As soon as you start using this new phrase—"women's labor *made* cheap"—you find yourself motivated to ask another new question: by whom?

Your curiosity now is being energized. You are inspired to ask even deeper questions. Digging deeper, you start asking: How? How is any woman's labor made cheap?

Now you are on an analytical roll. There is no dampening your feminist curiosity. You have lots of new questions to pose about globalized (or local) women's factory work. Making—and keeping—women's labor "cheap" does not look so easy anymore. It looks as though it takes effort by myriad actors. And so the international practice of using women's skills, talents, attentiveness, and energies begins to seem more political, more dependent on the wielding of power—psychological, cultural, legal, economic, and (as we will see) maybe even militarized power—by various people and institutions. Militarized police being called in by employers and government officials to quell a labor demonstration organized by women factory workers who have decided that their labor should not be "cheap" is a common occurrence in this age of globalization.

The low wages paid to women working on an assembly line no longer look "natural." Anything that is described as "natural" thus should be carefully examined under the feminist curiosity microscope, because anything that is labeled "natural" is something you are being encouraged *not* to explain. If it is labeled "natural," allegedly, it took no effort to make it that way: "Today thousands of women in factories all over Asia stitch Nike sneakers. So what? What is interesting about that? Women stitch. Women have always stitched. Sewing, it's just what women naturally do." . . .

So the first assumption to investigate in any examination of women in globalized factory work is the assumption that the women in the factories are there because they are doing naturally what women always do. Who benefits from this widespread assumption? It will probably turn out to be an alliance of diverse beneficiaries: parents, boyfriends, government planners, local factory managers, foreign corporate executives, overseas retailers, and shoppers hoping for bargains.

This act of feminist curiosity will prompt you to be skeptical about three additional common assumptions that are made today by "experts" in international political economy: first, the assumption that no government official (in alliance with company executives) ever had to think about ways to put the women there on that factory floor; second, the assumption that no government official (or company executive) ever had to think about how to *keep* women there; and third, the assumption that no company executives ever had to sit around the table and devise strategies to create and sustain an alliance with local government officials for the sake of making (and keeping) women's pay low and their labor thereby "cheap." Three assumptions. Three failures of curiosity creating three dangerous analytical traps.

A *non*feminist investigator of globalized capitalism assumes that no corporate executives ever had to hold a serious business strategy session to figure out how to keep women's labor cheap. That same investigator of international capitalism also imagines — lazily — that no corporate manager ever had to strategize about how to work with local government officials in order to get the "kind" of women — or girls — they wanted: old or young? urban or rural? local or migrant? married or unmarried? ethnicity A or ethnicity B?

The analysts who make these lazy assumptions usually are not challenged by anyone. They are thus allowed — by their supervisors, by their clients, by us — to go on making these flawed assumptions about women who work in international trade. Unchallenged, they continue talking about "cheap labor." They continue to discuss globally competitive trade or export processing zones, *as if* their expert understanding of international politics were rational, complete, reliable, and realistic.

It is not.

In reality, this widely used approach to the politics of global business, with its lack of a feminist curiosity, is too simplistic. It is an approach that hides power. Once you adopt a new questioning feminist curiosity, you begin to notice how many decisions, how many calculations, how many strategy changes it actually took to get those women into that factor. Suddenly you realize it took a lot more resources, and the wielding of a lot more power to get that woman to do (and to keep doing) the allegedly "natural" work she is doing — stitching a sneaker, assembling a microchip — for lower pay than the casual users of the phrase "cheap labor" have been willing to admit.

When I gave a talk in Tokyo a couple of years ago, I asked everyone in the audience to take off their shoes and to look at the labels inside to see where their shoes were made. I deliberately wore my sneakers that night. Professor Chizuko Ueno, the evening's discussant, and Professor Yumiko Mikanagi, our moderator, two well-known Japanese feminist scholars, both joined our collective investigation. We began with Professor Ueno. She found that though she'd purchased her fashionable, shiny black Reebok sneakers in New York, they had been made in the Philippines. Professor Ueno exclaimed, "So, actually I have caved in to exploitation!"

I tried to reassure her: "You have a lot of company. That is why I wore my sneakers tonight. I thought that I could not talk about how women's pay is made so low and pretend that I am not taking part in it too." My sneakers that night were New Balance — made in China. Others in the audience, doing research on their own shoes, started calling out the countries listed on the labels inside their shoes: "Brazil." "China." "China." "China." "Thailand." "Thailand." "Brazil." "Argentina." "Germany." "Japan." "China." "Thailand." "Indonesia." "Indonesia." "Vietnam."

In which of these countries have women been sewing these shoes with little right to create their own independent unions? In which of these countries do executives and government officials agree that using armed force to intimidate women labor organizers is necessary for company and national pro-ductivity? In which of these countries are women persuaded that they don't deserve promotions because they will be quitting paid work once they get married and become unpaid housewives? In which of these countries are women employees afraid to demand better working conditions (e.g., less forced overtime) because they believe their primary duty as good daughters is to keep sending money home to their impoverished rural parents?

That is, there are questions to ask, country by country, company by company. One shouldn't assume that every company or every country is iden-tical, even if they share broad similarities. Curiosity is crucial. Close attention to women factory workers and their relationships to their parents, to their fellow women workers, to their boyfriends or husbands, to their managers, to their government officials, and to foreign corporate executives thousands of miles away is called for.

Here is another research report "from the field." While still in Tokyo, I started going into the brightly lit sneaker shops along Tokyo's busy Takeshita Street. Here are my informal research findings: Converse low-top sneakers— so popular today in Japan and the United States—now are being made by women in Indonesia. Converse was recently bought by Nike but still markets its own distinctive styles. You can conduct your own research by reading sneaker labels in shops near you—in Durham or San Diego, in Leeds or Lon-don, in Santiago or St. Louis.

Style is political. In today's highly competitive globalized sneaker indus-try, the more elaborate the stitching, the more incentive corporate executives have to *make* the stitchers' labor "cheap." For example, envision the popular, multicolored Converse low-tops. They are among the least fancy of sneakers. "Hip," yes, but not fancy in either their materials or their stitching. Compare those low-tops now with the sneakers favored by soccer or basketball stars and the shoppers who admire their style. The fancier the stitching, the more nec-essary it will be for a sneaker executive to keep the stitchers' wages low in order to keep profits high. The more pressure factory managers and their cor-porate clients feel to keep the wages they pay their female workers low, the more tempting it will be for those same managers and corporate clients to tol-erate militarized intimidation of their workers. Highly styled, complexly stitched sneakers—those sneakers for export whose profits depend on keeping workers unorganized—are more likely to carry a militarized price tag.

It was largely because the low-tops were designed with so little stitching that Converse kept its low-top factories in the United States, primarily in North Carolina, until recently. Although Converse executives decided to pro-duce these low-tops in the United States, where wages are generally higher and safety regulations are generally more demanding, they chose a state whose local lawmakers have given local factory workers only limited rights to orga-nize labor unions. Furthermore, Converse's own personnel officers seemed (we do not know this for sure because no one has yet done a gender and racial study of a Converse factory in the United States) to prefer African American women factory workers. These are women who, due to North Carolina's longtime racialized gender politics, have limited job opportunities and thus have been least able to protest their low wages.

But my research along Tokyo's bustling Takeshita Street revealed that Converse executives based in Andover, Massachusetts, recently changed their gendered global strategy. They moved their low-top sneaker production from North Carolina to Indonesia. Why? Was it just a calculation of kilometers? Indonesia is closer to Japanese teenage shoppers than is North Carolina. Or did the women working in Converse's North Carolina factories start organizing? And what gendered sales pitch did the Converse executives back in the United States hear from Indonesia's male government officials? What gendered message about Indonesian women did Converse strategists hear from rival sneaker makers already manufacturing in Indonesia that made the labor of *Indonesian women* seem so economically and politically appealing?

In 2003, Nike bought Converse. There was some speculation that Nike, known worldwide for its very intricate sneaker designs—designs dependent on elaborate and complicated stitching by its Asian women employees—would push Converse to abandon its simple styles. But three years later, Nike's executives decided to keep the traditional styles because Converse sales were rising, as young consumers from Tokyo to Oslo, London to Chicago adopted the multicolored low-tops and high-tops as their symbols of counterculture (Kang 2006). Young sneaker buyers were wearing Converse to announce that they were off the Nike global fashion grid, perhaps not realizing that Nike now was banking the profits of their Converse purchases.

The corporate decision makers of New Balance, headquartered in Boston (my current hometown), adopted a different feminized (reliant on women) geographic strategy. Until four or five years ago, New Balance executives marketed their global brand as "made in the USA," hiring mainly new immigrant women living in the Boston area to stitch their sneakers. They seemed to think that consumers would view New Balance as a more socially responsible company if they kept producing their sneakers in a country and a region that allowed its mainly female workforce to unionize. This practice also allowed the mail-order retailer L.L. Bean to feature New Balance sneakers in their popular catalogs with a good conscience. But since 2000, New Balance can no longer make that claim. New Balance executives moved most of their manufacturing operations from Boston to China and Vietnam. Hoping consumers will understand, New Balance now inserts a card into each sneaker box explaining that they try to produce as many of their sneakers in the United States as possible.

Dates matter. Historical development matters. Gendered uses of power, which push certain women to stitch sneakers in certain countries more than in others, are not stagnant. A feminist curiosity is a historically lively curiosity. With a feminist curiosity, one keeps track of diverse women and ideas about diverse women around the world over time. The gendered global politics of sneakers—like all forms of gendered international politics—therefore has to be historicized.

So, open your closet and look at all your shoes. Now line up all your sneakers according to the year in which you think they were made. Borrow your mother's and father's oldest pairs of sneakers, too, so that you will have a longer historical time line to work with. You will be prompted now to start asking feminist questions about the time-specific dynamics of women's labor, women's hopes, women's organizing, governments' competing industrial policies, and corporate executives' changing geographic calculations about how to make women's labor cheap.

The recent history of South Korean women working in sneaker factories makes this clear. According to investigations by women's studies researcher Seung-Kyung Kim, executives of American, European, and Japanese sneaker companies and electronics companies were deliberately wooed, starting in the 1960s, by South Korea's then-military government led by the authoritarian president Chung Hee Park, who was eager to achieve rapid industrialization and compete in the emerging global economy (1997). In crafting their strategy, General Park and his military and civilian economic advisors did not rely on the widespread flawed assumption that it was "natural" for Korean women to stitch sneakers or to assemble delicate electronics products. These economic-policy strategists did, however, assume that women—especially young women—would be better stitchers than their Korean brothers. But they realized that sewing in their parents' homes and sewing in a Nike factory were very different ideologically. Thus, in the 1960s and early 1970s, the military government of Chung Hee Park launched a calculated campaign to change Korean citizens' image of the "respectable" Korean young woman. Conflating the concepts of "national security," "national pride," "modernization," and "industrial growth," this military government set about to persuade the parents of daughters to radically alter their own definitions of what was "natural" for "decent" ("marriageable") South Korean young women to do outside their homes. The government's campaigners argued that a young unmarried woman who stitched, not under her parents' careful supervision, but instead under the supervision of a foreman in a factory miles away from home, could be endowed with a "respectable" femininity and an appealing feminized morality that would still make her attractive on the Korean marriage market.

Nike, Reebok, and Adidas could not be lured to South Korean factories in the 1960s and 1970s *unless* the Park regime could transform Korean parents' ideas about what is "natural" and what is "respectable" behavior for "dutiful daughters." If we are not curious about mothers' and fathers' changed ideas of daughterhood, respectability, and marriageability, we will become *un*reliable analysts of the "Korean economic miracle."

So now dig deeper back into your family's closet. Pull out your oldest, most worn-out sneakers. If you can excavate a pair from the 1960s or early 1980s, most likely you will discover that the label says "made in Korea." behind that label is a lot more decision making and a lot more power wielding than nonfeminist analysts imagine. For behind that label is an entire state ideological campaign to alter citizens' definitions of "femininity," and "feminine respectability." The state's goal: to make young, unmarried South Korean women's "daughterly" labor available—cheaply—to foreign corporations.

Nike was the first sneaker company to shed its own factories and to start relying on subcontractors to own and to manage the factories producing Nike sneakers. Consequently, the Korean young women mobilized in the 1960s and 1970s to work as patriotic dutiful daughters in sneaker factories were not hired—or fired—directly by Nike. They were hired, disciplined, paid, and fired by the Korean male entrepreneurs with whom Nike signed contracts. The masculinized sneaker company executives from the United States and Europe were in part attracted by the fact that many of these factoryowning Korean men—subcontractors for Nike and later for Reebok and Adidas— enjoyed close political relationships with the militarized South Korean political elite. No matter what bright color sneakers had on the outside, by the 1970s sneakers were turning a distinctive shade of khaki underneath.

Threaded through virtually every sneaker you own is some relationship to masculinized militaries. Locating factories in South Korea was a good strategic decision in the eyes of those Oregon-headquartered male Nike executives because of the close alliance between male policymakers in Washington and Seoul. It was a relationship—unequal but intimate—based on their shared anticommunism, their shared commitment to waging the Cold War, and their shared participation in an ambitious international military alliance.

Pusan, a major Korean port and industrial city, became, by the late 1970s, the "sneaker capital of the world." By then, other sneaker companies had copied the Nike model. Here are the key elements of this globalizing industrial model that made Pusan so central to the world's sneaker industry: (1) close the company's own factories; (2) put the women employees who make the sneakers at arm's length by hiring local male subcontractors to run the factories and to make cozy alliances with the local male political elites; (3) view shared anticommunist ideologies as good for profitable manufacturing; (4) take comfort in a Cold War military alliance, as imagined by the U.S.-based company executives between "your" government and "their" government; (5) design corporate strategies to exploit local sexist ideas about femininity in order to justify low wages paid to young women workers; (6) depend on the local regime to craft a national ideology of "feminine respectability" that will enable your subcontractors to have a seemingly endless line of willing and unorganized women workers; (7) encourage consumers—women and men—in Japan, the United States, and Europe to imagine that *they* are "empowered" when they purchase and wear your high-priced sneakers; and

(8) persuade these same consumers *not* to be curious about whether the Asian women stitching their sneakers also feel "empowered" when they go to work in Pusan's modern factories.

Any investigator of global political economy (or "development") who lacks a feminist curiosity will not even see half of the building blocks it has taken to create and sustain this popular formula.

This potent international formula was crafted in the 1960s and 1970s and continued to "work" for South Korean and U.S. and European policymakers into he mid-1980s. Despite significant changes in South Korea's political culture, especially the rise of a lively civil society, many elements of this gendered — militarized — neoliberal industrial formula still operate today in the early 2000s. To tell whether — and why — any elements of this global sneaker industry formula have genuinely changed requires curiosity about the politics (local, national, and international) of both femininity and masculinity. Here is just a sampling of some feminist questions we need to find the answers to:

- To what extent do Nike's American male executives and their Korean (or Indonesian or Chinese or Vietnamese) male factory managers (subcontractors) use their shared masculinity to build trust between each other in what is a highly stressful global economic climate?

- Do today's Indonesian, Vietnamese, and Chinese women sneaker workers all have identical ideas about being "feminine" or being "dutiful daughters"?

- Do Chinese, Korean, Vietnamese, and Indonesian government officials promote the same feminized idea about the "model woman worker"?

In the early 1980s, a prodemocracy movement gathered steam in South Korea. Its chief goal was to force the twenty-year-old military-centered regime to turn over power to a popularly elected civilian government. At the outset of the movement, students at prestigious Korean universities provided the ideas, leadership, and members. But soon women and men working in factories began to take part. Participation in any prodemocracy movement is gendered — the risks taken, the nature of the consciousness change, the sorts of political influence gained and the goals set by the movement, as well as the rewards, are likely to be different for (and thus differently weighed by) women and men. Again, feminist researcher Seung-Kyung Kim (1997) provides us with insights into these often-ignored gendered realities of a prodemocracy movement's evolution. Many thousands of South Korean women working in sneaker, electronics, and garment factories in the early to mid-1980s began to imagine something new: that when they were working in these factories, they were acting as citizens. They began to believe that they—as low-paid factory workers—were not just "dutiful daughters," they were not just future wives; they were *citizens*.

How do companies and governments keep any woman's labor "cheap"? Policymakers encourage that woman to imagine that she is not a citizen when she is in the factory working those long hours, stitching Nikes and Reeboks on the assembly line, but rather a dutiful daughter. Dutiful daughters obey supervisors; dutiful daughters think first of their parents' needs (and of their brothers' needs) and second about saving money for a future husband.

Therefore, if enough women on the sneaker assembly line begin to imagine that, as they stitch Nike sneakers, they are doing it not as dutiful daughters but as full citizens—that is, individuals invested with rights—policymakers in corporate and government offices are going to have a harder time keeping the labor of women "cheap." In European and North American countries, as well as in Asian, Middle Eastern, Latin American, and African countries, whole political cultures and legal systems have been cultivated over generations to discourage women from thinking of themselves as citizens. The reason it took decades of women's gutsy organizing to simply win the right to vote was that the men who ran governments, schools, newspapers, and churches stubbornly clutched onto he masculinist idea that the proper place for women was in the home, imagining them first and foremost as wives, daughters, or mothers, not as citizens (even if, in reality, many women were working in fields, in textile and garment factories, and in the kitchens and laundry rooms of wealthier people's homes). So the claim that they were citizens when they were sewing high-priced sneakers for export, not just daughters or would-be wives, was not a claim unique to Korean women workers. It was a claim that had to be developed and asserted by women in most countries.

Despite the risks, many South Korean women workers—though not all—did develop a new consciousness during the upheavals of the mid-1980s. It was this change in factory women's sense of who they were that then enabled a student-led prodemocracy movement to burst out of its own narrow middle-class confines and make alliances with working-class women and men.

We cannot just note this transformation that was to alter the global politics of the sneaker industry and then move on. We need to *explain* it. And that can be accomplished only using a feminist curiosity. Without posing serious feminist questions, we will fail to adequately explain the success of the historic South Korean prodemocracy movement of the 1980s. Furthermore, if we don't look closely at the hopes, dreams, skills, fears, and strategies of these Korean women working in sneaker (and electronics and garment) factories, we will fail to see the causal connections between the ouster of the Seoul generals and the departure of Nike from Pusan. We will fail to see that individual women's rethinking of "respectable femininity," and "daughterhood" and their reimaging of themselves as "citizens" not only can bring down state regimes but can alter the calculus on which contemporary international political economies rely. A citizen-worker is no longer an easily cheapened worker. One might try to picture conversations in Nike's Oregon headquarters in the mid-1980s as so many South Korean women struggled to see themselves as citizens: "Get out the map, Charlie, we're packing up in Pusan. Where is Jakarta?"

There was an opportunity in the late 1980s for the sneaker industry to remain globalized and feminized (reliant on women's assembly work) but become less militarized. If Nike and the other international sneaker companies had decided that the ouster of the generals and the success of the pro-democracy movement was "good for business" and thus stayed in Pusan, the sneaker industry would have remained global—headquarters in one country, factory managers and assembly workers in another country, and customers buying their products around the world—but it would have adapted to South Korea's new partially demilitarized political culture and relationships (including the newly energized labor movement and the increasingly vibrant women's movement). But that was not the decision that the sneaker executives headquartered in the United States and Europe made. They had gotten used to the business advantages offered by a militarized regime. If South Korea was going to roll back its own militarization even somewhat (not completely, as many Korean antimilitarist analysts are quick to point out), then the sneaker companies would move to another country where militarized politics were still entrenched. Indonesia looked appealing.

Capitalism (local and global) is not just about modernity. The architects of late-twentieth- and early-twenty-first-century capitalism have deliberately decided to exploit a false notion of tradition. In practice, this has proved a very tricky game to play. It takes clever footwork by state and company strategists to promote a capitalist brand of modernity by entrenching traditional daughterhood and traditional wifehood. Reread this previous sentence. Slow down when you get to "by." "By" is the strategic "trick" here. One might think this "by" is easy to accomplish, that it's quite simple to entrench traditional ideas and practices of daughterhood and wifehood—or one might imagine that these overseas-investing capitalists are just in a muddle. Not so. Patriarchy routinely tries to hide its confusion. One of the tasks of researchers is to pull back the curtain of alleged coherence and rationality to reveal the confusion operating just behind it. How that modernizing patriarchal capitalist confusion—evidenced by contradictions, mixed messages, ambivalence—is superficially rationalized and disguised is a question for any analyst who seeks to make sense of the contemporary international political economy. Thus we need to investigate both government officials' and company executives' mixed messages about daughters and marriage and simultaneously pay careful attention to girls' and women's own efforts to untangle and use these mixed messages. We have to craft the feminist curiosity and feminist skills to do both, because it is the dynamic intertwining of the two that helps shape what the globalized sneaker industry is today and what it is soon to become. We dare not be satisfied with a single still photograph. And we dare not let our attention wander.

In the late 1980s a major migration of an entire industry occurred. In search of the next population of "dutiful daughter" employees (in the name of industrial modernity)—and of a regime that would use its own authority to promote a revised "traditional" ideology of dutiful daughterhood—Nike, Reebok, Adidas, and other sneaker companies moved to Indonesia. They brought their Korean male factory-owning subcontractors with them, too. Indonesia's president was then General Suharto, head of a "New Order" militarized regime. Like General Chung Hee Park of South Korea twenty years earlier, General Suharto and his Indonesian male civilian economists, in pursuit of rapid industrialization fueled by foreign investment, set about to modernize the Indonesian idea of a respectable, dutiful daughter, though perhaps the Suharto officials took less initiative, instead following the lead of the foreign investors and their factory managers, who had their own clear ideas of what was "men's work" and what was "women's work" (Caraway 2007). Once again, with the aid of the popular media, mothers and fathers were convinced that letting a daughter move away from home to work in a sneaker (or electronics or garment) factory would not compromise that daughter's respectability or jeopardize her chances for a decent marriage.

By 2000, Nike and other global sneaker companies had (through their subcontractors) hired 100,000 Indonesian women employees. The government's military and the militarized police have helped keep these thousands of Indonesian young women unorganized and therefore their labor "cheap." The Indonesians' nationwide prodemocracy movement did not end this practice But it hasn't just been the military. It has taken a complex, often unstable, combination of myths about "traditional Indonesian femininity" and media journalists' and editors' narratives, along with personal dreams of achieving a "good marriage," individual strategies for sustaining one's reputation as a "respectable woman," and state militarism to keep Indonesian sneaker workers' labor cheap. Just like the sneakers made in South Korea in the 1970s, sneakers being produced today in Indonesia may be threaded with militarism.

When any government calls in security forces to put down labor protests by women sneaker workers (protests for decent wages, for the right to organize, for the end of forced overtime, for the end of sexual harassment by male supervisors), there is a gendered politics going on—on all sides. It is not just the women workers who are gendered. The men in the police and army who confront them with shields and batons and guns are also gendered insofar as they see their wielding of instruments of intimidation as expressions of their own manliness. In other words, whenever women workers are confronted by male security forces, we are witnessing feminized labor being deliberately intimidated with masculinized force. We need to direct our feminist curiosities *both* to the women working in the factories *and* to the uniformed men ordered by the government to keep them in line. At present, we know startlingly little about how these security forces and how these women experience—and strategize about—these sharply gendered confrontations at the sneaker factory gates. . . .

Before one imagines that there is no alternative to this widely entrenched system for making and keeping women sneaker workers' labor "cheap," it is worth looking at a small but imaginative experiment: a private company called No Sweat. On the company's website the owners state their philosophy concerning globalization:

> We believe that the only viable response to globalization is a global labor movement. No Sweat defines the market for goods that support independent trade unions—the only historically proven solution to sweatshops. (No Sweat)

And printed inside each No Sweat sneaker is the company's motto: "100% union made."

The company was founded in 2004 by Jeff Ballinger, an American labor rights consultant and monitor, together with three others. For years, Ballinger had been charting the practices of the sneaker industry, especially the use of factories in Indonesia. During the 1990s, while the Suharto regime was still in power, Ballinger regularly published a four-page newsletter exposing the labor practices used in Indonesian sneaker factories to keep women's labor "cheap." He called his modest publication *Nike in Indonesia*. Gradually, this slim newsletter made its way into the hands of American op-ed journalists and even of Gary Trudeau, the politically minded cartoonist whose "Doonesbury" strip appears in newspapers across the United States. Nike executives began to feel pressure from consumers. Even some of their highly paid sports-star endorsers became defensive when asked why they were supporting exploitive labor practices.

Then came the 1998 prodemocracy movement in Indonesia, which toppled the Suharto regime. Regime change did not instantly lead to better working conditions for Indonesian women sneaker workers. But the political system opened up enough to permit some local labor unions to become more assertive on behalf of workers and to stop functioning merely as passive instruments of the government.

It was in this new less militarized political climate that Ballinger and his partners decided to launch No Sweat. They stayed in Indonesia. They were committed to proving that it was possible to create non-exploitation-reliant sneakers in Indonesia. They used their familiarity with the country's shoe business and relied on help from Indonesian labor advocates to compare factories. Were there any factories whose managers and owners were producing shoes without exploiting their workers? They finally decided on a factory owned by Bata, one of the world's biggest shoe manufacturers. They determined that Bata, which had a multigenerational history of paternalistic policies toward its employees, allowed their largely female workforce to join an autonomous labor union. That was No Sweat's core criterion. They also determined that Bata would provide workers stitching No Sweat's classic low-top black-and-white and red-and-white sneakers with decent, livable wages and employee benefits.

No Sweat inserts into each of its sneaker boxes a card summarizing the pay and benefits its Indonesian workers receive. For instance:

Hospitalization: Employee—100 percent coverage; Family—100 percent onsite, 80 percent offsite

Maternity (for female employee or wife of a male employee)—first child—225 rupees; second child—200 rupees; third child—150 rupees

Shift allowance: first and second shifts—175 rupees per hour; third shift (night shift)—200 rupees per hour

Working clothes (leather and canvas): two pairs per employee

Rice allowance: 30 liters per month

Ramadan bonus (most Indonesian employees are Muslim): eight weeks' salary.

Pension: 3 percent contribution by the employee; 7 percent by the company.

This does not mean that there is no room for exercising a feminist curiosity about this small innovative experiment in alternative sneaker globalization. Jeff Ballinger himself is candid about the limitations of the Bata/No Sweat labor union, SPSI, to which their employees belong. In the past many of the male leaders of Indonesian labor unions have been more eager to protect male workers' benefits than to extend those of women workers, often seeing women workers as a threat to their male members' wages because they imagined factory managers were enamored with the strategy of substituting women for men in certain assembly line jobs where they could pay women less (Caraway 2007). This perception of women workers as a threat to male workers' pay rates has been commonplace among all too many male union leaders in many countries Ballinger gives credit, however, to the activists inside the SPSI's Women's Bureau, an office created by women union members to focus especially on women workers' concerns and to monitor the union leaders' attentiveness to those concerns, for working against corruption and oppression and working for a decent national minimum wage. It is the combination of Bata's particular corporate philosophy, the evolving democratizing culture in post-Suharto Indonesia, and the work of SPSI's own women activists that has made No Sweat's anti-cheap-labor global business experiment possible. Using a feminist curiosity, we still need to know what the women stitching these No Sweat sneakers think about their working conditions and their union membership: do they feel as though the large national union's leaders are paying enough attention to their concerns? And we need to know more about whether working in a factory with such relatively good benefits and pay has altered these women's relationships with their parents, their brothers, their boyfriends, the police, the military, and Indonesia's civilian government officials. If in fact this anti-cheap-labor experiment has brought about meaningful change, then the relationships experienced by these women should be different from those experienced by their counterparts stitching sneakers in a Nike or Adidas factory across town.

Furthermore, as innovative as the No Sweat experiment is, it needs to be watched over time, just as the practices of sneaker companies, and women's responses to those practices, have to be watched over time. If faced with growing international competition, will Bata's managers, in whom the No Sweat owners have placed their trust, be tempted to cut back on the pension plan or on maternity leave? In the future, might some of the women stitching No Sweat sneakers begin to find the union too timid or too male dominated and seek to switch their membership to a more assertive labor union?

Neither globalization nor militarization is an inevitable process. Each can be stalled or even occasionally reversed. This is why using a feminist curiosity takes stamina. One has to stay attentive.

Delving into the globalized and often-militarized evolution of the production politics of just one product, the sneaker, has shown us that we have to direct our curiosities to more than simply business and the state governments. We need to demonstrate how difficult it is to construct—and sustain—a kind of femininity that allows women's hard work to be cheapened, a kind of femininity that serves both corporate profit and a masculinized state development strategy. Fashioning and deploying an energetic feminist curiosity will enable us to pose those questions with which we can reveal the confusion hidden behind the patriarchy's facade of rationality, as well as the calculation and coercion that is required to get one woman to accept low wages and meager benefits in exchange for stitching one pair of globalized sneakers.

REFERENCES

Barkawi, Tarak. 2006. *Globalization and War*. Lanham, MD: Rowman & Littlefield.

Caraway, Teri L. 2007. *Assembling Women: The Feminization of Global Manufacturing*. Ithaca: Cornell University Press.

Cockburn, Cynthia. 2007. *From Where We Stand: War, Women's Activism, and Feminist Analysis*. London: Zed Books.

Domosh, Mona. 2006. *American Commodities in an Age of Empire*. New York: Routledge.

Enloe, Cynthia. 1980. *Ethnic Soldiers: State Security in Divided Societies*. London: Penguin.

Giles, Wenona, Malathi de Alwis, Edith Klein, and Neluka Silva, eds. 2003. *Feminists Under Fire: Exchanges Across War Zones*. Toronto: Between the Lines.

Gillan, Audrey. 2005. "The Great Gurkha Race." *Guardian* (London), June 12.

Holmquist, Caroline. 2005. *Private Security Companies: The Case for Regulation.* Stockholm: Stockholm International Peace Research Institute.

Kang, Stephanie. 2006. "The Swoosh Treads Lightly at Chic Converse." *Globe and Mail* (Toronto), June 23.

Kim, Seung-Kyung. 1997. *Class Struggle or Family Struggle: The Lives of Women Factory Workers in South Korea.* London: Cambridge University Press.

Koonz, Claudia. 2003. *The Nazi Conscience.* Cambridge, MA: Harvard University Press.

No Sweat. www.nosweatapparel.com.

Stiehm, Judith Hicks. 2006. *Champions for Peace: Women Winners of the Nobel Peace Prize.* Lanham, MD: Rowman & Littlefield.

Wayne, Leslie. 2006. "British Arms Merchant with Passport to the Pentagon." *New York Times*, August 16.

Women in Black. 2005. *Women for Peace.* Belgrade: Women in Black.

ANNE FAUSTO-STERLING
The Five Sexes, Revisited

Anne Fausto-Sterling, an eminent biologist and social scientist, is Professor of Biology and Gender Studies at Brown University. For more, visit her homepage at http://bms .brown.edu/faculty/f/afs/afs_home.html.

The emerging recognition that people come in bewildering sexual varieties is testing medical values and social norms.

As Cheryl Chase stepped to the front of the packed meeting room in the Sheraton Boston Hotel, nervous coughs made the tension audible. Chase, an activist for intersexual rights, had been invited to address the May 2000 meeting of the Lawson Wilkins Pediatric Endocrine Society (LWPES), the largest organization in the United States for specialists in children's hormones. Her talk would be the grand finale to a four-hour symposium on the treatment of genital ambiguity in newborns, infants born with a mixture of both male and female anatomy, or genitals that appear to differ from their chromosomal sex. The topic was hardly a novel one to the assembled physicians.

Yet Chase's appearance before the group was remarkable. Three and a half years earlier, the American Academy of Pediatrics had refused her request for a chance to present the patients' viewpoint on the treatment of genital ambiguity, dismissing Chase and her supporters as "zealots." About two dozen intersex people had responded by throwing up a picket line. The Intersex Society of North America (ISNA) even issued a press release: "Hermaphrodites Target Kiddie Docs."

It had done my 1960s street-activist heart good. In the short run, I said to Chase at the time, the picketing would make people angry. But eventually, I assured her, the doors then closed would open. Now, as Chase began to address the physicians at their own convention, that prediction was coming true. Her talk, titled "Sexual Ambiguity: The Patient-Centered Approach," was a measured critique of the near-universal practice of performing immediate, "corrective" surgery on thousands of infants born each year with ambiguous genitalia. Chase herself lives with the consequences of such surgery. Yet her audience, the very endocrinologists and surgeons Chase was accusing of reacting with "surgery and shame," received her with respect. Even more remarkably, many of the speakers who preceded her at the session had already spoken of the need to scrap current practices in favor of treatments more centered on psychological counseling.

What led to such a dramatic reversal of fortune? Certainly, Chase's talk at the LWPES symposium was a vindication of her persistence in seeking attention for her cause. But her invitation to speak was also a watershed in the evolving discussion about how to treat children with ambiguous genitalia. And that discussion, in turn, is the tip of a biocultural iceberg—the gender iceberg—that continues to rock both medicine and our culture at large.

Chase made her first national appearance in 1993, in these very pages, announcing the formation of ISNA in a letter responding to an essay I had written for The Sciences, titled "The Five Sexes" (March/April 1993). In that article I argued that the two-sex system embedded in our society is not adequate to encompass the full spectrum of human sexuality. In its place, I suggested a five-sex system. In addition to males and females, I included "herms" (named after true hermaphrodites, people born with both a testis and an ovary); "merms" (male pseudohermaphrodites, who are born with testes and some aspect of female genitalia); and "ferms" (female pseudohermaphrodites, who have ovaries combined with some aspect of male genitalia).

I had intended to be provocative, but I had also written with tongue firmly in cheek. So I was surprised by the extent of the controversy the article unleashed. Right-wing Christians were outraged and connected my idea of five sexes with the United Nations–sponsored Fourth World Conference on Women, held in Beijing in September 1995. At the same time, the article delighted others who felt constrained by the current sex and gender system.

Clearly, I had struck a nerve. The fact that so many people could get riled up by my proposal to revamp our sex and gender system suggested that change—as well as resistance to it—might be in the offing. Indeed, a lot has changed since 1993, and I like to think that my article was an important stimulus. As if from nowhere, intersexuals are materializing before our very eyes. Like Chase, many have become political organizers, who lobby physicians and politicians to change current treatment practices. But more generally, though perhaps no less provocatively, the boundaries separating masculine and feminine seem harder than ever to define.

Some find the changes under way deeply disturbing. Others find them liberating.

Who is an intersexual—and how many intersexuals are there? The concept of intersexuality is rooted in the very ideas of male and female. In the idealized, Platonic, biological world, human beings are divided into two kinds: a perfectly dimorphic species. Males have an X and a Y chromosome, testes, a penis and all of the appropriate internal plumbing for delivering urine and semen to the outside world. They also have well-known secondary sexual characteristics, including a muscular build and facial hair. Women have two X chromosomes, ovaries, all of the internal plumbing to transport urine and ova to the outside world, a system to support pregnancy and fetal development, as well as a variety of recognizable secondary sexual characteristics.

That idealized story papers over many obvious caveats: some women have facial hair, some men have none; some women speak with deep voices, some men veritably squeak. Less well known is the fact that, on close inspection, absolute dimorphism disintegrates even at the level of basic biology. Chromosomes, hormones, the internal sex structures, the gonads and the external genitalia all vary more than most people realize. Those born outside of the Platonic dimorphic mold are called intersexuals.

In "The Five Sexes" I reported an estimate by a psychologist expert in the treatment of intersexuals, suggesting that some 4 percent of all live births are intersexual. Then, together with a group of Brown University undergraduates, I set out to conduct the first systematic assessment of the available data on intersexual birthrates. We scoured the medical literature for estimates of the frequency of various categories of intersexuality, from additional chromosomes to mixed gonads, hormones and genitalia. For some conditions we could find only anecdotal evidence; for most, however, numbers exist. On the basis of that evidence, we calculated that for every 1,000 children born, seventeen are intersexual in some form. That number—1.7 percent—is a ballpark estimate, not a precise count, though we believe it is more accurate than the 4 percent I reported.

Our figure represents all chromosomal, anatomical and hormonal exceptions to the dimorphic ideal; the number of intersexuals who might, potentially, be subject to surgery as infants is smaller—probably between one in 1,000 and one in 2,000 live births. Furthermore, because some populations possess the relevant genes at high frequency, the intersexual birthrate is not uniform throughout the world.

Consider, for instance, the gene for congenital adrenal hyperplasia (CAH). When the CAH gene is inherited from both parents, it leads to a baby with masculinized external genitalia who possesses two X chromosomes and the internal reproductive organs of a potentially fertile woman. The frequency of the gene varies widely around the world: in New Zealand it occurs in only forty-three children per million; among the Yupik Eskimo of southwestern Alaska, its frequency is 3,500 per million.

Intersexuality has always been to some extent a matter of definition. And in the past century physicians have been the ones who defined children as intersexual—and provided the remedies. When only the chromosomes are unusual, but the external genitalia and gonads clearly indicate either a male or a female, physicians do not advocate intervention. Indeed, it is not clear what kind of intervention could be advocated in such cases. But the story is quite different when infants are born with mixed genitalia, or with external genitals that seem at odds with the baby's gonads. Most clinics now specializing in the treatment of intersex babies rely on case-management principles developed in the 1950s by the psychologist John Money and the psychiatrists Joan G. Hampson and John L. Hampson, all of Johns Hopkins University in Baltimore, Maryland. Money believed that gender identity is completely malleable for about eighteen months after birth. Thus, he argued, when a treatment team is presented with an infant who has ambiguous genitalia, the team could make a gender assignment solely on the basis of what made the best surgical sense. The physicians could then simply encourage the parents to raise the child according to the surgically assigned gender. Following that course, most physicians maintained, would eliminate psychological distress for both the patient and the parents. Indeed, treatment teams were never to use such words as "intersex" or "hermaphrodite"; instead, they were to tell parents that nature intended the baby to be the boy or the girl that the physicians had determined it was. Through surgery, the physicians were merely completing nature's intention.

Although Money and the Hampsons published detailed case studies of intersex children who they said had adjusted well to their gender assignments, Money thought one case in particular proved his theory. It was a dramatic example, inasmuch as it did not involve intersexuality at all: one of a pair of identical twin boys lost his penis as a result of a circumcision accident. Money recommended that "John" (as he came to be known in a later case study) be surgically turned into "Joan" and raised as a girl. In time, Joan grew to love wearing dresses and having her hair done. Money proudly proclaimed the sex reassignment a success.

But as recently chronicled by John Colapinto, in his book *As Nature Made Him*, Joan—now known to be an adult male named David Reimer— eventually rejected his female assignment. Even without a functioning penis and testes (which had been removed as part of the reassignment) John/Joan sought masculinizing medication, and married a woman with children (whom he adopted).

Since the full conclusion to the John/Joan story came to light, other individuals who were reassigned as males or females shortly after birth but who later rejected their early assignments have come forward. So, too, have cases in which the reassignment has worked—at least into the subject's mid-twenties. But even then the aftermath of the surgery can be problematic. Genital surgery often leaves scars that reduce sexual sensitivity. Chase herself had a complete clitoridectomy, a procedure that is less frequently performed on intersexuals today. But the newer surgeries, which reduce the size of the clitoral shaft, still greatly reduce sensitivity.

The revelation of cases of failed reassignments and the emergence of intersex activism have led an increasing number of pediatric endocrinologists, urologists and psychologists to reexamine the wisdom of early genital surgery. For example, in a talk that preceded Chase's at the LWPES meeting, the medical ethicist Laurence B. McCullough of the Center for Medical Ethics and Health Policy at Baylor College of Medicine in Houston, Texas, introduced an ethical framework for the treatment of children with ambiguous genitalia. Because sex phenotype (the manifestation of genetically and embryologically determined sexual characteristics) and gender presentation (the sex role projected by the individual in society) are highly variable, McCullough argues, the various forms of intersexuality should be defined as normal. All of them fall within the statistically expected variability of sex and gender. Furthermore, though certain disease states may accompany some forms of intersexuality, and may require medical intervention, intersexual conditions are not themselves diseases.

McCullough also contends that in the process of assigning gender, physicians should minimize what he calls irreversible assignments: taking steps such as the surgical removal or modification of gonads or genitalia that the patient may one day want to have reversed. Finally, McCullough urges physicians to abandon their practice of treating the birth of a child with genital ambiguity as a medical or social emergency. Instead, they should take the time to perform a thorough medical workup and should disclose everything to the parents, including the uncertainties about the final outcome. The treatment mantra, in other words, should be therapy, not surgery.

I believe a new treatment protocol for intersex infants, similar to the one outlined by McCullough, is close at hand. Treatment should combine some basic medical and ethical principles with a practical but less drastic approach to the birth of a mixed-sex child. As a first step, surgery on infants should be performed only to save the child's life or to substantially improve the child's physical well-being. Physicians may assign a sex—male or female—to an intersex infant on the basis of the probability that the child's particular condition will lead to the formation of a particular gender identity. At the same time, though, practitioners ought to be humble enough to recognize that as the child grows, he or she may reject the assignment—and they should be wise enough to listen to what the child has to say. Most important, parents should have access to the full range of information and options available to them.

Sex assignments made shortly after birth are only the beginning of a long journey. Consider, for instance, the life of Max Beck: born intersexual, Max was surgically assigned as a female and consistently raised as such. Had her medical team followed her into her early twenties, they would have deemed her assignment a success because she was married to a man. (It should be noted that success in gender assignment has traditionally been defined as living in that gender as a heterosexual.) Within a few years, however, Beck had come out as a butch lesbian; now in her mid-thirties, Beck has become a man and married his lesbian partner, who (through the miracles of modern reproductive technology) recently gave birth to a girl.

Transsexuals, people who have an emotional gender at odds with their physical sex, once described themselves in terms of dimorphic absolutes—males trapped in female bodies, or vice versa. As such, they sought psychological relief through surgery. Although many still do, some so-called transgendered people today are content to inhabit a more ambiguous zone. A male-to-female transsexual, for instance, may come out as a lesbian. Jane, born a physiological male, is now in her late thirties and living with her wife, whom she married when her name was still John. Jane takes hormones to feminize herself, but they have not yet interfered with her ability to engage in intercourse as a man. In her mind Jane has a lesbian relationship with her wife, though she views their intimate moments as a cross between lesbian and heterosexual sex.

It might seem natural to regard intersexuals and transgendered people as living midway between the poles of male and female. But male and female, masculine and feminine, cannot be parsed as some kind of continuum. Rather, sex and gender are best conceptualized as points in a multidimensional space. For some time, experts on gender development have distinguished between sex at the genetic level and at the cellular level (sex-specific gene expression, X and Y chromosomes); at the hormonal level (in the fetus, during childhood and after puberty); and at the anatomical level (genitals and secondary sexual characteristics). Gender identity presumably emerges from all of those corporeal aspects via some poorly understood interaction with environment and experience. What has become increasingly clear is that one can find levels of masculinity and femininity in almost every possible permutation. A chromosomal, hormonal and genital male (or female) may emerge with a female (or male) gender identity. Or a chromosomal female with male fetal hormones and masculinized genitalia—but with female pubertal hormones—may develop a female gender identity.

The Medical and Scientific Communities have yet to adopt a language that is capable of describing such diversity. In her book *Hermaphrodites and the Medical Invention of Sex*, the historian and medical ethicist Alice Domurat Dreger of Michigan State University in East Lansing documents the emergence of current medical systems for classifying gender ambiguity. The current usage remains rooted in the Victorian approach to sex. The logical structure of the commonly used terms "true hermaphrodite," "male pseudohermaphrodite" and "female pseudohermaphrodite" indicates that only the so-called true hermaphrodite is a genuine mix of male and female. The others, no matter how confusing their body parts, are really hidden males or females. Because true hermaphrodites are rare—possibly only one in 100,000—such a classification system supports the idea that human beings are an absolutely dimorphic species.

At the dawn of the twenty-first century, when the variability of gender seems so visible, such a position is hard to maintain. And here, too, the old medical consensus has begun to crumble. Last fall the pediatric urologist Ian A. Aaronson of the Medical University of South Carolina in Charleston organized the North American Task Force on Intersexuality (NATFI) to review the clinical responses to genital ambiguity in infants. Key medical associations, such as the American Academy of Pediatrics, have endorsed NATFI. Specialists in surgery, endocrinology, psychology, ethics, psychiatry, genetics and public health, as well as intersex patient-advocate groups, have joined its ranks.

One of the goals of NATFI is to establish a new sex nomenclature. One proposal under consideration replaces the current system with emotionally neutral terminology that emphasizes developmental processes rather than preconceived gender categories. For example, Type I intersexes develop out of anomalous virilizing influences; Type II result from some interruption of virilization; and in Type III intersexes the gonads themselves may not have developed in the expected fashion.

What is clear that since 1993, modern society has moved beyond five sexes to a recognition that gender variation is normal and, for some people, an arena for playful exploration. Discussing my "five sexes" proposal in her book *Lessons from the Intersexed*, the psychologist Suzanne J. Kessler of the State University of New York at Purchase drives this point home with great effect:

> The limitation with Fausto-Sterling's proposal is that . . . [it] still gives genitals . . . primary signifying status and ignores the fact that in the everyday word gender attributions are made without access to genital inspection. . . . What has primacy in everyday life is the gender that is performed, regardless of the flesh's configuration under the clothes.

I now agree with Kessler's assessment. It would be better for intersexuals and their supporters to turn everyone's focus away from genitals. Instead, as she suggests, one should acknowledge that people come in an even wider assortment of sexual identities and characteristics than mere genitals can distinguish. Some women may have "large clitorises or fused labia," whereas some men may have "small penises or misshapen scrota," as Kessler puts it, "phenotypes with no particular clinical or identity meaning."

As clearheaded as Kessler's program is—and despite the progress made in the 1990s—our society is still far from that ideal. The intersexual or transgendered person who projects a social gender—what Kessler calls "cultural genitals"—that conflicts with his or her physical genitals still may die for the transgression. Hence legal protection for people whose cultural and physical genitals do not match is needed during the current transition to a more gender-diverse world. One easy step would be to eliminate the category of "gender" from official documents, such as driver's licenses and passports. Surely attributes both more visible (such as height, build and eye color) and less visible (fingerprints and genetic profiles) would be more expedient.

A more far-ranging agenda is presented in the International Bill of Gender Rights, adopted in 1995 at the fourth annual International Conference on Transgender Law and Employment Policy in Houston, Texas. It lists ten "gender rights," including the right to define one's own gender, the right to change one's physical gender if one so chooses and the right to marry whomever one wishes. The legal bases for such rights are being hammered out in the courts as I write and, most recently, through the establishment, in the state of Vermont, of legal same-sex domestic partnerships.

No one could have foreseen such changes in 1993. And the idea that I played some role, however small, in reducing the pressure—from the medical community as well as from society at large—to flatten the diversity of human sexes into two diametrically opposed camps gives me pleasure.

Sometimes people suggest to me, with not a little horror, that I am arguing for a pastel world in which androgyny reigns and men and women are boringly the same. In my vision, however, strong colors coexist with pastels. There are and will continue to be highly masculine people out there; it's just that some of them are women. And some of the most feminine people I know happen to be men.

MARJORIE GARBER
The Return to Biology

Marjorie Garber is Professor of English and American Literature at Harvard University, where she is also Chair of the Department of Visual and Environmental Studies and Director of the Carpenter Center for the Visual Arts. A prominent cultural critic, Garber has published twelve books on topics from Shakespeare to real estate, and the following selection is from her book, Vice Versa: Bisexuality and the Eroticism of Everyday Life *(1995; 2000).*

> Whether or not we find what we are seeking
> Is idle, biologically speaking.
> —Edna St Vincent Millay,
> "I Shall Forget You Presently"

OVER SEXED

"Dear Ann Landers," wrote "A Concerned Father in Ukiah, California,"

> My teenage son came home the other day with a story that floored me. One of his high school teachers is teaching the students that there are five sexes in the human race—male, female, homosexual, bisexual, and asexual. . . .
>
> I told my son that the teacher is wrong, that there are only TWO sexes, male and female, and the other categories are sexual practices.
>
> Ann, I'm disturbed by this misinformation. . . . What do the experts say about this? Do they claim there are five sexes nowadays? Things are changing so fast that it's hard to keep up.

Rising to the occasion, Ann Landers hastened to set the record straight: "There are only two sexes—male and female. Recent studies indicate that homosexuality, bisexuality and asexuality are not the result of something that has gone wrong with the sex organs, but rather a biochemical-genetic alteration that no one has been able to explain."[1]

This exchange, printed under the pedagogically disturbing but culturally reassuring headline "Teacher Needs to Learn Lesson—There Aren't Five Sexes," is a fairly characteristic signpost of the increasing desire to categorize and "explain" the vagaries of human sexuality in popular terms. What is sometimes called sexual preference (implying a choice) and sometimes called sexual orientation (implying a destiny) are in this schoolroom example—at least as reported, third hand, by the teenager's father—equated with "sex." "Sex" (biology) and "gender" (sociology, anthropology, and culture) are here silently and unhelpfully conflated. The result is to "save" heterosexuality, pointedly not listed as one of the "sexes," as the "natural" province of the first two delineated "sexes," male and female. Ann Landers's reply, addressing in telescoped terms both the list of five sexes and the implied critique, asserts that bi-, homo-, and asexuality are not "wrong" but different. They aren't wrong; but they aren't sexes.

This would seem perfectly straightforward, so to speak, in the everyday commerce of the newspaper advice page and perhaps even self-evident, if there had not appeared three months later in the respected journal *The Sciences* an article by geneticist Anne Fausto-Sterling, called "The Five Sexes," with the provocative subhead, "Why Male and Female Are Not Enough."[2]

Fausto-Sterling describes the legal erasure and medical reassignment of intersexed persons, those whose bodies are, biologically, anatomically, or chemically, a mixture of male and female.

The deep commitment of Western culture to the idea that there are only two sexes, exemplified in the limitations of language (Fausto-Sterling has to have recourse to *s/he* and *his/her* to describe some of her subjects) and law (over the past century, rights and obligations like the vote, the military draft, marriage, and private, consensual sex have all been governed by state or national laws about males and females), has led to a cultural resistance to openly intersexed individuals, called by Fausto-Sterling "herms" (true hermaphrodites, with one testis and one ovary), "merms" (male pseudohermaphrodites, with testes, some aspects of female genitalia, but no ovaries), and "ferms" (female pseudohermaphrodites, with ovaries and some aspects of male genitalia but no testes).

Doctors have translated the bodies of such persons into some semblance of "normality," reclassifying children who, as they grew older, developed sexual characteristics (an organ on a "female" that looks more like a penis than a clitoris; a "male" with an X and Y chromosome who develops breasts and begins to menstruate) that marked them as other than they had at first been regarded. "The aims of the policy," she stresses, "are genuinely humanitarian, reflecting the wish that people be able to 'fit in' both physically and psychologically. In the medical community, however, the assumptions behind the wish—that there be only two sexes, that heterosexuality alone is normal, that there is one true model of psychological health—have gone virtually unexamined."[3]

It is almost as if, in the story of the Ugly Duckling, veterinary intervention (and concomitant counselling) had translated the undiagnosed cygnet into a cosmetic mallard for his (or her?) own good.

"Hermaphrodites," Fausto-Sterling asserts with eloquence, "have unruly bodies. They do not fall naturally into a binary classification; only a surgical shoehorn can put them there. But why should we care if a 'woman,' defined as one who has breasts, a vagina, a uterus and ovaries and who menstruates, also has a clitoris large enough to penetrate the vagina of another woman? Why should we care if there are people whose biological equipment enables them to have sex 'naturally' with both men and women? The answers seem to lie in a cultural need to maintain clear distinctions between the sexes. Society mandates the control of intersexual bodies because they blur and bridge the great divide. Inasmuch as hermaphrodites literally embody both sexes, they challenge traditional beliefs about sexual difference: they possess the irritating ability to live sometimes as one sex and sometimes as another, and they raise the spectre of homosexuality."[4]

Of homosexuality — or of bisexuality? "To have sex 'naturally' with both men and women." This geneticist's fearless and provocative vision of a society, perhaps many generations from now, in which "sexuality is something to be celebrated for its subtleties and not something to be feared or ridiculed" opens the door not only to a fuller acceptance of homosexuality but also to the inclusion of bisexuals, transgenderists, and others who do not neatly fit into older preconceptions of social "normality."

Needless to say, such a visionary view of science and society did not go unchallenged. A briefer version of Fausto-Sterling's article appeared on the op-ed page of the *New York Times* under the title "How Many Sexes Are There?" and elicited a predictable range of commentary. One letter writer asked, plaintively, "What is it about human sexuality that leads people to engage in extraordinarily fuzzy thinking?"[5] British geneticist Winston Holt's book on *The Sexual Continuum* was cited to suggest that "each of us to some degree is both heterosexual and homosexual, and therefore bisexual," and Alfred Kinsey was quoted as saying that "The only abnormal sex act is the one you can't do."[6] *Times* readers were also reminded that "Native Americans believe that there are four sexes: men who love women, men who love men, women who love women and women who love men; and since men who love men and women who love women are fewer in number, they must be blessed by the gods."[7] (This cross-cultural point is one often made in bisexual 'zines and newsletters.)

What is especially striking about this cultural moment, however, is the way in which the 1990s seem to be re-creating the 1890s. Biologistic arguments explaining homosexuality are again in force, in contention, and in vogue; studies of hereditary family linkages are once again being undertaken, as they were a hundred years ago, in quest of an answer to the riddle of human sexuality that can be grounded in ascertainable "fact" — in science rather than in cultural influence. And once again, as was the case a hundred years ago, the quest for the biological truth of homosexuality, and thus of heterosexuality, is foundering on another inconvenient "fact" — the fact of bisexuality as a mode of human behavior. For bisexuality queers the pitch, messes up the neat double columns of figures: straight and gay.

Bi for biology, from *bios*, life. Bi for bisexuality, from *bis*, two.

THE QUESTION OF BIOLOGY

Biology is back. After decades of disfavor as an explanation for homosexual behavior (what used to be called, with finger-pointing disparagement, "homosexual tendencies"), biology is now making a major comeback. The "gay gene," the "gay brain," and the biological imperative—not a "lifestyle choice" but a DNA blueprint, a "fact" of life—are now the focus of studies by clinicians and investigators.[8] The politics of these new (or rather, renewed) claims has, in effect, come full circle. As the *Wall Street Journal* noted, "the discovery of a definitive biological cause of homosexuality could go a long way toward advancing the gay-rights cause. If homosexuality were found to be an immutable trait, like skin color, then laws criminalizing homosexual sex might be overturned."[9] Same-sex marriage, job protection, antidiscrimination in housing laws—all of these could hinge on the redefinition of homosexuality as biologically caused rather than socially and culturally chosen.

Dr. Paul Cameron, the chairman of the Family Research Institute, a conservative lobbying group that sails under the slogan "Scientists Defending Traditional Family Values," offered the following political advice to gay-rights activists: "If I were a gay-rights manager, I'd say, 'Guys, whatever we do, we have to make them believe we were born that way.' If they can get a majority of Americans believing it, they're home free."

But the political stakes for gays and lesbians are complex: If science can "prove" that homosexuality isn't a choice, what is to prevent its being repathologized and either "cured" or therapeutically aborted after prenatal testing discloses the presence of the gay gene? Tying the rights discourse to science opens the possibility of devaluing choice as somehow illegitimate. It also tacitly reaffirms the either/or nature of the heterosexual–homosexual split. What would happen if the "gay gene" were detected in routine testing of heretofore impeccably heterosexual men and women? Would that mean they were "really" gay? Would it suggest that they should be therapeutically resocialized as gay in order to be true to their genes?

"A biological explanation of homosexuality simultaneously explains heterosexuality," write Michael Bailey and Richard Pillard in an article welcoming Simon LeVay's research on the brain as good news for gays and lesbians. They note that "homophobia remains the one form of bigotry that respectable people can express in public," and suggest that the scientific study of the origins of sexual orientation will open up public debate and lead to breakthroughs of "self-discovery."[10] To track the genetic origins of homosexuality, they claim, is no more stigmatizing than to seek out the genetic causes of traits like extroversion or intelligence, which are regarded as positive rather than negative qualities. (How dubiously uncontroversial such other quests would prove was demonstrated by the clamorous reception of Richard Herrnstein and Charles Murray's *The Bell Curve*.)

The quest for a "scientific" explanation (or should that be scientific "explanation"?) of homo- and heterosexuality has been much on the minds of gender critics, as well as of biological scientists, in recent years. "Nobody knows how sexual orientation is in fact determined," Mariana Valverde observed in 1987, insisting that one reason for this failure was that almost all research to date had concentrated on finding "the causes" of homosexuality "as if heterosexuality had no cause."[11] Research like that of Bailey and Pillard, LeVay, and Dean H. Hamer attempts to redress that unequal balance, but in doing so it creates a new one. By seeking to resist ambiguity, their research models inevitably write out bisexuality.

The old biology of nineteenth-century sexologists (and, subsequently, the racial "hygienics" of Nazism, a "scientific" view that saw homosexuals as genetically flawed and logically subject to extermination) had maintained that homosexuals could be recognized by certain stigmata, from beardlessness and "limp wrists" in men to enlarged clitorises and short haircuts in women. By this biological logic, Jewish men, for example, were associated with women and with homosexuals; they were "oriental," "soft," high-voiced, degenerate, circumcised (and thus already self-castrated), and extravagant of gesture. According to sexologist Richard von Krafft-Ebing, the most identifiable "sexual inverts" were congenital, and could be recognized by the high voice, small waist, and wide pelvis in men, or, conversely, by the low voice, small breasts, and narrow pelvis in women.[12] Thus the form of the body represented the "inverted" desire: If a man desired a man, he would, according to this theory of "ideal" congenital sexual inversion, look not like a man but like a woman. Heterosexuality was thereby retained as the model. A male–female pair was envisaged, even if the "male" was a lesbian in trousers or the "female" a man in skirts.

The diagnosis of homosexuality as a perversion with biological roots and clinical and behavioural symptoms (women who wore trousers, smoked, chose not to marry; men who as children played with dolls and grew up to be hairdressers, ballet dancers, or interior decorators) was set aside by liberal psychology and psychoanalysis.

Thus Freud's initial insistence on the "bisexual disposition" of all human beings was grounded in an early faith in biology. By "bisexual," Freud meant a wide range of things, from what we would call explicit homosexuality to same-sex friendship, identification with the "opposite sex," cross-gender behaviour (men acting "effeminate"; "masculine" women), the undifferentiated tissues of the embryo, and the vestigial presence in the adult of tissues and organs of what, once again, he and his successors would call the "opposite sex." But Freud's early attempts to find a biological and anatomical basis for what he variously characterized as the "bisexual disposition," the "bisexual constitution," and the "bisexual organization" of all human beings bears a striking resemblance to recent claims, almost a hundred years later, that again seek an answer in biology.

"We're mixed bags, all of us," declared a professor directing research on androgens and women's health.[13] Yet even when modern science confronts the fact that "the borders between classic maleness and femaleness are much grayer than people realized," with the increasing awareness that male sex hormones like testosterone play a crucial part in women's bodies, the implications go unexplored. "Male Hormone Molds Women Too, in Mind and Body," announced the *New York Times*. "What society says is normal and what is normal for women can be very different," observes another medical researcher. "Women can have a full beard and still be breast-feeding."[14]

But though the debate about how androgens affect the brains as well as the bodies of women has begun to heat up—are androgenized women in fact "more mathematical, more aggressive, more sexually active, more enamored of guns and computers"?[15]—it does not seem to include the suggestion that the "mixed bags" might (bio)logically include "mixed" desires. That is to say, bisexual desires.

"The theory of bisexuality," Freud wrote, "has been expressed in its crudest form by a spokesman of the male inverts: 'a feminine brain in a masculine body.' But we are ignorant of what characterizes a feminine brain." Krafft-Ebing, he says, also puts forward such a theory, one perhaps not quite so crude: that "every individual's bisexual disposition endows him with masculine and feminine brain centres as well as with somatic organs of sex." And here, too, Freud is sceptical: "But what has just been said of masculine and feminine brains applies equally to masculine and feminine 'centres' " within the brain.[16]

Later gender theorists, like the psychoanalyst Robert J. Stoller, would challenge this on the basis of new scientific research even as they praised Freud's vision: "the brain is female," Stoller asserted, "in that *in both sexes* feminine behavior results if male hormones are not added."[17] And the media fanfare surrounding Simon LeVay's 1991 research on the hypothalamus revisits this territory of the "sexual brain" with the object of demonstrating that homosexuality is biologically produced.

According to LeVay—who examined the brains of forty-one men and women, many of them gay men who died of AIDS, and included no lesbian women in his research sample—the hypothalamus, the "part of the brain that produces sexual feelings," is much smaller in gay men than in straight men. As a result, he claims, it is possible to argue for a genetic and biological basis to male homosexuality. Gay men may after all be born rather than made. Even hairdressers and flower arrangers, he provocatively told the gay and lesbian newsmagazine *The Advocate*, might be biologically determined, identifiable by the size of their hypothalamic nuclei.[18] (Questions of larger and smaller size are not unfamiliar in sex discourse, as the *Advocate* headline "And How Big Is Yours?" wryly conceded.)

What advantage was there in grounding sexuality in biology? Hadn't some gay people objected to the idea that they were programmed for life by their brain structure? LeVay, himself a gay man, offered a by now familiar political analogy with the civil rights movement of the sixties. If gay identity were innate rather than chosen, genetic rather than optional and capricious, biological rather than behavioural, laws restricting equal opportunity for homosexuals would be prohibited by the courts. Surveys had shown, LeVay noted, that people were more tolerant of gays and lesbians when they thought they "were born that way" than when they thought it was "a lifestyle choice."

LeVay returns not only to biology but, in fact, to sociobiology. His remarks are characteristically full of analogies to male lions, lesbian seagulls, and the evolutionary strategies of the mammalian male animal, whose promiscuity is seen as ensuring the propagation of the species; hence gay men are living out a biological dictum for multiple partners which is inhibited in straight men by "the reluctance of women to be promiscuous." Thus, with the return to biology, the liberal move of Freud and his followers appears to have come full circle.

But what place has *bisexuality* in a medical research project like Simon LeVay's? If the hypothalamus of gay men is smaller than that of straight men, what size hypothalamus should bisexuals have? Are they to be imagined, like the furnishings of Goldilocks's third bear, to be neither too big nor too small, but just right—middle-sized glands for the excluded middle of sexual orientation? Might bisexuals have even smaller hypothalamuses than gay men—or larger ones, even, than straights? Or would medical science support the convictions of those psychologists and psychiatrists who think bisexuality is a mirage? Are all hypothalamuses either gay or straight? Is there such a thing as a "bi brain"? And if not, how do we account for bisexuality? The many political critiques of LeVay's study, which took him to task for everything from removing sexual desire from the realm of culturally constructed behavior to facilitating a eugenic campaign to eliminate homosexuals *in utero*, do not focus on this key question.

Critics of LeVay's research pointed out that (1) his hypothesis claimed a symmetry based upon the object of attraction, with those attracted to men (gay men and heterosexual women) having smaller hypothalamic nuclei than those attracted to women (heterosexual men and lesbians), but because his study contained no brain tissue from lesbians he was unable to test that part of his hypothesis; that (2) according to his own data the *range* of sizes of hypothalamic nuclei was virtually the same for homosexuals and heterosexuals, with some homosexuals having larger nuclei than many heterosexuals, and some heterosexuals having smaller nuclei than many homosexuals, so that "though the groups showed some difference as groups, there was no way to tell anything about an individual's sexual orientation by looking at his hypothalamus";[19] and that (3) since all his subjects were cadavers, there was no way of verifying the range or extent of their sexual behaviors.

This last point is the most relevant to charting bisexuality. LeVay describes his subjects as follows: "[N]ineteen subjects were homosexual men who died of complications of acquired immunodeficiency syndrome (AIDS) (one bisexual man was included in this group). Sixteen subjects were presumed heterosexual men; six of these subjects died of AIDS and ten of other causes. Six subjects were presumed heterosexual women. One of these women died of AIDS and five of other causes."[20]

The word "presumed" in the phrase "presumed heterosexual men" is marked by a footnote: "Two of these subjects (both AIDS patients) had denied homosexual activity. The records of the remaining 14 patients contained no information about their sexual orientation; they are assumed to have been mostly or all heterosexual on the basis of the numerical preponderance of heterosexual men in the population [A. C. Kinsey, W. B. Pomeroy, C. E. Martin, *Sexual Behavior in the Human Male* (Saunder, Philadelphia, 1948)]."

This strikes me as extraordinary "scientific" information. LeVay's category of "heterosexual men," the functional basis of his comparison study ("A Difference . . . Between Heterosexual and Homosexual Men") turns out to be almost entirely based on inference, guesswork, or statistical percentages drawn from a social science study which, however prestigious or canonical in the field, was completed more than forty years ago. To "presume" that the percentages remain the same over time, and that Kinsey's percentages are authoritative enough in 1991 to allow the "assumption" of heterosexuality in fourteen men about whose sexual orientation in fact nothing is known, seems not only stunningly inexact but also to be positing the very thing that LeVay wants to prove: namely, that homosexuality and heterosexuality are biological, perhaps innate, rather than social and cultural. For if "homosexuality" and "heterosexuality"—or, to use Kinsey's much less problematic terms, homosexual and heterosexual *behavior*—were in fact substantially produced or altered by cultural factors, we would have no reason to think that 1948's "numerical preponderance" would hold today.

Then there is the matter of the AIDS patients who "had denied homosexual activity"—itself a phrase of some interest, since it seems to imply that the investigators or doctors attending on the case initially "presumed" them homosexual—and of the "one bisexual man" who was included, by LeVay, in his homosexual sample. Why not include him, with equal logic, in the *heterosexual* group? Or indeed in *both* groups? "Homosexual" here becomes in effect a "default" category meaning "anything but straight."

Either LeVay regarded bisexuality as a euphemistic cover for gay identity, so that a "bisexual" in the terms of his study was really a gay man who had not come out to himself or to others, or else he hypothesized that having any sexual interest in men, even if he also had a sexual interest in women, would affect a man's hypothalamus in ways that would make him look, under the microscope, more gay than straight. In either case, bisexuality as· a scientifically determinable category once again disappears, is subsumed. The "bisexual individual" is counted among the homosexual men "for statistical purposes," while the "presumed heterosexuals," about whose sex lives in fact nothing is known, are counted among the straights.

LeVay begins his paper in *Science* by noting that sexual orientation has traditionally been studied on the level of psychology, anthropology, or ethics,[21] with the clear implication that he is going to move the discourse in the direction of biological evidence, of ascertainable scientific fact. He ends it by reviewing problems in interpreting his data, including the fact, already noted above, that his "ability to make correlations between brain structure and the diversity of sexual behavior that undoubtedly exists within the homosexual and the heterosexual populations" was limited—one might use a stronger word—by the "use of postmortem material." Dead men tell no tales.

The telltale word here is "undoubtedly" ("the diversity of sexual behavior that undoubtedly exists"), a word that, casually introduced into the text, becomes in effect the paper's bisexual ghost (here, there, and everywhere)—or, if you like, the bisexual skeleton in its half-opened closet. For what can this undoubted diversity of behavior be, in the context of an article that is only concerned with the sexual object (men or women) and not with the sexual aim (oral, anal, or genital sex)[22]—what can this "diversity" be except bisexuality? How much "diversity" makes a straight into a gay, or a gay into a straight, according to the either/or logic of LeVay's classification?

LeVay himself, challenged to explain how "a 40-year-old guy who's married and with children" can one day come out as gay, compares the gayness of such men to other genetic traits, like that for adult diabetes, that do not manifest themselves until later in life. "Their sexuality is probably just as genetically loaded as are kids' who realize they are gay when they are 12 years old."[23] Thus, for LeVay, such instances of sequential bisexuality are indices of a kind of latency; these men are genetically homosexual, not bisexual, although their homosexuality may not be apparent to them early on. Bisexuality here disappears into a kind of genetic false consciousness.

In the contrary case, that of a person who had early sexual experiences with same-sex partners and then switched to exclusive other-sex relations (the "it's a phase" or boys-will-be-boys theory of bisexuality, Freud's "contingent inverts"), should we expect that the hypothalamus would give the answer "straight"? And what is to be said about the individual, male or female, who is genetically programmed for gayness but dies before the program kicks in? Would the gland of such a person disclose this future identity? Would he or she be "really" *potentially* gay? LeVay's study had at least six variables: gay/straight, male/female, died of AIDS/died of other causes. Bisexuality here would be an inconvenient further complication, whether the size of the hypothalamus is a product of innate genetic design or, as has also been conjectured, a result of lived experience as a gay—or straight—person.

Furthermore, the absence of lesbians from his study makes the question of bisexuality's place even more acute. LeVay subsequently apologized for perpetuating "the tradition of ignoring women in biomedical research," explaining that he couldn't find "brains of women whose sexual orientation is known," since that information doesn't usually appear on medical charts. Because so many of his subjects were gay men with AIDS, their sexuality became part of their etiology of disease. They were "known" to be gay. The women, by contrast, were apparently "known" to be straight. But how do we "know"? How much gay sex, or straight sex, makes a person gay or straight? Bear in mind the spectre of the "bisexual AIDS carrier," that bogeyman of the eighties, whose secret life was said to be itself a cause of infection, and whose personality was conjectured to be duplicitous, cowardly, self-indulgent, or self-hating. Were any of them among the AIDS casualties in LeVay's study? If so— or even if not—would he mark them down as "gay"?

"This way of categorizing people obscure[s] the hitherto accepted fact that many people do not have sexual relations exclusively with one or the other sex," biologist Ruth Hubbard observes trenchantly, reflecting on the nineteenth-century turn of inquiry by which "homosexuality stopped being what people did and became who they were."[24] At what point does the politics of identity, necessary for the attainment of equal rights, come into conflict with the political incorrectness of human desire?

Some people are only attracted to redheads, or to people with muscular bodies, or to rich people. Do we call them roussophiles, or biceptophiles, or plutophiles? Do we examine their brains or their genes for the cause? When a young and beautiful woman marries an elderly and wealthy husband we may call her a fortune-hunter or a trophy wife or a society matron, but we do not, usually, describe her as having a perversion, or as choosing a way of life contrary to the will of God—at least not to her face. Indeed, the Bible might well be called in as evidence for sanctioning just such an arrangement. What if the same woman has previously been married to a man her own age, or if a woman who marries a blond had previously married a man with black hair? Is she to be questioned closely about why she has changed her mind?

But blond hair and black hair do not affect the economic structure, it will be objected. They do not enforce the institution of marriage and patriarchy, so there is no real analogy to be made. Well, then, what if a white woman marries a black man? We used to have a name for this unlawful practice— miscegenation. But black–white marriages are no longer against the law, at least in the United States, and while many people, black and white, may privately question it even today, "intermarriage"—between blacks and whites, between Christians and Jews—has become a much more culturally accepted practice now than it was fifty years ago. The term for such arrangements these days is not "intermarriage" or "mixed marriage" or "miscegenation" but "marriage."

Why do we resist the idea that erotic life is all part of the same set of pleasures, that there is only one sexuality, of which the "sexualities" we have so effectively and efficiently defined are equally permissible and gratifying aspects?

Because to do so would threaten the social structures on which "civiliza-tion" and "society" are built. And because much modern eroticism depends, in part, precisely upon transgression, upon the sensation or perception of dar-ing, of breaking a law or flauting a taboo. Like Robert Frost's famous defini-tion of free verse as "playing tennis with the net down," what used to be called "free love" (extramarital, nonmonogamous, ambisexual) needs rules to break.

GAY GENES

Simon LeVay, who has now given up science for a career in adult education at the West Hollywood Institute of Gay and Lesbian Education, gave the media the "gay gland." Other researchers—Michael Bailey and Richard Pillard in one study, Dean H. Hamer and associates at the National Cancer Institute in another—have given us the "gay gene." Hamer's investigation, results of which were published in *Science* in July 1993 (two years after LeVay's research appeared in the same journal), examined forty pairs of gay brothers and deter-mined that identical pieces of the end tip of the X chromosome (inherited from the mother) appeared in thirty-three pairs to predispose them genetically to homosexuality. Again, the immediate nonscientific fallout was political, and the findings were once more appropriated to a discourse of rights.

If homosexuality was proved to be largely inborn, gay people would be protected by the courts from discrimination. The same fears—of experimen-tation to eliminate potential homosexuals from the population, in this case by gene therapy—and the same doubts—about drawing a firm distinction be-tween gay and straight—were voiced. Anne Fausto-Sterling, who had been critical of earlier attempts to study human behavior through genetic research, praised the caution of Hamer's conclusions, which allowed for an interplay of the genes, the brain, and the environment in the molding of human behavior. As for LeVay, the *New York Times* described him as "ecstatic." He was quoted as calling Hamer's results "the most important scientific finding ever made in sexual orientation."[25]

Once again, though, the question of bisexuality might be said to com-plicate the equation, if not to queer the results. What Hamer's team did was to scrutinize the life histories of 114 men who identified themselves as homosex-ual. They then discovered a surprising number of homosexual males on the maternal side of the family, and, turning to brothers as most likely to be genet-ically linked, scrutinized their X chromosomes through a procedure known as linkage mapping. It was this procedure that revealed the surprising consonance of DNA markers on the tip of the X chromosome.

How did the study know these men were gay? Because they said so. No men who said they were heterosexual—or bisexual—were included, and although a parallel study of lesbians (again, self-identified) is under way, no results have yet appeared. "Sexual orientation is too complex to be determined by a single gene," said Hamer. But if the presence or absence of this genetic marker indicates either a direct relationship to sexual object choice or (as is also conjectured) a "temperamental" predisposition to homosexuality, what is the status of the bisexual? Is he to be thought of as resisting (heroically or perversely) the message of his genes when he has relationships with women? Should genetic factors be thought of as options or as limits? We are once again here on the terrain of the "natural" and the "original."

Hamer and his team of researchers at the National Cancer Institute begin their paper on genetics and male homosexuality with a stylish reference to homosexuality as a "naturally occurring variation," thus whisking it under the big tent of Darwinism. Their study of forty pairs of homosexual brothers, like Michael Bailey and Richard Pillard's earlier twins study, "recruited" subjects "through advertisements in local and national homophile publications."[26]

They end with a cautionary note on medical ethics that looks forward to Jonathan Tolins's play *The Twilight of the Golds,* in which a couple is told that genetic testing has proved their unborn child will be gay. Should they have the child or abort it and try again for a straight one?

"We believe," writes Hamer and his colleagues with admirable directness, "that it would be fundamentally unethical to use such information to try to assess or alter a person's current or future sexual orientation, either heterosexual or homosexual or other normal attributes of human behavior."[27] The zinger here is "other normal attributes" which closes the parentheses begun by "naturally occurring variation" to establish that both in the language of biology and in the language of psychology homosexuals are as "normal" and "natural" as hets.

But who are Hamer's either/or homo- and heterosexuals? Using the Kinsey scale of 0 to 6, Hamer finds that his straights are very straight (Kinsey 0s and 1s) and his gays are very gay (Kinsey 5s and 6s) in self-identification, attraction, and fantasy. "Only the sexual *behavior* scale gave a small overlap between the two groups largely because of adolescent and early adult experiences" (my emphasis).[28] So at least a small number of persons said one thing about their sexuality(ies) and did another. Yet by discounting these early experiences as insignificant, the researchers were able to conclude that sexual orientation was a "dimorphic rather than a continuously variable trait." That is, they were able to omit consideration of bisexuality. ("Dimorphic" means existing or occurring in two distinct forms.) "Heterosexuals" who had sex with men, and "homosexuals" who had sex with women, were part of this "dimorphic" sample.

Furthermore, when participants were asked about their family histories, they were requested to rate their male relatives as either "definitely homosexual" or "not definitely known to be homosexual (heterosexual, bisexual, or unclear)." Checking with the relatives in question, researchers confirmed these opinions, except for one person who said he was asexual and two who refused to answer. (The total number of participants and relatives in the study was 166.) In this context, then, bisexual was determined to mean, for statistical purposes, "not homosexual," rather than "homosexual." Thus, while the default category for LeVay was homosexual, for Hamer it is "not homosexual."

Hamer et al. were, perhaps deservedly, rather defensive about this flattening out of the sample: "[D]escribing individuals as either homosexual or nonhomosexual," they declare, "while undoubtedly overly simplistic, appears to represent a reliable categorization of the population under study." Here is the word "undoubtedly" again, a word that in the narrative of LeVay's hypothalamic study played the role of the bisexual ghost. We could say that it does the same in Hamer's gene study, for what is "undoubtedly overly simplistic" is in fact the elimination of bisexuality as a category of analysis. To prove a point about the scientific relationship of homosexuality to genetics it is apparently necessary to remove distractions like "bisexual," "asexual," or the extremely provocative "unclear."

In other words, in the interests of science, bisexuality has been made to disappear. But not completely.

In their peroration, which we have already noted to be both hortatory and political in tone, Hamer et al. suggest a broadening of linkage studies beyond "males who self-identified as predominantly or exclusively homosexual" to include "individuals who identity as bisexual or ambisexual." Self-identification rather than behaviour thus becomes the key to the scientific analysis of sexual orientation. What does this tell us about the relationship of ideas to acts?

By taking self-description as the ground of fact, rather than tracing sexual contacts as systematically as it traced family trees and DNA markers, Hamer's study may be said to repeat what it finds: that men who say they are gay are gay. The *Times* qualifies its own noncommittal response to the news ("Report Suggests Homosexuality is Linked to Genes") by raising the question of "ambiguity," but in what might be regarded as the wrong place. "So far the study has been limited to men who said they were gay, eliminating the ambiguity that would come from considering the genes of men who called themselves heterosexual." The real "ambiguity" here is, we may say, itself ambiguous, doubly located in the careful phrasing of "men who *said* they were gay . . . men who *called themselves* heterosexual" and in the intrinsic ambiguity of sexuality and eroticism especially when regarded over the span of a lifetime. The "bi" at the center of "ambiguity" is more than just a coincidental felicity for my argument; rather, it is a linguistic tag, like the genetic tag at the end tip of the chromosome, indicating a potential and posing a question. Is it possible to "eliminate ambiguity," or desirable to do so? What does science mean when it claims to know the truth about sexual desire? Does X really mark the spot?

Many of the scientists who are conducting studies on genetics and gay identity are, like Simon LeVay, themselves gay. This should not in itself suggest bias, any more than does the heterosexual identity of past sex researchers, but it does suggest a certain overdetermination of interest. Like so many researchers, in any discipline, scientific or humanistic, they are looking to find themselves. The popular response to their work has been a response consonant with identity politics. Whether "good news" or "bad news" for gays, it affirms essential identities rather than fluid constructions. Should we now look forward to a cadre of bisexual scientists searching for a bi gland, a bi gene, or, perhaps, a bisexually identified male research subject with a small hypothalamus and an unmarked X chromosome? Or vice versa?

OFF THE CHARTS

The social scientists' quest to locate sexualities on a quantifiable continuum and the geneticists' attempt to fix and determine gay identity through the microscope have in common a desire to *see*: to see clearly who is gay, who is straight, and who might cross those boundaries without showing or knowing it. Since the discourse of rights, at least in the United States, depends upon the identity of personhood—the U.S. constitution protects only persons, not acts—bisexuals have, following the lead of gays and lesbians in quest of civil rights, sought to establish themselves as a visible and definable group. Just as some gays believe that scientific evidence of their existence will aid them in their quest for equal treatment under the law, so some bisexuals seek a parallel equality through visibility: the model here clearly is identity politics, which has enabled not only interest-group lobbying but also historical self-awareness and individual pride for African Americans; women; Asian, Latino, and Native Americans; and, in the past decade, gays and lesbians.

But bisexuality will not readily fit this model. Defining the set as broadly as possible for both political and humane reasons as those who have or have had any degree of attraction to men and to women, bisexual activists and organizers come up, for example, against the real differences between what social scientists call "concurrent" and "sequential" bisexual behaviour.

If "sequential" bisexuals are categorized as "really" gay or "really" straight depending on the nature of their present relationships ("coming out to themselves" on the one hand or "going straight" and getting beyond an adolescent "phase" on the other) then not only the definition of "bisexuality" but also those of "homosexuality" and "heterosexuality" are at stake.

For "homo" and "hetero" define themselves as opposites, however social science instruments like the Kinsey scale and the Klein grid keep demonstrating that such "purity" is a cultural artefact. And identity politics as well as science has an interest in keeping them opposite. To add "bisexuality" as a third category here is not in fact to refine the terms of analysis but instead to expose the radical limitations of rights-based arguments when linked to a concept of fixed identity. This is one reason why "reclaiming" historical personages and contemporary celebrities as bisexual rather than gay—Oscar Wilde, Virginia

Woolf, David Bowie, Martina Navratilova — has stirred such a fuss in both the gay and the bisexual communities.

Biologists don't see bisexuality through their instruments and social scientists only see it as a composite of elements. Yet it exists, in other mammals as well as in humans, in ordinary people as well as in the famous, in adults as well as in children. If the subjects of social science analysis come uncannily to life in the talk-show medium, provoking the inevitable discussion of whether they are being used by the media or are using it for their own ends, the dispassionate categories of the Kinsey scale have likewise been taken over by today's gay and bisexual activists.

As bisexual writer Amanda Udis-Kessler notes, "phrases such as 'one in ten' and 'Kinsey 6' are probably as ingrained in queer culture as Judy Garland, Oscar Wilde, leather, *Desert Hearts*, Provincetown and Ferron."[29] In choosing "Kinsey 6" (or "Kinsey 3," defined as "equally heterosexual and homosexual") as a T-shirt slogan mode of self-identification, the successors of Kinsey's abstract "males" and "females" reclaim the territory of the survey, infusing it with personality, irony, and wit. But in giving life to these abstractions they also give them reality. To think in terms of categories is to categorize. It is no accident that gay and lesbian visibility gave rise to "gay and lesbian chic" as well as to campaigns to liberalize or repress gay and lesbian rights.

Thus, when a scale making use of the terms "concurrent" and "sequential" bisexuality came to the attention of a bisexual feminist writer, she was quick to "predict" that this "new jargon" would "find its way into many a bi circle."[30] No matter that the terms were not new;[31] a new use would be found for them in mirroring and "scientifically" validating their existence. Like Rock Hudson reading the Kinsey Report, like Simon LeVay charting the biology of gay identity, bisexuals also seek to read the face of nature, to find themselves already written there.

Ultimately, however, the object of scrutiny will escape even the most vigilant and searching eyes. Bisexuality undoes statistics, confounds dimorphism, creates a volatile set of subjects who will not stay put in neat and stable categories. No calipers will fit the shape of desire, which remains, thankfully, unquantifiable by even the most finely tested instruments.

NOTES

1. Ann Landers, "Teacher Needs to Learn Lesson — There Aren't Five Sexes," *Miami Herald*, 21 December 1992, p. 2C.
2. Anne Fausto-Sterling, "The Five Sexes," *The Sciences*, March/April 1993, pp. 20–4. A briefer version of this article appeared on the *New York Times* op-ed page under the title "How Many Sexes Are There?" (*New York Times*, 12 March 1993, p. A29).
3. Fausto-Sterling, "The Five Sexes," p. 22.
4. Ibid., p. 24.

5. Steve Wolfe, letter to the *New York Times*, 26 March 1993, p. AI2.

6. Gary Fairmount Filosa, letter to the *New York Times*, 26 March 1993, p. A12.

7. Ibid.

8. Simon LeVay, "A Difference in Hypothalamic Structure between Heterosexual and Homosexual Men," *Science*, vol. 253 (30 August 1991), pp. 1034–7.

9. David J. Jefferson, "Science Besieged: Studying the Biology of Sexual Orientation has Political Fallout," *Wall Street Journal*, 12 August 1993, p. 1.

10. Michael Bailey and Richard Pillard, "Are Some People Born Gay?" *New York Times*, 17 October 1991, p. A21.

11. Mariana Valverde, *Sex, Power, and Pleasure* (Philadelphia: New Society Publishers, 1987), p. 112.

12. Richard von Krafft-Ebing, *Psychopathia Sexualis*, 7th edn, trans. Franklin Klaf (New York: Stein & Day, 1965) pp. 221–2.

13. Robert A. Wild, quoted in Natalie Angier, "Male Hormone Molds Women, Too, in Mind and Body," *New York Times*, 3 May 1994, p. Cl3.

14. Roger S. Rittmaster, quoted in ibid.

15. Angier, "Male Hormone Molds Women, Too," p. C13.

16. Sigmund Freud, "Three Essays on the Theory of Sexuality" (1905), *Standard Edition*, 7: 140. The "spokesman of the male inverts" is Karl Heinrich Ulrichs.

17. Robert J. Stoller, "Facts and Fancies: An Examination of Freud's Concept of Bisexuality," in *Women and Analysis: Dialogues on Psychoanalytic Views of Femininity*, ed. Jean Strouse (New York: Grossman Publishers, 1974), p. 345.

18. Joe Dolce, "And How Big Is Yours?" *The Advocate*, 1 June 1993, p. 40.

19. Ruth Hubbard and Elijah Wald, *Exploding the Gene Myth* (Boston: Beacon Press, 1993), p. 96.

20. LeVay, "A Difference in Hypothalamic Structure," p. 1035.

21. Ibid., p. 1034.

22. LeVay mentions the possibility that his sample may be unrepresentative, since gay male AIDS patients might be thought of as belonging to a "subset of gay men, characterized, for example, by a tendency to engage in sexual relations with large numbers of different partners or by a strong preference for the receptive role in anal intercourse" but he refutes this by noting that "the majority of homosexual men who acquired HIV infection during the Multicenter AIDS Cohort Study reported that they took both the insertive and the receptive role in intercourse and the same is likely to be true of the homosexual subjects in my study" ("A Difference in Hypothalamic Structure," p. 1036). This is the only mention of sexual roles or aims in the paper, and it is clearly intended to be discounted rather than counted as a differential factor.

23. Dolce, "And How Big Is Yours?" p. 40.

24. Hubbard and Wald, *Exploding the Gene Myth*, p. 94.

25. Natalie Angier, "Report Suggests Homosexuality is Linked to Genes," *New York Times*, 16 July 1993, p. A12.

26. Dean H. Hamer, Stella Hu, Victoria L. Magnuson, Nan Hu, Angela M. L. Pattatucci, "A Linkage between DNA Markers on the X Chromosome and Male Sexual Orientation," *Science*, vol. 261, no. 5119 (16 July 1993), p. 321; J. Michael Bailey and Richard C. Pillard, "A Genetic Study of Male Sexual Orientation," *Archives of General Psychiatry*, vol. 48 (1991), pp. 1089–96.

27. Hamer et al. "Linkage between DNA Markers," p. 326.

28. Ibid., pp. 321–2.

29. Amanda Udis-Kessler, "Appendix: Notes on the Kinsey Scale and Other Measures of Sexuality," in *Closer to Home: Bisexuality and Feminism,* ed. Elizabeth Reba Weise (Seattle: The Seal Press, 1992), p. 316.

30. Ibid., p. 317.

31. In their article on "The Multidimension Scale of Sexuality," authors Braden Robert Berkey, Terri Perelman-Hall, and Lawrence A. Kurdek cite J. P. Paul's use of "sequential bisexual" and "contemporaneous bisexual" in 1984, and G. Zinik's terms "serial" and "concurrent" in 1985. See *Journal of Homosexuality*, vol. 19, no. 4 (Winter 1990), p. 68; J. P. Paul, "The Bisexual Identity: an Idea Without Social Recognition," *Journal of Homosexuality*, vol. 9, nos. 2–3 (1983–4), pp. 45–63; G. Zinik, "Identity Conflict or Adaptive Flexibility? Bisexuality Reconsidered," in Fritz Klein, MD, and Timothy J. Wolf, MD, *Two Lives to Lead: Bisexuality in Men and Women* (New York and London: Harrington Park Press, 1985), pp. 7–18.

DAVID GREVEN

Dude, Where's My Gender?: Contemporary Teen Comedies and New Forms of American Masculinity

David Greven is Professor of English at Connecticut College and writes widely on American literature, film, and culture. This selection first appeared in the film journal Cinéaste *in 2002.*

Gleefully vulgar celebrations of the sexual antics of youth and other raucous rites of puberty, contemporary American teen comedies—such as *American Pie* (1999), *Dude, Where's My Car?* (2000), *Loser* (2000), *American Pie 2* (2001), and *Saving Silverman* (2001)—usually fall below the radar of middlebrow moviegoing tastes and are rarely subjected to critical analysis. While they perpetuate the critically disreputable nature of the genre, established by earlier entries such as *Porky's* (1981), *Screwballs* (1983), and *Revenge of the Nerds* (1984), a closer look reveals that there's a lot more going on in these films than we might think.

Indeed, this latest wave of teen comedies offers a fascinating record of the fluctuations and new currents in the shaping of masculine identity in post-Clinton America. In surprising ways—often reflecting the impact of the feminist and gay-rights movements—they portray new visions of gender, mapping emergent sexualities, reshaping conventional notions of manhood, and helping to redefine gender identity as such.

This is not to suggest that these commercial entertainments are consciously making progressive statements, or that, in seismically monitoring changes in conventional sexual and gender codes, they are part of the feminist and gay movements' efforts to challenge the dominant culture. They are neither completely progressive nor devoid of political implications. While they might occasionally engage in a conscious, if humorously-motivated, socio-cultural critique, they also often display a troubling, reactionary dimension. Some of the representations of gender and sexuality in these comedies, which reveal the effect of radical changes in our culture, simultaneously evince a deep hostility to these changes. In fact, the comedies can be seen as an attack on the very forces they reflect. Yet what's interesting is that they don't merely counterattack perceived threats to stable gender and sexual stereotypes. The new teen comedies offer both reaction and representation, and thereby sometimes even sympathy for sexual transgression.

199

Ashton Kutcher, left, and Seann William Scott in *Dude, Where's My Car? (Photo by Tracy Bennett, courtesy of Photofest)*

Male teenagers are a distinct field of cultural inquiry—neither men nor boys, both childlike beings and adult men, blurring the boundaries of both categories. In his 1993 study *American Manhood*, E. Anthony Rotundo discusses the "free nation" of nineteenth-century American boy culture as "a distinct cultural world, with its own rituals and its own symbols and values. As a social sphere, it was separate both from the domestic world of women, girls, and small children, and from the public world of men and commerce. In this privileged space of their own, boys were able to play outside the rules of the home and the marketplace." Teen boys in a world of their own, playing outside the rules.

The new teen comedies exploit this special zone of identity, amounting to veritable pageants of boys in men's drag, donning and discarding codes of manhood that have dominated our culture for so long that they seem "natural." In this sense, the films remain thoroughly conventional in suggesting that boyhood—sustained pubescence—remains a period of romantic idealization in American culture: the perpetual antics of Huck Finn and Tom Sawyer.

Do teen comedies merely forestall the inevitable social definition of boys to men, acting as last-chance respites against complete male socialization, or can they be considered as serious challenges to dominant male codes? And how do girls and women figure in this special, distinct world of "boys"? In

Jim's dad (Eugene Levy) witnesses another of his son Jim's spectacular humiliations in *American Pie 2. (Photo by Vivian Zink, courtesy of Photofest)*

terms of film history, how do the contemporary teen comedies' occasional gender-bending characterizations relate to teen comedies from the Eighties such as *Porky's, Risky Business, Losin' It, Revenge of the Nerds,* and others that foreground male sexuality?

The new teen comedies treat male friendship as a primary social model under-pinned by the demands of two key compulsory aspects of American man-hood: the successful pursuit of marriage, a metonym for heterosexual relations, home, family, and work; and the successful formation of same-sex ties in the homosocial sphere. The term "homosocial," popularly used in academia since the Eighties, succinctly describes the sphere and realms of same-sex relations—the relationships and spaces in which both male power and intimacy are con-centrated. Homosocial relations may include homosexual ones, but, in our homophobic culture, they are not meant to. Teen comedies depict intense same-sex intimacies that are always informed—i.e., curtailed—by the threat of homosexual ardor or eroticism. The realms of the homosocial—public places where members of the same sex share intimacies—are just as important as the intimacies they facilitate. In the comedies, these locations include pizza parlors, dorm rooms, parent-free houses, luxury summer resorts. The rein-forced suggestion is that even the more overtly public realms truly are private, special, enclosed—the teen boys are both cut off from the world of adults and deliberately sequestered in a zone of intimacy in which they are safe to be themselves.

Although there is a strong female presence in *American Pie*—with Natasha Lyonne's frizzy-haired, seen-it-all Jessica, and Alyson Hannigan's flighty, geeky, but sexually rapacious band-camper Michelle, among others—the film focuses on male experiences. The four friends are a mixture of stalwart male types that suggest the motley fraternal crews of wartime movies such as Howard Hawks's *Air Force*: Jim (Jason Biggs), a sexual novice and smart goof; Oz (Chris Klein), a big jock with a sensitive side; Finch (Eddie Kaye Thomas), a fussy, vaguely effete intellectual-poseur; and affable, smooth Kevin (Thomas Ian Nicholas). Other players include Stifler (Seann William Scott), a Wild Man-monster whose lubricity and penchant for uproarious insensitivity knows no bounds, and Sherman (Chris Owen), the "Shermanator," who parodistically describes himself as a Terminator of heterosexual prowess, and whose intense undesirability is parodied throughout the film.

Jim's nebbishy dad (Eugene Levy) offers his son, much to Jim's discomfort, relentlessly "supportive" insights on sexual matters. Jim's overbearing dad confirms the film's relegation of adult men to the Other World of life experiences and sexuality—as much of an alien threat as he is a (sympathetic) boob. Jim's dad wanders in periodically to remind the audience of the distracting strangeness of adult life, and to provide the anticipatory terror of becoming an adult male. Made to look as unattractive as possible, Levy's dad provides a stark, hirsute counterbalance to the smooth, virginal sleekness of the boys, collectively on the verge of a manhood contingent upon achieving mastery over the mysteries of sex. Thus does sex become both a rapaciously sought goal and a terrible anxiety to be delayed, stalled, avoided—lest the sleek boys become, and start to look like, their fathers.

American Pie 2 is much more squarely, in every way, a guy's movie. Even the Sherminator "scores" in this one. The vital female presences from the first film are muted. The film affirms that male friendship provides an invaluable social base for teen males as they prosper experientially, financially, and sexually. Though now in college, the *American Pie* pals still consider themselves a tightly bound unit—no new college buddies intrude on their special world, which remains hermetically sealed, though the sequel folds Stifler more prominently into the mix. Rising above the pizza parlor where they congregated in *American Pie*, the boys of *American Pie 2* rent a plush summer beach house for the staging of their shenanigans. This lavish house buttresses their closed-world bonds in a luxuriousness that suggests a perpetually upward social and sexual mobility. As they refine their sexual prowess, the boys will always have each other, in increasingly prosperous surroundings.

In his classic study *Love and Death in the American Novel*, Leslie Fiedler argues that American men want to escape "the gentle tyranny of home and woman," and thus pursue male friendship as an escape from the domestic sphere. But *American Pie* (which features lavish house parties) and its sequel

Jessica (Natasha Lyonne, left) and Vicky (Tara Reid) discuss how to stay in control of the romantic relationships with the guys in their lives in *American Pie. (Photo courtesy of Photofest)*

(with its summer-house pleasure dome) suggest that men want homes all their own — the visible consolidation of male power and intimacy. An interesting complement to the *American Pie* films' use of the homosocial is *Saving Silverman*, which makes it clear that the homosocial has its own demands and needs. This time, Jason Biggs's male friends take revenge against the sphere of heterosexual love: they kidnap his snooty shrink fiancée because she isn't, they claim, good enough for him — they want him all to themselves. *Saving Silverman* explicitly defines the homosocial's interest in saving one of its own from the adulthood-conferring rigors of heterosexuality. The kidnapping of the hero's girlfriend is staged not as an act of malevolence but as the bound girlfriend's systematic humiliation of her captors. The movie never invites any sympathy for the captured woman — so confidently derisive and dismissive is she that we're invited to pity her captors as we castigate her. The film ensures, as well, that her wild beastliness will be tamed, since she ends up a nice, loving woman who marries one of her kidnappers.

But *Saving Silverman* muddies the waters of class that are so languidly still in *American Pie*. Biggs's goofy, shaggy Neil Diamond-worshipping friends, living together in a big but messy house, are the burnout freaks the suburban boys of *American Pie* shun. *Loser*, another Biggs film (he has become the male Muse of the teen comedy), inverts *Saving Silverman*'s class and homosocial schemas: Biggs plays a Midwestern rube in the Big Apple exploited by his dormmates, who are depicted as unremittingly cruel rich kids out to thwart the innocent yokel. Yet the theme of preventing sexual consummation endures—their efforts to stall his romantic bliss with Mena Suvari's daffy ingenue amounts, however inadvertently, to another homosocial "save."

The racially mixed cast of *Scary Movie* reminds us of how homogeneously white the casts of almost all of the teen comedies are. White male friendship becomes a self-contained realm, ruthlessly policing the intrusion of any foreign element, racial or sexual. *Dude, Where's My Car?* literalizes the foreign quality of hetero sex—its two best male friends repeatedly run into a horde of alien women who promise them hot sex that is never consummated. The domain of male friendship, color-coordinated and organized by coherent heterosexual desire (however problematic to male unity), buttresses the boys from all outside threat.

In terms of consummating heterosexual desire, the movies suggest that, in canine fashion, boys just want each other—females represent an alien mystery that threatens to disrupt the boys' bonds. Yet this strain in the films is too dangerous to be allowed to flourish unchecked; the films self-reflexively ensure that sexual relations surpass the ardent homosocial ties. The homosocial in these films militates against, yet also relentlessly strives toward, the procurement of boy-girl sex. If these films privilege male friendship (even *Loser* does—though the male group opposes Biggs's solitary loser-character, it functions as a cohesive whole) and depict the ways the boys cleave to their own collective companionship, the drive to seek out and achieve heterosexual intercourse looms as their primary quest-objective. In fact, male friendship seems to be the dugout where the boys catch their breath during the game of heterosexual conquest.

In this regard, the character of Kevin (Thomas Ian Nicholas) in *American Pie* and *American Pie 2* is, in many ways, the most interesting. Desperate to consummate his romance with his blonde, nervously virginal girlfriend, Vicky (Tara Reid), he is shown to be even more desperately obsessed with getting his fraternal crew to lose their virginities along with—although not along*side*—him. Kevin makes them all take a pact with him that, by prom night, they will each have lost their virginity. In our omnisexual era, the quest to lose one's virginity wouldn't seem to be as mythically arduous as *American Pie* depicts it, but it comprises the entire film. Kevin's bland, smooth affability transforms into an almost sinister coldness by the end of the film: his insistence that all of the guys get laid by prom night becomes rabid, unyielding. It's little surprise when Jason Biggs's Jim snaps at him during the prom, when all their sexual prospects begin to look dim, "I haven't even had sex yet and I hate it!" All of the other guys walk off at this point, leaving Kevin to contemplate his junior-league-Ahab manias. When Kevin and Vicky do consummate their relationship, the film goes to considerably length to depict it as an uncomfortable, joyless experience, focusing especially on the complete lack of fun in it for Vicky.

Kevin insists on implementing and maintaining a compulsory manhood within the group. Sex before marriage isn't marriage, but in white, middle-class suburbia it's the signpost up ahead on the route to the Marriage Zone—or so these films claim. Kevin brilliantly fuses the two bonds of male gender—marriage and male friendship—by insisting that the friendship the guys share be solidified by and organized around shared heterosexual experiences. Kevin's edicts confirm the biological and social imperatives toward heterosexual couplings, which the new teen comedies endorse, even though they also carnivalize them. Kevin's obsessive interest in the guys' productive, efficient, "normal" sex drives makes him a heterosexual slave driver, insisting on the compulsory performance of male virility—what evidently makes boys men.

If in *American Pie* Kevin is interestingly depicted as an oppressor of the other boys, and the disappointingly hollow sex he has with Vicky comes to seem a moralistic punishment, the film nevertheless allies itself to his campaign. After they shun him at the prom, the boys seek out Kevin, whom they find alone, brooding over his now publicly exposed manias. They comfort him, their unity is reaffirmed, and the film proceeds to make sure each of the boys finds sexual fulfillment. (Chris Klein's bland, dream-hunk Oz and his good-girl girlfriend cuddle under the stars, which, instead of seeming like a respite against the push towards heterosexual productivity, appears to confer a prepubescent, nonphallic sexuality on him for being such a nice guy.) Kevin may get a diegetic comeuppance, but the movie strives to realize his vision.

The efforts of Eugene Levy's dad to help his son be sexually successful—met with groans and exasperatedly raised eyes by Jim—remind us that a great deal rides on Jim's ability to be an effective, efficient lover. The movie, *Carrie*-style, turns sexual anxieties into hugely public displays of humiliation: Jim's disastrous efforts to get sexy, foreign-exchange student Nadia (Shannon Elizabeth) in bed—broadcast via hidden Webcam to the entire school—climax, so to speak, in his premature orgasm. He them prematurely ejaculates *again*, as the entire school watches this spectacle of male performance-failures. This scene becomes a treatise on male performance anxiety. The huge pressures put on the American male to be successfully virile are no excuse for this shambles of a sex act, the movie implies. *American Pie* also suggests that male heterosexual performance is no less rigidly compulsory for guys than it is for girls.

If Jim's male-performance anxiety suggests that the problem of achieving adult sexual potency is central to the teen comedy, *Dude, Where's My Car?* ingeniously solves the problem by depicting two male best friends whose sexuality is so hidden beneath their childlike goofiness that such problematic questions never arise. Starring Seann William Scott and *That 70s Show*'s Ashton Kutcher, *Dude* gives us a kinder, gentler, dreamier Stifler, and, in Kutcher, who's like a boy Marilyn—the American male as polymorphous-perverse infant—an appropriate accomplice. Both Scott and Kutcher play men here who are amazingly childlike, almost to the point of not seeming capable of sexual expression (truer in Kutcher's case, since Scott's manic energy retains its feral edge). In this manner, *Dude* allows homosocial ardor to flourish while reinforcing the sheer wonder and constant appeal of heterosexuality. The non-phallic innocence of the boys plays like arrested sexual development, while their wide-eyed reactions to the recurring promises of heterosexual intercourse make sure we understand its potent allure and necessity.

Loser would also appear to employ *Dude*'s solution. In making Biggs's character so aw-shucks nice in comparison to the mean homosocial order that excludes him, so attentive to the heroine (almost like the gay best friend stock character), and surrounding him with sick animals to nurture, *Loser* appears to be dispensing with both homosocial allegiances and the fulfillment of mature heterosexual love—not having to grapple, then, with the problem of the teen boy's potency. Yet *Loser* ultimately confirms Biggs's virility, having him knock out one of his rivals and get the girl. *Loser* shortcuts its way to the goal of manhood—it dispenses with male friendship, butches up its hero, and insures his union with the girl.

Given that the teen comedy both foregrounds male sexual-performance anxieties and resolves them through a final realization of "manly" sexual prowess; and given that this genre also affirms homosocial ardor while suggesting that it must ultimately be renounced, repudiated, and transcended in order for teen boys to achieve coherent, properly heterosexual manhood, the relationships these films and their boy protagonists establish with girls, women, femaleness, and femininity becomes especially interesting. The new teen comedies are all distinguished by an interest in women who wield sexual power and who, like the queen heroine of H. Rider Haggard's *She*, tower over the men they enslave.

For such deeply male-oriented entertainments, the *American Pie* films feature remarkably distinct and memorable female characters. The women—save for tense Vicky—are sexual dynamos with breezy airs of confidence, an avid appetite for sex, and no compunctions about discussing or satisfying their sexual needs. Hannigan's Michelle reveals herself to be a brazen proponent of wild sex. When Jim feels particularly hopeless about his sexual chances at the end of the film, Michelle, as the conclusion to one of her incessant, innocuous stories, says, "And then I stuck a flute in my pussy!" It's the sheer unselfconsciousness with which Michelle announces her adventure—in sharp juxtaposition to the inefficacy of Jim's sexual performance—that produces shocked laughter in the audience. The shock becomes sheer wonderment when Michelle says, with now characteristic blitheness, "So, are we going to fuck anytime soon?"

The shock of this scene comes from the surprise that this seemingly dizzy, clueless girl has steel-trap control over the entire sexual proceedings. Far from being a hopeless sexual prospect for Jim, Michelle controls the entire situation; it is she who impatiently awaits Jim's sexual performance. In both films,

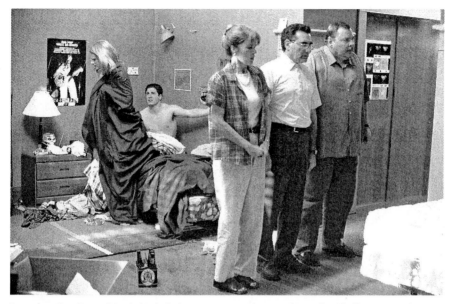

Just when Jim (Jason Biggs) thinks he's getting somewhere with Natalie (Joelle Carter), their parents decide to visit his college dorm room, in *American Pie 2*. *(Photo courtesy of Photofest)*

she routinely calls him her "bitch." Neither clueless nor frigid, Michelle is a sexual sorceress who controls all aspects of the sexual performance. But merely presenting strong female characters does not automatically constitute a challenge to dominant male culture. Reinforcing the cultural myth that women alone decide when sex happens, movies like *American Pie* continue to defer all the possession of the secrets of (hetero) sexual fulfillment to the women. Even tense Vicky, so plaintively uncomfortably, maintains tight control over the time and place she and Kevin will have sex. Even if sexualized and presented as the stuff wet dreams are made of, the teen girls of *American Pie* are miniature Dark Continents, to use Freud's rather infamous metaphor for female sexuality, or, in *Dude*-speak, they are from another planet.

Lyonne's Jessica, figured as a cross between wise-woman village crone and matchmaking *yenta*, is a sexual double agent—she gives advice to women on how to make men crazy; she tells men how to make women their sexual slaves. Again, like Michelle, she confirms the movie's gendered schema—it is the women who control and create the realm of sex. And Elizabeth's tall, sexy Nadia—who manages to be thin and voluptuous at once, Amazonian in the way she towers over Jim—attests to the sexual confidence of the women here. Left alone in Jim's room while she changes—Jim means only to film her undressing, not his subsequent failed sexual performance—Nadia rifles through his drawers and finds the sex magazines that Jim's dad has given him.

They went thataway, say the Dudes and their girlfriends, Wilma (Maria Sokoloff, left) and Wanda (Jennifer Garner) in *Dude, Where's My Car? (Photo by Tracy Bennett, courtesy of Photofest)*

She begins to masturbate, moaning audibly, remarkably relaxed about satiating her own desires. When Jim walks in on her, she seductively requests that he enhance her onanistic mission. The juxtaposition between her sexual fearlessness and Jim's pathetic premature orgasms provides the fiendish humor of the scene.

Like *American Pie* and its sequel, *Dude* fetishizes the sorceresslike power of women over men, a notion that is just as much a part of dominant male culture as the image of the virginal "good girl." The Dudes are in constant terror over displeasing their glowering girlfriends. The girlfriends wield all of the sexual power in the film, deciding when they will allow the Dudes to have sex with them. Almost as if fantasizing about entry into some sexual Heaven, the Dudes wonder aloud, with zonked faces, if the girlfriends are summoning them over for sex. Solidifying the movie's thematic assignment of all sexual power to women, that cadre of black-on-black, female alien hotties periodically appear. Obviously inspired by *The Matrix*, these chic dominatrix types are cold, deadly, demanding, and implacable in their relentless campaign to turn the Dudes into slaves. They're like Fembots, the mechanical killer women from the Seventies' TV shows, *The Six Million Dollar Man* and *The Bionic Woman*, only scarier, funnier, and more explicitly sexually charged. They manifest the theme of women's sexual power over men by embodying a militaristic image of that ideal.

Sexual sorceresses also wield power in *Scary Movie*, made the same year as *Dude*. Directed by Keenan Ivory Wayans, *Scary Movie*, a parody of parodistic teen horror films such as *Scream* (and hence a copy of a copy), is a shockingly violent and unappealingly cruel movie. As if in response to the female sexual authority of other teen comedies, not to mention the 'Final Girl' character— so brilliantly analyzed by Carol Glover in her book *Men, Women, and Chainsaws*—of the horror movies it spoofs, *Scary Movie* features feisty women who receive brutal punishments for their feistiness. A young, loud, obnoxious black woman finds herself beaten, stabbed, slashed, and slaughtered by hordes of angry white patrons. Shannon Elizabeth, *American Pie*'s Nadia, in a real comedown role, plays an indestructible woman whom the joking killer annihilates—or tries to. He hacks at bits of her, but she continues to taunt him with derisive comments meant to signal her awareness of her role as female victim. "Oooh, is this the part where I break my leg?," she shrieks, and then does so, graphically. We watch as tendons tear, sinews split, and blood gushes forth. Finally, the killer decapitates her and stuffs her still babbling, jeering head into the garbage.

These murdered-women scenes are particularly nasty modern movie sequences. The sexually powerful woman of the contemporary teen comedy pays quite a price for her gendered hubris. Hacked at but resisting destruction, she continues to spew vile sexual taunts and threats even as the film disposes of her. Seeing a crowd of white moviegoers annihilate a black woman would be shocking to watch in any film—much more so in one made by black filmmakers. *Scary Movie* is deeply reactionary.

Still, *Scary Movie* only makes especially apparent the deep ambivalence with which the new teen comedy beholds the girl and womanhood. The lively women of *American Pie* become much more muted, more drably peripheral, in the sequel. Even Lyonne's acerbic Jessica lacks bite here. Hannigan's band-campy Michelle gradually loses her eccentric edge and daffy conversational rhythms as she gains a moony romantic ardor for Jim. (This process happens all too often in Hollywood movies, which force women to give up their distinctiveness in order to realize romantic love.) Vicky, not an especially compelling character in *American Pie*, is revealed to be much more sexually confident in the sequel, but barely figures in it at all. Her contributions here consist mainly of glaring at Kevin—reduced to the status of blank worrywart—while he fumbles his way toward man-woman friendship with her. Nadia, such a tempting tigress in *American Pie*, in the sequel becomes neurotic and uncertain, duped, and dumped by Jim, who now realizes that he loves Michelle. And while her interest in coaxing Oz into phone-sex is intriguing, Mena Suvari's good-girl Heather, relegated to a year abroad in Europe, barely registers as a presence in the sequel.

Though a big hit (its source material, Austen's *Emma*, adding to its cachet), *Clueless* (1995), a teen comedy that focuses on girls, has not been widely emulated, even if its sardonic rhythms continue to circulate in pop-culture products like the WB's girl-ensemble shows and the Reese Witherspoon surprise smash, *Legally Blonde* (2001). Most teen comedies privilege male experience, this year even having the "girls" played by *Sorority Boys*. The kind of romantic friendship shared by Jodie Foster and Scott Jacoby in the 1976 B-movie classic, *The Little Girl Who Lives Down the Lane*, is quite rare in the new teen comedy, where boys collectively converge around iconic female statuary.

Herein lies the female bind of these films—they depict strong, confident females yet keep them at a chilly remove. The girls in these movies, largely free of the anxieties with which the boys are riddled, are in the paralytic position of being simultaneously powerful and unreal. Allocated all the sexual knowledge of the films, they wield power over boys yet remain largely outside the narrative. In this fashion, the girls become remote goddesses who exert a smug influence over the proceedings, while the boys get to have complex, problematic life experiences, and their characters show growth in narrative arcs. Assigning all the sexual power to the women and girls, then, becomes a means of containing and entrapping female experience—their confidence in these films serves as consolation prizes, concessions to the rising social prominence of women that yet manage to keep femaleness out of the narrative trajectory of individual life. In other words, these films allow us to watch boys turn into men, but girls have no access to such *bildungsromans*.

If feminism has made it more difficult to represent women in films as weak, irrelevant creatures, the teen comedies have found an ingenious compromise between earlier cinematic modes of femininity and current views—their depiction of strong women concedes the legitimacy of the advances of feminism, while their relegation of these strong women to the sidelines allows men to maintain preeminent control. Analogously, the comedies' expressions of gay awareness allow—even if in occluded ways—gay sensibility to lend its voice to the depiction of conventional manhood, while always reaffirming the normality (i.e., the heterosexuality) of the boys' sexual aims.

In *Saving Silverman*, one of the kidnapped psychiatrist's ploys is to diagnose one of her kidnappers as a repressed homosexual—thereby (mysteriously) bending him to her will. This seems a key move in the teen comedy. Homosexuality—and the threat of its manifestation—underlies the teen comedy, especially in terms of its fixation on straight male friendship, and thematically relates to its depiction of women as both symbolically powerful and narratively powerless.

American Pie registers not only an awareness of the gay sensibility that has reshaped mainstream culture but also the anxieties that attend that awareness, a simultaneous fascination and repulsion. In one striking scene, Stifler, the gonzo horny Wild Man, drinks another man's semen—surely a first in Hollywood movies. Indebted to the gross-out esthetic popularized by the Farrelly Brothers, this scene remarkably encapsulates the capacity for disgust still thoroughly in place within the relationship heterosexual culture has to homosexuality. As

Stifler retches copiously, Kevin jabs at him—'Hey, how'd you like that pale ale!"—generating wild crowd laughter.

In her essay on the calumniation of the maternal in horror films, "The Monstrous-Feminine," Barbara Creed discusses the centrality of establishing borders to the genre. It is the very crossing of those borders—human/monster, outside the body/inside the body, normal gender identity/abnormal gendered identity—that constitutes horror. Increasingly, the genre that, in the Farrelly Brothers era, most transgressively crosses these crucial borders is the (teen) comedy. Even today, with new treatments against AIDS available, the exchange of bodily fluids between men can only be the stuff of horror (alien contagion, vampirism) or gross-out comedy. The threat to the heterosexual male of contagion from the sexual energy of other men—in other words, the threat of being forced into homoerotic situations—is explicitly addressed in this moment. That it becomes a public spectacle of humiliation suggests the fear of the Secret being let out—sexual contact with other men, even if rendered in so baroque a fashion, could only cause excruciating embarrassment to those involved.

Unlike Eighties comedies such as *Revenge of the Nerds* (1984), neither *American Pie* nor its sequel has any explicitly queer characters—but they don't need them, in a sense, because a recognition of a pervasive gay threat to conventional masculinity permeates both films. Stifler becomes the battleground for the films' warring impulses between interest in homoeroticism and revulsion from it. Stifler has a much more expanded role in *American Pie 2*. It is important to contextualize Stifler's increased visibility within the film's much bolder interest in the graphic suggestion of the boys as purveyors and objects of sexual desire. *American Pie 2* takes all of the big setpieces from the original—the sex-object Jim's public humiliation, the homo-threat "pale ale" scene—and reimagines them in grander terms, upping the sexual ante. So, Jim's parents walk in on him *in flagrante delicto* with a woman; Stifler is luxuriantly urinated upon by a guy at a party; Jim performs his sex dance in front of a large public crowd (at Michelle's mythic band camp); Jim Krazy Glues himself when, while masturbating, he mistakes the adhesive agent for lubricant; sensitive-jock Oz fondles his organ during a comically interrupted phone sex scene; and so on.

Stifler's sexuality becomes one of the major motifs of *American Pie 2*. Though depicted as a kind of heterosexual satyr in *American Pie*, violently cheerful in his sexual pursuits, in the sequel he comes to seem a polysexual Pan. Stifler, savagely heterosexual in appetite but always suggestive of rampant sexual appetites inclusive of the homosexual, is like a character in a *Saturday Night Live* sketch about a homophobe who's actually just closeted: he blithely repels Oz's rebukes with the line, "I'm going to give you a spoon to eat my ass!" The film's use of Stifler—what a perfect name!—culminates in the movie's loony *pièce de résistance*, involving two "lesbians." Once they see that Jim, Finch, and Stifler want them to "prove" that they're real lesbians through

Jon Abrahams, Shawn Wayans and Marlon Wayans star in *Scary Movie*. *(Photo courtesy of Photofest)*

depictions of sapphic sex, the women decide to put one over on the guys, whom they've caught hiding out in their room. (Ladder-clenching Oz and Kevin voyeuristically observe from outside.) For every fake lesbian kiss, they request a complementary gay kiss from the guys. Stifler is shown to be the most animatedly willing to endure these trials in order to experience vicarious lesbian sex. Stifler even allows the men to bring him to climactic fruition — a last-straw prospect from which Jim and Finch flee, shrieking.

The complexities of this scene are rich. Once again, women are in sexual control, devising ways in which men can perform sexually for their delectation. The men are forced into homoerotic contact by women who want to beat them at their own game. And Stifler is so overcome by the promise of male-fantasy lesbian titillation that he even becomes excited at the prospect of group gay sex. Textually, it is impossible to determine whether or not the prankster women here are razzing the boys for their own homophobia or trapping the boys into homo-hijinks in order to humiliate them. Finch and Jim's terrified escape from the revelation of Stifler's willingness to engage in gay sex (albeit in the service of watching lesbian sex) would also seem to suggest the movie's hurried determination to reestablish the essentially disgusting nature of gay sex. Still, the sheer length of the scene implies an interest in pushing past the borders of straight male sexual taste.

Dude makes male sexuality and gender identity elastic and pliable categories. In one scene, the Dudes are driving around and come to a red light,

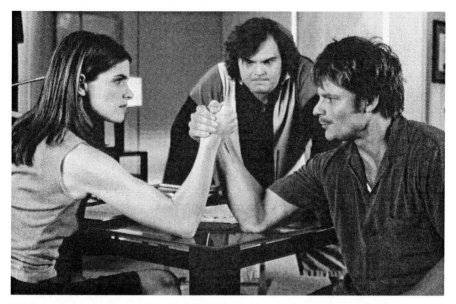

J.D. (Jack Black, center) and Wyne (Steve Zahn) struggle with Judith (Amanda Peet) over the future of their best friend in *Saving Silverman.* *(Photo by Joseph Lederer, courtesy of Photofest)*

as does a car with Fabio, the cartoon hunk, and a lady companion. To compete with Fabio, the Dudes end up passionately making out. It's hard to know exactly what's going on in this scene, where the radicalism ends and the homophobia begins, or whether either figures into it at all. Nevertheless, this scene suggests a new willingness in American males to adopt an increased tolerance — if not an all-out embrace — of homosexual identity, which, of course, they can discard at any moment. It suggests a comfort with homosexuality in mainstream culture that is in itself radical — the movie pushes a corner of the sexual envelope that still hasn't quite been pried open in social life. By assigning the obligatory gross-out to Fabio's vacuous lady friend, but not to either of the Dudes, the movie also suggests that homophobic reaction belongs to the enemy. Yet the film's depiction of the Dudes as nearly prepubescent in their innocence divests any homoeroticism between them of the threat of mature gay male sexuality. The homoeroticism becomes simply another aspect of their infantile manhood.

Dude also has a running gag involving a pre-op transsexual with a womanly body, a male-organ bulge revealed in close-up, and an alarmingly deep, monster voice. Like the alien dominatrices, she hounds the Dudes all through the movie. Having cornered them, she displays her lover, who appears to be a mustachioed woman, whom the transsexual woman kisses passionately. "Should we be grossed out by this?," one of the Dudes asks the other. The innocent way in which the question is posed lightly masks the obvious revulsion the movie feels towards the transsexual villainness. Without doubt, the film's depiction of the transsexual is offensive. Yet there's something else going on here, too—a kind of genuinely puzzled ambivalence over the rise of new forms of gendered identity. While it would be wrong to call this ambivalence a progressive statement, it would also be wrong to call it purely reactionary. In its own clumsy, dumb way, *Dude* labors on behalf of the youth culture it reflects and services, asking, "Dudes, *should* we be grossed out by this?" The movie leaves the Dudes and the teen audience in an ambiguous position— exposed to queer sexuality with no clear indication of how to respond.

Like *Dude*, *Scary Movie* represents queer concerns—including monstrous transsexuals and the fear of homosexuality—but only in service to an overall design of cruelty and phobia. Managing to be misogynistic, homophobic, racist, and unimaginative all at once may be a feat of some kind, but not one I wish to celebrate. *Scary Movie* threatens, at times, to be an interesting satire of the codes of white-teen privilege that provide the logic of teen horror films and most teen comedies, but its brutal mass slaughter of the black woman cancels out the possibility of such pointed satire.

The themes of homoeroticism that permeate the *American Pie* films and *Dude* achieve a grotesque realization here. In one scene, the character everyone believes is secretly gay goes into the restroom and finds a "glory hole," from which an extremely lifelike member pokes through. Intrigued, the closet case bends down to examine it, and the penis bursts through one ear and out the other. (He appears, however, to suffer only a mild earache.) The killers are revealed as queer, though the closet case violently denies it. It is of interest that the killer who denies being queer—Shawn Wayans's Ray—is African-American, while the one who affirms his queerness (only to have that affirmation mocked by Ray), Jon Abrahams's Bobby, is white. This uneasy moment in a film that is queasily full of them seems to suggest that homosexuality is a white boys' disease; it reaffirms conventional pop fantasies about the virility of black manhood by locating "actual" homosexuality in white rather than black men.

Scary Movie's ultimate allocation of homosexuality squarely to white males is suggestive. In terms of the homoerotic themes that circulate in them, the new teen comedies reflect the incoherence of the current state of that most controversial of social identities, white manhood. The films seem to be saying that—under pressure from feminism, racial tensions, emergent sexualities, and revisions in conventional codes of gender—white manhood is in a state of profound flux. The special world of boys depicted in these films then becomes a perfect arena in which these myriad tensions can battle—after all, the transitional state of teen manhood means nothing ever has to "stick."

To return to *American Pie*, the scene in which Nadia orders Jim to do a striptease for her bespeaks the incoherent state of white movie manhood. Jim's striptease—exuberant if gangly—signifies a new moment in American masculinity. Yes, Tom Cruise did dance in his underwear in *Risky Business* (1983), but Cruise gyrates in autoerotic isolation. In contrast, Jim gyrates for

NYU student Paul (Jason Biggs) and fellow student Dora (Mena Suvari) fall for each other in *Loser*. *(Photo by Gail Harvey, courtesy of Photofest)*

an audience—for Nadia and, unbeknownst to him, for the entire high school. The comedic edge of Biggs's dancing whittles down the sexually threatening nature of the scene. But the sheer energy and gusto of the striptease—at Nadia's behest—confirms his willing participation in the movie's construction of him as the object of Nadia's—and our—gaze. He has to strut his stuff and turn *us* on. No longer does Man wait to be turned on by what *he* gazes upon. Jim's striptease is a willing, and enthusiastic, recognition of men as the new sexual objects of our culture.

Jim's dancing for Nadia and the high-school audience (males and females) reflects the influence of a certain gay sensibility that has become more familiar since the politicized late Eighties and Nineties. The awareness that men can be perceived as objects of erotic contemplation—displayed by Jim's manic public display of his own sex-object status—is a gay idea that white, heterosexual, mainstream culture has now assimilated to some degree. Books, magazines, academic studies, and mass media are scrambling now to make up for the lack of a historical beauty culture for men.

Likewise, movies such as *There's Something About Mary* (1998) fore-grounds male sexuality through its ample discussions of messy orgasms and spewed semen (which Cameron Diaz mistakes for and uses as hair gel), or a scene in which crowds gather to watch Ben Stiller squirm in discomfort when his genitals are ensnared in his zipper. While such moments are not exactly paeans to homosexuality, they have facilitated a new openness about sexuality, the male body, and gender, which gay culture has traditionally expressed in its own folklore.

Yet straight male sexuality and bodies, despite their cinematic absorption of the new tensions and threats that surround them, remain, for all of these excesses, sacrosanct, hygienically cut off from the growing interest in their graphic representation. Two notable art-house films from last year—*Intimacy* and *Fat Girl*—not only featured nude men but also revealed their erect penises. Yet such displays are unimaginable in American cinema. Even an American film that obsessively privileges the white male body—last year's *Memento*, which fetishistically roams the expanse of Guy Pearce's extensively tattooed body—would never show full frontal male nudity.

This point is important as evidence that adult, white, heterosexual men remain—for all of the developments in male beauty culture, straight borrow-ings from gay culture, feminism, and so forth—cut off from the multifarious gazes of culture. Although Laura Mulvey's classic theory about the primacy of the "male gaze" may have to undergo some revision in the face of Jim's striptease, it remains relevant for the general, heterosexually oriented depic-tion of men in the cinema and on network TV. Herein lies the essential, inescapable conservatism of the teen comedies. Crammed with disorienting, occasionally bracing and shocking forays into socially perverse sexual and gen-dered territories, they nevertheless squarely situate these forays in the primeval forest of teendom, from which boys emerge as men. Kevin's strained attempts in *American Pie 2* to develop a mature friendship with Vicky, firmly entrenched in her cultural role as the aloof Woman, evinces not so much sensitivity and respect for women as it does an implicit acceptance of the inevitability of het-erosexual consummation—Kevin had better learn to treat women right if he's going to master them. The older, less boylike males of *American Pie 2* no longer need Kevin's vigilant prodding to seek out the successfully achieved adult heterosexuality that will confirm them as men.

The contemporary teen comedies have come to represent an infantile stage in American manhood—thus the preoccupation with bodily functions endemic to the current wave of gross-out humor. The boys in the teen comedies are really *boys*, not even proto-men, and are therefore allowed to grapple with the massive forces of cultural change that threaten conventional notions of white manhood without succumbing to them. The new American teen comedies, then, serve as consolatory catharses for white manhood. They suggest that exposure to homosexuality and the disabling power of strong women belong to the white male past — to that arrested but bygone period in which everything was up for grabs and the world had not yet been mastered. The teen comedies, therefore, incorporate as much sexual perversity and transgression as possible in order to make their ultimate evacuation of these perversities and transgressions total. For all of the impudence of the new American teen comedies, they amount to little more than a collective yearning for a discarded, amorphous age in the development of white manhood.

ELLEN GRUENBAUM

Female Genital Cutting: Culture and Controversy

Ellen Gruenbaum is Professor of Anthropology and Women's Studies at California State University, Fresno. Her research is in medical anthropology, and she is currently focusing on the rural communities of Sudan. She serves as a research consultant to UNICEF and CARE on the topic of female genital circumcision.

"Get away! What's the matter with you? You kids are behaving like a bunch of animals!" an older Sudanese woman yelled from inside the adobe brick room where the circumcision was to take place. She slapped the wire netting that screened the window and stomped outside to chase the small throng of laughing, curious children away from the window where they were peeking inside. She rounded the corner of the well-built rectangular adobe house and accosted the boys and girls at the window in a high-pitched, agitated voice, "Move on! See this switch? Let's go!" She smacked the ground threateningly with her long, thin stick, the sort commonly used to prod a wayward donkey or goat.

The children scattered. An older, more sensible boy took up a position near the window where he could keep the others away. The woman adjusted her long tobe, the over garment that covers the hair and body but not the face, and returned to the other women inside, who were preparing for the circumcisions. They had already moved one bed, made of wood and woven rope, into the center of the room where the trained midwife would have good light. The cotton mattresses on three beds where the children would recuperate were covered with clean cotton sheets and pillows. The midwife directed them to cover the bed for the surgeries with a red oilcloth over a cotton pillow and a pile of clean cloth scraps that could support a girl gently, and wash it with soap and water. They boiled water in a kettle on the charcoal fire, and the midwife prepared her instruments to be sterilized in an enamel bowl: a hypodermic, two sharp new razors, a curved suture needle, suturing thread, and a small scissors.

"Come, sit right close to me so you can see everything!" the midwife urged, motioning me to a small, low stool beside her. I hesitated, wondering if I would be able to watch the little girls experience the cutting that awaited them, known locally as "Pharaonic circumcision." But as an anthropologist doing research on rural health services and women's roles in this Sudanese village, I wanted this opportunity to observe, to be better able to understand and describe this important experience in the lives of girls. What I was about to witness was the most severe form of female genital cutting and closure (infibulation) found anywhere in Africa.

CLITORIDECTOMY, EXCISION, AND INFIBULATION

The term "female genital mutilation," or FGM, has been widely used in recent years, to describe various forms of "female circumcision" that are found in many countries. "Mutilation" is technically accurate for most variants of the practices since they entail damage to or removal of healthy tissues or organs. The provocative term, as well as the realities it conveys, has stimulated great international concern and action against the practices.

But since "mutilation" connotes intentional harm, its use is tantamount to accusing the women who do it of harmful intent. Some people, even those who favor stopping the practices, have been deeply offended by the term FGM, arguing that it is not women's intent to mutilate their daughters but to give them proper, socially expected treatment. Their intent is simply to "circumcise" or "purify." The words commonly used for female genital cutting in Arabic-speaking countries, *tahur* or *tahara*, means "purification," that is, the achievement of cleanliness through a ritual activity. "Female circumcision," however, echoes the term for the removal of the foreskin in the male, which has been considered non-mutilating (Toubia 1993:9) — at least until the recent movement to end that practice as well (see the work of the organization NOCIRC) — and is therefore rejected by many people, since it seems to trivialize the damage done and the huge scale of the practices. I prefer the term "Female Genital Cutting," or "FGC," which has become well established in international discourse: it avoids disparaging the practitioners yet does not minimize the seriousness of the issue.

There are several types of cutting and removal of tissues of genitalia of young girls and women, done to conform to social expectations in communities of many different religions and ethnicities. The form varies not only from one sociocultural context to another but even within a single village, such as the Sudanese village just described, where different ethnic groups do different types of cutting. Forms vary between families, too, with some preferring their ethnic group's traditional forms while other families seek less harmful forms. Also, trained midwives and other practitioners (including traditional birth attendants, other older women, barbers, and even medical doctors) have their own individual techniques of doing the procedures, resulting in varying amounts of tissue taken and various levels of hygiene. (In most countries, medical doctors are now strongly discouraged or forbidden by their professional organizations and governments from doing *any* form of FGC.)

In some cultural contexts, it is very young children who are cut, including infants or toddlers (Shandall 1967, Toubia 1993, 1994, Abdal Rahman

1997). Anne Jennings reported southern Egyptian girls undergoing genital cutting at age 1 or 2 (1995:48) Most commonly, it is done to young girls between the ages of 4 and 8. But in some cultural contexts (e.g. the Maasai of East Africa), cutting is delayed until a young woman is in her teens and about to be married (14–15 or even older).

In the past few years the World Health Organization has developed a comprehensive typology that technical experts use for the different types. People who practice female genital cutting have their own terms for different types in their many languages, of course, which mayor may not fit well with the World Health Organization's four types. Researchers can, however, place the range of the practices into the following categories.

Clitoridectomy. The World Health Organization's Type I includes both the partial and total removal of the clitoris, called clitoridectomy, and also the less severe forms of the operations, such as the cutting away of part or all of the clitoral prepuce, or "hood," analogous to the foreskin removal of male circumcision. Removal of only the prepuce seems to be very rare, but partial removal of the clitoris is fairly common.

Clitoridectomy, whether partial or total, is often referred to by Muslims and others as "*sunna* circumcision" or "*sunna* purification." In my experience doing ethnographic research in Sudan, the term "*sunna* circumcision" was in fact applied to a wide variety of surgeries, perhaps because of the positive association between that word and Muslim religious values.

Excision. The World Health Organization's Type II is called "excision." In this type, the cutting goes further than clitoridectomy to include removal of the prepuce, the entire clitoris, and partial or total excision of the labia minora (the smaller inner lips of the vaginal opening). In Sudan this form is usually also called "*sunna*," even though it is more damaging than what some people mean by "*sunna*." They are grouped in common parlance because there are just two basic folk terms—*sunna* and pharaonic circumcision— and they use the "*sunna*" terminology for both clitoridectomy and excision. In fact, it is often applied to any circumcisions that are not "pharaonic." Imprecise terms (such as *nuss* for "half") are also used for some of the in-between forms that would be included in Type II.

Infibulation and reinfibulation. The most severe cutting occurs with Type III, or infibulation. It is the main type in Sudan, where it is commonly called "pharaonic circumcision." People think it dates back to the days of the Pharaohs. In Egypt, where this severe infibulation is rare, it is called "Sudanese circumcision." In this type, part or all of the external genitalia— prepuce, clitoris, labia minora, and all or part of the labia majora—are removed and the raw edges are infibulated (held together by stitching or thorns). When healed, infibulation leaves a perfectly smooth vulva of skin and scar tissue with only a single tiny opening for urination and menstrual flow, preserved during healing by the insertion of a small object such as a piece of straw, In a variation of infibulation that is slightly less severe, the trimmed labia minora are sewn shut but the labia majora are left alone. In either case. it is essential that a midwife be present for childbirth to make an incision in the tissue to allow the baby to be born, The new mother often asks the midwife to make the opening very small, "like a virgin," to enhance her husband's sexual pleasure. This is analogous to, although more severe than, what some North American obstetricians do: take an extra stitch, called "the husband's stitch," when doing an episiotomy, for the purpose of restoring tightness to the opening.

Other variations. Others that do not include tissue removal are grouped as Type IV. This includes practices such as pricking, piercing, incision, stretching of the clitoris or labia, cauterization, cuts or scrapes on the genitalia, or the use of harmful substances in the vagina. Labia stretching to pursue culturally preferred aesthetics of the body is not particularly harmful, but other variations can be painful or damaging. In some East African countries, some men's preference for "dry sex" has resulted in the introduction of dangerous or uncomfortable astringents into the vagina to dry it out before intercourse, which is included in Type IV. In Europe and North America, the fad of labia piercing could be included as a Type IV practice.

HARMFUL EFFECTS

The harmful effects of these forms differ, but all forms—from clitoridectomy to infibulation—create risks for the girls at the time of cutting. Medical reports document cases of excess bleeding (hemorrhage), infections, blood poisoning (septicemia), retention of urine, or shock. Such complications can be life-threatening. Later on, the infibulated state sometimes results in retention of menses (if the vagina is blocked by scar tissue), difficulty in urination (if there is excess scar tissue around or over the urethra), and a high incidence of urinary tract and chronic pelvic infections. At first intercourse, the extremely small size of the opening created by infibulation presents a barrier which can make first sexual intercourse very difficult or impossible. Often the scar tissue around the opening must be painfully ruptured or is cut by the husband, a midwife, or a doctor. During childbirth, the inelastic scar tissue of infibulation must be cut by the birth attendant at the right time so labor will not be obstructed. Not only is obstructed labor dangerous to the baby, but also the mother's internal tissues can be damaged, creating a fistula (opening in the tissue separating the vagina from the urinary bladder), which can result in an embarrassing condition with constantly leaking urine (Shandall 1967, Shell-Duncan & Hernlund 2000b:14–18, Gruenbaum 2001, Toubia 1994).

The psychological effects are less well understood, not systematically researched, and no doubt differ a great deal from one situation to another. There is anecdotal evidence of adverse psychological effects, perhaps particularly if it comes without warning and seems a betrayal of trust. Yet many women simply accept the experience as just part of becoming a woman.

Damage to sexual responsiveness is suspected for many women, yet there is also data that suggests the frequency and extent of problems vary greatly. Many women do not lose sexual interest and retain the ability to achieve sexual satisfaction and orgasms, even among the infibulated (Gruenbaum 2001, chapter 5, and Lightfoot-Klein 1989). Sexual responsiveness could be affected differently depending on which tissues are cut and how, whether the surrounding or underlying tissues retain sensitivity, whether there is severe infibulation, and of course whether the emotional attachment of the partners is strong and the relationship loving and supportive. Some midwives have been careful to avoid cutting too much of the sensitive tissue (clitoris and erectile tissue) hoping to preserve sensitivity, but still make the result look like an infibulation by joining the labia across the opening.

It is therefore erroneous to assume that all women who have been cut have lost their sexual responsiveness. Similarly, although many experience very harmful medical consequences, many do not, so one cannot generalize about the effects without reference to the specific practices and circumstances.

But Why?

Indeed, the world wonders how loving parents can allow their daughters to be held down and cut, usually causing fear, pain, and possible major damage to health and physical functions, immediate or long-term. It seems incongruous and shocking to imagine a six-year-old girl enduring such pain and indignity, particularly at the hands of those she trusts.

Yet current estimates are that somewhere between 200,000 and a million girls experience some form of female genital cutting each year (Yoder 2003), mostly in 28 countries in Africa, and many millions of women and girls are living with FGC's life-long effects. In addition, the practices are found in other countries where they have spread by immigration or due to adoption of genital cutting if they believe it is associated with their religion. Why do women continue to arrange for these practices to be done to their daughters?

Is it because of any particular religion? No. The practices are found in many countries and among people of widely different ethnic groups and religions, including Judaism, Christianity, Islam, and traditional African religions. Yet it often happens that people who follow circumcision traditions often *do* associate the practices with their own religious beliefs.

For example, although many learned religious scholars have declared that infibulation has no place in Islam, and others say that no form whatsoever should be permitted, other teachers consider female circumcision as an "ennobling" act that is very proper for Muslims, so long as they don't go beyond clitoridectomy, which is usually called "*sunna* circumcision." The basic meaning of the Arabic word "*sunna*" is "tradition," which usually connotes the traditions of the Prophet Mohammed, i.e., those things that he did or advocated during his lifetime (570–622 C.E.), handed down through oral tradition and the writings know as the *Hadith*. Muslims believe the Holy Qur'an to be God's direct revelation, and the first source of guidance for righteous living, and it is silent on female circumcision. But Muslims also respect the sayings and actions attributed to the Prophet Mohammed during his lifetime as a secondary source of guidance. Although disputes remain among Muslims about which stories and quotations offer the most reliable versions of the Prophet's advice and how the sayings and stories should be interpreted, many Muslims have concluded that the Prophet Mohammed's words on the subject—"Reduce but do not destroy"—mean that only the less severe cutting is acceptable, though not required. Others believe the Prophet actually advocated it, making it either an obligation or at least a blessing to do it. Others believe Muslims should avoid female circumcision completely, since it is not mentioned in the Qur'an as a duty of the faithful. Using the term *sunna*, then, seems to imply that it is expected of Muslims, and while the term may help convince Muslims to give up infibulation, it may reinforce their continuing clitoridectomy. No doubt there will be many lively discussions among Muslim scholars in the coming years!

How about male dominance—is that the cause of this practice? Many analysts have noted that female genital cutting forms a part of the subordination of women where it is found. While of course not all strongly patriarchal societies of the world utilize female genital cutting, where it is found it is indeed embedded in the patriarchal structures of male domination of the lives of women and girls (Gruenbaum 2001, Shell-Duncan & Hernlund 2000a, Assaad 1980, Hayes 1975, El Saadawi 1980). That is not to say that women do not have any control or influence on the decisions, types, and timing of the cutting. And that does not mean it is always men who are pushing for it. Rather, the conditions of women's lives often encourage their participation in and celebration of the cutting, their advocacy or their tolerance of the rituals, and their willingness to endure or accept the health risks.

In analysis of several case examples, including my Sudanese research, the manifestation of male dominance is primarily in disparate economic and social circumstances of women and men. While women are usually economically productive (whether for the market economy or for subsistence), carry out important services in the domestic sphere, and have some distinctive rights in each of the different cultures of Africa, most societies nevertheless accord greater political and economic power to men, especially older and more dominant and successful men. Economic and social situations of women vary a great deal—traders/market women have their own incomes to spend and farming women may have sources of income they use to help support their families or provide for their personal needs, but in many cultures, a woman's access to economic resources is mediated by men. In Islamic law, Muslim women are entitled to own and manage property, but the inheritance rules favor men—a daughter receives half the share of a son, for example. Even then, local groups often expect daughters not to claim shares, so that their brothers can be more secure, arguing that women are entitled to rely on husbands and male kin for support and should not need separate holdings. In other cultures, women may be dependent on men for access to land, livestock, foodstuffs, a share of a husband's income, and old-age support by sons. But women are vulnerable to divorce or polygyny that might reduce their security. If economic security and socially-approved reproduction are mediated by the dominant roles of men, women dearly need to conform to whatever rules the culture requires, including varying expectations for virginity, excision, or infibulation in order to have successful marriages and child-bearing. Their enculturation process must prepare girls for their subordinate roles.

Women's consciousness regarding their positions may range from strong belief in the moral superiority of men, to wry acceptance of the role disparity, to willingness to challenge the status quo in favor of better futures. But given the power of social pressure and the rewards of acceptance of genital cutting—propriety, marriage, children, and financial support—it should not be surprising that most women have not yet jumped on the bandwagon of abandoning female genital cutting.

CULTURAL CONTEXTS AND PEOPLE'S REASONS

The explicit reasons people give for circumcising their daughters are varied, depending on the cultural contexts in which FGC practices occur. For some, genital cutting is a rite of passage to marriageable womanhood. The Maasai of Kenya, for example, usually wait until a girl's marriage has been arranged, and she is then excised (Type II) and her head is shaved during the weeks of marriage preparations. After she has healed she goes to her husband and new home ready for womanhood.

Female genital cutting often plays a role in gender identity. Some even use terms like "male parts" for the clitoris and labia, saying removal of them results in a more feminine and aesthetically pleasing body. In many of the Nile Valley cultures of Egypt and Sudan, genital cutting helps to define feminine gender and is considered an essential prerequisite to marriage. Nile Valley girls are cut at earlier ages, so that they will be known to be virgins and ready for socially approved marriage when old enough.

The type of circumcision done sometimes defines ethnic identity. Even within a single village, such as the Sudanese village described above, different ethnic groups do different types of cutting. Thus, the Zabarma and Hausa minorities who have immigrated to Sudan anywhere from a century ago to more recent decades have usually resisted adopting infibulation, yet some have also adopted it along with other changes as part of their cultural and linguistic acculturation to the dominant Arab-Sudanese culture.

Some practitioners in Sudan advocated genital cutting as a way to preserve virginity. Not only is cutting expected to reduce some sexual sensitivity, thought to help girls and wives resist improper sexual relationships by taming what are thought to be overly powerful female sexual impulses, but also the infibulation is an actual barrier to penetration, preventing pre-marital pregnancy. People have even speculated, without any confirmation, that the practice may have developed in ancient times as a measure to prevent rape by strangers passing through on trade routes.

The Big Day

The morning cool was beginning to fade, and the day promised to be hot and dry, as usual. The midwife washed her hands thoroughly with soap and water, shook off the water, and let them dry. The two pretty little girls were guided through the door by their mother. Recently bathed, hair freshly plaited and dotted with some henna paste, the girls wore colorful new dresses and special ornaments known as *jirtig*, as protection against excessive blood loss or the harm that might be done by spirits (*jinn*). The family's gold jewelry was ready for them to put on during recovery. They looked proud, though a little anxious, about this first time to be treated as such special people.

Their male cousin, about 7, lay silently on a bed in the corner, his face to the wall. Earlier in the morning he had been taken by car to the small hospital in a town several kilometers away to be circumcised by a medical assistant. When he returned, he was greeted with celebratory ululations and helped into a bed in the corner of this room to recover.

As the dozen women present greeted the mother and girls with smiles and encouragement, the mother hesitated, reconsidering the wisdom of doing the younger, who looked to be only about four years old. The other was six, the best age to be able to complete healing before starting school. But there were many advantages to cutting three children the same day, since the families could share the expenses of the celebration and not have to do it again in two years for the younger one. The midwife and the others quickly overcame the mother's hesitation, urging her to do it right away. Don't worry, it will soon be over, she's already prepared, and, as the saying goes, "You grow up, you forget" (*Tekbara, tensa*). Outside, other relatives and neighbors were cooking over charcoal fires, preparing a dried meat and yogurt stew, beans, bread, tea, and sweets for the well-wishers expected to begin arriving soon. The ceremony would not be easily delayed.

So, both girls were cut, the younger first. Thankfully the midwife's methods were fairly hygienic, not like the old methods, when the cutting was done using broken glass or an unsterilized knife with thorns for sutures. This midwife's better techniques were respected, as her patients usually avoided the worst complications. The first girl was washed carefully, held by loving but firm arms of the women, and injected—painfully—with the local anesthetic xylocaine into her clitoris, prepuce, and labia to deaden the feeling. A few minutes later, she was cut carefully, avoiding major arteries. She did not feel any pain when her prepuce, clitoris, and labia minora (inner lips) were cut off with one of the sterilized razor blades. Her labia majora (outer lips) were trimmed slightly and the two sides sutured together with the curved needle so they could heal with a smooth surface, leaving just one opening for urine and future menstrual flow. The second girl was done the same way, and after each cutting, the midwife rinsed the wound with an antiseptic, sprinkled the wound with antibiotic powder, and gave the girl some aspirin. Amid celebratory ululating, each girl was moved to a side bed to recover.

As soon as the work was completed, the bed cleaned up, and bowl with the discarded tissues carried out, adult well-wishers, both men and women, began arriving. They congratulated each child and tucked a little money under their pillows, then moved outside to share in the breakfast meal that the families had prepared. It was a joyful occasion of visiting and drinking tea. Meanwhile, as the local anesthetic wore off, the newly circumcised children endured their pain with aspirin and loving mothers.

But What About Girls' and Women's Human Rights?

Did these young girls consent to this cutting? They appeared to be willing. Of course in other places where girls are not informed beforehand, the practice is to surprise the girl and circumcision is carried out by force (see for example El-Saadawi for Egypt) it is obvious that such girls did not consent. But it is also quite common in Sudan and other countries for older girls to make fun of younger uncircumcised girls, teasing them with peer pressure until the younger girls' enviousness of being a big girl (i.e., circumcised) leads them to nag their mothers to let them be cut. Or suppose you grow up simply knowing that it will happen, and when your mother prepares the new dress, fusses over getting you ready, and tells you the big day has arrived, you go willingly, trusting your mother that it is for the best? Have you given your informed consent?

People concerned about the human rights of children would say no. At 5 or 6 years of age, one is by no means fully informed about the risks and consequences. A girl probably has no idea about sexual pleasure or infections or childbirth. Similarly, if you live in a culture where arranged marriages are common, and at 13 your father and mother arrange for you to get married to a groom they have selected for you, would you be able to speak up for yourself? Like so many other girls, you would probably feel you had no choice, or you would trust that your parents know best and accept the situation.

Both are violations of what have come to be understood as human rights for girls—the right to bodily integrity (that is, not to have her body permanently altered) and the right to consent to or decline to marry. Both of these clearly have not always been accepted as rights and certainly are not yet accepted in many societies. But should they be rights? The international community increasingly agrees that they should be, although there is no general agreement on what the age of consent should be: 16? 18? Most of the world's countries are signatories to agreements like the Convention on Elimination of All Forms of Discrimination Against Women, the Convention on the Rights of the Child, and other international agreements that stand against violations of girls' and women's rights, but not all enforce them.

Bodily integrity is something an adult woman can decide for herself. In the United States or Europe, it is accepted that someone over 18 is free to get tattoos or consent to having her labia pierced if she wishes. But to impose a decision on a child that will permanently alter her body, even if she is passively acquiescing, is to deny her right to make that decision when she is old enough to understand the consequences.

So, What's Being Done About Female Genital Cutting?

As you might expect, many who learn about female genital cutting practices respond with outrage and take strong positions against the practices. Outsiders often have evoked horrible stereotypes of malicious intent, condemning the people who practice such genital cutting of girls as intending to "torture" females or "deprive women of their sexuality."

Local reformers sometimes engage in similar strongly worded condemnations in international discourse. But grassroots change agents realize that inflammatory rhetoric and "preaching" alone are not likely to change strongly held values and traditions. Reformers recognize that it may take some time to enlist local practitioners in the change process, so they have patiently promoted health education that they hope will lead people to voluntarily abandon female genital cutting. Others have introduced alternate rituals that contribute to the social goals, for example a rite of passage for maturing girls that substitutes for a traditional ritual of circumcision, but without the physical harm of cutting. Meanwhile, a large number of countries are also pursuing legal reforms and policy changes to criminalize or otherwise discourage the cutting of underage girls. (See Rahman and Toubia, 2000, for an international comparison of laws and policies on female genital cutting.)

But the first step in changing anything is to understand what it means to the people who do it. With more insight, we can better understand why people have resisted widespread change and why some are now pursuing change. Many writers, particularly social scientists and public health researchers, have tried to improve the understanding of people's reasons for genital cutting without condemning the people who have followed their traditional practices (Boddy 1982, Cloudsley 1983, Gruenbaum 1982, 1996, 2001, El Dareer 1982, Obermeyer 2003).

In the Sudanese villages I studied, female genital cutting still persists, but change is in progress. In one village in the Gezira area, over the past twenty years female circumcision has become an increasingly important topic for discussions. Some mothers have quietly arranged to have their daughters be cut less severely, moving from severe infibulation to preserving more of the tissue and not closing the opening as much. Others have gone further, dropping infibulation and doing only Type II or Type I, resisting the social pressure to conform.

A few years later, when I interviewed the midwife from the descriptions above on a return visit, she said she hoped to change over to doing only the milder *sunna*, but the vast majority of her clients still wanted infibulations. Her changing attitude was encouraged by the government trained medical assistant at their local clinic, who was taking an active role in persuading people to stop infibulating. The public health discussions that have been held separately among the women, among the men, among school boys, and among girls, have resulted in greater willingness to talk about modification, a moderate change, though not total abandonment. Throughout the country, doctors and other medical personnel have decided to actively oppose all forms of female genital cutting. A law against the severe form, dating back to 1946, had seldom been enforced, but recently, the government of Sudan is showing renewed interest in enforcement of the laws against all forms of female genital cutting.

Stated intentions, of course, are not always realized, especially when there is such opposition. Nevertheless it is encouraging that grassroots developments, education, and organized public health education are having an effect to reduce the incidence of new cases.

SOCIAL MOVEMENTS FOR CHANGE

Successful social change requires widespread support, not merely written laws and policies. How will that support be won? Reformers need to endeavor to fully understand people's reasons. As Gerry Mackie has noted, "The followers of mutilation are good people who love their children; any campaign that insinuates otherwise is doomed to provoke defensive reaction" (Mackie 1996: 1015).

But remaining detached and uninvolved with this serious problem tests the ethical limits of "cultural relativism" (the respect that anthropologists use to try to understand each culture in its own terms rather than to judge it ethnocentrically by the values of another culture). The World Health Organization, the United Nations Children's Fund (UNICEF) and United Nations Population Fund issued a joint statement in 1996:

It is unacceptable that the international community remain passive in the name of a distorted vision of multiculturalism. Human behaviours and cultural values, however senseless or destructive they may appear from the personal and cultural standpoint of others, have meaning and fulfil a function for those who practise them. However, culture is not static but it is in constant flux, adapting and reforming. People will change their behaviour when they understand the hazards and indignity of harmful practices and when they realize that it is possible to give up harmful practices without giving up meaningful aspects of their culture.

Both elements are necessary to a successful change effort aimed at a cultural practice: a deep understanding of people's reasons and motivations for keeping a practice, yet recognition of the flexibility of culture. People have demonstrated many times that cultures can adapt, and people can make changes when convinced of the need without losing cultural identity and meaning. Ultimately, it is up to them to decide when the time is ripe, but can efforts within a cultural group and efforts from outside accelerate the process?

Opinion leaders and grassroots activists, working in different ways, are vital to social change, An outspoken critic of the Islamist government of Sudan and a long-time supporter of the leftist movement there, Fatima Ibrahim challenged the government's interpretation of Islam, and argued that the Islamic religion can be used to *support* women's rights and social justice. The Medical Assistant who holds discussions about FGC in the village where he works, the doctor who studies Islamic texts to help her clarify the limits of *sunna* circumcision to the medical establishment, the midwife who tries to convince her clients to do milder forms or none at all—all of these that I observed in Sudan are helping to prepare for change.

In the past two decades organized efforts for change throughout the African countries affected have accelerated dramatically, as international and non-governmental organizations have become involved and as African women have moved into leadership positions in speaking out about female genital cutting. International organizations, such as the InterAfrican Committee Against Harmful Traditional Practices, have taken a lead role in conducting public health education by organizing discussion groups in towns and villages. The World Health Organization has taken on the anti-circumcision work, as have other international organizations. Can such a message be carried forward effectively, so that female circumcision might actually be ended soon?

OBSTACLES TO CHANGE: RISK OF *NOT* CUTTING

The social conditions that act as barriers to parents taking the risk of leaving their daughters uncircumcised help to explain resistance to change (Gruenbaum 1990). No matter how clever the public health education message on the hazards of cutting or how authoritative the religious sources that say it is unnecessary, parents know that it *is* necessary if it is the prerequisite for their daughter's marriageability and long-term social and financial security. Even when the religious authorities speak against the practices and medical risks are known, these may not be sufficient reasons for parents to risk their daughters' marriageability and long-term security.

To counteract the social risks there are a number of possible directions for policymakers and change agents to address. One is to reduce the economic dependency of women. Better educational opportunities and employment opportunities would allow young women and their families to see delayed marriage as something other than a disaster. Daughters could be encouraged more in their education and careers, secure in the knowledge that although marriage is desirable, failure to marry or loss of spouse will not necessarily result in penury and dependence on male relatives. Better support for inheritance rights of women might help.

This is indeed a part of the change process that I have observed in Sudan. The teachers, professors, public health workers, students and other activists now working on reform are, as a result of their awareness, literacy, and cosmopolitan outlook, better able to confidently state that female circumcision can be left behind, that it is both harmful to health and not Islamic. Such women are confident that they will have a say in the decision on the circumcision of daughters, and they endeavor to provide their daughters with the educational opportunities needed to be self-reliant.

But even educated and confident women cannot be certain their uncircumcised daughters will be marriageable. If the young men in the community remain committed to marrying infibulated brides, a daughter's education may preserve her from poverty, but it will not assure her of marriage and children. The risk is lessened if there are social and familial ties to progressive families where men prefer *sunna* or no circumcision.

But as this cultural debate unfolds (Gruenbaum 1996), it is encouraging that some young men do state their preference for uninfibulated brides. One educated young man I knew in Khartoum told me he had insisted that the family not infibulate his sister, and he swore he would not marry an infibulated woman, even if she were a cousin. But will he or others like him actually refuse to marry a cousin the family expects him to marry? Or would he refuse to marry the young woman who has caught his eye, simply because she is infibulated? And can young men effectively prevent their sisters' circumcisions? How do families cope with the risk that there may not be men like this for their daughters to marry?

Risk avoidance remains the most significant factor to explaining why otherwise well informed families cling to female genital cutting practices. Gerry Mackie offered a provocative exploration of the risks involved in such social changes by comparing efforts to end infibulation and excision in Africa with the process of ending the painful, crippling footbinding of girls (i.e., tightly binding their small feet so they would not grow) practiced in China for centuries. Footbinding, which lasted until the early 20th century, was also related to making daughters marriageable (Mackie 1996).

While there had been efforts to change footbinding historically, parents were afraid to be the first to change, since men sought to marry women with tiny feet only. However, once a critical mass of people was persuaded of its harm through educational campaigns, they found they could take the risk of change when, with other parents, they pledged not to let their daughters' feet be bound nor let their sons marry women with bound feet. The movement led to wholesale abandonment of footbinding in a single generation (Mackie 1996:1001). Pledge groups do function in African societies for various purposes, so now that there is growing awareness of the risks of female genital cutting, perhaps people will develop this pledge idea for female genital cutting as well.

Thus, despite the spread of female genital cutting and its tenacity, there is no reason to conclude that it cannot change rapidly in the coming years, when people have learned enough about the issue and when they believe the risks of not doing it are not too high. The conditions are ripe for change in infibulation and excision practices in Africa. The international activism, the efforts at culturally appropriate approaches, and the emergence of, and a degree of support for, indigenous leaders of the movement make this an excellent time, if the additional resources can be mobilized, for rapid change to occur. Indeed, the World Health Organization, UNICEF, and the United Nations Population Fund have announced a joint plan to "significantly curb female genital mutilation over the next decade and completely eliminate the practice within three generations" (Reaves 1997).

To mobilize the Islamic religious arguments against infibulation—i.e., claiming only *sunna* is permitted for Muslims—often results in people favoring *sunna*, allowing them to continue to reject total abandonment of all forms. Reformers debate the wisdom of this: although abandoning infibulation constitutes a definite improvement in the health of women and girls, what public health officials have often advocated as "harm reduction," it might result in even stronger belief in the Islamic rightness of the remaining form, clitoridectomy, which might delay the demise of *all* forms.

ALTERNATIVE RITES

Even where circumcisions continue in Sudan, the celebration of it has lessened. Whether that indicates a decline in importance of the event or is due to harsh economic conditions is not clear, but even wealthy families have curtailed the celebrations. Reduction in celebrations suggests that cutting is beginning to lose its symbolic power, and might in a few years decline.

An extremely positive development in the last few years has been even more explicit changes in the way circumcision is celebrated in several areas where activists have been at work. Recognizing that circumcision is a rite of passage in many of the places where it is practiced, reformers have begun to introduce alternative ways to mark these important life transitions without involving the usual genital cutting. One good example comes from Kenya, where rural families have been adopting an alternative rite to circumcision over the last few years, known as "Circumcision Through Words" (*Ntanira na Mugambo*). As described by Malik Stan Reaves (1997), groups of families have participated in bringing together their appropriate-aged daughters to spend a week of seclusion learning their traditions concerning women's roles as adults and as future parents. The Kenyan national women's group, Maendeleo ya Wanawake Organization, worked with international collaborators to develop this program to include self-esteem and dealing with peer pressure, along with traditional values, as well as messages on personal health and hygiene, reproductive issues, and communications skills. At the end of the week of seclusion, a community celebration of feasting, singing, and dancing affirms the girls' transition to their new status.

Such approaches recognize that female circumcision has deep cultural significance, and if that significance can be preserved while the actual cutting is discontinued, there is strong hope that change can be rapid. Indeed, Reaves quotes the Chair of the Maendeleo ya Wanawake Organization, Zipporah Kittonysaid, as saying she was "overjoyed" to see the positive response and believes it was a critical achievement toward the eradication of female circumcision (Reaves 1997). This project serves as an excellent example of combining local initiative, international expertise, preparatory research and community discussion, and support from private foundations (including the Moriah Fund, Ford, Population Action International/Wallace Global Fund, and Save the Children–Canada) to accomplish a culturally sensitive alternative to female circumcision.

PUBLIC HEALTH EDUCATION

Poster campaigns, teachers on lecture tours, training for health workers, and public health announcements in the media have all been used at various times and places for several decades to spread the word on the dangers of female genital cutting. In the past two decades, the movement has accelerated, with more respectful and effective teaching tools and methods available. The Inter-African Committee, for example, uses a technique that involves sending a woman health worker into a marketplace where women are found, and striking up a discussion. She asks questions like "What do you think, is female circumcision a good tradition?" Rather than preaching, she listens to what they have to say, what their beliefs are. "Are you aware of the hazards?" leads to a discussion of the short and long term complications.

The educator encourages women to bring up their beliefs and then discusses them respectfully. For example, there is an erroneous belief in some countries that if the clitoris touches the baby's head at birth the baby will die. An educator brought the idea up in one such discussion filmed by the Inter-African Committee for their film *Female Circumcision: Beliefs and Misbeliefs* (1992), and the health worker explained that that was not possible. She also discussed other potentially harmful traditional practices such as nutritional taboos and marrying too young, encouraging the women to offer opinions and discuss their ideas with each other.

The work of national women's organizations in the countries affiliated with the Inter-African Committee is having a positive effect. Through such means as community discussions, formal classes with anatomical teaching aids, and organizing in villages willing to undergo friendly "inspections" of their baby girls, to show the success of the message, each national committee is reporting progress. The Sudan National Committee for Traditional Harmful Practices, for example, has many rural branches now, and although their efforts were met with resistance initially, their work is now better received according to the Executive Secretary, Amna Abdel Rahman Hassan (2002). Rogaia Abusharaf noted that the Sudan National Committee consistently avoids making female circumcision a separate issue, but always discusses it as one among several reproductive health issues (1999). Discussing child spacing, contraceptive use, and maternal and child health first, women are better prepared to consider not only the anti-circumcision message but also their well-being and rights.

TAKING A STANCE?

Regardless of the emotional or moral response one may feel about these situations, it is my opinion that those who are committed to improving the lives of women and girls must channel their responses into change efforts that are culturally informed and socially contextualized if they are to be effective. Anthropologists commonly advocate using cultural relativism to encourage people to overcome their prejudicial and ethnocentric tendencies and learn to understand cultures in their own terms. People who have been raised with the values and practices of their own culture, values and practices that have developed in adaptation to their own environment and social experiences, can be expected to have great faith in their own traditions. People are usually very unwilling to be judged according to, or expected to conform to, some other culture's values. So anthropologists rely on the mental exercise and teaching tool of cultural relativism to cultivate respect for cultural difference and enhance our ability to be analytical rather than ethnocentrically judgmental.

But that does not mean that we cannot discuss cultural practices in terms of their consequences, whether apparently neutral, helpful to some (e.g., to the preservation of identity), or harmful in certain respects (e.g., resulting in increased rates of infections). Indeed, most cultural practices are contested even within a cultural group: women and men may see things differently. Calm elders and testosterone-influenced youth may differ on when to fight. Men of a culture may like the "double standard" of sexual liberty for themselves but faithfulness for their wives, while the women have a different view of this.

As our human dialogs among cultures expand among societies and we humans try to agree on health protection measures or human rights protections, each culture must stretch a little as new information, experiences, and knowledge affect them. Once we have accepted that culture is dynamic and each of us is a citizen of a multi-cultural planet, it becomes easier to engage in respectful discussion, rather than the denunciation or preaching that often results from those who take a strong, absolute position in their interactions.

What feminist does not have respect for women's voices and their process of setting their own priorities, whether it be to end a war, get clean water, or change a traditional practice they have been questioning? What humanist can refuse to listen to the voices of women telling us of *their* priorities? And often anthropologists and public health workers, aware of possible harm from a practice, conduct a respectful dialog about it with people of another culture? Many anthropologists choose to advocate respectfully for change, and that is entirely in keeping with professional work in applied anthropology. But at other times an anthropologist steps back to observe, understand, and analyze in a non-interfering fashion, knowing that could be useful both for promoting mutual understanding and for assisting change agents.

As I see it, female genital cutting practices are changing and appear to be on their way to eventual abandonment as people become more knowledgeable, have alternative options that serve the same identity goals and promote values concerning morality, and become better able to resist the risks of change. Outsiders can help most effectively by offering understanding, respect, and support for grassroots and international change efforts, not only on female genital cutting but also on the *many* issues faced by the women and children of poor countries. It's fine to take a strong position ("I think people should stop doing this!"). But it's equally important to learn respectful dialog for those who do not see it your way.

My personal view is one of respectful challenge. As an anthropologist, my first commitment is to research and promote understanding, but as a humanist, I do not recoil from engagement in fostering improvements of the human condition. Female genital cutting practices vary so much that they clearly are not equally harmful. But because they are performed on non-consenting children, the human rights stance of total opposition to all forms, based on a right to bodily integrity, is ultimately hard to refute. [That principle would also prohibit male infant circumcision and ear-piercing of babies and toddlers, perhaps even extraction of a 12-year-old's teeth for orthodontia, so there are many ethical discussions to be had!] At the same time, my cultural relativism leads me to respect the values people choose to live by, recognizing that people themselves will make their future and choose when and how to change.

Thus, for outsiders, it has little practical consequence whether one is "for it" or "against it," since it is only the practitioners themselves who are in a position to abandon female genital cutting. What really matters is that we engender the respect and understanding for dialog to take place. That requires a respectful "cultural relativist" understanding on which to build the dialog for change, but anthropologists also recognize that "culture" is always contested and changing. Change is inevitable, and the world community should offer practitioners of female genital cutting not racist or ethnocentric condemnation, but understanding and listening. The international community can foster respectful dialog, help deliver information, and offer help with alternatives and improvement of underlying conditions that perpetuate the practices. Women and children living in poverty or marginal economic circumstances without the comforts of clean water, decent housing, adequate food resources, educational opportunities, job opportunities, electricity, or immunizations and basic health services may have social change agendas for their lives that do not list ending female genital cutting as their top priority. The international community would be wise to listen to African women and offer international assistance for their highest priorities as well.

While students, policy-makers, and the general public engage in disputes about female genital cutting, listening to the ideas of those affected and including attention to questions of context, motive, perspective, and the process of persuasion can only help. Change will need deep thinkers with passionate hearts and caring words.

BIBLIOGRAPHY

Abdalla, Raqiya Haji Dualeh. 1982. *Sisters in Affliction: Circumcision and Infibulation of Women in Africa.* London: Zed Press.

Abdal Rahman, Awatif. 1997. Member of the Sudan National Committee on Harmful Traditional Practices, quoted in Reuter report, "Sudan Tackles 'Silent Issue' of Female Circumcision," Feb. 20.

Abusharaf, Rogaia. 1999. Personal communication, Nov. 18.

Assaad, Marie Bassili. 1980. "Female Circumcision in Egypt: Social Implications, Current Research, and Prospects for Change." *Studies in Family Planning* 11, No. 1:3–16.

Cloudsley, Anne. 1983. *Women of Omdurman: Life, Love, and the Cult of Virginity.* London: Ethnographia.

Boddy, Janice. 1989. *Wombs and Alien Spirits: Women, Men, and the Zar Cult in Northern Sudan.* Madison: University of Wisconsin Press.

El Dareer, Asma. 1982. *Woman, Why Do You Weep? Circumcision and Its Consequences.* London: Zed Press.

El Sadaawi, Nawal. 1980a. "Creative Women in Changing Societies: A Personal Reflection." *Race and Class* 22, No. 2:159–82.

————. 1980b. *The Hidden Face of Eve: Women in the Arab World*. London: Zed Press.

Gruenbaum, Ellen. 1982. "The Movement Against Clitoridectomy and Infibulation in Sudan. *Medical Anthropology Newsletter* 13, no. 2:4–12. (Reissued in 1997 in *Gender in Cross-Cultural Perspective*, 2d ed., ed. Caroline Brettell and Carolyn Sargent, pp. 441–53. Upper Saddle River, NJ.: Prentice Hall.)

Gruenbaum, Ellen. 1996. "The Cultural Debate Over Female Circumcision: The Sudanese Are Arguing This One Out for Themselves." *Medical Anthropology Quarterly* 10, no. 4:455–75.

————. 2001. *The Female Circumcision Controversy: An Anthropological Perspective*. Philadelphia: University of Pennsylvania Press.

Hassan, Amna Abdal Rahman, Executive Secretary of the Sudan National Committee Against Harmful Traditional Practices, personal communication, 2002.

Jennings, Anne. 1995. *The Nubians of West Aswan: Village Women in the Midst of Change*. Boulder, CO: Lynne Rienner.

Mackie, Gerry. 1996. "Ending Footbinding and Infibulation." *American Sociological Review* 61: 991–1017.

————. 2000. "Female Genital Cutting: The Beginning of the End." *In* Shell-Duncan and Hernlund 2000: 253–281.

Obermeyer, Carla Maklouf. 2003. "The Health Consequences of Female Circumcision: Science, Advocacy, and Standards of Evidence," *Medical Anthropology Quarterly*.

Rahman, Anika, and Nahid Toubia. 2000. *Female Genital Mutilation: A Guide to Worldwide Laws and Policies*. London: Zed Press.

Reaves, Stanley. 1997. "Alternative Rite to Female Circumcision Spreading in Kenya." Africa News Services. Nov. 19.

Shandall, Ahmed Abu El Futuh. 1967. "Circumcision and Infibulation of Females." *Sudan Medical Journal* 5, no. 4:178–212.

Shell-Duncan, Bettina, and Ylva Hernlund, eds. 2000a. *Female "Circumcision" in Africa: Culture, Controversy, and Change*. Boulder, CO: Lynne Rienner.

Shell-Duncan, Bettina, and Ylva Hernlund. 2000b. "Female 'Circumcision' in Africa: Dimensions of the Practice and Debates." *In* Shell-Duncan and Hernlund, eds., 2000a:1–40.

Toubia, Nahid. 1993. *Female Genital Mutilation: A Call for Global Action*. New York: Women, Ink.

————. 1994. "Female Circumcision as a Public Health Issue." *New England Journal of Medicine* 331, no. 11 (Sept. 15):712–16.

————. 1996. Interview on "Fresh Air." National Public Radio.

Yoder, Stan. 2003. Personal communication, July 29.

RUTH HUBBARD
Rethinking Women's Biology

Ruth Hubbard is Professor Emerita of Biology at Harvard University. In 1967, she became the first woman to be awarded a tenured biology professorship at Harvard. The following selection is from her book, The Politics of Women's Biology *(1990).*

Women's biology is a social construct, and a political concept, not a scientific one, and I mean that in at least three ways. The first can be summed up in Simone de Beauvoir's (1953) dictum "One isn't born a woman, one becomes a woman." This does not mean that the environment shapes us, but that the concept, woman (or man), is a socially constructed one that little girls (or boys) try to fit as we grow up. Some of us are better at it than others, but we all try, and our efforts have biological as well as social consequences (a false dichotomy because our biological and social attributes are related dialectically). How active we are, what clothes we wear, what games we play, what we eat and how much, what kinds of schools we go to, what work we do, all affect our biology as well as our social being in ways we cannot sort out. So, one isn't born a woman (or man), one becomes one.

The concept of women's biology is socially constructed, and political, in a second way because it is not simply women's description of our experience of our biology. We have seen that women's biology has been described by physicians and scientists who, for historical reasons, have been mostly economically privileged, university-educated men with strong personal and political interests in describing women in ways that make it appear "natural" for us to fulfill roles that are important for their well-being, personally and as a group. Self-serving descriptions of women's biology date back at least to Aristotle. But if we dismiss the early descriptions as ideological, so are the descriptions scientists have offered that characterize women as weak, overemotional, and at the mercy of our raging hormones, and that construct our entire being around the functions of our reproductive organs. No one has suggested that men are just walking testicles, but again and again women have been looked on as though they were walking ovaries and wombs.

In the nineteenth century, when women tried to get access to higher education, scientists initially claimed we could not be educated because our brains are too small. When that claim became untenable, they granted that we could be educated the same as men but questioned whether we should be, whether it was good for us. They based their concerns on the claim that girls need to devote much energy to establishing the proper functioning of their ovaries and womb and that if they divert this energy to their brains by studying, their reproductive organs will shrivel, they will become sterile, and the race will die out.

This logic was steeped in race and class prejudice. The notion that women's reproductive organs need careful nurturing was used to justify excluding upper-class girls and young women from higher education but not to spare the working-class, poor, or black women who were laboring in the factories and homes of the upper class. If anything, these women were said to breed too much. In fact, their ability to have many children despite the fact that they worked so hard was taken as evidence that they were less highly evolved than upper-class women; for them breeding was "natural," as for animals.

Finally, and perhaps most importantly, our concept of ourselves is socially constructed and political because our society's interpretation of what is and is not normal and natural affects what we do. It therefore affects our biological structure and functioning because . . . what we do and how our bodies and minds function are connected dialectically. Thus norms are self-fulfilling prophecies that do not merely describe how we are but prescribe how we should be.

BODY BUILD AND STRENGTH

Let us consider a few examples. We can begin with a few obvious ones, such as height, weight, and strength. Women and men are physically not very different. There are enormous overlaps between women and men for all traits that are not directly involved with procreation.

For example, there is about a two-foot spread in height among people in the United States, but a difference of only three to five inches between the average heights of women and men. When we say men are taller than women, what we really mean is that the abstraction *average (or mean) height* is a few inches greater for men than women. Overall, women and men are about the same height, with many women as tall as, or taller than, lots of men. The impression that women are shorter than men is enhanced by our social convention that when women and men pair off it is considered preferable for the man to be taller than the woman. In some countries, such as Bali, differences in height and, indeed, overall body build are much smaller than in the United States (Lowe, 1982).

Clearly, height is affected by social factors, such as diet. In the early part of this century, English working-class men were significantly shorter, on average, than men from the upper class, and this difference in height was due to differences not just in the adequacy but in the composition of their diets—proportions of carbohydrates, proteins, fats, vitamins. In the United States we are familiar with a similar phenomenon when comparing the heights of immigrants and their U.S.-born children. We have tended to think that the U.S.-born children are taller than their immigrant parents because they get a better diet. But now that we are learning more about the health hazards of the typical U.S. diet, with its excessive fat and protein content, we should probably defer value judgments and just acknowledge that the diets are different.

Sex differences in height probably also arise from the differences in growth patterns between girls and boys. Until early adolescence, girls, on average, are taller than boys, but girls' growth rates tend to decrease after they begin to menstruate, whereas, boys continue to grow throughout their teens. It is generally assumed that this difference is due to the fact that the increase in estrogen levels after the onset of menstruation tends to slow the growth of girls' long bones. But the age of onset of menstruation, hence of increased estrogen secretion, depends on a number of social factors, such as diet, exercise and stress (Frisch, 1988). For example, female swimming champions, who, because of their intense, early training, tend to begin to menstruate later than most girls, tend also to be taller than average. We might therefore expect factors that delay the onset of menstruation to decrease the difference in average height between women and men, those that hasten the onset of menstruation to increase it.

It is probably not that simple because the factors that affect the onset of menstruation may also affect height in other ways. All I want to suggest is that height, in part, is a social variable and that differences in the average height of women and men vary with the social environment.

Weight clearly has considerable social components. Different societies have different standards of beauty for women, and many of these involve differences in desirable weight. Today we call the women in Rubens's paintings fat and consider Twiggy anorexic. In our society changes in style not just of clothing but of body shape are generated, at least in part, because entire industries depend on our not liking the way we look so that we will buy the products that promise to change it. To some extent this is true also for men: Padded shoulders are not that different from padded bras. But there is more pressure on women to look "right," and what is "right" changes frequently and sometimes quite drastically. At present, U.S. women are obsessed by concerns about their weight to the point where girls and young women deliberately eat less than they need for healthy growth and development.

Although we may inherit a tendency toward a particular body shape, most women's weight can change considerably in response to our diets, levels of physical activity, and other patterns of living. These also affect physical fitness and strength. When women begin to exercise or engage in weight training and body building, we often notice surprisingly great changes in strength in response to even quite moderate training. Here again, what is striking is the variation among women (and among men).

People ask whether there are "natural" limits to women's strength and therefore "natural" differences in strength between women and men. In

Europe and the United States women and men are far more similar in lower body strength than in the strength of our upper bodies. This fact is not surprising when we consider the different ways girls and boys are encouraged to move and play from early childhood on. We tend to use our legs much more similarly than our arms. Both girls and boys tend to run a lot, and hopscotch and skipping rope are considered girls' games. But when it comes to carrying loads, playing baseball, and wrestling and other contact sports, all of which strengthen the arms and upper body, girls are expected to participate much less than boys are. In general, male/female comparisons are made between physically more highly trained men and less trained women so that so-called sex differences at least in part reflect this difference in activity levels. More and less active men also differ in strength, and so do more and less active women.

If we compare the records of male and female marathon runners, we find that in 1963, when women were first permitted to run the Boston marathon, their record was 1 hour 20 minutes slower than the men's record. Twenty years later, Joan Benoit won in 2 hours, 22 minutes, and 43 seconds, a record that was only about fifteen minutes slower than the record of that year's male winner. And she ran the course in over an hour less time than the female winner in 1963 (Fausto-Sterling, 1985). The dramatic improvement women runners made in those twenty years clearly came with practice but no doubt also required changes in their expectations of what they could achieve. Men's records have improved by less than fifteen minutes during the entire time since modern marathon competitions began in 1908. Again the question: Are there "natural" limits and "natural" differences between women and men? Only time and opportunities to train and to participate in athletic events will tell. Note that in the 1988 Olympics, the woman who won the hundred-meter sprint took less than one second longer than the male winner, and he set a new world record. This feat is especially remarkable because women are said to compare with men much more favorably in long runs than in sprints.

WORK

The stratification of the work force is often explained as though it reflected inherent biological differences between women and men. Women have been disqualified from construction and other relatively well-paid heavy labor because they are said to be too weak for it. But the most prestigious men's jobs and those that pay most, in general, do not require physical strength, while much of women's traditional, unpaid or underpaid work involves strenuous physical labor. Nurses must sometimes lift heavy, immobilized people, and housework frequently involves carrying and pushing heavy, awkward loads. In many cultures women are responsible for providing the firewood and water, which usually means carrying heavy loads for long distances, often with small children tied to their chests or backs. In the United States, where men are expected to carry the heaviest loads, most men have "bad backs," which is why occupational health advocates argue that loads that are considered too heavy for women should be rated too heavy for everyone.

At present, there is an overemphasis on the reproductive hazards of employment for women and an underemphasis on comparable hazards for men, to the detriment of women, men, and children. Women have been barred from some higher-paying jobs unless they could prove they were sterile, while men in those very jobs, and in others, continue to be exposed to preventable chemical and radiation hazards (Stellman and Henifin, 1982). Women, too, continue to be exposed to reproductive hazards in traditional women's work, such as nursing and housework, and as x-ray technicians, beauticians, and hairdressers.

In other words, biological differences between women and men are used to rationalize the stratification of the labor force by sex; they do not explain it. One can readily find women or men who qualify for every kind of paid work, except that of sperm donor and what has come to be called surrogate mother. If society instead stratifies the work force into women's and men's jobs, it does so for economic, social, and political reasons. Such stratification is not mandated by biology.

MENSTRUATION

Let us leave these biosocial examples and look at menstruation, which most people would consider purely biological. A good way to begin is by asking, What is a normal woman's normal menstrual pattern? The standard answer is a twenty-eight-day cycle with five days of menstruation that begins at age twelve or thirteen and ends at about fifty. Yet that pattern does not reflect most women's actual experience. Until recently, we have had little information about the normal range of variation in age of onset, frequency, regularity, discomfort, and cessation of menstruation. Little information has been shared among women, and there has been almost no research on our routine experiences. Women have learned about menstruation mostly from their mothers or other female relatives or, if they had problems, from physicians — most of them men, who learn what they know from textbooks written by other men or from their "clinical experience," which means from women with problems.

In recent years, women's health activists and feminist medical and social scientists have finally begun to give us a sense of the variety of women's normal experiences of menstruation (Boston Women's Healthbook Collective, 1984; Martin, 1987). We are also beginning to learn about the experiences in other times and cultures. Rose Frisch (1988) has shown that, during the last century, the age of onset of menstruation has gone down and the age of cessation has gone up in both Europe and the United States. From this change and from studies of the menstrual patterns of athletes, she has concluded that nutrition and exercise strongly affect these parameters, probably by influencing the amounts of stored body fat. She suggests that women need to accumulate a threshold amount of fat in order to establish the hormonal cycles that regulate menstruation. As European and American diets have become richer in fats, girls reach the critical level earlier, and older women maintain it longer. Participation in vigorous sports affects menstrual patterns because athletes convert more of the food they eat into muscle (protein) and store less of it as fat.

Anthropologists observing the !Kung, a group of foragers living in the Kalahari desert in southern Africa, have noted that their menstrual and reproductive histories are quite different from what we in the West think of as "normal" (Howell, 1979; Konner and Worthman, 1980; Shostak, 1981). !Kung women and men collect their food, and as is true in most foraging societies, women provide most of it, which involves a good deal of walking and carrying. The !Kung diet is plentiful and nutritionally adequate but very different from ours because it is relatively high in complex carbohydrates and plant proteins but low in animal proteins and fats.

Presumably because of their high activity levels and their diet young !Kung women do not begin to menstruate until they are about eighteen years old, by which time they already tend to be heterosexually active. Like girls in the West, they tend not to ovulate during their first few cycles. They therefore experience their first pregnancy when they are about nineteen and have a first child at perhaps twenty. They nurse that child for two or three years but quite differently from the way many of us do. They suckle their babies as often as the infant wants to nurse, which can be several times an hour, albeit briefly. Melvin Konner and Carol Worthman (1980) have postulated that because of the frequent nursing, !Kung women tend not to menstruate or ovulate for almost the entire time they suckle their children. This experience contrasts with that of Western women, who tend to resume menstruation within a year after a birth, even when they nurse their children for several years, because they let them suck much less frequently and tend to supplement their diet with other foods. Thus, Western babies suckle less intensely and frequently than !Kung babies do.

!Kung women tend to wean a child sometime during its third year. By this time they may be pregnant, without having resumed menstruation, or they may menstruate and ovulate a few times before they become pregnant again. This pattern repeats until the women reach menopause, which they tend to do in their late thirties or early forties.

The menstrual and reproductive experience of !Kung women therefore is entirely different from what we take to be "normal." They have a shorter reproductive span, during which they tend to bear no more than four or five children, quite without contraception, and they experience few menstruations. But when the !Kung move into towns and live more as we do, their menstrual and reproductive patterns change to the ones we are used to seeing. So the difference between their experience and ours is not genetic.

Clearly it is meaningless to specify norms for even such a normal, biological function as menstruation without considering how women live. For !Kung women it is normal to menstruate rarely and have few children without using birth control. For us it is normal to menstruate every twenty-eight or so days and to get pregnant within a year after a birth, if we are heterosexually active without using birth control. Thus, even such biological events as menstruation and fecundity are strongly influenced by sociocultural factors.

WOMEN'S BIOLOGY IN CONTEXT

How had we best take these influences into consideration? Clearly we need to think about women's biology in its social context and consider how it interacts with culture. We need to get information directly from women and not rely on so-called experts, who are often male and whose knowledge tends to be based on the experience of "patients"—that is, of women with problems. Only when women have the opportunity to share experiences and when scientists collect the experiences of women of different ages and from different classes, races, and cultural groups can we get a sense of the texture and variety of women's biology (Martin, 1987).

We need to pay attention to the obvious contradictions between stereotypic descriptions of women's biology and the realities of women's lives. For example, women's reputed "maternal instinct" needs to be looked at in light of some women's desperate efforts to avoid having children, while society persuades or forces them to have children against their wills. Similarly, descriptions of women's frailty, passivity, and weakness need to be juxtaposed with the reality of women as providers and workers who in most societies, including our own, tend to work harder and for longer hours than most men.

Women's work histories are often obscured by the fact that work has been defined so that it excludes much of their daily work load. Indeed, whereas most of what men do is called work, much of what women do has been interpreted as the natural manifestation of our biology. How often do we hear people say, "My mother didn't work when I was growing up"? If she didn't work, how did we manage to grow up? Even women usually refer to what we do as work only when we get paid for it, implying that what we do at home and in our neighborhoods and communities is not work. This misrepresentation of work sets up the vicious circle whereby women are thought to be less good workers in the workplace when we have family and community obligations and less good housewives and mothers when we work outside the home.

No question, we are biological organisms like other animals, and women and men have different procreative structures and functions. But to try to find the biological basis of our social roles or to sort people by sex when it comes to strength, ability to do math, or other intellectual or social attributes is a political exercise, not a scientific one.

THE MEANING OF DIFFERENCE

That said, I want to stress that we need have no ideological investment in whether women and men exhibit biological differences, aside from the obvious ones involved with procreation. I have argued that we cannot know whether such biological differences exist because biology and society (or environment) are interdependent and cannot be sorted out. And in any gender-dichotomized society, the fact that we are born biologically female or male means that our environments will be different: We will live different lives. Because our biology and how we live are dialectically related and build on one another, we cannot vary gender and hold the environment constant. Therefore, the scientific methodology of sex-differences research is intrinsically flawed if scientists try to use it to sort effects of biology and society. Scientists can catalog similarities and differences between women and men but cannot establish their causes.

There are other problems with research on differences. One is that it is in the nature of scientific research that if we are interested in differences, we will go on looking until we find them. And if we do not find any, we will assume that our instruments were wrong or that we looked in the wrong place or at the wrong things. Another problem is that most characteristics vary continuously in the population rather than placing us into neat groups. To compare groups, however defined, we must use such concepts as the "average," "mean," or "median" in order to characterize each group by a single number. Yet these constructed, or reified, numbers obscure the diversity that exists within the groups (say, among women and among men) as well as the overlaps between them. That is why statisticians have invented the concept of the standard deviation from the mean to reflect the spread of the actual numbers around the reified average. This problem is obvious when we think about research into differences between blacks and whites. Just to do it, we have to agree on social definitions of who will count as black and who as white because after several centuries of mixing, the biological characteristic, skin color, varies continuously. Research comparing blacks and whites must first generate the group differences it pretends to catalog or analyze.

Differences, be they biological or psychological, become scientifically interesting only when they parallel differences in power. We do not frame scientific questions about differences between tall people and short people, although folk wisdom suggests there may be some. Nor do we, in this society, pursue differences between blue-eyed, blond people and dark-haired, dark-eyed ones. Yet the latter were scientifically interesting differences under the Nazis.

Sex differences are interesting in sexist societies that value one group more highly than the other. Because the overlaps are so large for all the characteristics that are not directly involved with procreation, it is easy to find women and men to perform any task we value. The existence of average sex differences is irrelevant to the way we organize society. To achieve an egalitarian division of labor requires political will and action, not changes in our biology. There is enough variability among us to let us construct a society in which people of both sexes contribute to whatever activities are considered socially useful and are rewarded according to their talents and abilities.

BIBLIOGRAPHY

Boston Women's Healthbook Collective. 1984. *The* New *Our Bodies, Ourselves.* New York: Simon & Schuster.

Fausto-Sterling, Anne. 1985. *Myths of Gender.* New York: Basic Books.

Frisch, Rose. 1988. "Body Fat, Menarche, Fitness and Fertility." *Human Reproduction* 2: 421–533.

Howell, Nancy. 1979. *Demography of the Dobe !Kung.* New York: Academic Press.

Konner, Melvin, and Carol Worthman. 1980. "Nursing Frequency, Gonadal Function, and Birth Spacing among !Kung Hunter-Gatherers." *Science* 207: 788–790.

Lowe, Marian. 1982. "Social Bodies: The Interaction of Culture and Women's Biology." In Ruth Hubbard, Mary Sue Henifin, and Barbara Fried, eds., *Biological Woman — The Convenient Myth.* Cambridge, Mass.: Schenkman.

Martin, Emily. 1987. *The Woman in the Body.* Boston: Beacon Press.

Shostak, Marjorie. 1981. *Nisa.* Cambridge: Harvard University Press.

Stellman, Jeanne M., and Mary Sue Henifin. 1982. "No Fertile Women Need Apply: Employment Discrimination and Reproductive Hazards in the Workplace." In Ruth Hubbard, Mary Sue Henifin, and Barbara Fried, eds. *Biological Woman — The Convenient Myth.* Cambridge, Mass.: Schenkman.

ALLAN G. JOHNSON

What Is This Thing Called Patriarchy?

Allan G. Johnson is a sociologist who writes and speaks about social inequality, privilege, and oppression. His books include, The Gender Knot: Unraveling Our Patriarchal Legacy *(1997; 2005), from which the following selection is drawn, and* Privilege, Power, and Difference *(2005).*

WHERE ARE WE?

Twenty-five men and women gather for a workshop on gender issues in the workplace. In a simple opening exercise, they divide into small single-gender groups and brainstorm four lists: the advantages and disadvantages their own gender has in the workplace, and their perception of the advantages and disadvantages the other gender has. The women dive into the task with energy to spare that gets more intense as their lists of women's disadvantages and men's advantages spill over onto second and third flip-chart pages. Sometimes the energy comes in waves of laughter that roll out into the room and wash up on the still quiet shore of the men's groups. At other times it's felt simply in women's furious scribbling of one item after another: paid less, held to higher or double standards, worked harder, granted little power or respect, judged on physical attractiveness more than performance or ability, confined by glass ceilings, not taken seriously, harassed, given little support or mentoring, allowed little space or privacy, excluded from informal networks, patronized, expected to do "housekeeping" chores from taking notes to getting coffee, treated as weaker and less intelligent, often denied credit for ideas appropriated by men, and treated without recognition of the family roles that also claim their time and energy in a society that makes few such demands on men.

On it goes. The men work in tight-knit little groups on the fringes of the women's energy. Surprisingly for many, their lists are quite similar to the women's lists, if a bit shorter. Men miss many of the forms that advantage and disadvantage take, but in a basic sense, they know very well what's going on. They know what they've got and what women don't.

When the men are done, they stand in awkward silence and watch the women, still at work. After a while each group shares what it's come up with. There is some good-natured if somewhat nervous laughter over the inevitable throw-away items: men don't have to wait in line to use the bathroom; men can get away with simpler wardrobes. But there soon follows a steady stream of undisputed facts about how gender shapes the lives of women and men in the workplace and beyond.

246

The accumulated sum hangs heavy in the air. There are flashes of anger from some of the women, but many don't seem to know what to do with how they feel. The men just stand and listen, muted, as if they'd like to find a safe place to hide or some way to defend themselves, as if all of this is about them personally. In response to questions about how the lists make them feel, one man says that he wants to hang on to the advantages without being part of their negative consequences for women. "Depressed" is a frequent response from the women.

In the silence that falls over the room, two things become clear: The lists say something powerful about people's lives. And we don't know how to talk about the lists. If we don't know how to talk about them, we certainly don't know what to do about them.

The result is a kind of paralysis that reflects not only where this particular group—and countless others like it—finds itself as it confronts the reality of gender inequality, but where entire societies are in relation to these issues. Where we are is stuck. Where we are is lost. Where we are is deep inside an oppressive gender legacy, faced with the knowledge that what gender is about is tied to a great deal of suffering and injustice. But we don't know what to do with the knowledge, and this binds us in a knot of fear, anger, and pain, of blame, defensiveness, guilt, and denial. We're unsure of just about everything except that something is wrong and we're in it up to our necks. The more we pull at the knot, the tighter it gets.

Patriarchy

We are trapped inside a legacy and its core is patriarchal. To understand it and take part in the journey out, we have to find ways to unravel the knot, and this begins with getting clear about what it means to be inside a patriarchal legacy. To get clear, we first have to get past the defensive reaction of many people—men in particular—to the word "patriarchy" itself, which they routinely interpret as a code word for "men." Patriarchy is *not* simply another way of saying "men." Patriarchy is a kind of society, and a society is more than a collection of people. As such, "patriarchy" doesn't refer to me or any other man or collection of men, but to a kind of society in which men *and* women participate. By itself this poses enough problems without the added burden of equating an entire society with a group of people.

What is patriarchy? A society is patriarchal to the degree that it promotes male privilege★ by being *male dominated, male identified,* and *male centered.* It is also organized around an obsession with control and involves as one of its key aspects the oppression of women.

★I use the term *privilege* according to the definition developed by Peggy McIntosh in her classic article, "White Privilege and Male Privilege," in *Gender Basics: Feminist Perspectives on Women and Men,* 2nd ed., edited by Anne Minas (Belmont, CA: Wadsworth, 2000). Privilege refers to any unearned advantage that is available to members of a social category while being

MALE DOMINANCE Patriarchy is male dominated in that positions of authority — political, economic, legal, religious, educational, military, domestic — are generally reserved for men. Heads of state, corporate CEOs and board members, religious leaders, school principals, members of legislatures at all levels of government, senior law partners, tenured professors, generals and admirals, and even those identified as "head of household" all tend to be male under patriarchy. When a woman finds her way into such positions, people tend to be struck by the exception to the rule and wonder how she'll measure up against a man in the same position. It's a test rarely applied to men ("I wonder if he'll be as good a president as a woman would be") except, perhaps, on those rare occasions when men venture into the devalued domestic and other "caring" work typically done by women. Even then, men's failure to measure up can be interpreted as a sign of superiority, a trained incapacity that actually protects their privileged status ("You change the diaper. I'm no good at that sort of thing").

In the simplest sense, male dominance creates power differences between men and women. It means, for example, that men can claim larger shares of income and wealth. It means they can shape culture in ways that reflect and serve men's collective interests by, for example, controlling the content of films and television shows, or handling rape and sexual harassment cases in ways that put the victim rather than the defendant on trial.

Male dominance also promotes the idea that men are superior to women. In part this occurs because we don't distinguish between the superiority of *positions* in a hierarchy and the kinds of people who usually occupy them.[1] This means that if men occupy superior positions, it's a short leap to the idea that *men must be superior*. If presidents, generals, legislators, priests, popes, and corporate CEOs are all men (with a few token women as exceptions to prove the rule), then men as a group become identified with superiority even though most men aren't powerful in their individual lives. In this sense, *every* man's standing in relation to women is enhanced by the male monopoly over authority in patriarchal societies.

Note that male dominance does not mean that all men are powerful. Most men in patriarchies are not powerful individuals, and spend their days doing what other men tell them to do whether they want to or not. Male dominance does mean that where there is a concentration of power, men are the ones most likely to have it — they are the default.

---

systematically denied to others. In patriarchy, for example, what men say tends to have greater credibility than what women say, even when they're saying the same thing. Access to privilege depends on the prevailing definition of categories such as "male" and "female" and the advantages and disadvantages socially attached to them. It also depends on related characteristics — a man's access to male privilege, for example, will vary according to other status characteristics such as race, sexual orientation, disability status, and social class. McIntosh's approach is important to any understanding of privilege because it refers not to individuals, but to the organization of social systems in which people live.

Nor does male dominance mean that all women are powerless. Supreme Court Justices Sandra Day O'Connor and Ruth Bader Ginsberg, for example, or National Security Advisor Condoleezza Rice or Hewlett-Packard Chair and CEO Carelton "Carly" Fiorina, are all far more powerful than most men will ever be. But, they stand out as exceptions because male dominance is the rule. Like all subordinate groups, women also manage to have some power by making the most of what is left to them by men. Just as patriarchy turns women into sex objects who are supposed to organize their lives around men's needs, for example, so, too, does this arrangement grant women the power to refuse to grant men sexual access.[2]

MALE IDENTIFICATION Patriarchal societies are *male identified* in that core cultural ideas about what is considered good, desirable, preferable, or normal are associated with how we think about men and masculinity. The simplest example of this is the still widespread use of male pronouns and nouns to represent people in general. When we routinely refer to human beings as "man" or to doctors as "he," we construct a symbolic world in which men are in the foreground and women are in the background, marginalized as outsiders and exceptions to the rule.[3] (This practice can back people into some embarrassingly ridiculous corners, as in describing man as a "species that breast-feeds his young.")

But male identification amounts to much more than this, for it also takes men and men's lives as the standard for defining what is normal. The idea of a career, for example, with its sixty-hour weeks, is defined in ways that assume the career holder has something like a wife at home to perform the vital support work of taking care of children, doing laundry, and making sure there's a safe, clean, comfortable haven for rest and recuperation from the stress of the competitive male-dominated world. Since women generally don't have wives, they find it harder to identify with and prosper within this male-identified model.

Another aspect of male identification is the cultural description of masculinity and the ideal man in terms that closely resemble the core values of society as a whole. These include qualities such as control, strength, competitiveness, toughness, coolness under pressure, logic, forcefulness, decisiveness, rationality, autonomy, self-sufficiency, and control over any emotion that interferes with other core values (such as invulnerability). These male-identified qualities are associated with the work valued most in patriarchal societies — business, politics, war, athletics, law, and medicine — because this work has been organized in ways that require such qualities for success. In contrast, qualities such as cooperation, mutuality, equality, sharing, compassion, caring, vulnerability, a readiness to negotiate and compromise, emotional expressiveness, and intuitive and other nonlinear ways of thinking are all devalued *and* culturally associated with femininity and femaleness.

Of course, femaleness isn't devalued entirely. Women are often prized for their beauty as objects of male sexual desire, for example, but as such they are often possessed and controlled in ways that ultimately devalue them. There is also a powerful cultural romanticizing of women in general and mothers in particular, but it is a tightly focused sentimentality (as on Mother's Day or Secretary's Day) that has little effect on how women are regarded and treated on a day-to-day basis. And, like all sentimentality, it doesn't have much weight when it comes to actually doing something to support women's lives by, for example, providing effective and affordable child day-care facilities for working mothers, or family-leave policies that allow working women to attend to the caring functions for which we supposedly value them so highly, without compromising their careers.

Because patriarchy is male identified, when most women look out on world they see themselves reflected as women in a few narrow areas of life such as "caring" occupations (e.g., teaching, nursing, child care) and personal relationships. To see herself as a leader, for example, a woman must first get around the fact that leadership itself has been gendered through its identification with maleness and masculinity as part of patriarchal culture. While a man might have to learn to see himself as a manager, a woman has to be able to see herself as a *woman* manager who can succeed in spite of the fact that she isn't a man.

As a result, any woman who dares strive for standing in the world beyond the sphere of caring relationships must choose between two very different cultural images of who she is and who she ought to be. For her to assume real public power—as in politics, corporations, or her church—she must resolve a contradiction between her culturally based identity as a woman, on the one hand, and the male-identified *position* that she occupies on the other. For this reason, the more powerful a woman is under patriarchy, the more "unsexed" she becomes in the eyes of others as her female cultural identity recedes beneath the mantle of male-identified power and the masculine images associated with it. With men the effect is just the opposite: the more powerful they are, the more aware we are of their maleness. In other words, power looks sexy on men but not on women.

But for all the pitfalls and limitations, some women do make it to positions of power. What about Margaret Thatcher, for example, or Queen Elizabeth I, Catherine the Great, Indira Gandhi, and Golda Meir? Doesn't their power contradict the idea that patriarchy is male dominated? The answer is that patriarchy can accommodate a limited number of powerful women so long as the society retains its essential patriarchal character, especially its male identification. Although a few individual women have wielded great power in patriarchal societies, each has been surrounded by powerful men—generals, cabinet ministers, bishops, and wealthy aristocrats or businessmen—whose collective interests she must support by embracing core patriarchal values. Indeed, part of what makes these women stand out as so exceptional is their ability to embody values culturally defined as masculine: they've been tougher, more decisive, more aggressive, more calculating, and more emotionally controlled than most men around them.[4]

These women's power, however, has nothing to do with whether women in general are subordinated under patriarchy. It also doesn't mean that putting more women in positions of authority will by itself do much for women unless we also change the patriarchal character of the systems in which they operate. Indeed, without such change, the Margaret Thatchers and Condoleezza Rices of the world tend to affirm the very systems that subordinate women by fostering the illusion of gender equality and by embracing the patriarchal values on which male power and privilege rest. This does *not* mean we shouldn't try to get women into positions of power, only that making some women powerful will not be enough to bring about fundamental change.

Since patriarchy identifies power with men, the vast majority of men who aren't powerful but are instead dominated by other men can still feel some connection with the idea of male dominance and with men who *are* powerful. It is far easier, for example, for an unemployed working-class man to identify with male leaders and their displays of patriarchal masculine toughness than it is for women of any class. When upper-class U.S. President George Bush "got tough" with Saddam Hussein, for example, men of all classes could identify with his acting out of basic patriarchal values. In this way, male identification gives even the most lowly placed man a cultural basis for feeling some sense of superiority over the otherwise most highly placed woman (which is why a construction worker can feel within his rights as a man when he sexually harasses a well-dressed professional woman who happens to walk by).[5] . . .

When a society identifies a particular group such as men as the standard for human beings in general, it follows that men will be seen as superior, preferable, and of greater value than women. Not only will maleness be culturally defined as superior, but whatever men do will tend to be seen as having greater value. Occupations performed primarily by men, for example, will tend to be more highly regarded and better paid than occupations done primarily by women even when women's jobs require the same or even higher levels of skill, training, and responsibility. In the nineteenth century, most secretaries, telephone operators, librarians, and nurses were men and those occupations consequently commanded higher pay and status than they do now when most are performed by women.[6]

And just as what men do tends to be valued more highly than what women do, those things that are valued in a social system's culture will tend to be associated with men more than with women. God, for example, is of enormous importance in human life, and so it should come as no surprise that every monotheistic patriarchal religion worships a male-identified God gendered as masculine. As Mary Daly argues in her book, *Beyond God the Father*, this, in turn, puts men in the highly favorable position of having God identified with *them*, which further reinforces the position of women as "other" and the legitimacy of men's claim to privilege and dominance.[7]

· · ·

THE OBSESSION WITH CONTROL   As with any system of privilege that elevates one group by oppressing another, control is an essential element of patriarchy: men maintain their privilege by controlling women and anyone else who might threaten it. Given the primacy of control, it becomes the cultural standard for a truly superior human being, which is then used to justify men's privileged position. Men are assumed (and expected) to be in control at all times, to be unemotional (except for anger and rage), to present themselves as invulnerable, autonomous, independent, strong, rational, logical, dispassionate, knowledgeable, always right, and in command of every situation, especially those involving women. These qualities, it is assumed, mark them as superior and justify their privilege. Women, in contrast, are assumed (and expected) to be just the opposite, especially in relation to men.

It would be misleading to suggest that control is inherently bad or inevitably leads to oppression. Control is, after all, one of the hallmarks of our species. It is our only hope to bring some order out of chaos or to protect ourselves from what threatens our survival. We imagine, focus, and act — from baking bread to composing music to designing a national health plan — and all of this involves control. Even small children delight in a sense of human agency, in being able to make things happen. Under patriarchy, however, control is more than an expression of human essence or a way to get things done. It's valued and pursued to a degree that gives social life an oppressive form by taking a natural human capacity to obsessive extremes.

Under patriarchy, control shapes not only the broad outlines of social life but also men's inner lives. The more men see control as central to their sense of self, well-being, worth, and safety, the more driven they feel to go after it and to organize their inner and outer lives around it. This takes men away from connection to others and themselves and toward disconnection. This is because control involves a relationship between controller and controlled and disconnection is an integral part of that relationship. In order to control something, we have to see it as a separate "other." Even if we're controlling ourselves, we have to mentally split ourselves into a "me" that's being controlled and an "I" that's doing the controlling. And if we're controlling other people, we have to justify the control and protect ourselves from an awareness of how our control affects them.

As a result, controllers come to see themselves as subjects who intend and decide what will happen, and to see others as objects to act upon. The controlled are seen without the fullness and complexity that define them as human beings. They have no history, no dimensions to give them depth or command the controllers' *attention* or *understanding* except by interfering with control. When parents control small children, for example, they often act as though children aren't full human beings, and justify punishment by saying that children can't reason and don't understand anything else. As children grow older, it becomes more difficult to see them as "other" and control becomes more difficult, especially in that memorable moment when a parent looks at a maturing child and sees a person looking back. Suddenly, control that once seemed justified may feel awkward, inappropriate, or even foolish.

Because patriarchy isn't organized around simply an obsession with control, but around an obsession with *male* control, the more men participate in the system, the more likely they are to see themselves as separate, autonomous, and disconnected from others. They may become versions of the western hero who rides into town from nowhere, with no past, and leaves going nowhere, with no apparent future. Women's lives, of course, also involve control, especially in relation to children. But the idea and practice of control as a core principle of social life is part of what defines patriarchal *man*hood, not womanhood, and so women are discouraged from pursuing it and criticized if they do. A woman perceived as controlling a man is typically labeled a "castrating bitch" or a "ball buster," and the man she supposedly controls is looked down upon as "henpecked," "pussy whipped," and barely a man at all. But there are no insulting terms for a man who controls a woman—by having the last word, not letting her work outside the home, deciding when she'll have sex, or limiting her time with other women—or for the woman he controls. There is no need for such words because men controlling women is a core aspect of patriarchal manhood.

Women and Patriarchy

An inevitable consequence of patriarchy is the oppression of women, which takes several forms. Historically, for example, women have been excluded from major institutions such as church, state, universities, and the professions. Even when they've been allowed to participate, it's generally been at subordinate, second-class levels. Marilyn French goes so far as to argue that historically women's oppression has amounted to a form of slavery:

> What other term can one use to describe a state in which people do not have rights over their own bodies, their own sexuality, marriage, reproduction or divorce, in which they may not receive education or practice a trade or profession, or move about freely in the world? Many women (both past and present) work laboriously all their lives without receiving any payment for their work.[8]

Because patriarchy is male identified and male centered, women and the work they do tends to be devalued, if not made invisible, and women are routinely repressed in their development as human beings through neglect and discrimination in schools[9] and in occupational hiring, development, promotion, and rewards. Anyone who doubts that patriarchy is an oppressive system need only consult the growing literature documenting not only economic, political, and other institutionalized sexism, but pervasive violence, from pornography to the everyday realities of wife battering, sexual harassment, and sexual assault.[10] And there are also the daily headlines—such as recent revelations of a long history of sexual assault at the U.S. Air Force Academy that was allowed to continue for years before a public scandal forced corrective action.

This is not to deny that much has changed in women's position over the last hundred years — from the appointment of women to the U.S. Supreme Court to assigning women to combat zones during the Iraq War. There is less tolerance for overt sexist behavior toward women in many settings. An elite of women has managed to enter the professions and, to a degree, upper levels of corporate management. And most laws that blatantly discriminate against women have been repealed.

To a great degree, however, such highly publicized progress supports an illusion of fundamental change. In spite of new laws, for example, violence and sexual harassment against women are as pervasive as ever, if not more so. Inequality of income and wealth has not changed much from the 1950s, and women are still heavily concentrated in a small number of low-level service and pink-collar occupations. In spite of the huge influx of married women, many of them mothers, into the paid labor force, and in spite of a great deal of talk about the joys of fatherhood, there's been no substantial increase in men's sense of responsibility for domestic labor or their willingness to actually participate.[11] And women's share of authority in major institutions — from the state to organized religion to corporations to science, higher education, and the mass media — remains low.[12] . . .

Thus far, mainstream women's movements have concentrated on the liberal agenda, whose primary goal has been to allow women to do what men do in the ways that men do it, whether in science, the professions, business, or government. More serious challenges to patriarchy have been silenced, maligned, and misunderstood for reasons that aren't hard to fathom. As difficult as it is to change overtly sexist sensibilities and behavior, it is much harder to raise critical questions about how sexism is embedded in major institutions such as the economy, politics, religion, and the family. . . .

Like all movements that work for basic change, women's movements have come up against the depth to which the status quo is embedded in virtually every aspect of social life. The power of patriarchy is especially evident in the ongoing backlash against even the liberal agenda of women's movements — including the Supreme Court's retreat on abortion rights, the widespread effort to discredit feminism resulting in women's growing reluctance to embrace or identify with it, and the emergence of a vocal movement of men who portray themselves as victims not only of the sex/gender system but of women's struggle to free themselves from their own oppression under it.

· · ·

Deep Structures and the Way Out

Over the last century or so, a lot has happened around the subject of male privilege and patriarchy. There's been an enormous amount of feminist writing and social action in Western industrial societies. And for the first time, the potential exists to challenge patriarchy in a serious and sustained way. Most people's attention is on the surface storms raging around particular issues such as abortion, pornography, sexual harassment and violence, and political and economic discrimination. But these struggles rarely if ever raise critical questions about the nature of patriarchy itself. In spite of the important feminist work being done on the patriarchal roots of pornography and men's violence against women, for example, public discussion rarely gets beyond issues of free speech, constitutional rights, and individual psychopathology.[13] In part this is because we don't know how to get beyond such questions to explore the trunk and roots of patriarchal society, but it is also a way to avoid going deeper into our own lives and the world that shapes them.

. . .

We're as stuck as we are primarily because we can't or won't acknowledge the roots of patriarchy and our involvement in it. We show no enthusiasm for going deeper than a surface obsession with sex and gender. We resist even saying things like "patriarchy" or "male privilege" in polite conversation. . . .

We shouldn't be too hard on ourselves for hanging on to denial and illusions about patriarchy. Letting go is risky business, and patriarchy is full of smoke and mirrors that make it difficult to see what has to be let go of. It's relatively easy to accept the idea of patriarchy as male dominated and male identified, for example, and even as male centered. Many people, however, have a much harder time seeing women as oppressed.[14] This is a huge issue that sparks a lot of argument. Still, it's worthwhile outlining a basic response here.

The reluctance to see women as oppressed has several sources. The first is that many women have access to privilege based on race, class, disability status or status or sexual orientation and it's difficult for many to see women as oppressed without insulting "truly oppressed" groups such as the lower classes or racial minorities.[15] How, for example, can we count upper-class women among the oppressed and lower-class men among their oppressors?

Although this objection has a certain logic to it, it rests on a confusion between the position of women and men as groups and their experience as individuals. Identifying "female" as an oppressed status under patriarchy doesn't mean that every woman suffers its consequences to an equal degree, just as living in a racist society doesn't mean that every person of color suffers equally or that every white person shares equally in the benefits of white privilege. Living in patriarchy does mean, however, that every woman must come to grips with an inferior gender *position* and that whatever she achieves will be *in spite of* that position. With the exception of child care and other domestic work and a few paid occupations related to it, women in almost every field of adult endeavor must labor under the presumption that they are inferior to men, that they are interlopers from the margins of society who must justify their participation. Men may have such experiences because of their race or other subordinate standing, but rarely if ever because they're men.

It is in this sense that patriarchies are male dominated even though most individual men may not *feel* dominant, especially in relation to other men. This is a crucial insight that rests on the fact that when we talk about societies, words like *privilege* and *oppression* describe relations between categories of people such as whites and people of color, lower and upper classes, or women and men. How privilege and oppression actually play out among individuals is another issue. Depending on other social factors such as race or class, individual men will vary in their access to male privilege. We can make a similar argument about women and the price they pay for belonging to a subordinate group. Upper-class women, for example, may be insulated to some degree from the oppressive effects of being women under patriarchy, such as discrimination in the workplace. Their class privilege, however, exists *in spite of* their subordinate standing as women, which they can never completely overcome, especially in relation to husbands.[16] No woman is immune, for example to the cultural devaluing of women's bodies as sexual objects to be exploited in public and private life, or the ongoing threat of sexual and domestic violence. . . .

Along with not seeing women as oppressed, we resist seeing men as a privileged oppressor group. This is especially true of men who are aware of their own suffering, who often argue that both men and women are oppressed because of their gender and that neither oppresses the other. Undoubtedly men do suffer because of their participation in patriarchy, but it isn't because men are oppressed *as men*. For women, gender oppression is linked to a cultural devaluing of femaleness itself. Women are subordinated and treated as inferior because they are culturally defined as inferior *as women*. Men, however, do not suffer because maleness is a devalued, oppressed status in relation to some higher, more powerful one. Instead, to the extent that men suffer as men — and not because they're also gay or of color — it's because they belong to the dominant gender group in a system of gender oppression, which both privileges them and exacts a price in return. . . .

WHY PATRIARCHY?

Perhaps more than anything else, what drives patriarchy as a system — what fuels competition, aggression, and oppression — is a dynamic relationship between control and fear.[1] Patriarchy encourages men to seek security, status, and other rewards through control, to fear other men's ability to control and harm them, and to identify being in control as both their best defense against loss and humiliation and the surest route to what they need and desire. In this sense, although we usually think of patriarchy in terms of women and men, it is more about what goes on *among men*. The oppression of women is certainly an important part of patriarchy, but, paradoxically, it may not be the *point* of patriarchy. . . .

Men's participation in patriarchy tends to lock them in an endless pursuit of and defense against control, for *under patriarchy, control is both the source of and the only solution offered for their fear.* The more invested a man is in the control–fear spiral, the worse he feels when he doesn't feel in control. And so on some level he's always on the lookout for opportunities to renew his sense of control while protecting himself from providing that same kind of opportunity for others, especially men. As each man pursues control as a way to defend and advance himself, he fuels the very same response in *other* men. This dynamic has provided patriarchy with an escalating driving force for thousands of years.

Men pay an enormous price for participating in patriarchy. The more in control men try to be, for example, the less secure they feel. They may not know it because they're so busy trying to be in control, but the more they organize their lives around being in control, the more tied they are to the fear of *not* being in control. As Marilyn French put it, "A religion of power is a religion of fear, and . . . those who worship power are the most terrified creatures on the earth."[2] Dig beneath the surface appearance of "great men," and you'll often find deep insecurity, fear, and a chronic need to prove themselves to other men. As president of the United States, for example, one of the most powerful positions on Earth, George H. W. Bush was obsessed that people might think he was a "wimp." Before him, President Lyndon Johnson continued the Vietnam War in part because he was afraid of being considered "less than manly" if he didn't.[3] Rather than making men feel safe, great power makes them need still greater control to protect themselves from still more powerful men locked into the same cycle. To make matters worse, control itself is a fleeting, momentary experience, not a natural, stable state. And so, as Marilyn French and Simone Weil argue, control is always on the edge of slipping away or falling apart:

> Power is not what we think it is. Power is not substantial; not even when it takes substantive form. The money you hold in your hand can be devalued overnight. . . . A title can be removed at the next board meeting. . . . A huge military establishment can disintegrate in a few days . . . a huge economic structure can collapse in a few weeks.[4]
>
> All power is unstable. . . . There is never power, but only a race for power. . . . Power is, by definition, only a means . . . but power seeking, owing to its essential incapacity to seize ahold of its object, rules out all consideration of an end, and finally comes . . . to take the place of all ends.[5]

The religion of fear and control also blocks men's need for human connection by redefining intimacy. Men are encouraged to see everything and everyone as other, and to look on every situation in terms of how it might enhance or threaten their sense of control. Every opportunity for control, however, can also be an occasion for a failure of control, a fact that can inject issues of control and power into the most unlikely situations. Intimacy is lost as a chance to be open and vulnerable on the way to a deeper connection. Sexual intimacy in particular can go from pleasure in a safe place to a male performance laced with worry about whether the penis—that notorious and willful "other" that so often balks at men's efforts at control—will "perform" as it's supposed to. Dictionaries typically define impotence as a man's *inability to achieve or sustain an erection*, as if an erection were something a man *did* and not something he experienced, like sweating or having his heart beat rapidly or feeling happy. The more preoccupied with control men are, the more lovers recede as full people with feelings, thoughts, will, and soul, and become vehicles for bolstering manhood and relieving anxiety. And even though a woman's opinion of a man's sexual "performance" may seem to be what matters, her words of reassurance are rarely enough, for it's always a patriarchal male gaze that's looking at him over her shoulder and judging him. . . .

Patriarchy as a Men's Problem

Patriarchy is usually portrayed as something that's primarily between women and men. At first blush this makes a lot of sense given that "male" and "female" define each other and that women occupy an oppressed position in relation to male privilege. Paradoxically, however, the cycle of control and fear that drives patriarchy has more to do with relations among men than with women, for it is men who control men's standing *as men*. With few exceptions, men look to other men—not women—to affirm their manhood, whether as coaches, friends, teammates, co-workers, sports figures, fathers, or mentors.

This contradicts the conventional wisdom that women hold the key to heterosexual men's sense of manhood. It's true that men often use women to show they measure up—especially by controlling women sexually—but the standards that are used are men's, not women's. Men also may try to impress women as "real men" in order to start and keep relationships with them, to control them, or to get sexual access and personal care. This isn't enough to prove they're real men, however. For affirmation of that, they have to go to a larger male-identified world—from the local bar to sports to work—which is also where they're most vulnerable to other men. Whether in locker rooms or the heat of political campaigns, when a man is accused of being a "wimp" or of otherwise failing to measure up, it almost always comes from another man. And when a man suspects *himself* of being less than a real man, he judges himself through a patriarchal male gaze, not from a woman's perspective.

Although men often use women as scapegoats for their bad feelings about themselves, women's role in this is indirect at most. If other men reject a man's claim to "real man" standing, how his wife or mother sees him usually makes little difference, and if women's opinions *do* matter to him, his manhood becomes all the more suspect to other men.[6] Women's marginal importance in the manhood question is plain to see in the risks men take to prove themselves in spite of objections from wives, mothers, and other women who find them just fine the way they are. The record books are full of men who seize upon *anything*—from throwing Frisbees to extreme sports to being the first to get somewhere or discover something—as a way to create competitive arenas in which they can jockey for position and prove themselves among men.[7] If a man must choose between men's and women's views of what makes a real man, he'll choose men's views most of the time. "A man's gotta do what a man's gotta do," is typically spoken by a man to a women (often as he goes off to do something with other men). And just what it is he's got to do is determined by men and patriarchy, not by women. It isn't up to women to decide what a real man is. Her role is to reassure men that they meet the standards of a male-identified patriarchal culture.

When a woman does question or attack a man's masculinity, the terms of the attack and the power behind it are based on men's standards of patriarchal manhood. She's not going to attack his manhood, for example, by telling him he isn't caring enough. When she uses what are culturally defined as *women's* terms—"You're not sensitive, nurturing, open, or vulnerable and you're *too* controlling"—the attack has much less weight and produces far less effect. But when women don't play along—when they criticize or question or merely lose enthusiasm for affirming patriarchal manhood—they risk the wrath of men, who may feel undermined, abandoned, and even betrayed. Men may not like being criticized for failing to measure up to "women's" ideas of what men should be, but it's nothing compared to how angry and violent men can be toward women who dare to use "men's" weapons against them by questioning their manhood.

In the patriarchal cycle of control and fear, no man is safe from challenges to his real-man standing, which is why even the rich and powerful can be so quick to defend themselves. In his analysis of John F. Kennedy's presidency, for example, David Halberstam argues that Kennedy initiated U.S. involvement in the Vietnamese civil war in part because he failed to appear sufficiently tough and manly at his 1961 Vienna summit meeting with Soviet Premier Nikita Khrushchev. Khrushchev challenged Kennedy from the start, and Kennedy, surprised, responded in kind only toward the end. Upon returning home, he felt the need for an opportunity to right the impression he'd made and remove any doubts about his manhood. "If he [Khrushchev] thinks I'm inexperienced and have no guts," Kennedy told *New York Times* reporter James Reston, ". . . we won't get anywhere with him. So we have to act . . . and Vietnam looks like the place."[8] And so the horror of U.S. involvement in Vietnam turned on a political system organized in part around men's ability to impress one another with their standing as real men. And this no doubt played a prominent role in the tortured progress of that war and the stubborn refusal of all sides to compromise or admit defeat.

In addition to what Kennedy's dilemma says about patriarchal politics, it also challenges the stereotype that macho displays of manhood are largely confined to lower- and working-class subcultures. The roots of men proving their manhood run deep in the upper classes from President George W. Bush taunting and daring Iraqi guerrillas to "bring it on" and attack U.S. troops to the enthusiastic stampede of Britain's elite to the killing fields of World War I to the sexually compulsive behavior of Bill Clinton and John Kennedy to the San Francisco Bohemian Grove retreats where captains of business and government gather to make deals, mock women in cross-dressing skits, and otherwise relax in the comfort of male privilege.[9] Men, of course, aren't born to this. They must be trained and given ongoing incentives.

In the early 1960s, for example, I was a middle-class first-year student at an all-male Ivy League college, a training ground for the sons of the elite. Among my classmates' fathers were prominent figures in business, government, and the professions, who fully expected their sons to follow in their footsteps. In late fall, dorm residents who'd been accepted to fraternities prepared for "sink night," a time to celebrate their newfound "brotherhood" by getting very drunk. Before they went off, they warned freshmen not to lock our doors when we went to bed because they intended to pay us a visit later on and didn't expect to be stopped by a locked door. We didn't know what was coming, but there was no mistaking the dense familiar weight of men's potential for violence.

When they returned that night, screaming drunk, they went from door to door, rousting us from our beds and herding us into the hall. They lined us up and ordered us to drop our pants. Then one held a metal ruler and another a *Playboy* magazine opened to the centerfold picture, and the two went down the line, thrusting the picture in our faces, screaming "Get it up!" and resting our penises on the ruler. The others paced up and down the hall behind them, yelling, screaming, and laughing, thickening the air with a mixture of alcohol and held violence. None of us protested, and of course none of us "measured up." We weren't supposed to (any man who'd managed an erection would have become a legend on the spot). That, after all, was the point: to submit to the humiliation, to mirror (like women) men's power to control and terrorize in what we later learned was a rite of passage known as "the peter meter."

For them, perhaps, it was a passage to a fraternal bond forged in their shared power over the "others." For us, it was a grant of immunity from having to submit again, at least in this place, to these men, in this way. But our lack of outrage and the general absence of talk about it afterward suggest we got something else as well. As outrageous as the peter meter was, it touched a core of patriarchal truth about men, power, and violence that, as men, we found repellant and yet ultimately acceptable. The truth is, we, too, got a piece of real-man standing that night, for by deadening and controlling ourselves in the face of an assault, we showed that we had the right stuff. Had anyone protested, he wouldn't have been seen as the more manly for his courage. More likely, he'd have been called a sissy, a pussy, a little mama's boy who couldn't take it. And so we both lost and gained during our late-night dip in the patriarchal paradox of men competing and bonding at the same time.[10]

What about Women?

In one sense, women, like all else under patriarchy, are something for men to control. The consequences of this are enormous because of the damage it does to women's lives, but controlling women is neither the point of patriarchy nor the engine that drives it. This means that women's place is more complicated than it might seem, especially in relation to competition among men.[11]

This works in several ways. First, heterosexual men are encouraged to use women as badges of success to protect and enhance their standing in the eyes of other men. People routinely compliment a man married to a beautiful woman, for example, not because he had a hand in making her beautiful but because he has proprietary rights of access to her. In contrast, people are much less likely to compliment a man whose wife is financially successful—especially if she earns more than he does—because this threatens rather than enhances his status as a real man.

Men's use of women as badges of success is a prime example of how men can compete and ally with one another at the same time.[12] On the one hand, they may compete over who has the highest standing and is therefore least vulnerable to other men's control, as when they vie for a specific woman or use women in general as a way to keep score on their manhood. A man who lacks enthusiasm for pursuing women may have his masculinity questioned, if not attacked, especially by being "accused" of being gay. In this sense, "getting laid" is more than a badge of success. It's also a safe-conduct pass through perpetually hostile territory.

At the same time that men may compete with one another, they're also encouraged to bond around a common view of women as objects to be competed for, possessed, and used. When men tell sexist jokes, for example, or banter about women's bodies, they usually can count on other men to go along (if only in silence), for a man who objects risks becoming an outcast. Even if the joke is directed at his wife or lover, he's likely to choose his tie to men over loyalty to her by letting it pass with a shrug and perhaps a good-natured smile that leaves intact his standing as one of the guys.

In this sense, the competitive dynamic of patriarchal heterosexuality brings men together and promotes feelings of solidarity by acting out the values of control and male domination. This is partly why there is so much male violence against gay men: Since gays don't use women in this way, their sexual orientation challenges not so much heterosexuality per se but *male solidarity* around the key role of control and domination in *patriarchal* heterosexuality.[13] John Stoltenberg argues that violence against gays also protects male solidarity by protecting men from sexual aggression at the hands of other men.

> Imagine this country without homophobia: There would be a woman raped every three minutes and a man raped every three minutes. Homophobia keeps that statistic at a manageable level. The system is not fool-proof. It breaks down, for instance, in prison and in childhood—when men and boys are often subject to the same sexual terrorism that women live with almost

all the time. But for the most part homophobia serves male supremacy by keeping males who act like real men safe from sexual assault.[14]

A second part that women play in men's struggle for control is to support the idea that men and women are fundamentally different, because this gives men a clear and unambiguous turf—masculinity—on which to pursue control in competition with one another.[15] Women do this primarily by supporting (or at least not challenging) femininity as a valid view of who women are and how they're supposed to be. The idea that male sexuality is inherently aggressive, predatory, and heterosexual, for example, defines a common ground for men in relation to both women and other men. To protect this, it's important that women *not* be sexually aggressive or predatory because this would challenge the idea of a unique male sexuality as a basis for male solidarity, competition, and dominance. . . .

In a third sense, a woman's place is to support the key patriarchal illusion that men are independent and autonomous. An unemployed wife who sees herself as dependent, for example, props up images of male independence that mask men's considerable dependence on women for emotional support, physical comfort, and a broad range of practical services. On the average, for example, men tend to have a much harder time adjusting to the loss of a spouse than women do, especially at older ages. And the standard model for a career still assumes a wife at home to perform support work, putting any man (or woman) who doesn't have one at a disadvantage.[16]

The illusion of male independence and female dependence is amplified whenever men complain about the burdens of the provider role. In fact, however, most husbands would have it no other way, because for all its demands, the provider role brings with it power and status and exempts men from domestic work such as cleaning and child care. As a result, many men feel threatened when their wives earn as much or more than they do. They cling to the idea that earning a living is a man's responsibility that anchors male gender identity, and that women are little more than helpers in that role[17] if not "little women" waiting for a man to bring home the bacon. This arrangement, however, was created largely by working- and middle-class white men who fought for the "family wage" in the early 1900s. This enabled them to support their families by themselves and justified keeping wives at home, where they would be financially dependent and available to provide personal services.[18]

You might think that such arrangements are a thing of the past, that with so many married women working outside the home, the provider role is no longer male-identified. But the superficial appearance of gender equity and balance masks a continuing imbalance that's revealed when we consider how men and women would be affected by leaving paid employment. If the woman in a two-earner household were to give up her job, it might create hardships and negative feelings, but these probably wouldn't include making her feel less than a real woman. But for a man to give up his job, he'd have to contend with far more serious threats to his sense of himself as a real man, and both women and men know it. This is why, when someone in a marriage has to leave paid employment—to take care of children or ailing relatives, for example—it is generally understood that it will be the woman, regardless of who earns more.[19]

A fourth aspect of women's place is to help contain men's resentment over being controlled *by other men* so that it doesn't overpower the male solidarity that is essential to patriarchy. Most men are dominated by other men, especially at work, and yet judge their manhood by how much control they have in their own lives. It's a standard against which they're bound to fall short. If they rebel against other men—as when workers go on strike—the risks can be huge and the gains short-lived. A safer alternative is compensation in the form of social support to control and feel superior to women. This provides both individual men and patriarchy with a safety valve for the frustration and rage that might otherwise be directed toward other men and at far greater risk to both individuals and the system as a whole. No matter what other men do to a man or how deeply they control his life, he can always feel culturally superior to women and entitled to take out his anger and frustration on them.[20]

In this way, men are allowed to dominate women as compensation for their being subordinated to other men because of social class, race, or other forms of inequality. Ironically, however, their dominance of women supports the same principles of control that enable other men to subordinate them, a contradiction that is typical of systems of privilege. Men may buy into this so long as they can, in turn, enjoy the dominance that comes with applying those principles to women. The use of such compensation to stabilize systems also works with race and class inequality where one oppression is used to compensate for another. Working-class people, for example, can always look down on people receiving welfare, just as lower-class whites can feel superior to people of color. The playing off of one oppression against another helps explain why overt prejudice is most common among the most disadvantaged groups— because these are the people most in need of some kind of compensation.[21]

Related to men's use of women as compensation is the expectation that women will take care of men who have been damaged by other men. When he comes home from work, her role is to greet and take care of him, whether or not she's been at work all day herself. On a deeper level, she is supposed to make him feel whole again, to restore what he loses through his disconnected pursuit of control, to calm his fears—all, of course, without requiring him to face the very things about himself and patriarchy that produce the damage in the first place. When women fail to "make it better"—and they are bound to fail eventually—they are also supposed to be there to accept the blame and receive men's disappointment, pain, and rage. Men who feel unloved, incomplete, disconnected, battered, humiliated, frightened, and anxious routinely blame women for not supporting or loving them enough. It's a responsibility women are encouraged to accept, which is one reason so many victims of domestic violence stay with the men who abuse them.[22]

Misogyny

These days, even the slightest criticism of men or male dominance can prompt accusations of "man hating" or "male bashing." But only feminists seem to care about the woman hating that's been around for thousands of years as part of everyday life under patriarchy.[23]

The cultural expression of *misogyny*—the hatred (*mis-*) of femaleness (*gyny*)—takes many forms.[24] It's found in ancient and modern beliefs that women are inherently evil and a primary cause of human misery—products of what the Greek philosopher and mathematician Pythagoras called the "evil principle which created chaos, darkness, and woman.[25] There is misogyny in pornography that portrays women as willing victims of exploitation and abuse, in jokes about everything from mothers-in-law to the slapping around or "good fuck" that some women supposedly "need." Misogyny shaped the historical transformation of ancient wise-women healers into modern-day images of witches who roast and eat children. It has been the basis for the torture and murder of millions of women from the witch hunts of the Middle Ages to Serb terrorism in Bosnia. It is reflected in the everyday reality of sexual coercion, abuse, violence, and harassment, in the mass media display of women's bodies as objects existing primarily to please men and satisfy the male gaze, in cultural ideals of slenderness that turn women against their own bodies and inspire self-hatred and denial, and in the steady stream of sensationalized and sexualized mass media "entertainment" in which men terrorize, torture, rape, and murder women.[26]

Not to be overlooked is the insulting of males with names that link them to females—sissy (sister), girl, son of a bitch, mama's boy. Notice, however, that the worst way to insult a woman isn't to call her a man or a "daddy's girl." It's to *still* call her a woman but by names that highlight or malign femaleness itself—bitch, whore, pussy, cunt.[27] The use of such words as insults is made even worse by the fact that prior to patriarchy, many had neutral or positive meanings for women. A "whore" was a lover of either sex, "bitch" was associated with the pre-Christian goddess of the hunt, Artemis-Diana, and "cunt" derives from several sources, including the goddesses Cund and Kunda, the universal sources of life.[28]

It's difficult to accept the idea that in the midst of wanting, needing, and loving women, men are involved—if only as sons in relation to mothers—in a system that makes misogynist feelings, thoughts, and behavior paths of least resistance. Most men would probably deny this affects them in any way. Often the most sexist men are among the first to say how much they love women. But there's no escaping misogyny, because it isn't a personality flaw. It's part of patriarchal culture. We're like fish swimming in a sea laced with it, and we can't breathe without passing it through our gills.[29] Misogyny infuses into our cells and becomes part of who we are because by the time we know enough to reject it, it's too late. As with everything else in a culture, some people are exposed to more of it than others, but to suppose that anyone escapes untouched is both wishful and disempowering. It's wishful because it goes against what we know about socialization and the power of culture to shape reality. It's disempowering because if we believe that misogyny doesn't involve us, we won't feel compelled to do anything about it.

Misogyny plays a complex role in patriarchy. It fuels men's sense of superiority, justifies male aggression against women, and works to keep women on the defensive and in their place. Misogyny is especially powerful in encouraging women to hate their own femaleness, an example of internalized oppression. The more women internalize misogynist images and attitudes, the harder it is to challenge male privilege or patriarchy as a system. In fact, women won't tend to see patriarchy as even problematic since the essence of self-hatred is to focus on the self as the sole cause of misery, including the self-hatred.

In another sense, patriarchy promotes the hatred of women as a reaction to men's fear of women. Why should men fear women? Because every system of privilege depends to some degree on subordinate groups going along with their own subordination. The other side of this, however, is the potential to undermine and rebel by not going along. This makes privilege inherently unstable, which makes dominant groups vulnerable. Throughout the slave-holding South, for example, white people's fear of slave revolts was woven into the fabric of everyday life and caused many a restless night. And I suspect that much of the discomfort that whites typically feel around blacks today, especially black men, also reflects a fear that the potential for challenge and rebellion is never far from the surface.[30] In a patriarchal system the fear for men is that women will stop playing the complex role that allows patriarchy to continue, or may even go so far as to challenge male privilege directly. Women's potential to disrupt patriarchy and make men vulnerable is why it's so easy for women to make men feel foolish or emasculated through the mildest humor that focuses on maleness and hints at women's power to stop going along with the status quo. Making fun of men, however, is just the tip of the iceberg of what women can do to disturb the patriarchal order, and on some level most men know this and have reason to feel threatened by it.

In more subtle ways, misogyny arises out of a system that offers women to men as a form of compensation. Because patriarchy limits men's emotional and spiritual lives, and because men rarely risk being vulnerable with other men, they often look to women as a way to ease the resulting sense of emptiness, meaninglessness, and disconnection. However, the patriarchal expectation that "real men" are autonomous and independent sets men up to both want and resent women at the same time. This is made all the worse by the fact that women can't possibly give men what they want, since autonomy and independence are illusions. Caught in this bind, men could face the truth of the system that put them there in the first place. They could look at patriarchy and how their position in it creates this dilemma. The path of least resistance, however, is to resent and blame women for what men lack, by accusing women of not being loving or sexual enough, of being manipulative, with-holding, selfish bitches who deserve to be punished.[31]

In a related sense, misogyny can reflect male envy of the human qualities patriarchy encourages men to devalue and deny in themselves as they avoid association with anything remotely female. Under patriarchy, women are viewed as trustees of all that makes a rich emotional life possible—of empathy and sympathy, vulnerability and openness to connection, caring and nurtur-ing, sensitivity and compassion, emotional attention and expressiveness—all of which tend to be driven out of men's lives by the cycle of control and fear. On some level, men know the value of what they don't have and see women as privileged for being able to hold on to it. As a result, women live a double bind: The patriarchal ideology that supports male privilege and women's oppression devalues the human qualities associated with being female, yet it also sets men up to envy and resent women for being able to weave those same qualities into their lives.[32] . . .

As a mainstay of patriarchal culture, misogyny embodies some of the most contradictory and disturbing aspects of male privilege, When love and need are bound up with fear, envy, resentment, and the obsession with con-trol, the result is an explosive mixture that can twist our sense of ourselves and one another beyond recognition, If misogyny were merely a problem of bad personal attitudes, it would be relatively easy to deal with. But its close con-nection to the cycle of control and fear that makes patriarchy work will make it part of human life as long as patriarchy continues.

NOTES

Where Are We?

1. See Marilyn French, *Beyond Power: On Men, Women, and Morals* (New York: Sum-mit Books, 1985), 303.

2. For more on gender and dominant/subordinate relationships, see Jean Baker Miller, *Toward a New Psychology of Women*, 2nd ed. (Boston: Beacon Press, 1986).

3. There is a lot of research that shows how such uses of language affect people's per-ception. See, for example, Mykol C. Hamilton, "Using Masculine Generics: Does Generic 'He' Increase Male Bias in the User's Imagery?" *Sex Roles* 19, nos. 11/12 (1988): 785–799; Wendy Martyna, "Beyond the 'He/Man' Approach: The Case for Nonsexist Language," *Signs* 5 (1980): 482–493; Casey Miller and Kate Swift, *Words and Women*, updated ed. (New York: HarperCollins, 1991); and Joseph W. Schneider and Sally L. Hacker, "Sex Role Imagery in the Use of the Generic 'Man' in Introductory Texts: A Case in the Sociology of Sociology," *American Soci-ologist* 8 (1973): 12–18.

4. See, for example, Carole Levin's *The Heart and Stomach of a King: Elizabeth I and the Politics of Sex and Power* (Philadelphia: University of Pennsylvania Press, 1994).

5. See Carol Brooks Gardner, *Passing By: Gender and Public Harassment* (Berkeley: University of California Press, 1995).

6. See Paula England and D. Dunn, "Evaluating Work and Comparable Worth," *Annual Review of Sociology* 14 (1988): 227–248.

7. Mary Daly, *Beyond God the Father: Toward a Philosophy of Women's Liberation* (Boston: Beacon Press, 1973).

8. French, *Beyond Power*, 132.

9. See American Association of University Women, *How Schools Shortchange Girls; Gender Gaps: Where Schools Still Fail Our Children; A License for Bias: Sex Discrimination, Schools, and Title IX*; and Sadker and Sadker, *Failing at Fairness*.

10. See Susan Brownmiller, *Against Our Will: Men, Women, and Rape* (New York: Simon and Schuster, 1975); Andrea Dworkin, *Woman Hating* (New York: E. P. Dutton, 1974); Susan Faludi, *Backlash: The Undeclared War Against American Women* (New York: Crown Publishers, 1991); Marilyn French, *The War Against Women* (New York: Summit Books, 1992); Gardner, *Passing By*; Laura Lederer, ed., *Take Back the Night: Women on Pornography* (New York: William Morrow, 1980); Catharine MacKinnon, *Only Words* (Cambridge: Harvard University Press, 1993); Catherine MacKinnon, *Sex Equality: Rape Law* (New York: Foundation Press, 2001); "Medical News and Perspectives," *Journal of the American Medical Association* 264, no. 8 (1990): 939; Diana E. H. Russell, *Rape in Marriage* (New York: Macmillan, 1982); Idem, *Sexual Exploitation: Rape, Child Sexual Abuse, and Workplace Harassment* (Beverly Hills, CA: Sage Publications, 1984); Diana E. H. Russell, ed., *Making Violence Sexy; Feminist Views on Pornography* (New York: Teachers College Press, 1993); Diana E. H. Russell and Roberta A. Harmes, *Femicide in Global Perspective*. (New York: Teachers College Press, 2001).

11. This is true even in socialist societies such as Sweden. For research on men and domestic work, see R. L. Blumberg, ed., *Gender, Family, and Economy: The Triple Overlap* (Newbury Park, CA: Sage Publications, 1991); C. Goldin, *Understanding the Gender Gap: An Economic History of American Women* (New York: Oxford University Press, 1990); L. Haas, *Equal Parenthood and Social Policy: A Study of Parental Leave in Sweden* (Albany: State University of New York Press, 1992); Arlie Hochschild, *The Second Shift* (New York: Viking, 1989); M. J. Intons-Peterson, *Gender Concepts of Swedish and American Youth* (Hillsdale, NJ: Lawrence Erlbaum Associates, 1988); and J. R. Wilkie, "changes in U.S. Men's Attitudes Towards the Family Provider Role," *Gender and Society* 7, no. 2 (1993): 261–279.

12. For thorough accounts, see Faludi, *Backlash*, and French, *War Against Women*. For more recent information, see Women's Action Coalition, *WAC Stats: The Facts about Women* (New York: New Press, published annually).

13. For a provocative and insightful argument about what becomes of the values supporting free speech and those opposed to oppression and inequality, see MacKinnon, *Only Words*.

14. For more on this, see Marilyn Frye, *The Politics of Reality: Essays in Feminist Theory* (Freedom, CA: Crossing Press, 1983).

15. Sam Keen, *Fire in the Belly: On Being a Man* (New York: Bantam, 1991), 203.

16. See, for example, Susan Ostrander, *Women of the Upper Class* (Philadelphia: Temple University Press, 1984).

Why Patriarchy?

1. The following discussion draws on many sources, especially Robert Connell, *Gender and Power: Society, the Person, and Sexual Politics* (Stanford: Stanford University Press, 1987); Eisler, *The Chalice and the Blade*; Fisher, *Woman's Creation*; French, *Beyond Power*; David D. Gilmore, *Manhood in the Making: Cultural Concepts of Masculinity* (New Haven: Yale University Press, 1990); Miriam M. Johnson, *Strong Mothers, Weak Wives: The Search for Gender Equality* (Berkeley: University of California Press, 1988); Lee and Daly, "Man's Domination"; and Lerner, *The Creation of Patriarchy*.

2. French, *Beyond Power*, 337.

3. See Doris Kearns Goodwin, *Lyndon Johnson and the American Dream* (New York: St. Martin's Press, 1991).

4. French, *Beyond Power*, 508.

5. Simone Weil, "Analysis of Oppression," in *Oppression and Liberty*, translated by Arthur Wills and John Petrie (Amherst: University of Massachusetts Press, 1973), quoted in French, *Beyond Power*, 508.

6. Anyone who doubts this needs look no further than the nearest school playground and the persecution endured by boys who show any interest in playing with girls. Among adults, woe betide the man who openly prefers the company of women. See Barrie Thorne, *Gender Play: Girls and Boys in School* (New Brunswick, NJ: Rutgers University Press, 1993).

7. I haven't done the research, but I'd guess that men comprise the overwhelming majority of entries in the *Guinness Book of World Records*.

8. David Halberstam, *The Best and the Brightest* (New York: Random House, 1972), 76.

9. See William G. Domhoff, *The Bohemian Grove and Other Retreats* (New York: Harper and Row, 1974).

10. Women in this position, of course, would only lose.

11. See Joseph H. Pleck, "Men's Power with Women, Other Men, and Society: A Men's Movement Analysis," in *Men's Lives*, 2nd ed. edited by Michael S. Kimmel and Michael A. Messner (New York: Macmillan, 1992), 25.

12. See Johnson, *Strong Mothers, Weak Wives*, 117–118; and Pleck, "Men's Power with Women," 22–25.

13. See, for example, Frank Browning, *The Culture of Desire: Paradox and Perversity in Gay Lives Today* (New York: Crown Publishers, 1993); Tim Carrigan, Robert Connell, and John Lee, "Hard and Heavy: Toward a New Sociology of Masculinity," in *Beyond Patriarchy*, edited by Michael Kaufman, 139–192; and Suzanne Pharr, *Homophobia: A Weapon of Sexism*, exp. ed. (Inverness, CA: Women's Project, 1997).

14. John Stoltenberg, "Pornography and Freedom," in *Men's Lives*, edited by Michael S. Kimmel and Michael A. Messner (New York: Macmillan, 1989), 482–488.

15. This is a confused area of thinking about gender.

16. See J. M. Golding, "Division of Household Labor, Strain, and Depressive Symptoms among Mexican American and Non-Hispanic Whites," *Psychology of Women*

Quarterly 14, no. 1 (1990): 103–117; E. Litwak and P. Messeri, "Organizational Theory, Social Supports, and Mortality Rates," *American Sociological Review* 54, no. 1 (1989): 49–66; and J. Mirowksy and C. E. Ross, *Social Causes of Psychological Distress* (New York: Aldine de Gruyter, 1989).

17. See, for example, Jessie Bernard, "The Good Provider Role," *American Psychologist* 36, no. 1 (1981); R. C. Kessler and J. A. McRae, Jr., "The Effects of Wives' Employment on the Mental Health of Married Men and Women," *American Sociological Review* 47 (April 1982): 216–227; W. Michelson, *From Sun to Sun: Daily Obligations and Community Structure in the Lives of Employed Women and Their Families* (Totowa, NJ: Rowman and Allanheld, 1985); and J. R. Wilkie, "Changes in U.S. Men's Attitudes Towards the Family Provider Role, 1972–1989," *Gender and Society* 7, no. 2 (1993): 261–279.

18. See Heidi I. Hartmann, "The Unhappy Marriage of Marxism and Feminism: Towards a More Progressive Union," in *Women and Revolution*, edited by Lydia Sargent (Boston: South End Press, 1981), 1–41.

19. For some revealing case studies of how this works, see Arlie Hochschild, *The Second Shift: Working Parents and the Revolution at Home* (New York: Viking/Penguin, 1989).

20. This phenomenon is part of most oppressive systems, including racist ones. See Gerda Lerner, "Reconceptualizing Differences Among Women," in *Feminist Frameworks*, edited by Alison M. Jaggar and Paul S. Rothenberg, 3rd ed. (New York: McGraw-Hill, 1993), 237–248.

21. See David R. Roediger, *The Wages of Whiteness: Race and the Making of the American Working Class* (New York: Verso, 1991).

22. See Ann Jones, *Next Time She'll Be Dead: Battering and How to Stop It* (Boston: Beacon Press, 2000).

23. See Andrea Dworkin, *Woman Hating* (New York: E. P. Dutton, 1974); Susan Faludi, *Backlash: The Undeclared War Against Women* (New York: Crown Publishers, 1991); Marilyn French, *The War Against Women* (New York: Summit Books, 1992); and Catharine A. MacKinnon, *Only Words* (Cambridge: Harvard University Press, 1993).

24. It is notable that although a word for the hatred of maleness exists—*misandry*—it wasn't included in most dictionaries until very recently. The closest the English language comes to the hatred of males is *misanthropy*, which actually refers to the hatred of people in general. Once again, patriarchal culture identifies males as the standard of humanity while women are marginalized as a hate-worthy "other."

25. See B. Dijkstra, *Idols of Perversity: Fantasies of Feminine Evil* (New York: Oxford University Press, 1987); and S. Pomeroy, *Goddesses, Whores, Wives, and Slaves* (New York: Schocken, 1975).

26. See N. Ben-Yehuda, "The European Witch Craze of the 14th and 17th Centuries: A Sociologist's Perspective," *American Journal of Sociology* 86, no. 1 (1980): 1–31; Kim Chernin, *The Obsession: Reflections on the Tyranny of Slenderness* (New York: Harper and Row, 1981); C. P. Christ, "Heretics and Outsiders: The Struggle over Female Power in Western Religion," in *Feminist Frontiers*, edited by L. Richardson and V. Taylor (Reading, MA: Addison-Wesley, 1983), 87–94; Dworkin, *Woman*

Hating; Barbara Ehrenreich and Deidre English, *For Her Own Good: 150 Years of Experts' Advice to Women* (New York: Anchor Books/Doubleday, 1989); Faludi, *Backlash*; French, *War Against Women*; and MacKinnon, *Only Words*.

27. It's true that "prick" is a form of insult, but it doesn't have nearly the weight of likening men to women.

28. Barbara G. Walker, *The Woman's Encyclopedia of Myths and Secrets* (San Francisco: Harper and Row, 1983).

29. A metaphor I first heard from Nora L. Jamieson.

30. For some accounts of how this works, see Studs Terkel, *Race* (New York: New Press, 1992).

31. It should come as no surprise that abusive men tend to be very emotionally dependent on the women they abuse. See Ann Jones, *Next Time She'll Be Dead*; and Thomas J. Scheff and Suzanne M. Retzinger, *Emotions and Violence: Shame and Rage in Destructive Conflicts* (Lexington MA: Lexington, 1991). See also Claire M. Renzetti, *Violent Betrayal: Partner Abuse in Lesbian Relationships* (Newbury Park, CA: Sage, 1992).

32. I suspect a similar phenomenon occurs in other forms of oppression. Whites, for example, often look upon stereotypical characteristics of people of color with a mixture of contempt and envy. I've heard some whites say they would like to have the feeling of strength and wisdom that many African Americans have developed in order to survive in a racist society.

MICHAEL S. KIMMEL
From Manhood in America

Michael Kimmel is Professor of Sociology at Stony Brook University. His work explores men and masculinity from a feminist perspective and his many highly-acclaimed books include, The Politics of Manhood *(1996) and* The Gender of Desire *(2005). This selection is from his definitive book about masculinity:* Manhood in America: A Cultural History *(1996; 2005).*

MASCULINITY ON DISPLAY IN THE NEW MILLENNIUM

As the dawn of the millennium approached and then passed, American men still felt an urgent need to prove their masculinity. The ground may have been shifting under their feet and old structural buttresses eroding or disappearing, but men remained faithful to the traditional recipe for masculinity. And they searched again through the time-tested ways men had always searched: self-control, exclusion, and escape. A spate of new magazines and TV shows celebrated "men behaving badly"—without apology. *Maxim* and *FHM*, among others, sought to grab the ever-elusive younger men's attention with inviting hotties on every cover. (They boast of 2.5 million and 1 million subscribers, respectively.[1]) The most successful issue of a "sports" magazine is the one with the near-nude pinups. By the summer of 2003, TNN reinvented itself as "Spike TV—The First Network for Men" (just in case domination of virtually every television network but Lifetime, Oxygen, and WE weren't enough). It's filled with extreme sports, adult-themed cartoons such as *Striperella* (featuring the voice of Pamela Anderson), pro-wrestling, titillation, and movie reruns. *The Man Show*, originally hosted by Jimmy Kimmel (no relation), featured bikini-clad buxom babes jumping on trampolines, while guys offered up inane locker room humor. Here is *The Man's Show's* theme song, an unabashed and ironic invitation to masturbation:

> Grab a beer and drop your pants
> Send the wife and kids to France
> It's the Man Show!!
>
> Quit your job and light a fart
> Yank your favorite private part
> It's the Man Show!!

Such loutish resurgence, however unapologetic or ironic it appeared on the surface, revealed a desperate anxiety lurking just underneath. Men could no longer take their entitlement to ogle for granted; after four decades of feminist critique, it had to be reasserted loudly, angrily, with more than just a whiff of sadness.

After all, men were no longer the only ones looking. Feminism had empowered women to look at men's bodies, and those bodies — perfectly sculpted, hairless, tan, and muscular — were displayed everywhere. From the famous 1983 Calvin Klein underwear ad featuring a photograph of Olympic pole-vaulter Tom Hintinauss splayed languidly against a white phallic spire on the Greek Island of Santorini to Marky Mark and a host of perfectly sculpted and well-endowed models, men's eroticized bodies have been on parade. No wonder that most men actually believe their penises are underaverage in size![2]

It makes some sense that men's efforts to prove masculinity through bodily display would reach a fever pitch in the 1990s and into the new millennium. The relentless economic squeeze of working men was now coupled with an economic squeeze on middle- and even upper-middle-class men — the cutbacks, layoffs, outsourcing, and downsizing — meant that those bodies were of decreasing utility, replaced by what Susan Faludi decried as "the ornamental culture." And just as every other generation of American men sought to demonstrate their masculinity through bodily display, so too has this one.

One of the most successful new magazines in history was *Men's Health*, launched in 1988, which seemed to equate physical or psychological health with erections, abdominal muscles, and sexual performance. "Whether you're a lumberjack or a hard-driving CEO," its promotional flyer reads, "[T]oday's man really does care about his health, his good looks, his waistline, his emotional well-being, and his sexuality — just as much as the women in his life care about theirs — *if not more so*."[3]

Ministering to men's sexual anxieties also took on new meanings since 1998, when Viagra hit the market. The most successful new drug ever launched in the United States — over 35,000 prescriptions were filled in the first two weeks alone, and millions since — Viagra, and its recent competitors Cialis and Levitra, is designed to treat "erectile dysfunction" (the current term for what used to be called "impotence") by enabling men to achieve and sustain erections. Viagra is not an aphrodisiac, creating the desire in the first place, but is designed to work only when there is adequate sexual desire, that is, when the men want to have sex and are aroused. And what therapists call "inhibited sexual desire" or "low sexual interest" (once interestingly called frigidity in women) is now the leading sexual problem among men.[4]

No sooner did Viagra appear than it was misunderstood — or misrepresented. One Pfizer sales representative made it sound like the Fountain of Sexual Youth, a performance enhancer, not a medical treatment for a physiological problem. Although the medical treatment is "what it's intended to be used for," he told an interviewer, "I think the real use of Viagra is, say, for the guy who is probably forty-plus to age sixty-five that just isn't what he used to be and . . . Viagra is a real enhancer to, uh, I hate the word 'performance' but . . .

it will make it like he was when he was twenty." And millions of men gobbled the pills up. Men were eager—indeed, desperate—to see these problems as physiological even though most also experience "morning erections," which suggests that their problems are more psychological in origin. Many men crowed that they had found the "magic bullet" that enabled them to reclaim something they had lost—their potency, their power, their manhood. "You just keep going all night," gushed one man. "The performance is unbelievable." America had created "a masculinity pill."[5]

The stakes seem higher and the lengths (literally) to which men will go seem to be more extreme, but this may be more a matter of quantity than quality. Excessive bodybuilding and the use of chemical enhancements are, after all, nothing new in men's quest to be the hardest, strongest, and most powerful—or at least to appear to be so. The tonics and elixirs men consumed, and the "peniscope" and other contraptions from a century ago, seem both familiar and tame when placed next to contemporary iterations. Standards of muscularity have now increased so that many men experience what some researchers have labeled "Muscle Dysmorphia," the belief that one is insufficiently muscular. Harrison Pope and his colleagues call it the "Adonis Complex": the belief that men must look like Greek gods, with perfect chins, thick hair, rippling muscles, and washboard abdominals.[6] As an example, in 1999, he took G. I. Joe's proportions and translated them into real-life statistics. In 1974, G. I. Joe was 5 feet 10 inches tall and had a 31-inch waist, a 44-inch chest, and 12-inch biceps. Strong and muscular, it's true, but at least within the realm of the possible. By 2002, he was quite different: He's still 5 feet 10 inches tall, but his waist has shrunk to 28 inches, his chest as expanded to 50 inches, and his biceps are now 22 inches (almost the size of his waist). Such proportions would make one a circus freak, not a role model.[7]

As role models, they make many men feel they don't measure up. Nearly half of all men in one survey reported significant body image disturbance. A 1997 study reported in *Psychology Today* found 43 percent of the men were dissatisfied with their appearance, compared with only 15 percent twenty-five years earlier. As one college student told a journalist:

> When I look in the mirror, I see two things: what I want to be and what I'm not. I hate my abs. My chest will never be huge. My legs are too thin. My nose is an odd shape. I want what *Men's Health* pushes. I want to be the guy in the Gillette commercials.[8]

And just as women have resorted to increasingly dangerous surgical and prosthetic procedures, such as having silicone-filled baggies placed in their breasts or being given mild localized doses of botulism to paralyze facial muscles and thereby "remove" wrinkles, so too are men resorting to increasingly dramatic efforts to get large. The use of anabolic steroids has mushroomed. While chemically enhanced athletes steal most of the nation's outraged headlines, it's college-aged men who have become the primary consumers of steroids. Legal prescriptions for steroids have doubled since 1997, to more than 1.5 million, and countless more illegal sources provide less regulated doses. Steroids enable men to increase muscle mass quickly and dramatically so that they look incredibly big. Prolonged use also leads to dramatic mood changes, increased uncontrolled rage, and a significant shrinkage in the testicles.[9]

In their efforts to appear strong and healthy, fit and trim, men have followed women under the cosmetic surgeon's scalpel. Male patients now make up about 20 percent of all procedures. "More men are viewing cosmetic surgery as a viable way of looking and feeling younger," observed ASPRS President Dennis Lynch, MD, "especially, to compete in the workplace." Such a comment underscores the homosociality of men's demonstration of manhood: It is performed before the evaluative eyes of other men. Nowhere is this more painfully revealed than in a more extreme example of cosmetic surgery: Penile enhancement. This is a dramatic (and expensive) procedure — every year about 15,000 men pay about $6,000 to have it done — by which the penis can be lengthened by about two inches.[10]

While one might think that men undergo this painful procedure to become "better" lovers or to please women more, the primary motivation is that the men suffer from what one physician called "locker room syndrome" — the fear of being judged as inadequately masculine *by other men*. Take, for example, the testimonial letter from a satisfied customer:

> I was always afraid to get into a situation where I would have to shower with other men or be seen by anyone. I can remember avoiding many of the sports and activities I loved dearly, all because I was afraid that I would be seen and made fun of . . . I even avoided wearing shorts and tight clothes because of my fear that others would notice me.

"The thing I missed most was the changing room camaraderie and male bonding associated with these sports, which was always something I enjoyed," writes another. "I felt ashamed to even go to the urinals in a public place and have made sure I never use these whilst other men are there too."[11]

Men's bodies have long been symbols of masculinity in America. They reveal (or at least they signify) manhood's power, strength, and self-control. As the functional economic utility of that strong, hard body has virtually disappeared, its association with masculinity remains as firm as ever. Maybe it's no longer through doing hard work but by working out, and maybe now it is chemically or surgically enhanced, but still men believe the title of that feminist health classic: Our bodies are ourselves.

HERE, QUEER AND EVER SO TRENDY

The traditional big, buff, and brawny image of muscular masculinity has also come in for his share of criticism by women who found him an insensitive lout, boorish and boring. "Chick flicks" such as *My Best Friend's Wedding* and *The Object of My Affection* imagined straight guys as clueless clods, while in both films it was gay men who were suddenly the men whom women wanted to be around. All the gal pals of the hit HBO comedy *Sex and the City* had good gay male friends and hoped that their boyfriends could become "gay straight men" (heterosexuals who exhibited gay affect and style) as opposed to "straight gay men" (who were simply closeted gay men). "Why can't you be more like him?" whispered many a straight woman to her boyfriend, nudging him the ribs and pointing to Rupert Everett or Eric MacCormack in the hit sitcom *Will and Grace*. The message was simple: Gay men know what straight women want. And if straight men could just be a "little bit gay," they'd do very well among women.

Enter the "metrosexual." He's manicured, pedicured, buffed, and shined. His clothes are tailored. He knows all the latest hair care and skin care products. He pumps up and shops 'til he drops. He cooks, cleans, and preens. Oh, and by the way, he's straight.

The term *metrosexual* was coined by British journalist Mark Simpson in 1994 to describe a decidedly urban, and urbane, new man who was emerging in the cosmopolitan centers of Europe and the United States (To Simpson, international soccer star David Beckham was the prototype metrosexual: An urban dandy, wearing nail polish, married to a former Spice Girl.) *New York Times* writer Warren St. John recognized a version of him in upscale eateries and boutiques in New York in the summer of 2003. According to Simpson, the "typical metrosexual is a young man with money to spend, living in or within easy reach of a metropolis—because that's where all the best shops, clubs, gyms and hairdressers are."

Fashionable, preoccupied with proper skin and hair care, he represented the return of a newly masculinized dandy or fop. As such, he expressed the acceptance of at least one expression of the urban gay male sensibility; the emergence of the metrosexual is predicated on the partial decline in homophobia among heterosexual men. But the metrosexual is just as much a meditation about class as he is a new embodiment of manhood. It's a particular type of manhood: trim and fit, to be sure, but hardly pumped, and far more urbane and stylish than those hulking steroid-enhanced ectomorphs. The metrosexual promised an alternate route to the achievement of masculinity through high-end consumerism. The metrosexual was promoted as an upwardly mobile aspiration—middle-class guys dressing and accessorizing for success.

But even these metrosexual pioneers were riffing off the "liberated" masculinity of the late 1950s and early 1960s, described by journalist Barbara Ehrenreich in her book *The Hearts of Men* (1987). Ehrenreich claimed that several cultural trends in the 1960s enabled a group of middle-class white men to reject the traditional definition of masculinity (the stable, suburban, married breadwinner) and express a cheerful narcissism as they pampered themselves with high-end stereo equipment, sports cars, and wine cellars.

As the older action heroes were increasingly laughed off as cartoons — Vin Diesel and The Rock are pale substitutes for Arnold Schwarzenegger and Bruce Willis — metrosexuals began turning up as a happy compromise: Still secure in his masculinity, he has little to prove to anyone, yet he is equally comfortable expressing emotions and dispensing advice about hair care products. In the popular TV show, *Will and Grace*, Will is a model, not for gay men but for straight men — exactly the men who really want to know what will captivate beautiful, sexy, and interesting women like Grace. (He's set off against Jack, the flaming queen, so that we're able to accept Will as a "good gay," maybe even a "straight gay," and laugh at Jack, the "fey gay," or maybe even the "gay gay.")

One startling example has been the surprising success of the television show *Queer Eye for the Straight Guy*, which debuted in 2003. In it, the "Fab 5" (five clever, campy, and culturally sophisticated gay men) target a forlorn, disheveled straight guy and give him (and his apartment) a total makeover. Each of the five has a specialty: food and wine, home décor, hair styles, clothing, and interpersonal manners. And each works his transformative magic with wit and flair. In the debut episode, they transformed an aspiring artist named Brian into someone who actually looked like his nickname "Butch." When he first appeared, Brian looked like he had just returned from the Altamont concerts — in 1970! Dirty brown overalls, long stringy hair, unkempt beard, and an apartment just one slight move up from cantaloupe crates for records and concrete blocks and boards for books. One half-hour later (in TV time, of course), he looks fabulous. His beard is now a goatee, his hair shaped and stylish, his clothing elegantly dressed-down chic, and his apartment the well-appointed home of a bachelor. That evening, women are so stunned by his transformation that their sexual interest oozes from every gaping stare. He's become a babe magnet — dashing, well mannered, utterly sexy.

Many critics argue that the metrosexual was hardly a progressive step toward a new masculinity but instead represented simply a narcissistic unapologetic consumer. And some felt *Queer Eye* only reinforced stereotypes of gay men as self-absorbed fashion plates. On the other hand, for once the stereotypes seem to work the other way: At the same time that gay men and lesbians are counseled that through "conversion therapy" they can become straight, in this "reality" show, the straight guy is transformed into an almost-gay guy. In that sense *Queer Eye* depends at least in part on the erosion of homophobia among straight men. Imagine such a show in 1993, not 2003. Most viewers would have thought a show with the title *A Queer Eye for the Straight Guy* was about gay men hitting on straight men in a bar. The second episode would have been called *A Black Eye for the Gay Guy*.

Yet a steady weekly parade of straight guys have invited the Fab 5 into their homes and let them rifle through their closets while launching cutting campy barbs about their lifestyle. The men touch each other affectionately and make caustic remarks dripping with sexual innuendo. And by the end of the show, the straight guy . . . hugs them! He thanks them! He realizes he needs them! Ironically, it's the insecurity of heterosexuality that begins to erode homophobia. "We're here, we're queer, we're fabulous, and we know what women want" is the message of *Queer Eye*. And if you're going to make it with the *Sex and the City* type of sexy single modern woman, the show seems to say, you'll need us to show you how.

Of course, metrosexuality is not for every man, let alone Everyman. Many younger men remain insecure about their sexuality and are unwilling to be mistaken for gay. "I don't want to be associated with some pansy wearing Kenneth Cole," one young man explained. After all, "That's so gay" continues to be the single most common putdown in middle schools and high schools in the nation. Metrosexuals are also mostly white men. Some wealthier and older black men can and do represent themselves as metrosexuals, such as K-Street's Roger G. Smith. Others choose an urban aesthetic that is less demonstrably gay, less feminine, and much less white. A *New York Times Magazine* article examining black men's lives "on the down low" revealed that many black men having sex with other black men refused to call themselves gay, not just because of the stigma of gayness and the loss of masculinity they associate with it, but because of gayness' association with whiteness.

Metrosexuality expresses many of the tensions among contemporary American men. It's playful in its gender bending and sexual tolerance and in its depoliticized consumerism masquerading as freedom. At its best, metrosexuality may promote reconciliation between straight and gay men. "Gay guys and straight guys may do things a little differently in the bedroom," says *Queer Eye* creator David Collins, "but in the end, we're all just guys."[12] Since our culture had devalued "feminine" men for so long, metrosexuality offers a sense of vindication for some men. As one women exclaimed, "there have always been guys like these, but it wasn't the popular thing. . . . Guys who are acting this way today are considered attractive." It may be liberating to "bend it like Beckham"—gender, that is. . . .

DEFENDING THE CAVEMAN: THE NEW MALE BASHERS

Traditional definitions of masculinity have their supporters. As has always been the case throughout American history, when masculinity is perceived as in crisis, there are those who defend a nostalgic traditional vision of gender relations that would return men to their "rightful" position of dominance. In the nineteenth century, this defense relied on theological arguments; by the turn of the twentieth century, biological arguments had supplanted religion as the dominant defensive discourse. Today it's both biology *and* theology—even if they do make rather strange bedfellows. In fact, defenders of traditional masculinity will use virtually any rhetorical means they can find. Many recapitulate backlash arguments from the 1970s and 1980s, blaming feminism for the gender "inversion" that has created men's plight. The sustained "assaults" by feminism and multiculturalism have made a biological imperative into a political liability. A few now go as far as to claim that in promoting girls and women, American society had swung the pendulum so far that we were making male biology a political "problem." Yet, in the guise of promoting and defending men and masculinity, these defenders actually celebrated a definition of masculinity that was far more insulting and "male bashing" than anything ever promulgated by feminists.

Take, for starters, the new academic field of "evolutionary psychology," which offers a pseudo-biological argument for male dominance. Taking up where sociobiology left off in the 1970s, evolutionary psychology sees men behaving badly as men behaving naturally, the way men are biologically programmed to behave. In the evolutionary psychological worldview, all human nature and all gender-based differences are encapsulated in the differences between males and females in the mating game. Males and females, we learn, have different reproductive "strategies" based on the size and number of their reproductive cells. From the cellular (sperm and egg), we get the psychological (namely, motivation, intention, perhaps even cognition). Male reproductive success comes from impregnating as many females as possible; females' success comes from enticing a male to provide and protect the vulnerable and dependent offspring. Sex is "something females have that males want," according to Donald Symons.[13] Thus males have a natural predisposition toward promiscuity, sex without love, and parental indifference; females have a natural propensity for monogamy, love as a precondition of sex, and parental involvement. "It is possible to interpret *all* other differences between the sexes as stemming from this one basic difference," writes Richard Dawkins in his celebrated work *The Selfish Gene*. "Female exploitation begins here."[14]

These arguments have been effectively exposed as ideology masquerading as science by primatologist Sarah Blaffer Hrdy, who has used the exact same empirical observations to construct an equally plausible case for females' natural propensity toward promiscuity (to seduce many males into believing the offspring is theirs and thus ensure survival by increasing food and protection from those males) and males' natural propensity toward monogamy (to avoid being run ragged providing for offspring that may — or may not — be their own). If I were a female at the mythic Darwinian moment of origin, Hrdy suggests, and if I knew that I had to invest a lot of time and energy in reproduction, I'd do the following: I'd "decide" to conceal ovulation so that any males I mate with would believe he is the father of my children and would then have to protect and provide for the reproduction of his genetic material. Then I'd promptly go out and have sex with as many males as possible so that each would believe the offspring to be his, and then each would run himself ragged feeding and protecting all the children who might — or might not — be his. Hoggamus higgamous, woman's polygamous! Female exploitation actually *ends* there; that is, it's a present day phenomenon read back into a mythic history, a faux-Darwinian "just-so" story.

In an effort to ensure successful reproduction, a reasonable man, by contrast, probably calculates the likelihood of any particular mating resulting in a healthy live offspring. Do the math, as journalist Natalie Angier does in her marvelous book *Woman, An Intimate Geography*. Let's say that I am able, somehow, to know when a woman is ovulating (unlike other mammals that go into heat, human females conceal ovulation, thus masking their periods of fertility) and therefore is likely to conceive. The odds are still nearly two to one against fertilization *on the day she is ovulating*, Even if conception occurs, the embryo still has nearly a one-third chance of miscarrying at some point. Thus, as Angier puts it, "[E]ach episode of fleeting sex has a remarkably small probability of yielding a baby—no more than 1 or 2 percent at best." But if a man were to invest a lot more time with one woman, mating with her often and preventing her from possible matings with others (what animal behaviorists call "mate guarding"), then his odds of successful reproduction would significantly increase. Higgamus hoggamus, it's man who's monogamous! And just to keep her in her place, he would surround his sexual control over her with an ideological veneer (let's call it "love") and by legally sanctioning it by church and state (let's call that "marriage"). What gender invented love anyway? And given that men control all other arenas of social, economic, and political life, why would they ever cede the single most important arena—successful reproduction, the raison d'etre of all life—to women?

While the feminist critique exposes evolutionary psychology's ideological view of women, its view of men is even more noxious. "Human males are by nature oppressive, possessive, flesh-obsessed pigs," writes Robert Wright. "Giving them advice on successful marriage is like offering Vikings a free booklet titled 'How Not to Pillage,'" he writes in his best-selling book *The Moral Animal*.[15] It would be hard to find a more insulting view of masculinity than Randy Thornhill and Craig Palmer's *A Natural History of Rape* (1999), which goes so far as to claim that rape is "a natural, biological phenomenon that is a product of human evolutionary heritage."[16]

Since, they argue, each male's biological predisposition is to reproduce, and reproductive success comes from spreading his seed as far and wide as possible, women are actually the ones with the power, since they get to choose which males will be successful. "But getting chosen is not the only way to gain sexual access to females," they write, "In rape, the male circumvents the females' choice."[17] Rape is the evolutionary mating strategy of losers, males who cannot otherwise get a date. Rape is an alternative to romance; if you can't always have what you want, you take what you need. As they write:

> [H]uman males in all societies so far examined in the ethnographic record possess genes that can lead, by way of ontogeny, to raping behavior when the necessary environmental factors are present, and that the necessary environmental factors are sometimes present in all societies studied to date.[18]

All men have the "motivation" to rape; all they need is social permission. Who says no one in his or her right mind could possibly believe that all men are rapists? Since "selection favored males who mated frequently," they argue, then "rape increased reproductive success.[19] But why should this be true? Might it not also be the case that being hardwired to be good lovers and devoted fathers enabled us to be reproductively successful? One might argue that selection did not favor males who mated frequently but those who mated *well*, since successful mating is more than spreading of seed. Being an involved father may ensure reproductive success far better than rape.

Thornhill and Palmer offer a far more "misandrous" account of rape than anything offered by radical feminists. To them, men are driven by evolutionary imperatives to rape, pillage, and destroy in order to ensure that they are still reproductively successful. This view is echoed by several neo-conservative thinkers who, in their effort to discredit feminism and gay liberation, actually end up insulting men.

The argument begins as a critique of feminism. By abandoning their natural roles as wives and mothers in the home and seeking satisfaction in the workplace in some vain imitation of men, women (encouraged by feminism) have reversed nature's plan and wreaked social havoc. Women's naturally demure sexual purity no longer tames men. Absentee fathers, sexual promiscuity, gang rape, and homosexuality are the inevitable results. George Gilder's 1986 *Men and Marriage* (the republication of his 1973 book *Sexual Suicide*) offers a Hobbesian view of masculinity: "solitary, poor, nasty, brutish and short."[20]

Men are, by nature, violent, sexually predatory, and irresponsible:

> Men lust, but they know not what for; they wander, and lose track of the goal; they fight and compete, but they forget the prize; they spread seed, but spurn the seasons of growth; they chase power and glory, but miss the meaning of life.[21]

An "importunate, undifferentiated lust . . . infects almost all men." Male sexuality is haphazard, irresponsible, non-procreative; intercourse is "the only male sex act."[22] Sexually inferior, men compensate with sexual aggression and predation. Gilder reserves his fiercest animus for younger men and boys who are, in his eyes, untamed beasts:

> Every society, each generation, faces an invasion by barbarians. They storm into the streets and schools, businesses and households of the land, and, unless they are brought to heel, they rape and pillage, debauch and despoil the settlements of society.[23]

Who are they? "These barbarians are young men and boys," Gilder informs us, who are "entirely unsuited for civilized life." Without marriage, the single man is "poor and neurotic. He is disposed to criminality, drugs and violence. He is irresponsible about his debts, alcoholic, accident prone, and susceptible to disease."[24] These young men, single and unattached, must be brought into the civilizing project by women. It is women's job to "transform male lust into love; channel male wanderlust into jobs, homes, and families." It is women who "conceive the future that men tend to flee: . . . [and] feed the children that men ignore."[25]

Gilder suggests if men stay single, the sexual demons reign, leading to the worst scourge of all: homosexuality. In an interesting reversal of stereotypes, gay men are, in Gilder's view, untamed sexual beasts: "[W]ith their compulsive lust and promiscuous impulses [gay men] offer a kind of caricature of typical single male sexuality."[26] Gay men are real men after all; in fact they're more "real" than straight men.

Other conservative policy analysts continue to build on Gilder's shaky foundation. For example, Charles Murray, coauthor of *The Bell Curve*, holds that young males are "essentially barbarians for whom marriage . . . is an indispensable civilizing force." Christina Hoff Sommers, author of *Who Stole Feminism?* and *The War Against Boys,* told an audience that "masculinity without morality is dangerous and destructive." And sociologist David Popenoe warns that "[e]very society must be wary of the unattached male, for he is universally the cause of numerous social ills."[27]

Popenoe is one of the chief academic proponents of a position that holds that irresponsible men are the cause of a current crisis in the institution of marriage. Fathers must remain attached to their families. "Men are not biologically as attuned to being committed fathers as women are to being committed mothers. Left culturally unregulated, men's sexual behavior can be promiscuous, their paternity casual, their commitment to families weak," he writes.[28]

Pundit David Blankenhorn makes a similar case in his near-hysterical book *Fatherless America* (1995), a collection of specious correlations that together blame virtually every social pathology on absent fathers. Often the correlations simply have it backward: Fatherlessness is more often the *consequence* of poverty than it is the cause.[29] Instead of a clarion call for a new fatherhood, based on emotional receptivity and responsiveness, compassion and patience, care and nurture, though, Blankenhorn actually despises that model of a "nurturing" man who "expresses his emotions," is "a healer, a companion, a colleague," a "deeply involved parent." He has little use for a father who "changes diapers, gets up at 2:00 a.m. to feed the baby, goes beyond 'helping out' in order to share equally in the work, joys, and responsibilities of domestic life."[30]

In Blankenhorn's view, this sensitive New Age father does all this because he "reflects the puerile desire for human omnipotentiality in the form of genderless parenthood, a direct repudiation of fatherhood as a gendered social role for men."[31] So the *real* father is neither nurturing nor expressive; he is neither a partner nor a friend to his wife, and he sleeps through most of the young baby's infantile helplessness, oblivious to the needs of his wife and child. Men are fathers, but they are not parents; they don't actually have to do any child care at all. The father "protects his family, provides for its material needs, devotes himself to the education of his children, and represents his family's interests in the larger world" — all valuable behaviors, to be sure, but also behaviors that do not require that he ever set foot in his child's room.[32] The notion that men should be exempt from mundane housework and child care, which should be left to their wives, is, of course, insulting to women. But it's also insulting to men because it assumes that the caring and nurturing of life itself cannot be men's province; give how clumsy and aggressive men are, all that had better be done at a distance.

It's not men's fault, of course; it's women's. As at every turn in American history, some version of antifeminism has masqueraded as a defense of masculinity. This agenda is most simply made by Harvey Mansfield, Harvard political scientist, in a 1997 op-ed essay in the *Wall Street Journal*. "The protective element of manliness is endangered by women who have equal access to jobs outside the home," he writes. "Women who do not consider themselves feminist often seem unaware of what they are doing to manliness when they work to support themselves. They think only that people should be hired and promoted on merit, regardless of sex."[33] Lionel Tiger claims that "the principal victims of moving toward a merit-based society have been male." Imagine that: Feminists actually believe in meritocracy, while those who would support men want to keep that playing field as uneven as possible. Tiger's most recent book, *The Decline of Males* (1999), argues, topsy-turvy, that "the male and female sex in industrial societies are slowly but inexorably moving apart," just at the moment when all available evidence — epidemiological, economic, social, and psychological — suggests precisely the opposite.[34] Males are in decline because women now control sexuality. By gaining control over birth control, they claimed all the sexual power. Now that women are the captains of the social ship, men are listing badly.[35]

And that's where the pop psychologists come in. Both "Dr." Laura Schlessinger and "Dr." John Gray have become modest-sized industries that manufacture light equipment for successful relationships, building multi-million-dollar psychological empires by scolding women into scaling back their expectations and accepting men just as they are — the lunks.[36] Schlessinger, the nationally syndicated talk show host, has made her mark by dispensing pop psychological bromides like bitter little pills. She confronts her listeners, yells at them, and makes fun of their foibles. And they love it! Her advice book for women, *The Stupid Things Women Do to Mess Up Their Lives* (1995), was a best-seller, another on an already sagging shelf of volumes that blame women for the inconstancies, infidelities, and inadequacies of the men in their lives. Its companion volume, *Ten Stupid Things Men Do to Mess Up Their Lives* (1998), also spends a good amount of time chastising seemingly smart women for their foolish choices, as does the final volume in the trilogy, *Ten Stupid Things Couples Do to Mess Up Their Relationships* (2001).

Basically, she argues, men are total losers, but they can't help it, the lovable oafs. They're biologically driven toward violence, aggression, and dumb choices in love.[37] In one of the most brilliant rhetorical strategies this side of

Jonathan Swift, she dispenses classically feminist advice to men in the guise of bashing those awful feminist harpies who are so bitter and angry all the time. She goes out of her way to bash "overgeneralizing, incredibly negative, hysterical, man-loathing" feminist ideas held by "insanely radical contemporary feminists."[38] Dr. Laura offers exactly the same critique of men that radical feminists have given for the past thirty years: Men are not caring, nurturing, loving, attentive, and emotional enough with their wives, their children, and their friends. She urges men to end rape, to stop beating up their wives, and to be more present in the home. But whose fault is that really? "Men would not do half of what they do if women didn't let them," she told an interviewer for *Modern Maturity* magazine recently. "That a man is going to do bad things is a fact. That you keep a man who does bad things in your life is your fault."[39]

John Gray may be the most successful self-help author of all time. His eight self-help books have sold tens of millions of copies worldwide; the flagship book, *Men Are from Mars, Women Are from Venus*, has sold more than 10 million copies in the United States alone. His central conceit is that men and women are completely different. To read *Men Are from Mars* or its identical cousins, you'd think we were different species, like, say, lobsters and giraffes are. Gray believes that not only do women and men communicate differently, but they also "think, feel, perceive, react, respond, love, need, and appreciate differently [and are] from different planets, speaking different languages, and needing different nourishment."[40]

The interplanetary differences in Gray's astronomy are hardwired into maleness and femaleness, the result, he says, of "DNA programming."[41] To demonstrate this, Gray recites a list of physical differences, aside from the rather obvious ones. Among other things, men have thicker skin, longer vocal cords, and heavier blood with more oxygen (to enable them to breathe more deeply). His books are liberally sprinkled with statements about how men "automatically" do some things and women "instinctively" do something else and how our "natural cycles" make communication difficult.

These biological differences are the origin of the fundamentally different personalities that men and women everywhere have. For example, men value power, competency, efficiency, and achievement; women value love, communication, beauty, and relationships. Women are "more intuitive, are more interested in love and relationships, and experience difference reactions to stress," while men have a "greater interest in producing results, achieving goals, power, competition, work, logic, and efficiency."[42] In relationships, a man is like a rubber band: He pulls away, stretching only so far and then springing back; he "automatically alternates between needing intimacy and autonomy." A woman is like a wave, her self-esteem rising and falling depending upon whether she feels loved.[43] Women are afraid of receiving; men are afraid of giving. "Women have an incredible capacity to give without getting back"; men, on the other hand, "are not instinctively motivated to offer their support: they need to be asked."[44]

Communication problems are inevitable. Men "silently 'mull over' or think about what they have heard or experienced"; women gab about it with everyone in sight. Or, from a Venusian perspective, she knows to sensibly talk things through while he becomes an uncommunicative rock.[45] Perhaps the best one can hope for is a sort of interplanetary détente in which women simply accept that Martians are impatient, inexpressive slobs who hog the remote control. At the seminars and lectures I've attended, I've noticed that the men were significantly older than the women, old enough, perhaps, to be their fathers. Gray's message seems to appeal to younger women, between ages 20 and 35, trying to initiate and sustain romantic relationships with men as they're pulled between family and career. His message also appeals to somewhat older men, in their late 40s and early 50s trying to make their second marriage work better than the first. There "post-feminist" women and "pre-feminist" men get the same basic message: Women must abandon any idea of changing him. "The secret of empowering a man is never to try to change or improve him."[46]

That message has become staple fodder of women's magazines and reaches its apotheosis in *The Rules*,[47] a guide that promises to help women land a husband through a step-by-step retreat through the 1950s and back to the 1840s, when Catherine Ward Beecher, Sarah Hale, and others articulated the need for separate spheres and for women to be "the angel of the house," in Virginia Woolf's memorable phrase. Women's problem is that they can't find husbands, and the reason for that is that women have been too busy being men's equal to connive to trap men in the time-tested ways that our grandmothers did, by holding out through manipulative coquetry. The most successful rule: "[T]reat the men we *wanted* like the men we *didn't* want."[48]

If our man is a couch potato, here's what *The Rules* would counsel:

> When he watches the ballgame on TV all afternoon instead of helping you clean the house, don't zap the tube off in a moment of anger. Nicely tell him you need his help. If he still insists on watching the game, leave him alone. Tell yourself "No big deal."[49]

Though the book is intended to be read by women, it's an important book for men to read as well, especially because it tells men what conniving, manipulative women those *Rules* gals are being counseled to be! But also consider what such behavior by women actually says about men. Men are "born to respond to challenge," biologically "the aggressor" who must pursue the women. Men love to be treated badly—treated as though they were not wanted—because that will only prime that testosterone to pump up their competitive hunting urges and really go after their prey. Men are overgrown babies who want everything their own way, who want "constant attention and companionship" as well as someone to clean up after them. Peter Pan is the icon for an entire gender: They won't grow up! And if you treat men like adults, they will run away and hide in their cave with John Gray.[50]

So the message here is simple: Women, your unhappiness is your own fault. For men, the message is far more insidious: You're fine just as you are; you don't have to change at all. "Don't try to change him because men never really change," write Fein and Schneider.[51] They're incapable of real change, and so fragile that they must be constantly coddled with kid gloves. But they're also destined to be unemotional grunters, at home nowhere in the world except their individually constructed caves. The best women can hope for is to come home, play by the rules, land a man of her very own, and hope he treats her well. Now *that's* insulting to men.

WHAT ABOUT THE BOYS?[52]

One of the primary arenas of rhetorical struggle has been in the classroom. At the turn of the last century, you will recall, cultural observers worried that the dominance of female teachers, female Sunday School teachers, and especially mothers was emasculating young boys, turning hardy, robust boyhood into "a lot of flat-chested cigarette smokers with shaky nerves and doubtful vitality," as you'll recall Boy Scout founder Ernest Thompson Seton put it. Just as American men were now leaving home and heading off to work, becoming virtual absentee landlords in their own homes, critics found a way to blame women for their sons' enervation and emasculation.

Today, the argument is slightly different in origin but has a remarkably similar tone. The dramatic successes of feminist-inspired educational policy reforms initiated since the 1980s—policies to reduce the "chilly classroom climate," the dominance of boys and the prevalence of sexual harassment of girls—have now rebounded to the detriment of boys, we are told. Boys, we hear, are the new victims of gender discrimination in schools. After all, what happens to boys in schools? They have to sit quietly, take naps, raise their hands, be obedient—all of which do extraordinary violence to their "natural" testosterone-inspired rambunctious playfulness. "Schools for the most part are run by women for girls. To take a high spirited second or third grade boy and expect him to behave like a girl in school is asking too much," comments Christina Hoff Sommers, author of *The War Against Boys.* The effect of education is "pathologizing boyhood." While we've been paying all this attention to girls' experiences—raising their self-esteem, enabling them to take science and math, deploring and preventing harassment and bullying—we've ignored the boys.[53]

On college campuses, the gender disparities also seem to indicate a reversal of fortunes between women and men. Women now constitute the majority of students on college campuses (passing men in 1982), so by 2010 women will earn 58 percent of bachelor's degrees in U.S. colleges and there are three women for every two men at the nation's community colleges. One reporter, obviously a terrible statistics student, tells us that if present trends continue,

"[T]he graduation line in 2068 will be all females." (That's like saying that if the enrollment of black students at Ol' Miss was 1 in 1964, 24 in 1968, and 400 in 1988, by 1994 there would have been no white students there.) Women now outnumber men in the social and behavioral sciences by about three to one, and they've invaded such traditionally male bastions as engineering, where they now make up about 20 percent of all students, and biology and business, where the genders are virtually on a par.[54]

But the numbers cited by critics just don't add up. For one thing, more *people* are going to college than ever before. In 1960, 54 percent of boys and 38 percent of girls went directly to college; today the numbers are 64 percent of boys and 70 percent of girls. Much of the gender disparity is actually what sociologist Cynthia Fuchs Epstein calls a "deceptive distinction," a difference that appears to be about gender but is actually about something else—in this case, class or race. The shortage of male college students is also actually a shortage of *nonwhite* males. The gender gap between college-age white males and white females is rather small, 51 percent women to 49 percent men. But only 37 percent of black college students are male and 63 percent are female, and 45 percent of Hispanic students are male, compared with 55 percent female.

Of course, boys do merit attention. In primary school, boys are more likely to be sent to child psychologists (by about four to one) and far more likely to be diagnosed with dyslexia and attention deficit disorder (ADD) than are girls. Throughout their schooling, boys receive poorer report cards: they are far more likely to repeat a grade. Nine times more boys than girls are diagnosed as hyperactive; boys represent 58 percent of those in special education classes for the mentally retarded, 71 percent of the learning disabled, and 80 percent of the emotionally disturbed. Nearly three-fourths of all school suspensions are of boys. By adolescence, boys are more likely to drop out, flunk out, and act out in class.[55]

But the recent research into the inner lives of boys indicates that the problem has far less to do with feminist-inspired education reforms and far more to do with the very definitions of masculinity that these new boyhood defenders are defending. Young girls, assertive, confident, and self-aware, psychologist Carol Gilligan found, tend to "lose their voice" when they hit adolescence.[56] By contrast, boys become more confident, even beyond their abilities. Just at the moment that girls lost their voices, boys *find* one—but it is the inauthentic voice of bravado, of constant posturing, of foolish risk-taking and gratuitous violence. According to psychologist William Pollack, boys learn that they are supposed to be in power and thus begin to act like it. "Although girls' voices have been disempowered, boy's voices are strident and full of bravado," he observes. "But their voices are disconnected from their genuine feelings." Thus, he argues, the way we bring boys up leads them to put on a "mask of masculinity," a posture, a front. They "ruffle in a manly pose," as the poet William Butler Yeats put it, "for all their timid heart."[57]

It turns out that it is not the school experience that "feminizes" boys but rather the ideology of traditional masculinity that keeps boys from wanting to

succeed. Boys see academic success itself as a disconfirmation of their masculinity. "reading is lame; sitting down and looking at words is pathetic," commented one boy to a researcher.

"Most guys who like English are faggots," commented another. The traditional liberal arts curriculum is seen as feminizing by boys. "The work you
do here is girls' work," one boy commented to a researcher. "It's not real work."
Such comments echo the consistent findings of social scientists since James
Coleman's path-breaking 1961 study that identified the "hidden curriculum"
among adolescents in which good-looking and athletic boys were consistently
more highly rated by their peers than were good students.[58] Or, as the feminist
critic Catharine Stimpson put it sarcastically, "[R]eal men don't speak French."[59]

Those who suggest that feminist-inspired reforms have been to the detriment of boys believe that gender relations are a zero-sum game and that if girls
and women gain, boys and men lose. But the reforms that have been initiated
to benefit girls in class—individualized instruction, attention to different
learning pathways, new initiatives, classroom configurations, teacher training,
and more collaborative team-building efforts—have also been to the benefit
of boys as well, as such methods would also target boys' specific experiences.
And the efforts to make the classroom safer and more hospitable to girls have
also redounded to boy's benefit. Take, for example, classroom decorum. In
1940, the top disciplinary problems identified by high-school teachers were
(in order): talking out of turn, chewing gum, making noise, running in the
hall, cutting in line, violating dress code, and littering. In 1990, the top disciplinary problems were (again, in order): drug abuse, alcohol abuse, pregnancy,
suicide, rape, robbery, and assault.[60] Challenging stereotypes and having
decreased tolerance for school violence and bullying enable both boys and girls
to feel safer at school. Those who would simply throw up their hands in resig-
nation and sigh that "boys will be boys" would have you believe that nothing
can or should be done to make those classrooms safer. In my estimation, those
four words, "boys will be boys," may be the most depressing words in educational policy circles today.[61] Consider instead an editorial in the Amherst
College newspaper, *The Amherst Student*, when the school first debated coedu-
cation at the turn of the twentieth century: "Every step in the advancement of
women has benefited our own sex no less than it has elevated her."[62]

ANGRY BOYS

Just because the right-wing rescuers of traditional masculinity and untram-
meled boyhood have it entirely backward doesn't mean that boys are not in
trouble. What many of the recent spate of books about boys has revealed is
that the pressures to live up to the "boy code" leave many boys suppressing
emasculating emotions like vulnerability, dependency, and compassion and
effecting, instead, a hypermasculine unemotional pose.[63] Proving masculinity
remains vitally important to young men, even as the opportunities to do so

seem to be shrinking. Boys look to their fathers, public figures, athletes, and other media-created heroes, and they evaluate—constantly, relentlessly—each other's performance. Anyone who doubts one of this book's central arguments—that the testing and proving of masculinity is a "homosocial" experience, performed before and evaluated by the eyes of other men—need look no further than adolescent peer culture. And one of the central markers of American manhood has, for many decades, been the capacity of violence.

Recall the turn of the last century when fears of enervated and emasculated boyhood led to the promotion of rough-and-tumble boyhood, schoolyard fistfighting, and organized sports. Today, the capacity for violence is a marker of authentic masculinity (as in *Fight Club*), a test of manhood. Just about every boy and man in American has some experience with violence, either using it himself, having it used against him, or being threatened with its use if he steps out of line or crosses someone. American men learn from an early age to fight back and that there are few expressions more legitimate than retaliatory violence. Violence is immoral if you use it first, but it is redemptive if you use it second. Moral men don't get mad but get even; men don't start fights, but they are eager to finish them.

At no time in life is violence more prevalent than among boys and young men. Stated most baldly, young American men are the most violent group of people in the industrial world. The age group sixteen to twenty-four commits *most* of the violent crime in America. Our homicide rate is much higher than that of any other industrial country; in 1992, young men between fifteen and twenty-four had a homicide rate of 37.2 per 100,000. This is ten times higher than the next highest, that of Italy, and sixty times higher than Britain's.

And it's getting worse. Between 1985 and 1994, the number of homicides by fourteen- to seventeen-year-old males more than tripled. According to the California Highway Patrol, nine out of ten of those arrested for drunk driving are men; 84 percent of those jailed for fatal accidents resulting from drunk driving are men, and 86 percent of arson crimes are committed by men. Nationwide, nine of ten (nonparking) driving infractions are committed by men; 93 percent of all road rage accidents are caused by men.

One needn't look very far to see the real "boy crisis" in America. Ask any kid in middle school or high school anywhere in the country what is the most common putdown in his or her school. The answer is, "That's so gay." The fear of being tainted with homosexuality—the fear of emasculation— has morphed into a generic putdown. These days, "That's so gay" has far less to do with aspersions of homosexuality and far more to do with "gender policing," making sure that no one contravenes the rules of masculinity. Listen, for example, to that eminent gender theorist Eminem as he defended the constant homophobic references to "fags" in his raps. In an interview on MTV, he explained that the ubiquitous gay-baiting and calling other guys "faggots" were not slurs on their sexuality but a challenge to their masculinity. "The lowest degrading thing that you can say to a man . . . is to call him a faggot and try to take away his manhood. Call him a sissy. Call him a punk. 'Faggot' to me doesn't mean gay people. 'Faggot' just means taking away your manhood."[64]

High schools have become far more than academic testing grounds; they're the central terrain on which gender identity is tested and demonstrated. And unlike the standardized tests for reading and arithmetic, the tests of adequate and appropriate gender performance are administered and graded by your peers, by grading criteria known only to them. Bullying has become a national problem in high schools, in part because of the relentlessness and the severity of the torments. Verbal teasing and physical bullying exist along a continuum stretching from using hurtful language through shoving and hitting to criminal assaulting and school shootings. Harmful teasing and bullying happen to more than one million schoolchildren a year.

If bullying creates hostile high-school hallways, those homosocial preserves within the school can be even more terrifying. Locker rooms, sports teams, and even the school band are plagued by increasingly dangerous and harmful incidents of hazing. There were over one hundred hazing-related deaths on high-school and college campuses between 1995 and 2005. A national survey of high-school students found that hazing is ubiquitous. Nearly half (48 percent) of all students who belong to a group reported being subjected to hazing; 43 percent were subjected to humiliating activities and fully 30 percent performed possibly illegal acts as part of their initiation. Hazing was so universal that there were virtually no groups that were safe. One-fourth of all students involved in church groups were subjected to hazing. Substance abuse in hazing is prevalent in high school (23 percent) and increases in college, where over half of all hazing activities (51 percent) involve substance abuse.

Most of the kids who are targeted manage to cope; they're resilient enough or have enough emotional resources to survive reasonably intact. Many try valiantly, and often vainly, to fit in, to conform to these impossible standards that others set for them. Some carry psychological or even physical scars for the rest of their lives. Some withdraw and become depressed, alienated, or despondent. Some self-medicate with drugs or alcohol, and a few explode. As every adolescent knows, "doing a Columbine" means exploding in a murderous rage—and taking as many classmates and teachers as you can with you.

Since 1992, there have been twenty-eight cases of random school violence in which a young boy (or boys) opened fire on classmates;[65] all twenty-eight were committed by boys. Contrary to many stereotypes, all but one of those cases took place in a rural or suburban school, not an inner-city school, and all but one of the shooters were white. Yet we seem to have missed this in all the discussion about these school shootings. We continue to call the problem "teen violence," "youth violence," "gang violence," "suburban violence," "violence in the schools." Just who do we think is doing it—girls? Imagine if the shooters in schools in Littleton, Colorado; Pearl, Mississippi; Paducah, Kentucky; Springfield, Oregon; and Jonesboro, Arkansas were instead black girls from poor families who lived in New Haven, Newark, Detroit, Compton, or South Boston. *Then* we'd notice race and class and gender! We'd likely hear about the culture of poverty, life in the inner city, and racial violence. Someone, I'd bet, would blame feminism for encouraging girls to become violent in vain imitation of boys.[66] Yet the obvious fact that these school killers were all middle-class white boys seems to have escaped almost everyone's notice.

More startlingly, though, is not that they were all middle-class white boys but that so many also had the same story. Virtually every single one of the shooters had a story about being targeted for gay baiting, bullied, and harassed—not every now and then but constantly, daily. Why? It was *not* because they were gay (at least there is no evidence to suggest that any of them were gay) but because they were *different* from the other boys—shy, bookish, academically talented, artistic, musical, theatrical, nonathletic, "geekish," or weird. It was because they were not athletic, were overweight or underweight, or wore glasses.

Take Luke Woodham, a bookish, overweight sixteen-year old in Pearl, Mississippi. An honor student, he was part of a little group that studied Latin and read Nietzsche. Students teased him constantly for being overweight and a nerd and taunted him as "gay" or "fag." Even his mother called him fat, stupid, and lazy. Other boys bullied him routinely, and, according to one fellow student, he "never fought back when other boys called him names." On October 1, 1997, Woodham stabbed his mother to death in her bed before he left for school. He then drove her car to school, carrying a rifle under his coat. He opened fire in the school's common area, killing two students and wounding seven others. After being subdued, he told the Assistant Principal, "The world has wronged me." Later, in a psychiatric interview, he said, "I am not insane. I am angry . . . I am not spoiled or lazy; for murder is not weak and slow-witted; murder is gutsy and daring. I killed because people like me are mistreated every day. I am malicious because I am miserable."

Or recall Michael Carneal, a fourteen-year-old freshman at Heath High School in Paducah, Kentucky. Shy and skinny, Carneal was barely five feet tall and weighed about one hundred and ten pounds. He wore thick glasses and played in the high school band. He felt alienated, pushed around, picked on. Boys stole his lunch and constantly teased him. In middle school, someone pulled down his pants in front of his classmates. He was so sensitive and afraid that others would see him naked that he covered the air vents in the bathroom and was devastated when students called him a "faggot" and the school gossip sheet labeled him as "gay." On Thanksgiving 1997, he stole two shotguns, two semiautomatic rifles, a pistol, and seven hundred rounds of ammunition, and after a weekend of showing them off to his classmates, he brought them to school hoping that they would bring him some instant recognition. "I just wanted the guys to think I was cool," he said. When the cool guys ignored him, he opened fire on a morning prayer circle, killing three classmates and wounding five others. Now serving a life sentence in prison, Carneal told psychiatrists weighing his sanity, "[P]eople respect me now."[67]

At Columbine High School, the site of the nation's most infamous school shooting, this connection was not lost on Evan Todd, a 255-pound defensive lineman on the Columbine football team, an exemplar of the jock culture that Dylan Klebold and Eric Harris found to be such an interminable torment. "Columbine is a clean, good place, except for those rejects," Todd said. "Sure we teased them. But what do you expect with kids who come to school with weird hairdos and horns on their hats? It's not just jocks; the whole school's disgusted with them. They're a bunch of homos. . . . If you want to get rid of someone, usually you tease 'em. So the whole school would call them homos." Ben Oakley, a soccer player, agreed. "[N]obody liked them," he said. "[T]he majority of them were gay. So everyone would make fun of them." Athletes taunted them; they would throw rocks and bottles at them from moving cars. The school newspaper had recently published a rumor that Harris and Klebold were lovers.[68]

Actually, both appeared to be reasonably well-adjusted kids. Harris's parents were a retired Army officer and a caterer, decent well-intentioned people. Klebold's father was a geophysicist who had recently moved into the mortgage services business, and his mother worked in job placement for the disabled. Harris had been rejected by several colleges; Klebold was due to enroll at Arizona in the fall. But the jock culture was relentless. "Every time someone slammed them against a locker and threw a bottle at them, I think they'd go back to Eric or Dylan's house and plot a little more — at first as a goof, but more and more seriously over time," said one friend.[69]

The rest is now painfully familiar. Harris and Klebold brought a variety of weapons to their high school and proceeded to walk through the school, shooting whoever they could find. Students were terrified and tried to hide. Many students who could not hide begged for their lives. The entire school was held under siege until the police secured the building. In all, twenty-three students and faculty were injured and fifteen died, including one teacher and the perpetrators.

Of course, these explosions are rare; most bullying victims manage to survive reasonably intact. But what is pervasive, and what does seem to be notably elevated, is the level of anger expressed by and experienced by boys and young men. It's everywhere they turn. Older teenage boys spend countless hours blowing up the galaxy, graphically splattering their computer screens in violent video games. Teenage boys splay violent pornography everywhere in their dorm rooms; indeed, pornographic pictures are the most popular screen savers on their computers. They listen to imbecilically juvenile shock jocks on the radio when they aren't listening to hate-filled enraged musicians screaming venom at them; they're laughing at cable-rated T&A or guffawing to the sophomoric body-fluid humor of Beavis and Butthead. The Southern Poverty Law Center reports that racist hate activity among kids "has probably never been more widespread, or more violent." Racist graffiti, swastika tattoos, and Confederate T-shirts abound in American small-town and suburban high schools.

And, as we've seen, they're learning all this from their fathers. Today's angry men are raising a generation of angry boys.

SPORTS CRAZY

The world of sports has long been a masculine refuge, a pristine homosocial world of male bonding. At the turn of the last century, participation in sports was prescribed by those cultural observers who saw both American boyhood wracked by indolence and emasculated by overdominance of women and American manhood enervated into lassitude by office work and modern life.

So, too, it is with sports today, at least in part. While the professional ranks remain sex-segregated, it's also true that the increase in female participation and female competence has been extraordinary. Today, in every high school and college, there are plenty of girls who can run circles around many of the boys on soccer fields and tennis courts. Perhaps that's one reason for the increased popularity of football, as feminist writer and former Sanford basketball player Mariah Burton Nelson noted when she titled her first book *The Stronger Women Get, the More Men Love Football*. It may also be a reason for the exponential growth in one aspect of the sporting life. It's not *doing* sports that seems to have increased among guys because the ranks of American men are pretty divided, as we have been for some time, between ascetic, health-conscious jogging junkies and drinking and smoking coach potatoes. No, it's *talking* about sports that has ballooned into a steady stream of 24-7 television, radio, fantasy leagues, and Internet sites. Women may be doing sports almost as much as men are, but they don't like to talk about it very much. Maybe the stronger women get, the more men love *to talk about* football. In classrooms and around water coolers, men's sports talk is hardly harmless banter; it's a mechanism for the political exclusion of women. Like conducting business meetings at Hooters or local upscale strip clubs or hosting power breakfasts at 7 A.M., the emphasis on sports talk redraws the boundaries of sex segregation and keeps women out.

Not only do men talk about it with a vengeance, but they keep consuming every more "extreme" sports, in some cases, extreme "sports" like professional wrestling, which offers hypermuscular caricatures of masculine icons locked in a timeless Manichean struggle between absolute good and absolute evil. (Professional wrestling, NASCAR races, and golf have moved into the top five sports on television, having edged baseball out.)

Perhaps one of the reasons sports has become contemporary American men's dominant institution is that it embraces all three strategies men have historically employed to prove their manhood. Participation in sports builds the body; it requires strength, skill, size, and stamina—and self-control. It's also, at least in principle, an all-male preserve, excluding those feminizing "others" from its hallowed fields. It's both the exclusion of others and a manly escape from them. Take, for example, the dramatic rise in golf among middle-class men. Their working world is increasingly heterogeneous: few can "escape" female colleagues, coworkers, supervisors, even bosses. Their home life is increasingly "androgynous": They have to cook, clean, and take care of the kids just like their working wives do. But on that golf course, that pristine field of masculine dreams, guys hang with other guys; it's a frat house and locker rook for middle-aged middle-class men. No wonder Hootie Johnson, Chairman of Augusta National, was so adamant about refusing to admit women. But, more importantly, no wonder so many otherwise sensible family men become apoplectically defensive about separate tee times for women and men. At least the golf course can remain a homosocial preserve, and the nineteenth hole a man's lair.

Another arena in which men's defensive anger is evident is the debate about the implementation of Title IX. When Title IX legislation was enacted by Congress as part of the 1964 Civil Rights Act, its intent was to alleviate the dramatic inequalities in educational opportunities afforded women and men. It's been especially useful in leveling the athletic playing field. No sooner was it implemented, though, than the backlash began. Several prominent universities (Brown, for example, among them) went to court to try and prevent full implementation, and several wrestling teams attempted to file federal sex discrimination suits with the Justice Department's Civil Rights Division, claiming "equal protection" violation. Once again, boys — white boys — were claiming to be the victims of reverse discrimination. (The Justice Department declined to take up any of these cases, since, as one of the department's lawyers explained it to me, "there is no constitutionally protected right to wrestle.")

FROM THE MASCULINITY OF POLITICS TO MASCULINITY AS POLITICS

Even before the terrorist attacks of 9-11, masculinity was intimately connected to American politics. Since the founding of the country, the electorate had always been assessing the manly strength and conviction of its leaders. A strong hand and firm resolve as well as virile restraint and a calm judiciousness, especially in the event of or the threat of war, have been seen as necessary to steer the ship of state. And while this has led, in part, to the exclusion of women from the pinnacles of power in the United States (compared to, for example, Israel, Britain, India, Pakistan, and other less bellicose nations), it has also enabled America to remain a beacon of hope to millions around the world.

That beacon had most often a decidedly parental (that is, a paternal) glow. It was not simply a man's guiding hand but that of an older man, a father figure, who could embody both comfort and strength. Ronald Reagan exuded those qualities in abundance and was perhaps the most popular president in the twentieth century. Even his more feckless successor, George H. W. Bush, while a bit more patrician than paternal, still projected a sagacious calm.

The election of 1992 proved a generational watershed as well as a changing of political parties. Just as John F. Kennedy had announced his administration as the first of a generation born "in this century," so too did Bill Clinton represent the first generation born after World War II, for whom Vietnam was the defining war and who grew up amid the unparalleled prosperity of the 1950s. Clinton's manhood was always in doubt and always on display. He didn't serve in the military, and his wife was hardly the subservient but gracious hostess we had come to expect from First Ladies; he expressed his feelings and felt our pain. Depicted by his enemies as alternately conniving and gay (in both cases, Hillary was depicted as a demonically masculinized hydra), he was also beloved by his admirers as deeply compassionate and politically astute. The revelations of a sexual liaison with Monica Lewinsky, a White House intern, seem to have confirmed rumors of is habitual skirt-chasing, and his subsequent impeachment trial was discrediting, if not dethroning.[70] Now satirized as a satyr, he had little political capital to spend on his successor and spent the campaign of 2000 on the sidelines.

The campaign featured two literal as well as symbolic sons. George W. Bush and Al Gore were both the namesake sons of venerated political fathers and had been carefully groomed for elective office. Yet Gore could not shake his image as a ruling-class wimp when compared to the equally preppy, equally Ivy League, and equally entitled Bush. No matter how Gore tried to "butch" it up and present the male toughness of an alpha male, as he was advised by feminist writer Naomi Wolf, he seemed officious, elite, and effete. It was as if Gore presented an image of the man who had never been a boy; Bush, by contrast, appeared as the boy who had never grown up, a good-time frat boy Peter Pan. And white men, who voted overwhelmingly for Bush, made clear whom they would rather have hanging out in the White House.

And yet Gore won the election—that is, he won the popular vote and probably would have won the Electoral College had not the Supreme Court intervened to stop the recount of the popular vote in Florida. Riddled with fraud, those votes were never counted, and Bush was crowned as president under a cloud of suspicion. America was deeply divided politically, but also about gender. Red states and blue states signified something important about images of masculinity as well: gun owners vs. gun controllers, aggressive military vs. conciliatory and diplomatic corps, environmentally rapacious policies vs. environmental stewardship, tax-cutting free marketeers who run up the debt vs. fiscal conservatives who are prudent in both taxation and spending.

Bush's first term of office steered the nation hard to the right. Already by September 11, 2001, there were policies to open wilderness to oil exploration and real estate development, to cut taxes and social services, and to curtail the rights of women, gays and lesbians, and other minorities. Bush's avowed religiosity harked back to the Muscular Christianity of the previous century. Gone was the forgiveness of Christian compassion; in its stead was the angry and vindictive God whose wrath was boundless against His enemies.

MASCULINITY AND 9-11

September 11, 2001, changed America — and the world. Indeed, it is often hard to recall the America before we were attacked by terrorists. In the years following the terrorist attacks on New York City and Washington, D.C., masculinity — both "ours" and that of the terrorists — has been very much debated and discussed. In a constructed cartoon version of good versus evil, masculinity versus cowardice, masculinity has been bandied about in contradictory ways: The terrorists are cowardly and diabolical; American men are courageous but peace-loving. Both cultural critic Susan Sontag and television commentators Bill Maher were vilified for daring to suggest that whatever else they were, the terrorists of 9-11 were not cowardly. (The fact that Maher's show was called "Politically Incorrect" did not dissuade the Manichean calls for his hide.)

On September 10, 2001, you may recall, firefighters, police officers, and soldiers represented some of the last remaining resisters of gender equality. Firehouses especially were bastions of men behaving badly, citadels of unreconstructed chauvinism. Photos of the fire department's graduating class every year looked more like the graduating class of the Citadel in 1964. How had New York City's fire department come to resemble a southern military school on the eve of integration? It's not that firefighters were the "bad guys" — one always distinguishes between the actual individual firefighters and the structure of their organization — but they were hardly the swoon-at-their-feet heroes they became on September 12.

Witness the divided fortunes of the two musical genres I discussed earlier: country and rap. Since 9-11, country music's been "firemanized," with its celebration of police, firefighters, and soldiers and its near-hysterical promotion of war against all comers. But rap's lost its focus; its anger feels almost sacrilegious. Eminem's most recent album is demonstrably tamer; groups like Outkast, Kanye West, or even Twista present a musical style more lovable than dangerous.

The nation's White Wing was politically divided by September 11. On one side were those who saw nonwhites, aliens, attacking America; they proclaimed the moment of holy war to have arrived and urged their followers to pick up their weapons and start killing immigrants. On the other hand, others marveled at the blow struck against America's Zionist Occupied Government and the symbols of global capitalism and governmental corruption, the World Trade Center and Pentagon. "We could work with those Islamic guys," one Alabama Klansman told a journalist. They "all feel the same way we do about who controls the world." Some even said they admired the terrorists' "testicular fortitude." "It's a disgrace that in a population of at least 150 million White/Aryan Americans, we provide so few that are willing to do the same," bemoaned Rocky Suhayda, Nazi Party chairman from Eastpointe, Michigan. "A bunch of towel head/sand niggers put our great White Movement to shame.[71]

On the other side of the class divide, on September 10, the newly installed global image of corporate masculinity was still riding high, despite the bursting of the dot-com bubble and the economic plunge into recession and the complicity of some of its most prominent high flyers in corporate scandals, the scale of which make Teapot Dome look increasingly like a tempest in a teapot. This globalized businessman became recognizable as a type in the late 1980s, and by 2001 had become the dominant image of a new class of corporate men around the world. He's readily identifiable: He sits in first-class waiting rooms or in the lobbies of elegant business hotels the world over in a designer business suit, speaking English, eating "continental" cuisine, talking on his cell phone, plugging his laptop computer into any electrical outlet in the world while he watches CNN International on television. Temperamentally, he is increasingly cosmopolitan, with liberal tastes in consumption (and sexuality) and conservative political ideas of limited government control of the economy.

The events of 9-11 reversed the fortunes of both images of masculinity. The rehabilitation of heroic masculinity among the firefighters, police, and other rescue workers was immediate. A headline in *The New York Times* proclaimed "Heavy Lifting Required: The Return of Manly Men," and a photo of brawny rescue workers, police, and firefighters reminded readers that "the attacks of Sept. 11 have brought more than a few good men back into the cultural limelight." A "Calendar of Heroes" with beefcake-like pinups of real firefighters sold sensationally. Even those few writers and pundits who managed to notice that there were female firefighters, police, and rescue workers among the heroes of 9-11 trumpeted the revival of traditional masculinity. "A certain kind of woman is tired of the dawdlers, melancholics and other variants of genius who would not know what to do with a baseball mitt or a drill press," gushed one female journalist. Real men were back—and we were safer for it. Some even proclaimed the crisis of masculinity over.[72]

The global business class has fared less well. Just as he was reeling from the bursting dot-com bubble, his masculinity quotient seems to be tumbling alongside the NASDAQ. Still connected to transnational institutions like the global marketplace, the European Union, and the United Nations, he's now seen as a dandified slave to the fashion designers of "Old Europe" (Secretary of Defense Donald Rumsfeld's term for those EU nations that had the temerity to oppose the U.S. invasion of Iraq). It is suspected he may even speak French. Globalization's well-dressed *Homo economicus* as been pushed aside by the reemergence of *Homo Reaganomicus*—the recharged militarized masculinity that proudly proclaims the United States not only as the world's only true superpower but as the axis of an emerging global empire. Beholden to no one and accountable to no one, U.S. foreign policy can be summed up simply: "Our way or the highway."

President George W. Bush is the icon of this new-old masculinity, a cowboy iteration derived less from the real western frontier than from cinematic westerns. (His wife calls him a "windshield cowboy," since he doesn't ride horses and surveys his ranch from a pickup truck.) Bush and his advisors clearly understand how masculinity is a "social construction" and forgo few opportunities to construct their man as a real man. Recall, for example, the image of the president, in military flight fatigues, staging a photo op to announce the end of the war against Iraq. Not only was he the first president in the twentieth or twenty-first century to don military attire (even Eisenhower restrained himself, and he was a general!), but the entire event was a staged pseudo-event, taking place a mile off the San Diego coast with the boat positioned to obscure the view of the coastline. This charade, "a masculine drag performance," was widely ridiculed, especially by real generals such as Wesley Clark, who scoffed at Bush "prancing on the deck of an aircraft carrier." But he was the first president to become an action figure![73]

Others are equally iconic. New York's then–Mayor Rudy Guiliani's belligerent authoritarianism was suddenly transformed into a laudatory steadfastness in the face of danger. Secretary of Defense Rumsfeld and his coterie of battle-pristine hawks in control of American foreign policy (who have not one day of actual military service among them) swagger into battle. *People* magazine called Rumsfeld one of the "sexiest Americans alive," CNN called him "a virtual rock star." Fox News labeled him a "babe magnet," and the president even began to call him "Rumstud." With testosterone-drenched rhetoric, American policy makers strut like bullies through the halls of the middle school—pushing inferior wimps out of the way, flouting the law, ignoring the fact that no one especially likes them, defying teachers, and daring the administration to do something about it. And it's probably not the last we'll see of this. One senior official made clear that masculinity was wrapped up in this ever-escalating military escapade. "Anyone can go to Baghdad," he said. "Real men go to Tehran."[74]

The new American unilateralism is pitted against Old Europe's reliance on cooperative institutions and its promotion of social welfare and peace. The invasion of Iraq, the prosecution of terrorism in places both real and imagined, and the stewardship of the economy have been the dominant political issues of the post-9-11 era. These issues dominated the presidential campaign of 2004, offering America a new choice of heroes.

ELECTION OF 2004 AND BEYOND

Rarely has a national election been more saturated with contested images of masculinity than the presidential election of 2004. Not since the election of 1840, when William Henry Harrison wimp-baited President Martin Van Buren, had masculinity been the axis around which the election was to revolve. In that election, the handlers and operatives for Harrison, Van Buren's Whig opponent, crafted an entire campaign to avoid any political issues and focused instead on Van Buren's gendered shortcomings.

Although we have discussed this campaign earlier, it might be useful to refresh the memory. In 1840, political songs chastised "Little Van" the "used up man," who "wore corsets, put cologne on his whiskers, slept on French beds, and rode in a British coach." One Harrison supporter declared van Buren's White House to be staffed by "French cooks" who furnished the president's table with "massive gold plate and French sterling silver services." (It is true that Van Buren presided over the installation of indoor plumbing in the White House.) Davy Crockett, he of unimpeachable masculinity, declared that "it would be difficult to say," from Van Buren's appearance, "whether he was man or woman." And it was rumored that when Van Buren read about these scandalous attacks, "he burst his corset." Campaign posters depicted Harrison, his sleeves rolled up and spade in hand, in front of his log cabin. In fact, none of it was true. Van Buren was a capable administrator, the son of an upstate New York innkeeper; Harrison was an aristocratic scion, bred in a three-story manor on a Virginia plantation. But the campaign worked. Over 80 percent of the eligible white male voters turned out for the election, and Harrison won in a landslide.

As in 1840, in the campaign of 2004 an aristocratic blueblood—prep school, Ivy League, summers in Kennebunkport—cast himself as a virtual log-cabin-born Everyman who raised himself by his bootstraps. And he cast his opponent, a sage and sober bureaucrat, as soft and sensitive, under the thumb of an emasculating wife. Bush snickered as Kerry windsurfed and waffled. Arnold Schwarzenegger, our own contemporary Davy Crockett, calls Kerry a girlie man. What might have been seen as "manly reticence" was sneered at as "patrician aloofness." Kerry, we heard, "looks French." Kerry and John Edwards, his running mate, were called "the first metrosexual presidential hopefuls." Edwards's styled hair brought him the label "the Breck Girl."[75]

More than representing two contrasting masculine styles, Kerry and Bush also embodied two competing masculine visions. President Bush embodies an older version of nineteenth-century manhood, hale and hardy, more comfortable clearing brush than debating policy. He offers casual swagger coupled with obstinate certainty, a resolute resistance to accepting blame for failures—the buck stops somewhere else. You know where he stands, even if it's in quicksand. Bush's election was understood by one reporter as "one of the last convulsions of angry, real American men, fighting desperately (and well) to hold back the time and tide of the new—the un-white and the un-Christian, and girlie-men too, who sooner or later will be America."[76]

John Kerry fought bravely in a war and, following his experience in Vietnam, did the unthinkable for a man: He changed his mind. He then fought bravely against it. This was, of course, used against him, proof that he waffled and flip-flopped in a feminine way. (Rarely has an election so denigrated femininity as a liability.) On Memorial Day weekend, one New York tabloid published the fictitious menus of the two candidates. For Bush it was sausages and beer (nonalcoholic, of course), and for Kerry it was frogs' legs, chardonnay, and crème brulee. It was parodies like these, and not his meritorious service or economic policies, that seemed to resonate with white male voters, who turned out overwhelmingly for Bush. Former President Bill Clinton summed up this new collective gendered psychology when he observed that when people feel uncertain or afraid, "they'd rather have somebody who's strong and wrong than somebody who's weak and right."[77]

While some think of the Republicans as the "Daddy Party" and the Democrats as the "Mommy Party," it is probably more accurate to se them representing two different visions of paternal masculinity. What sort of American father do we want, asked the linguist George Lakoff, a "nurturing parent" or a "strict father"? Democrats such as Bill Clinton nurtured; they felt our pain. George W. Bush offered a harsher, punitive style but promised safety and security under his wing. (In this analysis, it may be that Al Gore's and John Kerry's fatal mistake was not that they were not strict enough but that they were not nurturing enough!) And ironically, despite their link to myriad corporate scandals, libelous attacks on their opponents and fudging of Bush's elusive military service record, the Republicans became associated with the party of "moral values" in their steadfast opposition to abortion, gay marriage, and stem cell research and other scientific advances. (Such a position is doubly ironic because morality itself has so long been associated with femininity; real men typically chafe at the constraints opposed by such girlie virtues as fairness and compassion.)

The long-noted and oft-studied gender gap in politics often misses the point because it is typically expressed as the gap in women's voting patterns between the two major parties, that is, as Republicans' inability to appeal to women. However, women's voting patterns are only part of the picture. As Everett C. Ladd of the Roper Center explained, "[W]omen are not really more Democratic than they were fifteen years ago." The real story is that "men have become more Republican."[78]

The election also witnessed a divergence in cultural trends. True to political form, Bruce Springsteen gathered a team of contemporary pop stars (James Taylor, R. E. M., Dixie Chicks, and Dave Matthews, among others) to tour swing states; Sean Combs (aka Puff Daddy, P. Diddy, and a gaggle of other monikers) mobilized the inner-city youth vote. Toby Keith penned a bevy of boosterish country songs, praising Bush, the war effort, and heartland values. One song, "Courtesy of the Red, White and Blue (The Angry American)" makes promises:

> This big dog will fight
> When you rattle his cage
> And you'll be sorry that you messed with the U.S. of A
> 'Cause we'll put a boot in your ass
> It's the American way.

Contrast this knee-jerk jingoism to Eminem's surprising campaign anthem, "Mosh" released just prior to the election. In it, the black-hooded rapper calls the president himself a "Weapon of Mass Destruction" and leads a growing army of multicultural discontents. He chants:

Let him impress daddy that way
No more blood for oil, we got our own battles to fight on our own soil
No more psychological warfare to trick us to thinking that we ain't
    loyal
If we don't serve our country, we're patronizing our hero
Look in his eyes, it's all lies
The stars and stripes have been swiped
Washed out and wiped and replaced with his own face
Mosh now or die.[79]

In the end, Bush's election confirmed that his image of masculinity would remain the dominant image in the first decade of the new century. But it also left an America deeply divided over that legacy, a country in which half the population was left singing the blue state blues while the other half was seeing red in Iraq. The election contained some ironic twists. Bush's campaign rested on the reassertion of traditional masculinity as the best way to combat the terrorists who would impose traditional masculinity because they, the terrorists, believed that America had fallen prey to such secular and modern trends as female suffrage and employment! In a world being propelled forward so rapidly, the clash between these two fundamentalist ideals of masculinity seems to pivot on which version would move more quickly forward, into the past.

NOTES

1. See David Brooks, "The Return of the Pig," in *Atlantic Monthly*, April 2003; available at www.theatlantic.com/issues/2003.

2. This is, of course, statistically impossible; it is simply the flip side of Lake Wobegon, where, as Garrison Keilor reminds us, everyone is above average.

3. Cited in Stephen J. Ducat, *The Wimp Factor: Gender Gaps, Holy Wars and the Politics of Anxious Masculinity* (Boston: Beacon Press, 2004, p. 54.

4. See Bruce Handy, "The Viagra Craze," in *Time*, May 4, 1998, pp. 50–57; Christopher Hitchens, "Viagra Falls," in *The Nation*, May 25, 1998, p. 8; see also Meika Loe, *The Rise of Viagra: How the Little Blue Pill Changed Sex in America* (New York: New York University Press, 2004).

5. Cited in Susan Bordo, *The Male Body* (New York: Farrar Straus, and Giroux, 2000), p. 61. Loe, *The Rise of Viagra*, pp. 59, 78. There is actually some evidence of Viagra-related violence against women and a sort of sexual "road rage."

6. See Susan Bordo, *The Male Body*.

7. Harrison Pope, Katharine Phillips, and Roberto Olivardia, *The Adonis Complex: The Secret Crisis of Male Body Obsession* (New York: Free Press, 2000).

8. Cited in Richard Morgan, "The Men in the Mirror," in *Chronicle of Higher Education*, September 27, 2002, p. A 53.

9. Gina Kolata, "With No Answers on Risks, Steroid Users Still Say 'Yes,' " in *New York Times*, December 2, 2002, pp. A-1, 19.

10. The average flaccid penis is about 3.5 inches long; erect, it's about 5.1 inches long. In one of the few studies that rely on data and not anecdotal evidence and thrilled testimonials, psychologist Randy Klein found that the average penile length before surgery was 2.6" (flaccid) and 5.4" (erect); after the surgery, penile length was 3.8" (flaccid) and 5.7" (erect). The only significant difference in length was when the penis was flaccid. See Sam Fields, "Penis Enlargement Surgery," at www.4-men.org/penisenlargementsurgery.html; Randy Klein, "Penile Augmentation Surgery," In *Electronic Journal of Human Sexuality* 2, March 1999, Chapter 2, p. 1, and Chapter 5, pp. 8–9.

11. Testimonial letters to Dr. E. Douglas Whitehead; available at www.penile-enlargement-surgeon.com/diary.html.

12. Robin Finn, "Public Lives: The Queer Brown Behind Queer Eye" *New York Times*, November 21. 2003, B-2.

13. Cited in Randy Thornhill and Craig T. Palmer, "Why Men Rape," in *The Sciences*, January 2000, p. 33.

14. Richard Dawkins, *The Selfish Gene* (New York: Oxford Univ. Press, 1990), pp. 153, 162.

15. Robert Wright, *The Moral Animal* (New York: Vintage, 1995), p. 71.

16. Randy Thornhill and Craig T. Palmer, *A Natural History of Rape: Biological Bases of Sexual Coercion* (Cambridge: MIT Press, 1999); quote from Thornhill and Palmer, "Why Men Rape," p. 30.

17. Thornhill and Palmer, *A Natural History of Rape*, p. 53.

18. Ibid., p. 142.

19. Thornhill and Palmer, "Why Men Rape," pp. 32, 34.

20. George Gilder, *Men and Marriage* (Gretna, La.: Pelican, 1993). The current edition comes with a ringing endorsement from Rush Limbaugh.

21. Ibid., p. 5.

22. Ibid., pp. 11, 45.

23. Ibid. p. 39.

24. Ibid., pp. 39, 62.

25. Ibid., p. 5.

26. Ibid., p. 73

27. Charles Murray, *The Emerging British Underclass* (London: IEA Health and Welfare Unit, 1990), cited in Richard Collier, *Masculinities, Crime and Criminology* (London: Sage Publications, 1998), p. 129; Christina Hoff Sommers, comment at Symposium on "Reconnecting Males to Liberal Education," (Morehouse College, April 4–5, 2001; David Popenoe, *Life Without Father* (New York: Free Press, 1996), p. 12.

28. Popenoe, *Life Without Father*, p. 4.

29. David Blankenhorn, *Fatherless America* (New York: Basic Books, 1995).

30. Ibid., p. 96.

31. Ibid., p. 102.

32. Ibid., p. 122.

33. Harvey Mansfield, "Why a Woman Can't Be More Like a Man," in *Wall Street Journal*, November 3, 1997, p. A 22.

34. Lionel Tiger, *The Decline of Males* (New York: Golden Books, 1999), p. 90.

35. In one of his more bizarre arguments, Tiger suggests that women's use of barbiturates during pregnancy in the 1950s and 1960s caused the spike of male homosexuality in the 1960s and 1970s. "The sons of women using barbiturates are much more likely to be 'feminized,' to display bodies and behavior more typically female than male. Millions of American mothers of boys, an estimated eleven million in the 1950s and 60s, used barbiturates, and millions still do. A compelling thought is that this may have something to do with the evident increase in the number, or at least prominence, of male homosexuals" (p. 95). Although there is not a scintilla of evidence that those same women who took barbiturates had gay sons, nor even a correlation between barbiturate use and *having* a gay son, Tiger goes even further than a simple "correlation does not imply causation" fallacy. He thinks barbiturates explain not only the cause but the "prominence" of gay men. One can only imagine that causal reasoning: Gay sons of barbiturate-using mothers support liberalized drug laws, which bring them into public policy arenas and make them more prominent?

36. Schlessinger has no formal training as a psychologist; her degree is in kinesthesiology. And Columbia Pacific University, where Gray received his graduate "training," was a correspondence school offering degrees via what is called "distant learning," in which students receive course packets, read the materials, and then take open-book exams and receive degrees — until it was shut down, that is, by California's Department of Consumer Affairs, which called it a "giant scam" and a "diploma mill." See *San Francisco Chronicle*, March 14, 2001.

37. Laura Schlessinger, *Ten Stupid Things Women Do to Mess Up Their Lives* (New York: HarperCollins, 1995); *Ten Stupid Things Men Do to Mess Up Their Lives* (New York: HarperCollins, 1998); and *Ten Stupid Things Couples Do to Mess Up Their Relationships* (New York: HarperCollins, 2001).

38. Schlessinger, *Ten Stupid Things Men Do to Mess Up Their Lives*, pp. 194, 273.

39. Susan Goodman, "Dr. No," in *Modern Maturity*, September–October 1999, p. 68.

40. John Gray, *Men Are from Mars, Women Are from Venus* (New York: HarperCollins, 1992), p. 5.

41. John Gray, *Men, Women, and Relationships* (New York: HarperCollins, 1993), p. 53.

42. Ibid., pp. 52, 84.

43. Ibid., p. 95.

44. Ibid., pp. 27, 246.

45. Gray, *Men Are from Mars*, p. 68.

46. Ibid., pp. 146, 148, 78.

47. Ellen Fein and Sherrie Schneider, *The Rules: Time-Tested Secrets for Capturing the Heart of Mr. Right* (New York: Warner Books, 1995).

48. Ibid., p. 14.

49. Ibid., p. 167.

50. Ibid., pp. 7, 9, 28, 127, 157.

51. Ibid., p. 90.

52. This section summarizes the case I make in " 'What About the Boys?' What the Current Debates Tell us—and Don't Tell Us—About Boys in School," in *Michigan Feminist Studies*, 14, 1999–2000.

53. Christine Hoff Sommers, *The War Against Boys* (New York: Scribners, 1999). Sommers, cited in Debra Viadero, "Behind the 'Mask of Masculinity,' " in *Education Week*, May 13, 1998; Thompson cited in Margaret Combs, "What About the Boys?" in *Boston Globe*, July 26, 1998. For more of this backlash argument, see Michael Gurian, *The Wonder of Boys* (New York: Jeremy Tarcher/Putnam, 1997) and Judith Kleinfeld, "Student Performance: Male Versus Female," in *The Public Interest*, Winter 1999. For dissenting opinions, see my review of Gurian, "Boys to Men," in *San Francisco Chronicle*, January 12, 1997, and R. W. Connell, "Teaching the Boys," in *Teachers College Record*, 98(2), Winter, 1996.

54. Brendan Koerner, "Where the Boys Aren't," in *U.S. News & World Report*, February 8, 1999; Tamar Lewin, "American Colleges Begin to Ask, Where Have All The Men Gone?" in *New York Times*, December 6, 1998; Michael Fletcher, "Degrees of Separation," in *Washington Post*, June 25, 2002; Jamilah Evelyn, "Community Colleges Start to Ask, Where Are the Men?" in *Chronicle of Higher Education*, June 28, 2002; Ridger Doyle, "Men, Women and College," in *Scientific American*, October 1999.

55. See, for example, William Pollack, *Real Boys: Rescuing Our Sons from the Myths of Boyhood* (New York: Random House, 1998).

56. Carol Gilligan, *In a Different Voice*; Lyn Mikel Brown and Carol Gilligan, *Meeting at the Crossroads* (New York: Ballantine, 1992).

57. Pollack, cited in Debra Viadero, "Behind the Mask."

58. Martain Mac an Ghaill, *The Making of Men: Masculinities, Sexualities and Schooling* (Buckingham: Open University Press, 1994), p. 59; David Gillborne, *Race, Ethnicity and Education* (London: Unwin Hyman, 1990), p. 63; James Coleman, *The Adolescent Society* (New York: Harper and Row, 1961).

59. Wayne Martino, "Masculinity and Learning: Exploring Boys' Underachievement and Underrepresentation in Subject English," in *Interpretation*, 27(2), 1994; "Boys and Literacy: Exploring the Construction of Hegemonic Masculinities and the Formation of Literate Capacities for Boys in the English Classroom," in *English in Australia*, 112, 1995; "Gendered Learning Experiences: Exploring the Costs of Hegemonic Masculinity for Girls and Boys in Schools," in *Gender Equity: A Framework for Australian Schools* (Canberra: Publications and Public Communications, Department of Urban Services, ACT Government, 1997). Catharine Stimpson, quoted in Tamar Lewin, "American Colleges Begin to Ask, Where Have All the Men Gone?" in *New York Times*, December 6, 1998.

60. From the American Psychological Association, "All That Violence Is Numbing"; available at www.apa.org; statistics first appeared in 1992 in *U.S. News & World Report*.

61. "Boys will be boys" are, not so incidentally, the last four words of Hoff Sommers's antifeminist creed.

62. Cited in Michael S. Kimmel, "The Struggle for Gender Equality: How Men Respond," in *Thought and Action: The NEA Higher Education Journal* 8(2), 1993.

63. See, for example, William Pollack, *Real Boys* (New York: Henry Holt, 1998); Dan Kindlon and Michael Thompson, *Raising Cain* (New York: Ballantine, 2000, 1999); Eli Neuberger, *The Men They Will Become* (Cambridge: Perseus, 1999); and Paul Kivel, *Boys Will Be Men* (Philadelphia: New Society Press, 1999).

64. Cited in Richard Kim, "Eminem—Bad Rap?" in *The Nation*, March 13, 2001, p. 4. It's also true that in *8 Mile*, Eminem goes out of his way to defend a gay man from a gay-bashing assault, as if to undermine the charges of homophobia.

65. This section draws on Michael Kimmel and Matthew Mahler, "Adolescent Masculinity, Homophobia, and Violence: Random School Shootings, 1982–2001," in *American Behavioral Scientist*, 46(10), June 2003, pp. 1439–1458.

66. Actually, somebody did. Tom DeLay, the Texas Congressman, blamed day care, the teaching of evolution, and "working mothers who take birth control pills." See "The News of the Weak in Review," in *The Nation*, November 15, 1999, p. 5.

67. J. Adams and J. Malone, "Outsider's Destructive Behavior Spiraled into Violence," in *Louisville Courier Journal*, March 18, 1999; J. Blank, "The Kid No One Noticed," in *U.S. News & World Report*, December 16, 1998, p. 27.

68. N. Gibbs and T. Roche, "The Columbine Tapes," in *Time*, December 20, 1999, p. 40; D. Cullen, "The Rumor That Won't Go Away," in *Salon*, April 24, 1999; available at http://www.salon.com/news/feature/1999/04/24/rumors/index.html.

69. Eric Pooley, "Portrait of a Deadly Bond," in *Time*, May 10, 1999, pp. 26–7.

70. His impeachment trial came because he was accused of lying to the Special Prosecutor of the case when he said that he "did not have sexual relations with that woman." However, it appears that President Clinton and Monica Lewinsky's sexual trysts involved "everything but" sexual intercourse and instead were based on other sexual acts. In a survey published by the *Journal of the American Medical Association*, most Americans apparently agreed with him, saying that "sex" is defined only by penile-vaginal intercourse. Therefore, it appears that he was telling the truth, at least according to public opinion, if not according to the spirit of the law (cf. Stephanie A. Sanders and June Machover Reinisch, "Would You Say You 'Had Sex' If . . . ?" in *JAMA*, 281, 1999, p. 275–277.

71. Cited in James Ridgeway, "Osamas' New Recruits": *The Village Voice*, November 6, 2001, p. 41.

72. Richard Goldstein, "Neo-Macho Man," in *The Nation*, March 24, 2003; available at http://www.thenation.com/doc.mhtml?i=20030324&s=goldstein. The *American Enterprise* magazine trumpeted their return in a special issue: "Real Men, They're Back"; Patricia Leigh Brown, "Heavy Lifting Required: The Return of Manly Men," in *New York Times*, October 28, 2001, section K, p. 5. Some cheerleaders were just silly; see, for example, Charlotte Allen's paean to real guys in "Return of the Guy," in *Women's Quarterly*, 30, Winter 2002, pp. 9–11. Let me be clear: I share the reverence for those people who were willing to run into burning and collapsing skyscrapers to save others; they did behave heroically. But heroic actions in one arena should not blind us to unheroic behavior in other arenas.

73. See, for example, David Ford, "Shrinking Bush: S. F. Psychologist Argues That Hyper-Masculinity Is Undermining the American Political Culture," in *San Francisco Chronicle*, September 17, 2004; Lexington, "It's a Man's World," in *The Economist*, August 7, 2004, p. 28. The costuming was also noted by gay columnists such as Richard Goldstein; see "Bush's Basket," in *Village Voice*, May 21–27, 2003; available at http://www.villagevoice.com/print/issues/0321/Goldstein.php.

74. See, for example, www.ruminatethis.com/archives/001256.html accessed 6/25/05.

75. Front page headline in *New York Sun*, July 13, 2004; see also Katha Pollitt, "The Girlie Vote," in *The Nation*, September 27, 2004, p. 12; Kenneth Walsh, "What the Guys Want," in *U.S. News & World Report*, September 20, 2004, pp. 22–23; Frank Rich, "How Kerry Became a Girlie-Man," in *New York Times*, September 5, 2004, section 2, pp. 1, 18.

76. Richard Reeves, "The Chosen People," in *New York*, September 25, 2004, p. 26.

77. Cited in Richard Goldstein, "Neo-Macho Man." See also Frank Rich, "How Kerry Became a Girlie-Man"; Kenneth Walsh, "What the Guys Want."

78. Cited in Stephen J. Ducat, *The Wimp Factor*, p. 174.

79. Eminem, "Mosh" lyrics available at http://www.sing365.com.

EILEEN B. LEONARD

Household Labor and Technology in a Consumer Culture

Eileen B. Leonard is Professor of Sociology and Director of the Women's Studies Program at Vassar College. The following is from her book, Women, Technology, and the Myth of Progress *(2003).*

> The real liberators of American women were not the feminist noise-makers, they were the automobile, the supermarket, the shopping center, the dishwasher, the washer-dryer, the freezer.
>
> —Pat Buchanan

One of the most appealing images of household technology is that it single-handedly liberates women by automating the burdens of housework right out of existence. Many are convinced that technology makes housework easier, less time consuming, and perhaps even more equitably distributed in the home. These ideas hold so much power that traditional social research took them for granted instead of proving or disproving them empirically. Now, however, we know that the effects of washers, dryers, and microwaves on women have not been uniformly beneficial—and housework is far from a thing of the past. Any fair assessment of household technology indicates mixed blessings, striking patterns of both change and non-change. Many of the changes have been welcome, and the drudgery that has been left behind is all to the good. But there is another side to this story. Empirical research continues to document that American housewives spend about 33 hours a week on household chores, excluding child care. Women working full time outside the home do about 72 percent of the unpaid labor in the house.[1] How could this be, given all the advantages of technology and the supposed changes in gender roles? Several factors explain the apparent paradox, but first and foremost—and despite any new technology—housework is still largely designated as women's work.[2]

THE MORE THINGS CHANGE . . .

Households are significant sites of technological knowledge and artifacts in terms of food preparation, cleaning, caring for others, and even entertainment.[3] Crucial developments have included the transition from kitchen heating to central heating, outdoor to indoor plumbing, and the shift from

306

homemade to store bought clothes and food. Before industrialization, most housework entailed producing the goods and services that were then used within one's household. Housewives worked hard, but husbands and children also helped. With industrialization, however, women began to bear the burden of housework themselves while, for husbands and children, the home slowly became a place of leisure.[4] As increasing numbers of men and single women entered factory work, housewives began to assume the work of the household, and they began consuming as well as producing the bounty of American industrialization. By 1920, for example, most clothes were no longer made by women in the home, thus eliminating the tasks of sewing, knitting, and so forth; but the new tasks of shopping for and cleaning the clothing were done solely by women.

Ruth Cowan[5] argues that the commonplace notion that the household simply shifted from a unit of production to consumption is misleading. It not only fails to consider new tasks but it ignores other factors, such as the loss of servants and rising expectations, as well as the fact that mechanization took place in an isolated, private home. In a comprehensive fashion, Cowan analyzes household technology in terms of eight interlocking systems: food, clothing, health care, transportation, water, gas, electricity, petroleum. Food, clothing, and health care fit the model of production to consumption but transportation, for example, indicates a very different pattern of *increasing* work as delivery services disappeared and shopping tasks increased. Judy Wajcman[6] observes that "To argue that domestic labor time has been reduced is only meaningful if it means that leisure or discretionary free time has increased. If, however, mechanization results in less physical work but more 'personal services' work in the sense of increased time and quality of child care, then surely this does not mean a real decrease in work."

As men's share in domestic activity began to disappear, housework truly became "women's work." Some of the physical labor associated with housework was reduced, but the considerable work that remained shifted onto the individual housewife. Consider, for example, gas stoves. They are labor-saving devices, but the labor they eliminated was chopping and gathering of wood to fuel the stove (tasks men performed), not cooking the food or cleaning the stove (work designated for women). Similarly, washing machines made it far easier to clean clothes, but women remained largely responsible for performing this work. Machines thus reorganized the process of work, rather than saving the labor of women. "Industrialization, at least in these its earliest phases, had in fact created the material conditions under which the doctrine of separate spheres could take root and flourish."[7] Men learned the skills to work for wages, while relinquishing the tasks done at home.

There has been a great deal of optimism that household appliances would somehow free women. Yet technology has not been the liberator it is portrayed as being nor has it been the solution to gender inequality in the home. . . . In fact, the households they describe are remarkably traditional.

Contemporary research continues to demonstrate that women—even when employed outside the home—do at least twice as much household labor as men. Wives spend an average of 33 hours in household labor per week, while their husbands average about 14 hours.[8] Husbands consistently make only modest contributions to housework;[9] "on average, women are responsible for 75 percent of the work.[10] Since the 1960s much less work is being done in American homes, and more reliance is being placed on the service economy (such as fast food) and family standards of cleanliness are simply declining.[11] Nonetheless, the person doing the housework is still usually female. An adult son who lives at home increases the housework of the women, while an adult daughter reduces the labor of both the other women and men.[12]

Women and men also do quite different household chores: Wives do the daily chores, husbands assume responsibility for the less frequent repairs and the labor that comes up outside and around the house.[13] Even the tasks done by children are segregated by gender: "While differences in individual resources within the family influence the allocation of housework, gender influences it more; women from outside the household are hired, daughters are given more housework than sons, and employed women reduce their own housework more easily than they seek or obtain increases in their husbands' contributions."[14] . . .

In sum, increasing work for women *outside* the home has not resulted in a more equitable distribution of labor *inside* the home, despite the belief that this is the case. Social changes that have begun with paid labor for women need to be completed by men doing more of the unpaid labor. Chafetz and Hagan[15] pointedly summarize the pattern of change as "a major shift in the gender division of labor by which women have come increasingly to resemble men in their rates of labor force participation, within a context where men have not come to resemble women in their domestic/familial work." In fact, married women with children spend more hours at housework than do single mothers with the same number of children. Such factors led economist Heidi Hartmann[16] to speculate that "husbands may require more housework than they contribute," and indeed, when couples marry, women's housework hours increase while men's decline.[17] Women who work part-time, or part of the year, and those who do shift work frequently spend more time doing house-work,[18] but these forms of paid labor are also more insecure, provide fewer benefits, and are often poorly paid. Women seem to be at a crucial transition point: They recognize the unfairness of the current situation but have yet to see change.[19]

Orbuch and Eyster[20] note that discussions of gender inequality in terms of housework frequently refer only to the dominant white culture. Household roles vary, however, in many respects. Their research documents, for example, that "black couples are more egalitarian than white couples in their attitudes toward women's work and the division of household labor" and, moreover, that "blacks are more likely than whites to criticize gender inequality and traditional views of masculinity and femininity." Their analysis of newly married black and white couples in Michigan supports earlier studies and indicates that "black wives report greater participation from their husbands in female-type tasks than do white wives." Hispanic women and men are more inclined to accept a traditional division of household labor and less likely to see it as unfair to women.[21] Nonetheless, Stohs reports that almost two-thirds of all multicultural women in her study (including African-American, Asian, Hispanic, and Middle Eastern women) reported some conflict with their partners during the week regarding housework, specifically when they feel they are doing too much of the housework relative to others.

The gender gap in housework is greatest among married couples, as compared to cohabitants or those who have never married.[22] The distribution of household labor appears to be more equitable among remarried couples, in large measure because of the woman's prior experiences with housework and her demands for change.[23]

Housework remains extremely time consuming, in part because even as technology began to ease some arduous tasks, new ones were defined that transformed housework rather than eliminating it. For example, hot and cold running water ended pumping, hauling, and heating water, while washing machines eliminated scrubbing clothes. But women still do the bulk of the laundry and cooking, in addition to much of the shopping, chauffeuring, hostessing, and child care. Household tasks may be less taxing, but in some respects they have proliferated.

To elaborate on this, drudgery may have disappeared but the laundry has not. By the 1980s and with the help of technology, the American housewife "was processing roughly ten times (by weight) the amount of laundry that her mother had been accustomed to . . . The average time spent on this chore in 1925 had been 5.8 hours per week; in 1964 it was 6.2"[24] Appliances have also had mixed results: Storing, cleaning, and repairing them means new forms of labor. It makes sense to assume that industrialization made life easier for the average American woman, but empirical research tells a very different and unexpected story. As Ruth Cowan[25] puts it: "What a strange paradox that in the face of so many labor-saving devices, little labor appears to have been saved." . . .

Housework remains time consuming because of increasing expectations; women use technology to pursue ever-rising standards. Late nineteenth-century germ theory played a part in encouraging increasing cleanliness and more frequent changing and washing of clothes. Standards of nutrition have also risen, giving women more work in terms of providing quality meals. Rugs were previously beaten once a year as part of ritual spring cleaning (a task assigned to children); vacuuming, however, became a weekly chore typically done by women. In addition, higher expectations regarding child care (in terms of time, energy, and results) came to be widely accepted and made further demands on women's time in the home.

Thus, monumental technological changes took place that permitted many families to live "at a level of health and comfort that not so long ago was reserved only for those who were very rich,"[26] but these innovations did not serve to shorten a woman's work day. Rather, they raised American living standards while keeping homemakers isolated and relatively inefficient. Technology allowed individual labor to substitute for the loss of servants and other female helpers and raised the standards of living, but women have not been released from expectations regarding their role in the household. While some hail the machine age as causing a "household revolution" that freed women from toil, technology did more to *change* labor than to *save* it.

CONSUMERISM

The increasing standards of household labor associated with new technology and the drive for more household appliances did not develop by happenstance. Instead, the centrality of consumerism and a consumer economy must be acknowledged. Women were educated to new standards through advertising, media, and domestic science classes, which played a significant role in defining housework at the beginning of this century. The role of the housewife and mother was idealized, and women were assured that their work was important and emotionally rewarding. The vision of women as guardians of the family was used to promote increasing standards of cleanliness and nutrition, but it also promoted the growing consumption of commodities for the household. Women were taught to be good managers and consumers, and buying household appliances was part of this.[27] The early twentieth century marked the shift to a new kind of consumer and a new form of advertising. Susan Strasser[28] illuminates the scope of the changes:

> Advertisers came to see women as their audience; home economists taught women how to shop and how to plan for shopping; new, interrelated products like washing machines and soap powders appeared on the market, each encouraging the use of another; mail-order houses, department stores, supermarkets, and chain stores, emphasizing impersonal relationships between buyer and seller and dominated by large corporations, replaced small shops, country stores, and public markets.

With new technology, the home was envisioned as a well-run machine and the homemaker as not only a moral guardian but, more in tune with modern industrial society, as "a lab assistant and efficiency expert who knew how to manage modern technology."[29] Assumptions about the role of women reflected and reinforced the design and marketing of household machines.[30] Manufacturers and public utilities also used domestic science classes to assist them in marketing since the interests of appliance manufacturers and the ideology of domestic science coincided: Both maintained that women belonged in the home, with appliances designed for their individual use—not communally shared. Collectivist movements of the late nineteenth century, which advocated more communal solutions to the work of the household—including communal child care, laundry, and food preparation—had been defeated,[31] and household products began to be actively marketed by the 1920s and 1930s. Culture industries "mobilized female desire for commodity goods and have constructed notions of femininity which are complicit with consumption.[32] Automatic laundry equipment, for example, was used in commercial establishments in the nineteenth century, but then transferred to the home in the 1920s. "Rather than selling a few large machines to centralized businesses, manufacturers sought to sell many smaller units to private households. The return of laundry to the home affirmed women's roles as consumers of individual products instead of shared central services.[33] Cynthia Cockburn notes that the focus of the industry remains on "stand-alone" appliances that bring the most profit and reflect the absence of any overall planning regarding the development and marketing of household technologies. "Competition produces an appearance of great choice in the market economies; there are scores of models of each item available . . . But they are not always designed to answer user needs."[34] Lupton[35] is even more forthright: "In a consumer economy, objects are manufactured primarily to be sold, and only secondarily to satisfy a human need." Wajcman[36] provides an illustration: "The drive to motorize all household tasks—including brushing teeth, squeezing lemons, and carving meat—is less a response to need than a reflection of the economic and technical capacity for making motors."

Both advertising and the corporations producing household products encouraged the view of housework as women's work that expressed family love and devotion. "Housework became conceptualized as a personal task made easier by the purchase of an ever-increasing array of products which women bought because they wished to care for their families in the best, most modern way possible."[37] Researchers vary in their interpretations of the precise relationship between advertising messages regarding household technology and their impact on women, but there is general agreement that advertisers aimed "to fashion the housewife into the ultimate consumer in order to sell their products."[38] In an analysis of advertisements in *The Ladies' Home Journal* from 1910 to 1980, Bonnie J. Fox[39] found that ads consistently advocated housework as women's work and as private work. This reflected and reinforced the association of women with household labor, despite the fact that this labor continues to be unpaid or low-paid and devalued.

Although advertisers are interested in anyone who might buy the products they promote, their decision to focus their efforts on women reinforced women's role as the primary consumers. Time spent on consumption only added to women's responsibilities in the home: "Advertisements used guilt and fear to promote dependence on products, creating artificial burdens to substitute for the disappearing real ones. (Women, it seems, were meant to be burdened)."[40]

Many argue that advertising campaigns, rather than being relatively straightforward, are manipulative. Marketing strategies create needs, rather than meet them, and intentionally encourage the purchase of more and more unnecessary products. In the advertisements of the 1920s, for example, appliances became equated with freedom: Toasters and washing machines meant liberation for women. According to Ewen,[41] this illustrates "how the feminist demand for equality and freedom for women was appropriated into the jargon of consumerism." New "corporate diseases" began to emerge: underarm offense, sneaker smell, ashtray breath.[42] These developments were designed to increase the profits of business and advertising—more "time-saving" devices, more specialized products, and more products to enhance self-esteem. Technologies were developed and marketed to individual housewives, who were targeted as the ones buying and using these items. "The very activity of buying came to represent happiness, and perhaps indeed to produce it, if only temporarily . . . The expandable task of consumption, like the other new task of motherhood, capable of taking up whatever time the new products released, became ever more necessary as families adapted their daily lives to manufactured existence."[43] Appliances were also explicitly portrayed as relieving women of work. A 1946 Bendix advertisement for automatic washing machines, for example, shows a smiling woman seated on a stool next to her washer claiming, "It's Wonderful! -how my BENDIX does all the work of washing."[44]

Wajcman[45] makes the point that the relationship between technology and change is fundamentally indeterminate and cannot be completely predicted. She provides the example of the telephone, which was initially designed as a business machine, but telephone executives resisted its use for what they termed "trivial gossip." As Lupton[46] puts it, they "dismissed women's talk as 'idle chatter' that tied up the lines." By the late 1920s, however, AT&T began to see the financial advantages of encouraging women to use the telephone, and during the depression, Bell began targeting women in their advertising.

Advertising is a powerful U.S. industry, with domestic ad spending reaching $200 billion in 1998.[47] It continues to portray housework as easy and fulfilling, creating the impression that homes require relatively little care, given available technology. Likewise, it still implies that buying more products makes people happier.[48] But, to the extent that domestic technologies are "designed to support the home system, and thereby keep women economically marginal to the larger society, they may actually increase dissatisfaction with housework."[49] In addition, the privacy, freedom, and individualism symbolized in the single family home and its extensive technology is paradoxical in modern society. As Spigel[50] points out: "Consumer products promised people the everyday experience of liberation in return for their increasing dependence on corporate production." Freedom, it seems, is a microwave oven, which in turn presupposes a consumer society . . . which may be anything but freeing.

. . .

GENDER, RACE, AND CLASS INEQUALITIES

Household technology has eased some of the most physically demanding forms of household labor, and it has raised the standards of living for many people. In the United States, the living conditions of most people have improved significantly in the past fifty years. Ruth Cowan[51] argues that we tend to forget just how well off we have become: As recently as 1940, one-third of Americans were still carrying water in buckets, two-thirds had no central heating, and only 53 percent had built-in bathroom equipment. These amenities are now regarded as basic standards in the United States. Nonetheless, when we use a lens of gender, race, and class to examine household technology, we see that once again the larger (non-egalitarian) social context has constrained the development and use of technology even within our households. Gender inequality, for example, has been crucial in shaping household technology and its use. Although this technology has become increasingly sophisticated and powerful, it has not reduced the time spent in household labor: Women have assumed new tasks, new expectations, new standards of cleanliness, which effectively eroded any extra time technology may have permitted. Many improvements in the twentieth century have been accomplished largely through the increased productivity of individual women. According to Cowan,[52] Modern technology enabled the American housewife of 1950 to produce single-handedly what her counterpart of 1850 needed a staff of three or four to produce: a middle-class standard of health and cleanliness for herself, her spouse, and her children." Despite technology, households remain places of intensive domestic labor.

Moreover, technology has been unable to change the allocation of labor by gender. The work of women and men remain sharply segregated: Most women still do the bulk of the housework and child care, men contribute modest amounts. Far from being "revolutionary," the development and marketing of household technology reflects and reinforces a specific middle-class ideal of a single-family household, with a wife responsible for the household labor. Thus gender inequality has, in significant ways, dictated who will use household technology. In many ways, technology has been used to reinforce the gender division of labor, not to undermine it. It may even have made it increasingly difficult to dislodge some household tasks from the home. Bose, Bereano, and Malloy[53] give three reasons for this:

> First, the small scale of household work and technologies are labor intensive. Second, the work has become so laden with emotion that attaining a more communalized form may be impossible. Finally, since women's labor at

home is unpaid and this is seen as "cheap," it could be indefinitely used for these tasks, retaining the specialization of labor within the home and keeping housework structurally separated from the paid labor market.

Increasing numbers of women are employed outside the home, but the inequitable distribution of housework remains. Empirical studies consistently demonstrate that even women employed full-time outside the home continue to bear responsibility for most of the housework, daughters do more housework than sons, and when someone outside the family is paid to do the work, the employee is typically a woman. Even specific tasks are influenced by gender. And technology has been unable to alter any of this.

Our social understanding that women are primarily responsible for household labor has had important design consequences. Washing machines, vacuum cleaners, and refrigerators have all been designed and marketed for use by individual women, in individual homes. Household labor, and certainly large appliances, could have been shared, but given the isolated and gendered understanding of housework, such alternatives failed. Women remain the targets of advertising and consumerism for all manner of household items. Their responsibilities in the home are glorified, and traditional gender roles are bolstered in the process. When men are found in advertisements for household technology, they are often portrayed as incompetent. Only a woman *really* knows how to vacuum a living room rug. Put differently, housework is women's work. Household technology may have modified, but it did not fundamentally alter, the gender division of household labor.

Not only gender inequality, but racism has penetrated the organization of our households and household labor. At the most basic level, some have access to household technology that is unavailable to others. This includes home computers which have been hailed as revolutionizing households. But Julianne Malveaux[54] points out that given existing social and racial inequalities, certain groups simply lack the money to get computers and communication tools for the home. Technology cannot enhance or alter the lives of those who cannot afford it, and recent discussions of the "digital divide" have barely begun to address this issue.

In her groundbreaking work on household technology, Ruth Cowan[55] wisely suggests that we revise some of the unwritten rules about housework, including our high standards and our notions of who is responsible for this work. She aims to neutralize the association of gender and housework, as well as neurotic ideas of cleanliness, and enable us to exert control over household technology instead of it controlling us. Her argument is compelling regarding middle-class, white women, but if we think of household technology and household labor in broader, less individualistic terms, this type of privatized solution is inadequate. Women do an unequal share of the unpaid labor in the home as a result of gender inequality, but some women are able to shift the burden of housework onto paid domestic workers, typically lower-class minority women. When we consider paid domestic labor, the liberatory vision of household technology becomes increasingly suspect. It is misguided, at best, to revel in the liberating effects of household technology with a tense and exhausted professional woman shouldering a double day, but for a weary domestic worker earning $15 a day and then trudging home to do more housework, it may be absurd. Moreover, social inequalities both connected with and beyond gender inequality become vividly apparent.

Widening our analysis of domestic labor and including paid as well as unpaid work in the home, raises a considerably different set of concerns. It becomes evident that household labor is structured in our society in terms of class and race as well as gender inequality. All women lack economic rewards as well as security or prestige for the household labor they perform. As paid employment, domestic work is extremely low-paid and devalued, and working conditions tend to be unacceptable to anyone with decent alternatives. Thus the ranks of domestic workers are filled by impoverished women of color, those with the fewest options. This includes U.S. citizens as well as a global trade in live-in minority women workers.

Evelyn Nakano Glenn[56] observes that the activities and relationships involved in maintaining people, such as cooking, cleaning, and caring for children and other adults, are typically defined as women's work. But she argues that the *racial* division of this labor "is key to the distinct exploitation of women of color and is a source of both hierarchy and interdependence among white women and women of color." Racist beliefs confirm the suitability of certain women for paid domestic work, although the particularities of the stereotypes conveniently shift depending on the racial group — we are told that Asians are quiet and thus suited to work in the home whereas African Americans are dependent and thus need such employment.[57] Researchers have implicated racism in the way household workers are treated including poor pay, demands for deference, and the manipulation of them as "one of the family."

The current division of household labor not only reinforces gender, class, and racial divisions within the United States, but highlights global inequalities as well. Heart-rending stories of immigrant women from Mexico, Jamaica, the Philippines, and the Caribbean demonstrate the gendered and racist nature of household labor, and technology has apparently been powerless to undermine the status quo in this regard.

Glenn[58] argues that sexist notions of women's place in the home are in fact bolstered by racialized ideas that permit women of color to be used to do the most degrading work, thus protecting the gendered division of labor: "By providing them an acceptable self-image, racial constructs gave the white housewives a stake in the system that ultimately oppressed them." The racial division of labor also protects the position of white men because opposition between white women and men can be redirected to clashes among women. Thus with domestic workers, race and class divisions pit groups of women against one another and, as Glenn astutely observes, maintain gender inequality in the process since what is uncontested is the assumption that, paid or unpaid, housework is *women's* work.

Class divisions are also crucial. They affect what technology individuals can afford to purchase for the home, but more significantly, the apparent advantages of household technology conceal the ways in which they serve capitalist production far more than they serve the traditional housewife. Household technology is a profit-making enterprise, and consumers only get to choose between profitable alternatives. Our corporate economy develops technology not simply to meet household needs but to foster consumerism. With the help of advertising, the public is educated to new standards of consumption and new products to buy for the household. Large appliances are designed for use in individual households, again assuring the purchase of as many items as possible. Thus the centrality of consumerism and profit-making fuels the development of many household technologies, not an effort to free women from labor nor any genuine human need. The consumerism and proliferation of household gadgets is also jarring in a context of global hunger and increasing homelessness among U.S. women.

The targeting of women as the primary consumers of household technology plays a significant role in relegating women to the home and maintaining their place in the gender division of unpaid labor. This also keeps them economically marginal, given that the heavy responsibilities they assume for the care of the home and its dependents hinders their ability to assume certain positions in the paid labor force. Advertising glorifies and mystifies the role of the housewife as guardian of the home and premier consumer, thus binding women ideologically to the home.

Paid household labor illustrates class divisions even more vividly, given the profound economic disadvantages confronting domestic workers. When a household becomes a site of paid employment, class divisions necessarily separate the interests of employers and employees.[59] But whether household labor is paid or unpaid, the technology in the home has not simply freed women, but operates instead within class constraints and illustrates both hierarchy and interdependence among women.

None of this is intended to idealize a less industrialized past. Some women may have lost the satisfactions of their labor and the intimacy of work with others in the home, but as Susan Strasser[60] reminds us, "Craft satisfaction, intimacy, and community went along with grueling amounts of heavy labor, a lack of privacy that most modern Americans would find intolerable, and the oppression of women on both individual and social levels." Technological changes in the twentieth century have benefited many women. Judy Wajcman[61] criticizes the emphasis some feminists put on the negative effects of domestic technology and the assumption that women are worse off now because of technology. She believes this has led to the view that women have simply been duped. She argues instead that, "Once we recognize that the mechanization of the home did bring substantial improvements to women's domestic working conditions, even while it introduced new pressures, women seem less irrational." Wajcman notes that women blame themselves for the failure of technology to ease the work of the home, rather than recognizing the design of the technologies and the social relations in the home. Her point is well taken, but while we acknowledge the considerable benefits of technology, let's not ignore the lack of change and the persistent inequalities of race, class, and gender that remains a significant and unacceptable part of the picture.

CONCLUSION

What we have seen from our discussion not only of household technology but reproductive and office technology as well, is that none of these technologies have functioned in a truly revolutionary way to dislodge the inequality of women or to challenge the traditional divisions of paid and unpaid labor. None of them have been "progressive" in the sense of undermining the structural inequality that impinges on the lives of so many.

Instead, gender, race, and class inequalities shape the conditions of women's lives and their experiences with technology. Thus, technology is not the independent or neutral instrument it may appear to be, but is instead deeply affected by the larger social and political context. Certainly it can be co-opted or used for more progressive purposes, as will be discussed in our final chapter, but more significant social change will not come without directly addressing the very purpose of technology and the way in which it currently supports rather than undermines hierarchy.

NOTES

1. Theodore N. Greenstein, "Gender Ideology and Perception of the Fairness of the Division of Household Labor: Effects on Marital Quality," *Social Forces*, Vol. 74, (March 1996): 1029.

2. Suzanne Bianchi et al., "Is Anyone Doing the Housework? Trends in the Gender Division of Household Labor," *Social Forces*, Vol. 79 (September 2000): 191.

3. Cynthia Cockburn, "Domestic Technologies: Cinderella and the Engineers," *Women's Studies International Forum*, Vol. 20 (1997): 361–371.

4. Ruth Schwartz Cowan, *More Work for Mother: The Ironies of Household Technology from the Open Hearth to the Microwave* (New York: Basic Books, 1983), 47.

5. Ibid.

6. Judy Wajcman, *Feminism Confronts Technology* (University Park, PA: The Pennsylvania State University Press, 1991), 93–94.

7. Cowan, *More Work for Mother*, 66–67.

8. Greenstein, "Gender Ideology."

9. Richard A. Feinberg, " 'Man May Work From Sun to Sun But Woman's Work Is Never Done': A Short Note on Why the Issue of Household Work Is Important Socially, Economically, and Politically," *Family and Consumer Sciences Research Journal*, Vol. 24 (June 1996): 355.

10. Toni Calasanti and Carol Bailey, "Gender Inequality and the Division of Household Labor in the United States and Sweden: A Socialist-Feminist Approach" *Social Problems*, Vol. 38 (February 1991): 35.

11. Bianchi et al., "Is Anyone Doing the Housework?"

12. Scott J. South and Glenn Spitze, "Housework in Marital and Nonmarital Households," *American Sociological Review*, Vol. 59 (June 1994): 327.

13. Sampson Blair and Michael Johnson, "Wives' Perceptions of the Fairness of the Household Division of Labor: The Intersection of Housework and Ideology," *Journal of Marriage and the Family*, Vol. 54 (August 1992): 570; John P. Robinson and Geoffrey Godbey, *Time for Life* (University Park, PA: Pennsylvania State University Press, 1997).

14. Myra Marx Ferree, "Beyond Separate Spheres: Feminism and Family Research," *Journal of Marriage and the Family*, Vol. 52 (November 1990): 877.

15. Janet Saltzman Chafetz and Jacqueline Hagan, "The Gender Division of Labor and Family Change in Industrial Societies: A Theoretical Accounting." *Journal of Comparative Family Studies*, Vol. 29 (Summer 1996): 187–188.

16. Heidi Hartmann, "The Family as the Locus of Gender, Class and Political Struggle: The Example of Housework," *Signs*, Vol. 6 (Spring 1981): 383.

17. Sanjiv Gupta, "The Effects of Transitions in Marital Status on Men's Performance of Housework," *Journal of Marriage and the Family*, Vol. 61 (1999): 700–711.

18. Hilary Silver and Frances Goldscheider, "Flexible Work and Housework: Work and Family Constraints on Women's Domestic Labor," *Social Forces*, Vol. 72 (June 1994): 1103–1119.

19. Joanne Hoven Stohs, "Predictions of Conflict Over the Household Division of Labor Among Women Employed Full Time," *Sex Roles*, Vol. 33 (1995): 257–275.

20. Terri L. Orbuch and Sandra Eyster, "Division of Household Labor Among Black Couples and White Couples," *Social Forces*, Vol. 76 (September 1997): 301–332.

21. Joanne Hoven Stohs, "Multicultural Women's Experience of Household Labor, Conflicts, and Equity," *Sex Roles: A Journal of Research*, March 2000, 339.

22. South and Spitze, "Housework."

23. Oriel Sullivan, "The Division of Housework Among 'Remarried' Couples," *Journal of Family Issues*, Vol. 18 (March 1997): 205.

24. Ruth Schwartz Cowan, "Less Work for Mother?" Invention and Technology, Spring 1987, 61.

25. Cowan, *More Work for Mother*, 44.

26. Cowan, "Less Work for Mother?" 63.

27. Joanne Vanek, "Household Technology and Social Status: Rising Living Standards and Status and Residence Differences in Housework," *Technology and Culture*, Vol. 19 (July 1978): 367–368.

28. Susan Strasser, *Never Done: A History of American Housework* (New York: Pantheon Books, 1982), 243.

29. Lynn Spigel, *Make Room for TV: Television and the Family Ideal in Postwar America* (Chicago: University of Chicago Press, 1992), 22.

30. Ellen Lupton, *Mechanical Brides: Women and Machines from Home to Office* (New York: Cooper-Hewitt National Museum of Design Smithsonian Institute and Princeton Architectural Press, 1993), 4.

31. Harriet Rosenberg, "The Kitchen and the Multinational Corporation: An Analysis of the Links Between the Household and Global Corporations," *Journal of Business Ethics*, Vol. 6 (1987): 179–194.

32. Lynn Spigel and Denise Mann, "Women and Consumer Culture: A Selective Bibliography," *Quarterly Review of Film and Video*, Vol. 11 (1989): 85.

33. Lupton, *Mechanical Brides*, 15.

34. Cockburn, "Domestic Technologies," 366.

35. Lupton, *Mechanical Brides*, 10.

36. Wajcman, *Feminism Confronts Technology*, 100.

37. Rosenberg, "The Kitchen," 184.

38. Bonnie J. Fox, "Selling the Mechanized Household: 70 Years of Ads in *Ladies Home Journal*," *Gender and Society*, Vol. 4 (March 1990): 26–27.

39. Ibid.

40. Strasser, *Never Done*, 8.

41. Stuart Ewen, *Captains of Consciousness: Advertising and the Social Roots of the Consumer Culture* (New York: McGraw-Hill Book Company, 1976), 160.

42. Strasser, *Never Done*, 253.

43. Ibid., 262.

44. Lupton, *Mechanical Brides*, 19.

45. Wajcman, *Feminism Confronts Technology*, 104.

46. Lupton, *Mechanical Brides*, 38.

47. Gary Ruskin and Robert Weissman, "The Cost of Commercialism," *Multinational Monitor*, Vol. 20 (January–February 1999): 9.

48. Ibid.

49. Christine Bose, Philip Bereano, and Mary Malloy, "Household Technology and the Social Construction of Housework," *Technology and Culture*, Vol. 25 (January 1984): 64.

50. Spigel, *Make Room for TV*, 21.

51. Cowan, *More Work for Mother*.

52. Ibid., 100.

53. Bose, Bereano, and Malloy, "Household Technology," 77.

54. Julianne Malveaux, "Will Technology Bridge the Gap Between Black and White?" *Black Issues in Higher Education*, Vol. 13 (22 August 1996): 48.

55. Cowan, *More Work for Mother*.

56. Evelyn Nakano Glenn, "From Servitude to Service Work: Historical Continuities in the Racial Division of Paid Reproductive Labor," *Signs*, Vol. 18 (Autumn 1992): 3.

57. Ibid.

58. Ibid., 34.

59. Abigail B. Bakan and Daiva K. Stasiulis, "Making the Match: Domestic Placement Agencies and the Racialization of Women's Household Work," *Signs*, Vol. 20 (Winter 1995): 303–335.

60. Strasser, *Never Done*, 8.

61. Wajcman, *Feminism Confronts Technology*, 82.

MARCIA R. LIEBERMAN

"Some Day My Prince Will Come":
Female Acculturation Through
the Fairy Tale

This selection by Marcia R. Lieberman was a groundbreaking and controversial essay when originally published in College English *in 1971. Lieberman was Professor of English at the University of Connecticut.*

In a review of children's stories for a Christmas issue of *The New York Review of Books*, Alison Lurie praised traditional fairy and folk tales as

> One of the few sorts of classic children's literature of which a radical feminist would approve . . . These stories suggest a society in which women are as competent and active as men, at every age and in every class. Gretel, not Hansel, defeats the Witch; and for every clever youngest son there is a youngest daughter equally resourceful. The contrast is greatest in maturity, where women are often more powerful than men. Real help for the hero or heroine comes most frequently from a fairy godmother or wise woman, and real trouble from a witch or wicked stepmother. . . . To prepare children for women's liberation, therefore, and to protect them against Future Shock, you had better buy at least one collection of fairy tales. . . .[1]

Radical feminists, apparently, bought neither Ms. Lurie's ideas nor the collections of fairy tales. It is hard to see how children could be "prepared" for women's liberation by reading fairy tales; an analysis of those fairy tales that children actually read indicates instead that they serve to acculturate women to traditional social roles.

Ms. Lurie has now repeated her argument in a recent article, in which she objects to the opinion that feminists actually have of such stories as "Cinderella" and "Snow White":

> It is true that some of the tales we know best, those that have been popularized by Disney, have this sort of heroine. But from the point of view of European folklore they are a very unrepresentative selection. They reflect the taste of the refined literary men who edited the first popular collections of fairy tales for children during the Victorian era. Andrew Lang, for instance, chose the tales in his *Blue Fairy Book* (first published in 1889) from

---

[1] Alison Lurie, "Fairy Tale Liberation," *The New York Review of Books*, December 17, 1970, p. 42.

among literally thousands known to him as a folklorist; and he chose them . . . partly for their moral lesson. Folk tales recorded in the field by scholars are full of everything Lang leaves out: sex, death, low humor, and female initiative.

In the other more recent collections of tales—as well as in Lang's later collections—there are more active heroines. . . .[2]

No one would disagree with Ms. Lurie that Andrew Lang was very selective in choosing his tales, but to a feminist who wishes to understand the acculturation of women, this is beside the point. Only the best-known stories, those that everyone has read or heard, indeed, those that Disney has popularized, have affected masses of children in our culture. Cinderella, the Sleeping Beauty, and Snow White are mythic figures who have replaced the old Greek and Norse gods, goddesses, and heroes for most children. The "folk tales recorded in the field by scholars," to which Ms. Lurie refers, or even Andrew Lang's later collections, are so relatively unknown that they cannot seriously be considered in a study of the meaning of fairy tales to women.

In this light, *The Blue Fairy Book* is a very fruitful book to analyze, for it contains many of the most famous stories, and has perhaps been the best-known and hence most influential collection of tales. It was compiled by Andrew Lang and first published by Longman's Green, and Co. in London in 1889. It was followed by *The Red Fairy Book*, and then the *Green*, and then by many others, the *Yellow*, the *Brown*, the *Rose*, the *Violet*, etc. In the preface to *The Green Fairy Book*, in 1892, Lang noted that the stories were made not only to amuse children, but also to teach them. He pointed out that many of the stories have a moral, although, he wrote, "we think more as we read them of the diversion than of the lesson."[3] The distinction that Lang drew between diversions and lessons is misleading, for children do not categorize their reading as diverting or instructive, but as interesting or boring. If we are concerned, then, about what our children are being taught, we must pay particular attention to those stories that are so beguiling that children think more as they read them "of the diversion than of the lesson"; perhaps literature is suggestive in direct proportion to its ability to divert. We know that children are socialized or culturally conditioned by movies, television programs, and the stories they read or hear, and we have begun to wonder at the influence that children's stories and entertainments had upon us, though we cannot now measure the extent of that influence.

Generations of children have read the popular fairy books, and in doing so may have absorbed far more from them than merely the outlines of the various stories. What is the precise effect that the story of "Snow-White and the Seven Dwarfs" has upon a child? Not only do children find out what happens

---

[2]Lurie, "Witches and Fairies: Fitzgerald to Updike," *The New York Review of Books*, December 2, 1971, p. 6.

[3]Andrew Lang, ed., *The Green Fairy Book* (New York: McGraw-Hill, 1966), pp. ix–xi.

to the various princes and princesses, wood-cutters, witches, and children of their favorite tales, but they also learn behavioral and associational patterns, value systems, and how to predict the consequences of specific acts or circumstances. Among other things, these tales present a picture of sexual roles, behavior, and psychology, and a way of predicting outcome or fate according to sex, which is important because of the intense interest that children take in "endings"; they always want to know how things will "turn out." A close examination of the treatment of girls and women in fairy tales reveals certain patterns which are keenly interesting not only in themselves, but also as material which has undoubtedly played a major contribution in forming the sexual role concept of children, and in suggesting to them the limitations that are imposed by sex upon a person's chances of success in various endeavors. It is now being questioned whether those traits that have been characterized as feminine have a biological or a cultural basis: discarding the assumptions of the past, we are asking what is inherent in our nature, and what has become ours through the gentle but forcible process of acculturation. Many feminists accept nothing as a "given" about the nature of female personality; nearly all the work on that vast subject is yet to be done. In considering the possibility that gender has a cultural character and origin we need to examine the primary channels of acculturation. Millions of women must surely have formed their psycho-sexual self-concepts, and their ideas of what they could or could not accomplish, what sort of behavior would be rewarded, and of the nature of reward itself, in part from their favorite fairy tales. These stories have been made the repositories of the dreams, hopes, and fantasies of generations of girls. An analysis of the women in *The Blue Fairy Book* presents a picture that does not accord with Ms. Lurie's hypothesis.

Certain premises and patterns emerge at once, of which only the stereotyped figure of the wicked step-mother has received much general notice. The beauty-contest is a constant and primary device in many of the stories. Where there are several daughters in a family, or several unrelated girls in a story, the prettiest is invariably singled out and designated for reward, or first for punishment and later for reward. Beautiful girls are never ignored; they may be oppressed at first by wicked figures, as the jealous Queen persecutes Snow-White, but ultimately they are chosen for reward. Two fundamental conventions are associated here: the special destiny of the youngest child when there are several children in a family (this holds true for youngest brothers as well as for youngest sisters, as long as the siblings are of the same sex), and the focus on beauty as a girl's most valuable asset, perhaps her only valuable asset. Good-temper and meekness are so regularly associated with beauty, and ill-temper with ugliness, that this in itself must influence children's expectations. The most famous example of this associational pattern occurs in "Cinderella," with the opposition of the ugly, cruel, bad-tempered older sisters to the younger, beautiful, sweet Cinderella, but in *The Blue Fairy Book* it also occurs in many other stories, such as "Beauty and the Beast" and "Toads and Diamonds." Even when there is no series of sisters (in "Snow-White and Rose-Red" both girls are beautiful and sweet) the beautiful single daughter is nearly always noted for her docility, gentleness, and good temper.

This pattern, and the concomitant one of reward distribution, probably acts to promote jealousy and divisiveness among girls. The stories reflect an intensely competitive spirit: they are frequently about contests, for which there can be only one winner because there is only one prize. Girls win the prize if they are the fairest of them all; boys win if they are bold, active, and lucky. If a child identifies with the beauty, she may learn to be suspicious of ugly girls, who are portrayed as cruel, sly, and unscrupulous in these stories; if she identifies with the plain girls, she may learn to be suspicious and jealous of pretty girls, beauty being a gift of fate, not something that can be attained. There are no examples of a crossed-pattern, that is, of plain but good-tempered girls. It is a psychological truth that as children, and as women, girls fear homeliness (even attractive girls are frequently convinced that they are plain), and this fear is a major source of envy and discord among them. Girls may be predisposed to imagine that there is a link between the lovable face and the lovable character, and to fear, if plain themselves, that they will also prove to be unpleasant, thus using the patterns to set up self-fulfilling prophecies.

The immediate and predictable result of being beautiful is being chosen, this word having profound importance to a girl. The beautiful girl does not have to *do* anything to merit being chosen; she does not have to show pluck, resourcefulness, or wit; she is chosen because she is beautiful. Prince Hyacinth chooses the Dear Little Princess for his bride from among the portraits of many princesses that are shown to him because she is the prettiest; the bear chooses the beautiful youngest daughter in "East of the Sun & West of the Moon"; at least twenty kings compete to win Bellissima in "The Yellow Dwarf"; the prince who penetrates the jungle of thorns and briars to find the Sleeping Beauty does so because he had heard about her loveliness; Cinderella instantly captivates her prince during a ball that amounts to a beauty contest; the old king in "The White Cat" says he will designate as his heir whichever of his sons brings home the loveliest princess, thereby creating a beauty contest as a hurdle to inheriting his crown; the prince in "The Water-Lily or The Gold-Spinners" rescues and marries the youngest and fairest of the three enslaved maidens; the King falls in love with Goldilocks because of her beauty; the enchanted sheep dies for love of the beautiful Miranda in "The Wonderful Sheep"; Prince Darling pursues Celia because she is beautiful; the young king in "Trusty John" demands the Princess of the Golden Roof for her beauty, and so on. This is a principal factor contributing to the passivity of most of the females in these stories (even those few heroines who are given some sort of active role are usually passive in another part of the story). Since the heroines are chosen for their beauty (*en soi*), not for anything they do (*pour soi*), they seem to exist passively until they are seen by the hero, or described to him. They wait, are chosen, and are rewarded.

Marriage is the fulcrum and major event of nearly every fairy tale; it is the reward for girls, or sometimes their punishment. (This is almost equally true for boys, although the boy who wins the hand of the princess gets power as well as a pretty wife, because the princess is often part of a package deal including half or all of a kingdom). While it would be futile and anachronistic to suppose that these tales could or should have depicted alternate options or rewards for heroines or heroes, we must still observe that marriage dominates them, and note what they show as leading to marriage, and as resulting from it. Poor boys play an active role in winning kingdoms and princesses; Espen Cinderlad, the despised and youngest of the three brothers in so many Norwegian folk tales, wins the Princess on the Glass Hill by riding up a veritable hill of glass. Poor girls are chosen by princes because they have been seen by them.

Marriage is associated with getting rich: it will be seen that the reward basis in fairy and folk tales is overwhelmingly mercenary. Good, poor, and pretty girls always win rich and handsome princes, never merely handsome, good, but poor men. (If the heroine or hero is already rich, she or he may marry someone of equal rank and wealth, as in "The White Cat," "Trusty John," "The Sleeping Beauty," etc.; if poor, she or he marries someone richer.) Since girls are chosen for their beauty, it is easy for a child to infer that beauty leads to wealth, that being chosen means getting rich. Beauty has an obviously commercial advantage even in stories in which marriage appears to be a punishment rather than a reward: "Bluebeard," in which the suitor is wealthy though ugly, and the stories in which a girl is wooed by a beast, such as "Beauty and the Beast," "East of the Sun & West of the Moon," and "The Black Bull of Norroway."

The bear in "East of the Sun & West of the Moon" promises to enrich the whole family of a poor husbandman if they will give him the beautiful youngest daughter. Although the girl at first refuses to go, her beauty is seen as the family's sole asset, and she is sold, like a commodity, to the bear (the family does not know that he is a prince under an enchantment). "Beauty and the Beast" is similar to this part of "East of the Sun," and the Snow-White of "Snow-White and Rose-Red" also becomes rich upon marrying an enchanted prince who had been a bear.[4] Cinderella may be the best-known story of this type.

Apart from the princesses who are served out as prizes in competitions (to the lad who can ride up a glass hill, or slay a giant, or answer three riddles, or bring back some rarity), won by lucky fellows like Espen Cinderlad, a few girls in *The Blue Fairy Book* find themselves chosen as brides for mercantile

---

[4]In these stories, the girl who marries a beast must agree to accept and love a beast as a husband; the girl must give herself to a beast in order to get a man. When she is willing to do this, he can shed his frightening, rough appearance and show his gentler form, demonstrating the softening agency of women (as in the story of Jane Eyre and Mr. Rochester). These heroines have an agentive role, insofar as they are responsible for the literal reformation of the male.

reasons, such as the girl in "Toads and Diamonds" who was rewarded by a fairy so that flowers and jewels dropped from her mouth whenever she spoke. In "Rumpelstiltzkin," the little dwarf helps the poor miller's daughter to spin straw into gold for three successive nights, so that the King thinks to himself, " 'She's only a miller's daughter, it's true . . . but I couldn't find a richer wife if I were to search the whole world over,' " consequently making her his queen.[5] The system of rewards in fairy tales, then, equates these three factors: being beautiful, being chosen, and getting rich.

Alison Lurie suggests that perhaps fairy tales are the first real women's literature, that they are literally old wives' tales: "throughout Europe . . . the storytellers from whom the Grimm Brothers and their followers heard them were most often women; in some areas they were all women."[6] She wonders if the stories do not reflect a matriarchal society in which women held power, and she mentions Gretel as an example of an active, resourceful young heroine (I will set aside the problem of the power of older women for the moment). An examination of the best-known stories shows that active resourceful girls are in fact rare; most of the heroines are passive, submissive, and helpless. In the story of "Hansel and Gretel" it is true that Gretel pushes the witch into the oven; Hansel is locked up in the stable, where the witch has been fattening him. At the beginning of the story, however, when the children overhear their parents' plan to lose them in the forest, we read that "Gretel wept bitterly and spoke to Hansel: 'Now it's all up with us.' 'No, no, Gretel,' said Hansel, 'don't fret yourself, I'll be able to find a way of escape, no fear.' " (p. 251) It is Hansel who devises the plan of gathering pebbles and dropping them on the path as they are led into the forest. "Later, in the dark forest, Gretel began to cry, and said: 'How are we ever to get out of the wood?' But Hansel comforted her. 'Wait a bit,' he said, 'till the moon is up, and then we'll find our way sure enough.' And when the full moon had risen he took his sister by the hand and followed the pebbles, which shone like new threepenny bits, and showed them the path." (p. 252)

After they get home, they overhear their parents scheming to lose them again. Gretel weeps again, and again Hansel consoles her. Gretel does perform the decisive action at the end, but for the first half of the story she is the frightened little sister, looking to her brother for comfort and help.

Even so, Gretel is one of the most active of the girls, but her company is small. The heroines of the very similar "East of the Sun" and "The Black Bull of Norroway" are initially passive, but then undertake difficult quests when they lose their men. The heroine of "East of the Sun" succumbs to curiosity (the common trap for women: this story is derived from the myth of Cupid and Psyche), and attempts to look at her bear-lover during the night, and the

---

[5]Lang, ed., *The Blue Fair Book* (New York: McGraw-Hill, 1966), p. 98. All quotations are from this edition.

[6]Lurie, "Fairy Tale Liberation," *loc. cit.*

second heroine forgets to remain motionless while her bull-lover fights with the devil (good girls sit still). The lovers disappear when their commands are broken. The girls travel to the ends of the earth seeking them, but they cannot make themselves seen or recognized by their men until the last moment. The Master-maid, in a story whose conclusion resembles these other two, is concealed in a backroom of a giant's house. A prince, looking for adventure, comes to serve the giant, who gives him tasks that are impossible to accomplish. The Master-maid knows the giant's secrets and tells the prince how to do the impossible chores. She knows what to do, but does not act herself. When the giant tells her to kill the prince, she helps the prince to run away, escaping with him. Without her advice the escape would be impossible, yet apparently she had never attempted to run away herself, but had been waiting in the back room for a prince-escort to show up.

Most of the heroines in *The Blue Fairy Book*, however, are entirely passive, submissive, and helpless. This is most obviously true of the Sleeping Beauty, who lies asleep, in the ultimate state of passivity, waiting for a brave prince to awaken and save her. (She is like the Snow-White of "Snow-White and the Seven Dwarfs," who lies in a death-like sleep, her beauty being visible through her glass coffin, until a prince comes along and falls in love with her.) When the prince does penetrate the tangle of thorns and brambles, enters the castle, finds her chamber, and awakens her, the princess opens her eyes and says, " 'Is it you, my Prince? You have waited a long while.' " (p. 59) This is not the end of the story, although it is the most famous part. The Sleeping Beauty, who was, while enchanted, the archetype of the passive, waiting beauty, retains this character in the second part, when she is awake. She marries the prince, and has two children who look savory to her mother-in-law, an Ogress with a taste for human flesh. While her son is away on a hunting trip the Ogress Queen orders the cook to kill and serve for dinner first one child and then the other. The cook hides the children, serving first a roast lamb and then a kid, instead. When the Ogress demands that her daughter-in-law be killed next, the cook tells her the Queen-mother's orders. The young Queen folds up at once: " 'Do it; do it' (said she, stretching out her neck). 'Execute your orders, and then I shall go and see my children . . . whom I so much and so tenderly loved.' " (p. 62) The compassionate cook, however, decides to hide her too, and the young King returns in time to save them all from the Ogress' wrath and impending disaster

Cinderella plays as passive a role in her story. After leaving her slipper at the ball she has nothing more to do but stay home and wait. The prince has commanded that the slipper be carried to every house in the kingdom, and that it be tried on the foot of every woman. Cinderella can remain quietly at home; the prince's servant will come to her house and will discover her identity. Cinderella's male counterpart, Espen Cinderlad, the hero of a great many Norwegian folk tales, plays a very different role. Although he is the youngest of the three brothers, as Cinderella is the youngest sister, he is a Cinderlad by choice. His brothers may ridicule and despise him, but no one forces him to sit by the fire and poke in the ashes all day; he elects to do so. All the while, he knows that he is the cleverest of the three, and eventually he leaves the fireside and wins a princess and half a kingdom by undertaking some adventure or winning a contest.

The Princess on the Glass Hill is the prototype of female passivity. The whole story is in the title; the Princess has been perched somehow on top of a glass hill, and thus made virtually inaccessible. There she sits, a waiting prize for whatever man can ride a horse up the glassy slope. So many of the heroines of fairy stories, including the well-known Rapunzel, are locked up in towers, locked into a magic sleep, imprisoned by giants, or otherwise enslaved, and waiting to be rescued by a passing prince, that the helpless, imprisoned maiden is the quintessential heroine of the fairy tale.

In the interesting story of "The Goose-Girl," an old Queen sends off her beautiful daughter, accompanied by a maid, to be married to a distant prince. The Queen gives her daughter a rag stained with three drops of her own blood. During the journey the maid brusquely refuses to bring the Princess a drink of water, saying " 'I don't mean to be your servant any longer.' " The intimidated Princess only murmurs, " 'Oh! heaven, what am I to do?' " (p. 266) This continues, the maid growing ruder, the Princess meeker, until she loses the rag, whereupon the maid rejoices, knowing that she now has full power over the girl, "for in losing the drops of blood the Princess had become weak and powerless." (p. 268) The maid commands the Princess to change clothes and horses with her, and never to speak to anyone about what has happened. The possession of the rag had assured the Princess' social status; without it she becomes *déclassée*, and while her behavior was no less meek and docile before losing the rag than afterwards, there is no formal role reversal until she loses it. Upon their arrival the maid presents herself as the Prince's bride, while the Princess is given the job of goose-girl. At length, due solely to the intervention of others, the secret is discovered, the maid killed, and the goose-girl married to the Prince.

The heroine of "Felicia and the Pot of Pinks" is equally submissive to ill-treatment. After their father's death, her brother forbids her to sit on his chairs:

> Felicia, who was very gentle, said nothing, but stood up crying quietly; while Bruno, for that was her brother's name, sat comfortably by the fire. Presently, when suppertime came, Bruno had a delicious egg, and he threw the shell to Felicia, saying:
> 'There, that is all I can give you; if you don't like it, go out and catch frogs; there are plenty of them in the marsh close by.' Felicia did not answer but she cried more bitterly than ever, and went away to her own little room. (p. 148)

The underlying associational pattern of these stories links the figures of the victimized girl and the interesting girl; it is always the interesting girl, the special girl, who is in trouble. It needs to be asked whether a child's absorption of the associational patterns found in these myths and legends may not sensitize the personality, rendering it susceptible to melodramatic self-conceptions and expectations. Because victimized girls like Felicia, the Goose-girl, and Cinderella are invariably rescued and rewarded, indeed glorified, children learn that suffering goodness can afford to remain meek, and need not and perhaps should not strive to defend itself, for if it did so perhaps the fairy godmother would not turn up for once, to set things right at the end. Moreover, the special thrill of persecution, bordering at once upon self-pity and self-righteousness, would have to be surrendered. Submissive, meek, passive female behavior is suggested and rewarded by the action of these stories.

Many of the girls are not merely passive, however; they are frequently victims and even martyrs as well. The Cinderella story is not simply a rags-to-riches tale. Cinderella is no Horatio Alger; her name is partly synonymous with female martyrdom. Her ugly older sisters, who are jealous of her beauty, keep her dressed in rags and hidden at home. They order her to do all the meanest housework. Cinderella bears this ill-treatment meekly: she is the patient sufferer, an object of pity. When the older sisters go off to the ball she bursts into tears; it is only the sound of her weeping that arouses her fairy godmother. Ultimately, her loneliness and her suffering are sentimentalized and become an integral part of her glamor. "Cinderella" and the other stories of this type show children that the girl who is singled out for rejection and bad treatment, and who submits to her lot, weeping but never running away, has a special compensatory destiny awaiting her. One of the pleasures provided by these stories is that the child-reader is free to indulge in pity, to be sorry for the heroine. The girl in tears is invariably the heroine; that is one of the ways the child can identify the heroine, for no one mistakenly feels sorry for the ugly older sisters, or for any of the villains or villainesses. When these characters suffer, they are only receiving their "just deserts." The child who dreams of being a Cinderella dreams perforce not only of being chosen and elevated by a prince, but also of being a glamorous sufferer or victim. What these stories convey is that women in distress are interesting. Fairy stories provide children with a concentrated early introduction to the archetype of the suffering heroine, who is currently alive (though not so well) under the name of Jenny Cavilleri.

The girl who marries Blue Beard is a prime example of the helpless damsel-victim, desperately waiting for a rescuer. She knows that her husband will not hesitate to murder her, because she has seen the corpses of his other murdered wives in the forbidden closet. The enraged Blue Beard announces that he will cut off her head; he gives her fifteen minutes to say her prayers, after which he bellows for her so loudly that the house trembles:

> The distressed wife came down, and threw herself at his feet, all in tears, with her hair about her shoulders.

'This signifies nothing,' said Blue Beard: 'you must die': then, taking hold of her hair with one hand, and lifting up the sword with the other, he was going to take off her head. The poor lady, turning about to him, and looking at him with dying eyes, desired him to afford her one little moment to recollect herself.

'No, no,' said he, 'recommend thyself to God,' and was just about to strike. . . . (p. 295)

'At this very instant,'' as the story continues, her brothers rush in and save her.

It is worth noticing that the one Greek legend that Lang included in *The Blue Fairy Book* is the Perseus story, which Lang entitled "The Terrible Head." It features two utterly helpless women, the first being Danae, who is put into a chest with her infant son, Perseus, and thrown out to sea, to drown or starve or drift away. Fortunately the chest comes to land, and Danae and her baby are saved. At the conclusion of the story, as the grown-up Perseus is flying home with the Gorgon's head, he looks down and sees "a beautiful girl chained to a stake at the high-water mark of the sea. The girl was so frightened or so tired that she was only prevented from falling by the iron chain about her waist, and there she hung, as if she were dead." (p. 190) Perseus learns that she has been left there as a sacrifice to a sea-monster; he cuts her free, kills the monster, and carries her off as his bride.

Few other rescues are as dramatic as that of Blue Beard's wife or of Andromeda, but the device of the rescue itself is constantly used. The sexes of the rescuer and the person in danger are almost as constantly predictable; men come along to rescue women who are in danger of death, or are enslaved, imprisoned, abused, or plunged into an enchanted sleep which resembles death. Two well-known stories that were not included in *The Blue Fairy Book*, "Snow-White and the Seven Dwarfs" and "Rapunzel," are notable examples of this type: Snow-White is saved from a sleep which everyone assumes is death by the arrival of a handsome prince; Rapunzel, locked up in a tower by a cruel witch, is found and initially rescued by her prince.

Whatever the condition of younger women in fairy tales, Alison Lurie claims that the older women in the tales are often more active and powerful than men. It is true that some older women in fairy tales have power, but of what kind? In order to understand the meaning of women's power in fairy tales, we must examine the nature, the value, and the use of their power

There are only a few powerful good women in *The Blue Fairy Book*, and they are nearly all fairies: the tiny, jolly, ugly old fairy in "Prince Hyacinth," the stately fairies in "Prince Darling," "Toads and Diamonds," and "Felicia," and of course Cinderella's fairy godmother. They are rarely on the scene; they only appear in order to save young people in distress, and then they're off again. These good fairies have gender only in a technical sense; to children, they probably appear as women only in the sense that dwarfs and wizards appear as men. They are not human beings, they are asexual, and many of them are old. They are not examples of powerful women with whom children can identify as role models; they do not provide meaningful alternatives to the stereotype of the younger, passive heroine. A girl may hope to become a princess, but can she ever become a fairy?

Powerful, bad, older women appear to outnumber powerful, good ones. A certain number of these are also not fully human; they are fairies, witches, trolls, or Ogresses. It is generally implied that such females are wicked because of their race: thus the young king in "The Sleeping Beauty" fears his mother while he loves her, "for she was of the race of the Ogres, and the King (his father) would never have married her had it not been for her vast riches; it was even whispered about the Court that she had Ogreish inclinations, and that, whenever she saw little children passing by, she had all the difficulty in the world to avoid falling upon them." (p. 60) Either extra-human race or extreme ugliness is often associated with female wickedness, and in such a way as to suggest that they explain the wickedness. The evil Fairy of the Desert in "The Yellow Dwarf" is described as a "tall old woman, whose ugliness was even more surprising than her extreme old age." (p. 39) The sheep-king in "The Wonderful Sheep" tells Miranda that he was transformed into a sheep by a fairy " 'whom I had known as long as I could remember, and whose ugliness had always horrified me.' " (p. 223) The bear-prince in "East of the Sun" is under a spell cast by a troll-hag, and the fairy who considers herself slighted by the Sleeping Beauty's parents is described as being old: the original illustration for Lang's book shows her to be an ugly old crone, whereas the other fairies are young and lovely.

In the case of wicked but human women, it is also implied that being ill-favored is corollary to being ill-natured, as with Cinderella's step-mother and step-sisters. Cinderella is pretty and sweet, like her dead mother. The step-mother is proud and haughty, and her two daughters by her former husband are like her, so that their ill-temper appears to be genetic, or at least transmitted by the mother. The circumstances in "Toads and Diamonds" are similar: the old widow has two daughters, of whom the eldest resembles her mother "in face and humour. . . . They were both so disagreeable and so proud that there was no living with them. The youngest, who was the very picture of her father for courtesy and sweetness of temper, was withal one of the most beautiful girls ever seen." (p. 274)

Powerful good women are nearly always fairies, and they are remote: they come only when desperately needed. Whether human or extra-human, those women who are either partially or thoroughly evil are generally shown as active, ambitious, strong-willed and, most often, ugly. They are jealous of any woman more beautiful than they, which is not surprising in view of the power deriving from beauty in fairy tales. In "Cinderella" the domineering step-mother and step-sisters contrast with the passive heroine. The odious step-mother wants power, and successfully makes her will prevail in the house; we are told that Cinderella bore her ill-treatment patiently, "and dared not tell her father, who would have rattled her off; for his wife governed him entirely."

The wicked maid in "The Goose-Girl" is not described as being either fair or ugly (except that the Princess appears to be fairer than the maid at the end), but like the other female villains she is jealous of beauty and greedy for wealth. She decides to usurp the Princess' place, and being evil she is also strong and determined, and initially successful. Being powerful is mainly associated with being unwomanly.

The moral value of activity thus becomes sex-linked.[7] The boy who sets out to seek his fortune, like Dick Whittington, Jack the Giant-Killer, or Espen Cinderlad, is a stock figure and, provided that he has a kind heart, is assured of success. What is praiseworthy in males, however, is rejected in females; the counterpart of the energetic, aspiring boy is the scheming, ambitious woman. Some heroines show a kind of strength in their ability to endure, but they do not actively seek to change their lot. (The only exceptions to this rule are in the stories that appear to derive from the myth of Cupid and Psyche: "East of the Sun" and "The Black Bull or Norroway," in which the heroines seek their lost lovers. We may speculate whether the pre-Christian origin of these stories diminishes the stress placed on female passivity and acceptance, but this is purely conjectural.) We can remark that these stories reflect a bias against the active, ambitious, "pushy" woman, and have probably also served to instil this bias in young readers. They establish a dichotomy between those women who are gentle, passive, and fair, and those who are active, wicked, and ugly. Women who are powerful and good are never human; those women who are human, and who have power or seek it, are nearly always portrayed as repulsive.

While character depiction in fairy tales is, to be sure, meagre, and we can usually group characters according to temperamental type (beautiful and sweet, or ugly and evil), there are a couple of girls who are not portrayed as being either perfectly admirable or as wicked. The princesses in "The Yellow Dwarf," "Goldilocks," and "Trusty John" are described as being spoiled, vain, and wilful: the problem is that they refuse to marry anyone. The Queen in "The Yellow Dwarf" expostulates with her daughter:

> 'Bellissima,' she said, 'I do wish you would not be so proud. What makes you despise all these nice kings? I wish you to marry one of them, and you do not try to please me.'
>
> 'I am so happy,' Bellissima answered: 'do leave me in peace, madam. I don't want to care for anyone.'
>
> 'But you would be very happy with any of these princes,' said the Queen, 'and I shall be very angry if you fall in love with anyone who is not worthy of you.'

---

[7]Ruth Kelso's *Doctrine for the Lady of the Renaissance* (Urbana: University of Illinois Press, 1956) demonstrates that "the moral ideal for the lady is essentially Christian . . . as that for the gentleman is essentially pagan. For him the ideal is self-expansion and realization. . . . For the lady the direct opposite is prescribed. The eminently Christian virtues of chastity, humility, piety, and patience under suffering and wrong, are the necessary virtues." (p. 36)

> But the Princess thought so much of herself that she did not consider any one of her lovers clever or handsome enough for her; and her mother, who was getting really angry at her determination not be married, began to wish that she had not allowed her to have her own way so much. (p. 31)

Princess Goldilocks similarly refuses to consider marriage, although she is not as adamant as Bellissima. The princess in the Grimms' story, "King Thrushbeard," which is not included in this collection, behaves like Bellissima; her angry father declares that he will give her to the very next comer, whatever his rank: the next man to enter the castle being a beggar, the king marries his daughter to him. This princess suffers poverty with her beggar-husband, until he reveals himself as one of the suitor kings she had rejected. Bellissima is punished more severely; indeed, her story is remarkable because it is one of the rare examples outside of H. C. Andersen of a story with a sad ending. Because Bellissima had refused to marry, she is forced by a train of circumstances to promise to marry the ugly Yellow Dwarf. She tries to avoid this fate by consenting to wed one of her suitors at last, but the dwarf intervenes at the wedding. Ultimately the dwarf kills the suitor, whom Bellissima had come to love, and she dies of a broken heart. A kind mermaid transforms the ill-fated lovers into two palm trees.

These princesses are portrayed as reprehensible because they refuse to marry; hence, they are considered "stuck-up," as children would say. The alternate construction, that they wished to preserve their freedom and their identity, is denied or disallowed (although Bellissima had said to her mother, " 'I am so happy, do leave me in peace, madam.' ") There is a sense of triumph when a wilful princess submits or is forced to submit to a husband.

The Blue Fairy Book is filled with weddings, but it shows little of married life. It contains thirty stories in which marriage is a component, but eighteen of these stories literally end with the wedding. Most of the other twelve show so little of the marital life of the hero or heroine that technically they too may be said to end with marriage. Only a few of the stories show any part of the married life of young people, or even of old ones. The Sleeping Beauty is a totally passive wife and mother, and Blue Beard's wife, like the Sleeping Beauty, depends on a man to rescue her. Whereas the Sleeping Beauty is menaced by her mother-in-law who, being an Ogress, is only half-human, Blue Beard's wife is endangered by *being* the wife of her ferocious husband. (Her error may be ascribed to her having an independent sense of curiosity, or to rash disobedience.) This widely-known story established a potent myth in which a helpless woman violates her husband's arbitrary command and then is subject to his savage, implacable fury. It is fully the counterpoise of the other stock marital situation containing a scheming, overbearing wife and a timid, hen-pecked husband, as in "Cinderella"; moreover, whereas the domineering wife is always implicitly regarded as abhorrent, the helpless, threatened, passive wife is uncritically viewed and thus implicitly approved of. As Andromeda,

Blue Beard's wife, or the imperiled Pauline, her function is to provide us with a couple of thrills of a more or less sadistic tincture.

The other peculiar aspect of the depiction of marriage in these stories is that nearly all the young heroes and heroines are the children of widows or widowers; only five of the thirty-seven stories in the book contain a set of parents: these include "The Sleeping Beauty," in which the parents leave the castle when the hundred-year enchantment begins, and the two similar tales of "Little Thumb" and "Hansel and Gretel," in both of which the parents decide to get rid of their children because they are too poor to feed them. (In "Little Thumb" the husband persuades his reluctant wife, and in "Hansel and Gretel" the wife persuades her reluctant husband.) Cinderella has two parents, but the only one who plays a part in the story is her stepmother. In general, the young people of these stories are described as having only one parent, or none. Although marriage is such a constant event in the stories, and is central to their reward system, few marriages are indeed shown in fairy tales. Like the White Queen's rule, there's jam tomorrow and jam yesterday, but never jam today. The stories can be described as being preoccupied with marriage without portraying it; as a real condition, it's nearly always off-stage.

In effect, these stories focus upon courtship, which is magnified into the most important and exciting part of a girl's life, brief though courtship is, because it is the part of her life in which she most counts as a person herself. After marriage she ceases to be wooed, her consent is no longer sought, she derives her status from her husband, and her personal identity is thus snuffed out. When fairy tales show courtship as exciting, and conclude with marriage, and the vague statement that "they lived happily ever after," children may develop a deep-seated desire always to be courted, since marriage is literally the end of the story.

The controversy about what is biologically determined and what is learned has just begun. These are the questions now being asked, and not yet answered: to what extent is passivity a biological attribute of females; to what extent is it culturally determined? Perhaps it will be argued that these stories show archetypal female behavior, but one may wonder to what extent they reflect female attributes, or to what extent they serve as training manuals for girls? If one argued that the characteristically passive behavior of female characters in fairy stories is a reflection of an attribute inherent in female personality, would one also argue, as consistency would require, that the mercantile reward system of fairy stories reflects values that are inherent in human nature? We must consider the possibility that the classical attributes of "femininity" found in these stories are in fact imprinted in children and reinforced by the stories themselves. Analyses of the influence of the most popular children's literature may give us an insight into some of the origins of psycho-sexual identity.

JUDITH LORBER

"Night to His Day":
The Social Construction of Gender

Judith Lorber is Professor of Sociology at Brooklyn College and the Graduate School, City University of New York. She is an acclaimed feminist and sociologist, and founding editor of the journal, Gender and Society. *The following is from her book,* Paradoxes of Gender *(1994).*

Talking about gender for most people is the equivalent of fish talking about water. Gender is so much the routine ground of everyday activities that questioning its taken-for-granted assumptions and presuppositions is like wondering about whether the sun will come up.[1] Gender is so pervasive that in our society we assume it is bred into our genes. Most people find it hard to believe that gender is constantly created and re-created out of human interaction, out of social life, and is the texture and order of that social life. Yet gender, like culture, is a human production that depends on everyone constantly "doing gender" (West and Zimmerman 1987).

And everyone "does gender" without thinking about it. Today, on the subway, I saw a well-dressed man with a year-old child in a stroller. Yesterday, on a bus, I saw a man with a tiny baby in a carrier on his chest. Seeing men taking care of small children in public is increasingly common — at least in New York City. But both men were quite obviously stared at — and smiled at, approvingly. Everyone was doing gender — the men who were changing the role of fathers and the other passengers, who were applauding them silently. But there was more gendering going on that probably fewer people noticed. The baby was wearing a white crocheted cap and white clothes. You couldn't tell if it was a boy or a girl. The child in the stroller was wearing a dark blue T-shirt and dark print pants. As they started to leave the train, the father put a Yankee baseball cap on the child's head. Ah, a boy, I thought. Then I noticed the gleam of tiny earrings in the child's ears, and as they got off, I saw the little flowered sneakers and lace-trimmed socks. Not a boy after all. Gender done.

Gender is such a familiar part of daily life that it usually takes a deliberate disruption of our expectations of how women and men are supposed to act to pay attention to how it is produced. Gender signs and signals are so ubiquitous that we usually fail to note them — unless they are missing or ambiguous. Then we are uncomfortable until we have successfully placed the other person in a gender status; otherwise, we feel socially dislocated. In our society, in addition to man and woman, the status can be *transvestite* (a person who dresses in opposite-gender clothes) and *transsexual* (a person who has had sex-change surgery). Transvestites and transsexuals carefully construct their gender status by dressing, speaking, walking, gesturing in the ways prescribed for women or men, whichever they want to be taken for—and so does any "normal" person.

For the individual, gender construction starts with assignment to a sex category on the basis of what the genitalia look like at birth.[2] Then babies are dressed or adorned in a way that displays the category because parents don't want to be constantly asked whether their baby is a girl or a boy. A sex category becomes a gender status through naming, dress, and the use of other gender markers. Once a child's gender is evident, others treat those in one gender differently from those in the other, and the children respond to the different treatment by feeling different and behaving differently. As soon as they can talk, they start to refer to themselves as members of their gender. Sex doesn't come into play again until puberty, but by that time, sexual feelings and desires and practices have been shaped by gendered norms and expectations. Adolescent boys and girls approach and avoid each other in an elaborately scripted and gendered mating dance. Parenting is gendered, with different expectations for mothers and for fathers, and people of different genders work at different kinds of jobs. The work adults do as mothers and fathers and as low-level workers and high-level bosses, shapes women's and men's life experiences, and these experiences produce different feelings, consciousness, relationships, skills—ways of being that we call feminine or masculine.[3] All of these processes constitute the social construction of gender.

Gendered roles change—today fathers are taking care of little children, girls and boys are wearing unisex clothing and getting the same education, women and men are working at the same jobs. Although many traditional social groups are quite strict about maintaining gender differences, in other social groups they seem to be blurring. Then why the one-year-old's earrings? Why is it still so important to mark a child as a girl or a boy, to make sure she is not taken for a boy or he for a girl? What would happen if they were? They would, quite literally, have changed places in their social world.

To explain why gendering is done from birth, constantly and by everyone, we have to look not only at the way individuals experience gender but at gender as a social institution. As a social institution, gender is one of the major ways that human beings organize their lives. Human society depends on a predictable division of labor, a designated allocation of scarce goods, assigned responsibility for children and others who cannot care for themselves, common values and their systematic transmission to new members, legitimate leadership, music, art, stories, games, and other symbolic productions. One way of choosing people for the different tasks of society is on the basis of their talents, motivations, and competence—their demonstrated achievements. The other way is on the basis of gender, race, ethnicity—ascribed membership in a category of people. Although societies vary in the extent to which they use one or the other of these ways of allocating people to work and to carry out other responsibilities, every society uses gender and age grades. Every society classifies people as "girl and boy children," "girls and boys ready to be married," and "fully adult women and men," constructs similarities among them and differences between them, and assigns them to different roles and responsibilities. Personality characteristics, feelings, motivations, and ambitions flow from these different life experiences so that the members of these different groups become different kinds of people. The process of gendering and its outcome are legitimated by religion, law, science, and the society's entire set of values.

Western society's values legitimate gendering by claiming that it all comes from physiology—female and male procreative differences. But gender and sex are not equivalent, and gender as a social construction does not flow automatically from genitalia and reproductive organs, the main physiological differences of females and males. In the construction of ascribed social statuses, physiological differences such as sex, stage of development, color of skin, and size are crude markers. They are not the source of the social statuses of gender, age, grade, and race. Social statuses are carefully constructed through prescribed processes of teaching, learning, emulation, and enforcement. Whatever genes, hormones, and biological evolution contribute to human social institutions is materially as well as qualitatively transformed by social practices. Every social institution has a material base, but culture and social practices transform that base into something with qualitatively different patterns and constraints. The economy is much more than producing food and goods and distributing them to eaters and users; family and kinship are not the equivalent of having sex and procreating; morals and religions cannot be equated with the fears and ecstasies of the brain; language goes far beyond the sounds produced by tongue and larynx. No one eats "money" or "credit"; the concepts of "god" and "angels" are the subjects of theological disquisitions; not only words but objects, such as their flag, "speak" to the citizens of a country.

Similarly, gender cannot be equated with biological and physiological differences between human females and males. The building blocks of gender are socially *constructed* statuses. Western societies have only two genders, "man" and "woman." Some societies have three genders—men, women, and *berdaches* or *hijras* or *xaniths*. Berdaches, hijras, and xaniths are biological males who behave, dress, work, and are treated in most respects as social women; they are therefore not men, nor are they female women; they are, in our language, "male women."[4] There are African and American Indian societies that have a gender status called *manly hearted women*—biological females who work, marry, and parent as men; their social status is "female men" (Amadiume 1987; Blackwood 1984). They do not have to behave or dress as men to have the social responsibilities and prerogatives of husbands and fathers; what makes them men is enough wealth to buy a wife.

Modern Western societies' *transsexuals* and *transvestites* are the nearest equivalent of these crossover genders, but they are not institutionalized as third genders (Bolin 1987). Transsexuals are biological males and females who have sex-change operations to alter their genitalia. They do so in order to bring their physical anatomy in congruence with the way they want to live and with their own sense of gender identity. They do not become a third gender; they change genders. Transvestites are males who live as women and females who live as men but do not intend to have sex-change surgery. Their dress, appearance, and mannerisms fall within the range of what is expected from members of the opposite gender, so that they "pass." They also change genders, sometimes temporarily, some for most of their lives. Transvestite women have fought in wars as men soldiers as recently as the nineteenth century; some married women, and others went back to being women and married men once the war was over.[5] Some were discovered when their wounds were treated; others not until they died. In order to work as a jazz musician, a man's occupation, Billy Tipton, a woman, lived most of her life as a man. She died recently at seventy-four, leaving a wife and three adopted sons for whom she was husband and father, and musicians with whom she had played and traveled, for whom she was "one of the boys" (*New York Times* 1989).[6] There have been many other such occurrences of women passing as men to do more prestigious or lucrative men's work (Matthaei 1982, 192–93).[7]

Genders, therefore, are not attached to a biological substratum. Gender boundaries are breachable, and individual and socially organized shifts from one gender to another call attention to "cultural, social, or aesthetic dissonances" (Garber 1992, 16). These odd or deviant or third genders show us what we ordinarily take for granted—that people have to learn to be women and men. Men who cross-dress for performances or for pleasure often learn from women's magazines how to "do" femininity convincingly (Garber 1992, 41–51). Because transvestism is direct evidence of how gender is constructed, Marjorie Garber claims it has "extraordinary power . . . to disrupt, expose, and challenge, putting in question the very notion of the 'original' and of stable identity" (1992, 16). . . .

FOR INDIVIDUALS, GENDER MEANS SAMENESS

Although the possible combinations of genitalia, body shapes, clothing, mannerisms, sexuality, and roles could produce infinite varieties in human beings, the social institution of gender depends on the production and maintenance of a limited number of gender statuses and of making the members of these statuses similar to each other. Individuals are born sexed but not gendered, and they have to be taught to be masculine or feminine.[8] As Simone de Beauvoir said: "One is not born, but rather becomes, a woman . . . ; it is civilization as a whole that produces this creature . . . which is described as feminine" (1952, 267). . . .

Many cultures go beyond clothing, gestures, and demeanor in gendering children. They inscribe gender directly into bodies. In traditional Chinese society, mothers once bound their daughters' feet into three-inch stumps to enhance their sexual attractiveness. Jewish fathers circumcise their infant sons to show their covenant with God. Women in African societies remove the clitoris of prepubescent girls, scrape their labia, and make the lips grow together to preserve their chastity and ensure their marriageability. In Western societies, women augment their breast size with silicone and reconstruct their faces with cosmetic surgery to conform to cultural ideals of feminine beauty. Hanna Papanek (1990) notes that these practices reinforce the sense of superiority or inferiority in the adults who carry them out as well as in the children on whom they are done: The genitals of Jewish fathers and sons are physical and psychological evidence of their common dominant religious and familial status; the genitals of African mothers and daughters are physical and psychological evidence of their joint subordination.[9]

Sandra Bem (1981, 1993) argues that because gender is a powerful "schema" that orders the cognitive world, one must wage a constant, active battle for a child not to fall into typical gendered attitudes and behavior. In 1972, *Ms.* magazine published Lois Gould's fantasy of how to raise a child free of gender-typing. The experiment calls for hiding the child's anatomy from all eyes except the parents' and treating the child as neither a girl nor a boy. The child, called X, gets to do all the things boys *and* girls do. The experiment is so successful that all the children in X's class at school want to look and behave like X. At the end of the story, the creators of the experiment are asked what will happen when X grows up. The scientists' answer is that by then it will be quite clear what X is, implying that its hormones will kick in and it will be revealed as a female or male. That ambiguous, and somewhat contradictory, ending lets Gould off the hook; neither she nor we have any idea what someone brought up in a totally androgynous manner would be like sexually or socially as an adult. The hormonal input will not create gender or sexuality but will only establish secondary sex characteristics; breasts, beards, and menstruation alone do not produce social manhood or womanhood. Indeed, it is at puberty, when sex characteristics become evident, that most societies put pubescent children through their most important rites of passage, the rituals that officially mark them as fully gendered—that is, ready to marry and become adults.

Most parents create a gendered world for their newborn by naming, birth announcements, and dress. Children's relationships with same-gendered and different-gendered caretakers structure their self-identifications and personalities. Through cognitive development, children extract and apply to their own actions the appropriate behavior for those who belong in their own gender, as well as race, religion, ethnic group, and social class, rejecting what is not appropriate. If their social categories are highly valued, they value themselves highly; if their social categories are of low status, they lose self-esteem (Chodorow 1974). Many feminist parents who want to raise androgynous children soon lose their children to the pull of gendered norms (Gordon 1990, 87–90). My son attended a carefully nonsexist elementary school, which didn't even have girls' and boys' bathrooms. When he was seven or eight years old, I attended a class play about "squares" and "circles" and their need for each other and noticed that all the girl squares and circles wore makeup, but none of the boy squares and circles did. I asked the teacher about it after the play, and she said, "Bobby said he was not going to wear makeup, and he is a powerful child, so none of the boys would either." In a long discussion about conformity, my son confronted me with the question of who the conformists were, the boys who followed their leader or the girls who listened to the woman teacher. In actuality, they both were, because they both followed same-gender leaders and acted in gender-appropriate ways. (Actors may wear makeup, but real boys don't.)

For human beings there is no essential femaleness or maleness, femininity or masculinity, womanhood or manhood, but once gender is ascribed, the social order constructs and holds individuals to strongly gendered norms and expectations. Individuals may vary on many of the components of gender and may shift genders temporarily or permanently, but they must fit into the limited number of gender statuses their society recognizes. In the process, they re-create their society's version of women and men: "If we do gender appropriately, we simultaneously sustain, reproduce, and render legitimate the institutional arrangements. . . . If we fail to do gender appropriately, we as individuals—not the institutional arrangements—may be called to account (for our character, motives, and predispositions)" (West and Zimmerman 1987, 146).

The gendered practices of everyday life reproduce a society's view of how women and men should act. Gendered social arrangements are justified by religion and cultural productions and backed by law, but the most powerful means of sustaining the moral hegemony of the dominant gender ideology is that the process is made invisible; any possible alternatives are virtually unthinkable (Foucault 1972; Gramsci 1971).[10]

FOR SOCIETY, GENDER MEANS DIFFERENCE

The pervasiveness of gender as a way of structuring social life demands that gender statuses be clearly differentiated. Varied talents, sexual preferences, identities, personalities, interests, and ways of interacting fragment the individual's bodily and social experiences. Nonetheless, these are organized in Western cultures into two and only two socially and legally recognized gender statuses, "man" and "woman."[11] In the social construction of gender, it does not matter what men and women actually do; it does not even matter if they do exactly the same thing. The social institution of gender insists only that what they do is *perceived* as different.

If men and women are doing the same tasks, they are usually spatially segregated to maintain gender separation, and often the tasks are given different job titles as well, such as executive secretary and administrative assistant (Reskin 1988). If the differences between women and men begin to blur, society's "sameness taboo" goes into action (Rubin 1975, 178). At a rock and roll dance at West Point in 1976, the year women were admitted to the prestigious military academy for the first time, the school's administrators "were reportedly perturbed by the sight of mirror-image couples dancing in short hair and dress gray trousers," and a rule was established that women cadets could dance at these events only if they wore skirts (Barkalow and Raab 1990, 53).[12] Women recruits in the U.S. Marine Corps are required to wear makeup—at a minimum, lipstick and eye shadow—and they have to take classes in makeup, hair care, poise, and etiquette. This feminization is part of a deliberate policy of making them clearly distinguishable from men Marines. Christine Williams quotes a twenty-five-year-old woman drill instructor as saying, "A lot of the recruits who come here don't wear makeup; they're tomboyish or athletic. A lot of them have the preconceived idea that going into the military means they can still be a tomboy. They don't realize that you are a Woman Marine" (1989, 76–77).[13]

If gender differences were genetic, physiological, or hormonal, gender bending and gender ambiguity would occur only in hermaphrodites, who are born with chromosomes and genitalia that are not clearly female or male. Since gender differences are socially constructed, all men and all women can enact the behavior of the other, because they know the other's social script: "'Man' and 'woman' are at once empty and overflowing categories. Empty because they have no ultimate, transcendental meaning. Overflowing because even when they appear to be fixed, they still contain within them alternative, denied, or suppressed definitions" (Scott 1988a, 49). Nonetheless, though individuals may be able to shift gender statuses, the gender boundaries have to hold, or the whole gendered social order will come crashing down. . . .

GENDER AS PROCESS, STRATIFICATION, AND STRUCTURE

As a social institution, gender is a process of creating distinguishable social statuses for the assignment of rights and responsibilities. As part of a stratification system that ranks these statuses unequally, gender is a major building block in the social structures built on these unequal statuses.

As a *process*, gender creates the social differences that define "woman" and "man." In social interaction throughout their lives, individuals learn what is expected, see what is expected, act and react in expected ways, and thus simultaneously construct and maintain the gender order: "The very injunction to be a given gender takes place through discursive routes: to be a good mother, to be a heterosexually desirable object, to be a fit worker, in sum, to signify a multiplicity of guarantees in response to a variety of different demands all at once" (Butler 1990, 145). Members of a social group neither make up gender as they go along nor exactly replicate in rote fashion what was done before. In almost every encounter, human beings produce gender, behaving in the ways they learned were appropriate for their gender status, or resisting or rebelling against these norms. Resistance and rebellion have altered gender norms, but so far they have rarely eroded the statuses.

Gendered patterns of interaction acquire additional layers of gendered sexuality, parenting, and work behaviors in childhood, adolescence, and adulthood. Gendered norms and expectations are enforced through informal sanctions of gender-inappropriate behavior by peers and by formal punishment or threat of punishment by those in authority should behavior deviate too far from socially imposed standards for women and men.

Everyday gendered interactions build gender into the family, the work process, and other organizations and institutions, which in turn reinforce gender expectations for individuals.[14] Because gender is a process, there is room not only for modification and variation by individuals and small groups but also for institutionalized change (Scott 1988, 7).

As part of a stratification system, gender ranks men above women of the same race and class. Women and men could be different but equal. In practice, the process of creating difference depends to a great extent on differential evaluation. As Nancy Jay (1981) says: "That which is defined, separated out, isolated from all else is A and pure. Not-A is necessarily impure, a random catchall, to which nothing is external except A and the principle of order that separates it from Not-A" (45). From the individual's point of view, whichever gender is A, the other is Not-A; gender boundaries tell the individual who is like him or her, and all the rest are unlike. From society's point of view, however, one gender is usually the touchstone, the normal, the dominant, and the other is different, deviant, and subordinate. In Western society, "man" is A, "woman" is Not-A. (Consider what a society would be like where woman was A and man Not-A.)

The further dichotomization by race and class constructs the gradations of a heterogeneous society's stratification scheme. Thus, in the United States, white is A, African American is Not-A; middle class is A, working class is Not-A, and "African-American women occupy a position whereby the inferior half of a series of these dichotomies converge" (Collins 1990,70). The dominant categories are the hegemonic ideals, taken so for granted as the way things should be that white is not ordinarily thought of as a race, middle class as a class, or men as a gender. The characteristics of these categories define the Other as that which lacks the valuable qualities the dominants exhibit.

Societies vary in the extent of the inequality in social status of their women and men members, but where there is inequality, the status "woman" (and its attendant behavior and role allocations) is usually held in lesser esteem than the status "man." Since gender is also intertwined with a society's other constructed statuses of differential evaluation — race, religion, occupation, class, country of origin, and so on — men and women members of the favored groups command more power, more prestige, and more property than the members of the disfavored groups. Within many social groups, however, men are advantaged over women. The more economic resources, such as education and job opportunities, are available to a group, the more they tend to be monopolized by men. In poorer groups that have few resources (such as working-class African Americans in the United States), women and men are more nearly equal, and the women may even outstrip the men in education and occupational status (Almquist 1987).

As a structure, gender divides work in the home and in economic production, legitimates those in authority, and organizes sexuality and emotional life (Connell 1987, 91–142). As primary parents, women significantly influence children's psychological development and emotional attachments, in the process reproducing gender. Emergent sexuality is shaped by heterosexual, homosexual, bisexual, and sadomasochistic patterns that are gendered — different for girls and boys, and for women and men — so that sexual statuses reflect gender statuses.

When gender is a major component of structured inequality, the devalued genders have less power, prestige, and economic rewards than the valued genders. In countries that discourage gender discrimination, many major roles are still gendered; women still do most of the domestic labor and child rearing, even while doing full-time paid work; women and men are segregated on the job and each does work considered "appropriate"; women's work is usually paid less than men's work. Men dominate the positions of authority and leadership in government, the military, and the law; cultural productions, religions, and sports reflect men's interests.

Gender inequality — the devaluation of "women" and the social domination of "men" — has social functions and a social history. It is not the result of sex, procreation, physiology, anatomy, hormones, or genetic predispositions. It is produced and maintained by identifiable social processes and built into the general social structure and individual identities deliberately and purposefully. The social order as we know it in Western societies is organized around racial ethnic, class, and gender inequality. I contend, therefore, that the continuing purpose of gender as a modern social institution is to construct women as a group to be the subordinates of men as a group. The life of everyone placed in the status "woman" is "night to his day — that has forever been the fantasy. Black to his white. Shut out of his system's space, she is the repressed that ensures the system's functioning" (Cixous and Clément [1975] 1986, 67). . . .

There is no core or bedrock human nature below these endlessly looping processes of the social production of sex and gender, self and other, identity and psyche, each of which is a "complex cultural construction" (Butler 1990, 36). For *humans, the social is the natural.* Therefore, "in its feminist senses, gender cannot mean simply the cultural appropriation of biological sexual difference.

Sexual difference is itself a fundamental—and scientifically contested—construction. Both 'sex' and 'gender' are woven of multiple, asymmetrical strands of difference, charged with multifaceted dramatic narratives of domination and struggle" (Haraway 1990, 140).

NOTES

1. Gender is, in Erving Goffman's words, an aspect of *Felicity's Condition*, "any arrangement which leads us to judge an individual's . . . acts not to be a manifestation of strangeness. Behind Felicity's Condition is our sense of what it is to be sane" (1983, 27). Also see Bern 1993; Frye 1983, 17–40; Goffman 1977.

2. In cases of ambiguity in countries with modern medicine, surgery is usually performed to make the genitalia more clearly male or female.

3. See Butler 1990 for an analysis of how doing gender is gender identity.

4. On the *hijras* of India, see Nanda 1990; on the *xaniths* of Oman, see Wikan 1982, 168–86; on the American Indian *berdaches*, see Williams 1986. Other societies that have similar institutionalized third-gender men are the Koniag of Alaska, the Tanala of Madagascar, the Mesakin of Nuba, and the Chukchee of Siberia (Wikan 1982, 170).

5. Durova 1989; Freeman and Bond 1992; Wheelwright 1989.

6. Gender segregation of work in popular music still has not changed very much, according to Groce and Cooper 1989, despite considerable androgyny in some very popular figures. See Garber 1992 on the androgyny. She discusses Tipton on pp. 67–70.

7. In the nineteenth century, not only did these women get men's wages, but they also "had male privileges and could do all manner of things other women could not: open a bank account, write checks, own property, go anywhere unaccompanied, vote in elections" (Faderman 1991, 44).

8. For an account of how a potential man-to-woman transsexual learned to be feminine, see Garfinkel 1967, 116–85, 285–88.

9. Paige and Paige (1981, 147–49) argue that circumcision ceremonies indicate a father's loyalty to his lineage elders—'visible public evidence that the head of a family unit of their lineage is willing to trust others with his and his family's most valuable political asset, his son's penis" (147). On female circumcision, see El Dareer 1982; Lightfoot-Klein 1987; van der Kwaak 1992; Walker 1992. There is a form of female circumcision that removes only the prepuce of the clitoris and is similar to male circumcision, but most forms of female circumcision are far more extensive, mutilating, and spiritually and psychologically shocking than the usual form of male circumcision. However, among the Australian aborigines, boys' penises are slit and kept open, so that they urinate and bleed the way women do (Bettelheim 1962, 165–206).

10. The concepts of moral hegemony, the effects of everyday activities (praxis) on thought and personality, and the necessity of consciousness of these processes before political change can occur are all based on Marx's analysis of class relations.

11. Other societies recognize more than two categories, but usually no more than three or four (Jacobs and Roberts 1989).

12. Carol Barkalow's book has a photograph of eleven first-year West Pointers in a math class, who are dressed in regulation pants, shirts, and sweaters, with short haircuts. The caption challenges the reader to locate the only woman in the room.

13. The taboo on males and females looking alike reflects the U.S. military's homophobia (Bérubé 1989). If you can't tell those with a penis from those with a vagina, how are you going to determine whether their sexual interest is heterosexual or homosexual unless you watch them having sexual relations?

14. On the "logic of practice," or how the experience of gender is embedded in the norms of everyday interaction and the structure of formal organizations, see Acker 1990; Connell 1987; Smith 1987.

REFERENCES

Acker, Joan. 1990. "Hierarchies, Jobs, and Bodies: A Theory of Gendered Organizations." *Gender and Society* 4, 139–58.

Almquist, Elizabeth M. 1987. "Labor Market Gendered Inequality in Minority Groups." *Gender and Society* 1, 400–414.

Amadiume, Ifi. 1987. *Male Daughters, Female Husbands: Gender and Sex in an African Society.* London: Zed Books.

Barkalow, Carol, with Andrea Raab. 1990. *In the Men's House.* New York: Poseidon Press.

Beauvoir, Simone de. 1953. *The Second Sex*, translated by H. M. Parshley. New York: Knopf.

Bern, Sandra Lipsitz. 1981. "Gender Schema Theory: A Cognitive Account of Sex Typing." *Psychological Review* 88, 354–64.

———. 1983. "Gender Schema Theory and Its Implications for Child Development: Raising Gender Aschematic Children in a Gender-Schematic Society." *Signs: Journal of Women in Culture and Society* 8, 598–616.

———. 1993. *The Lenses of Gender: Transforming the Debate on Sexual Inequality.* New Haven: Yale University Press.

Bérubé, Allan. 1989. "Marching to a Different Drummer: Gay and Lesbian GIs in World War II." In Duberman, Vicinus, and Chauncey, eds., *Hidden from History: Reclaiming the Gay and Lesbian Past.* New York: New American Library.

Bettelheim, Bruno. 1962. *Symbolic Wounds: Puberty Rites and the Envious Male.* London: Thames and Hudson.

Blackwood, Evelyn. 1984. "Sexuality and Gender in Certain Native American Tribes: The Case of Cross-Gender Females." *Signs: Journal of Women in Culture and Society* 10, 27–42.

Bolin, Anne. 1987. "Transsexualism and the Limits of Traditional Analysis." *American Behavioral Scientist* 31, 41–65.

Butler, Judith. 1990. *Gender Trouble: Feminism and the Subversion of Identity.* New York: Routledge.

Chodorow, Nancy. 1974. "Family Structure and Feminine Personality." In Rosaldo and Lamphere, eds., *Women, Culture and Society*. Stanford, Calif.: Stanford University Press.

Cixous, Hélène, and Catherine Clément. [1975] 1986. *The Newly Born Woman*, translated by Betsy Wing. Minneapolis: University of Minnesota Press.

Collins, Patricia Hill. 1990. *Black Feminist Thought: Knowledge, Consciousness, and the Politics of Empowerment*. Boston: Unwin Hyman.

Connell, R[obert] W. 1987. *Gender and Power: Society, the Person, and Sexual Politics*. Stanford, Calif.: Stanford University Press.

Duberman, Martin Bauml, Martha Vicinus, and George Chauncey Jr., eds. 1989. *Hidden from History: Reclaiming the Gay and Lesbian Past*. New York: New American Library.

Durova, Nadezhda. 1989. *The Cavalry Maiden: Journals of a Russian Officer in the Napoleonic Wars*, translated by Mary Fleming Zirin. Bloomington: Indiana University Press.

El Dareer, Asma. 1982. *Woman, Why Do You Weep? Circumcision and Its Consequences*. London: Zed Books.

Faderman, Lillian. 1991. *Odd Girls and Twilight Lovers: A History of Lesbian Life in Twentieth-Century America*. New York: Columbia University Press.

Foucault, Michel 1972. *The Archeology of Knowledge and the Discourse on Language*, translated by A. M. Sheridan Smith. New York: Pantheon.

Freeman, Lucy, and Alma Halbert Bond. 1992. *America's First Woman Warrior: The Courage of Deborah Sampson*. New York: Paragon.

Frye, Marilyn. 1983. *The Politics of Reality: Essays in Feminist Theory*. Trumansburg, N.Y.: Crossing Press.

Garber, Marjorie. 1992. *Vested Interests: Cross-Dressing and Cultural Anxiety*. New York and London: Routledge.

Garfinkel, Harold. 1967. *Studies in Ethnomethodology*. Englewood Cliffs, NJ.: Prentice-Hall.

Goffman, Erving. 1977. "The Arrangement between the Sexes." *Theory and Society* 4, 301–33. 1983. "Felicity's Condition." *American Journal of Sociology* 89, 1–53.

Gordon, Tuula. 1990. *Feminist Mothers*. New York: New York University Press.

Gould, Lois. 1972. "X: A Fabulous Child's Story." *Ms.*, December, 74–76, 105–106.

Gramsci, Antonio. 1971. *Selections from the Prison Notebooks*, translated and edited by Quintin Hoare and Geoffrey Nowell Smith. New York: International Publishers.

Groce, Stephen B., and Margaret Cooper. 1990. "Just Me and the Boys? Women in Local-Level Rock and Roll." *Gender and Society* 4, 220–29.

Haraway, Donna. 1990. "Investment Strategies for the Evolving Portfolio of Primate Females." In Jacobus, Keller, and Shuttleworth, eds., *Body/Politics: Women and the Discourses of Science*. New York: Routledge.

Jacobs, Sue-Ellen, and Christine Roberts. 1989. "Sex, Sexuality, Gender, and Gender Variance." In *Gender and Anthropology*, ed. Sandra Morgen. Washington, D.C.: American Anthropological Association.

Jacobus, Mary, Evelyn Fox Keller, and Sally Shuttleworth, eds. 1990. *Body/Politics: Women and the Discourses of Science*. New York and London: Routledge.

Jay, Nancy. 1981. "Gender and Dichotomy." *Feminist Studies* 7, 38–56.

Lightfoot-Klein, Hanny. 1989. *Prisoners of Ritual: An Odyssey into Female Circumcision in Africa*. New York: Harrington Park Press.

Matthaei, Julie A. 1982. *An Economic History of Women's Work in America*. New York: Schocken.

Nanda, Serena. 1990 *Neither Man nor Woman: The Hijiras of India*. Belmont, Calif.: Wadsworth.

New York Times. 1989. "Musician's Death at 74 Reveals He Was a Woman." February 2.

Paige, Karen Ericksen, and Jeffrey M. Paige. 1981. *The Politics of Reproductive Ritual*. Berkeley and Los Angeles: University of California Press.

Papanek, Hanna. 1990. "To Each Less Than She Needs, From Each More Than She Can Do: Allocations, Entitlements, and Value." In Tinker, ed., *Persistent Inequalities: Women and World Development*. New York: Oxford University Press.

Reskin, Barbara J. 1988. "Bringing the Men Back In: Sex Differentiation and the Devaluation of Women's Work." *Gender and Society* 7, 58–81.

Rosaldo, Michelle Zimbalist, and Louise Lamphere, eds. 1974. *Woman, Culture and Society*. Stanford, Calif.: Stanford University Press.

Rubin, Gayle. 1975. "The Traffic in Women: Notes on the Political Economy of Sex." In *Toward an Anthropology of Women*, edited by Rayna R[app] Reiter. New York: Monthly Review Press.

Scott, Joan Wallach. 1988. *Gender and the Politics of History*. New York: Columbia University Press.

Smith, Dorothy E. 1987. *The Everyday World as Problematic: A Feminist Sociology*. Toronto: University of Toronto Press.

Tinker, Irene, ed. 1990. *Persistent Inequalities: Women and World Development*. New York: Oxford University Press.

van der Kwaak, Anke. 1992. "Female Circumcision and Gender Identity: A Questionable Alliance?" *Social Science and Medicine* 35, 777–87.

Walker, Alice. 1992. *Possessing the Secret of Joy*. New York: Harcourt Brace Jovanovich.

West, Candace, and Don Zimmerman. 1987. "Doing Gender." *Gender and Society* 1, 125–51.

Wheelwright, Julie. 1989. *Amazons and Military Maids: Women Who Cross-Dressed in Pursuit of Life, Liberty and Happiness*. London: Pandora Press.

Wikan, Unni. 1982. *Behind the Veil in Arabia: Women in Oman*. Baltimore, Md.: Johns Hopkins University Press.

Williams, Christine L. 1989. *Gender Differences at Work: Women and Men in Nontraditional Occupations*. Berkeley: University of California Press.

Williams, Walter L. 1986. *The Spirit and the Flesh: Sexual Diversity in American Indian Culture*. Boston: Beacon Press.

KARIN A. MARTIN

Becoming a Gendered Body: Practices of Preschools

Karin Martin is Professor of Sociology at the University of Michigan whose research examines the intersections of gender, sexuality, and the body. This selection appeared in the journal American Sociological Review *in 1998.*

Social science research about bodies often focuses on women's bodies, particularly the parts of women's bodies that are most explicitly different from men's—their reproductive capacities and sexuality (E. Martin 1987; K. Martin 1996; but see Connell 1987, 1995). Men and women in the United States also hold and move their bodies differently (Birdwhistell 1970; Henley 1977; Young 1990); these differences are sometimes related to sexuality (Haug 1987) and sometimes not. On the whole, men and women sit, stand, gesture, walk, and throw differently. Generally, women's bodies are confined, their movements restricted. For example, women take smaller steps than men, sit in closed positions (arms and legs crossed across the body), take up less physical space than men, do not step, twist, or throw from the shoulder when throwing a ball, and are generally tentative when using their bodies (Birdwhistell 1970; Henley 1977; Young 1990). Some of these differences, particularly differences in motor skills (e.g., jumping, running, throwing) are seen in early childhood (Thomas and French 1985).[1] Of course, within gender, we may find individual differences, differences based on race, class, and sexuality, and differences based on size and shape of body. Yet, on average, men and women move differently.

Such differences may seem trivial in the large scheme of gender inequality. However, theoretical work by social scientists and feminists suggests that these differences may be consequential. Bodies are (unfinished) resources (Shilling 1993:103) that must be "trained, manipulated, cajoled, coaxed,

---

[1]There is little research on differences in things like step size and sitting positions among children; most of the traditional developmental research on children looks at motor skills and the outcomes of those skills. "Although the outcome reflects the movement process, it does not do so perfectly and does not describe this process" (Thomas and French 1985:277). I am just as interested in differences in the process as the outcome (also see Young 1990). For a review of the developmental psychology literature on gender differences in motor skills see Thomas and French 1985; for more recent examples in this literature, see Butterfield and Loovis 1993, Plimpton and Regimbal 1992, and Smoll and Schutz 1990.

organized and in general disciplined" (Turner 1992: 15). We use our bodies to construct our means of living, to take care of each other, to pleasure each other. According to Turner, ". . . social life depends upon the successful presenting, monitoring and interpreting of bodies" (p. 15). Similarly, according to Foucault (1979), controlled and disciplined bodies do more than regulate the individual body. A disciplined body creates a context for social relations. Gendered (along with "raced" and "classed") bodies create particular contexts for social relations as they signal, manage, and negotiate information about power and status. Gender relations depend on the successful gender presentation, monitoring, and interpretation of bodies (West and Zimmerman 1987). Bodies that clearly delineate gender status facilitate the maintenance of the gender hierarchy.

Our bodies are also one *site* of gender. Much postmodern feminist work (Butler 1990, 1993) suggests that gender is a performance. Microsociological work (West and Zimmerman 1987) suggests that gender is something that is "done." These two concepts, "gender performance" and "doing gender," are similar—both suggest that managed, adorned, fashioned, properly comported and moving bodies establish gender and gender relations.

Other feminist theorists (Connell 1987, 1995; Young 1990) argue that gender rests not only on the surface of the body, in performance and doing, but becomes *embodied*—becomes deeply part of whom we are physically and psychologically. According to Connell, gender becomes embedded in body postures, musculature, and tensions in our bodies.

> The social definition of men as holders of power is translated not only into mental body-images and fantasies, but into muscle tensions, posture, the feel and texture of the body. This is one of the main ways in which the power of men becomes naturalized. . . . (Connell 1987:85)

Connell (1995) suggests that masculine gender is partly a feel to one's body and that bodies are often a source of power for men. Young (1990), however, argues that bodies serve the opposite purpose for women—women's bodies are often sources of anxiety and tentativeness. She suggests that women's lack of confidence and agency are embodied and stem from an inability to move confidently in space, to take up space, to use one's body to its fullest extent. Young (1990) suggests "that the general lack of confidence that we [women] frequently have about our cognitive or leadership abilities is traceable in part to an original doubt of our body's capacity" (p. 156). Thus, these theorists suggest that gender differences in minute bodily behaviors like gesture, stance, posture, step, and throwing are significant to our understanding of gendered selves and gender inequality. This feminist theory, however, focuses on adult bodies.

Theories of the body need gendering, and feminist theories of gendered bodies need "childrening" or accounts of development. How do adult gendered bodies become gendered, if they are not naturally so? Scholars run the risk of continuing to view gendered bodies as natural if they ignore the processes that produce gendered adult bodies. Gendering of the body in child-hood is the foundation on which further gendering of the body occurs throughout the life course. The gendering of children's bodies makes gender differences feel and appear natural, which allows for such bodily differences to emerge throughout the life course.

I suggest that the hidden school curriculum of disciplining the body is gendered and contributes to the embodiment of gender in childhood, making gendered bodies appear and feel natural. Sociologists of education have demonstrated that schools have hidden curriculums (Giroux and Purpel 1983; Jackson 1968). Hidden curriculums are covert lessons that schools teach, and they are often a means of social control. These curriculums include teaching about work differentially by class (Anyon 1980; Bowles and Gintis 1976; Carnoy and Levin 1985), political socialization (Wasburn 1986), and training in obedience and docility (Giroux and Purpel 1983). More recently, some the-orists and researchers have examined the curriculum that disciplines the body (Carere 1987; Foucault 1979; McLaren 1986). This curriculum demands the practice of bodily control in congruence with the goals of the school as an institution. It reworks the students from the outside in on the presumption that to shape the body is to shape the mind (Carere 1987). In such a curricu-lum teachers constantly monitor kids' bodily movements, comportment, and practices.[2] Kids begin their day running wildly about the school grounds. Then this hidden curriculum funnels the kids into line, through the hallways, quietly into a classroom, sitting upright at their desks, focused at the front of the room, "ready to learn" (Carere 1987; McLaren 1986). According to Carere (1987), this curriculum of disciplining the body serves the curriculums that seek to shape the mind and renders children physically ready for cognitive learning.

I suggest that this hidden curriculum that controls children's bodily prac-tices serves also to turn kids who are similar in bodily comportment, move-ment, and practice into girls and boys, children whose bodily practices are different. Schools are not the only producers of these differences. While the process ordinarily begins in the family, the schools' hidden curriculum further facilitates and encourages the construction of bodily differences between the genders and makes these physical differences appear and feel natural. Finally, this curriculum may be more or less hidden depending on the particular pre-school and particular teachers. Some schools and teachers may see teaching children to behave like "young ladies" and "young gentlemen" as an explicit part of their curriculums.

---

[2]I use "kids" and "children" interchangeably; children themselves prefer the term "kids" (Thorne 1993:9).

DATA AND METHOD

The data for this study come from extensive and detailed semistructured field observations of five preschool classrooms of three- to five-year-olds in a midwestern city.[3] Four of the classrooms were part of a preschool (Preschool A) located close to the campus of a large university. A few of the kids were children of faculty members, more were children of staff and administrators, and many were not associated with the university. Many of the kids who attended Preschool A attended part-time. Although teachers at this school paid some attention to issues of race and gender equity, issues of diversity were not as large a part of the curriculum as they are at some preschools (Jordan and Cowan 1995; Van Ausdale and Feagin 1996). The fifth classroom was located at Preschool B, a preschool run by a Catholic church in the same city as Preschool A. The kids who attended Preschool B were children of young working professionals, many of whom lived in the vicinity of the preschool. These children attended preschool "full-time"—five days a week for most of the day.

The curriculums and routines of the two preschools were similar with two exceptions. First, there was some religious instruction in Preschool B, although many of the kids were not Catholic. Preschool B required children to pray before their snack, and the children's activities focused more on the religious aspects of Christian holidays than did the activities of children in Preschool A. For example, at Christmas, teachers talked to the kids about the birth of baby Jesus. At Preschool A there was little religious talk and more talk about decorating Christmas trees, making cards, and so on. The second difference between the two preschools is that Preschool B had some explicit rules that forbade violent actions at school. Posted on the wall of the playroom was the following sign (which few of the preschoolers could read):

1. No wrestling.
2. No violent play, killing games, kicking, karate, etc.
3. Bikes belong on the outside of the gym.
4. No crashing bikes.
5. Houses are for playing in not climbing on.
6. Older children are off bikes when toddlers arrive.
7. Balls should be used for catching, rolling, tossing—not slamming at people.
8. Adults and children will talk with each other about problems and not shout across the room.
9. Use equipment appropriately.

---

[3]There were three physical locations for the classrooms, but two of the classrooms had both morning and afternoon sessions with a different teacher and different student composition, resulting in five sets of teachers and students.

Such rules were usually directed at boys, although they were not enforced consistently. Preschool A also had some of these rules, but they were not as explicit or as clearly outlined for the teachers or the kids. For example, teachers would usually ask kids to talk about their problems or disputes (rule 8) at both schools. However, rule 2 was not in effect at Preschool A unless a game got "out of control"—became too loud, too disruptive, or "truly" violent instead of "pretend" violent. The data from these preschools represent some ways that schools may discipline children's bodies in gendered ways. As Suransky's (1982) study of five preschools suggests, the schools' and teachers' philosophies, and styles, and cultural context make dramatic differences in the content and experience of a day at preschool.

A total 112 children and 14 different teachers (five head teachers and nine aides) were observed in these classrooms.[4] All teachers were female. Forty-two percent of the kids were girls and 58 percent were boys, and they made up similar proportions in each classroom. There were 12 Asian or Asian American children, 3 Latino/a children, and 4 African American children. The remaining children were white. The children primarily came from middle-class families.

A research assistant and I observed in these classrooms about three times a week for eight months. Our observations were as unobtrusive as possible, and we interacted little with the kids, although on occasion a child would ask what we were doing or would sit next to us and "write" their own "notes." We varied our observation techniques between unstructured field observation, in which we observed the classroom in a holistic manner and recorded everyday behavior, and more structured techniques, in which we observed one part of the classroom (the block area, the dress-up area), one particular child (25 children were observed this way), one particular teacher (seven teachers were observed this way), or one set of children (boys who always play with blocks, the kids that play with the hamsters, the kids that played at the water table a lot—most children were observed this way). We observed girls and boys for equal amounts of time, and we heeded Thorne's (1993) caution about the "big man bias" in field research and were careful not to observe only the most active, outgoing, "popular" kids.

We focused on the children's physicality—body movement, use of space, and the physical contact among kids or between kids and teachers. Our field notes were usually not about "events" that occurred, but about everyday physical behavior and interaction and its regulation. Field notes were coded using the qualitative software program Hyper-Research. Categories that were coded emerged from the data and were not predetermined categories. Excerpts from field notes are presented throughout and are examples of representative patterns in the data. Tables presenting estimates of the numbers of

---

[4]Classrooms usually contained 15 to 18 children on a given day. However, since some kids came to preschool five days a week, some three, and some two, a total of 112 different kids were observed.

times particular phenomena were observed provide a context for the field note excerpts. The data are subject to the observers' attention and accurate descriptions in the field notes. For instance, most micro and "neutral" physical contact between kids or among teachers and kids is probably underestimated (e.g., shoulders touching during circle time, knees bumping under the snack table). Future research might use video recordings to assess such micro events.

RESULTS

Children's bodies are disciplined by schools. Children are physically active, and institutions like schools impose disciplinary controls that regulate children's bodies and prepare children for the larger social world. While this disciplinary control produces docile bodies (Foucault 1979), it also produces gendered bodies. As these disciplinary practices operate in different contexts, some bodies become more docile than others. I examine how the following practices contribute to a gendering of children's bodies in preschool: the effects of dressing-up or bodily adornment, the gendered nature of formal and relaxed behaviors, how the different restrictions on girls' and boys' voices limit their physicality, how teachers instruct girls' and boys' bodies, and the gendering of physical interactions between children and teachers and among the children themselves.

Bodily Adornment: Dressing Up

Perhaps the most explicit way that children's bodies become gendered is through their clothes and other bodily adornments. Here I discuss how parents gender their children through their clothes, how children's dressup play experiments with making bodies feminine and masculine, and how this play, when it is gender normative, shapes girls' and boys' bodies differently, constraining girls' physicality.

Dressing up (1). The clothes that parents send kids to preschool in shape children's experiences of their bodies in gendered ways.[5] Clothes, particularly their color, signify a child's gender; gender in preschool is in fact color-coded. On average, about 61 percent of the girls wore pink clothing each day (Table 1). Boys were more likely to wear primary colors, black, florescent green, and orange. Boys never wore pink.

> The teacher is asking each kid during circle (the part of the day that includes formal instruction by the teacher while the children sit in a circle) what their favorite color is. Adam says black. Bill says "every color that's not pink." (Five-year-olds)

---

[5]Parents are not solely responsible for what their children wear to preschool, as they are constrained by what is available and affordable in children's clothing. More important, children, especially at ages three to five, want some say in what they wear to preschool and may insist on some outfits and object to others.

Table 1. Observations of Girls Wearing Dresses and the Color Pink: Five Preschool Classrooms

Observation	N	Percent
Girls wearing something pink	54	61
Girls wearing dresses	21	24
3-year-old girls	6	14
5-year-old girls	15	32
Number of observations	89	100
3-year-old girls	42	47
5-year-old girls	47	53

Note: In 12 observation sessions, what the children were wearing, including color of their clothing, was noted. The data in Table 1 come from coded field notes. There were no instances of boys wearing pink or dresses, and no age differences among girls in wearing the color pink.

Fourteen percent of three-year-old girls wore dresses each day compared to 32 percent of five-year-old girls (Table 1). Wearing a dress limited girls' physicality in preschool. However, it is not only the dress itself, but knowledge about how to behave in a dress that is restrictive. Many girls already knew that some behaviors were not allowed in a dress. This knowledge probably comes from the families who dress their girls in dresses.

Vicki, wearing leggings and a dress-like shirt, is leaning over the desk to look into a "tunnel" that some other kids have built. As she leans, her dress/shirt rides up exposing her back. Jennifer (another child) walks by Vicki and as she does she pulls Vicki's shirt back over her bare skin and gives it a pat to keep it in place. It looks very much like something one's mother might do. (Five-year-olds)

Four girls are sitting at a table — Cathy, Kim, Danielle, and Jesse. They are cutting play money out of paper. Cathy and Danielle have on overalls and Kim and Jesse have on dresses. Cathy puts her feet up on the table and crosses her legs at the ankle; she leans back in her chair and continues cutting her money. Danielle imitates her. They look at each other and laugh. They put their shoulders back, posturing, having fun with this new way of sitting. Kim and Jesse continue to cut and laugh with them, but do not put their feet up. (Five-year-olds)

Dresses are restrictive in other ways as well. They often are worn with tights that are experienced as uncomfortable and constraining. I observed girls constantly pulling at and rearranging their tights, trying to untwist them or pull them up. Because of their discomfort, girls spent much time attuned to and arranging their clothing and/or their bodies.

Dresses also can be lifted up, an embarrassing thing for five-year-olds if done purposely by another child. We witnessed this on only one occasion — a boy pulled up the hem of a girl's skirt up. The girl protested and the teacher told him to stop and that was the end of it. Teachers, however, lifted up girls' dresses frequently — to see if a child was dressed warmly enough, while reading a book about dresses, to see if a child was wet. Usually this was done without asking the child and was more management of the child rather than an interaction with her. Teachers were much more likely to manage girls and their clothing this way — rearranging their clothes, tucking in their shirts, fixing a ponytail gone astray.[6] Such management often puts girls' bodies under the control of another and calls girls' attentions to their appearances and bodily adornments.

Dressing up (2). Kids like to *play* dressup in preschool, and all the classrooms had a dress-up corner with a variety of clothes, shoes, pocketbooks, scarves, and hats for dressing up. Classrooms tended to have more women's clothes than men's, but there were some of both, as well as some gender-neutral clothes — capes, hats, and vests that were not clearly for men or women — and some items that were clearly costumes, such as masks of cats and dogs and clip-on tails. Girls tended to play dress-up more than boys — over one-half of dressing up was done by girls. Gender differences in the amount of time spent playing dress-up seemed to increase from age three to age five. We only observed the five-year-old boys dressing up or using clothes or costumes in their play three times, whereas three-year-old boys dressed up almost weekly. Five-year-old boys also did not dress up elaborately, but used one piece of clothing to animate their play. Once Phil wore large, men's winter ski gloves when he played monster. Holding up his now large, chiseled looking hands, he stomped around the classroom making monster sounds. On another occasion Brian, a child new to the classroom who attended only two days a week, walked around by himself for a long time carrying a silver pocketbook and hovering first at the edges of girls' play and then at the edges of boys' play. On the third occasion, Sam used ballet slippers to animate his play in circle.

When kids dressed up, they played at being a variety of things from kitty cats and puppies to monsters and superheroes to "fancy ladies." Some of this play was not explicitly gendered. For example, one day in November I observed three girls wearing "turkey hats" they had made. They spent a long time gobbling at each other and playing at being turkeys, but there was nothing

---

[6]All of my observations of this uninteractional management were with three-year-olds. Teachers seemed to manage children's bodies more directly and with less interaction at this age than with the five-year-olds. perhaps because they could. Five-year-olds demanded explanations and interaction. This result may also be confounded with race. On at least two occasions when teachers treated girls this way. the girls were Asian students who understood little English. The teachers generally tended to interact less with non-English speaking kids and to talk about them as if they were not there more than they did with those who spoke English.

explicitly gendered about their play. However, this kind of adornment was not the most frequent type. Children often seemed to experiment with both genders when they played dress–up. The three–year–olds tended to be more experimental in their gender dress–up than the five–year–olds, perhaps because teachers encouraged it more at this age.

> Everett and Juan are playing dress–up. Both have on "dresses" made out of material that is wrapped around them like a toga or sarong. Everett has a pocketbook and a camera over his shoulder and Juan has a pair of play binoculars on a strap over his. Everett has a scarf around his head and cape on. Juan has on big, green sunglasses. Pam (teacher) tells them, "You guys look great! Go look in the mirror." They shuffle over to the full-length mirror and look at themselves and grin, and make adjustments to their costumes. (Three–year–olds)

The five–year–old children tended to dress–up more gender normatively. Girls in particular played at being adult women.

> Frances is playing dress–up. She is walking in red shoes and carrying a pocketbook. She and two other girls, Jen and Rachel, spend between five and ten minutes looking at and talking about the guinea pigs. Then they go back to dress–up. Frances and Rachel practice walking in adult women's shoes. Their body movements are not a perfect imitation of an adult woman's walk in high heels, yet it does look like an attempt to imitate such a walk. Jen and Rachel go back to the guinea pigs, and Frances, now by herself, is turning a sheer, frilly lavender shirt around and around and around trying to figure out how to put it on. She gets it on and looks at herself in the mirror. She adds a sheer pink and lavender scarf and pink shoes. Looks in the mirror again. She walks, twisting her body—shoulders, hips, shoulders, hips—not quite a (stereotypic) feminine walk, but close. Walking in big shoes makes her take little bitty steps, like walking in heels. She shuffles in the too big shoes out into the middle of the classroom and stops by a teacher. Laura (a teacher) says, "don't you look fancy, all pink and purple." Frances smiles up at her and walks off, not twisting so much this time. She's goes back to the mirror and adds a red scarf. She looks in the mirror and is holding her arms across her chest to hold the scarf on (she can't tie it) and she is holding it with her chin too. She shuffles to block area where Jen is and then takes the clothes off and puts them back in dress–up area. (Five–year–olds)

I observed not only the children who dressed up, but the reactions of those around them to their dress. This aspect proved to be one of the most interesting parts of kids' dress–up play. Children interpreted each others' bodily adornments as gendered, even when other interpretations were plausible. For instance, one day just before Halloween, Kim dressed up and was "scary" because she was dressed as a woman:

> Kim has worn a denim skirt and tights to school today. Now she is trying to pull on a ballerina costume—pink and ruffly—over her clothes. She has a hard time getting it on. It's tight and wrinkled up and twisted when she gets

it on. Her own clothes are bunched up under it. Then she puts on a mask—
a woman's face. The mask material itself is a clear plastic so that skin shows
through, but is sculpted to have a very Anglo nose and high cheek bones. It
also has thin eyebrows, blue eye shadow, blush, and lipstick painted on it.
The mask is bigger than Kim's face and head. Kim looks at herself in the
mirror and spends the rest of the play time with this costume on. Intermit-
tently she picks up a plastic pumpkin since it is Halloween season and carries
that around too. Kim walks around the classroom for a long time and then
runs through the block area wearing this costume. Jason yells, "Ugh! There's
a woman!" He and the other boys playing blocks shriek and scatter about
the block area. Kim runs back to the dress-up area as they yell. Then
throughout the afternoon she walks and skips through the center of the
classroom, and every time she comes near the block boys one of them yells,
"Ugh, there's the woman again!" The teacher even picks up on this and says
to Kim twice, "Woman, slow down." (Five-year-olds)

The boys' shrieks indicated that Kim was scary, and this scariness is linked in
their comments about her being a woman. It seems equally plausible that they
could have interpreted her scary dress as a "trick-o-treater," given that it was
close to Halloween and she was carrying a plastic pumpkin that kids collect
candy in, or that they might have labeled her a dancer or ballerina because she
was wearing a tutu. Rather, her scary dressup was coded for her by others as
"woman."

Other types of responses to girls dressing up also seemed to gender their
bodies and to constrain them. For example, on two occasions I saw a teacher
tie the arms of girls' dress-up shirts together so that the girls could not move
their arms. They did this in fun, of course, and untied them as soon as the girls
wanted them to, but I never witnessed this constraining of boys' bodies in play.

Thus, how parents gender children's bodies through dressing them and the
ways children experiment with bodily adornments by dressing up make girls'
and boys' bodies different and seem different to those around them. Adorning a
body often genders it explicitly—signifies that it is a feminine or masculine
body. Adornments also make girls movements smaller, leading girls to take up
less space with their bodies and disallowing some types of movements.[7]

Formal and Relaxed Behaviors

Describing adults, Goffman (1959) defines front stage and backstage behavior:

The backstage language consists of reciprocal first-naming, co-operative
decision making, profanity, open sexual remarks, elaborate griping, smoking, rough informal dress, "sloppy" sitting and standing posture, use of
dialect or substandard speech, mumbling and shouting, playful aggressivity
and "kidding," inconsiderateness for the other in minor but potentially sym-

---

[7]Although girls could take up *more* space with their dressing up—by twirling in a skirt or
wearing large brimmed hats or carrying large pocketbooks—we did not observe this behavior
at either preschool.

bolic acts, minor physical self-involvements such as humming, whistling, chewing, nibbling, belching, and flatulence. The front stage behavior language can be taken as the absence (and in some sense the opposite) of this. (p. 128)

Thus, one might not expect much front stage or formal behavior in preschool, and often, especially during parents' drop-off and pick-up time, this was the case. But a given region of social life may sometimes be a backstage and sometimes a front stage. I identified several behaviors that were expected by the teachers, required by the institution, or that would be required in many institutional settings, as formal behavior. Raising one's hand, sitting "on your bottom" (not on your knees, not squatting, not lying down, not standing) during circle, covering one's nose and mouth when coughing or sneezing, or sitting upright in a chair are all formal behaviors of preschools, schools, and to some extent the larger social world. Crawling on the floor, yelling, lying down during teachers' presentations, and running through the classroom are examples of relaxed behaviors that are not allowed in preschool, schools, work settings, and many institutions of the larger social world (Henley 1977). Not all behaviors fell into one of these classifications. When kids were actively engaged in playing at the water table, for example, much of their behavior was not clearly formal or relaxed. I coded as formal and relaxed behaviors those behaviors that would be seen as such if done by adults (or children in many cases) in other social institutions for which children are being prepared.

In the classrooms in this study, boys were allowed and encouraged to pursue relaxed behaviors in a variety of ways that girls were not. Girls were more likely to be encouraged to pursue more formal behaviors. Eighty-two percent of all formal behaviors observed in these classrooms were done by girls, and only 18 percent by boys. However, 80 percent of the behaviors coded as relaxed were boys' behaviors (Table 2).

These observations do not tell us *why* boys do more relaxed behaviors and girls do more formal behaviors. Certainly many parents and others would argue that boys are more predisposed to sloppy postures, crawling on the floor, and so on. However, my observations suggest that teachers help construct this gender difference in bodily behaviors.[8] Teachers were more likely to reprimand girls for relaxed bodily movements and comportment. Sadker and Sadker (1994) found a similar result with respect to hand-raising for answering teachers' questions—if hand raising is considered a formal behavior and calling out a relaxed behavior, they find that boys are more likely to call out without raising their hands and demand attention:

---

[8]Throughout the paper, when I use the term "constructed," I do *not* mean that preschools create these differences or that they are the only origins of these differences. Clearly, children come to preschool with some gender differences that were created in the family or other contexts outside of preschool. My argument is that preschools reinforce these differences and build (construct) further elaborations of difference upon what children bring to preschool.

Table 2. Observations of Formal and Relaxed Behaviors,
by Gender of Child: Five Preschool Classrooms

Type of Behavior	Boys		Girls		Total	
	N	Percent	N	Percent	N	Percent
Formal	16	18	71	82	87	100
Relaxed	86	80	21	20	107	100

Note: Structured/formal behaviors were coded from references in the field notes to formal postures, polite gestures, etc. Relaxed/informal behaviors were coded from references to informal postures, backstage demeanors, etc.

> Sometimes what they [boys] say has little or nothing to do with the teacher's questions. Whether male comments are insightful or irrelevant, teachers respond to them. However, when girls call out, there is a fascinating occurrence: Suddenly the teacher remembers the rule about raising your hand before you talk. (Sadker and Sadker 1994:43)

This gendered dynamic of hand-raising exists even in preschool, although our field notes do not provide enough systematic recording of hand-raising to fully assess it. However, such a dynamic applies to many bodily movements and comportment:

> The kids are sitting with their legs folded in a circle listening to Jane (the teacher) talk about dinosaurs. ("Circle" is the most formal part of their preschool education each day and is like sitting in class.) Sam has the ballet slippers on his hands and is clapping them together really loudly. He stops and does a half-somersault backward out of the circle and stays that way with his legs in the air. Jane says nothing and continues talking about dinosaurs. Sue, who is sitting next to Sam, pushes his leg out of her way. Sam sits up and is now busy trying to put the ballet shoes on over his sneakers, and he is looking at the other kids and laughing, trying to get a reaction. He is clearly not paying attention to Jane's dinosaur story and is distracting the other kids. Sam takes the shoes and claps them together again. Jane leans over and tells him to give her the shoes. Sam does, and then lies down all stretched out on the floor, arms over his head, legs apart. Adam is also lying down now, and Keith is on Sara's (the teacher's aide) lap. Rachel takes her sweater off and folds it up. The other children are focused on the teacher. After about five minutes, Jane tells Sam "I'm going to ask you to sit up." (She doesn't say anything to Adam.) But he doesn't move. Jane ignores Sam and Adam and continues with the lesson. Rachel now lies down on her back. After about ten seconds Jane says, "Sit up, Rachel." Rachel sits up and listens to what kind of painting the class will do today. (Five-year-olds)

Sam's behavior had to be more disruptive, extensive, and informal than Rachel's for the teacher to instruct him and his bodily movements to be quieter and for him to comport his body properly for circle. Note that the boys who were relaxed but not disruptive were not instructed to sit properly. It was also common for a teacher to tell a boy to stop some bodily behavior and for the boy to ignore the request and the teacher not to enforce her instructions, although she frequently repeated them.

The gendering of body movements, comportment, and acquisitions of space also happens in more subtle ways. For example, often when there was "free" time, boys spent much more time in child-structured activities than did girls. In one classroom of five-year-olds, boys' "free" time was usually spent building with blocks, climbing on blocks, or crawling on the blocks or on the floor as they worked to build with the blocks whereas girls spent much of their free time sitting at tables cutting things out of paper, drawing, sorting small pieces of blocks into categories, reading stories, and so on. Compared to boys, girls rarely crawled on the floor (except when they played kitty cats). Girls and boys did share some activities. For example, painting and reading were frequently shared, and the three-year-olds often played at fishing from a play bridge together. Following is a list from my field notes of the most common activities boys and girls did during the child-structured activity periods of the day during two randomly picked weeks of observing:

> BOYS: played blocks (floor), played at the water table (standing and splashing), played superhero (running around and in play house), played with the car garage (floor), painted at the easel (standing).
> GIRLS: played dolls (sitting in chairs and walking around), played dress-up (standing), coloring (sitting at tables), read stories (sitting on the couch), cut out pictures (sitting at tables).

Children sorted themselves into these activities and also were sorted (or not unsorted) by teachers. For example, teachers rarely told the three boys that always played with the blocks that they had to choose a different activity that day.[9] Teachers also encouraged girls to sit at tables by suggesting table activities for them—in a sense giving them less "free" time or structuring their time more.

> It's the end of circle, and Susan (teacher) tells the kids that today they can paint their dinosaur eggs if they want to. There is a table set up with paints and brushes for those who want to do that. The kids listen and then scatter

---

[9]Once a teacher put a line of masking tape on the floor to show where the "block corner" ended because the boys playing with the blocks took up one whole end of the classroom. However, this did not work. As the teacher was making the line on the floor, the boys told her to extend it further outward (which she did) so they could have room to play in an area in which they did not usually play, and in the end the line was ignored. The same teacher tried on another occasion to tell the boys who played with the blocks that they had to play with Legos instead. They did this, and two girls began playing with the blocks; but in short order two of the boys who were supposed to be playing Legos asked the girls if they could play with them, instead of asking the teacher. There was about 10 minutes of mixed gender play before the girls abandoned the blocks.

to their usual activities. Several boys are playing blocks, two boys are at the water table. Several girls are looking at the hamsters in their cage and talking about them, two girls are sitting and stringing plastic beads. Susan says across the classroom, "I need some painters, Joy, Amy, Kendall?" The girls leave the hamster cage and go to the painting table. Susan pulls out a chair so Joy can sit down. She tells them about the painting project. (Five-year-olds)

These girls spent much of the afternoon enjoying themselves painting their eggs. Simon and Jack joined them temporarily, but then went back to activities that were not teacher-structured.

Events like these that happen on a regular basis over an extended period of early childhood serve to gender children's bodies—boys come to take up more room with their bodies, to sit in more open positions, and to feel freer to do what they wish with their bodies, even in relatively formal settings. Henley (1977) finds that among adults men generally are more relaxed than women in their demeanor and women tend to have tenser postures. The looseness of body-focused functions (e.g., belching) is also more open to men than to women. In other words, men are more likely to engage in relaxed demeanors, postures, and behaviors. These data suggest that this gendering of bodies into more formal and more relaxed movements, postures, and comportment is (at least partially) constructed in early childhood by institutions like preschools.

Controlling Voice

Speaking (or yelling as is often the case with kids) is a bodily experience that involves mouth, throat, chest, diaphragm, and facial expression. Thorne (1993) writes that an elementary school teacher once told her that kids "reminded her of bumblebees, an apt image of swarms, speed, and constant motion" (p. 15). Missing from this metaphor is the buzz of the bumblebees, as a constant hum of voices comes from children's play and activities. Kids' play that is giggly, loud, or whispery makes it clear that voice is part of their bodily experiences.

Voice is an aspect of bodily experience that teachers and schools are interested in disciplining. Quiet appears to be required for learning in classrooms. Teaching appropriate levels of voice, noise, and sound disciplines children's bodies and prepares them "from the inside" to learn the school's curriculums and to participate in other social institutions.

The disciplining of children's voices is gendered. I found that girls were told to be quiet or to repeat a request in a quieter, "nicer" voice about three times more often than were boys (see Table 3). This finding is particularly interesting because boys' play was frequently much noisier. However, when boys were noisy, they were also often doing other behaviors the teacher did not allow, and perhaps the teachers focused less on voice because they were more concerned with stopping behaviors like throwing or running.

**Table 3. Observations of Teachers Telling Children to Be Quiet,
by Gender of Child: Five Preschool Classrooms**

Gender	N	Percent
Girls	45	73
Boys	16	26
Total	61	100

Note: Coded from references in the field notes to instances of teachers quieting children's voices.

Additionally, when boys were told to "quiet down" they were told in large groups, rarely as individuals. When they were being loud and were told to be quiet, boys were often in the process of enacting what Jordan and Cowan (1995) call warrior narratives:

> A group of three boys is playing with wooden doll figures. The dolls are jumping off block towers, crashing into each other. Kevin declares loudly, "I'm the grown up." Keith replies, "I'm the police." They knock the figures into each other and push each other away. Phil grabs a figure from Keith. Keith picks up two more and bats one with the other toward Phil. Now all three boys are crashing the figures into each other. making them dive off towers. They're having high fun. Two more boys join the group. There are now five boys playing with the wooden dolls and the blocks. They're breaking block buildings: things are crashing; they're grabbing each other's figures and yelling loudly. Some are yelling "fire, fire" as their figures jump off the block tower. The room is very noisy. (Five-year-olds)

Girls as individuals and in groups were frequently told to lower their voices. Later that same afternoon:

> During snack time the teacher asks the kids to tell her what they like best in the snack mix. Hillary says, "Marshmallows!" loudly, vigorously, and with a swing of her arm. The teacher turns to her and says, "I'm going to ask you to say that quietly," and Hillary repeats it in a softer voice. (Five-year-olds)

These two observations represent a prominent pattern in the data. The boys playing with the wooden figures were allowed to express their fun and enthusiasm loudly whereas Hillary could not loudly express her love of marshmallows. Girls' voices are disciplined to be softer and in many ways less physical—toning down their voices tones down their physicality. Hillary emphasized "marshmallows" with a large swinging gesture of her arm the first time she answered the teacher's question, but after the teacher asked her to say it quietly she made no gestures when answering. Incidents like these that are repeated often in different contexts restrict girls' physicality.

It could be argued that context rather than gender explains the difference in how much noise is allowed in these situations. Teachers may expect more formal behavior from children sitting at the snack table than they do during semistructured activities. However, even during free play girls were frequently told to quiet down:

> Nancy, Susan, and Amy are jumping in little jumps, from the balls of their feet, almost like skipping rope without the rope. Their mouths are open and they're making a humming sound, looking at each other and giggling. Two of them keep sticking their tongues out. They seem to be having great fun. The teacher's aide sitting on the floor in front of them turns around and says "Shhh, find something else to play. Why don't you play Simon Says?" All three girls stop initially. Then Amy jumps a few more times, but without making the noise. (Five-year-olds)

By limiting the girls' voices, the teacher also limits the girls' jumping and their fun. The girls learn that their bodies are supposed to be quiet, small, and physically constrained. Although the girls did not take the teacher's suggestion to play Simon Says (a game where bodies can be moved only quietly at the order of another), they turn to play that explores quietness yet tries to maintain some of the fun they were having:

> Nancy, Susan, and Amy begin sorting a pile of little-bitty pieces of puzzles, soft blocks, Legos, and so on into categories to "help" the teacher who told them to be quiet and to clean up. The three of them and the teacher are standing around a single small desk sorting these pieces. (Meanwhile several boys are playing blocks and their play is spread all over the middle of the room.) The teacher turns her attention to some other children. The girls continue sorting and then begin giggling to each other. As they do, they cover their mouths. This becomes a game as one imitates the other. Susan says something nonsensical that is supposed to be funny, and then she "hee-hees" while covering her mouth and looks at Nancy, to whom she has said it, who covers her mouth and "hee-hees" back. They begin putting their hands/fingers cupped over their mouths and whispering in each others' ears and then giggling quietly. They are intermittently sorting the pieces and playing the whispering game. (Five-year-olds)

Thus, the girls took the instruction to be quiet and turned it into a game. This new game made their behaviors smaller, using hands and mouths rather than legs, feet, and whole bodies. Whispering became their fun, instead of jumping and humming. Besides' requiring quiet, this whispering game also was gendered in another way: The girls' behavior seemed to mimic stereotypical female gossiping. They whispered in twos and looked at the third girl as they did it and then changed roles. Perhaps the instruction to be quiet, combined with the female role of "helping," led the girls to one of their understandings of female quietness—gossip—a type of feminine quietness that is perhaps most fun.

Finally, by limiting voice teachers limit one of girls' mechanisms for resisting others' mistreatment of them. Frequently, when a girl had a dispute with another child, teachers would ask the girl to quiet down and solve the problem nicely. Teachers also asked boys to solve problems by talking, but they usually did so only with intense disputes and the instruction to talk things out never carried the instruction to talk *quietly*.

> Keith is persistently threatening to knock over the building that Amy built. He is running around her with a "flying" toy horse that comes dangerously close to her building each time. She finally says, "Stop it!" in a loud voice. The teacher comes over and asks, "How do we say that, Amy?" Amy looks at Keith and says more softly, "Stop trying to knock it over." The teacher tells Keith to find some place else to play. (Five-year-olds)

> Cheryl and Julie are playing at the sand table. Cheryl says to the teacher loudly, "Julie took mine away!" The teacher tells her to say it more quietly. Cheryl repeats it less loudly. The teacher tells her, "Say it a little quieter," Cheryl says it quieter, and the teacher says to Julie, "Please don't take that away from her." (Three-year-olds)

We know that women are reluctant to use their voices to protect themselves from a variety of dangers. The above observations suggest that the denial of women's voices begins at least as early as preschool, and that restricting voice usually restricts movement as well.

Finally, there were occasions when the quietness requirement did not restrict girls' bodies. One class of three-year-olds included two Asian girls, Diane and Sue, who did not speak English. Teachers tended to talk about them and over them but rarely to them. Although these girls said little to other children and were generally quiet, they were what I term body instigators. They got attention and played with other children in more bodily ways than most girls. For example, Sue developed a game with another girl that was a sort of musical chairs. They'd race from one chair to another to see who could sit down first. Sue initiated this game by trying to squeeze into a chair with the other girl. Also, for example,

> Diane starts peeking into the play cardboard house that is full of boys and one girl. She looks like she wants to go in, but the door is blocked and the house is crowded. She then goes around to the side of the house and stands with her back to it and starts bumping it with her butt. Because the house is cardboard, it buckles and moves as she does it. The teacher tells her, "Stop — no." Diane stops and then starts doing it again but more lightly. All the boys come out of the house and ask her what she's doing. Matt gets right in her face and the teacher tells him, "Tell her no." He does, but all the other boys have moved on to other activities, so she and Matt go in the house together. (Three-year-olds)

Thus, Diane and Sue's lack of voice in this English-speaking classroom led to greater physicality. There may be other ways that context (e.g., in one's neighborhood instead of school) and race, ethnicity, and class shape gender and voice that cannot be determined from these data (Goodwin 1990).

Bodily Instructions

Teachers give a lot of instructions to kids about what to do with their bodies. Of the explicit bodily instructions recorded 65 percent were directed to boys, 26 percent to girls; and the remaining 9 percent were directed to mixed groups (Table 4). These numbers suggest that boys' bodies are being disciplined more than girls. However, there is more to this story—the types of instructions that teachers give and children's responses to them are also gendered.

First, boys obeyed teachers' bodily instructions about one-half of the time (48 percent), while girls obeyed about 80 percent of the time (Table 4).[10] Boys may receive more instructions from teachers because they are less likely to follow instructions and thus are told repeatedly. Frequently I witnessed a teacher telling a boy or group of boys to stop doing something—usually running or throwing things—and the teacher repeated these instructions several times in the course of the session before (if ever) taking further action. Teachers usually did not have to repeat instructions to girls—girls either stopped on their own with the first instruction, or because the teacher forced them to stop right then. Serbin (1983) finds that boys receive a higher proportion of teachers' ". . . loud reprimands, audible to the entire group. Such patterns of response, intended as punishment, have been repeatedly demonstrated to reinforce aggression and other forms of disruptive behavior" (p. 29).

Table 4. Observations of Teachers Giving Bodily Instructions to Children, by Gender of Child: Five Preschool Classrooms

Teacher's Instruction/ Child's Response	Boys		Girls		Mixed Groups	
	N	Percent	N	Percent	N	Percent
Bodily instructions from teachers[a]	94	65	39	25	13	9
Child obeys instructions[b]	45	48	31	80	—[c]	—[c]
Undirected bodily instructions from teachers[b]	54	57	6	15	5	55

Note: Bodily instructions are coded from references in the field notes to instances of a teacher telling a child what to do with his or her body.

[a]Percentages based on a total of 146 observations.

[b]Percentages based on a total of 94 observations for boys and 39 observations for girls.

[c]In the observations of mixed groups of girls and boys, usually some obeyed and some did not. Thus an accurate count of how the groups responded is not available.

---

[10]There were several cases for boys and girls in which the observer did not record the child's response.

Second, teachers' instructions directed to boys' bodies were less substantive than those directed to girls. That is, teachers' instructions to boys were usually to stop doing something, to end a bodily behavior with little suggestion for other behaviors they might do. Teachers rarely told boys to change a bodily behavior. A list of teachers' instructions to boys includes: stop throwing, stop jumping, stop clapping, stop splashing, no pushing, don't cry, blocks are not for bopping, don't run, don't climb on that. Fifty-seven percent of the instructions that teachers gave boys about their physical behaviors were of this undirected type, compared with 15 percent of their instructions to girls (Table 4). In other words, teachers' instructions to girls generally were more substantive and more directive, telling girls to do a bodily behavior rather than to stop one. Teachers' instructions to girls suggested that they alter their behaviors. A list of instructions to girls includes: talk to her, don't yell, sit here, pick that up, be careful, be gentle, give it to me, put it down there. Girls may have received fewer bodily instructions than did boys, but they received more directive ones. This gender difference leaves boys a larger range of possibilities of what they might choose to do with their bodies once they have stopped a behavior, whereas girls were directed toward a defined set of options.

Physical Interaction between Teachers and Children

Teachers also physically directed kids. For example, teachers often held kids to make them stop running, tapped them to make them turn around and pay attention, or turned their faces toward them so that they would listen to verbal instructions. One-fourth of all physical contacts between teachers and children was to control children's physicality in some way, and 94 percent of such contacts were directed at boys.

Physical interaction between teachers and children was coded into three categories: positive, negative, or neutral. Physical interaction was coded as positive if it was comforting, helpful, playful, or gentle. It was coded as negative if it was disciplining, assertive (not gentle), restraining, or clearly unwanted by the child (e.g., the child pulled away). Physical interaction was coded as neutral if it seemed to have little content (e.g., shoulders touching during circle, legs touching while a teacher gave a group of kids directions for a project). About one-half of the time, when teachers touched boys or girls, it was positive. For example, the teacher and child might have bodily contact as she tied a shoe, wiped away tears, or tickled a child, or if a child took the teacher's hand or got on her lap. For girls, the remaining physical interactions included 15 percent that were disciplining or instructing the body and about one-third that were neutral (e.g., leaning over the teacher's arm while looking at a book). For boys, these figures were reversed: Only 4 percent of their physical interactions with teachers were neutral in content, and 35 percent were negative and usually included explicit disciplining and instructing of the body (see Table 5).

Table 5. Observations of Physical Interaction between Teachers and Children, by Gender of Child: Five Preschool Classrooms

Type of Contact	Boys		Girls	
	N	Percent	N	Percent
Positive	41	60	21	54
Negative	24	35	6	15
Neutral	3	4	12	31
Total	68	99	39	100

Note: Coded from references in field notes to bodily contact between teachers and children. Percentages may not sum to 100 due to rounding.

This disciplining of boys' bodies took a particular form. Teachers usually attempted to restrain or remove boys who had "gone too far" in their play or who had done something that could harm another child:

> Irving goes up to Jack, who is playing dressup, and puts his arms up, makes a monster face and says, "Aaarhhh!" Jack looks startled. Irving runs and jumps in front of Jack again and says "Aaaarrhh!" again. Marie (teacher) comes from behind Irving and holds him by the shoulders and arms from behind. She bends over him and says, "Calm down." He pulls forward, and eventually she lets him go. He runs up to Jack again and growls. Marie says, "He doesn't want you to do that." (Three-year-olds)

> Jane (teacher) tells Jeff to pick up the blocks. He says, "I won't." She catches him and pulls him toward her by the arm. She holds him by the arm. He struggles and gets away. He jumps up and down. Other kids put the blocks away. Jane ignores Jeff. (Several minutes later:) Jeff has been throwing the blocks and now Jane pries the blocks from him and grabs him by the wrist and drags him away from the blocks by his shirt arm. He is looking up at her and pointing his finger at her and saying, "No, cut it out!" in a mocking tone. Jane is angry, but she talks to him calmly but sternly telling him he can't throw the blocks. Jeff is struggling the entire time. Jane lets go of his arm, and Jeff runs right back to the block area and walks on the blocks that are still on the floor. (Five-year-olds)

As Serbin (1983) suggests, frequent loud reprimands of boys may increase their disruptive behavior; more frequent physical disciplining interactions between teachers and boys may do so as well. Because boys more frequently than girls experienced interactions in which their bodies were physically restrained or disciplined by an adult who had more power and was angry, they may be more likely than girls to associate physical interaction with struggle and anger, and thus may be more likely to be aggressive or disruptive.

Physical Interaction among Children

Thorne (1993) demonstrates that children participate in the construction of gender differences among themselves. The preschool brings together large groups of children who engage in interactions in which they cooperate with the hidden curriculum and discipline each others bodies in gendered ways, but they also engage in interactions in which they resist this curriculum.

Girls and boys teach their same-sex peers about their bodies and physicality. Children in these observations were much more likely to imitate the physical behavior of a same-sex peer than a cross-sex peer. Children also encourage others to imitate them. Some gendered physicality develops in this way. For example, I observed one boy encouraging other boys to "take up more space" in the same way he was.

> James (one of the most active boys in the class) is walking all over the blocks that Joe, George, and Paul have built into a road. Then he starts spinning around with his alms stretched out on either side of him. He has a plastic toy cow in one hand and is yelling, "Moo." He spins through half of the classroom, other children ducking under his arms or walking around him when he comes near them. Suddenly he drops the cow and still spinning, starts shouting, "I'm a tomato! I'm a tomato!" The three boys who were playing blocks look at him and laugh. James says, "I'm a tomato!" again, and Joe says, "There's the tomato." Joe, George, and Paul continue working on their block road. James then picks up a block and lobs it in their direction and then keeps spinning throughout this half of the classroom saying he's a tomato. Joe and George look up when the block lands near them and then they get up and imitate James. Now three boys are spinning throughout much of the room, shouting that they are tomatoes. The other children in the class are trying to go about their play without getting hit by a tomato. (Five-year-olds)

The within-gender physicality of three-year-old girls and boys was more similar than it was among the five-year-olds. Among the three-year-old girls there was more rough and tumble play, more physical fighting and arguing among girls than there was among the five-year-old girls.

> During clean up, Emily and Sara argue over putting away some rope. They both pull on the ends of the rope until the teacher comes over and separates them. Emily walks around the classroom then, not cleaning anything up. She sings to herself, does a twirl, and gets in line for snack. Sara is behind her in line. Emily pushes Sara. Sara yells, "Aaahh," and hits Emily and pushes her. The teacher takes both of them out of line and talks to them about getting along and being nice to each other. (Three year-olds)

> Shelly and Ann have masks on. One is a kitty and one is a doggy. They're crawling around on the floor, and they begin play wrestling—kitties and doggies fight. The teacher says to them, "Are you ok?" They stop, lift up their masks, and look worried. The teacher says, "Oh, are you wrestling? It's ok, I just wanted to make sure everyone was ok." The girls nod; they're ok.

Then, they put their masks back on and crawl on the floor some more. They do not resume wrestling. (Three-year-olds)

From lessons like these, girls have learned by age five that their play with each other should not be "too rough." The physical engagement of girls with each other at age five had little rough-and-tumble play:

> Three girls leave the dress-up corner. Mary crawls on the floor as Naomi and Jennifer talk. Jennifer touches Naomi's shoulder gently as she talks to her. They are having quite a long conversation. Jennifer is explaining something to Naomi. Jennifer's gestures are adult-like except that she fiddles with Naomi's vest buttons as she talks to her. Her touching and fiddling with Naomi's clothes is very gentle, how a child might fiddle with a mom's clothing while talking to her—doing it absent-mindedly. Mary, on the floor, is pretending to be a kitty. Then Jennifer gets on the floor and is a kitty too. They are squeaking, trying to mimic a cat's meow. Naomi then puts her arm around Susan's shoulder and leads her to play kitty too. Naomi seems to be a person still, not a kitty. She is in charge of the kitties. (Five-year-olds)

> Two girls are playing with the dishes and sitting at a table. Keisha touches Alice under the chin, tickles her almost, then makes her eat something pretend, then touches the corners of her mouth, telling her to smile. (Five-year-olds)

I do not mean to suggest that girls' physical engagement with each other is the opposite of boys' or that all of boys' physical contacts were rough and tumble. Boys, especially in pairs. hugged, gently guided, or helped each other climb or jump. But often, especially in groups of three or more and especially among the five-year-olds, boys' physical engagement was highly active, "rough," and frequent. Boys experienced these contacts as great fun and not as hostile or negative in any way:

> Keith and Lee are jumping on the couch, diving onto it like high jumpers, colliding with each other as they do. Alan watches them and then climbs onto the back of the couch and jumps off. Keith takes a jump onto the couch, lands on Lee, and then yells, "Ouch, ouch—I hurt my private," and he runs out of the room holding onto his crotch. The teacher tells them to stop jumping on the couch. (Five-year-olds)

> A group of boys is building and climbing on big, hollow, tall blocks. They're bumping into each other, crawling and stepping on each other and the blocks as they do it. They begin yelling, "Garbage can," and laughing. They put little blocks inside the big hollow ones, thus "garbage can." Mike pushes Steve away from the "garbage can" and says, "No that's not!" because he wanted to put a block that was too big into the "can." Steve quits trying and goes to get another block. (Five-year-olds)

The physical engagement of boys and girls *with each other* differed from same-sex physical engagement. Because girls' and boys' play is semi-segregated, collisions (literal and figurative) in play happen at the borders of

Table 6. Observations of Physical Interactions among Children, by Gender of Children: Five Preschool Classrooms

| | Interactions between: | | | | | |
| | Boys | | Girls | | Boys and Girls | |
Type of Interaction	N	Percent	N	Percent	N	Percent
Positive	46	70	42	66	20	18
Negative	19	29	20	31	68	60
Neutral	1	2	2	3	26	23
Total	66	101	64	100	114	101

Note: Physical interaction was coded from references in the field notes to bodily inter-action between children. Bodily contact that was minor and seemingly meaningless was not recorded in field notes. For example, children brushing against each other while picking up toys was not recorded if both children ignored the contact and did not alter their actions because of it. Percentages may not sum to 100 due to rounding.

these gender-segregated groups (Maccoby 1988; Thome 1993). As Thorne (1993) demonstrates, not all borderwork is negative—40 percent of the physical interactions observed between girls and boys were positive or neutral (Table 6).

> Ned runs over to Veronica, hipchecks her and says "can I be your friend?" and she says "yes." Ned walks away and kicks the blocks again three to four times. (Five-year-olds)

However, cross-gender interactions were more likely to be negative than same-sex interactions. In fact, physical interactions among children were twice as likely to be a negative interaction if they were between a girl and boy than if they were among same-gender peers. Approximately 30 percent of the inter-actions among girls and among boys were negative (hostile, angry, controlling, hurtful), whereas 60 percent of mixed-gender physical interactions were nega-tive. Sixty percent of 113 boy-girl physical interactions were initiated by boys, 39 percent were initiated by girls, and only 1 percent of these interactions were mutually initiated.

At the borders of semi-segregated play there are physical interactions about turf and toy ownership:

> Sylvia throws play money on the floor from her play pocketbook. Jon grabs it up. She wrestles him for it and pries it from his hands. In doing this she forces him onto the floor so that he's hunched forward on his knees. She gets behind him and sandwiches him on the floor as she grabs his hands and gets the money loose. Then two minutes later, she's giving money to kids, and she gives Jon some, but apparently not enough. He gets right close to her face, inches away and loudly tells her that he wants more. He scrunches up his face, puts his arms straight down by his sides and makes fists. She steps back; he steps up close again to her face. She turns away. (Five-year-olds)

Negative interactions occur when there are "invasions" or interruptions of play among children of one gender by children of another:

> Courtney is sitting on the floor with the girls who are playing "kitties." The girls have on their dress-up clothes and dress-up shoes. Phil puts on big winter gloves and then jumps in the middle of the girls on the floor. He lands on their shoes. Courtney pushes him away and then pulls her legs and clothes and stuff closer to her. She takes up less space and is sitting in a tight ball on the floor. Phil yells, "No! Aaarrhh." Julie says, "It's not nice to yell." (Five-year-olds)

As Thorne (1993) suggests, kids create, shape, and police the borders of gender. I suggest that they do so physically. In this way, they not only sustain gender segregation, but also maintain a sense that girls and boys are physically different, that their bodies are capable of doing certain kinds of things. This sense of physical differences may make all gender differences feel and appear natural.

CONCLUSION

Children also sometimes resist their bodies being gendered. For example, three-year-old boys dressed up in women's clothes sometimes. Five-year-old girls played with a relaxed comportment that is normatively (hegemonically) masculine when they sat with their feet up on the desk and their chairs tipped backward. In one classroom when boys were at the height of their loud activity—running and throwing toys and blocks—girls took the opportunity to be loud too as the teachers were paying less attention to them and trying to get the boys to settle down. In individual interactions as well, girls were likely to be loud and physically assertive if a boy was being unusually so:

> José is making a plastic toy horse fly around the room, and the boys playing with the blocks are quite loud and rambunctious. José flies the toy horse right in front of Jessica's face and then zooms around her and straight toward her again. Jessica holds up her hand and waves it at him yelling, "Aaaarrrh." José flies the horse in another direction. (Five-year-olds)

These instances of resistance suggest that gendered physicalities are not natural, nor are they easily and straightforwardly acquired. This research demonstrates the many ways that practices in institutions like preschools facilitate children's acquisition of gendered physicalities.

Men and women and girls and boys fill social space with their bodies in different ways. Our everyday movements, postures, and gestures are gendered. These bodily differences enhance the seeming naturalness of sexual and reproductive differences, that then construct inequality between men and women (Butler 1990). As MacKinnon (1987) notes, "Differences are inequality's post hoc excuse . . ." (p. 8). In other words, these differences create a context for social relations in which differences confirm inequalities of power.

This research suggests one way that bodies are gendered and physical differences are constructed through social institutions and their practices. Because this gendering occurs at an early age, the seeming naturalness of such differences is further underscored. In preschool, bodies become gendered in ways that are so subtle and taken-for-granted that they come to feel and appear natural. Preschool, however, is presumably just the tip of the iceberg in the gendering of children's bodies. Families, formal schooling, and other institutions (like churches, hospitals, and workplaces) gender children's physicality as well.

Many feminist sociologists (West and Zimmerman 1987) and other feminist scholars (Butler 1990, 1993) have examined how the seeming naturalness of gender differences underlies gender inequality. They have also theorized that there are no meaningful natural differences (Butler 1990, 1993). However, how gender differences come to feel and appear natural in the first place has been a missing piece of the puzzle.

Sociological theories of the body that describe the regulation, disciplining, and managing that social institutions do to bodies have neglected the gendered nature of these processes (Foucault 1979; Shilling 1993; Turner 1984). These data suggest that a significant part of disciplining the body consists of gendering it, even in subtle, micro, everyday ways that make gender appear natural. It is in this sense that the preschool as an institution genders children's bodies. Feminist theories about the body (Bordo 1993; Connell 1995; Young 1990), on the other hand, tend to focus on the adult gendered body and fail to consider how the body becomes gendered. This neglect may accentuate gender differences and make them seem natural. This research provides but one account of how bodies become gendered. Other accounts of how the bodies of children and adults are gendered (and raced, classed, and sexualized) are needed in various social contexts across the life course.

REFERENCES

Anyon, Jean. 1980. "Social Class and the Hidden Curriculum of Work." *Journal of Education* 162:67–92.

Birdwhistell, Ray. 1970. *Kinesics and Contexts.* Philadelphia, PA: University of Pennsylvania Press.

Bordo, Susan. 1993. *Unbearable Weight.* Berkeley, CA: University of California Press.

Bowles, Samuel, and Herbert Gintis. 1976. *Schooling in Capitalist America.* New York: Basic Books.

Butler, Judith. 1990. *Gender Trouble.* New York: Routledge.

———. 1993. *Bodies That Matter.* New York: Routledge.

Butterfield, Stephen, and E. Michael Loovis. 1993. "Influence of Age, Sex, Balance, and Sport Participation on Development of Throwing by Children in Grades K-8." *Perceptual and Motor Skills* 76:459–64.

Carere, Sharon. 1987. "Lifeworld of Restricted Behavior." *Sociological Studies of Child Development* 2: 105–38.

Carnoy, Martin, and Henry Levin. 1985. *Schooling and Work in the Democratic State.* Stanford, CA: Stanford University Press.

Connell. R. W. 1987. *Gender and Power.* Stanford, CA: Stanford University Press.

———. 1995. *Masculinities.* Berkeley, CA: University of California Press.

Foucault, Michel. 1979. *Discipline and Punish: The Birth of the Prison.* New York: Vintage Books.

Giroux, Henry, and David Purpel. 1983. *The Hidden Curriculum and Moral Education.* Berkeley, CA: McCutchan.

Goffman, Erving. 1959. *The Presentation of Self in Everyday Life.* Garden City, NY: Doubleday.

Goodwin, Marjorie Harness. 1990. *He-Said-She-Said: Talk as Social Organization among Black Children.* Bloomington, IN: Indiana University Press.

Haug, Frigga. 1987. *Female Sexualization: A Collective Work of Memory.* London, England: Verso.

Henley, Nancy. 1977. *Body Politics.* New York: Simon and Schuster.

Jackson, Philip W. 1968. *Life in Classrooms.* New York: Holt, Rinehart, and Winston.

Jordan, Ellen, and Angela Cowan. 1995. "Warrior Narratives in the Kindergarten Classroom: Renegotiating the Social Contract." *Gender and Society* 9:727–43.

Maccoby, Eleanor. 1988. "Gender as a Social Category." *Developmental Psychology* 24:755–65.

MacKinnon, Catharine. 1987. *Feminism Unmodified.* Cambridge, MA: Harvard University Press.

Martin, Emily. 1987. *The Woman in the Body.* Boston, MA: Beacon Press.

Martin, Karin. 1996. *Puberty, Sexuality, and the Self: Boys and Girls at Adolescence.* New York: Routledge.

McLaren, Peter. 1986. *Schooling as a Ritual Performance: Towards a Political Economy of Educational Symbols and Gestures.* London, England: Routledge and Kegan Paul.

Plimpton, Carol E., and Celia Regimbal. 1992. "Differences in Motor Proficiency According to Gender and Race." *Perceptual and Motor Skills* 74:399–402.

Sadker, Myra, and David Sadker. 1994. *Failing at Fairness: How America's Schools Cheat Girls.* New York: Charles Scribner and Sons.

Serbin, Lisa. 1983. "The Hidden Curriculum: Academic Consequences of Teacher Expectations." Pp. 18–41 in *Sex Differentiation and Schooling*, edited by M. Marland. London, England: Heinemann Educational Books.

Shilling, Chris. 1993. *The Body and Social Theory.* London, England: Sage.

Smoll, Frank, and Robert Schutz. 1990. "Quantifying Gender Differences in Physical Performance: A Developmental Perspective:' *Developmental Psychology* 26:360–69.

Suransky, Valerie Polakow. 1982. *The Erosion of Childhood.* Chicago, IL: University of Chicago Press.

Thorne, Barrie. 1993. *Gender Play: Girls and Boys in School*. New Brunswick, NJ: Rutgers University Press.

Thomas, Jerry, and Karen French. 1985. "Gender Differences across Age in Motor Performance: A Meta-Analysis." *Psychological Bulletin* 98: 260–82.

Turner, Bryan S. 1984. *The Body and Society: Explorations in Social Theory*. New York: Basil Blackwell.

———. 1992. *Regulating Bodies: Essays in Medical Sociology*. London, England: Routledge.

Van Ausdale, Debra, and Joe R. Feagin. 1996. "Using Racial and Ethnic Concepts: The Critical Case of Very Young Children." *American Sociological Review* 61: 779–93.

Wasburn, Philo C. 1986. "The Political Role of the American School." *Theory and Research in Social Education* 14:51–65.

West, Candace, and Don Zimmerman. 1987. "Doing Gender." *Gender and Society* 1:127–51.

Young, Iris. 1990. *Throwing Like a Girl*. Bloomington, IN: Indiana University Press.

SARAH McCORMIC

Hoovers and Shakers:
The New Housework Workout

Sarah McCormic is a freelance writer and editor living in Seattle, Washington. For more, visit http://www.sarahmccormic.com.

The other day, my neighbor Kathy stopped by and witnessed an unusual sight: me pushing a vacuum cleaner around my living room. She nodded enthusiastically at my upright Hoover. "Did you know that vacuuming burns almost two hundred calories an hour?"

I looked down at a week's worth of cat hair and dirt tracked in from the yard. "No, I did not know that."

"You can also do lunges to burn even more calories," Kathy said, grabbing the handle away from me to demonstrate. Taking a giant step forward, she bent her other knee almost to the ground while thrusting the vacuum handle forward in a move worthy of one of the Three Musketeers. "It's a killer thigh workout. You should really try it."

After she left, I did. But I felt ridiculous, and the lunges only prolonged one of my least favorite activities. Despite the very real threat of flabby thighs, I vowed to continue vacuuming as infrequently and as quickly as possible.

A few days after Kathy's visit, I came across an article on the popular women's site iVillage.com that called my decision into question. In order to stay fit and trim, it suggested, women should "turn vacuuming into a race, wash windows with plenty of elbow grease, or scrub floors until you work up a sweat."

A quick web search turned up several similar articles in newspapers around the country, all touting this new housework–centric exercise regimen. In March 2004, a *Chicago Sun-Times* headline suggested that you "Scrub, mop your way to fitness." In April, the Louisville, Kentucky, *Courier-Journal* announced that "ordinary chores can promote health and burn calories."

From these and other articles, I learned that while making the bed burns a measly 136 calories an hour, washing windows takes care of a more respectable 204, and scrubbing floor knocks off a full 258. But if you really want to shed those pounds, you should consider rearranging the furniture (408 calories) or carrying a small child up and down stairs (578 calories per hour). An April 2004 *Atlanta Journal-Constitution* article recommended that you "intensify cleaning and outdoor tasks to improve fitness" and offered suggestions such as using shopping bags as weights for biceps curls or doing squats while dusting.

The Boston Globe went a step further in a March 2004 piece suggesting that in order to maximize the slimming benefits of housework, you should try to be less efficient when doing chores. It suggested "taking multiple trips upstairs with the laundry or other clutter instead of one trip" and ended with an ominous warning: "Hiring a cleaning service and gardener is attractive when you're too busy or can't be bothered to do it yourself, but it doesn't help your waistline one bit."

Since I can't afford to pay someone else to clean my house, I figured my figure was safe, but then I came across an article that implied cleaning just one house might not be enough to keep off the pounds. Under the headline "Grab a duster and lose some weight," a newspaper in England's Wiltshire County recounted the success story of Emma Langley, a young woman who shed her pregnancy weight by cleaning houses. After just a few months of scrubbing other people's floors, the article gushed, Ms. Langley "saw immediate health benefits."

I doubted that we were hearing Ms. Langley's whole story (perhaps a pressing need for money had something to do with her activities?). But it occurred to me that no matter where you find yourself on the socioeconomic scale, the message is the same. On the upper end of the economic ladder, women in Boston are being told not to hire someone to clean their homes for the very same reasons that middle-class British women are being schooled in the benefits of scrubbing someone else's toilets: Doing housework is healthy for women.

And, apparently, only women. Not surprisingly, none of these articles profiled men who were taking advantage of the new domestic athleticism. Indeed, it's hard to imagine entreaties like "Wash windows for killer biceps!" or "Lose that gut with a little mopping!" appearing in the likes of *Men's Health*. The trend of housework-as-workout pairs two of the classic standards used to measure a woman's value. My own mother taught me from an early age that being a "good" woman meant steering clear of both extra flab and a messy house; combining these two sources of female shame in a self-help message is as ingenious as it is cruel.

Despite my annoyance with the retrograde messages of this new domestic weight-loss plan, when I thought about my neighbor Kathy—fit, upbeat, healthy Kathy—I realized that you can't argue with its basic premise: Staying active (whether by doing yoga or lugging loads of laundry) burns calories and builds muscles. And that can't be a bad thing in our couch-potato culture, right? But then I read something that upped the stakes considerably.

The March 29, 2004, BBC News headline read "Housework 'reduces cancer risk.'" The story that followed described how researchers at Vanderbilt University had found a decreased risk for a form of uterine cancer in women who do four or more hours of housework a day compared with women who do fewer than two. This study, picked up by Reuters, made headlines in newspapers from Chicago to London to New Delhi. At its most stark, the message was this: If women don't do enough housework, we're not just going to get fat—we're going to die. What those headlines didn't bother to mention, however, is that the study had also found that women who spent an hour walking each day were at lower risk for the same kind of cancer.

Although you probably don't need a study to tell you this, recent research shows that women are still doing much more housework than men. A 2002 study at the University of Michigan found that, on average, American men do sixteen hours a week of housework; women do twenty-seven. This eleven-hour gap actually represents some progress. Between 1965 and 1985, men's share of the housework increased by a whopping four hours. At the same time, women's share dropped, from forty to thirty-one hours, reflecting the fact that more women were working outside the home. After 1985, women's weekly average dropped by another four hours, but after climbing slowly for two decades, men's share skidded to a halt in 1985 and hasn't budged since.

It's no coincidence that the 1980s also gave birth to Martha Stewart's homemaking empire. A rising nostalgia for domesticity has brought with it a slew of recent books and magazine articles promising women fulfillment through a return to the most time-consuming forms of homemaking. Cheryl Mendelson's bestselling *Home Comforts: The Art and Science of Keeping House* puts even Martha to shame in its painstaking attention to the most minute details of housekeeping, instructing readers in the proper method for folding socks and the correct distance between place settings. Nigella Lawson, bodacious TV chef and author of *How to Be a Domestic Goddess*, argues on her website that "many of us have become alienated from the domestic sphere, and . . . it can actually make us feel better to claim back some of that space," which she calls "reclaiming our lost Eden."

The new housework workout passes itself off as an ideal health plan for the busy modern woman, but it's another permutation of this resurgence in nostalgia for more traditional gender roles. It's a new and compelling justification to make the daily drudgery bearable: It's good for us. It will ward off a fat butt, flabby arms, and deadly disease. And it's man's best friend, too, allowing him to keep his housework hours minimal while women mop and scrub their way to tight abs and unmutated uterine cells.

But is the road to health really paved with dust rags? While some chores surely do burn calories and tone muscles, that's not the whole story. A 2002 study conducted by Nanette Mutrie, professor of exercise and sport psychology at the University of Strathclyde, looked at the effects of various forms of exercise—including housework—on depression in both women and men. As she told Scotland's *Sunday Herald:* "With vigorous exercise, the effect is clear: The more you do, the better it is for well-being. With housework, it is the opposite. The more you do, the more depression you report."

I made a mental note to share this information with Kathy next time I saw her. Maybe then she'd think twice about spreading the gospel of aerobic vacuuming. Then again, it might be hard to convince her that housework isn't healthy, since the depression study had barely registered in the media. I couldn't find it reported in a single American newspaper: While stories about housework's cancer-fighting qualities zipped around the globe, almost no one seemed interested in the inconvenient news that the unpaid, tedious, and necessary drudgery performed largely by the world's women might be making them depressed.

And it's not so hard to guess why. If we were to acknowledge that housework, rather than constituting an all-purpose female health tonic, might actually be *harmful* to women, we might find ourselves faced with an uncomfortably strong case for major social change: Men might be asked to take on a larger portion of the housework and child care. Companies might come under increased pressure to offer their employees—both male and female—more flexible, family-friendly schedules. Martha might even see sales go down for her Tuscan table linens and make-your-own-wrapping-paper kits.

The housework workout, on the other hand, asks nothing of men, employers, the government, or corporate America—its message is for women alone. It knows you're tired, overworked, and overscheduled, and let's face it, the men in your life aren't likely to help out anytime soon. It's a tool to balance all the competing demands on your time without inconveniencing anyone else. Its time-tested advice? Adapt. Multitask. Try harder. And remember what your mother (or popular culture) taught you: Keep up your body and your home, or risk everything.

FATEMA MERNISSI
Size 6: The Western Women's Harem

Fatema Mernissi is a writer and sociologist whose work examines the lives of women in Morocco. Her highly acclaimed books include Scheherazade Goes West: Different Cultures, Different Harems *(2001), in which the following selection first appeared.*

It was during my unsuccessful attempt to buy a cotton skirt in an American department store that I was told my hips were too large to fit into a size 6. That distressing experience made me realize how the image of beauty in the West can hurt and humiliate a woman as much as the veil does when enforced by the state police in extremist nations such as Iran, Afghanistan, or Saudi Arabia. Yes, that day I stumbled onto one of the keys to the enigma of passive beauty in Western harem fantasies. The elegant saleslady in the American store looked at me without moving from her desk and said that she had no skirt my size. "In this whole big store, there is no skirt for me?" I said. "You are joking." I felt very suspicious and thought that she just might be too tired to help me. I could understand that. But then the saleswoman added a condescending judgment, which sounded to me like an imam's fatwa. It left no room for discussion:

"You are too big!" she said.

"I am too big compared to what?" I asked, looking at her intently, because I realized that I was facing a critical cultural gap here.

"Compared to a size 6," came the saleslady's reply.

Her voice had a clear-cut edge to it that is typical of those who enforce religious laws. "Size 4 and 6 are the norm," she went on, encouraged by my bewildered look. "Deviant sizes such as the one you need can be bought in special stores."

That was the first time that I had ever heard such nonsense about my size. In the Moroccan streets, men's flattering comments regarding my particularly generous hips have for decades led me to believe that the entire planet shared their convictions. It is true that with advancing age, I have been hearing fewer and fewer flattering comments when walking in the medina, and sometimes the silence around me in the bazaars is deafening. But since my face has never met with the local beauty standards, and I have often had to defend myself against remarks such as *zirafa* (giraffe), because of my long neck, I learned long ago not to rely too much on the outside world for my sense of self-worth. In fact, paradoxically, as I discovered when I went to Rabat as a student, it was the self-reliance that I had developed to protect myself against

379

"beauty blackmail" that made me attractive to others. My male fellow students could not believe that I did not give a damn about what they thought about my body. "You know, my dear," I would say in response to one of them, "all I need to survive is bread, olives, and sardines. That you think my neck is too long is your problem, not mine."

In any case, when it comes to beauty and compliments, nothing is too serious or definite in the medina, where everything can be negotiated. But things seemed to be different in that American department store. In fact, I have to confess that I lost my usual self-confidence in that New York environment. Not that I am always sure of myself, but I don't walk around the Moroccan streets or down the university corridors wondering what people are thinking about me. Of course, when I hear a compliment, my ego expands like a cheese soufflé, but on the whole, I don't expect to hear much from others. Some mornings, I feel ugly because I am sick or tired; others, I feel wonderful because it is sunny out or I have written a good paragraph. But suddenly, in that peaceful American store that I had entered so triumphantly, as a sovereign consumer ready to spend money, I felt savagely attacked. My hips, until then the sign of a relaxed and uninhibited maturity, were suddenly being condemned as a deformity. . . .

"And who says that everyone must be a size 6?" I joked to the saleslady that day, deliberately neglecting to mention size 4, which is the size of my skinny twelve-year-old niece.

At that point, the saleslady suddenly gave me an anxious look. "The norm is everywhere, my dear," she said. "It's all over, in the magazines, on television, in the ads. You can't escape it. There is Calvin Klein, Ralph Lauren, Gianni Versace, Giorgio Armani, Mario Valentino, Salvatore Ferragamo, Christian Dior, Yves Saint-Laurent, Christian Lacroix, and Jean-Paul Gaultier. Big department stores go by the norm." She paused and then concluded, "If they sold size 14 or 16, which is probably what you need, they would go bankrupt."

She stopped for a minute and then stared at me, intrigued. "Where on earth do you come from? I am sorry I can't help you. Really, I am." And she looked it too. She seemed, all of a sudden, interested, and brushed off another woman who was seeking her attention with a cutting, "Get someone else to help you, I'm busy." Only then did I notice that she was probably my age, in her late fifties. But unlike me, she had the thin body of an adolescent girl. Her knee-length, navy blue, Chanel dress had a white silk collar reminiscent of the subdued elegance of aristocratic French Catholic schoolgirls at the turn of the century. A pearl-studded belt emphasized the slimness of her waist. With her meticulously styled short hair and sophisticated makeup, she looked half my age at first glance.

"I come from a country where there is no size for women's clothes," I told her. "I buy my own material and the neighborhood seamstress or craftsman makes me the silk or leather skirt I want. They just take my measurements each time I see them. Neither the seamstress nor I know exactly what size my new skirt is. We discover it together in the making. No one cares about my size in Morocco as long as I pay taxes on time. Actually, I don't know what my size is, to tell you the truth."

The saleswoman laughed merrily and said that I should advertise my country as a paradise for stressed working women. "You mean you don't watch your weight?" she inquired, with a tinge of disbelief in her voice. And then, after a brief moment of silence, she added in a lower register, as if talking to herself: "Many women working in highly paid fashion-related jobs could lose their positions if they didn't keep to a strict diet."

Her words sounded so simple, but the threat they implied was so cruel that I realized for the first time that maybe "size 6" is a more violent restriction imposed on women than is the Muslim veil. Quickly I said good-bye so as not to make any more demands on the saleslady's time or involve her in any more unwelcome, confidential exchanges about age-discriminating salary cuts. A surveillance camera was probably watching us both.

Yes, I thought as I wandered off, I have finally found the answer to my harem enigma. Unlike the Muslim man, who uses space to establish male domination by excluding women from the public arena, the Western man manipulates time and light. He declares that in order to be beautiful, a woman must look fourteen years old. If she dares to look fifty, or worse, sixty, she is beyond the pale. By putting the spotlight on the female child and framing her as the ideal of beauty, he condemns the mature woman to invisibility. In fact, the modern Western man enforces Immanuel Kant's nineteenth-century theories: To be beautiful, women have to appear childish and brainless. When a woman looks mature and self-assertive, or allows her hips to expand, she is condemned as ugly. Thus, the walls of the European harem separate youthful beauty from ugly maturity.

These Western attitudes, I thought, are even more dangerous and cunning than the Muslim ones because the weapon used against women is time. Time is less visible, more fluid than space. The Western man uses images and spotlights to freeze female beauty within an idealized childhood, and forces women to perceive aging—that normal unfolding of the years—as a shameful devaluation. "Here I am, transformed into a dinosaur," I caught myself saying aloud as I went up and down the rows of skirts in the store, hoping to prove the saleslady wrong—to no avail. This Western time-defined veil is even crazier than the space-defined one enforced by the ayatollahs.

The violence embodied in the Western harem is less visible than in the Eastern harem because aging is not attacked directly, but rather masked as an aesthetic choice. Yes, I suddenly felt not only very ugly but also quite useless in that store, where, if you had big hips, you were simply out of the picture. You drifted into the fringes of nothingness. By putting the spotlight on the pre-pubescent female, the Western man veils the older, more mature woman, wrapping her in shrouds of ugliness. This idea gives me the chills because it tattoos the invisible harem directly onto a woman's skin. Chinese foot-binding worked the same way: Men declared beautiful only those women who had small, childlike feet. Chinese men did not force women to bandage their feet to keep them from developing normally—all they did was to define the beauty ideal. In feudal China, a beautiful woman was the one who voluntarily sacrificed her right to unhindered physical movement by mutilating her own feet, and thereby proving that her main goal in life was to please men. Similarly, in the Western world, I was expected to shrink my hips into a size 6 if I wanted to find a decent skirt tailored for a beautiful woman. We Muslim women have only one month of fasting, Ramadan, but the poor Western woman who diets has to fast twelve months out of the year. *"Quelle horreur,"* I kept repeating to myself, while looking around at the American women shopping. All those my age looked like youthful teenagers. . . .

Now, at last, the mystery of my Western harem made sense. Framing youth as beauty and condemning maturity is the weapon used against women in the West just as limiting access to public space is the weapon used in the East. The objective remains identical in both cultures: to make women feel unwelcome, inadequate, and ugly.

The power of the Western man resides in dictating what women should wear and how they should look. He controls the whole fashion industry, from cosmetics to underwear. The West, I realized, was the only part of the world where women's fashion is a man's business. In places like Morocco, where you design your own clothes and discuss them with craftsmen and -women, fashion is your own business. Not so in the West. . . .

But how does the system function? I wondered. Why do women accept it?

Of all the possible explanations, I like that of the French sociologist Pierre Bourdieu the best. In his latest book, *La Domination Masculine*, he proposes something he calls *"la violence symbolique"*: "Symbolic violence is a form of power which is hammered directly on the body, and as if by magic, without any apparent physical constraint. But this magic operates only because it activates the codes pounded in the deepest layers of the body.[1] Reading Bourdieu, I had the impression that I finally understood Western man's psyche better. The cosmetic and fashion industries are only the tip of the iceberg, he states, which is why women are so ready to adhere to their dictates. Something else is going on on a far deeper level. Otherwise, why would women belittle themselves spontaneously? Why, argues Bourdieu, would women make their lives more difficult, for example, by preferring men who are taller or older than they are? "The majority of French women wish to have a husband who is older and also, which seems consistent, bigger as far as size is concerned," writes Bourdieu.[2] Caught in the enchanted submission characteristic of the symbolic violence inscribed in the mysterious layers of the flesh, women relin-

---

[1]Pierre Bourdieu, *La Domination Masculine* (Paris: Editions du Seuil, 1998), p. 44.
[2]Ibid., p. 41.

quish what he calls "les signes ordinaires de la hiérarchie sexuelle," the ordinary signs of sexual hierarchy, such as old age and a larger body. By so doing, explains Bourdieu, women spontaneously accept the subservient position. It is this spontaneity Bourdieu describes as magic enchantment.[3]

Once I understood how this magic submission worked, I became very happy that the conservative ayatollahs do not know about it yet. If they did, they would readily switch to its sophisticated methods, because they are so much more effective. To deprive me of food is definitely the best way to paralyze my thinking capabilities. . . .

"I thank you, Allah, for sparing me the tyranny of the 'size 6 harem,'" I repeatedly said to myself while seated on the Paris-Casablanca flight, on my way back home at last. "I am so happy that the conservative male elite does not know about it. Imagine the fundamentalists switching from the veil to forcing women to fit size 6."

How can you stage a credible political demonstration and shout in the streets that your human rights have been violated when you cannot find the right skirt?

---

[3]Ibid., p. 42

●
○ ───

MICHAEL A. MESSNER
Barbie Girls Versus Sea Monsters: Children Constructing Gender

Michael A. Messner is Professor of Sociology at the University of Southern California, and is widely-published researcher of masculinity whose work has played a significant role in bringing men's issues to the forefront of gender studies. His many books and articles have focused on politics, youth, and sports as domains of masculine formation. For more on Michael Messner, including further readings, visit his homepage at http://www-rcf.usc.edu/~messner/.

In the past decade, studies of children and gender have moved toward greater levels of depth and sophistication (e.g., Jordan and Cowan 1995; McGuffy and Rich 1999; Thorne 1993). In her groundbreaking work on children and gender, Thorne (1993) argued that previous theoretical frameworks, although helpful, were limited: The top-down (adult-to-child) approach of socialization theories tended to ignore the extent to which children are active agents in the creation of their worlds—often in direct or partial opposition to values or "roles" to which adult teachers or parents are attempting to socialize them. Developmental theories also had their limits due to their tendency to ignore group and contextual factors while overemphasizing "the constitution and unfolding of *individuals* as boys or girls" (Thorne 1993, 4). In her study of grade school children, Thorne demonstrated a dynamic approach that examined the ways in which children actively construct gender in specific social contexts of the classroom and the playground. Working from emergent theories of performativity, Thorne developed the concept of "gender play" to analyze the social processes through which children construct gender. Her level of analysis was not the individual but *"group life*—with social relations, the organization and meanings of social situations, the collective practices through which children and adults create and recreate gender in their daily interactions" (Thorne 1993, 4).

A key insight from Thorne's research is the extent to which gender varies in salience from situation to situation. Sometimes, children engage in "relaxed, cross sex play"; other times—for instance, on the playground during boys' ritual invasions of girls' spaces and games—gender boundaries between boys and girls are activated in ways that variously threaten or (more often) reinforce and clarify these boundaries. However, these varying moments of gender salience are not free-floating; they occur in social contexts such as schools and in which gender is formally and informally built into the division of labor, power structure, rules, and values (Connell 1987).

The purpose of this article is to use an observation of a highly salient gendered moment of group life among four- and five-year-old children as a point of departure for exploring the conditions under which gender boundaries become activated and enforced. I was privy to this moment as I observed my five-year-old son's first season (including weekly games and practices) in organized soccer. Unlike the long-term, systematic ethnographic studies of children conducted by Thorne (1993) or Adler and Adler (1998), this article takes one moment as its point of departure. I do not present this moment as somehow "representative" of what happened throughout the season; instead, I examine this as an example of what Hochschild (1994, 4) calls "magnified moments," which are "episodes of heightened importance, either epiphanies, moments of intense glee or unusual insight, or moments in which things go intensely but meaningfully wrong. In either case, the moment stands out; it is metaphorically rich, unusually elaborate and often echoes [later]." A magnified moment in daily life offers a window into the social construction of reality. It presents researchers with an opportunity to excavate gendered meanings and processes through an analysis of institutional and cultural contexts. The single empirical observation that serves as the point of departure for this article was made during a morning. Immediately after the event, I recorded my observations with detailed notes. I later slightly revised the notes after developing the photographs that I took at the event.

I will first describe the observation — an incident that occurred as a boys' four- and five-year-old soccer team waited next to a girls' four- and five-year-old soccer team for the beginning of the community's American Youth Soccer League (AYSO) season's opening ceremony. I will then examine this moment using three levels of analysis.

> *The interactional level*: How do children "do gender," and what are the contributions and limits of theories of performativity in understanding these interactions?
>
> *The level of structural context*: How does the gender regime, particularly the larger organizational level of formal sex segregation of AYSO, and the concrete, momentary situation of the opening ceremony provide a context that variously constrains and enables the children's interactions?
>
> *The level of cultural symbol*: How does the children's shared immersion in popular culture (and their differently gendered locations in this immersion) provide symbolic resources for the creation, in this situation, of apparently categorical differences between the boys and the girls?

Although I will discuss these three levels of analysis separately, I hope to demonstrate that interaction, structural context, and culture are simultaneous and mutually intertwined processes, none of which supersedes the others.

Barbie Girls Versus Sea Monsters

It is a warm, sunny Saturday morning. Summer is coming to a close, and schools will soon reopen. As in many communities, this time of year in this small, middle- and professional-class suburb of Los Angeles is marked by the beginning of another soccer season. This morning, 156 teams, with approximately 1,850 players ranging from 4 to 17 years old, along with another 2,000 to 3,000 parents, siblings, friends, and community dignitaries have gathered at the local high school football and track facility for the annual AYSO opening ceremonies. Parents and children wander around the perimeter of the track to find the assigned station for their respective teams. The coaches muster their teams and chat with parents. Eventually, each team will march around the track, behind their new team banner, as they are announced over the loudspeaker system and are applauded by the crowd. For now though, and for the next 45 minutes to an hour, the kids, coaches, and parents must stand, mill around, talk, and kill time as they await the beginning of the ceremony.

The Sea Monsters is a team of four- and five-year-old boys. Later this day, they will play their first-ever soccer game. A few of the boys already know each other from preschool, but most are still getting acquainted. They are wearing their new uniforms for the first time. Like other teams, they were assigned team colors—in this case, green and blue—and asked to choose their team name at their first team meeting, which occurred a week ago. Although they preferred "Blue Sharks," they found that the name was already taken by another team and settled on "Sea Monsters." A grandmother of one of the boys created the spiffy team banner, which was awarded a prize this morning. As they wait for the ceremony to begin, the boys inspect and then proudly pose for pictures in front of their new award-winning team banner. The parents stand a few feet away—some taking pictures, some just watching. The parents are also getting to know each other, and the common currency of topics is just how darned cute our kids look, and will they start these ceremonies soon before another boy has to be escorted to the bathroom?

Queued up one group away from the Sea Monsters is a team of four- and five-year-old girls in green and white uniforms. They too will play their first game later today, but for now, they are awaiting the beginning of the opening ceremony. They have chosen the name "Barbie Girls," and they also have a spiffy new team banner. But the girls are pretty much ignoring their banner, for they have created another, more powerful symbol around which to rally. In fact, they are the only team among the 156 marching today with a team float—a red Radio Flyer wagon base, on which sits a Sony boom box playing music, and a 3-foot-plus-tall Barbie doll on a rotating pedestal. Barbie is dressed in the team colors—indeed, she sports a custom-made green-and-white cheerleader-style outfit, with the Barbie Girls' names written on the skirt. Her normally all-blonde hair has been streaked with Barbie Girl green and features a green bow, with white polka dots. Several of the girls on the team also have supplemented their uniforms with green bows in their hair.

The volume on the boom box nudges up and four or five girls begin to sing a Barbie song. Barbie is now slowly rotating on her pedestal, and as the girls sing more gleefully and more loudly, some of them begin to hold hands and walk around the float, in sync with Barbie's rotation. Other same-aged girls from other teams are drawn to the celebration and, eventually, perhaps a dozen girls are singing the Barbie song. The girls are intensely focused on Barbie, on the music, and on their mutual pleasure.

As the Sea Monsters mill around their banner, some of them begin to notice, and then begin to watch and listen as the Barbie Girls rally around their float. At first, the boys are watching as individuals, seemingly unaware of each other's shared interest. Some of them stand with arms at their sides, slack-jawed, as though passively watching a television show. I notice slight smiles on a couple of their faces, as though they are drawn to the Barbie Girls' celebratory fun. Then, with side-glances, some of the boys begin to notice each other's attention on the Barbie Girls. Their faces begin to show signs of distaste. One of them yells out, "NO BARBIE!" Suddenly, they all begin to move—jumping up and down, nudging and bumping one another—and join into a group chant: "NO BARBIE! NO BARBIE! NO BARBIE!" They now appear to be every bit as gleeful as the girls, as they laugh, yell, and chant against the Barbie Girls.

The parents watch the whole scene with rapt attention. Smiles light up the faces of the adults, as our glances sweep back and forth, from the sweetly celebrating Barbie Girls to the aggressively protesting Sea Monsters. "They are SO different!" exclaims one smiling mother approvingly. A male coach offers a more in-depth analysis: "When I was in college," he says, "I took these classes from professors who showed us research that showed that boys and girls are the same. I believe it, until I had my own kids and saw how different they are." "Yeah," another dad responds, "Just look at them! They are so different!"

The girls, meanwhile, show no evidence that they hear, see, or are even aware of the presence of the boys who are now so loudly proclaiming their opposition to the Barbie Girls' songs and totem. They continue to sing, dance, laugh, and rally around the Barbie for a few more minutes, before they are called to reassemble in their groups for the beginning of the parade.

After the parade, the teams reassemble on the infield of the track but now in a less organized manner. The Sea Monsters once again find themselves in the general vicinity of the Barbie Girls and take up the "NO BARBIE!" chant again. Perhaps put out by the lack of response to their chant, they begin to dash, in twos and threes, invading the girls' space, and yelling menacingly. With this, the Barbie Girls have little choice but to recognize the presence of the boys—some look puzzled and shrink back, some engage the boys and chase them off. The chasing seems only to incite more excitement among the boys. Finally, parents intervene and defuse the situation, leading their children off to their cars, homes, and eventually to their soccer games.

THE PERFORMANCE OF GENDER

In the past decade, especially since the publication of Judith Butler's highly influential *Gender Trouble* (1990), it has become increasingly fashionable among academic feminists to think of gender not as some "thing" that one "has" (or not) but rather as situationally constructed through the performances of active agents. The idea of gender as performance analytically foregrounds the agency of individuals in the construction of gender, thus highlighting the situational fluidity of gender: here, conservative and reproductive, there, transgressive and disruptive. Surely, the Barbie Girls versus Sea Monsters scene described above can be fruitfully analyzed as a moment of crosscutting and mutually constitutive gender performances: The girls—at least at first glance—appear to be performing (for each other?) a conventional four- to five-year-old version of emphasized femininity. At least on the surface, there appears to be nothing terribly transgressive here. They are just "being girls," together. The boys initially are unwittingly constituted as an audience for the girls' performance but quickly begin to perform (for each other?—for the girls, too?) a masculinity that constructs itself in opposition to Barbie, and to the girls, as not feminine. They aggressively confront—first through loud verbal chanting, eventually through bodily invasions—the girls' ritual space of emphasized femininity, apparently with the intention of disrupting its upsetting influence. The adults are simultaneously constituted as an adoring audience for their children's performances and as parents who perform for each other by sharing and mutually affirming their experience-based narratives concerning the natural differences between boys and girls.

In this scene, we see children performing gender in ways that constitute themselves as two separate, opposed groups (boys vs. girls) and parents performing gender in ways that give the stamp of adult approval to the children's performances of difference, while constructing their own ideological narrative that naturalizes this categorical difference. In other words, the parents do not seem to read the children's performances of gender as social constructions of gender. Instead, they interpret them as the inevitable unfolding of natural, internal differences between the sexes. That this moment occurred when it did and where it did is explicable, but not entirely with a theory of performativity. As Walters (1999, 250) argues,

> The performance of gender is never a simple voluntary act. . . . Theories of gender as play and performance need to be intimately and systematically connected with the power of gender (really, the power of male power) to constrain, control, violate, and configure. Too often, mere lip service is given to the specific historical, social, and political configurations that make certain conditions possible and others constrained.

Indeed, feminist sociologists operating from the traditions of symbolic interactionism and/or Goffmanian dramaturgical analysis have anticipated the recent interest in looking at gender as a dynamic performance. As early as 1978, Kessler and McKenna developed a sophisticated analysis of gender as an everyday, practical accomplishment of people's interactions. Nearly a decade later, West and Zimmerman (1987) argued that in people's everyday interactions, they were "doing gender" and, in so doing, they were constructing masculine dominance and feminine deference. As these ideas have been taken up in sociology, their tendencies toward a celebration of the "freedom" of agents to transgress and reshape the fluid boundaries of gender have been put into play with theories of social structure (e.g., Lorber 1994; Risman 1998). In these accounts, gender is viewed as enacted or created through everyday interactions, but crucially, as Walters suggested above, within "specific historical, social, and political configurations" that constrain or enable certain interactions.

The parents' response to the Barbie Girls versus Sea Monsters performance suggests one of the main limits and dangers of theories of performativity. Lacking an analysis of structural and cultural context, performances of gender can all too easily be interpreted as free agents' acting out the inevitable surface manifestations of a natural inner essence of sex difference. An examination of structural and cultural contexts, though, reveals that there was nothing inevitable about the girls' choice of Barbie as their totem, nor in the boys' response to it.

THE STRUCTURE OF GENDER

In the entire subsequent season of weekly games and practices, I never once saw adults point to a moment in which boy and girl soccer players were doing the *same* thing and exclaim to each other, "Look at them! They are so *similar!*" The actual similarity of the boys and the girls, evidenced by nearly all of the kids' routine actions throughout a soccer season — playing the game, crying over a skinned knee, scrambling enthusiastically for their snacks after the games, spacing out on a bird or a flower instead of listening to the coach at practice — is a key to understanding the salience of the Barbie Girls versus Sea Monsters moment for gender relations. In the face of a multitude of moments that speak to similarity, it was this anomalous Barbie Girls versus Sea Monsters moment — where the boundaries of gender were so clearly enacted — that the adults seized to affirm their commitment to difference. It is the kind of moment — to use Lorber's (1994, 37) phrase — where "believing is seeing," where we selectively "see" aspects of social reality that tell us a truth that we prefer to believe, such as the belief in categorical sex difference. No matter that our eyes do not see evidence of this truth most of the rest of the time.

In fact, it was not so easy for adults to actually "see" the empirical reality of sex similarity in everyday observations of soccer throughout the season. That is due to one overdetermining factor: an institutional context that is characterized by informally structured sex segregation among the parent coaches and team managers, and by formally structured sex segregation among the children. The structural analysis developed here is indebted to Acker's (1990) observation that organizations, even while appearing "gender neutral," tend to reflect, re-create, and naturalize a hierarchical ordering of gender. Following Connell's (1987, 98–99) method of structural analysis, I will examine the "gender regime"—that is, the current "state of play of sexual politics"— within the local AYSO organization by conducting a "structural inventory" of the formal and informal sexual divisions of labor and power.[1]

Adult Divisions of Labor and Power

There was a clear—although not absolute—sexual division of labor and power among the adult volunteers in the AYSO organization. The Board of Directors consisted of 21 men and 9 women, with the top two positions— commissioner and assistant commissioner—held by men. Among the league's head coaches, 133 were men and 23 women. The division among the league's assistant coaches was similarly skewed. Each team also had a team manager who was responsible for organizing snacks, making reminder calls about games and practices, organizing team parties and the end-of-the-year present for the coach. The vast majority of team managers were women. A common slippage in the language of coaches and parents revealed the ideological assumptions underlying this position: I often noticed people describe a team manager as the "team mom." In short, as Table 1 shows, the vast majority of the time, the formal authority of the head coach and assistant coach was in the hands of a man, while the backup, support role of team manager was in the hands of a woman.

These data illustrate Connell's (1987, 97) assertion that sexual divisions of labor are interwoven with, and mutually supportive of, divisions of power and authority among women and men. They also suggest how people's choices to volunteer for certain positions are shaped and constrained by previous institutional practices. There is no formal AYSO rule that men must be the leaders, women the supportive followers. And there are, after all, *some* women coaches and *some* men team managers.[2] So, it may appear that the division of labor among adult volunteers simply manifests an accumulation of individual choices and preferences. When analyzed structurally, though, individual men's

Table 1. Adult Volunteers as Coaches and Team Managers, by Gender (in percentages) (N = 156 teams)

	Head Coaches	Assistant Coaches	Team Managers
Women	15	21	86
Men	85	79	14

apparently free choices to volunteer disproportionately for coaching jobs, alongside individual women's apparently free choices to volunteer dispropor-tionately for team manager jobs, can be seen as a logical collective result of the ways that the institutional structure of sport has differentially constrained and enabled women's and men's previous options and experiences (Messner 1992). Since boys and men have had far more opportunities to play organized sports and thus to gain skills and knowledge, it subsequently appears rational for adult men to serve in positions of knowledgeable authority, with women serving in a support capacity (Boyle and McKay 1995). Structure—in this case, the his-torically constituted division of labor and power in sport—constrains current practice. In turn, structure becomes an object of practice, as the choices and actions of today's parents re-create divisions of labor and power similar to those that they experienced in their youth.

The Children: Formal Sex Segregation

As adult authority patterns are informally structured along gendered lines, the children's leagues are formally segregated by AYSO along lines of age and sex. In each age-group, there are separate boys' and girls' leagues. The AYSO in this community included 87 boys' teams and 69 girls' teams. Although the four- to five-year-old boys often played their games on a field that was con-tiguous with games being played by four- to five-year-old girls, there was never a formal opportunity for cross-sex play. Thus, both the girls' and boys' teams could conceivably proceed through an entire season of games and prac-tices in entirely homosocial contexts.[3] In the all-male contexts that I observed throughout the season, gender never appeared to be overtly salient among the children, coaches, or parents. It is against the backdrop that I might suggest a working hypothesis about structure and the variable salience of gender: The formal sex segregation of children does not, in and of itself, make gender overtly salient. In fact, when children are absolutely segregated, with no opportunity for cross-sex interactions, gender may appear to disappear as an overtly salient organizing principle. However, when formally sex-segregated children are placed into immediately contiguous locations, such as during the opening ceremony, highly charged gendered interactions between the groups (including invasions and other kinds of border work) become more possible.

Although it might appear to some that formal sex segregation in chil-dren's sports is a natural fact, it has not always been so for the youngest age-groups in AYSO. As recently as 1995, when my older son signed up to play as a five-year-old, I had been told that he would play in a coed league. But when he arrived to his first practice and I saw that he was on an all-boys team, I was told by the coach that AYSO had decided this year to begin sex segregating all age-groups, because "during half-times and practices, the boys and girls tend to separate into separate groups. So the league thought it would be better for team unity if we split the boys and girls into separate leagues." I suggested to some coaches that a similar dynamic among racial ethnic groups (say, Latino kids and white kids clustering as separate groups during halftimes) would not similarly result in a decision to create racially segregated leagues. That this comment appeared to fall on deaf ears illustrates the extent to which many adults' belief in the need for sex segregation—at least in the context of sport—is grounded in a mutually agreed-upon notion of boys' and girls' "separate worlds," perhaps based in ideologies of natural sex difference.

The gender regime of AYSO, then, is structured by formal and informal sexual divisions of labor and power. This social structure sets ranges, limits, and possibilities for the children's and parents' interactions and performances of gender, but it does not determine them. Put another way, the formal and informal gender regime of AYSO made the Barbie girls versus Sea Monsters moment possible, but it did not make it inevitable. It was the agency of the children and the parents within that structure that made the moment happen. But why did this moment take on the symbolic forms that it did? How and why do the girls, boys, and parents construct and derive meanings from this moment, and how can we interpret these meanings? These questions are best grappled within the realm of cultural analysis.

THE CULTURE OF GENDER

The different between what is "structural" and what is "cultural" is not clear-cut. For instance, the AYSO assignment of team colors and choice of team names (cultural symbols) seem to follow logically from, and in turn reinforce, the sex segregation of the leagues (social structure). These cultural symbols such as team colors, uniforms, songs, team names, and banners often carried encoded gendered meanings that were then available to be taken up by the children in ways that constructed (or potentially contested) gender divisions and boundaries.

Team Names

Each team was issued two team colors. It is notable that across the various age-groups, several girls' teams were issued pink uniforms—a color commonly recognized as encoding feminine meanings—while no boys' teams were issued pink uniforms. Children, in consultation with their coaches, were asked to choose their own team names and were encouraged to use their assigned team colors as cues to theme of the team name (e.g., among the boys, the "Red Flashes," the "Green Pythons," and the blue-and-green "Sea Monsters"). When I analyzed the team names of the 156 teams by age-group and by sex, three categories emerged:

1. Sweet names: These are cutesy team names that communicate small stature, cuteness, and/or vulnerability. These kinds of names would most likely be widely read as encoded with feminine meanings (e.g.,

"Blue Butterflies," "Beanie Babes," "Sunflowers," "Pink Flamingos," and "Barbie Girls").

2. Neutral or paradoxical names: Neutral names are team names that carry no obvious gendered meaning (e.g., "Blue and Green Lizards," "Team Flubber," "Galaxy," "Blue Ice"). Paradoxical names are girls' team names that carry mixed (simultaneously vulnerable *and* powerful) messages (e.g., "Pink Panthers," "Flower Power," "Little Tigers").

3. Power names: These are team names that invoke images of unambiguous strength, aggression, and raw power (e.g., "Shooting Stars," "Killer Whales," "Shark Attack," "Raptor Attack," and "Sea Monsters").

As Table 2 illustrates, across all age-groups of boys, there was only one team name coded as a sweet name—"The Smurfs," in the 10- to 11-year-old league. Across all age categories, the boys were far more likely to choose a power name than anything else, and this was nowhere more true than in the youngest age-groups, where 35 of 40 (87 percent) of boys' teams in the four-to-five and six-to-seven age-groups took on power names. A different pattern appears in the girls' team name choices, especially among the youngest girls. Only 2 of the 12 four- to five-year-old girls' teams chose power names, while 5 chose sweet names and 5 chose neutral/paradoxical names. At age six to seven, the numbers begin to tip toward the boys' numbers but still remain different, with half of the girls' teams now choosing power names. In the middle and older girls' groups, the sweet names all but disappear, with power names dominating, but still higher proportion of neutral/paradoxical names than among boys in those age-groups.

Table 2. Team Names, by Age-Groups and Gender

	4–5		6–7		8–13		14–17		Total	
	n	%	n	%	n	%	n	%	n	%
Girls										
Sweet names	5	42	3	17	2	7	0	0	10	15
Neutral/ paradoxical	5	42	6	33	7	25	5	45	23	32
Power names	2	17	9	50	19	68	6	55	36	52
Boys										
Sweet names	0	0	0	0	1	4	0	0	1	1
Neutral/ paradoxical	1	7	4	15	4	12	4	31	13	15
Power names	13	93	22	85	29	85	9	69	73	82

Barbie Narrative versus Warrior Narrative

How do we make sense of the obviously powerful spark that Barbie provided in the opening ceremony scene described above? Barbie is likely one of the most immediately identifiable symbols of femininity in the world. More conservatively oriented parents tend to happily buy Barbie dolls for their daughters, while perhaps deflecting their sons' interest in Barbie toward more sex-appropriate "action toys." Feminist parents, on the other hand, have often expressed open contempt—or at least uncomfortable ambivalence—toward Barbie. This is because both conservative and feminist parents see dominant cultural meanings of emphasized femininity as condensed in Barbie and assume that these meanings will be imitated by their daughters. Recent developments in cultural studies, though, should warn us against simplistic readings of Barbie as simply conveying hegemonic messages about gender to unwitting children (Attfield 1996; Seiter 1995). In addition to critically analyzing the cultural values (or "preferred meanings") that may be encoded in Barbie or other children's toys, feminist scholars of cultural studies point to the necessity of examining "reception, pleasure, and agency," and especially "the fullness of reception contexts" (Walters 1999, 246). The Barbie Girls versus Sea Monsters moment can be analyzed as a "reception context," in which differently situated boys, girls, and parents variously used Barbie to construct pleasurable intergroup bonds, as well as boundaries between groups.

Barbie is plastic both in form and in terms of cultural meanings children and adults create around her (Rogers 1999). It is not that there are not hegemonic meanings encoded in Barbie: Since its introduction in 1959, Mattel has been successful in selling millions[4] of this doll that "was recognized as a model of ideal teenhood" (Rand 1998, 383) and "an icon—perhaps *the* icon—of true white womanhood and femininity" (DuCille 1994, 50). However, Rand (1998) argues that "we condescend to children when we analyze Barbie's content and then presume that it passes untransformed into their minds, where, dwelling beneath the control of consciousness or counterargument, it generates self-image, feelings, and other ideological constructs." In fact, people who are situated differently (by age, gender, sexual orientation, social class, race/ethnicity, and national origin) tend to consume and construct meanings around Barbie variously. For instance, some adult women (including many feminists) tell retrospective stories of having rejecting (or even mutilated) their Barbies in favor of boys' toys, and some adult lesbians tell stories of transforming Barbie "into an object of dyke desire" (Rand 1998, 386).

Mattel, in fact, clearly strategizes its marketing of Barbie not around the imposition of a singular notion of what a girl or woman should be but around "hegemonic discourse strategies" that attempt to incorporate consumers' range of possible interpretations and criticisms of the limits of Barbie. For instance, the recent marketing of "multicultural Barbie" features dolls with different skin colors and culturally coded wardrobes (DuCille 1994). This strategy broadens the Barbie market, deflects potential criticism of racism, but still "does not boot blond, white Barbie from center stage" (Rand 1998, 391). Similarly, Mattel's marketing of Barbie (since the 1970s) as a career woman raises issues concerning the feminist critique of Barbie's supposedly negative effect on girls. When the AAUW recently criticized Barbie, adult collectors defended Barbie, asserting that "Barbie, in fact, is a wonderful role model for women. She has been a veterinarian, an astronaut, and a soldier—and even before real women had a chance to enter such occupations" (Spigel forthcoming). And when the magazine *Barbie Bazaar* ran a cover photo of its new "Gulf War Barbie," it served "as a reminder of Mattel's marketing slogan: 'We Girls Can Do Anything'" (Spigel forthcoming). The following year, Mattel unveiled its "Presidential Candidate Barbie" with the statement "It is time for a woman president, and Barbie had the credentials for the job." Spigel observes that these liberal feminist messages of empowerment for girls run—apparently unambiguously—alongside a continued unspoken understanding that Barbie must be beautiful, with an ultraskinny waist and long, thin legs that taper to feet that appear deformed so that they may fit (only?) into high heels.[5] "Mattel does not mind equating beauty with intellect. In fact, so long as the 11½ inch Barbie body remains intact, Mattel is willing to accessorize her with a number of fashionable perspectives—including feminism itself" (Spigel forthcoming).

It is this apparently paradoxical encoding of the all-too-familiar oppressive bodily requirements of feminine beauty alongside the career woman role modeling and empowering message that "we girls can do anything" that may inform how and why the Barbie Girls appropriated Barbie as their team symbol. Emphasized femininity—Connell's (1987) term for the current form of femininity that articulates with hegemonic masculinity—as many Second Wave feminists have experienced and criticized it, has been characterized by girls' and women's embodiments of oppressive conceptions of feminine beauty that symbolize and reify a thoroughly disempowered stance vis-à-vis men. To many Second Wave feminists, Barbie seemed to symbolize all that was oppressive about this femininity—the bodily self-surveillance, accompanying eating disorders, slavery to the dictates of the fashion industry, and compulsory heterosexuality. But Rogers (1999, 14) suggests that rather than representing an unambiguous image of emphasized femininity, perhaps Barbie represents a more paradoxical image of "emphatic femininity" that

> takes feminine appearances and demeanor to unsustainable extremes. Nothing about Barbie ever looks masculine, even when she is on the police force. . . . Consistently, Barbie manages impressions so as to come across as a proper feminine creature even when she crosses boundaries usually dividing women from men. Barbie the firefighter is in no danger, then, of being seen as "one of the boys." Kids know that; parents and teachers know that; Mattel designers know that too.

Recent Third Wave feminist theory sheds light on the different sensibilities of younger generations of girls and women concerning their willingness to display and play with this apparently paradoxical relationship between bodily experience (including "feminine" displays) and public empowerment. In Third Wave feminist texts, displays of feminine physical attractiveness and empowerment are not viewed as mutually exclusive or necessarily opposed realities, but as lived (if often paradoxical) aspects of the same reality (Heywood and Drake 1997). This embracing of the paradoxes of post–Second Wave femininity is manifested in many punk, or Riot Grrrl, subcultures (Klein 1997) and in popular culture in the resounding late 1990s' success of the Spice Girls' mantra of "Girl Power." This generational expression of "girl power" may today be part of "the pleasures of girl culture that Barbie stands for" (Spigel forthcoming). Indeed, as the Barbie Girls rallied around Barbie, their obvious pleasure did not appear to be based on a celebration of quiet passivity (as feminist parents might fear). Rather, it was a statement that they—the Barbie Girls—were here in this public space. They were not silenced by the boys' oppositional chanting. To the contrary, they ignored the boys, who seemed irrelevant to their celebration. And, when the boys later physically invaded their space, some of the girls responded by chasing the boys off. In short, when I pay attention to what the girls *did* (rather than imposing on the situation what I *think* Barbie "should" mean to the girls), I see a public moment of celebratory "girl power."

And this may give us better basis from which to analyze the boys' oppositional response. First, the boys may have been responding to the threat of displacement they may have felt while viewing the girls' moment of celebratory girl power. Second, the boys may simultaneously have been responding to the fears of feminine pollution that Barbie had come to symbolize to them. But why might Barbie symbolize feminine pollution to little boys? A brief example from my older son is instructive. When he was about three, following a fun day of play with the five-year-old girl next door, he enthusiastically asked me to buy him a Barbie like hers. He was gleeful when I took him to the store and bought him one. When we arrived home, his feet had barely hit the pavement getting out of the car before an eight-year-old neighbor boy laughed at and ridiculed him: "A *Barbie*? Don't you know that Barbie is a *girl's toy*?" No amount of parental intervention could counter this devastating peer-induced injunction against boys' playing with Barbie. My son's pleasurable desire for Barbie appeared almost overnight to transform itself into shame and rejection. The doll ended up at the bottom of a heap of toys in the closet, and my son soon became infatuated, along with other boys in his preschool, with Ninja Turtles and Power Rangers.

Research indicates that there is widespread agreement as to which toys are appropriate for one sex and polluting, dangerous, or inappropriate for the other sex. When Campenni (1999) asked adults to rate the gender appropriateness of children's toys, the toys considered most appropriate to girls were those pertaining to domestic tasks, beauty enhancement, or child rearing. Of the 206 toys rated, Barbie was rated second only to Makeup Kit as a female-only toy. Toys considered most appropriate to boys were those pertaining to sports gear (football gear was the most masculine-rated toy, while boxing gloves were third), vehicles, action figures (G. I. Joe was rated second only to football gear), and other war-related toys. This research on parents' gender stereotyping of toys reflects similar findings in research on children's toy preferences (Bradbard 1985; Robinson and Morris 1986). Children tend to avoid cross-sex toys, with boys' avoidance of feminine-coded toys appearing to be stronger than girls' avoidance of masculine-coded toys (Etaugh and Liss 1992). Moreover, preschool-age boys who perceive their fathers to be opposed to cross-gender-typed play are more likely than girls or other boys to think that it is "bad" for boys to play with toys that are labeled as "for girls" (Raag and Rackliff 1998).

By kindergarten, most boys appear to have learned—either through experiences similar to my son's, where other male persons police the boundaries of gender-appropriate play and fantasy and/or by watching the clearly gendered messages of television advertising—that Barbie dolls are not appropriate toys for boys (Rogers 1999, 30). To avoid ridicule, they learn to hide their desire for Barbie, either through denial and oppositional/pollution discourse and/or through sublimation of their desire for Barbie into play with male-appropriate "action figures" (Pope et al. 1999). In their study of a kindergarten classroom, Jordan and Cowan (1995, 728) identified "warrior narratives . . . that assume that violence is legitimate and justified when it occurs within a struggle between good and evil" to be the most commonly agreed-upon currency for boys' fantasy play. They observe that the boys seem commonly to adapt story lines that they have seen on television. Popular culture—film, video, computer games, television, and comic books—provides boys with a seemingly endless stream of Good Guys versus Bad Guys characters and stories—from cowboy movies, Superman and Spiderman to Ninja Turtles, Star Wars, and Pokémon—that are available for the boys to appropriate as the raw materials for the construction of their own warrior play.

In the kindergarten that Jordan and Cowan studied, the boys initially attempted to import their warrior narratives into the domestic setting of the "Doll Corner." Teachers eventually drove the boys' warrior play outdoors, while the Doll Corner was used by the girls for the "appropriate" domestic play for which it was originally intended. Jordan and Cowan argue that kindergarten teachers' outlawing of boys' warrior narratives inside the classroom contributed to boys' defining schools as a feminine environment, to which they responded with a resistant, underground continuation of masculine warrior play. Eventually though, boys who acquiesce and successfully sublimate warrior play into fantasy or sport are more successful in constructing what Connell (1989, 291) calls "a masculinity organized around themes of rationality and responsibility [that is] closely connected with the 'certification' function of the upper levels of the education system and to a key form of masculinity among professionals."

In contrast to the "rational/professional" masculinity constructed in schools, the institution of sport historically constructs hegemonic masculinity as *bodily superiority* over femininity and nonathletic masculinities (Messner 1992). Here, warrior narratives are allowed to publicly thrive—indeed, are openly celebrated (witness, for instance, the commentary of a televised NFL [National Football League] football game or especially the spectacle of televised professional wrestling). Preschool boys and kindergartners seem already to know this, easily adopting aggressively competitive team names and an us-versus-them attitude. By contrast, many of the youngest girls appear to take two or three years in organized soccer before they adopt, or partially accommodate themselves to, aggressively competitive discourse, indicated by the 10-year-old girls' shifting away from the use of sweet names toward more power names. In short, where the gender regime of preschool and grade school may be experienced as an environment in which mostly women leaders enforce rules that are hostile to masculine fantasy play and physicality, the gender regime of sport is experienced as a place where masculine styles and values of physicality, aggression, and competition are enforced and celebrated by mostly male coaches.

A cultural analysis suggests that the boys' and the girls' previous immersion in differently gendered cultural experiences shaped the likelihood that they would derive and construct different meanings from Barbie—the girls through pleasurable and symbolically empowering identification with "girl power" narratives; the boys through oppositional fears of feminine pollution (and fears of displacement by girl power?) and with aggressively verbal, and eventually physical, invasions of the girls' ritual space. The boys' collective response thus constituted them differently, *as boys*, in opposition to the girls' constitution of themselves *as girls*. An individual girl or boy, in this moment, who may have felt an inclination to dissent from the dominant feelings of the group (say, the Latina Barbie Girl who, her mother later told me, did not want the group to be identified with Barbie, or a boy whose immediate inner response to the Barbie Girls' joyful celebration might be to join in) is most likely silenced into complicity in this powerful moment of border work.

What meanings did this highly gendered moment carry for the boys' and girls' teams in the ensuing soccer season? Although I did not observe the Barbie Girls after the opening ceremony, I did continue to observe the Sea Monsters' weekly practices and games. During the boys' ensuring season, gender never reached this "magnified" level of salience again—indeed, gender was rarely raised verbally or performed overtly by the boys. On two occasions, though, I observed the coach jokingly chiding the boys during practice that "if you don't watch out, I'm going to get the Barbie Girls here to play against you!" This warning was followed by gleeful screams of agony and fear, and nervous hopping around and hugging by some of the boys. Normally, though, in this sex-segregated, all-male context, if boundaries were invoked, they were not boundaries between boys and girls but boundaries between the Sea Monsters and other boys' teams, or sometimes age boundaries between the Sea Monsters and a small group of dads and older brothers who would engage them in a mock scrimmage during practice. But it was also evident that when the coach was having trouble getting the boys to act together, as a group, his strategic and humorous invocation of the dreaded Barbie Girls once again served symbolically to affirm their group status. They were a team. They were the boys.

CONCLUSION

The overarching goal of this article has been to take one empirical observation from everyday life and demonstrate how a multilevel (interactionist, structural, cultural) analysis might reveal various layers of meaning that give insight into the everyday social construction of gender. This article builds on observations made by Thorne (1993) concerning ways to approach sociological analyses of children's worlds. The most fruitful approach is not to ask why boys and girls are so different but rather to ask how and under what conditions boys and girls constitute themselves as separate, oppositional groups. Sociologists needs not debate whether gender is "there" — clearly, gender is always already there, built as it is into the structures, situations, culture, and consciousness of children and adults. The key issue is under what conditions it may be less salient. These are important questions, especially since the social organization of categorical gender difference has always been so clearly tied to gender hierarchy (Acker 1990; Lorber 1994). In the Barbie Girls versus Sea Monsters moment, the performance of gendered boundaries and the construction of boys' and girls' groups as categorically different occurred in the context of a situation systematically structured by sex segregation, sparked by the imposing presence of a shared cultural symbol that is saturated with gendered meanings, and actively supported and applauded by adults who basked in the pleasure of difference, reaffirmed.[6]

I have suggested that a useful approach to the study of such "how" and "under what conditions" questions is to employ multiple levels of analysis. At the most general level, this project supports the following working propositions.

Interactionist theoretical frameworks that emphasize the ways that social agents "perform" or "do" gender are most useful in describing how groups of people actively create (or at times disrupt) the boundaries that delineate seemingly categorical differences between male persons and female persons. In this case, we saw how the children and the parents interactively performed gender in a way that constructed an apparently natural boundary between the two separate worlds of the girls and the boys.

Structural theoretical frameworks that emphasize the ways that gender is built into institutions through hierarchical sexual divisions of labor are most useful in explaining under what conditions social agents mobilize variously to disrupt or to affirm gender differences and inequalities. In this case, we saw how the sexual division of labor among parent volunteers (grounded in their own histories in the gender regime of sport), the formal sex segregation of the children's leagues, and the structured context of the opening ceremony created conditions for possible interactions between girls' teams and boys' teams.

Cultural theoretical perspectives that examine how popular symbols that are injected into circulation by the culture industry are variously taken up by differently situated people are most useful in analyzing how the meanings of cultural symbols, in a given institutional context, might trigger or be taken up by social agents and used as resources to reproduce, disrupt, or contest binary conceptions of sex difference and gendered relations of power. In this case, we saw how a girls' team appropriated a large Barbie around which to construct a pleasurable and empowering sense of group identity and how the boys' team responded with aggressive denunciations of Barbie and invasions.

Utilizing any one of the above theoretical perspectives by itself will lead to a limited, even distorted, analysis of the social construction of gender. Together, they can illuminate the complex, multileveled architecture of the social construction of gender in everyday life. For heuristic reasons, I have falsely separated structure, interaction, and culture. In fact, we need to explore their constant interrelationships, continuities, and contradictions. For instance, we cannot understand the boys' aggressive denunciations and invasions of the girls' space and the eventual clarification of categorical boundaries between the girls and the boys without first understanding how these boys and girls have already internalized four or five years of "gendering" experiences that have shaped their interactional tendencies and how they are already immersed in a culture of gendered symbols, including Barbie and sports media imagery. Although "only" preschoolers, they are already skilled in collectively taking up symbols from popular culture as resources to be used in their own group dynamics—building individual and group identities, sharing the pleasures of play, clarifying boundaries between in-group and out-group members, and constructing hierarchies in their worlds.

Furthermore, we cannot understand the reason that the girls first chose "Barbie Girls" as their team name without first understanding the fact that a particular institutional structure of AYSO soccer preexisted the girls' entrée into the league. The informal sexual division of labor among adults, and the formal sex segregation of children's teams, is a preexisting gender regime that constrains and enables the ways that the children enact gender relations and construct identities. One concrete manifestation of this constraining nature of sex segregated teams is the choice of team names. It is reasonable to speculate that if the four- and five-year-old children were still sex integrated, as in the pre-1995 era, no team would have chosen "Barbie Girls" as its team name, with Barbie as its symbol. In other words, the formal sex segregation created the conditions under which the girls were enabled—perhaps encouraged— to choose a "sweet" team name that is widely read as encoding feminine meanings. The eventual interactions between the boys and the girls were made possible — although by no means fully determined — by the structure of the gender regime and by the cultural resources that the children variously drew on.

On the other hand, the gendered division of labor in youth soccer is not seamless, static, or immune to resistance. One of the few woman head coaches, a very active athlete in her own right, told me that she is "challenging the sexism" in AYSO by becoming the head of her son's league. As post–Title IX women increasingly become mothers and as media images of competent, heroic female athletes become more a part of the cultural landscape for children, the gender regimes of children's sports may be increasingly challenged (Dworkin and Messner 1999). Put another way, the dramatically shifting opportunity structure and cultural imagery of post–Title IX sports have created opportunities for new kinds of interactions, which will inevitably challenge and further shift institutional structures. Social structures simultaneously constrain and enable, while agency is simultaneously reproductive and resistant.

NOTES

1. Most of the structural inventory presented here is from a content analysis of the 1998–99 regional American Youth Soccer League (AYSO) yearbook, which features photos and names of all of the teams, coaches, and managers. I counted the number of adult men and women occupying various positions. In the three cases where the sex category of a name was not immediately obvious (e.g., Rene or Terry), or in the five cases where simply a last name was listed, I did not count it. I also used the AYSO yearbook for my analysis of the children's team names. To check for reliability, another sociologist independently read and coded the list of team names. There was disagreement on how to categorize only 2 of the 156 team names.

2. The existence of some women coaches and some men team managers in this AYSO organization manifests a less extreme sexual division of labor than that of the same community's Little League baseball organization, in which there are proportionally far fewer women coaches. Similarly, Saltzman Chafetz and Kotarba's (1999, 52) study of parental labor in support of Little League baseball in a middle-class Houston community revealed an apparently absolute sexual division of labor, where nearly all of the supportive "activities off the field were conducted by the women in the total absence of men, while activities on the field were conducted by men and boys in the absence of women." Perhaps youth soccer, because of its more recent (mostly post–Title IX) history in the United States, is a more contested gender regime than the more patriarchally entrenched youth sports like Little League baseball or youth football.

3. The four- and five-year-old kids' games and practices were absolutely homosocial in terms of the kids, due to the formal structural sex segregation. However, 8 of the 12 girls' teams at this age level had male coaches, and 2 of the 14 boys' teams had female coaches.

4. By 1994, more than 800 million Barbies had been sold worldwide. More than $1 billion was spent on Barbies and accessories in 1992 alone. Two Barbie dolls

were purchased every second in 1994, half of which were sold in the United States (DuCille 1994, 49).

5. Rogers (1999, 23) notes that if one extrapolates Barbie's bodily proportions to "real woman ones," she would be "33–18–31.5 and stand five feet nine inches tall, with fully half of her height accounted for by her 'shapely legs.' "

6. My trilevel analysis of structure, interaction, and culture may not be fully adequate to plumb the emotional depths of the magnified Barbie Girls versus Sea Monsters moment. Although it is beyond the purview of this article, an adequate rendering of the depths of pleasure and revulsion, attachment and separation, and commitment to ideologies of categorical sex difference may involve the integration of a fourth level of analysis: gender at the level of personality (Chodorow 1999). Object relations theory has fallen out of vogue in feminist sociology in recent years, but as Williams (1993) has argued, it might be most useful in revealing the mostly hidden social power of gender to shape people's unconscious predispositions to various structural contexts, cultural symbols, and interactional moments.

REFERENCES

Acker, Joan. 1990. Hierarchies, jobs, bodies: A theory of gendered organizations. *Gender & Society* 4:139–58.

Adler, Patricia A., and Peter Adler, 1998. *Peer power: Preadolescent culture and identity.* New Brunswick, NJ: Rutgers University Press.

Attfield, Judy. 1996. Barbie and Action Man: Adult toys for girls and boys, 1959–93. In *The gendered object*, edited by Pat Kirkham, 80–89. Manchester, UK, and New York: Manchester University Press.

Boyle, Maree, and Jim McKay. 1995. "You leave your troubles at the gate": A case study of the exploitation of older women's labor and "leisure" in sport. *Gender & Society* 9:556–76.

Bradbard, M. 1985. Sex differences in adults' gifts and children's toy requests. *Journal of Genetic Psychology* 145:283–84.

Butler, Judith. 1990. *Gender trouble: Feminism and the subversion of identity.* New York and London: Routledge.

Campenni, C. Estelle. 1999. Gender stereotyping of children's toys: A Comparison of parents and nonparents. *Sex Roles* 40:121–38.

Chodorow, Nancy J. 1999. *The power of feelings: Personal meanings in psychoanalysis, gender, and culture.* New Haven, CT, and London: Yale University Press.

Connell, R. W. 1987. *Gender and power.* Stanford, CA: Stanford University Press.

———. 1989. Cool guys, swots and wimps: The interplay of masculinity and education. *Oxford Review of Education* 15:291–303.

DuCille, Anne. 1994. Dyes and dolls: Multicultural Barbie and the merchandising of difference. *Differences: A Journal of Cultural Studies* 6:46–68.

Dworkin, Shari L., and Michael A. Messner. 1999. Just do . . . what?: Sport, bodies, gender. In *Revisioning gender*, edited by Myra Marx Ferree, Judith Lorber, and Beth B. Hess, 341–61. Thousand Oaks, CA: Sage.

Etaugh, C., and M. B. Liss. 1992. Home, school, and playroom: Training grounds for adult gender roles. *Sex Roles* 26:129–47.

Heywood, Leslie, and Jennifer Drake, Eds. 1997. *Third wave agenda: Being feminist, doing feminism*. Minneapolis: University of Minnesota Press.

Hochschild, Arlie Russell. 1994. The commercial spirit of intimate life and the abduction of feminism: Signs from women's advice books. *Theory, Culture & Society* 11:1–24.

Jordan, Ellen, and Angela Cowan. 1995. Warrior narratives in the kindergarten classroom: Renegotiating the social contract? *Gender & Society* 9:727–43.

Kessler, Suzanne J., and Wendy McKenna. 1978. *Gender: An ethnomethodological approach*. New York: John Wiley.

Klein, Melissa. 1997. Duality and redefinition: Young feminism and the alternative music community. In *Third wave agenda: Being feminist, doing feminism*, edited by Leslie Heywood and Jennifer Drake, 207–25. Minneapolis: University of Minnesota Press.

Lorber, Judith. 1994. *Paradoxes of gender*. New Haven, CT, and London: Yale University Press.

McGuffy, C. Shawn, and B. Lindsay Rich. 1999. Playing in the gender transgression zone: Race, class and hegemonic masculinity in middle childhood. *Gender & Society* 13:608–27.

Messner, Michael A. 1992. *Power at play: Sports and the problem of masculinity*. Boston: Beacon.

Pope, Harrison G., Jr., Roberto Olivarda, Amanda Gruber, and John Borowiecki. 1999. Evolving ideals of male body image as seen through action toys. *International Journal of Eating Disorders* 26:65–72.

Raag, Tarja, and Christine L. Rackliff. 1998. Preschoolers' awareness of social expectations of gender: Relationships to toy choices. *Sex Roles* 38:685–700.

Rand, Erica. 1998. Older heads on younger bodies. In *The children's culture reader*, edited by Henry Jenkins, 382–93. New York: New York University Press.

Risman, Barbara. 1998. *Gender vertigo: American families in transition*. New Haven and London: Yale University Press.

Robinson, C. C., and J. T. Morris, 1986. The gender-stereotyped nature of Christmas toys received by 36-, 48-, and 60-month-old children: A comparison between non-requested vs. requested toys. *Sex roles* 15:21–32.

Rogers, Mary F. 1999. *Barbie culture*. Thousand Oaks, CA: Sage.

Saltzman Chafetz, Janet, and Joseph A. Kotarba. 1999. Little League mothers and the reproduction of gender. In *Inside sports*, edited by Jay Coakley and Peter Donnelly, 46–54. London and New York: Routledge.

Seiter, Ellen. 1995. *Sold separately: Parents and children in consumer culture*. New Brunswick, NJ: Rutgers University Press.

Spigel, Lynn. Forthcoming. Barbies without Ken: Femininity, feminism and the art-culture system. In *Sitting room only: Television, consumer culture and the suburban home*, edited by Lynn Spigel. Durham, NC: Duke University Press.

Thorne, Barrie. 1993. *Gender play: Girls and boys in school*. New Brunswick, NJ: Rutgers University Press.

Walters, Suzanna Danuta. 1999. Sex, text, and context: (In) between feminism and cultural studies. In *Revisioning gender*, edited by Myra Marx Ferree, Judith Lorber, and Beth B. Hess, 222–57. Thousand Oaks, CA: Sage.

West, Candace, and Don Zimmerman. 1987. Doing gender. *Gender & Society* 1:125–51.

Williams, Christine. 1993. Psychoanalytic theory and the sociology of gender. In *Theory on gender, gender on theory*, edited by Paula England, 131–49. New York: Aldine.

MICHAEL MESSNER AND JEFFREY MONTEZ DE OCA

The Male Consumer as Loser: Beer and Liquor Ads in Mega Sports Media Events

Michael Messner is Professor of Sociology and Gender Studies at the University of Southern California, and Jeffrey Montez de Oca is Professor of Sociology at DePauw University. Their fields of research include the social construction of gender and sport, and this essay was first published in 2005 in Signs: Journal of Women in Culture and Society.

The historical development of modern men's sport has been closely intertwined with the consumption of alcohol and with the financial promotion and sponsorship provided by beer and liquor producers and distributors, as well as pubs and bars (Collins and Vamplew 2002). The beer and liquor industry plays a key economic role in commercialized college and professional sports (Zimbalist 1999; Sperber 2000). Liquor industry advertisements heavily influence the images of masculinity promoted in sports broadcasts and magazines (Wenner 1991). Alcohol consumption is also often a key aspect of the more dangerous and violent dynamics at the heart of male sport cultures (Curry 2000; Sabo, Gray, and Moore 2000). By itself, alcohol does not "cause" men's violence against women or against other men; however, it is commonly one of a cluster of factors that facilitate violence (Koss and Gaines 1993; Leichliter et al. 1998). In short, beer and liquor are central players in "a high holy trinity of alcohol, sports, and hegemonic masculinity" (Wenner 1998).

This article examines beer and liquor advertisements in two "mega sports media events" consumed by large numbers of boys and men—the 2002 and 2003 Super Bowls and the 2002 and 2003 *Sports Illustrated* swimsuit issues. Our goal is to illuminate tropes of masculinity that prevail in those ads. We see these ads as establishing a pedagogy of youthful masculinity that does not passively teach male consumers about the qualities of their products so much as it encourages consumers to think of their products as essential to creating a stylish and desirable lifestyle. These ads do more than just dupe consumers into product loyalty; they also work with consumers to construct a consumption-based masculine identity relevant to contemporary social conditions. Drawing on insights from feminist cultural studies (Walters 1999), we argue that these gendered tropes watched by tens of millions of boys and men offer a window through which we can broaden our understanding of contemporary continuities, shifts, and strains in the social construction of masculinities.

GENDER, MEN'S SPORTS, AND ALCOHOL ADS

Although marketing beer and liquor to men is not new, the imagery that advertisers employ to pitch their product is not static either. Our analysis of past Super Bowls and *Sports Illustrated* beer and liquor ads suggests shifting patterns in the gender themes encoded in the ads. Consistently, over time, the ads attempt not to simply "plug" a particular product but to situate products within a larger historically specific way of life. Beer and liquor advertisers normally do not create product differentiation through typical narratives of crisis and resolution in which the product is the rescuing hero. Instead, they paint a series of images that evoke feelings, moods, and ways of being. In short, beer and liquor advertising engages in "lifestyle branding." Rather than simply attaching a name to a product, the brand emanates from a series of images that construct a plausible and desirable world to consumers. Lifestyle branding—more literary and evocative than simple crisis/resolution narratives—theorizes the social location of target populations and constructs a desiring subject whose consumption patterns can be massaged in specific directions. As we shall see, the subject constructed by the beer and liquor ads that we examined is an overtly gendered subject.

Beer and alcohol advertising construct a "desirable lifestyle" in relation to contemporary social conditions, including shifts and tensions in the broader gender order. Ads from the late 1950s through the late 1960s commonly depicted young or middle-aged white heterosexual couples happily sharing a cold beer in their suburban backyards, in their homes, or in an outdoor space like a park.

In these ads, the beer is commonly displayed in a clear glass, its clean, fresh appearance perhaps intended to counter the reputation of beer as a working-class male drink. Beer in these ads symbolically unites the prosperous and happy postwar middle-class couple. By the mid-1970s, women as wives and partners largely disappeared from beer ads. Instead of showing heterosexual couples drinking in their homes or backyards, these ads began primarily to depict images of men drinking with other men in public spaces. Three studies of beer commercials of the 1970s and 1980s found that most ads pitched beer to men as a pleasurable reward for a hard day's work. These ads told men that "For all you do, this Bud's for you." Women were rarely depicted in these ads, except as occasional background props in male-dominated bars (Postman et al. 1987; Wenner 1991; Strate 1992).

The 1950s and 1960s beer ads that depicted happy married suburban couples were part of a moment in gender relations tied to postwar culture and Fordist relations of production. White, middle-class, heterosexual masculinity was defined as synonymous with the male breadwinner, in symmetrical relation to a conception of femininity grounded in the image of the suburban housewife. In the 1970s and early 1980s, the focus on men's laboring bodies, tethered to their public leisure with other men, expressed an almost atavistic view of hegemonic masculinity at a time when women were moving into public life in huge numbers and blue-collar men's jobs were being eliminated by the tens of thousands.

Both the postwar and the postindustrial ads provide a gendered pedagogy for living a masculine lifestyle in a shifting context characterized by uncertainty. In contrast to the depiction of happy white families comfortably living lives of suburban bliss, the postwar era was characterized by anxieties over the possibility of a postwar depression, nuclear annihilation, suburban social dislocation, and disorder from racial and class movements for social justice (Lipsitz 1981; May 1988; Spigel 1992). Similarly, the 1970s and 1980s beer ads came in the wake of the defeat of the United States in the Vietnam War, the 1972 gas crisis, the collapse of Fordism, and the turbulence in gender relations brought on by the women's and gay/lesbian liberation movements. All of these social ruptures contributed to produce an anxious white male subject (Connell 1995; Lipsitz 1998). Therefore, there is a sort of crisis/resolution narrative in these beer ads: the "crisis" lies broadly in the construction of white masculinities in the latter half of the twentieth century (Kimmel 1987), and the resolution lies in the construction of a lifestyle outside of immediate anxieties. The advertisements do not straightforwardly tell consumers to buy; rather, they teach consumers how to live a happy, stress-free life that includes regular (if not heavy) consumption of alcoholic beverages.

The 2002 and 2003 ads that we examine here primarily construct a white male "loser" whose life is apparently separate from paid labor. He hangs out with his male buddies, is self-mocking and ironic about his loser status, and is always at the ready to engage in voyeurism with sexy fantasy women but holds committed relationships and emotional honesty with real women in disdain. To the extent that these themes find resonance with young men of today, it is likely because they speak to basic insecurities that are grounded in a combination of historic shifts: deindustrialization, the declining real value of wages and the male breadwinner role, significant cultural shifts brought about by more than three decades of struggle by feminists and sexual minorities, and challenges to white male supremacy by people of color and by immigrants. This cluster of social changes has destabilized hegemonic masculinity and defines the context of gender relations in which today's young men have grown toward adulthood.

In theorizing how the loser motif in beer and liquor ads constructs a version of young white masculinity, we draw on Mikhail Bakhtin's (1981) concept of the chronotope. This is especially relevant in analyzing how lifestyle branding goes beyond the reiteration of a name to actually creating desirable and believable worlds in which consumers are beckoned to place themselves.

The term *chronotope*—literally meaning "time-space"—describes how time and space fuse in literature to create meaningful structures separate from the text and its representations (Bakhtin 1981). The ads that we looked at consistently construct a leisure-time lifestyle of young men meeting in specific sites of sports and alcohol consumption: bars, television rooms, and stadiums. This meeting motif gives a temporal and spatial plane to male fantasy where desire can be explored and symbolic boundaries can simultaneously be transgressed and reinscribed into the social world.

Two Mega Sports Media Events

This article brings focus to the commercial center of sports media by examining the gender and sexual imagery encoded in two mega sports media events: the 2002 and 2003 Super Bowls and the 2002 and 2003 *Sports Illustrated* swimsuit issues. (See the appendix for a complete list of the ads and commercials.)[1]

Mega sports media events are mediated cultural rituals (Dayan and Katz 1988) that differ from everyday sports media events in several key ways: sports media actively build audience anticipation and excitement throughout the year for these single events; the Super Bowl and the swimsuit issue are each preceded by major pre-event promotion and hype—from the television network that will broadcast the Super Bowl to *Sports Illustrated* and myriad other print and electronic media; the Super Bowl and the swimsuit issue are used as marketing tools for selling the more general products of National Football League (NFL) games and *Sports Illustrated* magazine subscriptions; the Super Bowl and the swimsuit issue each generate significant spin-off products (e.g., videos, books, "making of" TV shows, calendars, frequently visited Web pages); the Super Bowl and the swimsuit issue generate significantly larger audiences than does a weekly NFL game or a weekly edition of *Sports Illustrated*; and advertisements are usually created specifically for these mega sports media events and cost more to run than do ads in a weekly NFL game or a weekly edition of *Sports Illustrated*.

To be sure, the Super Bowl and the *Sports Illustrated* swimsuit issue are different in some fundamental ways. First, the Super Bowl is a televised event,

---

[1] We first conducted a content analysis of the Super Bowl tapes and the *Sports Illustrated* swimsuit issues to determine how many beer and liquor ads there were and where they were placed in the texts. Next, we employed textual analysis to identify common thematic patterns in the ads. We also sought to identify tensions, discontinuities, and contradictory gender themes in the ads. Finally, we examined the ways that the advertisements meshed with, respectively, the actual Super Bowl football game broadcast and the *Sports Illustrated* swimsuit issue text. We sought to understand how the intertextual cross-referencing of beer and liquor ads' gender themes with the game or the swimsuit models might variously create tensions in the dominant gender codings of the texts, reinforce these tensions, or both. In the absence of a systematic study of the various ways that audiences interpret and use these texts, our textual analysis is obviously limited.

while the swimsuit issue is a print event. Second, the Super Bowl is an actual sporting contest, while the swimsuit issue is a departure from *Sports Illustrated's* normal coverage of sports. However, for our purposes, we see these two events as comparable, partly because they are mega sports media events but also because their ads target young males who consume sports media.

SUPER BOWL ADS

Since its relatively modest start in 1967, the NFL Super Bowl has mushroomed into one of the most expensive and most watched annual media events in the United States, with a growing world audience (Martin and Reeves 2001), the vast majority of whom are boys and men. Increasingly over the past decade, Super Bowl commercials have been specially created for the event. Newspapers, magazines, television news shows, and Web sites now routinely run pre–Super Bowl stories that focus specifically on the ads, and several media outlets run post–Super Bowl polls to determine which ads were the most and least favorite. Postgame lists of "winners" and "losers" focus as much on the corporate sponsors and their ads as on the two teams that—incidentally?—played a football game between the commercials.

Fifty-five commercials ran during the 2003 Super Bowl (not counting pregame and postgame shows), at an average cost of $2.1 million for each thirty-second ad. Fifteen of these commercials were beer or malt liquor ads. Twelve of these ads were run by Anheuser-Busch, whose ownership of this Super Bowl was underlined at least twenty times throughout the broadcast, when, after commercial breaks, the camera lingered on the stadium score-board, atop which was a huge Budweiser sign. On five other occasions, "Bud" graphics appeared on the screen after commercial breaks, as voice-overs reminded viewers that the Super Bowl was "brought to" them by Budweiser. This represented a slight increase in beer advertising since the 2002 Super Bowl, which featured thirteen beer or malt liquor commercials (eleven of them by Anheuser-Busch), at an average cost of $1.9 million per thirty-second ad. In addition to the approximately $31.5 million that the beer companies paid for the 2003 Super Bowl ad slots, they paid millions more creating and testing those commercials with focus groups. There were 137.7 million viewers watching all or part of the 2003 Super Bowl on ABC, and by far the largest demographic group watching was men, aged twenty-five to fifty-five.

Sports Illustrated *Swimsuit Issue Ads*

Sports Illustrated began in 1964 to publish an annual February issue that featured five or six pages of women modeling swimsuits, embedded in an otherwise normal sixty-four-page magazine (Davis 1997). This modest format continued until the late 1970s, when the portion of the magazine featuring swimsuit models began gradually to grow. In the 1980s, the swimsuit issue morphed into a special issue in which normal sports coverage gradually disappeared. During this decade, the issue's average length had grown to 173 pages, 20 percent of which were focused on swimsuit models. By the 1990s the swimsuit issue averaged 207 pages in length, 31 percent of which featured swimsuit models. The magazine has continued to grow in recent years. The 2003 issue was 218 pages in length, 59 percent of which featured swimsuit models. The dramatic growth in the size of the swimsuit issue in the 1990s, as well as the dropping of pretence that the swimsuit issue had anything to do with normal "sports journalism," were facilitated by advertising that began cleverly to echo and spoof the often highly sexualized swimsuit imagery in the magazine. By 2000, it was more the rule than the exception when an ad in some way utilized the swimsuit theme. The gender and sexual themes of the swimsuit issue became increasingly seamless, as ads and *Sports Illustrated* text symbiotically echoed and played off of each other. The 2002 swimsuit issue included seven pages of beer ads and seven pages of liquor ads, which cost approximately $230,000 per full page to run. The 2003 swimsuit issue ran the equivalent of sixteen pages of beer ads and thirteen pages of liquor ads. The ad space for the 2003 swimsuit issue sold for $266,000 per full-page color ad.

The millions of dollars that beer and liquor companies spent to develop and buy space for these ads were aimed at the central group that reads the magazine: young and middle-aged males. *Sports Illustrated* estimates the audience size of its weekly magazine at 21.3 million readers, roughly 76 percent of whom are males.[2] Nearly half of the male audience is in the coveted eighteen-to thirty-four-year-old demographic group, and three quarters of the male *Sports Illustrated* audience is between the ages of eighteen and forty-nine. A much larger number of single-copy sales gives the swimsuit issue a much larger audience, conservatively estimated at more than 30 million readers.[3]

The Super Bowl and the *Sports Illustrated* swimsuit issue are arguably the biggest single electronic and print sports media events annually in the United States. Due to their centrality, size, and target audiences, we suggest that mega sports media events such as the Super Bowl and the swimsuit issue offer a magnified view of the dominant gender and sexual imagery emanating from the center of the sports-media-commercial complex. Our concern is not simply to describe the stereotypes of masculinity and femininity in these ads; rather, we use these ads as windows into the ways that cultural capitalism constructs

---

[2]*Sports Illustrated*'s rate card claims 3,137,523 average weekly subscribers and additional single-copy sales of 115,337. The company then uses a multiplier of 6.55 readers per issue to estimate the total size of its audience at 21,306,468.

[3]In addition to *Sports Illustrated*'s 3,137,523 average weekly subscribers, the company's rate card claims 1,467,228 single copy sales of the swimsuit issue. According to the same multiplier of 6.55 readers per magazine that *Sports Illustrated* uses for estimating the total size of its weekly audience, the swimsuit issue audience is over 30 million. More than likely, the multiplier for the swimsuit issue is higher than that of the weekly magazine, so the swimsuit issue audience is probably much larger than 30 million.

gender relationally, as part of a general lifestyle. In this article, we will employ thick description of ads to illuminate the four main gender relations themes that we saw in the 2002 and 2003 ads, and we will follow with a discussion of the process through which these themes are communicated: erotic and often humorous intertextual referencing. We will end by discussing some of the strains and tensions in the ads' major tropes of masculinity.

LOSERS AND BUDDIES, HOTTIES AND BITCHES

In the 2002 and 2003 beer and liquor ads that we examined, men's work worlds seem mostly to have disappeared. These ads are less about drinking and leisure as a reward for hard work and more about leisure as a lifestyle in and of itself. Men do not work in these ads; they recreate. And women are definitely back in the picture, but not as wives who are partners in building the good domestic life. It is these relations among men as well as relations between men and women that form the four dominant gender themes in the ads we examined. We will introduce these four themes by describing a 2003 Super Bowl commercial for Bud Lite beer.

Two young, somewhat nerdy-looking white guys are at a yoga class, sitting in the back of a room full of sexy young women. The two men have attached prosthetic legs to their bodies so that they can fake the yoga moves. With their bottles of Bud Lite close by, these voyeurs watch in delight as the female yoga teacher instructs the class to "relax and release that negative energy . . . inhale, arch, *thrust* your pelvis to the sky and exhale, *release* into the stretch." As the instructor uses her hands to push down on a woman's upright spread-eagled legs and says "focus, focus, focus," the camera (serving as prosthesis for male spectators at home) cuts back and forth between close-ups of the women's breasts and bottoms, while the two guys gleefully enjoy their beer and their sexual voyeurism. In the final scene the two guys are standing outside the front door of the yoga class, beer bottles in hand, and someone throws their fake legs out the door at them. As they duck to avoid being hit by the legs, one of them comments, "*She's* not very relaxed" (fig. 1).

We begin with this ad because it contains, in various degrees, the four dominant gender themes that we found in the mega sports media events ads:

1. Losers: Men are often portrayed as chumps, losers. Masculinity— especially for the lone man—is precarious. Individual men are always on the cusp of being publicly humiliated, either by their own stupidity, by other men, or worse, by a beautiful woman.

2. Buddies: The precariousness of individual men's masculine status is offset by the safety of the male group. The solidity and primacy— and emotional safety—of male friendships are the emotional center of many of these ads.

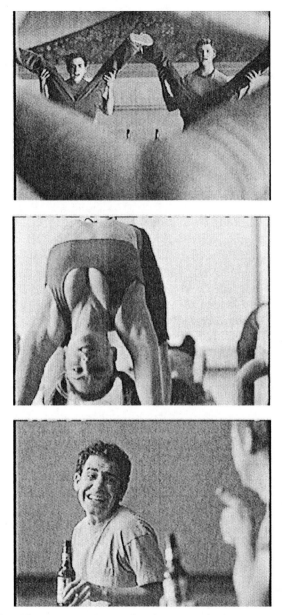

FIGURE 1 Budweiser, "Yoga Voyeurs," Anheuser-Busch, 2003 Super Bowl on ABC.

3. Hotties: When women appear in these ads, it is usually as highly sex-ualized fantasy objects. These beautiful women serve as potential prizes for men's victories and proper consumption choices. They sometimes serve to validate men's masculinity, but their validating power also holds the potential to humiliate male losers.

4. Bitches: Wives, girlfriends, or other women to whom men are emotionally committed are mostly absent from these ads. However, when they do appear, it is primarily as emotional or sexual blackmailers who threaten to undermine individual men's freedom to enjoy the erotic pleasure at the center of the male group.

To a great extent, these four gender themes are intertwined in the Super Bowl "Yoga Voyeurs" ad. First, the two guys are clearly not good-looking, high-status, muscular icons of masculinity. More likely they are intended to represent the "everyman" with whom many boys and men can identify. Their masquerade as sensitive men allows them to transgress the female space of the yoga class, but they cannot pull the masquerade off and are eventually "outed" as losers and rejected by the sexy women. But even if they realize that they are losers, they do not have to care because they are so happy and secure in their bond with each other. Their friendship bond is cemented in frat-boy-style hijinks that allow them to share close-up voyeurism of sexy women who, we can safely assume, are way out of these men's league. In the end, the women reject the guys as pathetic losers. But the guys do not seem too upset. They have each other and, of course, they have their beers.

Rarely did a single ad in our study contain all four of these themes. But taken together, the ads show enough consistency that we can think of these themes as intertwined threads that together make up the ideological fabric at the center of mega sports media events. Next, we will illustrate how these themes are played out in the 2002 and 2003 ads, before discussing some of the strains and tensions in the ads.

REAL FRIENDS, SCARY WOMEN

Five twenty-something white guys are sitting around a kitchen table playing poker. They are laughing, seemingly having the time of their lives, drinking Jim Beam whiskey. The caption for this ad reflects the lighthearted, youthful mood of the group: "Good Bourbon, ice cubes, and whichever glasses are clean." This ad, which appeared in the 2002 *Sports Illustrated* swimsuit issue, is one in a series of Jim Beam ads that have run for the past few years in *Sports Illustrated* and in other magazines aimed at young men.[4] Running under the umbrella slogan of "Real Friends, Real Bourbon," these Jim Beam ads hail a white, college-age (or young college-educated) crowd of men with the appeal of playful male bonding through alcohol consumption in bars or pool halls. The main theme is the safety and primacy of the male group, but the

---

[4]Most of the Jim Beam "Real Friends" ads discussed here did not appear in the two *Sports Illustrated* swimsuit issues on which we focus. However, it enhances our understanding of the gender themes in the Jim Beam ads to examine the thematic consistencies in the broader series of Jim Beam "Real Friends" ads.

accompanying written text sometimes suggests the presence of women. In one ad, four young white guys partying up a storm together and posing with arms intertwined are accompanied by the caption, "Unlike your girlfriend, they never ask where this relationship is going." These ads imply that women demand levels of emotional commitment and expression undesirable to men, while life with the boys (and the booze) is exciting, emotionally comfortable, and safe. The comfort that these ads suggest is that bonding and intimacy have clear (though mostly unspoken) boundaries that limit emotional expression in the male group. When drinking with the guys, a man can feel close to his friends, perhaps even drape an arm over a friend's shoulder, embrace him, or tell him that he loves him. But the context of alcohol consumption provides an escape hatch that contains and rationalizes the eruption of physical intimacy.

Although emotional closeness with and commitment to real women apparently are to be avoided, these ads also do suggest a role for women. The one ad in the Jim Beam series that includes an image of a woman depicts only a body part (*Sports Illustrated* ran this one in its 2000 swimsuit issue in 3-D). Four guys drinking together in a bar are foregrounded by a set of high-heeled legs that appear to be an exotic dancer's. The guys drink, laugh, and seem thoroughly amused with each other. "Our lives would make a great sitcom," the caption reads, and continues, "of course, it would have to run on cable." That the guys largely ignore the dancer affirms the strength and primacy of their bond with one another—they do not need her or any other women, the ad seems to say. On the other hand—and just as in the "Yoga Voyeurs" commercial—the female dancer's sexualizing of the chronotopic space affirms that the bond between the men is safely within the bounds of heterosexuality.

Although these ads advocate keeping one's emotional distance from women, a commitment to heterosexuality always carries the potential for developing actual relationships with women. The few ads that depict real women portray them consistently as signs of danger to individual men and to the male group. The ads imply that what men really want is sex (or at least titillation), a cold beer, and some laughs with the guys. Girlfriends and wives are undesirable because they push men to talk about feelings and demonstrate commitment to a relationship. In "Good Listener," a 2003 Super Bowl ad for Budweiser, a young white guy is sitting in a sports bar with his girlfriend while she complains about her best friend's "totally self-centered and insensitive boyfriend." As he appears to listen to this obviously boring "girl talk," the camera pulls to a tight close-up on her face. She is reasonably attractive, but the viewer is not supposed to mistake her for one of the model-perfect fantasy women in other beer ads. The close-up reveals that her teeth are a bit crooked, her hair a bit stringy, and her face contorts as she says of her girlfriend that "she has these *emotional* needs he can't meet." Repelled, the guy spaces out and begins to peer over her shoulder at the television. The camera takes the guy's point of view and focuses on the football game while the speaking woman is in the fuzzy margins of his view. The girlfriend's monologue gets transposed by a football announcer describing an exciting run. She stops talking, and just in time his gaze shifts back to her eyes. She lovingly says, "You're such a great listener." With an "aw-shucks" smile, he says "thanks," and the "Budweiser TRUE" logo appears on the screen (fig. 2). These ads suggest that a sincere face and a bottle of beer allow a guy to escape the emotional needs of his partner while retaining regular access to sex. But the apparent dangers of love, long-term commitment, and marriage remain. The most overtly misogynist ad in the 2003 Super Bowl broadcast was "Sarah's Mom." While talking on the phone to a friend, a young, somewhat nerdy-looking white guy prepares to meet his girlfriend's mother for the first time. His friend offers him this stern advice: "Well, get a good look at her. 'Cause in twenty years, that's what Sarah's gonna look like." The nerd expresses surprised concern, just as there is a knock on the door. Viewed through the door's peephole, the face of Sarah's mother appears as young and beautiful as Sarah's, but it turns out that Sarah's mother has grotesquely large hips, thighs, and buttocks. The commercial ends with the screen filled mostly with the hugeness of the mother's bottom, her leather pants audibly stretching as she bends to pet the dog, and Sarah shoveling chips and dip into her mouth, as she says of her mother, "Isn't she incredible?" The guy replies, with obvious skepticism, "yeah" (fig. 3).

The message to boys and men is disturbing. If you are nerdy enough to be thinking about getting married, then you should listen to your male friends' warnings about what to watch out for and what is important. If you have got to have a wife, make sure that she is, and always will be, conventionally thin and beautiful.

In beer ads, the male group defines men's need for women as sexual, not emotional, and in so doing it constructs women as either whores or bitches and then suggests ways for men to negotiate the tension between these two narrow and stereotypical categories of women. This, we think, is a key point of tension that beer and liquor companies are attempting to exploit to their advantage. They do so by creating a curious shift away from the familiar "madonna-whore" dichotomy of which Western feminists have been so critical, where wives/mothers/girlfriends are put on a pedestal and the women one has sex with are put in the gutter. The alcohol industry would apparently prefer that young men not think of women as madonnas. After all, wives and girlfriends to whom men are committed, whom they respect and love, often do place limits on men's time spent out with the boys, as well as limits on men's consumption of alcohol. The industry seems to know this: as long as men remain distrustful of women, seeing them either as bitches who are trying to ensnare them and take away their freedom or as whores with whom they can party and have sex with no emotional commitment attached, then men remain more open to the marketing strategies of the industry.

· · ·

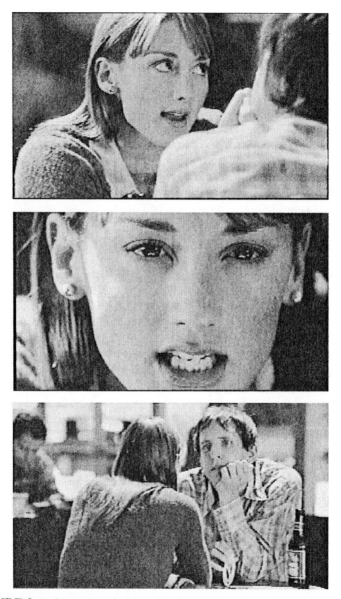

FIGURE 2 Bud Lite, "Good Listener," Anheuser-Busch, 2003 Super Bowl on ABC.

FIGURE 3 Bud Lite, "Sarah's Mom," Anheuser–Busch, 2003 Super Bowl on ABC.

REVENGE OF THE REGULAR GUYS

If losers are used in some of these ads to clarify the bounds of masculine normality, this is not to say that hypermasculine men are set up as the norm. To the contrary, overly masculine men, muscle men, and men with big cars who flash their money around are often portrayed as the real losers, against whom regular guys can sometimes turn the tables and win the beautiful women. In the ads we examined, however, this "regular guy wins beautiful fantasy woman" outcome was very rare. Instead, when the regular guy does manage to get the beautiful fantasy woman's attention, it is usually not in the way that he imagined or dreamed. A loser may want to win the attention of—and have sex with—beautiful women. But ultimately, these women are unavailable to a loser; worse, they will publicly humiliate him if he tries to win their attention. But losers can always manage to have another beer.

If white-guy losers risk punishment or humiliation from beautiful women in these ads, the level of punishment faced by black men can be even more severe. Although nearly all of the television commercials and print ads that we examined depict white people, a very small number do focus centrally on African Americans.[5] In "Pick-Up Lines," a Bud Lite ad that ran during the 2002 Super Bowl, two black males are sitting at a bar next to an attractive black female. Paul, the man in the middle, is obviously a loser; he's wearing a garish shirt, and his hair looks like an Afro gone terribly wrong. He sounds a bit whiny as he confides in his male friend, "I'm just not good with the ladies like you, Cedric." Cedric, playing Cyrano de Bergerac, whispers opening pickup lines to him. The loser turns to the woman and passes on the lines. But just then, the bartender brings another bottle of beer to Cedric, who asks the bartender, "So, how much?" Paul, thinking that this is his next pickup line, says to the woman, "So, how much?" Her smile turns to an angry frown, and she delivers a vicious kick to Paul's face, knocking him to the floor. After we see the Budweiser logo and hear the voice-over telling us that Bud Lite's great taste "will never let you down," we see a stunned Paul rising to his knees and trying to pull himself up to his bar stool, but the woman knocks him down again with a powerful backhand fist to the face (fig. 4).

This Bud Lite "Pick-Up Lines" ad—one of the very few ads that depict relations between black men and black women—was the only ad in which we saw a man being physically beaten by a woman. Here, the African American

---

[5] Of the twenty-six beer and malt liquor ads in the two Super Bowls, twenty-four depicted people. Among the twenty-four ads that depicted people, eighteen depicted white people only, three depicted groups that appear to be of mixed race, and three focused on African American main characters. Thirteen of the twenty-four beer and liquor ads in the two *Sports Illustrated* swimsuit issues depicted people: twelve depicted white people only, and one depicted what appears to be the silhouette of an African American couple. No apparent Latino/as or Asian Americans appeared in any of the magazine or television ads.

FIGURE 4 Bud Lite, "Pick-Up Lines," Anheuser-Busch, 2002 Super Bowl on ABC.

woman as object turns to subject, inflicting direct physical punishment on the African American man. The existence of these very few "black ads" brings into relief something that might otherwise remain hidden: most of these ads construct a youthful white masculinity that is playfully self-mocking, always a bit tenuous, but ultimately lovable. The screwups that white-guy losers make are forgivable, and we nearly always see these men, in the end, with at least a cold beer in hand. By contrast, the intersection of race, gender, and class creates cultural and institutional contexts of suspicion and punishment for African American boys and men (Ferguson 2000). In the beer ads this translates into the message that a black man's transgressions are apparently deserving of a kick to the face.

EROTIC INTERTEXTUALITY

One of the dominant strategies in beer and liquor ads is to create an (often humorous) erotic tension among members of a "threesome": the male reader/ viewer, a woman depicted as a sexy fantasy object, and a bottle of cold beer. This tension is accomplished through intertextual referencing between the advertising text and the sport text. For instance, on returning to live coverage of the Super Bowl from a commercial break, the camera regularly lingered on the stadium scoreboard, above which was a huge Budweiser sign. One such occasion during the 2003 Super Bowl was particularly striking. Coors had just run its only commercial (an episode from its successful "Twins" series) during this mega sports media event that seemed otherwise practically owned by Anheuser-Busch. Immediately on return from the commercial break to live action, the handheld field-level camera focused one by one on dancing cheer-leaders (once coming so close that it appears that the camera bumped into one of the women's breasts), all the while keeping the Budweiser sign in focus in the background. It was almost as though the producers of the Super Bowl were intent on not allowing the Coors "twins" to upstage Anheuser-Busch's ownership of the event.

Omnipresent advertising images in recent years have continued to obliterate the already blurry distinction between advertising texts and other media texts (Goldman and Papson 1996). This is surely true in the world of sport: players' uniforms, stadium walls, the corner of one's television screen, and even moments within telecasts are regularly branded with the Nike swoosh or some other corporate sign. Stephanie O'Donohoe argues that "popular texts have 'leaky boundaries,' flowing into each other and everyday life. . . . This seems especially true of advertising" (1997, 257–58). The "leakiness" of cultural signs in advertising is facilitated, O'Donohoe argues, "by increasing institutional ties between advertising, commercial media, and mass entertainment. . . . Conglomeration breeds intertextuality" (257–58). When ads appropriate or make explicit reference to other media (e.g., other ads, celebrities, movies, television shows, or popular music), they engage in what Robert Goldman and Stephen Papson call "cultural cannibalism" (1998, 10). Audiences are then invited to make the connections between the advertised product and the cultural meanings implied by the cannibalized sign; in so doing, the audience becomes "the final author, whose participation is essential" (O'Donohoe 1997, 259). As with all textual analyses that do not include an audience study, we must be cautious in inferring how differently situated audiences might variously take up, and draw meanings from, these ads. However, we suspect that experiences of "authorship" in the process of decoding and drawing intertextual connections are a major part of the pleasure of viewing mass media texts.

The 2002 and 2003 *Sports Illustrated* swimsuit issues offer vivid examples of texts that invite the reader to draw intertextual connections between erotically charged ads and other non-ad texts. Whereas in the past the *Sports Illustrated* swimsuit issue ran ads that were clearly distinct from the swimsuit text, it has recently become more common for the visual themes in the ads and the swimsuit text to be playfully intertwined, symbiotically referencing each other. A 2003 Heineken ad shows a close-up of two twenty-four-ounce "keg cans" of Heineken beer, side by side.

The text above the two cans reads, "They're big. And yeah, they're real." As if the reference to swimsuit models' breast size (and questions about whether some of the models have breast implants) were perhaps too subtle, *Sports Illustrated* juxtaposed the ad with a photo of a swimsuit model, wearing a suit that liberally exposed her breasts.

For the advertisers and for *Sports Illustrated*, the payoff for this kind of intertextual coordination is probably large: for the reader, the text of the swimsuit issue becomes increasingly seamless, as ads and swimsuit text melt into each other, playfully, humorously, and erotically referencing each other. As with the Super Bowl ads, the *Sports Illustrated* swimsuit issue ads become something that viewers learn not to ignore or skip over; instead, the ads become another part of the pleasure of consuming and imagining.

In 2003, Miller Brewing Company and *Sports Illustrated* further developed the symbiotic marketing strategy that they had introduced in 2002. The 2003 swimsuit issue featured a huge Miller Lite ad that included the equivalent of fourteen full pages of ad text. Twelve of these pages were a large, pull-out poster, one side of which was a single photo of "Sophia," a young model wearing a bikini with the Miller Lite logo on the right breast cup. On the opposite side of the poster were four one-page photos and one two-page photo of Sophia posing in various bikinis, with Miller Lite bottles and/or logos visible in each picture. As it did in the 2002 ad, Miller invites viewers to enter a contest to win a trip to the next *Sports Illustrated* swimsuit issue photo shoot. The site of the photo shoot fuses the text-based space of the magazine with the real space of the working models in exotic, erotic landscapes of desire that highlight the sexuality of late capitalist colonialism (Davis 1997). The accompanying text invites the reader to "visit http://www.cnnsi.com" to "check out a 360 degree view of the *Sports Illustrated* swimsuit photo shoot." And the text accompanying most of the photos of Sophia and bottles of Miller Lite teasingly encourages the reader to exercise his consumer power: "So if you had to make a choice, which one would it be?"

This expansive ad evidences a multilevel symbiosis between *Sports Illustrated* and Miller Brewing Company. The playful tease to "choose your favorite" (model, swimsuit, and/or beer) invites the reader to enter another medium—the *Sports Illustrated* swimsuit Web site, which includes access to a *Sports Illustrated* swimsuit photo shoot video sponsored by Miller. The result is a multifaceted media text that stands out as something other than mere advertisement and other than business-as-usual *Sports Illustrated* text. It has an erotic and commercial charge to it that simultaneously teases the reader as a sexual voyeur and hails him as an empowered consumer who can freely choose his own beer and whichever sexy woman he decides is his "favorite."

"LIFE IS HARSH": MALE LOSERS AND ALCOHOLIC ACCOMMODATION

In recent years, the tendency in the *Sports Illustrated* swimsuit issue to position male readers as empowered individuals who can "win" or freely choose the sexy fantasy object of their dreams has begun to shift in other directions. To put it simply, many male readers of the swimsuit issue may find the text erotically charged, but most know that these are two-dimensional images of sexy women who in real life are unavailable to them. In recent years, some swimsuit issue ads have delivered this message directly. . . . For instance, in the 1999 swimsuit issue, a full-page photo of a Heineken bottle included the written text "The only heiny in this magazine you could actually get your hands on."

These ads play directly to the male reader as loser and invite him to accommodate to his loser status, to recognize that these sexy fantasy women, though "real," are unavailable to him, and to settle for what he can have: a cold (rather than a hot) "Heiny." The Bud Lite Super Bowl commercials strike a similar chord. Many Bud Lite ads either titillate the viewer with sexy fantasy women, point to the ways that relationships with real women are to be avoided, or do both simultaneously. The break that appears near the end of each Bud Lite ad contrasts sharply with the often negative depiction of men's relations with real women in the ad's story line. The viewer sees a close-up of a bottle of Bud Lite. The bottle's cap explodes off, and beer ejaculates out, as a male voice-over proclaims what a man truly can rely on in life: "For the great taste that won't fill you up, and never lets you down . . . make it a Bud Lite."

REVENGE OF THE LOSERS

The accommodation theme in these ads may succeed, momentarily, in encouraging a man to shift his feelings of being a sexual loser toward manly feelings of empowerment through the consumption of brand-name beers and liquor. If the women in the ads are responsible for heightening tensions that result in some men's sense of themselves as losers, one possible outcome beyond simply drinking a large amount of alcohol (or one that accompanies the consumption of alcohol) is to express anger toward women and even to take revenge against them. This is precisely a direction that some of the recent ads have taken.

A full-page ad in the 2002 swimsuit issue showed a large photo of a bottle of Maker's Mark Whiskey. The bottle's reflection on the shiny table on which it sits is distorted in a way that suggests an hourglass-shaped female torso. The text next to the bottle reads, " 'Your bourbon has a great body and fine character. I WISH the same could be said for my girlfriend.' D. T., Birmingham, AL." This one-page ad is juxtaposed with a full-page photo of a *Sports Illustrated* model, provocatively using her thumb to begin to pull down the right side of her bikini bottom.

Together, the ad text and *Sports Illustrated* text angrily express the bitch-whore dichotomy that we discussed above. D. T.'s girlfriend is not pictured, but the description of her clearly indicates that not only does she lack a beautiful body; worse, she's a bitch. While D. T's girlfriend symbolizes the real woman whom each guy tolerates, and to whom he avoids committing, the juxtaposed *Sports Illustrated* model is the beautiful and sexy fantasy woman. She is unavailable to the male reader in real life; her presence as fantasy image highlights that the reader, like D. T., is stuck, apparently, with his bitchy girlfriend. But at least he can enjoy a moment of pseudo-empowerment by consuming a Maker's Mark whiskey and by insulting his girlfriend's body and character. Together, the Maker's Mark ad and the juxtaposed *Sports Illustrated* model provide a context for the reader to feel hostility toward the real women in his life.

.   .   .

TENSION, STABILIZATION, AND MASCULINE CONSUMPTION

We argued in our introduction that contemporary social changes have destabilized hegemonic masculinity. Examining beer and liquor ads in mega sports media events gives us a window into the ways that commercial forces have seized on these destabilizing tendencies, constructing pedagogical fantasy narratives that aim to appeal to a very large group—eighteen- to thirty-four-year-old men. They do so by appealing to a broad zeitgeist among young (especially white, heterosexual) men that is grounded in widespread tensions in the contemporary gender order.[6] The sexual and gender themes of the beer and liquor ads that we examine in this article do not stand alone; rather they reflect, and in turn contribute to, broader trends in popular culture and marketing to young white males. Television shows like *The Man Show*, new soft-core porn magazines like *Maxim* and *FHM*, and radio talk shows like the syndicated *Tom Leykus Show* share similar themes and are targeted to similar audiences of young males. Indeed, radio talk show hosts like Leykus didactically instruct young men to avoid "girlie" things, to eschew emotional commitment, and to think of women primarily as sexual partners (Messner 2002, 107–8). The chronotope of these magazines and television and radio shows constructs young male lifestyles saturated with sexy images of nearly naked, surgically enhanced women; unabashed and unapologetic sexual voyeurism shared by groups of laughing men; and explicit talk of sexual exploits with "hotties" or "juggies." A range of consumer products that includes—often centrally, as in *The Man Show*—consumption of beer as part of the young male lifestyle stitches together this erotic bonding among men. Meanwhile, real women are either absent from these media or they are disparaged as gold diggers (yes, this term has been resuscitated) who use sex to get men to spend money on them and trick them into marriage. The domesticated man is viewed as a wimpy victim who has subordinated his own pleasures (and surrendered his paychecks) to a woman. Within this framework, a young man should have sex with as many women as he can while avoiding (or at least delaying) emotional commitments to anyone woman. Freedom from emotional commitment grants 100 percent control over disposable income for monadic consumption and care of self. And that is ultimately what these shows are about: constructing a young male consumer characterized by personal and emotional freedom who can attain a hip lifestyle by purchasing an ever-expanding range of automobile-related products, snack foods, clothes, toiletries, and, of course, beer and liquor.

At first glance, these new media aimed at young men seem to resuscitate a 1950s "*Playboy* philosophy" of men's consumption, sexuality, and gender relations (Ehrenreich 1983). Indeed, these new media strongly reiterate the dichotomous bitch–whore view of women that was such a lynchpin of Hugh Hefner's "philosophy." But today's tropes of masculinity do not simply reiterate the past; rather, they give a postfeminist twist to the *Playboy* philosophy. A half-century ago, Hefner's pitch to men to recapture the indoors by creating (purchasing) one's own erotic "bachelor pad" in which to have sex with women (and then send them home) read as a straightforwardly masculine project. By contrast, today's sexual and gender pitch to young men is delivered with an ironic, self-mocking wink that operates, we think, on two levels. First, it appears to acknowledge that most young men are neither the heroes of the

---

[6]These same beer companies target different ads to other groups of men. Suzanne Danuta Walters (2001) analyzes Budweiser ads, e.g., that are aimed overtly at gay men.

indoors (as Hefner would have it) nor of the outdoors (as the 1970s and 1980s beer ads suggested). Instead, the ads seem to recognize that young white men's unstable status leaves them always on the verge of being revealed as losers. The ads plant seeds of insecurity on this fertile landscape, with the goal of creating a white guy who is a consistent and enthusiastic consumer of alcoholic beverages. The irony works on a second level as well: the throwback sexual and gender imagery—especially the bitch-whore dichotomization of women— is clearly a defensively misogynistic backlash against feminism and women's increasing autonomy and social power. The wink and self-mocking irony allow men to have it both ways: they can engage in humorous misogynist banter and claim simultaneously that it is all in play. They do not take themselves seriously, so anyone who takes their misogyny as anything but boys having good fun just has no sense of humor. The humorous irony works, then, to deflect charges of sexism away from white males, allowing them to define themselves as victims, as members of an endangered species. We suspect, too, that this is a key part of the process that constructs the whiteness in current reconstructions of hegemonic masculinity. As we have suggested, humorous "boys-will-be-boys" misogyny is unlikely to be taken ironically and lightly when delivered by men of color.

The white-guy-as-loser trope, though fairly new to beer and liquor ads, is certainly not new to U.S. media. Part of the irony of this character is not that he is a loser in every sense; rather he signifies the typical everyman who is only a loser in comparison to versions of masculinity more typical to beer and liquor ads past—that is, the rugged guys who regularly get the model-beautiful women. Caught between the excesses of a hyper-masculinity that is often discredited and caricatured in popular culture and the increasing empowerment of women, people of color, and homosexuals, while simultaneously being undercut by the postindustrial economy, the "Average Joe" is positioned as the ironic, vulnerable but lovable hero of beer and liquor ads. It is striking that the loser is not, or is rarely, your "José Mediano," especially if we understand the construction as a way to unite diverse eighteen- to thirty-four-year-old men. This is to say that the loser motif constructs the universal subject as implicitly white, and as a reaction against challenges to hegemonic masculinity it represents an ongoing possessive investment in whiteness (Lipsitz 1998).

Our analysis suggests that the fact that male viewers today are being hailed as losers and are being asked to identify with—even revel in—their loser status has its limits. The beer and liquor industry dangles images of sexy women in front of men's noses. Indeed, the ads imply that men will go out of their way to put themselves in position to be voyeurs, be it with a TV remote control, at a yoga class, in a bar, or on the *Sports Illustrated*/Miller Beer swimsuit photo shoot Web site. But ultimately, men know (and are increasingly being told in the advertisements themselves) that these sexy women are not available to them. Worse, if men get too close to these women, these women will most likely humiliate them. By contrast, real women—women who are not model-beautiful fantasy objects—are likely to attempt to ensnare men into a commitment, push them to have or express feelings that make them uncomfortable, and limit their freedom to have fun watching sports or playing cards or pool with their friends. So, in the end, men have only the safe haven of their male friends and the bottle.

This individual sense of victimization may feed young men's insecurities while giving them convenient scapegoats on which to project anger at their victim status. The cultural construction of white males as losers, then, is tethered to men's anger at and desire for revenge against women. Indeed, we have observed that revenge-against-women themes are evident in some of the most recent beer and liquor ads. And it is here that our analysis comes full circle. For, as we suggested in the introduction, the cultural imagery in ads aimed at young men does not simply come from images "out there." Instead, this imagery is linked to the ways that real people live their lives. It is the task of future research—including audience research—to investigate and flesh out the specific links between young men's consumption of commercial images, their consumption of beer and liquor, their attitudes toward and relationships with women, and their tendencies to drink and engage in violence against women.

APPENDIX

Commercials and Advertisements in the Sample

2002 Super Bowl:
  Michelob Lite, "Free to Be"
  Budweiser, "Robobash"
  Budweiser, "Pick-Up Lines"
  Bud Lite, "Hawk"
  Budweiser, "Clydesdales"
  Bud Lite, "Greeting Cards"
  Budweiser, "How Ya Doin'?"
  Bud Lite, "Black Teddy"
  Budweiser, "Meet the Parents"
  Budweiser, "History of Budweiser"
  Budweiser, "Designated Driver"
  Smirnoff Ice
	2002 *Sports Illustrated* swimsuit issue (no. of pages):
	  Miller Lite (2)
	  Jim Beam (1)
	  Miller Genuine Draft (2, plus card insert)
	  Heineken (1)
	  Budweiser (1)
	  Captain Morgan Rum (1)
	  Martell (1)
	  Sam Adams Utopia (1)
	  Maker's Mark Whiskey (1)
	  Bacardi Rum (1.25)
	  José Cuervo Tequila (1)
	  Crown Royal (1)
	  Chivas (1)

2003 Super Bowl:
  Budweiser, "Zebras"
  Bud Lite, "Refrigerator"
  Bud Lite, "Clown"
	2003 *Sports Illustrated* swimsuit issue (no. of pages):
	  Budweiser (1)
	  José Cuervo Tequila (1)

Bud Lite, "Rasta Dog"	Smirnoff Vodka (1)
Bud Lite, "Conch"	Captain Morgan Rum (4)
Bud Lite, "Date Us Both"	Seagrams (1)
Smirnoff Lite, "Blind Date"	Miller Lite (11, including
Bud Lite, "Sarah's Mom"	poster pullout)
Bud Lite, "Three Arms"	Crown Royal (1)
Coors, "Twins"	Heineken (1)
Budweiser, "Good Listener"	Skyy Vodka (1)
Budweiser, " 'How Ya Doin'?' Redux"	Knob Whiskey (1)
Michelob Ultra, "Low-Carb Bodies"	Chivas (1)
Bud Lite, "Yoga Voyeurs"	

REFERENCES

Bakhtin, Mikhail. 1981. "Forms of Time and the Chronotope in the Novel." In *The Dialogic Imagination: Four Essays,* trans. Caryl Emerson and Michael Holmquist, 84–258. Austin: University of Texas Press.

Collins, Tony, and Wray Vamplew. 2002. *Mud, Sweat, and Beers: A Cultural History of Sport and Alcohol.* New York: Berg.

Connell, R. W. 1995. *Masculinities.* Berkeley: University of California Press.

Curry, Timothy. 2000. "Booze and Bar Fights: A Journey to the Dark Side of College Athletics." In *Masculinities, Gender Relations, and Sport,* ed. Jim McKay, Donald F. Sabo, and Michael A. Messner, 162–75. Thousand Oaks, CA: Sage.

Davis, Laurel L. 1997. *The Swimsuit Issue and Sport: Hegemonic Masculinity in* Sports Illustrated. Albany, NY: SUNY Press.

Dayan, Daniel, and Elihu Katz. 1988. "Articulating Consensus: The Ritual and Rhetoric of Media Events." In *Durkheimian Sociology: Cultural Studies,* ed. Jeffrey C. Alexander, 161–86. Cambridge: Cambridge University Press.

Ehrenreich, Barbara. 1983. *The Hearts of Men: American Dreams and the Flight from Commitment.* New York: Anchor Doubleday.

Ferguson, Ann Arnett. 2000. *Bad Boys: Public Schools in the Making of Black Masculinity.* Ann Arbor: University of Michigan Press.

Goldman, Robert, and Stephen Papson. 1996. *Sign Wars: The Cluttered Landscape of Advertising.* New York: Guilford.

———. 1998. *Nike Culture: The Sign of the Swoosh.* Thousand Oaks, CA: Sage.

Kimmel, Michael S. 1987. "Men's Responses to Feminism at the Turn of the Century." *Gender and Society* 1(3):261–83.

Koss, Mary, and John A. Gaines. 1993. "The Prediction of Sexual Aggression by Alcohol Use, Athletic Participation, and Fraternity Affiliation." *Journal of Interpersonal Violence* 8(1):94–108.

Leichliter, Jami S., Philip W. Meilman, Cheryl A. Presley, and Jeffrey R. Cashin. 1998. "Alcohol Use and Related Consequences among Students with Varying Levels of Involvement in College Athletics." *Journal of American College Health* 46(6):257–62.

Lipsitz, George. 1981. *Class and Culture in Cold War America: "A Rainbow at Midnight."* New York: Praeger.

———. 1998. *The Possessive Investment in Whiteness: How White People Profit from Identity Politics.* Philadelphia: Temple University Press.

Martin, Christopher R., and Jimmie L. Reeves. 2001. "The Whole World Isn't Watching (but We Thought They Were): The Super Bowl and U.S. Solipsism." *Culture, Sport, and Society* 4(2):213–54.

May, Elaine Tyler. 1988. *Homeward Bound: American Families in the Cold War Era.* New York: Basic Books.

Messner, Michael A. 2002. *Taking the Field: Women, Men, and Sports.* Minneapolis: University of Minnesota Press.

O'Donohoe, Stephanie. 1997. "Leaky Boundaries: Intertextuality and Young Adult Experiences of Advertising." In *Buy This Book: Studies in Advertising and Consumption,* ed. Mica Nava, Andrew Blake, Ian McRury, and Barry Richards, 257–75. London: Routledge.

Postman, Neil, Christine Nystrom, Lance Strate, and Charlie Weingartner. 1987. *Myths, Men, and Beer: An Analysis of Beer Commercials on Broadcast Television,* 1987. Washington, DC: AAA Foundation for Traffic Safety.

Sabo, Don, Phil Gray, and Linda Moore. 2000. "Domestic Violence and Televised Athletic Events: 'It's a man thing.'" In *Masculinities, Gender Relations, and Sport,* ed. Jim McKay, Don Sabo, and Michael A. Messner, 127–46. Thousand Oaks, CA: Sage.

Sperber, Murray. 2000. *Beer and Circus: How Big-Time College Sports Is Crippling Undergraduate Education.* New York: Henry Holt.

Spigel, Lynn. 1992. *Make Room for TV: Television and the Family Ideal in Postwar America.* Chicago: University of Chicago Press.

Strate, Lance. 1992. "Beer Commercials: A Manual on Masculinity." In *Men, Masculinity, and the Media,* ed. Steve Craig, 78–92. Newbury Park, CA: Sage.

Walters, Suzanna Danuta. 1999. "Sex, Text, and Context: (In) Between Feminism and Cultural Studies." In *Revisioning Gender,* ed. Myra Marx Ferree, Judith Lorber, and Beth B. Hess, 222–57. Thousand Oaks, CA: Sage.

———. 2001. *All the Rage: The Story of Gay Visibility in America.* Chicago: University of Chicago Press.

Wenner, Lawrence A. 1991. "One Part Alcohol, One Part Sport, One Part Dirt, Stir Gently: Beer Commercials and Television Sports." In *Television Criticism: Approaches and Applications,* ed. Leah R. Vende Berg and Lawrence A. Wenner, 388–407. New York: Longman.

———. 1998. "In Search of the Sports Bar: Masculinity, Alcohol, Sports, and the Mediation of Public Space." In *Sport and Postmodern Times,* ed. Genevieve Rail, 303–32. Albany, NY: SUNY Press.

Zimbalist, Andrew. 1999. *Unpaid Professionals: Commercialism and Conflict in Big-Time College Sports.* Princeton, NJ: Princeton University Press.

LINDA MIZEJEWSKI

Queen Latifah, Unruly Women, and the Bodies of Romantic Comedy

Linda Mizejewski, Professor of Women's Studies at Ohio State University, has written three books on representations of women in film. For more on her work, visit http:// people.cohums.ohio-state.edu/Mizejewski1/.

BODIES, STARDOM, NARRATIVES

The questions that compel this essay concern the relationship between bodies and narratives: the narratives available to certain bodies and the disruptive impact of those bodies on narratives. My focus is the embodiment of the spunky heroine of the romantic comedy film—the feisty screwball leading lady whose excessive speech, aspirations, and energy have endeared her to generations of cinema lovers and to feminist film theory as well, which has celebrated her as woman-on-top and fast-talking dame. Earlier versions of this film character were played by the likes of Rosalind Russell, Barbara Stanwyck, Carole Lombard, and Katherine Hepburn, the later versions by Meg Ryan, Julie Roberts, Drew Barrymore, and Jennifer Aniston. As this list suggests, the excessiveness of this heroine is proscribed by the cultural ideals of white femininity, which in turn is pictured through very select bodies. While feminist film scholarship has long acknowledged the power of the unruly woman in comedy, this scholarship has glossed over the ways in which race in particular enables the unruliness of this character and intersects with class ideals in the picturing of this heroine. Using the star persona of Queen Latifah as a case study, this essay centers on how the romantic comedy narrative handles the sexuality of the unruly woman who is black, or conversely, the narratives available for racial unruliness when it is female.

The traditional romantic comedy ends in the coupling of the unlikely couple, but the pleasure of the narrative—and its feminist appeal—is the lively, quarrelsome give-and-take of the courtship, fired by the struggle for egalitarianism between the unruly woman and the man who is her match. This film genre has proven remarkably resilient since its formulation in the 1930s, retaining its original formula but shape-shifting to accommodate social change and contemporary issues (Krutnik 131–37; Paul 126–28; Preston 227–29). As a result, following a decline in the 1970s and early 1980s, romantic comedy has seen a steady resurgence since 1984, and it remains one of the most prevalent versions of heterosexual romantic ideology.

429

Stardom is a key issue here because these comedies register cultural wishes and fantasies about the bodies of heterosexuality. As popular culture's most salient narrative of marriage, it is no surprise that romantic comedy shares the ideals Chrys Ingraham describes in the representations of contemporary wedding culture: "what counts as beautiful is white, fair, thin, and female" (81). Confirming this configuration, the women of color who have starred in this genre — Halle Berry, Jennifer Lopez, Gabrielle Union, Nia Long, Sanaa Lathan — are light-skinned women with Caucasian features and the bodies of fashion models. When the Bridget Jones films came out (*Bridget Jones's Diary*, 2001; *Bridget Jones: The Edge of Reason*, 2004), there was nearly obsessive press attention to Rene Zellweger's weight gain for the roles, even though the extra thirty pounds put her at an average weight and size for most women (Brennan and Schwabauer). Another telling example is the 2002 runaway hit *My Big Fat Greek Wedding*, which begins with a heroine who does not fall into the classic romantic-body template. So the narrative is embedded with a makeover subplot that irons out her more stereotypically ethnic features — even though the narrative is focused on ethnic comedy. The popularity of this film, a low-budget venture that reaped unexpectedly large box-office returns, may have resided in the appeal of a star (Nia Vardalos) who was not Hollywood-style glamorous, but its romantic plot is triggered when she becomes not only thinner but less "Greek." Even lesbian romantic comedies, which have a better record with race, tend to rely on Hollywood's ideal for leading ladies in films such as *Better Than Chocolate* (1999), *Saving Face* (2004), *Chutney Popcorn* (1999), and *But I'm a Cheerleader* (1999).

The physical and racial profile of the romantic-comedy heroine and the whiteness of the romantic narrative itself may be obvious. More interesting is the testing of the body-narrative relationship through particular cases of stardom and celebrity, first of all because those cases foreground the bodies at stake in the cultural imagination of heterosexuality, and secondly because they delineate the genre's cultural work in articulating gender and race. The film career of Queen Latifah (Dana Owens), still very much in progress as I write this essay, provides a fascinating example of this intersection of body, cultural fantasy, and available narratives. Latifah has achieved stardom with a physique that is unconventional in star culture, but her films — with one exception — have so far resisted centering her as part of a romantic couple.

The exception, *Bringing Down the House*, her 2003 comedy with Steve Martin, is the focus of this study because it conspicuously twists the romantic-comedy narrative to avoid romance between the two main characters, suggesting the dissonance of the large, black female body in this cinema formula. In *Bringing Down the House*, Martin and Latifah are a classic screwball couple: he's the uptight lawyer who needs soul, and she's the funky homegirl who has been framed for a crime and needs him to clear her name. In the spirit of romantic comedy, they perform the requisite sparring and pratfalls, but then end up coupling with far less interesting characters. As Roger Ebert protested, this "violates all the laws of economical screenplay construction. . . . A comedy is not allowed to end with the couples incorrectly paired." The *New York Times* critic blamed it on squeamishness, claiming the film "doesn't have the nerve to follow through on what seems like its romantic-comedy setup" (Mitchell 15). Rachel Swan, the reviewer for *bitch*, put it even more bluntly: "Though *Bringing Down the House* is initially set up as a romance between Charlene and Peter, it becomes clear as the movie progresses that love would blossom only if Charlene were white" (27).

The assumption of these and other disappointed reviewers was that race is the obstacle preventing the romantic formula from playing out. Yet the success of an interracial comedy such as *Something New* (2006) indicates that mixed-race romance is hardly a screen taboo anymore. It is not simply race, but the raced body and persona of a particular star which is at stake here. In this conjunction of stardom and narrative, the unruly woman as progressive romantic heroine takes on particular racial implications. *Bringing Down the House* celebrates Latifah as a hip-hop version of this heroine, but it also reduces her to a series of racist stereotypes, revealing the axis of race upon which the unruly-woman figure revolves.

My aim in this essay is to frame Latifah's role in *Bringing Down the House* within the contexts of romantic comedy, the racial implications of that genre's unruly woman, and the histories of other popular unruly-woman actresses— Mae West, Josephine Baker, and Whoopi Goldberg—who have likewise tended to disrupt or be diminished in romantic-couple film narratives. In particular, *Bringing Down the House* repeats the narrative structure of a 1935 Josephine Baker film, *Princess Tam Tam*, which similarly posits a powerful African-American star as a romantic heroine and then erodes her subjectivity as she becomes a racial marker within a white, masculinist narrative. I am not claiming that romantic comedy is impossible for the black, non–glamorous female star, and in fact Whoopi Goldberg's foray into that genre, *Made in America* (1993), is discussed later in this essay. However, given Latifah's high-profile stardom in both hip-hop and mainstream popular cultures, the odd narrative twists in *Bringing Down the House* merit attention for their cultural implications. The following section rereads the overlapping histories of the unruly woman and romantic comedy as histories of racialized bodies, and examines the sexuality, race, and class of the female bodies of romantic comedy. The final section analyzes the narrative impact of the Queen Latifah persona on *Bringing Down the House*, in particular its racialized twist on an unruly-woman plot formula, and juxtaposes this film with the Josephine Baker vehicle *Princess Tam Tam*.

UNRULY WOMEN

To date, *Bringing Down the House* is Latifah's only film that draws on the romantic-comedy formula. Queen Latifah often plays characters who are overtly sexualized, but in her other comedies — *Taxi* (2004), *Beauty Shop* (2005); *Last Holiday* (2006) — her characters' romantic interests have been bracketed to the margins of the narrative, and in earlier films, she played powerful women who were not associated with men at all. Latifah was cast as a butch lesbian bank robber in her breakthrough film *Set It Off* (1996), a role with continuing implications for her career, and she was nominated for an Academy Award for her role in *Chicago* (2003) as a prison matron whose sex life is suggested, succinctly, by an unbuttoned blouse in a scene with Catherine Zeta Jones. In the successful television comedy series *Living Single* (1993–98), Latifah played the independent-minded editor of an urban magazine, coolly at odds with her man-crazy roommates and friends.

This cinema and television history of strong, non-traditional roles matches her outspoken star persona, originating in the male-dominated world of hip-hop music, where she debuted with a platinum-selling album, *All Hail the Queen*, in 1989. Equally unorthodox is Latifah's publicity, which aggressively foregrounds her size and a discourse of bodily acceptance. Because Latifah had breast-reduction surgery and had in fact lost weight in 2004, the bodily-acceptance discourse has at times contradicted her more conventional celebrity-body publicity. Her *Glamour* cover photo of May, 2004 carried the caption, "Enough with the unreal cover girls! Curvy, proud Queen Latifah," but the accompanying story included an account of her weight loss and a series of photos suggesting the requisite before-and-after effect (Childress 85). Nevertheless, a predominant theme of Latifah's stardom has been self-confidence about body-image, and her references to her size-16 frame are striking in the cultural "hegemony of the fat-free body," as Susan Bordo has put it (xxxi). A 2006 *Essence* article, challenging the reigning definitions of beauty, quoted Latifah as feeling fortunate "to be supported by people who like me for me and don't try to make me look like somebody else" (Robertson 103). The "somebody else" cited in this quotation is precisely the Hollywood body likely to be cast in a romantic comedy.

It is significant that *Bringing Down the House*, her only post-*Chicago* film to do well at the box office as of this writing, was also her only film promoted as a romantic comedy, suggesting that audiences were indeed ready for a screwball pairing of Latifah and Martin. The film was financially successful despite mixed reviews, which registered appreciation of the considerable comic talents of the stars but also uneasiness with the film's satire of racism and with its odd shirking of the romantic-comedy formula.

The failure of the film to follow through with Latifah's role as romantic heroine is especially ironic because by many accounts, romantic comedy is the site in Hollywood cinema where female unruliness has best been able to thrive.

In her pioneering work on women in film, Molly Haskell described the genre as "a world in which male authority, or sexual imperialism, is reduced or in abeyance, while the feminine spirit is either dominant or equal" (131). The formula itself requires the sparring of well-matched contenders, with "the couple meeting up, or ending up, as equals," thus fulfilling "their desires of equal standing and of equal motive power," as Deborah Thomas describes it (58–59). In their more recent incarnations, romantic comedies are more likely to stage cultural ambivalence about feminism and shifting gender roles (Cornut-Gentille 112–13; Tasker and Negra 171–73). But overall, romantic comedy remains the genre where women's issues and desires are likely to be prioritized.

In her book-length study of the unruly woman figure, Kathleen Rowe persuasively argues that romantic comedy, because of its inherently subversive nature, is one of the few popular narratives possible, in fact, for this comic, rebellious, and powerful female character who talks back, laughs loudly, and makes clear her own desires (101–02). The utopianism of romantic comedy— its projection of a younger, better generation—springs from this vetting of the couple whose union signifies a triumph over the old guard. Thomas Schatz goes even further in his description of the antiauthoritarian young couple in this genre, noting that their unconventional behavior in courtship precludes the possibility of settling into a staid, traditional marriage; in short, the genre promises marriage but also promises an unruly, unconventional couple (159).

Taking a different perspective on the spirited romantic-comedy heroine, Maria DiBattista emphasizes her verbal clout, arguing that the "fast-talking dames" of 1930s and 1940s comedy were characterized by their smart talk, verbal wit, and ability to use language to claim space and power—certainly characteristics shared by the Queen Latifah persona. DiBattista traces this strong tradition through dozens of films starring Irene Dunne, Jean Harlow, Myrna Loy, and others, all of them playing heroines "who balked at traditional gender roles and were insistent on self-rule" (11).

This rebellion against female gender roles is possible in romantic comedy because no matter how transgressive she may be, the unruly heroine's destiny is thoroughly conformist. The implication may be that the romantic couple will turn into unconventional citizens, as Schatz claims, but this will happen to them as a couple, securely under the sign of heterosexuality and within the social auspices of matrimony. The eccentricities of even the most "screwball" characters are, as genre critics repeatedly point out, tempered by their concurrence to the middle-class ideology of marriage (Neale and Krutnik 155–56; Schatz 159).

It is not simply that the ideologies of the unruly woman contradict those of romantic comedy, but that the genre staging this heroine thrives on this very tension, endlessly promising both glorified individualism and the bittersweet compromises of marriage. Addressing this tension, comedy scholar Geoff King claims that the contradiction is palatable because even though the heroine is "tamed" into bourgeois life at the end of the narrative, the assumption is that she never loses her rebellious elan (132). King makes a distinction, however, between this dynamic heroine of romantic comedy and the comedian whose stardom is based on the unruly-woman persona. The latter, he says, is a far greater risk in Hollywood cinema. Unlike her raucous male counterpart whose horseplay maintains male authority (Robin Williams, Adam Sandler, Ben Stiller), the unruly woman comic "represents a more serious challenge to the gender hierarchies on which so many social relationships are based" (133).

However, Rowe argues that the stakes are not just social relationships, but sexual difference itself. The woman who disrupts the status quo by talking back and laughing loudly enacts male privilege and thus posits a possible breakdown of sexual categories, a possibility at which romantic comedy occasionally hints before the couple is safely recontained into the heterosexual norm (43, 118). If the investment is sexual difference itself, then the conservative function of romantic comedy is spelled out as the popular narrative that disciplines a powerful female figure—a figure threatening to the very categories of sexuality—by positioning her within the heterosexual couple.

Certainly the absent terms in this history of unruly women in romantic comedy are race and queer or gay sexualities and bodies. For King, the Julia Roberts character Vivian in *Pretty Woman* (1990) is the primary example of the "tamed" woman whose rebelliousness is the powerhouse of the film. But it seems to me the powerhouse of that film is Julia Roberts herself and her status as the eponymous pretty woman—a woman who looks like a high-end fashion model (thin, white, or with white features). When King moves into a discussion of subversive women comic characters, he drops romantic comedy and instead uses as examples characters played by Whoopi Goldberg, Barbara Windsor, Julie Walker, and Marianne Sägebrecht.

Neither King nor Rowe specify that only a particular *feminine* version of female unruliness makes romantic comedy possible. Femininity is a concept inherently racialized, historically configured, and weighted with specific class connotations. Romantic comedy strikingly illustrates how the very categories "masculine" and "feminine" are imagined through these lenses. As Judith Halberstam puts it in her study of female masculinity, "femininity and masculinity signify as normative within and through white middle-class heterosexual bodies." Halberstam is particularly interested in Latifah's role as Cleo in *Set it Off* because it conforms to the stereotype of the inherent masculinity of African-American women and because it makes Cleo's performance of masculinity both edgy and attractive (29). These stereotypes of race and gender empower the performance, she argues, producing "credible butchness" (228).

The stereotype works both ways, as Ann M. Ciasullo has argued about the lesbian femme body in popular culture which, she says, "is nearly always a white, upper-middle class body" (578). For its heterosexual models, we can posit from this that the unruly woman of romantic comedy can be black only if she plays against the race/class stereotype—that is, if she looks like Gabrielle Union or Sanaa Lathan, whose bodies and demeanors reinforce rather than threaten middle-class concepts of the feminine, as we see in films such as *Love and Basketball* (2000) and *Deliver Us From Eva* (2003).

So in order to place Queen Latifah into this history of the unruly woman, the category itself needs more scrutiny in that it seems to signify both radical sex/gender transgression but also a conventional middle-class heroine. In her history of the unruly woman in popular culture, Rowe is in fact interested in subversive female bodies—androgynous, grotesque, excessive, masculine— but the structure of her argument separates the truly transgressive bodies from the ones in romantic comedy. The first part of the book focuses on Miss Piggy and Roseanne Arnold, or as one chapter is entitled, "Pig Ladies, Big Ladies, and Ladies With Big Mouths." Tracing these strong female personas to older literatures and folklores, Rowe describes the unruly woman as one who refuses her proper place and is associated with jokes and laughter, masculinity, androgyny, looseness, dirt, liminality, and excessiveness of body and speech (31). Using Mikhail Bakhtin's terms, Rowe demonstrates the unruly woman's association with the grotesque body, which emphasizes its "lower stratum" (belly, buttocks, genitals) as opposed to the classical body with its privileged "upper stratum" (head, face, eyes) (33).

The second part of the book focuses on the unruly woman in popular film narratives. Rowe begins with Mae West as the brassy unruly woman whose sexually-experienced persona (the prostitute with a heart of gold) was unsuitable for romantic comedy as it developed in the 1930s. Instead, Rowe suggests, the heiresses of West's legacy are Miss Piggy and Roseanne (117). Rowe then shifts to romantic comedy as the site where "the woman on top" tradition materializes in Hollywood, and the shape and look of the heroines shift, too: the primary examples are characters played by actresses such as Claudette Colbert, Katherine Hepburn, Barbara Stanwyck, Julia Roberts, and Cher, whose performances of subversive unruly-woman traits are embodied as white, middle-class femininity. Even Cher gets a bourgeois makeover in *Moonstruck* (1987). Rowe's point is that romantic-comedy heroines carry on the comic woman-on-top tradition in the only narrative available that allows them autonomy and individuality—and spares them the crueler fates of the *femme fatale* or the melodramatic victim, the other configurations of Hollywood heroines. But for this mainstream narrative as pictured by Hollywood, the bodies become petite and pretty, small-breasted, classical. The transgressive body has dropped out of the conversation.

And missing from the conversation entirely is race. The disruptiveness of the woman-on-top has a different effect if played by Katherine Hepburn or Meg Ryan instead of Queen Latifah. For the traditionally attractive white woman in white culture, unruliness can be a liberating quality of female individualism. For the black woman in white culture—someone who is already under suspicion as part of an "unruly" subculture—the opposite occurs: her subjectivity diminishes as she slides into racial stereotype. In his treatment of race and gender in comedy, Geoff King makes this point about Whoopi Goldberg's ability to play the disruptive comic: "To be a loud, crazy, unruly figure is to go against dominant stereotypes of 'acceptable' female behavior and is something of a rarity in film, even in the realm of comedy. The same qualities might fit more easily into the parameters of long-standing racial stereotypes, however, most notably that of the 'coon': the racist version of the African American as black buffoon" (143). For King, race both enables Goldberg's performance and positions it in a risky space where one possible interpretation is racist spectacle (145). This is exactly the risk of many of the jokes in *Bringing Down the House*. The final section of this essay treats in more detail the film's racial humor, but my point here is that the concept of "woman on top" assumes white privilege—the ability of disruptive behavior to be interpreted as laudable individualism.

The other significant aspect of Queen Latifah as unruly woman is her ability to perform female masculinity, as suggested by Halberstam. Rowe does not theorize certain masculinized unruly bodies as queer, but she does include two cases of "grotesque" or excessive bodies and campy performances which backfire for romantic comedy: Mae West in the 1930s and the Marilyn Monroe-Jane Russell combination in *Gentlemen Prefer Blondes* (1953). They are also the bodies engaged in the truly subversive tradition of camp, which, in its scorn of sentimentality and sexual categories, has no place in the middle-class pieties of romantic comedy. The example of Mae West is particularly relevant to Latifah. Although Rowe does not discuss masculinity as part of West's sexual/gender transgressions, the latter's physical heft and demeanor are intrinsic to what Rowe names as the subversive, "unruly woman" qualities of West's performance—the exaggerations of gender performance and inversion (119). West literally outsized most of her leading men, walked with a macho swagger, and dominated the space around her, even as she invoked feminine stereotypes. As Pamela Robertson Wojcik points out, West's masculinity was produced by her mimicry of female impersonators, so it always involved mixed gender codes (291). Rowe argues that West's dominating and highly sexualized presence, as well as her affinities to camp, limited her comic narratives to gold-digger films, resulting in "a single-note performance" (124).

The parallels with Latifah are striking. Like West, Latifah has strong affinities to gay culture. Especially because of her role as Cleo in *Set It Off*, gay rumors have haunted her publicity, so that "a decade later, she's still getting asked how much she and Cleo have in common," a 2006 article in *Essence* reports. Her reply in this interview is typical of what she has said over the years: "Latifah refuses to confirm or deny. She says she has plenty of gay friends, and to deny anything about her personal life would be an insult to them" (Amber 182). As Ciasullo reports, Latifah's remarks about lesbianism over the years have ranged from defiance ("I'd rather have you die wanting to know") to a cool distancing from the topic, with the effect of leaving the question ambiguous

(598). Discussing the strong, womanist character played by Latifah on *Living Single*, Krystal Zook argues that this ambiguity was a key to Latifah's power on that show, which played up her resistance to traditional sex and gender roles (68–74).

In addition to these biographical similarities, Latifah also shares West's proclivities for outrageous poses, costumes, and performances, most notably her over-the-top *Chicago* musical number "When You're Good to Mama," a *tour de force* tribute to camp divas such as Sophie Tucker, Eartha Kitt, Ethel Merman and of course West herself. In addition, Latifah sometimes uses her large body for the effect of female masculinity in her films, most obviously in *Set it Off,* but also in her dominating gestures and skillful driving (coded as "masculine") in *Taxi.* As Charlene, the tough ex-con in *Bringing Down the House,* she jumps into a fist fight with men twice her size and beats up a prissy white girl whose Tai Bo lessons are no match for what Charlene "learned in the hood," as she puts it.

As this suggests, the performance is not simply tough chick but tough chick from the 'hood, and here the class and racial issues overlapping with Mae West more pointedly delineate the female bodies excluded from romantic comedy. Mae West's success as a 1930s sex symbol was highly racialized, as Wojcik has shown, particularly in her screen relationships with subordinate black female characters. These relationships constructed, through contrast, "West's glowing whiteness" (290), but the films also emphasized West's intimacy and identification with these women as winking co-conspirators about sex with men, and also as possible lesbian interests. This association, claims Wojcik, constructed West's sexuality as working-class, an effect intensified by her appropriation of a "dirty blues" singing style that in the 1930s was associated with lower-class black culture (291–92). A similar set of class associations converge around the stardom of Latifah, whose associations with "the hood" are made not so much through her lower-middle-class background, but rather through her place in hip-hop culture and rap music, resulting in her public image as "New Jersey-bred bad girl" (Daniels), "the Jersey homegirl" (Amber 180), or "former tomboy from the 'hood" (Norment 130).

My interest here is how these class markers—"dirty blues" and "Jersey girl"—merge with racial markers in the production of an unruly woman who disrupts or simply does not fit the romantic comedy narrative. In her 2001 analysis "The Colour of Class," Ann DuCille uses the classic romantic comedy *The Philadelphia Story* (1940) as her primary example in arguing that "there is no space for a black middle or upper class in the American popular imagination" (409). In this film, she says, "the class signifiers . . . are so recognizably *haute couture* that the characters could only be imagined as white" (410), and she points to the failure of the 1996 romance *The Preacher's Wife,* a black re-make of a white romance, *The Bishop's Wife* (1947), as further evidence of the dissonance between "colour" and class. For DuCille, the issue is the American cultural positioning of the "coloured figure—the dark form, the black body" as "low-Other," to use the term Peter Stallybrass and Allon White have developed in accounting for marginalized configurations that support a status quo (412).

As DuCille's example suggests, the issue is also "the coloured figure" as the marginalized low-Other in romantic ideology. In popular culture, whiteness as a class signifier conveys the privileged status of the romantic heroine and hero. Analyzing the meanings of the "white wedding," Ingraham emphasizes the importance of race in the signification of class: "Whiteness, wealth, and wedding become central features of the ideology of romantic love, communicating a sign system that collapses them into one package" (88). It is not simply that DuCille's example happens to come from romantic comedy, but that romantic comedy exemplifies this race-class packaging of heterosexuality which, Ingraham argues, suppresses the "complicated ways institutionalized heterosexuality works in the interest of the dominant classes" (88).

My argument so far has focused on the relationship between the unruly woman and the bodies of romantic comedy in order to make the case that the Latifah persona, as "former tomboy from the 'hood'" is triply excluded (masculinized, black, lower class) from the cultural imagination of heterosexual romance. Moving now to a more detailed reading of *Bringing Down the House*, I want to explore how the coherency of this text is disrupted under the cultural weight of this particular unruly heroine and how, in the resulting narrative, Latifah functions as a racial/cultural signifier at the expense of the subjectivity and individuality usually accorded the romantic-comedy heroine.

ROMANCE AS SAFARI

A favorite plot for romantic comedy is the rescue of a stodgy and dreary man by the zany, unruly woman. Rowe discusses this pattern in classic comedies such as *The Lady Eve* (1941) and *Bringing Up Baby* (1938), and the formula continues in films such as *Pretty Woman*, *You've Got Mail* (1998), and *Along Came Polly* (2004). The possibility of this male redemption in romantic comedy is exactly what makes it such an ideal narrative for egalitarianism and the unruly woman; it gives the heroine agency, subjectivity, and license for gleeful chaos (Rowe 146–47). The 1992 screwball comedy *Housesitter* is an especially significant example of this plot in that this too was a Steve Martin vehicle, with Goldie Hawn playing the madcap woman who moves into the hero's house and eventually makes him realize she is more his match than the dowdy ex-fiancee for whom he yearns for most of the movie. *Housesitter* was cited in reviews of *Bringing Down the House* by critics displeased that the later film failed to follow through on the formula that succeeded in the earlier movie (Mitchell, Swan).

In *Bringing Down the House*, the racial twist on this formula works especially well for Steve Martin, whose inhibited WASP persona is one of his specialties and a signal that whiteness itself is being broadly satirized in this film. Here he plays Peter, the divorced, middle-aged tax lawyer losing his grip. A younger man is dating his ex-wife, another younger man is usurping his power at the law firm, and his kids are constantly disappointed by his lack of attention. Peter's life is suddenly rattled by Charlene, the character played by Latifah. Charlene is an obvious version of the Queen Latifah persona—tough, outrageous, excessive in body and style. Peter meets Charlene on an internet chat site where she has been posting as Lawyer Girl, leading him to believe she is the svelte blonde professional in the photo she sends. The joke is that Charlene is in the photo, but in the background, being handcuffed by cops; in actuality, she's broken out of prison and needs a lawyer to help prove her innocence. The photo startlingly captures the racialized sexual dynamics of mainstream visual culture: the blonde woman foregrounded as icon, the black woman's story nearly obscured in the distance—a pattern which the film at first seems to reverse.

As much as Peter is repulsed by Charlene and repeatedly ejects her from his house and life, she cons him into taking her in, bringing him jive, bling, dancing lessons, and soul food, as well as emotional support for his children. She teaches the younger one to read; she teaches the teenager to respect herself. Peter, in turn, learns that Charlene's ex-boyfriend is the one who framed her, and in the film's climactic scene, Peter disguises himself as a white rapper so he can infiltrate the bad boyfriend's club and manipulate a confession from him. In sum, Charlene gets legitimacy and Peter gets soul.

This so far adheres to the cultural exchange intrinsic to the romantic-comedy formula, which tends "to play both ends against the middle, to celebrate the contradictions within our culture while seeming to do away with them" (Schatz 159). The film up to this point strongly resembles *Housesitter*, setting up the expectation that Peter and Charlene will kiss, couple, and commit to a crazy future together as the main characters do in the earlier film.

However, the romantic comedy plot is hijacked, and the hijacking occurs in a cheesy turnaround that defies its own clichéd moment. During the melee at the black nightclub—a wild free-for-all fistfight pitting the bad boyfriend's heavies against Peter and his friends—Charlene is shot and seems to be dying. Peter rushes to take her into his arms. This is a standard melodramatic moment when, conventionally, the sparring couple realize what they mean to each other and succumb to the inevitable kiss. The camera moves in for a tight shot of the two, Peter tenderly touches her cheek, and since the bullet hit her titanium cellphone instead of her breast, Charlene comes miraculously back to life. But instead of the kiss, Peter turns around and calls to his sidekick Howie to tell him Charlene is alright. Howie (Eugene Levy) is the oddball Jewish lawyer besmitten by the "cocoa goddess," as he calls her. She calls him "freakboy." He has been courting her throughout the film with a deadpan appropriation of Charlene's hip-hop slang—"You got me straight trippin, Boo"—which instantly achieved eye-rolling notoriety in reviews. The upshot is that in the coda, we see Charlene with Howie, while Peter has reunited with his blonde ex-wife.

Ebert's review, emphasizing the wrongness of "the couples incorrectly paired" in a romantic comedy, points out that "There isn't a shred of chemistry between Latifah and Levy," while Peter's ex-wife "exists only so that he can go back to her." The film is sprinkled with hints that Peter misses his wife and desires the reunion, but Ebert here is referring to the film's lack of emotional investment in this reunion, as happens in the romantic comedy of remarriage, in which the story revolves around the *divorced* couple, as in *The Awful Truth* (1937) and *His Girl Friday* (1940). In this kind of comedy, the focus of the entire film is the reunion of a couple who should never have broken up. The stars are the separated main characters, and the dynamic between them is what keeps the film going.

In striking contrast, the reunion with the ex-wife at the end of *Bringing Down the House* repudiates the dynamic between Peter and Charlene—unless, that is, we recognize the racial dynamic that overrides the romantic one. The unruly woman who rescues the nerd may be standard for romantic comedy, but the *black* unruly woman in that position bears the pressure of another, specifically racial cultural narrative. As the reviewer for *The Boston Globe* put it, "it has always been in American pop culture that white people can only find validation, get crazy, get real if they hang with black folks" (Burr 1). This racial trajectory of white masculinity in crisis actually structures the film, despite the romantic-comedy formula recognized by many reviewers. The plot begins with Peter's emasculation at work and on the home front. It ends with him winning back his ex-wife, restoring a healed nuclear family, and gaining a multi-million dollar client so he can quit his stuffy law firm and open his own business. And it happens because of his journey into hip-hop culture via Charlene.

Peter's heroism occurs literally as the journey to the black club called the Down Low, which is urban slang for "secret" but also for the man with a homosexual life kept from his wife or girlfriend. This disavowal of attraction characterizes Peter's relationship to Charlene but also to black culture, which is portrayed throughout the film, by way of Charlene, as sexier and livelier than Peter's white suburban world. Peter borrows clothes from some brothers so he can slip into the club as a drugged-out, weirdo white rapper. In this way, he takes on a type of blackface that has the effect described by Michael Rogin in his treatment of blackface performances in Hollywood film: it frees the performer from rigid racial identity and allows sexual aggression (102–03, 184). Inside the club, Peter dances and jives with a variety of black women, and then boldly traps the bad boyfriend into a taped confession. The FBI agent who makes the arrest congratulates Peter for a job that was "pretty ballsy," as he puts it.

If this rings of colonial triumph, the white man on the jungle adventure to prove his stuff, it may be symptomatic of the larger cultural positioning of this story as a Disney film aimed at a predominantly white market. According to Latifah, Disney Studios approached her with the offer of the starring role and also the role of Executive Producer. "The studio felt the script needed not just a black voice, but because it was so racy and edgy, it also needed someone who could develop a different take on the characters" (Hart). As several reviewers pointed out, Disney was indeed anxious to channel a "black voice" for white audiences as a way to tap into the vast popularity of hip-hop culture. Steve Martin wearing a gangsta doo-rag and big jewelry, freaking on the dance floor, is comedy that both enacts and parodies white appropriation of hip-hop fashion and music. Typifying African-American cultural critics who are skeptical about the superficial and often racist dynamic of this culture-surfing, historian Kevin Powell argues that "all this fascination with hip-hop is just a cultural safari for white people" (Samuels 62).

In *Bringing Down the House*, the safari to the Down Low club is particularly rewarding for Peter because, in an unlikely scenario, this is where he bonds with the snooty, wealthy, and racist client Mrs. Arness (Joan Plowright), who has been brought to the club against her will by Charlene and Howie, has gotten stoned, and survives the brawl. After the police and FBI clean up the scene, Mrs. Arness asks Peter to take her to a diner because she has the munchies. She then withdraws her multi-million dollar account from Peter's law firm and as a private client directs it instead to Peter, so he is suddenly a tax lawyer with his own business. In short, in a comedy about restoring white masculinity, Charlene is the strategy that enables the restoration by serving as guide and translator through racial otherness.

Judith Mayne has described this cultural narrative as one in which "a black character functions centrally and crucially to enable the fantasy of the white participants" (143). As scholars have pointed out, a number of mainstream films attest to the popularity of this narrative: *Field of Dreams* (1989), *Ghost* (1990), *Shawshank Redemption* (1994), *The Family Man* (2000). Donald Bogle, historian of African-American cinema, comments that *Bringing Down the House* delivers "the typical depiction of blacks as the ones who come in to teach and help whites be all they can be" (Samuels 62). The black redeemer characters are thus positioned as versions of the faithful servant in relation to needy white characters—in this case, enabling the reunion of the white family and the re-masculinization of Peter. The Charlene character does attain her goal of clearing her police record, but along the way, she is subject to some humiliating humor, including a literal positioning as servant, and she's the one who takes the bullet, a traditional sign of selflessness in this kind of narrative.

Reception of this film, as gauged by reviewers from both the mainstream and African-American press, indicates considerable uneasiness about the racial humor centered on Latifah's character and disappointment about Latifah's involvement in this project. According to the *New York Beacon*, "the movie's racially insensitive subject matter . . . drew harsh reactions from the audience" at the media screening in New York (Daniels). The *Washington Post* reviewer observed that "Since [Latifah] has acknowledged cleaning up the crude script, she clearly read the thing and agreed to play a hip hop Aunt Jemima" (Kempley). Reviews frequently remarked on how, even with all Charlene's tough talk and charm, she is often positioned as butt of the joke. "The comedy of mismatched partners works only if the laughs are at each player's expense," the *Los Angeles Times* reviewer pointed out. "Charlene sasses [Peter] every which way, but somehow the joke is usually on her" (Dargis).

An ongoing gag — and the one reviewers noted most often — has Charlene posing as a nanny for Peter's children in order to save his reputation — that is, to explain his association with a loud black woman heavy on bling and cleavage. Charlene calls the nanny pose "that slave bit" and slathers on a fawning plantation accent to camp it up. In the most prolonged comic scene on this theme, Peter convinces Charlene to wear a maid's outfit and serve dinner in order to appease the visiting Mrs. Arness, who then reminisces fondly about black servants in her childhood household who were grateful for table scraps. She caps it by singing "a sad Negro spiritual" with the refrain, "Is massa gonna sell us tomorrow? Yes, yes, yes." Charlene's revenge for the dinner scene is to season a dish of food with Milk of Magnesia and hand it to Mrs. Arness — but it ends up being eaten by Peter instead. In the long run, neither Mrs. Arness nor the bigoted country-club types are ever made to suffer for their racism. The *Wall St. Journal* review claimed this takes racial satire "to a new level, allowing several characters to crack racial slurs, with no comeuppance" (T. King 6).

Charlene's tough, trash-talking posture and outrageous clothing are clearly meant to spark and satirize racist reactions from Peter and his horrified white neighbors and colleagues. She appears at the Beverly Hills country club in low-cut, thigh-high urban chic. She breaks into Peter's house to host a wild party around his pool, filling the BMW-laden neighborhood with the sound of rap music and with black partiers in scanty clothing. But this unruly-woman behavior takes on other connotations in relationship to black stereotypes. Reviewer Kam Williams of the *New York Beacon* says Charlene "behaves like a rap video ho' who finds fulfillment as a hyper-sexualized Mammy" (27).

The problem is that that these stereotypes are the film's sole markers of "authentic" blackness. The film takes care to recuperate Charlene from these stereotypes, showing that she was an astute reader of law books while she was in prison and is an astute reader of human nature with Peter's children. However, the uneasy reception of the racial humor indicates these more subtle characterizations are overshadowed by the troubling nature of the negative ones. The *Los Angeles Times* reviewer observed that the film "desperately wants her hip, her edge and mostly her blackness but doesn't know what to do with the human being who comes with the package" (Dargis). That is, the film has invested not in a character played by Latifah but in her cultural and commodified meanings as rap star and hip-hop diva.

Overall, Charlene functions as a racial signifier rather than a romantic heroine, a position usually privileged with far more subjectivity even in comedies. More specifically, as "former tomboy from the 'hood," Latifah enacts the type of unruly woman excluded from middle-class romance. Her size and toughness constitute one of the film's running jokes. After their disastrous blind date, Charlene cons Peter into giving her a bed for the night, but when he comes in to wake her up the next morning, she is startled awake still in prison-mode and punches him in the face, knocking him flat. When she shows up at Peter's country club to embarrass him, Peter considers calling the security guard. Then he looks at the comparatively diminutive guard and says, "No, she could probably take him." In a later scene at the club, Charlene gets into a brawl with a skinny white shrew (Missi Pyle) who doesn't stand a chance against Charlene's heft and street smarts. Upon learning that Peter's teen-aged daughter is being sexually harassed by her date, Charlene "bitch-slaps" him, as the daughter reports later, and then hangs him over a balcony by his feet until he apologizes. These physical scraps always position Charlene sympathetically as a kind of hip-hop wonder woman, and the joke is always on the white victim. But the cliché of the masculinized black woman is embedded in the text not as a joke but as a serious plot point. The bad boyfriend, it turns out, framed her by robbing the bank disguised as a woman. The video footage captured a figure that seems to be Charlene. Because we too see the video footage at one point, identified as Charlene, the implication is that Charlene herself looks like a man in drag.

My point is that this narrative struggles not simply with racial stereotypes but with the stardom of a popular female entertainer whose physical dimensions combined with her race defy the cultural profile of the heterosexual body in romantic comedy. As a thinly-disguised version of Latifah, Charlene is positioned ambivalently as a figure of fascination but also as a threatening cultural and sexual power that is fetishized and disavowed through various objectifications — rap video ho' — but also through the narrative of the masculine colonial voyage into the world of the exotic Other.

Understood in these terms, *Bringing Down the House* bears an uncanny resemblance to the Josephine Baker vehicle *Princess Tam Tam* (1935), one of two French films made by Baker at the height of her popularity in France. *Princess Tam Tam* is widely regarded as a colonialist fantasy about a white writer who regains his career, masculinity, and estranged wife through his relationship with the Baker character, Alwina, a "primitive" Tunisian shepherdess whom he meets when he travels to Africa for inspiration. Just as Charlene is a thinly-disguised version of the Latifah persona, the Alwina character is a thinly disguised version of the Josephine Baker persona — comic, spontaneous, outrageous, highly sexualized.

At the time *Princess Tam Tam* was made, Baker was lionized in France as *La Bakaire*, the fabulous Black Venus, a problematic embodiment of primitivism, the object of ceaseless scrutiny and fetishization. The French press adulated Baker's "primitive" beauty, obsessed about the darkness of her skin, and exclaimed about the grotesquery of her body and her dancing (Sweeney

56–61; Dalton and Gates 913–18). In France, her primary work was onstage, though she made, in addition to *Princess Tam Tam*, one other musical film, *Zouzou* (1934), which similarly gives her an interracial romance that goes astray. *Princess Tam Tam* reflects French culture's racialized idolization of Baker, and its object is to satirize the white man and his superficial world—similar to the satire in *Bringing Down the House*. But like the later film, *Tam Tam* gets entangled in its own racist biases. Critics have agreed that the satire never gets past its own fetishization of the Baker character as the exotic object of the colonialist gaze (Ezra 124–45; Coffman 380–83; Kalinak 319–21).

As in *Bringing Down the House*, the story opens with the hero symbolically castrated; his wife has thrown him out of the bedroom and his writing career is at a standstill. The answer, he believes, is to go "among the savages. The real savages! Yes, to Africa!" After Max discovers Alwina in Tunisia, he decides to take her home and pass her off as an African princess in the tradition of Eliza Doolittle, a good joke on Parisian culture. Just as the flirtation between Max and Alwina begins to get serious, we learn that the entire Pygmalion story was a fantasy and that Alwina has never left Africa. In short, the romantic-comedy trajectory is suddenly hijacked. But in writing the story about Alwina, Max has won back his wife and become a huge success as an author. As in *Bringing Down the House*, these plot twists come at the expense of coherency, logic, and generic formula. The revelation that most of the film has been Max's fiction is puzzling because there is no clear marker of a framework to the story-within-the-story. As critic Kathryn Kalinak puts it, "Race disturbs the very coherence of the narrative itself" (332).

The films are also parallel in their depiction of heroines representing "unruly" cultures positioned as exotic, sensual, and far more sexualized than the cultures of the white protagonist. This is demonstrated when, at a high-class Parisian ball, Alwina is tricked into breaking out of her carefully learned demeanor and throwing herself into a wild, captivating dance performance. The parallel moment in *Bringing Down the House* occurs when Charlene tries to teach Peter to freak on the dance floor of an upscale night club. The uncanny similarity is that Peter's ex-wife and sister-in-law, horrified, look down from a balcony at the couple on the dance floor, just as the uppity society women look down from a balcony at Alwina's dance. In both cases, the staging signifies the split between the bawdy physical "lower stratum" versus the refined "upper stratum." Alwina and Charlene also closely conform to Rowe's description of the unruly woman whose body and speech are excessive, whose "behavior is associated with looseness" and who is "associated with dirt, liminality" and pollution taboos (31). Alwina plays a trick on white tourists by filling their salt shakers with sand, similar to Charlene's trick of spicing a plate of food with a laxative. Both characters are associated with dancing, food, drink, the lower body, refusal of constrictive behavior and dress, and even crime—the writer meets Alwina when he catches her stealing oranges. Alwina's most charmingly subversive behaviors conform to white expectations of the colonial native: she won't wear shoes, she eats with her hands, and she refuses to obey clocks and schedules, positioning her, like Charlene, as a beguiling outsider to the boring orderliness of white culture.

Without losing the historical specificity of *Princess Tam Tam*—the French presence in Tunisia, Baker's stardom in France, French xenophobia in the 1930s—my case here is that the repetition of this story in *Bringing Down the House* suggests how Baker and Latifah, as black stars fetishized in white culture, disrupt and actually hijack a traditional white narrative, but then are themselves hijacked into demeaning roles, functioning as signs of racial/cultural difference rather than heroine. Kalinak's description of *Princess Tam Tam* could easily apply to the later Latifah film; *Tam Tam*, she says, is a film "genuinely fascinated and sympathetic to Baker on the surface, and one whose underlying structure marks her as a signifier of her race" (323).

The larger question is what, exactly, is being romanced in these films, which celebrate a larger-than-life black female stardom and its exotic culture, and then retreat to whiteness and the safety of the familiar and the status quo. In her well-known essay "Eating the Other," bell hooks describes this cultural use of "the body of the colored Other" as "unexplored terrain, a symbolic frontier that will be fertile ground for [the] reconstruction of the masculine norm" (24). Because Charlene functions as racial marker rather than subject, her sexuality is constantly deferred in *Bringing Down the House*, no matter how much cleavage squeezes out of her camisoles. As the *Boston Globe* reviewer points out, Howie's leering comments to Charlene are "as close as the movie gets to actual sex. Every time the script hints that she and Peter might possibly be physically attracted to each other, everyone involved dances skittishly away" (Burr).

Hortense Spillers wrote about this sexual displacement more than twenty years ago in analyzing the failure of the white cultural imagination to deal with black female sexuality. For whites, says Spillers, "sexual experience among black people (or sex between black and any other) is so boundlessly imagined that it loses meaning and becomes, quite simply, a medium through which the individual is suspended" (85). Thus in *Bringing Down the House*, the Eugene Levy character sexualizes Charlene constantly through a stream of suggestive comments and come-ons, but the sexual life of these two characters is an off-screen joke, "boundlessly imagined." Charlene as "rap video ho'" embodies an updated version of primitivism and the exotic Other, her sexuality a fantasy rather than a facet of personhood.

The one sexualized scene actually included in the plot is Charlene's comic attempt to teach Peter how to be a sexual tiger after they've both had too much to drink and Peter asks for advice about how to win back his ex-wife. As Ebert notes, this is a standard ploy in romantic comedy films and is in fact part of the formula which this film confounds: "they are constantly thrown together, they go from hate to affection, and they get drunk together one night and tear up the living room together, which in movies of this kind is usually the closer." Peter and Charlene drunkenly clamber all over each other, she puts his hands on her breasts, and they end up on the sofa poised for action. Instead, they are suddenly interrupted when the racist neighbor appears at the door—a metonym for the larger racist pressures looming at the perimeters of this film.

The door appears to mark the threshold of sexual possibility for this particular version of the unruly black woman in cinema. A strikingly similar moment occurs in Whoopi Goldberg's interracial romantic comedy, *Made in America*. When she and the Ted Danson character finally have the opportunity for a sex scene, it similarly morphs into physical comedy. They scramble through the house knocking over lamps and shattering knickknacks, but at the moment they get to the bed, a knock at the door downstairs interrupts them. Unlike *Bringing Down the House*, *Made in America* follows the screwball formula to its end, with the Danson character miraculously reformed of his drunken, redneck behavior and hooked up with the Goldberg character at the closure. That is, it doesn't escape the clichés of the black woman as savior. But neither does it allow the characters the requisite sexuality of romantic comedy.

Exemplifying the resistance to certain black unruly bodies in heterosexual narratives, Goldberg's films are curiously prudish in their representations of sex, as *Made in America* indicates. Even though Goldberg has often been paired romantically in her films, the camera each time turns tactfully away from sex scenes, so that even in a film such as *Fatal Beauty* (1987), the lovemaking scene is signified by a smiling Goldberg in a bathrobe the following morning. Goldberg has joked about the long lapse between her screen kisses in her debut, *The Color Purple* (1985), and her comedy with Danson eight years later. "My first screen kiss was with another woman, and I hadn't been kissed since" (Pickle 1).

Critics' comments on these deferrals of sexuality in Goldberg's films support my case about how the black unruly woman troubles the narratives of heterosexuality if she does not conform to white, middle-class ideals. Yvonne Tasker argues that Hollywood can't quite picture Goldberg as a woman, mainly because of the masculinity she projects in some of her roles. (172–73). Chris Holmlund includes Goldberg as one of the "impossible bodies" of Hollywood which "exceed the paramaters within which we think of 'ideal' or even 'normal' physiques" (4). Referring to Goldberg's role in *Ghost*, in which she channels a dead man so he can kiss his widow, Holmlund observes that "Whoopi is the first, and so far the only, black woman who 'becomes' a straight white man in mainstream movies" (133). The masculine poses are compounded by Goldberg's deliberately outrageous off-screen clothing which "effectively de-sexes her," claims critic Andrea Stuart (13), indicating the refusal of feminine norms.

The bracketing of Queen Latifah with Mae West, Josephine Baker, and Whoopi Goldberg foregrounds the problem of available romantic narratives for highly popular female stars whose "impossible bodies" and unruly-woman demeanors disrupt the norms of heterosexuality. My argument here has been that race complicates this problem as a primary inscription of the unruly-woman character, evident in the juxtaposition of *Bringing Down the House* and *Princess Tam Tam*. The startling similarities between these white masculinist fantasies, built around high-profile African-American female stars in two very different eras, delineate the racial contours of romantic comedy and its feisty traditional heroine. The unruly woman thrives in this narrative only to the extent that she conforms to racialized ideals of femininity, which can be pictured only through specific bodies and stars. Indeed, the figure of the unruly woman palpably reveals the impact of race in the conjunction of stardom and narrative, as well as its impact in the cinematic picturing of bodies within genres. Latifah's popularity as a hip-hop "crossover" star inevitably reveals racialized and contradictory cultural desires, including fascination with a black, full-figure body at odds with mainstream feminine ideals and thus at odds with heterosexuality's favorite stories.

WORKS CITED

Amber, Jeannine. "She's the Boss." *Essence* Oct. 2006: 180+.

Babbit, Jamie, dir. *But I'm a Cheerleader*. 1999. DVD. Lion's Gate, 2003.

Benjamin, Richard, dir. *Made in America*. 1993. DVD. Warner, 2004.

Bordo, Susan. *Unbearable Weight: Feminism, Western Culture, and the Body*. 1993. Tenth Anniversary Edition. Berkeley, Los Angeles, and London: U of California P, 2003.

Brennan, Sue and Barbara Schwabuer. " 'Just as You Are': Summoning and Erasing the Fat Female Body in *Bridget Jones's Diary* and *Bridget Jones: The Edge of Reason*." Seminar paper. Ohio State University, 2006.

Burr, Ty. Review of *Bringing Down the House*. *Boston Globe* 7 March 2003: C1.

Childress, Cindy. "Glamour's Portrayal of Queen Latifa: Another Unreal Ideal." *Feminist Media Studies* 5:1 (2005): 84–87.

Ciasullo, Ann M. "Making Her (In)Visible: Cultural Representations of Lesbianism and the Lesbian Body in the 1990s." *Feminist Studies* 27.3 (2001): 577–608.

Coffman, Elizabeth. "Uncanny Performances in Colonial Narratives: Josephine Baker in *Princess Tam Tam. Paradoxa* 3.3–4 (1997): 379–94.

Cornut-Gentille, Chantal. "*Working Girl*: A Case Study of Achievement by Women? New Opportunities, Old Realities." Evans and Deleyto, 111–28.

Cukor, George, dir. *The Philadelphia Story*. 1940. DVD. Warner, 2000.

Dalton, Karen C. C. and Henry Louis Gates, Jr. "Josephine Baker and Paul Colin: African-American Dance Seen Through Parisian Eyes." *Critical Inquiry* 24 (1998): 903–34.

Daniels, Karu F. "Queen Latifah Rules Hollywood's Royal Court." *New York Beacon* 19 March 2003: 3.

Darabont, Frank, dir. *The Shawshank Redemption*. 1994. DVD. Castle Rock, 1999.

Dargis, Manohla. Review of *Bringing Down the House*. *Los Angeles Times* 7 March 2003.

DiBattista, Maria. *Fast Talking Dames*. New Haven and London: Yale UP, 2001.

DuCille, Ann. "The Colour of Class: Classifying Race in the Popular Imagination." *Social Identities* 7.3 (2001): 409–19.

Ebert, Roger. Review of *Bringing Down the House*. *Chicago Sun Times*. 7 March 2003. *http://rogerebert.suntimes.com/apps/pbcs.dll/article*

Ephron, Nora, dir. *You've Got Mail*. 1998. DVD. Warner, 1999.

Evans, Peter William and Celestino Delyeto. *Terms of Endearment: Hollywood Romantic Comedy of the 1980s and 1990s*. Edinburgh: Edinburgh UP, 1998.

Ezra, Elizabeth. *The Colonial Unconscious: Race and Culture in Interwar France*. Ithaca and London: Cornell, 2000.

Ganatra, Nisha, dir. *Chutney Popcorn*. 1999. DVD. Wolfe, 2001.

Gray, Gary, dir. *Set it Off*. 1996. DVD. New Line, 1999.

Gréville, Edmond, dir. *Princess Tam Tam*. [*Princesse Tam Tam*]. 1935. DVD. Kino, 2005.

Halberstam, Judith. *Female Masculinity*. Durham and London: Duke UP, 1998.

Hamburg, John, dir. *Along Came Polly*. 2004. DVD. Universal, 2004.

Hamri, Sanaa, dir. *Something New*. 2006. DVD. Universal, 2006.

Hart, Hugh. "Her Hip Hop Majesty for the Oscar-Nominated Queen Latifah." *Boston Globe* 2 March 2003: N13.

Haskell, Molly. *From Reverence to Rape: The Treatment of Women in the Movies*. 1974. Chicago and London: U of Chicago P, 1987.

Hawkes, Howard, dir. *Bringing Up Baby*. 1938. DVD. Turner, 2005.

———, dir. *Gentlemen Prefer Blondes*. 1953. DVD. Fox, 2006.

———, dir. *His Girl Friday*. 1940. DVD. Sony, 2000.

Hirschberg, Lynn. "A Film of One's Own." *The New York Times Magazine*. 3 Sept. 2006. 31+.

Holland, Tom, dir. *Fatal Beauty*. 1987. DVD. MGM, 2001.

Holmlund, Chris. *Impossible Bodies: Femininity and Masculinity at the Movies*. London and New York: Routledge, 2002.

hooks, bell. "Eating the Other." *Black Looks*. Boston: South End, 1992. 21–40.

Ingraham, Chrys. *White Weddings: Romancing Heterosexuality in Popular Culture*. New York and London: Routledge, 1999.

Jewison, Norman, dir. *Moonstruck*. 1987. DVD. MGM, 1998.

Kalinak, Kathryn. "Disciplining Josephine Baker: Gender, Race, and the Limits of Disciplinarity." *Music and Cinema*. Eds. James Buhler et al. Hanover and London: UP of New England, 2000. 316–38.

Kempley, Rita. "Bringing Down the House & Moral Standards, Too." *Washington Post* 7 March 2003: C5.

Kidron, Beeban, dir. *Bridget Jones — The Edge of Reason*. 2004. DVD. Universal, 2005.

King, Geoff. *Film Comedy*. London and New York: Wallflower, 2002.

King, Tom. "Getting Down on 'House.'" *The Wall Street Journal* 28 March 2003: W6.

Koster, Henry. *The Bishop's Wife*. 1948. DVD. MGM, 2001.

Krutnik, Frank. "Conforming Passion?: Contemporary Romantic Comedy." Neale, 130–47.

Latifah, Queen. *All Hail the Queen*. CD. Tommy Boy, 1989.

Living Single. Fox. 1993–98. Complete First Season. DVD. Warner, 2006.

Maguire, Sharon, dir. *Bridget Jones's Diary*. 2001. DVD. Miramax, 2001.

Marshall, Garry, dir. *Pretty Woman*. 1990. DVD. Dimension, 2001.

Marshall, Penny, dir. *The Preacher's Wife*. 1996. DVD. Buena Vista, 2002.

Marshall, Rob, dir. *Chicago*. 2002. DVD. Miramax, 2003.

Mayne, Judith. *Cinema and Spectatorship*. New York and London: Routledge, 1993.

McCarey, Leo, dir. *The Awful Truth*. 1938. DVD. Sony, 2003.

Mitchell, Elvis. "How Out of It Can You Be? Here's Going All the Way." *New York Times* 7 March 2003: E15.

Neale, Steve, ed. *Genre and Contemporary Hollywood*. London: BFI, 2002.

——— and Frank Krutnik. *Popular Film and Television Comedy*. Routledge: London and New York, 1990.

Norment, Lynn. "Queen Latifah Changes Her Figure and Her Tune." *Ebony* Jan. 2005: 130+.

Oz, Frank, dir. *Housesitter*. 1992. DVD. Universal, 1998.

Paul, William. "The Impossibility of Romance: Hollywood Comedy, 1978–1999." Neale, 117–29.

Pickle, Betsy. "Whoopi & Ted: Only in America." *St. Louis Post-Dispatch* 4 June 1993: 1G.

Preston, Catherine L. "Hanging on a Star: The Resurrection of the Romance Film in the 1990s." *Film Genre 2000: New Critical Essays*. Ed. Wheeler Winston Dixon. Albany: State U of New York P, 2000. 227–43.

Ratner, Brett, dir. *The Family Man*. 2000. DVD. Universal, 2001.

Robertson, Regina R. "Lovin' the Skin They're In." *Essence* Jan. 2006: 103+.

Robinson, Phil Alden, dir. *Field of Dreams*. 1989. DVD. Universal, 2004.

Rogin, Michael. *Blackface, White Noise: Jewish Immigrants in the Hollywood Melting Pot*. 1996. Berkeley, Los Angeles, and London: U of California P, 1998.

Rowe, Kathleen. *The Unruly Woman: Gender and the Genres of Laughter*. Austin, Texas: U of Texas P, 1995.

Samuels, Allison. "Minstrels in Baggy Jeans? How to Sell a Hip Hop Movie: Make it About White People." *Newsweek* 5 May 2003: 62.

Schatz, Thomas. *Hollywood Genres: Formulas, Filmmaking, and the Studio System*. New York: Random House, 1981.

Shankman, Adam, dir. *Bringing Down the House*. 2003. DVD. Walt Disney Video, 2003.

Spielberg, Steven, dir. *The Color Purple*. 1985. DVD. Warner, 1997.

Spillers, Hortense J. "Interstices: A Small Drama of Words." *Pleasure and Danger: Exploring Female Sexuality*. Ed. Carole S. Vance. Boston, London, Melbourne and Henley: Routledge & Kegan Paul, 1984. 73–100.

Sturges, Preston, dir. *The Lady Eve*. 1941. DVD. Criterion, 2001.

Story, Tim, dir. *Taxi*. 2004. DVD. Fox, 2005.

Stuart, Andrea. "Making Whoopi." *Sight and Sound*. 3.2 (1993): 12–13.

Swan, Rachel. "The Queen's Gambit: The Underhanded Treatment of Race in *Bringing Down the House*." *bitch* 21 (2003): 25–28.

Sweeney, Carole. *From Fetish to Subject: Race, Modernism, and Primitivism, 1919–1935*. Westport, Conn. and London: Praeger, 2004.

Tasker, Yvonne. *Working Girls: Gender and Sexuality in Popular Cinema*. London and New York: Routledge, 1998.

———— and Diane Negra. "Postfeminism and the Archive for the Future." *Camera Obscura* 21.2 (2006): 170–76.

Thomas, Deborah. "*Murphy's Romance*: Romantic Love and the Everyday." Evans and Deleyto. 57–74.

Wang, Wayne, dir. *Last Holiday*. 2006. DVD. Paramount, 2006.

Williams, Kam. "Queen Latfiah and Martin 'Bringing Down the House.' " *The New York Beacon* 19 March 2003: 27.

Wheeler, Anne, dir. *Better Than Chocolate*. 1999. DVD. Lions' Gate, 1999.

KATHRYN PAULY MORGAN

Women and the Knife: Cosmetic Surgery and the Colonization of Women's Bodies

Kathryn Pauly Morgan is Professor of Philosophy, Women's Studies, and Gender Studies at the University of Toronto, and her current research is on gender and bioethics. This selection is from Hypatia, *a journal of feminist philosophy.*

Voice 1: (a woman looking forward to attending a prestigious charity ball): "There will be a lot of new faces at the Brazilian Ball" ("Changing Faces" 1989). [Class/status symbol]

Voice 2: "You can keep yourself trim. . . . But you have no control over the way you wrinkle, or the fat on your hips, or the skin of your lower abdomen. If you are *hereditarily predestined* to stretch out or wrinkle in your face, you will. If your parents had puffy eyelids and saggy jowls, you're going to have puffy eyelids and saggy jowls" ("Changing Faces" 1989). [Regaining a sense of control; liberation from parents; transcending hereditary predestination]

Voice 3: "Now we want a nose that makes a statement, with tip definition and a strong bridge line" ("Changing Faces" 1989). [Domination; strength]

Voice 4: "I've decided to get a facelift for my fortieth birthday after ten years of living and working in the tropics had taken its toll" ("Changing Faces" 1989). [Gift to the self; erasure of a decade of hard work and exposure]

Voice 5: "I've gotten my breasts augmented. I can use it as a tax write-off" ("Changing Faces" 1989). [Professional advancement; economic benefits]

Voice 6: "I'm a teacher and kids let schoolteachers know how we look and they aren't nice about it. A teacher who looks like an old bat or has a big nose will get a nickname" ("Retouching Nature's Way: Is Cosmetic Surgery Worth It?" 1990). [Avoidance of cruelty; avoidance of ageist bias]

Voice 7: "I'll admit to a boob job" (Susan Akin, Miss America of 1986 quoted in Goodman 1986). [Prestige; status; competitive accomplishments in beauty context]

Voice 8 (forty-five year old grandmother and proprietor of a business): "In my business, the customers expect you to look as good as they do"

451

(Hirschson 1987). [Business asset; economic gain; possible denial of grandmother status]

Voice 9: "People in business see something like this as showing an overall aggressiveness and go-forwardness *The trend is to, you know, be all that you can be*" ("Cosmetic Surgery for the Holidays" 1985). [Success; personal fulfillment]

Voice 10 (paraphrase): "I do it to fight holiday depression" ("Cosmetic Surgery for the Holidays" 1985). [Emotional control; happiness]

Voice 11: "I came to see Dr. X for the holiday season. I have important business parties, and the man I'm trying to get to marry me is coming in from Paris" ("Cosmetic Surgery for the Holidays" 1985). [Economic gain; heterosexual affiliation]

Women have traditionally regarded (and been taught to regard) their bodies, particularly if they are young, beautiful, and fertile, *as a locus of power* to be enhanced through artifice and, now, through artifact. In 1792, in *A Vindication of the Rights of Woman*, Mary Wollstonecraft remarked: "Taught from infancy that beauty is woman's scepter, the mind shapes itself to the body and roaming round its gilt cage, only seeks to adorn its prison." How ironic that the mother of the creator of *Frankenstein* should be the source of that quote. We need to ask ourselves whether today, involved as we are in the modern inversion of "our bodies shaping themselves to our minds," we are creating a new species of woman-monster with new artifactual bodies that function as prisons or whether cosmetic surgery for women does represent a potentially liberating field of choice.[1]

When Snow White's stepmother asks the mirror "Who is fairest of all?" she is not asking simply an empirical question. In wanting to continue to be "the fairest of all," she is striving, in a clearly competitive context, for a prize, for a position, for power. The affirmation of her beauty brings with it privileged heterosexual affiliation, privileged access to forms of power unavailable to the plan, the ugly, the aged, and the barren.

The Voices are seductive—they speak the language of gaining access to transcendence, achievement, liberation, and power. And they speak to a kind of reality. First, electing to undergo the surgery necessary to create youth and beauty artificially not only appears to but often actually does give a woman a sense of identity that, to some extent, she has chosen herself. Second, it offers her the potential to raise her status both socially and economically by increasing her opportunities for heterosexual affiliation (especially with white men). Third, by committing herself to the pursuit of beauty, a woman integrates her life with a consistent set of values and choices that bring her wide-spread approval and a resulting sense of increased self-esteem. Fourth, the pursuit of beauty often gives a woman access to a range of individuals who administer to her body in a caring way, an experience often sadly lacking in the day-to-day lives of many women. As a result, a woman's pursuit of beauty through transformation is often associated with lived experiences of self-creation, self-fulfillment, self-transcendence, and being cared for. The power of these experiences must not be underestimated.[2]

While I acknowledge that these choices can confer a kind of integrity on a woman's life, I also believe that they are likely to embroil her in a set of interrelated contradictions. I refer to these as "Paradoxes of Choice."

THREE PARADOXES OF CHOICE

In exploring these paradoxes, I appropriate Foucault's analysis of the diffusion of power in order to understand forms of power that are potentially more personally invasive than are more obvious, publicly identifiable aspects of power. In the chapter "Docile Bodies" in *Discipline and Punish*, Foucault (1979, 136–37) highlights three features of what he calls disciplinary power:

(1) The *scale* of the control. In disciplinary power the body is treated individually and in a coercive way because the body itself is the *active* and hence apparently free body that is being controlled through movements, gestures, attitudes, and degrees of rapidity.

(2) The *object* of the control, which involves meticulous control over the efficiency of movements and forces,

(3) the *modality* of the control, which involves constant, uninterrupted coercion.

Foucault argues that the outcome of disciplinary power is the docile body, a body "that may be subjected, used, transformed, and improved" (Foucault 1979, 136). Foucault is discussing this model of power in the context of prisons and armies, but we can adapt the central insights of this notion to see how women's bodies are entering "a machinery of power that explores it, breaks it down, and rearranges it" through a recognizably political metamorphosis of embodiment (Foucault 1979, 138).[3] What is important about this notion in relation to cosmetic surgery is the extent to which it makes it possible to speak about the diffusion of power throughout Western industrialized cultures that are increasingly committed to a technological beauty imperative. It also makes it possible to refer to a set of experts — cosmetic surgeons — whose explicit power mandate is to explore, break down, and rearrange women's bodies.

Paradox One: The Choice of Conformity —
Understanding the Number 10

While the technology of cosmetic surgery could clearly be used to create and celebrate idiosyncrasy, eccentricity, and uniqueness, it is obvious that this is not how it is presently being used. Cosmetic surgeons report that legions of women appear in their offices demanding "Bo Derek" breasts ("Cosmetic Surgery for the Holidays" 1985). Jewish women demand reductions of their noses so as to be able to "pass" as one of their Aryan sisters who form the dominant ethnic group (Lakoff and Scherr, 1984). Adolescent Asian girls who bring in pictures of Elizabeth Taylor and of Japanese movie actresses (whose faces have already been reconstructed) demand the "Westernizing" of their own eyes and the creation of higher noses in hopes of better job and marital prospects ("New Bodies for Sale" 1985). Black women buy toxic bleaching agents in hopes of attaining lighter skin. What is being created in all of these instances is not simply beautiful bodies and faces but white, Western, Anglo-Saxon bodies in a racist, anti-Semitic context.

More often than not, what appear at first glance to be instances of choice turn out to be instances of conformity. The women who undergo cosmetic surgery in order to compete in various beauty pageants are clearly choosing to conform. So is the woman who wanted to undergo a facelift, tummy tuck, and liposuction all in one week, in order to win heterosexual approval *from a man she had not seen in twenty-eight years* and whose individual preferences she could not possibly know. In some ways, it does not matter who the particular judges are. Actual men—brothers, fathers, male lovers, male beauty "experts"—and hypothetical men live in the aesthetic imaginations of women. Whether they are male employers, prospective male spouses, male judges in the beauty pageants, or male-identified women, these modern day Parises are generic and live sometimes ghostly but powerful lives in the reflective awareness of women (Berger, 1972). A woman's makeup, dress, gestures, voice, degree of cleanliness, degree of muscularity, odors, degree of hirsuteness, vocabulary, hands, feet, skin, hair, and vulva can all be evaluated, regulated, and disciplined in the light of the hypothetical often-white male viewer and the male viewer present in the assessing gaze of other women (Haug, 1987). Men's appreciation and approval of achieved femininity becomes all the more invasive when it resides in the incisions, stitches, staples, and scar tissue of women's bodies as women choose to conform. And, as various theorists have pointed out, women's public conformity to the norms of beauty often signals a deeper conformity to the norms of compulsory heterosexuality along with an awareness of the violence that can result from violating those norms.[4] Hence the first paradox: that what looks like an optimal situation of reflection, deliberation, and self-creating choice often signals conformity at a deeper level.

Paradox Two: Liberation into Colonization

As argued above, a woman's desire to create a permanently beautiful and youthful appearance that is not vulnerable to the threats of externally applied cosmetic artifice or to the natural aging process of the body must be understood as a deeply significant existential project. It deliberately involves the exploitation and transformation of the most intimately experienced domain of immanence, the body, in the name of transcendence: transcendence of hereditary predestination, of lived time, of one's given "limitations." What I see as particularly alarming in this project is that what comes to have primary significance is not the real given existing woman but her body viewed as a "primitive entity" that is seen only as potential, as a kind of raw material to be exploited in terms of appearance, eroticism, nurturance, and fertility as defined by the colonizing culture.[5]

But for whom is this exploitation and transformation taking place? Who exercises the power here? Sometimes the power is explicit. It is exercised by brothers, fathers, male lovers, male engineering students who taunt and harass their female counterparts, and by male cosmetic surgeons who offer "free advice" in social gatherings to women whose "deformities" and "severe problems" can all be cured through their healing needles and knives.[6] And the colonizing power is transmitted through and by those women whose own bodies and disciplinary practices demonstrate the efficacy of "taking care of herself" in these culturally defined feminine ways.

Sometimes, however, the power may be so diffused as to dominate the consciousness of a given woman with no other subject needing to be present. As Bartky notes, such diffused power also signals the presence of the colonizer:

> Normative femininity is coming more and more to be centered on woman's body. . . . Images of normative femininity . . . have replaced the religious oriented tracts of the past. The woman who checks her makeup half a dozen times a day to see if her foundation has caked or her mascara has run, who worries that the wind or the rain may spoil her hairdo, who looks frequently to see if her stockings have bagged at the ankle, or who, feeling fat, monitors everything she eats, *has become, just as surely as the inmate of the Panopticon, a self-policing subject, a self committed to a relentless self-surveillance. This self-surveillance is a form of obedience to patriarchy.* (Bartky 1988, 81; italics added)

As Foucault and others have noted, practices of coercion and domination are often camouflaged by practical rhetoric and supporting theories that appear to be benevolent, therapeutic, and voluntaristic. Previously, for example, colonizing was often done in the name of bringing "civilization" through culture and morals to "primitive, barbaric people," but contemporary colonizers mask their exploitation of "raw materials and human labor" in the name of "development." Murphy (1984), Piercy (1980), and I (Morgan, 1989) have all claimed that similar rhetorical camouflage of colonization takes place in the areas of women's reproductive decision–making and women's right to bodily self–determination. In all of these instances of colonization the ideological manipulation of technology can be identified, and, I would argue, in all of these cases this technology has often been used to the particular disadvantage and destruction of some aspect of women's integrity.[7]

In electing to undergo cosmetic surgery, women appear to be protesting against the constraints of the "given" in their embodied lives and seeking liberation from those constraints. But I believe they are in danger of retreating and becoming more vulnerable, at that very level of embodiment, to those colonizing forms of power that may have motivated the protest in the first place. Moreover, in seeking independence, they can become even more dependent on male assessment and on the services of all those experts they initially bought to render them independent.

Here we see a second paradox bound up with choice: that the rhetoric is that of liberation and care, of "making the most of yourself," but the reality is often the transformation of oneself as a woman for the eye, the hand, and the approval of the Other—the lover, the taunting students, the customers, the employers, the social peers. And the Other is almost always affected by the dominant culture, which is male-supremacist, racist, ageist, heterosexist, anti-Semitic, ableist and class-biased.[8]

Paradox Three: Coerced Voluntariness and the Technological Imperative

Where is the coercion? At first glance, women who choose to undergo cosmetic surgery often seem to represent a paradigm case of the rational chooser. Drawn increasingly from wider and wider economic groups, these women clearly make a choice, often at significant economic cost to the rest of their life, to pay the large sums of money demanded by cosmetic surgeons (since American health insurance plans do not cover this elective cosmetic surgery).

Furthermore, they are often highly critical consumers of these services, demanding extensive consultation, information regarding the risks and benefits of various surgical procedures, and professional guarantees of expertise. Generally they are relatively young and in good health. Thus, in some important sense, they epitomize relatively invulnerable free agents making a decision under virtually optimal conditions.

Moreover, on the surface, women who undergo cosmetic surgery choose a set of procedures that are, by definition, "elective." This term is used, quite straightforwardly, to distinguish cosmetic surgery from surgical intervention for reconstructive or health-related reasons (e.g., following massive burns, cancer-related forms of mutilation, etc.). The term also appears to distinguish cosmetic surgery from apparently involuntary and more pathologically transforming forms of intervention in the bodies of young girls in the form of, for example, foot-binding or extensive genital mutilation.[9] But I believe that this does not exhaust the meaning of the term "elective" and that the term performs a seductive role in facilitating the ideological camouflage of the *absence of choice*. Similarly, I believe that the word "cosmetic" serves an ideological function in hiding the fact that the changes are *noncosmetic*: they involve lengthy periods of pain, are permanent, and result in irreversibly alienating metamorphoses such as the appearance of youth on an aging body.

In order to illuminate the paradox of choice involved here, I wish to draw an analogy from the literature on reproductive technology. In the case of reproductive self-determination, technology has been hailed as increasing the range of women's choices in an absolute kind of way. It cannot be denied that due to the advances in various reproductive technologies, especially IVF and embryo freezing, along with various advances in fetology and fetal surgery, there are now women with healthy children who previously would not have had children. Nevertheless, there are two important ideological, choice-diminishing dynamics at work that affect women's choices in the area of the new reproductive technologies. These dynamics are also at work in the area of cosmetic surgery.

The first of these is the *pressure to achieve perfection through technology*, signaled by the rise of new forms of eugenicist thinking. More profoundly than ever before, contemporary eugenicists stigmatize potential and existing disabled babies, children, and adults. More and more frequently, benevolently phrased eugenicist pressures are forcing women to choose to submit to a battery of prenatal diagnostic tests and extensive fetal monitoring in the name of producing "perfect" (white) babies. As more and more reproductive technologies and tests are invented (and "perfected" in and on the bodies of fertile women), partners, parents, family, obstetricians, and other experts on fertility pressure women to submit to this technology in the name of "maximized choice" and "responsible motherhood." As Achilles (1988), Beck-Gernsheim (1989), Rothman (1984), Morgan (1989) and others have argued, women are being subjected to increasingly intense forms of coercion, a fact that is signaled by the intensifying *lack of freedom* felt by women to refuse to use the technology if they are pregnant and the technology is available. . . .

Increasingly, "fully responsible motherhood" is coming to be defined in technology-dependent terms and, in a larger cultural context of selective obligatory maternity, more and more women are "choosing to act" in accord with technological imperatives prior to conception, through conception, through maternity, and through birthing itself. Whether this is, then, a situation of increased choice is at the very least highly contestable. Moreover, in a larger ideological context of obligatory and "controlled" motherhood, I am reluctant simply to accept the reports of the technologists and fertility experts that their patients "want access" to the technology as a sufficient condition for demonstrating purely voluntary choice.[10]

A similar argument can be made regarding the significance of the pressure to be beautiful in relation to the allegedly voluntary nature of "electing" to undergo cosmetic surgery. It is clear that pressure to use this technology is on the increase. Cosmetic surgeons report on the wide range of clients who buy their services, pitch their advertising to a large audience through the use of the media, and encourage women to think, metaphorically, in terms of the seemingly trivial "nips" and "tucks" that will transform their lives. As cosmetic surgery becomes increasingly normal-ized through the concept of the female "make-over" that is translated into columns and articles in the print media or made into nationwide television shows directed at female viewers, as the "success stories" are invited on to talk shows along with their "makers," and as surgically transformed women win the Miss America pageants, women who refuse to submit to the knives and to the needles, to the anaesthetics and the bandages, will come to be seen as deviant in one way or another. Women who refuse to use these technologies are already becoming stigmatized as "unliberated," "not caring about their appearance," as "refusing to be all that they could be" or as "granola."

And as more and more success comes to those who do "care about themselves" in this technological fashion, more coercive dimensions enter the scene. In the past, only those women who were perceived to be *naturally* beautiful (or rendered beautiful through relatively conservative superficial artifice) had access to forms of power and economic social mobility closed off to women regarded as plain or ugly or old. But now womanly beauty is becoming technologically achievable, a commodity for which each and every woman can, in principle, sacrifice if she is to survive and succeed in the world, particularly in industrialized Western countries. Now technology is making obligatory the appearance of youth and the reality of "beauty" for every woman who can afford it. Natural destiny is being supplanted by technologically grounded coercion, and the coercion is camouflaged by the language of choice, fulfillment, and liberation. . . .

In the technical and popular literature on cosmetic surgery, what have previously been described as *normal* variations of female bodily shapes or described in the relatively innocuous language of "problem areas," are increasingly being described as "deformities," "ugly protrusions," "inadequate breasts," and "unsightly concentrations of fat cells"—a litany of descriptions designed to intensify feelings of disgust, shame, and relief at the possibility of recourse for these "deformities." Cosmetic surgery promises virtually all women the creation of beautiful, youthful-appearing bodies. As a consequence, more and more women will be labeled "ugly" and "old" in relation to this more select population of surgically created beautiful faces and bodies that have been contoured and augmented, lifted and tucked into a state of achieved feminine excellence.

NOTES

1. The desire to subordinate our bodies to some ideal that involves bringing the body under control is deeply felt by many contemporary women (apart from any religious legacy of asceticism). As Bartky (1988) and Bordo (1985, 1989a, 1989b) have noted, this is an aspect of the disembodying desires of anorexic women and women who "pump iron." In the area of cosmetic surgery, this control is mediated by the technology and expertise of the surgeons, but the theme is continually articulated.

2. A similar point regarding femininity is made by Sandra Bartky (1988) in her discussion of "feminine discipline." She remarks that women will resist the dismantling

of the disciplines of femininity because, at a very deep level, it would involve a radical alteration of what she calls our "informal social ontology":

> To have a body felt to be "feminine"—a body socially constructed through the appropriate practices—is in most cases crucial to a woman's sense of herself as female and, since persons currently can *be* only as male or female, to her sense of herself as an existing individual. . . . The radical feminist critique of femininity, then, may pose a threat not only to a woman's sense of her own identity and desirability but to the very structure of her social universe. (Bartky 1988, 78)

3. I view this as a recognizably *political* metamorphosis because forensic cosmetic surgeons and social archaeologists will be needed to determine the actual age and earlier appearance of women in cases where identification is called for on the basis of existing carnal data. See Griffin's (1978) poignant description in "The Anatomy Lesson" for a reconstruction of the life and circumstances of a dead mother from just such carnal evidence. As we more and more profoundly artifactualize our own bodies, we become more sophisticated archaeological repositories and records that both signify and symbolize our culture.

4. For both documentation and analysis of this claim, see Bartky (1988), Bordo (1985, 1989a, 1989b), and Rich (1980).

5. I intend to use "given" here in a relative and political sense. I don't believe that the notion that biology is somehow "given" and culture is just "added on" is a tenable one. I believe that we are intimately and inextricably encultured and embodied, so that a reductionist move in either direction is doomed to failure. For a persuasive analysis of this thesis, see Lowe (1982) and Haraway (1978, 1989). For a variety of political analyses of the "given" as primitive, see Marge Piercy's poem "Right to Life" (1980), Morgan (1989), and Murphy (1984).

6. Although I am cognizant of the fact that many women are entering medical school, the available literature is preponderantly authored by men most of whom, I would infer, are white, given the general demographics of specializations in medical school. I also stress the whiteness here to emphasize the extent to which white norms of beauty dominate the field. I think of these surgeons as akin to "fairy godfathers" to underscore the role they are asked to play to "correct," "improve," or "render beautiful" what girls and women have inherited from their mothers, who can only make recommendations at the level of artifice, not artifact.

7. Space does not permit development of this theme on an international scale but it is important to note the extent to which pharmaceutical "dumping" is taking place in the so-called "developing countries" under the ideological camouflage of "population control and family planning." See Hartman (1987) for a thorough and persuasive analysis of the exploitative nature of this practice.

8. The extent to which ableist bias is at work in this area was brought home to me by two quotations cited by a woman with a disability. She discusses two guests on a television show. One was "a poised, intelligent young woman who'd been rejected as a contestant for the Miss Toronto title. She is a paraplegic. The organizers' lame excuse for disqualifying her: 'We couldn't fit the choreography around you.' Another guest was a former executive of the Miss Universe contest. He declared, 'Her participation in a beauty contest would be like having a blind man compete in a shooting match'" (Matthews 1985).

9. It is important here to guard against facile and ethnocentric assumptions about beauty rituals and mutilation. See Lakoff and Scherr (1984) for an analysis of the relativity of these labels and for important insights about the fact that use of the term "mutilation" almost always signals a distancing from and reinforcement of a sense of cultural superiority in the speaker who uses it to denounce what other cultures do in contrast to "our culture."

10. For the most sustained and theoretically sophisticated analysis of pronatalism operating in the context of industrialized capitalism, see Gimenez (1984). Gimenez restricts her discussion to working-class women but, unfortunately, doesn't develop a more differentiated grid of pronatalist and antinatalist pressures within that economic and social group. For example, in Quebec there are strong pressures on Francophone working class women to reproduce, while there is selective pressure against Anglophone and immigrant working women bearing children. Nevertheless, Gimenez's account demonstrates the systemic importance of pronatalism in many women's lives.

REFERENCES

Achilles, Rona. 1988. What's new about the new reproductive technologies? *Discussion paper: Ontario Advisory Council on the Status of Women.* Toronto: Government of Ontario.

Bartky, Sandra Lee. 1988. Foucault, femininity, and the modernization of patriarchal power. In *Femininity and Foucault: Reflections of resistance.* Irene Diamond and Lee Quinby, eds. Boston: Northeastern University Press.

Beck-Gernsheim, Elisabeth. 1989. From the pill to test-tube babies: New options, new pressures in reproductive behavior. In *Healing technology: Feminist perspectives.* Kathryn Strother Ratcliff, ed. Ann Arbor: University of Michigan Press.

Berger, John. 1972. *Ways of seeing.* New York: Penguin Books.

Bordo, Susan R. 1985. Anorexia nervosa: Psychopathology as the crystallization of culture. *The Philosophical Forum* 2(Winter): 73–103.

———. 1989a. The body and the reproduction of femininity: A feminist appropriation of Foucault. In *Gender/body/knowledge: Feminist reconstructions of being and knowing.* Alison Jaggar and Susan Bordo, eds. New Brunswick, NJ: Rutgers University Press.

———. 1989b. Reading the slender body. In *Women, science and the body politic: Discourses and representations.* Mary Jacobus, Evelyn Fox Keller and Sally Shuttleworth, eds. New York: Methuen.

Changing Faces. 1989. *Toronto Star.* May 25.

Computer used to pick hairstyles. 1989. *Globe and Mail.*

Cosmetic surgery for the holidays. 1985. *Sheboygan Press.* New York Times News Service.

Diamond, Irene and Lee Quinby, eds. 1988. *Feminism and Foucault: Reflections on resistance.* Boston: Northeastern University Press.

Facial regeneration. 1990. *Health: A community education service of the Froedtert Memorial Lutheran Hospital.* Supplement to *Milwaukee Journal,* August 26.

Falling in love again. 1990. *Toronto Star.* July 23.

Foucault, Michel. 1979. *Discipline and punish: The birth of the prison.* Alan Sheridan, trans. New York: Pantheon.

———. 1988. Technologies of the self: The political technology of the individual. In *The technologies of the self.* Luther H. Martin, Huck Gutman and Patrick Hutton, eds. Amherst: University of Massachusetts Press.

Gimenez, Martha. 1984. Feminism, pronatalism, and motherhood. In *Mothering: Essays in feminist theory.* Joyce Trebilcot, ed. Totowa, NJ: Rowman and Allenheld.

Goodman, Ellen. 1989. A plastic pageant. *Boston Globe.* September 19.

Griffin, Susan. 1978. The anatomy lesson. In *Woman and nature: The roaring inside her.* New York: Harper and Row.

Haraway, Donna. 1978. Animal sociology and a natural economy of the body politic, Parts I, II. *Signs: Journal of Women in Culture and Society* 4(1): 21–60.

———. 1989. *Primate visions.* New York: Routledge.

Hartman, Betsy. 1987. *Reproductive rights and wrongs: The global politics of population control and contraceptive choice.* New York: Harper and Row.

Haug, Frigga, ed. 1987. *Female sexualization: A Collective work of memory.* Erica Carter, trans. London: Verso.

Jaggar, Alison, and Susan R. Bordo, eds. 1989. *Gender/body/knowledge: Feminist reconstructions of being and knowing.* New Brunswick, NJ: Rutgers University Press.

Lakoff, Robin Tolmach, and Raquel Scherr. 1984. *Face value: The politics of beauty.* Boston: Routledge and Kegan Paul.

Long, strong, perfect nails usually not nature's own. 1988. *Toronto Star.* August 18.

Looking for Mr. Beautiful. 1990. *Boston Globe.* May 7.

Lowe, Marion. 1982. The dialectic of biology and culture. In *Biological woman: The convenient myth.* Ruth Hubbard, Mary Sue Henifin, and Barbara Fried, eds. Cambridge, MA: Schenkman.

Madonna passionate about fitness. 1990. *Toronto Star.* August 16.

Matthews, Gwyneth Ferguson. 1985. Mirror, mirror: Self-image and disabled women. *Women and disability: Resources for feminist research* 14(1): 47–50.

Morgan, Kathryn Pauly. 1986. Romantic love, altruism, and self-respect: An analysis of Simone De Beauvoir. *Hypatia* 1(1): 117–48.

———. 1987. Women and moral madness. In *Science, morality and feminist theory.* Marsha Hanen and Kai Nielsen, eds. Special issue of the *Canadian Journal of Philosophy* Supplementary Volume 13: 201–26.

———. 1989. Of woman born: How old-fashioned! New reproductive technologies and women's oppression. In *The future of human reproduction.* Christine Overall, ed. Toronto: The Women's Press.

Murphy, Julie [Julien S]. 1984. Egg farming and women's future. In *Test-tube women: What future for motherhood?* Rita Arditti, Renate Duelli-Klein, and Shelley Minden, eds. Boston: Pandora Press.

New bodies for sale. 1985. *Newsweek.* May 27.

New profile took 3 years. 1989. *Toronto Star.* May 25.

Piercy, Marge. 1980. Right to life. In *The moon is always female.* New York: Alfred A. Knopf.

The quest to be a perfect 10. 1990. *Toronto Star.* February 1.

Ratcliff, Hathryn Strother, ed. 1989. *Healing technology: Feminist perspectives.* Ann Arbor: University of Michigan Press.

Raymond, Janice. 1987. Preface to *Man-made woman.* Gena Corea et al., eds. Bloomington: Indiana University Press.

Retouching nature's way: Is cosmetic surgery worth it? 1990. *Toronto Star.* February 1.

Rich, Adrienne. 1980. Compulsory heterosexuality and lesbian existence. *Signs: Journal of Women in Culture and Society* 5(4): 631–60.

Rothman, Barbara Katz. 1984. The meanings of choice in reproductive technology. In *Test-tube women: What future for motherhood?,* Rita Arditti, Renate Duelli-Klein, and Shelley Minden, eds. Boston: Pandora Press.

Woman, 43, dies after cosmetic surgery. 1989. *Toronto Star.* July 7.

KATHA POLLITT
Why Boys Don't Play with Dolls

Katha Pollitt's articles, essays, and reviews appear frequently in The New York Times, The New York Review of Books, The New Yorker, The New Republic, Harper's, *and a host of other major international newspapers and magazines. She is a regular columnist for* The Nation.

It's twenty-eight years since the founding of NOW, and boys still like trucks and girls still like dolls. Increasingly, we are told that the source of these robust preferences must lie outside society — in prenatal hormonal influences, brain chemistry, genes — and that feminism has reached its natural limits. What else could possibly explain the love of preschool girls for party dresses or the desire of toddler boys to own more guns than Mark from Michigan?

True, recent studies claim to show small cognitive differences between the sexes: He gets around by orienting himself in space; she does it by remembering landmarks. Time will tell if any deserve the hoopla with which each is invariably greeted, over the protests of the researchers themselves. But even if the results hold up (and the history of such research is not encouraging), we don't need studies of sex-differentiated brain activity in reading, say, to understand why boys and girls still seem so unalike.

The feminist movement has done much for some women, and something for every woman, but it has hardly turned America into a playground free of sex roles. It hasn't even got women to stop dieting or men to stop interrupting them.

Instead of looking at kids to "prove" that differences in behavior by sex are innate, we can look at the ways we raise kids as an index to how unfinished the feminist revolution really is, and how tentatively it is embraced even by adults who fully expect their daughters to enter previously male-dominated professions and their sons to change diapers.

I'm at a children's birthday party. "I'm sorry," one mom silently mouths to the mother of the birthday girl, who has just torn open her present — Tropical Splash Barbie. Now, you can love Barbie or you can hate Barbie, and there are feminists in both camps. But *apologize* for Barbie? Inflict Barbie, against your own convictions, on the child of a friend you know will be none too pleased?

Every mother in that room had spent years becoming a person who had to be taken seriously, not least by herself. Even the most attractive, I'm willing to bet, had suffered over her body's failure to fit the impossible American ideal.

463

Given all that, it seems crazy to transmit Barbie to the next generation. Yet to reject her is to say that what Barbie represents—being sexy, thin, stylish—is unimportant, which is obviously not true, and children know it's not true.

Women's looks matter terribly in this society, and so Barbie, however ambivalently, must be passed along. After all, there are worse toys. The Cut and Style Barbie styling head, for example, a grotesque object intended to encourage "hair play." The grown-ups who give that probably apologize, too.

How happy would most parents be to have a child who flouted sex conventions? I know a lot of women, feminists, who complain in a comical, eyeball-rolling way about their sons' passion for sports: the ruined weekends, obnoxious coaches, macho values. But they would not think of discouraging their sons from participating in this activity they find so foolish. Or do they? Their husbands are sports fans, too, and they like their husbands a lot.

Could it be that even sports-resistant moms see athletics as part of manliness? That if their sons wanted to spend the weekend writing up their diaries, or reading, or baking, they'd find it disturbing? Too antisocial? Too lonely? Too gay?

Theories of innate differences in behavior are appealing. They let parents off the hook—no small recommendation in a culture that holds moms, and sometimes even dads, responsible for their children's every misstep on the road to bliss and success.

They allow grown-ups to take the path of least resistance to the dominant culture, which always requires less psychic effort, even if it means more actual work: Just ask the working mother who comes home exhausted and nonetheless finds it easier to pick up her son's socks than make him do it himself. They let families buy for their children, without *too* much guilt, the unbelievably sexist junk that the kids, who have been watching commercials since birth, understandably crave.

But the thing the theories do most of all is tell adults that the *adult* world—in which moms and dads still play by many of the old rules even as they question and fidget and chafe against them—is the way it's supposed to be. A girl with a doll and a boy with a truck "explain" why men are from Mars and women are from Venus, why wives do housework and husbands just don't understand.

The paradox is that the world of rigid and hierarchical sex roles evoked by determinist theories is already passing away. Three-year-olds may indeed insist that doctors are male and nurses female, even if their own mother is a physician. Six-year-olds know better. These days, something like half of all medical students are female, and male applications to nursing school are inching upward. When tomorrow's three-year-olds play doctor, who's to say how they'll assign the roles?

With sex roles, as in every area of life, people aspire to what is possible, and conform to what is necessary. But these are not fixed, especially today. Biological determinism may reassure some adults about their present, but it is feminism, the ideology of flexible and converging sex roles, that fits our children's future. And the kids, somehow, know this.

That's why, if you look carefully, you'll find that for every kid who fits a stereotype, there's another who's breaking one down. Sometimes it's the same kid—the boy who skateboards *and* takes cooking in his afterschool program; the girl who collects stuffed animals *and* A-pluses in science.

Feminists are often accused of imposing their "agenda" on children. Isn't that what adults always do, consciously and unconsciously? Kids aren't born religious, or polite, or kind, or able to remember where they put their sneakers. Inculcating these behaviors, and the values behind them, is a tremendous amount of work, involving many adults. We don't have a choice, really, about *whether* we should give our children messages about what it means to be male and female—they're bombarded with them from morning till night.

CLAIRE M. RENZETTI AND DANIEL J. CURRAN
From Women, Men and Society

Claire Renzetti is Professor and Chair of the Department of Sociology at St. Joseph's University in Philadelphia, Pennsylvania. She has written extensively on marriage, family, romance, law, and violence against women. Daniel Curran, her collaborator in the following piece from Women, Men and Society *(1999), is a screenwriter and film theorist living in Los Angeles, California.*

GROWING UP FEMININE OR MASCULINE

If you ask expectant parents whether they want their baby to be a boy or a girl, most will say they don't have a preference (Steinbacher & Gilroy, 1985). The dominance of this attitude, though, is relatively recent; from the 1930s to the 1980s, most Americans expressed a preference for boys as only children and, in larger families, preferred sons to outnumber daughters (Coombs, 1977; Williamson, 1976). In some parts of the world today, boys are still strongly favored over girls. In fact, in some countries this preference has resulted in a population imbalance, with a disproportionate ratio of males to females.

Even though American parents do not express a strong sex preference, research shows that parents do have different expectations of their babies and treat them differently, simply on the basis of sex. It has even been argued by some researchers that gender socialization actually may begin in utero by those parents who know the sex of their child before it is born. As Kolker and Burke (1992, pp. 12–13) explain, "The knowledge of sex implies more than chromosomal or anatomical differences. It implies gender, and with it images of personality and social role expectations." Such a hypothesis is difficult, if not impossible to test, but what currently is known is that gender socialization gets underway almost immediately after a child is born. Research shows, for instance, that the vast majority of comments parents make about their babies immediately following birth concern the babies' sex (Woollett et al., 1982). Moreover, although there are few physiological or behavioral differences between males and females at birth, parents tend to respond differently to newborns on the basis of sex. For example, when asked to describe their babies shortly after birth, new parents frequently use gender stereotypes. Infant boys are described as tall, large, athletic, serious, and having broad, wide hands. In contrast, infant girls were described small and pretty, with fine, delicate features (Reid, 1994). These findings are quite similar to those obtained in a study conducted twenty years earlier (Rubin et al., 1974), indicating that there has been little change in parental gender stereotyping.

466

That parents associate their child's sex with specific personality and behavioral traits is further evidenced by the effort they put into ensuring that others identify their child's sex correctly. It's often difficult to determine whether a baby is a boy or a girl because there are no physical cues: Male and female infants overlap more than they differ in terms of weight, length, amount of hair, alertness, and activity level. Parents most often use clothing to avoid confusion (Shakin et al., 1985). Boys are typically dressed in dark or primary colors, such as red and blue. They wear overalls that are often decorated with sporting or military equipment, trucks and other vehicles, or superheros. Girls are typically dressed in pastels, especially pink and yellow. Their dresses and slacks sets are decorated with ruffles, bows, flowers, and hearts. Parents also often put satiny headbands on their baby daughters (despite their lack of hair) and have their ears pierced. Disposable diapers are even different for girls and boys, not only in the way they are constructed, which arguably might have a rational basis to it, but also in the way they are decorated: Girls' diapers often have pink flowers on them; boys' diapers are embellished with sailboats or cars and trucks. Thus, clothing usually provides a reliable clue for sex labeling, although mistakes do still occur, which often anger parents. As one new mother recently told us in frustration, "I dress her in pink and she always wears earrings, but people still look at her and say, 'Hey, big fella.' What else can I do?"

Clothing, then, plays a significant part in gender socialization in two ways. First, as children become mobile, certain types of clothing encourage or discourage particular behaviors or activities. Girls in frilly dresses, for example, are discouraged from rough-and-tumble play, whereas boys' physical movement is rarely impeded by their clothing. Boys are expected to be more active than girls, and the styles of the clothing designed for them reflect this gender stereotype. Second, by informing others about the sex of the child, clothing sends implicit messages about how the child should be treated. "We know . . . that when someone interacts with a child and a sex label is available, the label functions to direct behavior along the lines of traditional [gender] roles" (Shakin et al., 1985, p. 956).

Clothing clearly serves as one of the most basic ways in which parents organize their children's world along gender-specific lines. But do parents' stereotyped perceptions of their babies translate into differential treatment of sons and daughters? If you ask parents whether they treat their children differently simply on the basis of sex, most would probably say "no." However, there is considerable evidence that what parents *say* they do and what they *actually* do are frequently not the same.

Parent-Child Interactions

The word *interaction* denotes an ongoing exchange between people. This meaning is important to keep in mind when discussing parent-child interaction, for the relationship is not one-way—something parents do to their children—but rather two-way, a give-and-take between the parent and the child. Parents sometimes raise this point themselves when they are questioned about the style and content of their interactions with their children. Parents report that male infants and toddlers are "fussier" than female infants and toddlers; boys, they say, are more active and anger more easily than girls. Girls are better behaved and more easy going. So if we observe parents treating their sons and daughters differently, is it just because they are responding to biologically based sex differences in temperament? Perhaps, but research by psychologist Liz Connors (1996) indicates that girls may be better behaved than boys because their mothers expect them to be. In observing girls and boys three-and-a-half to fourteen months old, Connors found few differences in the children's behavior. However, she also found that the mothers of girls were more sensitive to their children, while the mothers of boys were more restrictive of their children. Connors reports that fourteen-month-old girls are more secure in their emotional attachment to their mothers than fourteen-month-old boys, and she attributes this difference to mothers' differential treatment of their children.

Additional research lends support to Connors's conclusion. For example, Fagot and her colleagues (1985) found that although thirteen- and fourteen-month-old children showed no sex differences in their attempts to communicate, adults tended to respond to boys when they "forced attention" by being aggressive, or by crying, whining, and screaming, whereas similar attempts by girls were usually ignored. Instead, adults were responsive to girls when they used gestures or gentle touching, or when they simply talked. Significantly, when Fagot and her colleagues observed these same children just eleven months later, they saw clear sex differences in their styles of communication; boys were more assertive, whereas girls were more talkative.

In studies with a related theme, researchers have found that parents communicate differently with sons and daughters. Parents use a greater number and variety of emotion words when talking with daughters than sons. They also talk more about sadness with daughters, whereas they talk more about anger with sons (Adams et al., 1995; Fivush, 1991; Kuebli et al., 1995). One outcome of this differential interaction is that by the age of six, girls use a greater number of and more specialized emotion words than boys (Adams et al., 1995; Kuebli et al., 1995). Researchers have found that preschoolers whose mothers engaged in frequent emotion talk with them are better able to understand others' emotions (Denham et al., 1994), and by first grade, girls are better at monitoring emotion and social behavior than boys (Davis, 1995). Certainly, it is not unreasonable to speculate that through these early socialization experiences, parents are teaching their daughters to be more attentive to others' feelings and to interpersonal relationships, while they are teaching boys to be assertive, but unemotional except when expressing anger. Is it any wonder that among adults, women are better able than men to interpret people's facial expressions and are more concerned about maintaining social connections (Erwin et al., 1992; Goleman, 1996; Schneider et al., 1994)?

Are there other ways in which parent-child interactions differ by sex of the child? Research indicates that parents tend to engage in rougher, more physical play with infant sons than with infant daughters (MacDonald & Parke, 1986). Interestingly, the sex of the parent also appears to be significant. Fathers usually play more interactive games with infant and toddler sons and also encourage more visual, fine-motor, and locomotor exploration with them, whereas they promote vocal interaction with their daughters. At the same time, fathers of toddler daughters appear to encourage closer parent-child physical proximity than fathers of toddler sons (Bronstein, 1988). Both fathers and mothers are more likely to believe — and to act on the belief — that daughters need more help than sons (Burns et al., 1989; Snow et al., 1983). In these ways, parents may be providing early training for their sons to be independent and their daughters dependent. Moreover, Weitzman and her colleagues (1985) found that mothers tend to teach and question boys more than girls, thereby providing their sons with more of the kind of verbal stimulation thought to foster cognitive development.

In their study, Weitzman and her colleagues included mothers who professed not to adhere to traditional gender stereotypes. Although the differential treatment of sons and daughters was less pronounced among these mothers, it was by no means absent. This is an important point because it speaks to the strength of gender bias in our culture, reminding us that gender stereotypes are such a taken-for-granted part of our everyday lives that we often discriminate on the basis of sex without intentionally trying. "Even when we don't think we are behaving in gender stereotyped ways, or are encouraging gender-typed behavior in our children, examination of our actual behavior indicates that we are" (Golombok & Fivush, 1994, p. 26; see also Lewis et al., 1992; Weisner et al., 1994).

Still, it is also important to keep in mind that, like the research we discussed earlier, these studies are based almost exclusively on White, middle-class, two-parent, heterosexual families. We must ask how the findings might be different if the samples were more diverse. There is evidence that Black parents stress heavily for both male and female children the importance of hard work, independence, and self-reliance. Available data also show that Black children, regardless of sex, are at an early age imbued with a sense of financial responsibility toward their families, and with racial pride and strategies for dealing with racism (Hale-Benson, 1986; Poussaint & Comer, 1993; Thornton, 1997). The nontraditional content of this gender socialization could contribute to less gender stereotyping among Black children, although Hale-Benson (1986) also points out that the socialization experiences of young Black males and females are not identical or equal. Other researchers report as much, if not more, gender stereotyping among Blacks as among Whites (Price-Bonham & Skeen, 1982).

Similarly, studies that have examined social class have found modest support for the hypothesis that gender-stereotyped interaction decreases as one moves up the social class hierarchy (Burns & Homel, 1989; Lackey, 1989; but for contradictory findings, see Bardwell et al., 1986). One study that looked at the interaction of social class with race and ethnicity showed that the latter is the more important variable; that is, race and ethnicity have a stronger influence on child-rearing practices than social class does, but this research did not focus on gender socialization specifically (Hale-Benson, 1986).

Finally, there is little research on gender socialization in gay and lesbian families, although available studies indicate that children reared in such families are no different in their gender role behavior than children reared in heterosexual families. However, most of these studies used samples of children who spent at least part of their early childhood in heterosexual families (Golombok & Fivush, 1994).

Clearly, much more research is needed to elucidate the rich diversity of parent-child interactions and their outcomes among not only gay and lesbian families, but also families of color and families of different social classes.

Toys and Gender Socialization

Say the word "toys" in the company of children and you are likely to generate a good deal of excitement. Children will eagerly tell you about their favorite toy or about a "cool" new toy they'd like to have. Toys are, without a doubt, a major preoccupation of most children because, as any child will tell you, they're fun. However, toys not only entertain children, they also teach them particular skills and encourage them to explore through play a variety of roles they may one day occupy as adults. Are there significant differences in the toys girls and boys play with? If so, are these different types of toys training girls and boys for separate (and unequal) roles as adults?

More than twenty years ago, two researchers actually went into middle-class homes and examined the contents of children's rooms in an effort to answer these questions (Rheingold & Cook, 1975). Their comparison of boys' and girls' rooms is a study of contrasts. Girls' rooms reflected traditional conceptions of femininity, especially in terms of domesticity and motherhood. They contained an abundance of baby dolls and related items (e.g., doll houses) as well as miniature appliances (e.g., toy stoves). Few of these items were found in boys' rooms, where, instead, there were military toys and athletic equipment. Boys also had building and vehicular toys (e.g., blocks, trucks, and wagons). In fact, boys had more toys overall as well as more types of toys, including those considered educational. The only items girls were as likely to have as boys were musical instruments and books.

A decade later, another group of researchers (Stoneman et al., 1986) replicated Rheingold and Cook's study and obtained similar findings: Toys for girls still revolved around the themes of domesticity and motherhood, while toys for boys focused on action and adventure. A quick perusal of most contemporary toy catalogs reveals that little has changed in this regard during the 1990s as well. The toys for sale in the catalogs are usually pictured with models, which can be taken as an indication of the gender appropriateness of the toy. In the catalogs we examined (Childcraft, 1997; F. A. O. Schwartz, 1997; and Just Pretend, 1997), most of the toys were obviously gender-linked. We found, for instance, that little girls were most frequently shown with dolls or household appliances. The "dolls" boys were pictured with were referred to as "action figures" and included superheros (Superman, Batman), G.I. Joe (in a variety of roles, such as General Patton and the Golden Knight army paratrooper), characters from the *Star Wars* film series, and monsters (Spawn Vandalizer, with "real jaw-chomping action," and Deathlock, who is "half-man and half-cyborg"). Costumes for dressing up were also gender-specific. Boys were shown modeling the "Bold and Brave Collection," for the child with "the soul of an explorer" and "the heart of a hero." The set included costumes for a knight, a ninja, a cyborg, a pirate, and even a vampire. Girls were shown modeling the "Satin and Lace Collection," which was "designed to honor those timeless fantasies of girls." This set contained costumes for a ballerina, a princess, a fairy, an angel, and a bride. Accessories for the bride's costume (sold separately, of course) included a "diamond-look ring" on a heart-shaped pillow, five fill-in-the-blank wedding announcements, and a gift bag with two champagne flutes. On other pages of the catalogs, a little girl was talking on a pink cordless telephone with the sound effects, "As if" and "Whatever" from the film, *Clueless*, while a boy dressed in black and wearing dark glasses talked on a black cordless "spy gear" phone that had a flashlight for "night operations." Girls were shown bathing a doll in an "infant care center," weaving hair extensions and attaching them with barrettes, and serving tea from a "teatime treasures" picnic hamper. Boys drove tractors, a train, and a rocket ship; worked in a fix-it shop; built a "space training center" out of snap-together plastic parts; played hockey and electric football; and hunted dinosaurs. Boys were shown with scientific toys in all but one instance (the "Science in the Kitchen" set) and with athletic equipment.

Of course, it may be argued that toy catalogs are directed primarily to parents, and parents usually claim that they buy gender-typed toys because that's what their children prefer. Research does show that children express gender-typed toy preferences as early as one year of age, but their toy "choices" may have been inspired even earlier by parental encouragement. For example, when adults were given the opportunity to interact with a three-month-old infant dressed in a yellow gender-neutral jumpsuit, they usually used a doll for play when they thought the infant was a girl, but chose a football and a plastic ring when they thought the infant was a boy (Seavey et al., 1975; see also Caldera et al., 1989; Fisher-Thompson et al., 1995). Parental encouragement of gender-typed toy choices are further reinforced by the toy catalogs (which children themselves spend a considerable time looking at), by television commercials, by the pictures on toy packaging, and by the way toy stores often arrange their stock in separate sections for boys and girls (Schwartz & Markham 1985; Shapiro 1990).

In considering the toys we've described, it is not difficult to see that they foster different traits and abilities in children, depending on their sex. Toys for boys tend to encourage exploration, manipulation, invention, construction, competition, and aggression. In contrast, girls' toys typically rate high on manipulability, but also creativity, nurturance, and attractiveness (see also Bradbard, 1985; Miller, 1987; Peretti & Sydney, 1985). As one researcher concluded, "These data support the hypothesis that playing with girls' vs. boys' toys may be related to the development of differential cognitive and/or social skills in girls and boys" (Miller, 1987, p. 485). Certainly, the toy manufacturers think so; the director of public relations for Mattel, Inc. (which makes the Barbie doll) stated in an interview that, "Girls' play involves dressing and grooming and acting out their future — going on a date, getting married — and boys' play involves competition and conflict, good guys versus bad guys" (quoted in Lawson, 1989, p. C1).

This attitude remains a major premise of the $15 billion-a-year toy industry, as evidenced by the new toys introduced annually at the American International Toy Fair. Among the offerings at the 1996 and 1997 toy fairs were "Tub Warriors," floating action figures armed with water-propelled weapons such as a cannon and missile launcher; and "Melanie's Mall," in which a doll with long, silky hair, dressed in a miniskirt goes shopping in stores ("Beauty World," "Glamour Gowns") that children collect. The stores have their own shopping bags and Melanie has her own gold credit card (Lawson, 1996; 1997). It is not difficult to figure out which of these toys is targeted at the male market and which is intended for the female market.

The most popular toy for girls continues to be Barbie, with annual sales of $1.7 billion. In recent years, Barbie has been given several nontraditional roles, including dentist and astronaut (although her space wardrobe includes silver lingerie). In 1997, Mattel introduced "Talk with Me Barbie," in which Barbie has her own computer work station that can be attached to a real personal computer with a CD-ROM. Although some observers might see this invention as progress since it at least encourages girls to use computers, the game still focuses on shopping, makeup, and parties. More progressive was Mattel's 1997 announcement that Barbie is being redesigned to have more realistic body proportions; for thirty-eight years, Barbie's figure has translated into proportions of 36–20–32 (that is, the bust of an adult woman, the waist of a child, and the hips of a teenager). In 1997, Mattel also introduced "Share a Smile Becky," Barbie's disabled friend in a wheelchair, although the new doll met with mixed reactions from disability groups ("New Friend for Barbie," 1997).

In short, with few exceptions, toys for young children tend to strongly reinforce gender stereotypes. The messages these toys—and the marketing and packaging for the toys—send to children is that what they *may* do, as well as what they *can* do, is largely determined and *limited* by their sex. Apart from toys, what other items are significant in early childhood gender socialization?

Gendered Images in Children's Literature

Traditionally, children's literature ignored females or portrayed males and females in a blatantly stereotyped fashion. In the early 1970s, for example, Lenore Weitzman and her colleagues (1972) found in an analysis of award-winning picture books for preschoolers that males were usually depicted as active adventurers and leaders, while females were shown as passive followers and helpers. Boys were typically rewarded for their accomplishments and for being smart; girls were rewarded for their good looks. Books that included adult characters showed men doing a wide range of jobs, but women were restricted largely to domestic roles. In about one third of the books they studied, however, there were no female characters at all.

Fifteen years later, Williams et al. (1987) replicated the Weitzman study and noted significant improvements in the visibility of females. Only 12.5 percent of the books published in the early 1980s that they examined had no females, while a third had females as central characters. Nevertheless, although males and females were about equal in their appearance in children's literature, the ways they were depicted remained largely unchanged. According to Williams et al. (1987, p. 155), "With respect to role portrayal and characterization, females do not appear to be so much stereotyped as simply colorless. No behavior was shared by a majority of females; while nearly all males were portrayed as independent, persistent, and active. Furthermore, differences in the way males and females are presented is entirely consistent with traditional culture."

In 1997, children's librarian Kathleen Odean reported that although over four thousand children's books are published each year, in the vast majority females are presented in supporting roles and very few female characters are brave, athletic, or independent. Out of the thousands of books available for children of all ages, from preschoolers to adolescents, she compiled a list of just six hundred that are about girls who go against feminine stereotypes: girls who take risks and face challenges without having to be rescued by a male, girls who solve problems rather than having the solutions given to them, and girls who make mistakes but learn from them. There are, she notes, few books about girls' sports teams, even though over 2 million girls play on such teams, and no animal fantasies analogous to the popular *Wind in the Willows* with female characters.

One recent study indicates that at least for children's picture books, the race of the illustrator might make a difference in the amount of gender stereotyping depicted. Roger Clark and his colleagues (1993) analyzed children's picture books that received awards during the years 1987 through 1991 and compared those illustrated by White illustrators with those illustrated by African American illustrators. Among their findings were that while all the recent children's picture books contained more female central characters who are depicted as more independent, creative, and assertive than those in the past, the books illustrated by African American artists (and written by African American authors) gave female characters the greatest visibility and were significantly more likely to depict these females as competitive, persistent, nurturant, aggressive, emotional, and active. Clark et al. (1993) argue that the recent books illustrated by White artists reflect the liberal feminist emphasis on more egalitarian depictions of female and male characters, whereas those illustrated by African American artists reflect the aims of Black feminist theorists who emphasize women's greater involvement in an ethic of care and an ethic of personal accountability.

There is no doubt, then, that children's literature is less sexist than it was when Weitzman carried out her research, but for the most part, the changes have been modest. But modest though they may be, the question remains as to what impact less stereotyped books have on children's thinking about gender. In one study that tried to answer this question, the researcher found that nontraditional gender messages may be lost on young children. Bronwyn Davies (1989) read storybooks with feminist themes to groups of preschool boys and girls from various racial and ethnic and social class backgrounds. She found that the majority of children expressed a dislike for and an inability to identify with storybook characters who were acting in nontraditional roles or engaged in cross-gender activities. By the time the children heard these stories (at the ages of four or five), "[t]he power of the pre-existing structure of the traditional narrative [prevented] a new form of narrative from being heard." There were no differences across racial, ethnic, or social class lines. What did emerge as significant was parents' early efforts to socialize their children in nonsexist, non-gender-polarizing ways. Thus, the two children in the study whose parents did not support polarized gender socialization did not see anything wrong with characters engaged in cross-gendered behaviors and had less difficulty identifying with these characters—an encouraging finding that not only offers support for Bern's theory of gender acquisition that we discussed earlier, but also shows that nonstereotyped gender socialization is possible with concerted effort.

This finding is also especially important in light of research that shows that when characters are depicted as genderless or gender-neutral, adults almost always label the characters in gender-specific ways. In 95 percent of these cases, the labeling is masculine (DeLoache et al., 1987). The only pictures that seem to prompt feminine labels are those showing an adult helping a child, an interpretation consistent with the gender stereotypes that females need more help than males and that females are more attentive to children. Based on this research, then, it appears that "picturing characters in a gender-neutral way is actually counterproductive, since the adult 'reading' the picture book with the child is likely to produce an even more gender-biased presentation than the average children's book does" (DeLoache et al., 1987, p. 176).

To summarize our discussion so far, we have seen that virtually every significant dimension of a child's environment—his or her clothing, toys, and, to a lesser extent, books—is structured according to cultural expectations of appropriate gendered behavior. If, as the cognitive developmental theorists maintain, young children actively try to organize all the information they receive daily, their parents and other adults are dearly providing them with the means. Despite their claims, even most parents who see themselves as egalitarian tend to provide their children with different experiences and opportunities and to respond to them differently on the basis of sex. Consequently, the children cannot help but conclude that sex is an important social category. By the time they are ready for school, they have already learned to view the world in terms of a dichotomy: his and hers.

Parents, though, are not the only socializers of young children. Research has also highlighted the importance of peers in early childhood socialization.

Early Peer Group Socialization

As we noted previously, socialization is not a one-way process from adults to children. Rather, childhood socialization is a collective process in which "children creatively appropriate information from the adult world to produce their own unique peer cultures" (Corsaro & Eder, 1990, p. 200). Indeed, according to Beverly Fagot (1985), children's same-sex peers are the most powerful agents of socialization.

Children socialize one another through their everyday interactions in the home and at play. Research indicates, for example, that one of young children's first attempts at social differentiation is through increasing sex segregation. Observations of young children at play show that they voluntarily segregate themselves into same-sex groups. This preference for play with same-sex peers emerges between the ages of two and three and grows stronger as children move from early to middle childhood (Feiring & Lewis, 1987; Serbin et al., 1991). Moreover, when compared with girls, boys tend to interact in larger groups, be more aggressive and competitive, and engage in more organized games and activities (Corsaro & Eder, 1990; Maccoby 1988; Sheldon, 1990).

Thorne (1993) is critical of much of this research for focusing solely on sex differences and ignoring sex similarities and cross-sex interaction. She gives a number of examples in which young children work cooperatively and amiably in sex-integrated groups (see also Goodenough, 1990). She also points out that children frequently engage in "borderwork"; that is, they attempt to cross over into the world of the other sex and participate in cross-gender activities. Nevertheless, there is considerable evidence that even very young children reward gender-appropriate behavior and show disapproval for cross-gender behavior in their peers (Fagot & Leinbach, 1983; Goodenough, 1990; Martin, 1989). In fact, research shows that preschoolers disapprove of gender-"inappropriate" behavior by their peers more so than by adults (Golombok & Fivush, 1994).

Both boys and girls who choose gender-appropriate toys are more liked by their peers and have a better chance of getting other children to play with them (Martin, 1989; Roopnarine 1984). However, boys are criticized more by their peers for cross-gender play, and boys who play with girls are rated unpopular by their peers (Lobel et al., 1993; Roopnarine, 1984). Fagot and Leinbach (1983) found that for boys, peers are often more powerful socializers than teachers. When boys in the day care center they observed received contradictory messages from peers and teachers about gender-typed play, the boys were more likely to respond to their peers; teachers' exhortations had little impact on their behavior.

By the Time a Child Is Five

In summary, during early childhood, boys and girls—at least those from White, middle-class, two-parent, heterosexual families—are socialized into separate and unequal genders. Little boys are taught independence, problem-solving abilities, assertiveness, and curiosity about their environment—skills that are highly valued in our society. In contrast, little girls are taught dependence, passivity, and domesticity—traits that our society devalues. Children themselves reinforce and respond to adults' socialization practices by socializing one another in peer groups.

May we conclude from all this that nonsexist socialization is impossible? Certainly not. Recall Davies's (1989) study showing that conscious efforts at nonsexist socialization by parents do have a positive impact on children's attitudes and behavior (see also Lorber, 1986). However, we must keep in mind that parents are not the only ones responsible for gender socialization. Indeed, schools and the media take up where parents leave off, and peers remain active socializers throughout our lives.

REFERENCES

Adams, S., Kuebli, J., Boyle, P. A., & Fivush, R. (1995). Gender differences in parent-child conversations about past emotions. A longitudinal investigation. *Sex Roles, 33*, 309–323.

Bardwell, J. R., Cochran, S. W., & Walker, S. (1986). Relationship of parental education, race, and gender to sex role stereotyping in five-year-old kindergartners. *Sex Roles, 15*, 275–281.

Bradbard, M. R. (1985). Sex differences in adults' gifts and children's toy requests at Christmas. *Psychological Reports, 56*, 969–970.

Bronstein, O. (1988). Father-child interaction. In P. Bronstein & C. P. Cowan (Eds.), *Fatherhood today: Men's changing role in the family* (pp. 107–124). New York: John Wiley.

Burns, A., & Homel, R. (1989). Gender division of tasks by parents and their children. *Psychology of Women Quarterly, 13*, 113–125.

Burns, A. L., Mitchell, G., & Obradovich, S. (1989). Of sex roles and strollers: Female and male attention to toddlers at the zoo. *Sex Roles, 20*, 309–315.

Caldera, Y. M., Huston, A. C., & O'Brien, M. (1989). Social interactions and play patterns of parents and toddlers with feminine, masculine, and neutral toys. *Child Development, 60*, 70–76.

Chodorow, N. (1989). *Feminism and psychoanalytic theory*. New Haven: Yale University Press.

Chodorow, N. J. (1994). *Femininities, masculinities, sexualities: Freud and beyond*. Lexington, KY: University of Kentucky Press.

Clark, R., Lennon, R. & Morris, L. (1993). Of Caldecotts and kings: Gendered images in recent American children's books by Black and non-Black illustrators. *Sex Roles, 7*, 227–245.

Connors, L. (1996). *Gender of infant differences in attachment: Associations with temperament and caregiving experiences*. Paper presented at the Annual Conference of the British Psychological Society, Oxford, England.

Coombs, L. C. (1977). Preferences for sex of children among U. S. couples. *Family Planning Perspectives, 9*, 259–265.

Corsaro, W. A., & Eder, D. (1990). Children's peer cultures. In W. R. Scott (Ed.), *Annual review of sociology, Volume 16* (pp. 197–220). Palo Alto, CA: Annual Reviews, Inc.

Davies, B. (1989). *Frogs and snails and feminist tales*. Sydney: Allen and Unwin.

Davis, T. L. (1995). Gender differences in masking negative emotions: Ability or motivation? *Developmental Psychology, 31*, 660–667.

DeLoache, J. S., Cassidy, D. J., & Carpenter, C. J. (1987). The three bears are all boys: Mothers' gender labeling of neutral picture book characters. *Sex Roles, 17*, 163–178.

Denham, S. A., Zoller, D., & Couchoud, E. A. (1994). Socialization of preschoolers' emotional understanding. *Developmental Psychology, 30*, 928–938.

Erwin, R. J., Gur, R. C., Gur, R. E., Skolnick, B., Mawhinney-Hee, M., & Smailis, J. (1992). Facial emotion discrimination: 1. Task construction and behavioral findings in normal subjects. *Psychiatry Research, 42*, 231–240.

Fagot, B. I. (1985). Beyond the reinforcement principle: Another step toward understanding sex role development. *Developmental Psychology, 21*, 1097–1104.

Fagot, B. I., Hagan, R., Leinbach, M. D., & Kronsberg, S. (1985). Differential reactions to assertive and communicative acts of toddler boys and girls. *Child Development, 56*, 1499–1505.

Fagot, B. I., & Leinbach, M. D. (1983). Play styles in early childhood: Social consequences for boys and girls. In M. B. Liss (Ed.), *Social and cognitive skills: Sex roles and children's play* (pp. 93–116). New York: Academic Press.

Fagot, B. I., & Leinbach, M. D. (1989). The young child's gender schema: Environmental input, internal organization. *Child Development, 60*, 663–672.

Feiring, C., Lewis, M. (1987). The child's social network: Sex differences from three to six years. *Sex Roles, 17*, 621–636.

Fisher-Thompson, D., Sausa, A. D., & Wright, T. F. (1995). Toy selection for children: Personality and toy request influences. *Sex Roles, 33*, 239–255.

Fivush, R. (1991). Gender and emotion in mother-child conversations about the past. *Journal of Narrative and Life History, 1*, 325–341.

Goleman, D. (1996). *Emotional intelligence*. New York: Bantam Books.

Golombok, S., & Fivush, R. (1994). *Gender development*. Cambridge: Cambridge University Press.

Goodenough, R. G. (1990). Situational stress and sexist behavior among young children. In P. R. Sanday & R. G. Goodenough (Eds.) *Beyond the second sex* (pp. 225–252). Philadelphia: University of Pennsylvania Press.

Hale-Benson, J. E. (1986). *Black children: Their roots, culture and learning styles* (rev. ed.). Provo, UT: Brigham Young University Press.

Kolker, A., & Burke, B. M. (1992). *Sex preference and sex selection: Attitudes of prenatal diagnosis clients*. Paper presented at the Annual Meeting of the American Sociological Association, Pittsburgh, PA.

Kuebli, J., Butler, S. A., & Fivush, R. (1995). Mother-child talk about past emotions: Relations of maternal language and child gender over time. *Cognition and Emotion, 9*, 265–283.

Lackey, P. N. (1989). Adult's attitudes about assignments of household chores to male and female children. *Sex Roles, 20*, 271–281.

Lawson, C. (1989, June 15). Toys: Girls still apply makeup, boys fight wars. *New York Times*, pp. C1, C10.

Lewis, C., Scully, D., & Condor, S. (1992). Sex stereotyping of infants: A re-examination. *Journal of Reproductive and Infant Psychology, 10*, 53–63.

Lobel, T. E., Bempechat, J., Gewirtz, J. C., Shoken-Topaz, T., & Bashe, E. (1993). The role of gender-related information and self-endorsements of traits in preadolescents' inferences and judgments. *Child Development, 64*, 1285–1294.

Maccoby, E. (1988). Gender as a social category. *Developmental Psychology, 24*, 755–765.

MacDonald, K., & Parke, R. D. (1986). Parent-child physical play: The effects of sex and age on children and parents. *Sex Roles, 15*, 367–378.

Martin, C. L. (1989). Children's use of gender-related information in making social judgments. *Developmental Psychology, 25*, 80–88.

Miller, C. L. (1987). Qualitative differences among gender-stereotyped toys: Implications for cognitive and social development in girls and boys, *Sex Roles, 16*, 473–488.

Odeon, K. (1997). *Great books for girls*. New York: Ballantine Books.

Peretti, P. O., & Sydney, T. M. (1985). Parental toy choice stereotyping and its effects on child toy preference and sex-role typing. *Social Behavior and Personality, 12,* 213–216.

Poussaint, A. F., & Comer, J. P. (1993). *Raising Black children.* New York: Plume.

Price-Bonham, S., & Skeen, P. (1982). Black and White fathers' attitudes toward children's sex roles. *Psychological Reports, 50,* 1187–1190.

Reid, G. M. (1994). Maternal sex-stereotyping of newborns. *Psychological Reports, 75,* 1443–1450.

Rheingold, H. L., & Cook, K. V. (1975). The content of boys' and girls' rooms as an index of parents' behavior. *Child Development, 46,* 459–463.

Roopnarine, J. L. (1984). Sex-typed socialization in mixed-age preschool classrooms. *Child Development, 55,* 1078–1084.

Rubin, J. Z., Provenzano, F. J., & Luria, Z. (1974). The eye of the beholder: Parents' views on sex of newborns. *American Journal of Orthopsychiatry, 44,* 512–519.

Schneider, F., Gur, R. C., Gur, R. E., & Muenz, L. R. (1994). Standardized mood induction with happy and sad facial expressions. *Psychiatry Research, 51,* 19–31.

Schwartz, L. A., & Markham, W. T. (1985). Sex stereotyping in children's toy advertisements. *Sex Roles, 12,* 157–170.

Seavy, A. A., Katz, P. A., & Zalk, S. R. (1975). Baby X: The effect of gender labels on adult responses to infants. *Sex Roles, 1,* 103–109.

Serbin, L. A., Moller, L., Powlishta, K., & Gulko, J. (1991). *The emergence of gender segregation and behavioral compatibility in toddlers' peer preferences.* Paper presented at the Annual Meeting of the Society for Research in Child Development, Seattle, WA.

Shakin, M., Shakin, D., & Sternglanz, S. H. (1985). Infant clothing: Sex labeling for strangers. *Sex Roles, 12,* 955–964.

Shapiro, L. (1990, May 28). Guns and dolls. *Newsweek,* pp. 56–65.

Sheldon, A. (1990). Pickle fights: Gendered talk in preschool disputes. *Discourse Processes, 13,* 5–31.

Snow, M. E., Jacklin, C. N., & Maccoby, E. E. (1983). Sex-of-child differences in father-child interaction at one year of age. *Child Development, 54,* 227–232.

Steinbacher, R., & Gilroy, F. D. (1985). Preference for sex of child among primiparous women. *The Journal of Psychology, 119,* 541–547.

Stoneman, Z., Brody, G. H., & MacKinnon, C. E. (1986). Same-sex and cross-sex siblings: Activity choices, roles, behavior, and gender stereotypes. *Sex Roles, 15,* 495–511.

Thorne, B. (1993). *Gender play: Girls and boys in school.* New Brunswick, NJ: Rutgers University Press.

Weisner, T. S., Garnier, H., Loucky, J. (1994). Domestic tasks, gender egalitarian values and children's gender typing in conventional and nonconventional families. *Sex Roles, 30,* 23–54.

Weitzman, L., & Rizzo, D. (1976). *Images of males and females in elementary school textbooks.* Washington, DC: Resource Center on Sex Roles in Education.

Weitzman, L. J. (1985). *The divorce revolution*. New York: Free Press.

Weitzman, L. J., Eifler, D., Hokada, E., & Ross, C. (1972). Sex-role socialization in picture books for pre-school children. *American Journal of Sociology, 77*, 1125–1150.

Weitzman, N., Birns, B., & Friend, R. (1985). Traditional and nontraditional mothers' communication with their daughters and sons. *Child Development, 56*, 894–896.

Williams, J. A., Jr., Vernon, J. A., Williams, M. C., & Malecha, K. (1987). Sex role socialization in picture books: An update. *Social Science Quarterly, 68*, 148–156.

Williamson, N. E. (1976). *Sons or daughters*. Beverly Hills, CA: Sage.

Woollett, A., White, D., & Lyon, L. (1982). Fathers' involvement with their infants: The role of holding. In N. Beail & J. McGuire (Eds.), *Fathers: Psychological perspectives* (pp. 72–91). London: Junction.

CARYL RIVERS
Superwomen and Twitching Wrecks

Caryl Rivers, Professor of Journalism at Boston University, is a scholar, journalist, novelist, and screenwriter who contributes frequently to the Los Angeles Times, *the* Boston Globe, *the* Philadelphia Inquirer, New York's Newsday, *and other major national newspapers. The following is from her book,* Selling Anxiety: How the News Media Scares Women *(2007).*

Working women in the news media come in two basic styles: Superwomen and Twitching Wrecks.

The former are often profiled in business pages, lifestyle pages, and TV features. They are accomplished, incredibly organized, and never seem to sweat. Since I've written a number of books, I have been the subject of such stories, and I rarely recognize the dynamo presented on the pages. It's what they *don't* report that intrigues me.

They do not say, for example, that there are so many dust kitties in my house that I am considering applying to the Department of Agriculture for a subsidy to raise them. I never even owned an iron until my kids were in their late teens. They wore stuff just the way it came out of the dryer. I never wrote thank you notes—or any kind of notes. My son forged his own "please excuse Steven's absence, he had the flu" notes to take to the principal. If you are my friend and you die, don't expect your heirs to hear from me. It's not that I don't care—I'm too busy and too disorganized to deal with it. The whole thrust of the Superwoman genre of story appears to present women who are so, well, super, in their entire lives that no ordinary woman can possibly hope to emulate them. On the surface such stories seem as if they are presenting role models, but the fact is they are presenting the very antithesis—women so far above the madding crowd that they intimidate rather than encourage.

On the other end of the media spectrum are the Twitching Wretches. They seem to inhabit every "working woman" trend story that rolls off the presses or onto videotape. Such women are endlessly miserable, eternally frazzled. Here's *U.S. News and World Report*: "The first time Kristen Garris, 29, dropped off her 10-week-old daughter, Bailey, at the day care center, she says, "I cried the whole way to work."[1]

And *Newsweek*:[2] "For the New York lawyer, it all hit home in the grocery store. She had stopped in with her six-year-old to pick up a few things. But since the babysitter normally did the shopping, she was unprepared for what was about to happen. Suddenly, there was her son, whooping and tearing around the store, skidding the length of the aisles on his knees. *This can't be my son* she thought in horror. Then the cashier gave a final twist of the knife. 'Oh,' she remarked, 'So you're the mother!' " The upshot? The mother leaves her good job to work part-time in a suburb. One does wonder, however, why she was so upset. Any mother of a six-year-old has seen the kid go wild in supermarket aisles. It's in their genes. I would, in fact, *worry* about a child so well behaved that he or she was able to resist using the aisles as a running track or grabbing produce from the shelves.

From my database surveys, the "twitching wrecks" news frame in the media far outnumber happy, competent women who like their jobs and manage well, except in specialized publications like *Working Mother*. Women are miserable at work, say the media, in such stories as these:

- The Majority of Working Women Are Stressed Out (UPI).[3]
- Female Managers Face Super Stress (*Chicago Tribune*).[4]
- Working Women Stressed Out (Reuters).[5]
- Life's a Nightmare for Today's Middle-Class Working Mothers (*Guardian*).[6]
- *Business Week* declared a blues epidemic among working women.[7]
- Are You Headed for Overload? (*Redbook*).[8]

You would think that something—or someone—was forcing all those miserable women to stay at their jobs, instead of running home where they would really be happy. But what does reliable social science research say? Dr. Rosalind Barnett and I examined the data in our book *She Works, He Works*.[9] Nearly two decades of well-designed, reliable research find working women consistently healthy—healthier, in fact, than homemakers. A national longitudinal study[10] analyzed at the University of Michigan found women who combined work and family had better physical health and fewer emotional problems than homemakers. A federally funded three-year study found working women emotionally healthier than those not employed.[11] According to a 22-year-long UC Berkeley study, at age 43, homemakers had more chronic conditions and were more disillusioned and frustrated than employed women.[12] The Framingham heart study finds no heart problems in most working women—it's only those in dead-end jobs with low pay, repetitive tasks, and little control over working conditions who have problems.[13] (It's a lousy job that offers high demand and low control that can literally be a killer, the study says, especially if you have little help at home. Many women have such jobs.) One major study found that having a baby did not increase psychological distress for a woman—*unless she dropped out of the workplace!*[14] A 2005 study of 1,053 mothers found that children of working mothers do not suffer socially or intellectually if their mothers work outside the home.[15]

A veritable Everest of research tells us that, on the whole, real women are doing well at work, facing stress but handling it well, especially if they have well-paid and challenging jobs. But in the media, the Twitching Wrecks are the story, especially the ones who give up and go home. After the *Boston Globe* ran a profile of an anchorwoman who had left her job, Associate Professor Jeff Melnick of Babson College wrote, in a letter to the editor, "So what's with the working mother guilt trip? I'm wondering if anyone at the *Globe* has noticed how many times in the past five years or so you have run approving Living/Arts features about mothers who have renounced the 'fast track' in order to stay home with their kids. The one about the TV news anchor was only the latest in what seems like an onslaught of 'backlash' pieces about the impossibility of balancing work life and home life."[16]

And it's usually stories about lawyers, brokers, managers, and other prestige workers that are featured in the newspapers and magazines, because that's who the desired readers are. Too little newsprint is wasted on the poor and working-class women who face the real problems at work that cause severe health risks. (See Barbara Ehrenreich's *Nickel and Dimed: On (Not) Getting By in America*, 2001.[17]) As a society, we are insisting that welfare mothers march off to jobs that are high-stress and low-paid, while their kids are either home alone or in the care of a neighbor. At exactly the same time, the media are lecturing women with good jobs and excellent child care that they are at risk for stress and are probably rotten mommies to boot. Does this make sense?

But no matter. The news media still insist that going home is what all women really want to do. I've followed several of the women-going-home news trendlets over the years, and you can almost hear the sigh of relief behind them. *Well, now they're doing it. Finally they are going home. (Where, of course we always knew they belonged.)*

But nearly all the trends are phony. In the early nineties, misreading of census data led to a whole spate of such stories, with headlines like these:

- More Supermoms Are Hanging Up Their Capes (*Orlando Sentinel*).[18]
- Is Superwoman Shedding Her Cape? (*Atlanta Constitution*).[19]
- The Failed Superwoman (*Ebony*).[20]
- Superwoman Has Had Enough (*The Independent*).[21]

What led to all this? A slight dip in the number of women in the workforce. But, in fact, the dip among *men* entering the workforce was greater than that of women. Were men going home to bake cookies, shedding their superheroes' capes, just longing for home and hearth? Hardly. Most likely, it was the sluggish economy at the time that led to the dip. Had the news media put the statistics in context, those stories would have fallen apart.

This "bad news" narrative, however, proved hard to dismiss. The *New York Times* highlighted it in a 2002 feature on female executives who had left their high-level jobs.[22] "They Conquered, They Left," announced the *Times*, and in a large black subhead added, "Some say women have less psychic investment in careers." When Jane Swift stepped down as Governor of Massachusetts,

Rosie O'Donnell left her talk show, and presidential aide Karen Hughes left the White House to go back to Texas, the news media used these particular women as archetypes for *all* women. The media almost never use individual men as archetypes for an entire gender, as they do with women. These kinds of stories never appear when powerful men leave jobs. When labor secretary Robert Reich quit the Clinton cabinet, saying he wanted to spend more time with his kids, there was no story about "men" leaving. No stories surfaced when senators Fred Thompson and Phil Gramm said they were calling it quits. But men do leave, of course. Jane Swift's old boss, Paul Cellucci, left the Massachusetts governor's job to take an ambassador's spot, a job with much less power and visibility. He is just one of a long list of such men. Men, in fact, leave good jobs all the time for a variety of reasons, including family, but you never read much about this, because it's not seen as a "trend."

But the women–going–home trend story rolls relentlessly on. *Time* magazine wrote of a "reluctant revolt" of mothers who are going home and the *New York Times Magazine* sounded this same theme in one of its most controversial cover articles, 2003's "The Opt-Out Revolution."[23] (The cover illustration shows a young woman with a toddler on her lap, sitting in front of a ladder.) The sweeping nature of the title and the placement of the article on the cover implies that the author, Lisa Belkin, is examining a pervasive national trend. "Many high–powered women today don't ever hit the glass ceiling, choosing to leave the workplace for motherhood. Is this the failure of one movement or the beginning of another?" asks the magazine.

Here is an example, all too common in today's news media, of the overhyping of a story to make it seem more important than it really is. This major article is based on no systematic research; rather it is a collection of anecdotes from a very nonrepresentative sample. Belkin based nearly her entire story on small groups of Princeton graduates who were members of book groups in several cities and who had husbands affluent enough to finance a comfortable lifestyle on one income. And even though these women were presented as opting out "by choice," that's not quite an accurate picture. One television news reporter, for example, had asked her station for a part-time contract, but was refused. They said it was all or nothing, so she left — and called it a wrenching decision. "It kills me that I'm not contributing to my 401(k) anymore," she said. Another woman, a lawyer, decided to leave her firm only after a judge made an arbitrary schedule change on a major case on which she had been working intensely for months — while nursing her daughter. The schedule change made her life nearly impossible.

Do these women in fact constitute a revolution? Are they even typical of their Princeton classes? We have no idea, because Belkin gives us little data. Are these women really "opting out?" One woman Belkin quotes says, "It's not black or white, it's gray. You're working. Then you're not working. Then you're working part time or consulting. Then you go back. This is a chapter, not the whole book." Another says, "I'm doing what is right for me at the moment. Not necessarily what is right for me forever." The author herself writes that all the professional women she has spoken to who made the choice to stay home say they have made a temporary decision for just a few years, not a permanent decision for the rest of their lives. They have not lost their skills, just put them on hold.

And one woman notes that, "The exodus of professional women from the workplace isn't really about motherhood at all. It is really about work." She adds, "There's a misconception that it's mostly a pull toward motherhood and her precious baby that drives a woman to quit her job . . . not that the precious baby doesn't magnetize many of us. Mine certainly did. As often as not, though, a woman would have loved to have maintained some version of a career, but that job wasn't cutting it anymore. Among women I know, quitting is driven as much from the job dissatisfaction side as from the pull to motherhood."

This would have been an interesting article about some educated women making individual career decisions if it hadn't been incredibly overplayed. Why did it need an exaggerated title, a cover graphic that shows a woman holding a baby with the abandoned career ladder in the background, and the simplistic headline suggesting that this issue is only about women "choosing" to leave work? The article's tagline also suggests, hyperbolically, that this may be a "failure" of feminism (though, later on, the author herself contradicts that idea.) In fact, wasn't feminism all about giving women more choices? Most important, what the article really shows is the inflexibility of the workplace. Many of these women didn't opt out. They in fact wanted to keep working, but were presented with impossible choices—either working insanely long hours or not working at all.

The Belkin article suggests that professional and management-level women are focusing more on home and hearth and abandoning serious careers. Is this in fact true? Does such a major trend really exist? No. Citing the *Times* article, sociologist Kathleen Gerson of NYU notes, "the media start their annual claim that the new generation of women is turning away from careers to care for their families."[24] This idea, Gerson says, is nonsense. "Over the past 30 years, reversing previous historical trends, highly educated, well-employed women have become more likely to marry and have a child than their counterparts with fewer educational credentials, even though they tend to start families later. Educated women are especially likely to be in the work force. A 2001 census survey of all mothers with children under six found that 68 percent of women with college degrees and 75 percent of women with postgraduate degrees are in the labor force. They are three times as likely to work full time as part time." In 2006, economist Heather Boushy analyzed the most recent data and wrote, "Contrary to conventional wisdom, highly educated mothers are MORE likely to be in the labor force than women with less education or less demanding careers. . . . Between 2000 and 2004, the labor force participation by mothers did go down—but so did the labor force participation of childless women and of men. In the recession of 2002 to 2005, mothers were not opting out of employment—they were simply not finding jobs. In the long run, the trend is for mothers to opt in when they can find jobs!"[25]

There's the truth. Women do not regularly opt out of demanding management jobs for home and hearth. And since the Labor Department reports that about 45 percent of all managerial posts are held by females, the tide of women running home must indeed be a trickle.[26]

One major study of high-level women failed to uncover an "Opt-Out" trend. Linda Stroh, Jeanne Brett, and Anne Reilly of Loyola studied 1,029 men and women managers who not only had the same level of jobs, but also the same levels of education and time in the workforce, and who had relocated for their careers.[27] Not only did these women *not* opt out of demanding jobs, they were as devoted to their jobs as the men were to theirs. When they left, it wasn't to go home, it was for the same reason men left: better jobs and more advancement. Since women in corporations are more likely to stall out at lower levels than men, it's no surprise that more of them get frustrated and leave. Many form their own businesses, where they won't run into glass walls and ceilings. Stroh, Brett, and Reilly say that this defection is not due to qualities women managers lack, or to anything they are doing wrong, but to persistent discrimination.

One female investment professional told the *New York Times* that she believed she was denied a promotion because she was a woman, but decided not to waste time trying to figure it out. Instead, she simply joined another firm.[28] And Janet Tiebout Hanson, who spent fourteen years at Goldman Sachs, asked, "Why spend ten or fifteen years hitting the glass ceiling? Why not go directly to Go and collect $200?" She left Goldman and founded her own investment firm, Milestone Capital Management.[29] Stroh, Brett, and Reilly say, flatly, "Corporate America has run out of explanations that attribute women's career patterns to women's own behavior. It is time for corporations to take a closer look at their own behavior."

Well, the fact is that every day thousands of women in important, well-paid jobs do not leave them. Thousands of women do their work, perform more than competently, and relate well to their kids. But that's rarely news. The women who stay in good jobs and do well are the huge majority—those who leave are in a small minority. It's the same old story as the "Superwoman Is Leaving" headlines of the nineties. A temporary weak labor market creates a slight downtick in the steady, upward march of women into the workplace and the media rush in with yet another fake trend.

When women do leave jobs, news stories imply that these women are returning to domesticity. But will we find then planting peonies in their back gardens? Hardly. Like accomplished men, they will go on to other achievements. Karen Hughes is back in DC, advising George W., her old boss. Rosie O'Donnell took the TV job in the first place for family reasons—she didn't have to travel the way she did playing the comedy clubs. She's now back on the popular ABC show *The View*. As for Jane Swift, she's the breadwinner in her family, so moved easily into the private sector. She stepped down because her polls were lousy and the state republicans were looking for a white knight—and found one in Mitt Romney. If Swift had wanted to depart for domestic reasons, she would have done so when she had twins while in office. If Mitt hadn't come riding through on his charger, grabbing up the republican big bucks, the political story in Massachusetts would have been "See Jane Run." But the news stories usually use the loaded words "going home," as if the women were about to put on their pearls and start vacuuming like June Cleaver on the old TV sitcom.

A corollary to the "going home" story" popped up in 2005 when a front page story in the *New York Times* reported "Many Women at Elite Colleges Set Career Path to Motherhood."[30] The article, by Louise Story, claimed to have found—through interviews and an e-mailed questionnaire—that 60 percent of women in two Yale dorms planned to jettison career plans in favor of being longtime at-home mothers.

As it turned out, the story was rather thin gruel. It was not written by a *Times* reporter, but by a Columbia journalism student doing her thesis for professor Sylvia Nasar. Critics immediately pounced. Slate media writer Jack Shafer found the "facts" in the story so flimsy that he said the reporter "deserves a week in the stockades. And her editor deserves a month."[31] He pointed out that the writer used the word "many" 12 times, in place of statistics. The e-mail survey she sent around hardly qualified as anything but anecdotal evidence, and it seems the writer edited out those people who didn't fit her thesis, or misrepresented those who appeared to fit. Writing in *The Nation* ("Desperate Housewives of the Ivy League"), Katha Pollitt said she had contacted a number of people at Yale, including professors and students who were interviewed, and "I didn't find one person who felt Story fairly represented women at Yale."[32] Many students said they'd thrown away Story's questionnaire in disgust. Physics professor Megan Urry polled the 45 female students in her class and only two said they planned to stay at home as the primary parent.

The *Times*, it seems, is addicted to the story of women going home—which it runs over and over. Shafer asks, "Is there a *New York Times* conspiracy afoot to drive feminists crazy and persuade young women that their place is in the home?" The real story about young women—which the writer could have told instead of straining to manufacture a fake trend—is that females at elite colleges want good jobs with reasonable hours, so that they can have adequate time with their families. (Men aged 20 to 39 said exactly the same thing in a survey by the Radcliff Public Policy Institute in 2000. Eighty-two percent put family first and 71 percent would sacrifice pay for family time.)[33] But that nuanced, contextual story would not have had much "buzz." It certainly would not have appeared on the front page of the *Times*. While the article was a journalistic failure, in the buzz department it was a big hit. It was the most e-mailed story on the paper's website in its time period. And that was why it was published.

Unfortunately, the paper is missing the real news because of what Pollitt calls its "obsessive focus on the most privileged as bellwethers of American womanhood." What may be truly surprising in the working woman saga is who really is at home. Education is playing a significant role in determining which mothers work and which don't. Among college-educated women, 68 percent of those who had a baby within the last year were employed, compared with only 38 percent of those who had not graduated from high school.[34] But the high-school-grad working mothers are not the desired demographic of elite publications and get little attention. This picture is almost exactly the opposite of the idea that has been popular in the media for years — that women wanted to stay home, and if they had the resources to do so, they would. The women who stayed in the workforce were supposed to be those with the least economic resources who *had* to work.

Demographic projections show that women are living very long lives, and will continue to do so. A 65-year-old woman today can expect to live, on average, 19 more years. An 85-year-old-woman can, on average, expect to live six-and-a-half more years. Some estimate that a white baby girl born today has a good chance of living for a century.[35]

All this raises the very real specter of a legion of older women facing dwindling resources. Those least educated and out of the work force for a significant period of time will be the most vulnerable. They will probably outlive their husbands — and their husbands' pension benefits. And even if they do have some retirement benefits of their own, those may be meager. The Heinz Foundation notes that women retirees receive only half the average pension benefits that men receive and that women's earnings average $.74 for every $1 earned by men — a lifetime loss of over $250,000.[36]

But that's not a sexy media story, and it gets little attention. What this all means is that we have to get the message out to young girls — especially those in poor and working-class families — that staying in school and getting as much education as possible is critical to their future well-being. Our idea that the typical at-home mom is the contented spouse of a high-earning male, baking cookies, lunching with friends, having time to drive her kids around the suburbs, is out of date.

The true picture may be of a woman living close to the economic edge — and very much at risk.

NOTES

1. "The Lies Parents Tell About Work, Kids, Day Care and Ambition," *U.S. News*, May 12, 1997.
2. Laura Shapiro, "The Myth of Quality Time," *Newsweek*, May 12, 1997.

3. "The Majority of Working Women Are Stressed Out," *UPI*, March 27, 1991.

4. "Female Managers Face Super Stress," *Chicago Tribune*, May 8, 1989.

5. "Working Women Stressed Out," Reuters, March 27, 1991.

6. "Life's a Nightmare for Today's Middle-Class Working Mothers," *The Guardian*, August 10, 2002.

7. "A Blues Epidemic," *Business Week*, September 26, 1988.

8. "Are You Headed for Overload?" *Redbook*, June 1990.

9. Rosalind C. Barnett and Caryl Rivers, *She Works/He Works: How Two Income Families Are Happier, Healthier, and Better Off* (San Francisco: Harper, 1996).

10. Elaine Wethington and Ronald Kessler, "Employment, Parental Responsibility and Psychological Distress," *Journal of Family Issues*, December 1989.

11. Grace Baruch, Rosalind Barnett, and Caryl Rivers, *Lifeprints: New Patterns of Love and Work for Today's Women* (New York: McGraw-Hill, 1983).

12. "Working Women Fare Better," *Boston Globe* (wire dispatch), September 17, 1995.

13. Susanna Haynes, "Work, Women and Coronary Heart Disease," *American Journal of Public Health* 70 (1980).

14. Wethington and Kessler, "Employment . . ."

15. Aletha C. Huston and Stacey Rosenkrantz Aronson, "Mothers' Time with Infant: Quality, Not Quantity, Most Important in Early Infant Development," summarized from *Child Development*, 6:2, Society for Research in Child Development, March 25, 2005.

16. Jeff Melnick, "Letters," *Boston Globe*, November 1, 2004.

17. Barbara Ehrenreich, *Nickel and Dimed: On (Not) Getting By in America* (New York: Metropolitan, May 2001).

18. "More Supermoms Are Hanging Up Their Capes," *Orlando Sentinel*, April 22, 1994.

19. "Is Superwoman Shedding Her Cape?" *Atlanta Constitution*, May 2, 1994.

20. "The Failed Superwoman," *Ebony*, May 1994.

21. "Superwoman Has Had Enough," *The Independent*, June 20, 1994.

22. Alex Kuczynski, "They Conquered, They Left," *New York Times*, March 24, 2002.

23. Lisa Belkin, "The Opt-Out Revolution," *New York Times Magazine*, October 26, 2003.

24. Kathleen Gerson, "Working Moms Heading Home? Not Likely," Listserv, Council on Contemporary Families, CCF@listserv.unh.edu.

25. Heather Boushy, "Are Mothers Really Leaving the Workplace?" Council on Contemporary Families website, March 28, 2006, www.contemporaryfamilies.org.

26. Rochelle Sharpe, "As Leaders, Women Rule," *Business Week*, November 20, 2000.

27. Linda K. Stroh, Jeanne M. Brett, and Anne H. Reilly, "All the Right Stuff: A Comparison of Female and Male Managers' Career Progression," *Journal of Applied Psychology*, 77:3 (1992).

28. Richard Abelson, "If Wall Street Is a Dead End, Do Women Stay to Fight or Go Quietly?" *New York Times*, August 3, 1999.

29. Ibid.

30. Louise Story, "Many Women at Elite Colleges Set Career Path to Motherhood," *New York Times*, September 20, 2005.

31. Jack Shafer, "A Trend So Old It's New," *Slate*, September 25, 2005.

32. Katha Pollitt, "Desperate Housewives of the Ivy League," *The Nation*, June 19, 2006.

33. Radcliffe Public Policy Center, *Life's Work: Generational Attitudes Towards Work and Life Integration* (Cambridge: Radcliffe Center for Advanced Study, 2000).

34. Gerson, "Working Moms . . ."

35. "HHS Issues Report Showing Dramatic Improvements in America's Health Over Past 50 Years," National Center for Health Statistics, September 12, 2002, www.hhs.gov.

36. Teresa and H. John Heinz III Foundation, The Women's Retirement Initiative, http://www.hfp.heinz.org/programs/.

FELICITY SCHAEFFER-GRABIEL

Planet-Love.com: Cyberbrides in the Americas and the Transnational Routes of U.S. Masculinity

Felicity Schaeffer-Grabiel is Professor of Feminist Studies and Latin American/Latino Studies at the University of California, Santa Cruz. Her research is on the ways global exchanges are changing gender dynamics within and outside the United States.

> I am an explorer in the undiscovered continent of love, a scientist in the laboratory of masculine longing. Can a middle-aged man, scarred by the sex wars at home, find a new beginning on a tropical island where women are still feminine?
>
> —Makow 2000, back cover

> My whole life is abstract. . . . I don't find myself feeling really close to people, I don't feel really close to my family. . . . I've realized I'm just sort of going through the motions, so on some level, going outside the country is an attempt to, you know, get past that cynical, detached experience that I have here.
>
> —Jason, interview, March 2005

When the mall-order bride industry shifted from using a magazine format to operating over the Internet during the 1990s, the number of companies providing matchmaking services exploded and spread from Russia and Asia into Latin America. Scholarship on the mail-order bride industry in Asia and Russia tends to emphasize the exploitation of poor women in developing countries by Western men as part of the sexual trafficking trade, an emphasis that reproduces binary relations of power between developing and first-world countries.[1] The emergence of agencies on the Internet with services in Latin America has resulted in attracting women from a mostly middle-class and/or professional clientele, although male participants come from various regional,

---

[1]Nicole Constable's book, *Romance on a Global Stage* (2003), is the only exception. While I am differentiating my work from traditional studies on the mail-order bride industry, there are many similarities in the ways women from Latin America are cast—as better mothers, as warmer, more sexual, and less outspoken than U.S. women—that resonate with how Asian women are popularly constructed within the global economy. See Glenn 1986; Parreñas 2001; Kang 2002.

491

economic, ethnic, and class backgrounds. In illuminating the process of finding a Mexican or Colombian bride, I argue that this industry does not merely
commodify relationships into binaries of the white male buyer and ethnic
female seller, as is often repeated in mail-order bride studies (Villipando 1989;
Glodava and Onizuka 1994; Tolentino 1999), but involves a more complex
and uneven historical moment of racial formation, nationhood, and understandings of masculinity and subjectivity. The more recent expansion of the
industry into Latin America also capitalizes on the language of morality in an
attempt to shore up the industry's (and men's) central role in forging a new
national family across borders.

In feminist writing on mail-order brides, women's and men's voices
remain absent. Instead, this scholarship assumes a one-to-one correspondence
between the male gaze on the Web sites and women's exploitation as domestic
laborers in the home. While this article focuses on the men, I discuss elsewhere the ways middle-class Mexican women interpret their desire to marry
U.S. men (see Schaeffer-Grabiel 2004). Men have few opportunities to understand women's perspectives, especially since Web sites promote stereotypical
information about women as more family oriented, accustomed to large age
differences, willing to please, and as sexual objects for men's pleasure. Women's
self-descriptions and their alluring photos (often requested by companies) as
well as media images, popular imaginaries, and language and cultural barriers
further perpetuate stereotypical renderings of differences across borders. Many
women perceive U.S. men (as opposed to local men) as more equitable com-
panions in marriage, who value women's contributions to the home and family and who offer women opportunities to enjoy a stable, middle-class lifestyle.
These contradictory imaginaries produce various outcomes when couples
marry and live together in the United States. While I center my critique on
discourses generated by the men and through company Web sites, I want to
point out that some men and women do form egalitarian and loving relationships. It is with the hope of avoiding a dichotomy between love and power
relations that I analyze the ways love is inseparable from labor relations, race,
gender, and the global economy.

In recent years, scholarship on the sex tourism trade has positioned men
as visible participants (see Truong 1990; Bishop and Robinson 1998, 2002).
There are similarities in both marriage and sex tourism, such as the sharing of
information via chat rooms and Web sites that lure men in with images of
overly sexualized Latin American women. Yet Web companies are careful to
"class up" the language of marriage—using labels such as *gentlemen* and *ladies*
and using discourses of courtship and romance rather than sex. Men's masculine identity is connected to class as travel to Latin America reflects men's
desire to "get more bang for your buck" (Bishop and Robinson 2002). While
the reference here is to sex, many of the men I interviewed repeatedly stated
that in Latin America they could date and potentially marry younger and more
beautiful women than in the United States. They hope for a fresh start in Latin

America through their search for better wives and mothers while constructing a heightened moral and class status within the global world order as the "good guys," heroes, or sensitive "new men" crafted against the macho Latin male stereotype.

It is through the Internet that men's quest for a bride takes on new dimensions. The Internet's connectivity and interactivity have intensified the speed, repetition, and self-formulation of discursive imaginings between participants (Caldwell 2000). Unlike other forms of media technology, the Internet not only offers images and narratives of otherness but also guarantees one's ability to actively participate with the fantasies of women seductively displayed on Web sites. Internet companies offer more than a forum for purchasing brides; they also sell women's e-mail addresses, "Vacation Romance" tours where men and women meet, and how-to guidebooks and videos, and provide chat room boards where men may share their experiences. In other words, men do not embark on a solitary journey in search of a wife. Chat room discussants on Planet-Love spend months, even years, sharing "travel reports," swapping dating and marital experiences, and discussing cultural differences and immigration procedures.[2]

In this article I demonstrate a contemporary way that empire and globalization resurface through men's everyday lives, practices, and forms of intimacy. In considering why, at this particular moment, transnational marriages are so alluring, I argue that outsourcing the family from developing nations follows the logic of the transnational economy and corporate multiculturalism. Many company Web sites and men idealize Latin American women as having better genes than U.S. women or, as Jason described, better "raw materials" (interview, March 2005). This neocolonial imaginary persists in contemporary globalization as Web sites herald the benefits of shifting the site of production for the family outside of the nation. Latin American women are imagined as untainted by modern capitalist relations while also in need of being saved from anachronistic nationalism. Men in the United States imagine themselves as the benevolent force saving globally "disadvantaged" middle-class women (docile laborers) abroad as well as saving the U.S. nation from the so-called disintegration of the family brought about by feminism, women's entrance into the labor force, and U.S. women of color, who are stereotyped as welfare recipients (viewed as unruly and lazy laborers). As Ana Teresa Ortiz and Laura Briggs describe, in the popular industry of adoption of children from Romania the "Third World poor are romanticized as malleable innocents who can take advantage of the opportunities passed up by the dysfunctional domestic underclass" (2003, 42). By analyzing race, gender, and the family in a transnational context, I hope to bring Latin American women into a relational framework with immigrant women and U.S. women of color, whose labor is

---

[2]There are three chat boards available for men seeking brides from Russia, Asia, and Latin America on Planet-Love, which can be found at http://www.planet-love.com.

envisioned as polluting and crippling the progress of U.S. nationalism and family values.

While men lament that U.S. women are overdetermined by their labor outside the home, Latin American women represent the utopian prospect of importing spiritual rejuvenation and purifying the boundaries of the self, the nuclear family, and the nation. Latin American women embody the "last frontier," merging colonial and new cyberfrontier possibilities.[3] Thus, finding a foreign bride converges with four discourses: colonialism, modern self-help movements, transnational capitalism, and futuristic ideals of flexibility, mobility, and a postracial society. These themes demonstrate the ways technology and ideas about globalization are incorporated into men's everyday lives as a yearning for a utopian, multiracial, postbody affinity to masculinity and citizenship, regardless of skin color, profession, or class affiliation.

In chat room discussions, men from various ethnicities, classes, and professions construct themselves through fantasies of colonialism and empire and as cosmopolitan citizens of the globe. I am concerned here with the role of the Internet in altering patterns of intimacy and subjectivity, as well as the labor Latin American women's bodies perform as reproducers of the new nation. The thousands of men who flee the United States for wives and adventures abroad reveal one way men transform their sense of victimhood into empowerment. Men in the United States elevate their value and social capital through their association with hegemonic masculinity predicated on a traditional wife and family and on heroic ideals of global adventure, risk, and self-exploration.

METHODOLOGY

In this article I combine chat room discussions, interviews with more than forty men at "Vacation Romance" tours, and guidebooks to show continuities between cyberspace discussions, face-to-face interactions, and Web site images and narratives.[4] I discovered that even as a lurker, or invisible voyeur, in Planet-Love, the stories men told me at the tours mimicked the stories repeated in Planet-Love's chat room. While I feared my identity as a mixed race Chicana from the United States would hinder the openness and sincerity during interviews with men at the tour in Guadalajara, Mexico, most men were eager to share their stories with me. The fact that I interviewed men and women, that I spoke Spanish, and that I had permission from company owners to conduct interviews at their tours contributed to my association by some of the men as "one of the guys." My willingness to listen to men's stories and the fact that I

---

[3]See Ehrenreich and Hochschild 2002.

[4]The Romance Tours are held at five-star hotels, and men usually pay steep prices to attend (from $500 to $1,200, plus travel expenses) while women are invited for free.

was racially visible as nonwhite (and to them, nonfeminist) contributed to my insider status.[5] While being one of the guys was neither my intent nor a position I felt comfortable with at all times, I was able to engage men in honest and open discussions to which, at times, I wished I was not privy. As an educated, confident, middle-class woman with knowledge of Mexican culture and language, I occupied a complicated position of power vis-à-vis the men I interviewed.

Unlike face-to-face interviews — carried out over a short period of time and with a limited number of people — chat room ethnography provides an unending dialogue among a rotating group of men. As people increasingly find intimacy and a sense of community through the Internet, this type of ethnography is an indispensable tool for following the ways men and women create consensus about their participation in this industry and how the boundaries of inclusion and exclusion are drawn. Rather than focusing on what is true versus what is false, ethnographic narratives are important in unraveling the trends and frameworks within which people tell the stories they wish to tell.[6]

GLOBAL MASCULINITIES

The formation of first-world masculinities in the bride industry must be situated within global economic restructuring. Recent changes affecting men in the United States include the perceived loss of authority in the family, their departure from families in mostly rural areas to cities with high-tech industries and finance (where populations are predominantly male), blue-collar unemployment, and changing media images redefining masculine attributes in the labor force (Runyan 1996; Faludi 1999; Hooper 2001). Charlotte Hooper (2001) argues that global restructuring in the 1970s softened the previously dominant image of postwar hypermasculinity based on the myth of toughness, power, and strength. She writes, "Activities and qualities which were previously defined as feminine or effeminate are being increasingly integrated into hegemonic masculinity" (63). For example, she states, "flexibility in job descriptions and career paths is being reinterpreted as 'masculine' risk taking and entrepreneurialism; and computers have lost their feminine associations

---

[5]Most men I interviewed equate feminism with white, upwardly mobile women and assume Latin American women and, to a lesser extent, U.S. women of color, to be more feminine and thus not feminist.

[6]In order to answer the question of whether Internet chat room observations are "legitimate" or accurate places to do research because of preoccupations with deception and identity play, scholars have conducted in-depth analysis comparing online and offline interactions. Like Lori Kendall (2002) and Constable (2003), I found that there was not much difference between online and face-to-face interviews and discussions. Even regarding face-to-face interviews, many have written about the varying degrees of exaggerated and false statements given by those hoping to tell the story they think we want to hear (Scott 1999).

with keyboard skills, now being marketed as macho power machines" (156). In labeling work attributes as masculine, men attain a higher pay scale than women, they naturalize their entrance into gender-appropriate careers, and they access a collective masculine imaginary that draws on previous historical narratives of masculine bravado in wars, colonizing projects, and as frontiersmen. R. W. Connell (1995) argues that hegemonic masculinities can only be established if there is some link between the cultural ideal and institutional power. Thus, for men in search of a bride, information technology combined with an adventurous frontier manhood provide both the cultural and institutional capital on which hegemony relies.

Cybermasculinities formed in chat room discussions are more complex than scholars of globalization and masculinity such as Connell (2000) and Hooper (2001) have theorized. Drawing on feminist postcolonial scholarship, Connell perceives legacies of colonialism and imperialism as formative to the making of gender, racial, and sexual hierarchies. European and Western dominance shaped the formation of a white male national citizenship through the extraction of labor and sexuality from native others.[7] Virile masculinity and citizenship were predicated on the separation of the public and private spheres. The purity and honor of the domesticated white woman at home were distinct from sexual conquests with the hypersexualized, racial, and/or lower-class "other" and from the hypersexualized colonized male subjects outside the nation. Connell elucidates the continuities and disjunctures between colonial masculinity and its hegemonic manifestation, "transnational business masculinity" (2000, 51). He describes this current world gender order as "the masculinity associated with those who control its dominant institutions: the business executives who operate in global markets, and the political executives who interact . . . with them" (51).

This new transnational business masculinity departs from traditional bourgeois masculinity "by its increasingly libertarian sexuality, with a growing tendency to commodify women" (Connell 2000, 52). New sexualized industries have cropped up within patterns of transnational business, which include hotel porn videos and sex tourism. Similarly, Hooper describes corporate manhood alongside a sexual imaginary described as a "rape script," including images of penetrating markets and male exploration and adventure in "virgin territories" (2001, 139–40). The Internet marriage industry utilizes similar discourses of adventure, with landscapes imagined as women's bodies. Despite similar racial and sexualized fantasies, these metaphors create a simplistic binary between the violent gaze of white men, on the one hand, and victimized women, on the other. These debates do not take into account how multicultural configurations of race, sexuality, class, and the nation are transplanted onto a global economy of desire. I depart from this linear narrative of colo-

---

[7]Connell relies on the work of scholars such as Anne McClintock (1995). See also Castañeda 1990; Limón 1998.

nization to globalization by arguing that this new transnational masculinity builds on previous colonialist fantasies and rewrites them by drawing from the discourse of corporate multiculturalism. In other words, masculinity is not associated with colonial constructions of Western whiteness in contrast to racialized, native "others" or with contemporary anti-immigration nativism and white supremacy.[8] Instead, men imagine themselves as the benevolent engineers who racially uplift the moral fabric of the national family by importing a superior breed of women. Furthermore, in both Connell and Hooper's theorizations, global manhood is characterized through images of white, male entrepreneurs, erasing the ways men of color collude, resist, and compete with this Western white male construct.[9] Men access a multicultural patriotic manhood through adherence to the ideal American values at the foundation of the immigrant's assimilation into the nation: hard work, traditional family values and gender roles, and notions of benevolence couched in romantic ethics of chivalry and the saving of women. Nationalism is founded on the preservation of an invented traditional past and a future vision of modernity.

For men who do not envision themselves on the cutting edge of global business culture, bride hunting in developing countries symbolizes men's entrance into the future. A former professor, Henry Makow, reflects on his search for a traditional Filipina in his book, *A Long Way to Go for a Date*. He writes, "All my life I have been like a man facing the rear on a speeding train. I have always had my back to the future. Although the future is unknown, at least now I feel I am facing forward" (2000, 12). For men eager to move forward and join the global economy, women's racial and sexual identities are critical to this Janus-faced masculine national identity between the past and future. While international dating and romance are not new, men insert themselves into the modern future as members of a global class where mobility is preconfigured by access to Internet technology, English, passports, and dollars, while women are conversely disadvantaged by their relative dependence on men in order to become mobile.

Contrary to Connell's association of business masculinity with men who enjoy a dominant position in the global marketplace, men's chat room discussions and interviews revealed their sense of disempowerment in the United States. Many felt alienated in some way from U.S. culture and society. Jason's quote, with which I began this article—"My whole life is abstract. . . . so on some level, going outside the country is an attempt to, you know, get past that cynical, detached experience that I have here"—demonstrates his exodus to Latin America as a way to, as he says, "break out of the mold" and leave behind relationships overdetermined by capitalist exchange (interview, March 28,

[8]For a discussion of U.S. nativism against immigrants, see Reimers 1985; Parea 1997; Chavez 2001.

[9]For an account of other versions of global manhood, see Kondo 1997; Ong 1999; Lu 2000.

2005). His career in computer programming left him feeling estranged and devoid of relationships outside the hegemony of exchange value. He realized he was replaceable in both his professional and intimate life. He was fed up with the highly competitive market of the Silicon Valley, a situation exacerbated by the influx of highly skilled and lower-paid technicians from South Asia. He had divorced his previous wife and had to work unfathomable hours to maintain a high quality of life in California, both of which prevented him from realizing the American dream of having a family and owning a home.

GLOBAL MULTICULTURALISM

Just as corporate multiculturalism promises new markets and the comparative advantage that will solve all business problems, so too are men turning to Latin America to renovate their image back home. In the Internet marriage industry, women from developing nations embody the frontier of the future; their bodies and the products they represent promise spiritual vitality, a connectedness to nature, and access to a new, rejuvenated self. This departure from understanding race as a marker of inequalities to a celebration of cultural difference speaks to the excess labor racialized bodies provide in revitalizing a dominant U.S. subject position and the economy more broadly.

Technology ads contribute to a vision of a world unencumbered by race. An example of this genre of advertising is an advertisement by MCI that promotes conservative multiculturalism through images of people across age, race, and gender. The ad states, "There is no race. There is no gender. There is no age. There are only minds. Utopia? No. The Internet" (Nakamura 2000, 15). While race is idealized as no longer a relevant category for the future of our technological world in the West, where everyone now supposedly has access to technology, Internet ads also project those outside of technology, in developing countries, as the place race now resides. Lisa Nakamura also discusses an IBM advertisement that uses an Egyptian man on a camel to reflect the idea that technological modernity has yet to spread to underdeveloped nations, which are thus in need of corporations to bring development to the rest of the world (20). A better future is equated with developmental capitalism and a future time when the entire world will have access to technology. Thus, the U.S. corporate empire is projected as a benevolent force that promises to spread democracy through worldwide access and to wipe out racial difference and inequality. Yet this presents a contradiction, because for bride-seeking men, women from "developing" countries are imagined to embody traditions felt to be lost in U.S. culture. Women represent the last pure space untainted by modern life and in opposition to the crisis of the domestic sphere in the United States. This is the context, I argue, in which men imagine Latin American women as the last pure frontier, bodies that promise to rectify a crisis in U.S. masculinity and the breakdown of middle-class family structures. They moralize the need for new genes and bodies and for a postnational family structure that will rejuvenate not only the U.S. domestic sphere but also their own inner journeys to selfhood.

For example, many Internet bride Web sites offer links to an array of guidebooks or how-to manuals on finding a bride in another country. These do-it-yourself books help men turn emasculating experiences with Western women into redemptive self-help narratives through the importation of a superior breed of women, Here is testimony from a male client who tells the story of why he is ready to find a mail-order wife. He describes his mother's "feminazi" thought process as the following:

> My final decision to pursue a foreign bride resulted from an argument I heard between my mother and her new husband, Mother was bitching moaning and carrying on about how her life was a drudgery and how she felt unappreciated. Her new husband got tired of her whining and shouted, "Fran, YOU have a brand new $250,000 dream home in the suburbs with every furnishing and knick knack you wanted, a new Isuzu Trooper, a healthy bank account, a very comfortable living, a husband who has bent over backwards to make you happy. . . . WHAT THE HELL MORE DO YOU WANT!" . . . This is when I realized that the odds are stacked against me finding happiness with an American wife, which has led me to say, "IT IS TIME FOR NEW GENES." (Clark, February 23, 2001, http://www.planetlove.com/gclark/gclark02/)

In the Oedipal cybernarrative above, the author envisions a better future by replacing his mother, rather than father, and infusing whiteness with "new genes" in a transracial family. The author degrades "spoiled" suburban white women who do not appreciate what they have, women who do not reciprocate with docile bodies in exchange for a capitalist and patriarchal order in the workplace and home. Earlier in the story he describes his mother's ideological participation in the feminist movement as the unhealthy "male-bashing environment" in which he unfortunately grew up. These women are labeled feminazis, women who are hyper-masculinized, driven to crush all opposition in their path toward power and success.[10] As a castrating force, feminazis create gender and sexual disorder within the family and nation. Male participants want a less liberated woman, someone less spoiled and materialistic than the women in their lives. In this excerpt, found on a link from Planet-Love's main Web page, the testimonial serves—intentionally or not—to provide men with the language and ideology from which to understand and justify their desire for a foreign bride. This focus on genes continually reemerges in various forms during interviews, chat room discussions, and on Web sites. Men with the same resentful feelings are prompted to take action against ungrateful women, to pick themselves up by the bootstraps and take charge of their lives through a foreign, less demanding, and more docile wife.

---

[10]In *Stiffed*, Susan Faludi (1999, 9) describes the term *feminazis* as used to apply to the radical feminists who men fear have gone beyond equal treatment and are now trying to take power away from and exercise control over them.

Many Latin American women I interviewed were aware that men wanted a woman who was more family oriented than U.S. women supposedly are. In fact, many rejected being labeled a feminist for fear of their association with white women popularly thought to be selfish, sexually loose, or too domineering. This did not mean, however, that women were not strong in their conviction that they wanted a man who respected them and who saw their contributions as carrying equal weight in the family.

While at a "Romance Vacation Tour" in Mexico, I was told by Blake, a forty-two-year-old Anglo club owner from Los Angeles with a muscular physique and a tanning-salon glow, that he was looking for a woman from Mexico because "I think these women are culturally grown to want what we also want" (interview, September 2001). Latin American and other "foreign" women are naturalized as having the right biological makeup and cultural grooming, making them more feminine, traditional, docile, and better mothers of the family. Unlike nineteenth-century constructions of racial mixing as degenerative, in this instance foreign genes are constructed as regenerative. This shift in racial construction connects with individualistic ideals of multiculturalism in the global marketplace. Once again, diversity and race are advertised as products that promise to bring one closer to nature, toward one's "true self," and to contribute to the making of "natural" gender and racial hierarchies. The idea of flexible genetic engineering emphasizes an understanding of women's bodies as mutable through the masculine hands and gaze of the Internet techie. Men imagine themselves as the heroic engineers of the family and nation (contradicting the popular image of them as outcasts), just as ethnic women embody the transformation. Even though suburban flight reflects the fleeing of whites from racial urban centers and the search for nature and purity they themselves have destroyed, these individualized interracial dramas remain at the level of the family. This personal lament connects with empire as chat room discussants reveal men's anxiousness to push into new frontiers, into countries with women less tainted by U.S. culture. These sentiments are echoed in the statement of a U.S. owner of a Colombian agency, Latin Life Mates, in an interview posted on his Web site: "Because of the drug wars . . . Colombia has been off the map for U.S. tourists for the past 15 years. During that period, the country experienced considerable economic growth. Now it is filled with well-educated women who have maintained 'pristine' values because they were isolated from U.S. tourists. . . . You used to think of drugs when you thought of Colombian exports. . . . But forget that. Now the big demand in the States is for Colombian women" (November 1998, http://www.latinlifemates.com/faq.stm). The malleability of people, commodities, and notions of space reflects the ways decentralized production infiltrates the intimate spheres and desires of men's everyday lives.

Men's concerns with "natural" gender differences are part of a wider ideology endemic in popular men's movements, such as those of Robert Ely and within the religious right, and even within academic debates. David Popenoe, a professor of sociology at Rutgers University, contributed a lengthy study on the deplorable state of marriage and the family in contemporary times that was designed to help reinvigorate a dying social institution. He writes, "In order to restore marriage and reinstate fathers into the lives of their children, we are somehow going to have to undo the cultural shift toward radical individualism and get people thinking again in terms of social purposes" (1996, 197). In Wendy Kline's book, *Building a Better Race*, she argues that if we replace the word *social* with *race*, then this statement resounds with the earlier project of David Popenoe's father, Paul Popenoe, who in the 1920s and 1930s warned of the threat of race suicide if eugenic projects to reproduce white middle-class families were not taken with utmost seriousness (Kline 2001, 164).

Many men I interviewed concurred that it was high time far a new kind of family in the United States. An agency owner from Mexico suggested I speak to Barry, a well-known advocate of international marriages. Referred to as a guru of the cyberbride industry, Barry himself married (and later divorced) a woman from Colombia and attempted to open an agency; he now counsels U.S.-Colombian married couples and is writing a book about the industry. Barry capitalizes on David Popenoe's marriage study and his "academic cachet" to argue for the need not for racially superior (or white) families but for men to go outside the nation to find more appropriate wives. Like Popenoe, Barry uses biological gender differences between men and women to argue that the market dictates demand. During a phone interview in 2003, he described to me the thesis of his forthcoming book, *The Marketplace of Love*. He said that when you combine U.S. men's frustration with their relationships with U.S. women, and women's dissatisfaction with the way they are treated in Latin America, you have a natural market exchange of supply and demand. In fact, he argues, no man looks overseas first, but "the marketplace drives men" (interview, February 2003). In describing the development of the marketplace as inevitable and as taking on a life of its own, Barry does not have to question historical processes such as colonialism and imperialism nor contemporary forms of global capitalism that contribute to the unequal distribution of resources within this "neutral" marketplace. The focus on genetics and evolution also mirrors popular conceptions of international business, where competition in the marketplace is described as a natural and inevitable Darwinian struggle for the survival of the fittest (Hooper 2001). Contemporary corporate multiculturalism both enables possibilities for love across borders and naturalizes inequalities between the kinds of labor men and women provide. Women continue to have value for their spiritual and domestic qualities while men provide the economic stability. At the macro level, the United States is constructed as a biologically masculine nation and Latin America as feminine in order to naturalize these kinds of transnational marriages.

Barry's forthcoming book and lifelong quest is to create a sense of normalcy in regard to the cyberbride business and, as Popenoe himself argues (through the lens of Kline), to create for the United States "a new, modern form of morality—a reproductive morality—[is] to counter the ever-increasing individualism in society and to build a better family" (Kline 2001, 164). In couching this moral quest as one in opposition to individualism, family values take on a social and even national imperative. Barry may support ethnic, religious, and class mixtures, but it is women's "differences" that ultimately support men's dominance and that of the United States more widely.

LATIN AMERICAN WOMEN AS THE "FINAL FRONTIER"

Latin American women's bodies are reconfigured within the global marketplace as young, untainted natural resources. For example, a former company out of San Diego called Sonoran Girls opened its Web site with a picture of smiling young women from the northern town of Sonora, Mexico; bold letters over the picture read: "Discover Mexico's Greatest Treasures."

These photos are of young Latinas positioned in front of the colors of the Mexican flag, as symbols of the nation. Young *Mexicanas* are the new resources, or as Barbara Ehrenreich and Arlie Hochschild (2002) describe them, the "new gold," whose laboring bodies are in need of men to import them to the United States where they will become fully realized.

Other Web sites depict women as cultural and biological *mestizas*, hybrid bodies that visually narrate the progression of history and the nation. Women's bodies mark the transition between the indigenous past and the modern future, and they are figured both as individuals yet simultaneously as overabundant and technologically reproducible (and thus expendable).

Figuring women's bodies as those of light-skinned *mestizas* also makes visible men's central role in neocolonial fantasies. Men take part in the colonial narrative of turning nature (raw materials) into culture (finished modern products). On these Web sites, women's bodies are young and pliable. . . . Many men and Web sites echo the idea that U.S. feminism is the polluting force of the family and nation. Henry Makow reiterates this point: "Today feminism has morphed into a potent and virulent disease attacking the biological and cultural foundations of society" (2000, 123). The contemporary use of the language of eugenics resembles the surge of biological theories of gender in the 1970s that followed on the heels of the women's liberation movements.

In contrast to the bodies of U.S. women, Latin American women's bodies continue to gain currency as workers in the global economy—as bodies that maintain domestic order, as docile and hardworking immigrants, as moral caretakers, as adaptable and elastic bodies, and as cheap, abundant natural resources.[11] The position of women in the cybermarriage industry resembles the subject position of women in the feminized global economy, where

---

[11]See Fernandez-Kelly 1983; Iglesias Prieto 1997; Chang 2000; Hondagneu-Sotelo 2001; Parreñas 2001; Ehrenreich and Hochschild 2002.

African-American women, feminists, and white women fall to the bottom rung as the least desirable bodies, as those who are imagined to be too outspoken, too demanding of their worth.[12] Yet Latin American women also hold a tenuous position, as they can easily be lowered to the same degraded category as U.S. women. Women who do not produce docile bodies for their husbands or proper sexual and gendered behavior can easily fall from grace. In chat room discussions, women who divorce men, who display acts of selfishness, or who are too resourceful (and thus "conniving") are labeled "green card sharks," lesbians, feminists, or too modern, and thus overly influenced by U.S. culture. By locating culture within the body, citizenship is imagined not by national or political participation but by women's self-sacrificial relationship to men through their reproductive sexual, racial, and gender position in the home and, by extension, in the global economy.

In many chat room and interview discussions, men described themselves as active participants in assimilating women into the "American dream" of upward mobility. At one of the agencies in Guadalajara, Mexico, I interviewed an energetic seventy-year-old man named Stuart (who told women he was fifty-five) about his marriage to a twenty-seven-year-old Colombian woman. She had a child and came from an abusive family whose socioeconomic status had dropped dramatically due to the social unrest plaguing the country. They divorced after living together in the United States for almost two years, even, Stuart tells me, after he gave his wife everything from plenty of spending money, English classes, and a membership to an exclusive gym.[13] He says, "All she needed to do was go to school, learn the culture, and be a mother and wife. I had yearly passes to the zoo, parks—I just wanted them to experience American life, the American dream."

Like the female missionaries of the twentieth century who fulfilled their duty as moral citizens of the world by "uplifting" the natives, men too take on this role of the moral "good guys" who teach Latinas how to assimilate into the dream of liberal capitalism.[14] Chat room discussions about women marveling over skyscrapers and washing machines in the United States and men's emphasis of women's "traditional" qualities easily slip into colonial ideas of the "natives" as backward, primitive, and uncivilized. Yet Latinas are also modern enough to appreciate technology when faced with its magnitude.

---

[12]This understanding of racial value in the global economy is strikingly similar to scholarship on the domestic service industry. See Hondagneu-Sotdo 2001.

[13]It is interesting that they divorced after two years, because in 1986 President Ronald Reagan signed the Immigration Marriage Fraud Amendment (IMFA) in hopes of decreasing marriage scams by imposing a two-year waiting period for women to obtain permanent residency status.

[14]There has been a great deal of feminist scholarship on women's role as missionaries in relation to British imperialism and U.S. empire. See Tyrrell 1991; Chaudhuri and Strobel 1992; Abraham 1996; Santiago-Valles 1999.

Stuart's philanthropic spirit, his desire to share the American dream with "less fortunate" women, was mirrored in his own personal genealogy as he described himself to me as not simply as a wealthy Anglo businessman but someone who came to the United States as a poor (and, at the time, racially marked) immigrant who worked his way up the social hierarchy.[15] For many men, the benefits of white masculinity can be tapped into through upward social and class mobility. Envisioning oneself as a self-made man elides privileges of race and the values of individualism and materialism that men consistently critiqued about U.S. women and U.S. culture in general. What Stuart had to do to gain his fortune as an insurance investor is less important here than his work ethic and desire to uplift others. Having a foreign wife reinvigorates the idea that the United States is an immigrant nation where those who work hard can make the American dream come true, while erasing the unequal system of power, slave labor, and colonial violence at the foundation of this nation's continuing global dominance. For those who do not achieve this dream, the blame falls on pathologizing the individual — which Stuart describes as his wife's "laziness" — rather than examining deeper structures of disempowerment.

SELF-HELP AND CHAT ROOMS

. . . While the majority of participants on Planet-Love are Anglo-Americans, there are increasingly more men of color as well as men from a variety of regions in the United States and from a variety of professional, class, and ethnic backgrounds. In a chat room discussion, a Peruvian American participant named Doug responds to another participant, "hombre rosas," about the need for him to sacrifice time and money to fly to Latin America to meet a woman with whom he has been corresponding. Doug acknowledges, "It's easier for some than others. . . . You'll do it because good guys can ALWAYS find a way. She's counting on you" (Planet-Love.com chat room, December 3, 2000). They bond on two levels, as U.S. Latinos who have had to struggle more than others, and as professionals and citizens who now enjoy upward mobility.

On Planet-Love there was often hostility directed at the few African American participants who brought up race as a marker of structural inequalities or oppression. Anglo participants refused to believe that race influenced why some African American men had less success than Anglo-Americans in dating women from various countries such as Mexico. Yet cultural differences, such as Latino participants' familiarity with Spanish and/or Latin culture, were interpreted as a positive asset. For Latino men, their travel back to Latin America resembled the cultural nationalist project, whereby Chicanos would harken

---

[15]For more on the historical whitening of the Polish, Germans, Italians, and Irish, see Jacobson 1998.

back to Mexican history and culture to authenticate and preserve a racial identity threatened by U.S. assimilation. Hombre rosas says:

> So here I am, turning to LW [Latin Women], turning inward, towards the center of who I am, where I came from, it has made me once again count the ways I value my latin culture. But again, I never used to openly celebrate latin values or compare and contrast them with American, out of respect for the general American public, my neighbors, friends and family. But these days I see that I'm not alone in many of my sentiments and there is a general atmosphere of criticism of AW [American Women] and their values, so I am less hesitant to celebrate being latino and saying where I'm from and all that. (Planet-Love.com chat room, December 2, 2000)

For hombre rosas, a critique of American women opens up a space to be critical of assimilation and U.S. values. Turning to "authentic" Latin American women (i.e., women closer to values of submission, unlike unruly Chicanas/ Latinas in the United States) signifies his journey to rediscovering his true self that he has had to hide in order to assimilate into Anglo culture. Situating Latin American women as the authentic other enables Latino men to construct an ethnic identity as white in relation to Latin American women, manual labor, and immigrants in general. Conversing on this board has connected hombre rosas to other professional Latinos — as well as to white men who appreciate Latin American culture — and it becomes a safe place for him to openly celebrate his cultural heritage. The act of revealing oneself personally serves as an initiation or a rite of passage where this new, "sensitive" masculinity is encouraged. In the world of self-help and male support groups, sharing one's experiences marks the journey of finding a bride, discovering one's self, and finding the "true man" one really is. Male camaraderie is founded on releasing the male energies participants believe are suppressed by domineering women from the United States and, for Latino men, by U.S. culture in general.

White men's self-conception as the good guy who is sensitive yet in control is fabricated alongside an idealized image of Latinas and in contest with hypermasculinized Mexican/Latino masculinities. Pierrette Hondagneu-Sotelo and Michael Messner (1994) argue that white, educated, middle-class constructions of the sensitive new male image must not be too quickly heralded. This image builds itself on the backs of poor, working-class, and ethnically subordinate men who are the projected targets of aggression, domination, and misogynistic attitudes. Often overlooked, however, is how Latin men reassert their masculinity by feminizing white, Anglo men. A respondent called "The Watcher" says: "If any of these guys put down Latin men, they have some damn nerve! When they finally realize that 99% of the reason that ANY foreign woman would want to marry them and come to this country is for HER OWN opportunity and benefit and that of HER family, and NOT because American men are so special, then maybe they will check their egos and see the light" (Planet-Love.com chat room, June 24, 1999). Through his critique of U.S. men, "The Watcher" offers a disruptive moment of competing mas-culinities. He diminishes U.S. men's status by elevating women as creative survivors, thus negating women's supposed adoration of U.S. men. He also suggests women use men to improve their lives and that of their families. He continues, "Latinas need strong men. Men who are macho, that's right, I said MACHO, but in a good way. They don't want a man who will beat them around and treat her like trash, but they don't want some pansy who acts like a femi-nist sympathizer either. They want a Man who is not afraid to be a MAN!" (Planet-Love.com chat room, June 24, 1999). "The Watcher's" hostility reveals a Latin male perspective regarding white U.S. men. He turns the tables on Anglo-Americans who go to Latin America by feminizing them as the sort of men who not only support feminism but who are also the ones who allowed women to take charge through feminism in the first place. By labeling feminist sympathizers as "pansies," he also implicates gay men and Anglo sexuality as feminized and overly domesticated, degrading the two alongside femininity. He also redefines his derogatory ethnic association with machismo from one that is undesirable to one that is highly desired by Latinas.

The discursive threat of white U.S. men's feminization in the United States has led to a refashioning of the cyberbride industry via popular culture. A cosmopolitan magazine, *Men's Journal*, disassociates men from domesticity and thus femininity by depicting them as travelers, adventurers, risk takers, and capitalists on the hunt for women in virgin markets. A recent article titled "Bride-Hunting in Russia/Project Wife" (Tayman 2000) captures this spirit of adventure and cosmopolitanism. It was placed alongside other articles on top-ics such as how to increase one's testosterone and exotic sporting adventures all over the world. The featured client in this article looking for a Russian bride is Spencer, who "flies planes and rock climbs, but he's lonely. He hasn't had a serious girlfriend in quite some time" (139). Couched in this quote is a critique of the dark side of wealth and success—loneliness and alienation. A dose of a third-world encounter, however, can offset this sense of feeling ungrounded, overworked, and lonely. In the article, the problem is not that Spencer works too much, is dissatisfied with his job, and participates in per-petuating the capitalist system but that he is undervalued in the United States. While structures of corporate white male masculinity may be perceived to be in decline in the United States, the average Joe, or José, is enticed to enjoy the comparative advantage of women who value his hard work ethic, find him attractive, and who are dying to marry men from the West. Interestingly, men are interpolated to understand themselves not only as consumers but also as prized commodities in the global marketplace.

· · ·

. . . John, who has participated in chat room discussions on Planet-Love for five years, talks about his ex-wife, whom he married in Colombia after know-ing her for five days: "One thing I notice is when we are in Colombia she always treats me better. It's like I get more respect from her because I get respect from her family. I'm sort of the main attraction, even with her friends that come over. . . . But back in San Jose [U.S.] back to the same old. . . . Two big things happened in 2002. She got a job. And she got her permanent residency card. Both made her feel a lot more independent" (Planet-Love.com chat room, October 10, 2003). John's statement raises the question of whether men's dominant position is more fragile than previous studies on the mail-order bride industry have purported. While men may enjoy a boost in status in Latin America, they may find this wears off once they return home. Similarly, women's subject positions and reasons for marrying U.S. men are also much more complex when examined from a transborder perspective.

CONCLUSION

The desire for a Latin American woman from outside the United States speaks to the power of the erotic imagination and the role of technology in transporting one's personal fantasies into a transnational social forum. . . . Men's search for a Latin American bride necessitates a critique of U.S. capitalist culture, yet men and industry Web sites ghettoize this critique onto U.S. feminist bodies rather than onto larger structures of power. In other words, men blame consumption, materialism, and even greed for high divorce rates, for the fact that women leave them for wealthier and younger men, or that women seek their own empowerment through entering the workforce. Mirroring the tension between the global economy and the state in protecting the unbounded needs of capitalism and, conversely, the bounded role of the state (Noble 2002), men justify their search outside the nation for foreign genes through a moral desire to improve the national family and, simultaneously, via fantasies of mobility through the tropes of empire and the heroics of global manhood. Through their desire to improve the culture of national family, they are caught in the dilemma of embracing ethnic, gender, religious, and national differences while maintaining global hierarchies.

The consequences of men's imaginaries are best reflected in an e-mail interview with Manuela, a *Mexicana* who participated in the *Latinaesposa/Latinawife* e-mail exchange for married women who moved to the United States to live with their husbands. She has been married to her Anglo husband for more than three years. In an e-mail interview she described to me one of the many contradictions discussed by women: "While men want a Latina because she is supposedly more passionate, when we have this passion, they don't know how to respond. Men prefer Internet pornography than to make love with us. They'd rather watch perfect women than normal and real women. All of us agree that we can't compete with these unreal bodies, that don't fight, that don't get angry, who don't veer from the norm. . . . It's easier for los gringos to masturbate in front of the computer, where they don't have to put forth any effort to satisfy anyone. Like many things here (in the U.S.),

[U.S. men are] . . . the most individualistic and self-absorbed" (interview, December 10, 2004). Manuela's theorizing of Western individualism, masculinity, and whiteness in relation to technological power ends up deflating Western fantasies as getting lost in the maze of their own simulations. The role of the Internet in facilitating visual and interactive fantasies and even marriage speaks to yet another way U.S. individualism and the capitalistic gaze turn a potentially powerful means for men to experience themselves as a decentered subject rather than the center. While many men turn to Latin American women and culture in hopes of living a life outside of the tyranny of capitalism, materialism, and rugged individualism, many simply seek a fantasy-ridden image of women as the object of change they seek to import back home without having to change anything about themselves.

REFERENCES

Abraham, Meera. 1996. *Religion, Caste and Gender: Missionaries and Nursing History in South India.* Bangalore: BI Publications.

Bishop, Ryan, and Lillian S. Robinson. 1998. *Night Market: Sexual Cultures and the Thai Economic Miracle.* New York: Routledge.

———. 2002. "How My Dick Spent Its Summer Vacation: Labor, Leisure, and Masculinity on the Web." *Genders* 35. Available online at http://www.genders.org/g35/g35_robinson.html.

Caldwell, John Thornton, ed. 2000. *Theories of the New Media: A Historical Perspective.* London: Athlone.

Calvo, Luz. 2001. "Border Fantasies: Sexual Anxieties and Political Passions in the Mexico-U.S. Borderlands." PhD dissertation, University of California, Santa Cruz.

Castañeda, Antonia I. 1990. "The Political Economy of Nineteenth-Century Stereotypes of Californians." In *Between Borders: Essays on Mexicana/Chicana History*, ed. Adelaida Del Castillo, 213–36. Encino, CA: Floricanto.

Chang, Grace. 2000. *Disposable Domestics: Immigrant Women Workers in the Global Economy.* Cambridge, MA: South End.

Chaudhuri, Nupur, and Margaret Strobel, eds. 1992. *Western Women and Imperialism: Complicity and Resistance.* Bloomington: Indiana University Press.

Chavez, Leo R. 2001. *Covering Immigration: Popular Images and the Politics of the Nation.* Berkeley: University of California Press.

Connell, R. W. 1995. *Masculinities.* Berkeley: University of California Press.

———. 2000. *The Men and the Boys.* Berkeley: University of California Press.

Constable, Nicole. 2003. *Romance on a Global Stage: Pen Pals, Virtual Ethnography, and "Mail Order" Marriages.* Berkeley: University of California Press.

Ehrenreich, Barbara, and Arlie Russell Hochschild, eds. 2002. *Global Woman: Nannies, Maids, and Sex Workers in the New Economy.* New York: Metropolitan Books.

Faludi, Susan. 1999. *Stiffed: The Betrayal of the American Man.* New York: Perennial.

Fernandez-Kelly, Maria Patricia. 1983. *For We Are Sold, I and My People: Women and Industry on Mexico's Frontier.* Albany, NY: SUNY Press.

Glenn, Evelyn Nakano. 1986. *Issei, Nisei, War Bride: Three Generations of Japanese American Women in Domestic Service.* Philadelphia: Temple University Press.

Glodava, Mila, and Richard Onizuka. 1994. *Mail-Order Brides: Women for Sale.* Fort Collins, CO: Alaken, Inc.

Hondagneu-Sotelo, Pierrette. 2001. *Doméstica: Immigrant Workers Cleaning and Caring in the Shadows of Affluence.* Berkeley: University of California Press.

Hondagneu-Sotelo, Pierrette, and Michael A. Messner. 1994. "Gender Displays and Men's Power: The 'New Man' and the Mexican Immigrant Man." In *Theorizing Masculinities*, ed. Harry Brod and Michael Kaufman, 200–218. Thousand Oaks, CA: Sage.

Hooper, Charlotte. 2001. *Manly States: Masculinities, International Relations, and Gender Politics.* New York: Columbia University Press.

Iglesias Prieto, Norma. 1997. *Beautiful Flowers of the Maquiladora: Life Histories of Women Workers in Tijuana.* Trans. Michael Stone and Gabrielle Winkler. Austin: University of Texas Press.

Inda, Jonathan Xavier. 2002. "Biopower, Reproduction, and the Migrant Woman's Body." In *Decolonial Voices: Chicana and Chicano Cultural Studies in the 21st Century*, ed. Arturo J. Aldama and Naomi H. Quiñonez, 98–112. Bloomington: Indiana University Press.

Jacobson, Matthew Frye. 1998. *Whiteness of a Different Color: European Immigrants and the Alchemy of Race.* Cambridge, MA: Harvard University Press.

Kang, Laura Hyun Yi. 2002. *Compositional Subjects: Enfiguring Asian/American Women.* Durham, NC: Duke University Press.

Kendall, Lori. 2002. *Hanging Out in the Virtual Pub: Masculinities and Relationships Online.* Berkeley: University of California Press.

Kline, Wendy. 2001. *Building a Better Race: Gender, Sexuality, and Eugenics from the Turn of the Century to the Baby Boom.* Berkeley: University of California Press.

Kondo, Dorinne. 1997. *About Face: Performing Race in Fashion and Theater.* New York: Routledge.

Limón, José E. 1998. *American Encounters: Greater Mexico, the United States, and the Erotics of Culture.* Boston: Beacon.

Lu, Sheldon H. 2000. "Soap Opera in China: The Transnational Politics of Visuality, Sexuality, and Masculinity." *Cinema Journal* 40(1):25–47.

Makow, Henry. 2000. *A Long Way to Go for a Date.* Winnipeg: Silas Green.

McClintock, Anne. 1995. *Imperial Leather: Race, Gender, and Sexuality in the Colonial Contest.* New York: Routledge.

Nakamura, Lisa. 2000. "'Where do you want to go today?' Cybernetic Tourism, the Internet, and Transnationality." In *Race in Cyberspace*, ed. Beth E. Kolko, Lisa Nakamura, and Gilbert B. Rodman, 15–26. New York: Routledge.

Noble, David W. 2002. *Death of a Nation: American Culture and the End of Exceptionalism.* Minneapolis: University of Minnesota Press.

Ong, Aihwa. 1999. *Flexible Citizenship: The Cultural Logics of Transnationality*. Durham, NC: Duke University Press.

Ortiz, Ana Teresa, and Laura Briggs. 2003. "The Culture of Poverty, Crack Babies, and Welfare Cheats: The Making of the 'Healthy White Baby Crisis.'" *Social Text* 21(3):39–57.

Parea, Juan F. 1997. *Immigrants Out! The New Nativism and the Anti-immigrant Impulse in the United States*. New York: New York University Press.

Parreñas, Rhacel Salazar. 2001. *Servants of Globalization: Women, Migration, and Domestic Work*. Stanford, CA: Stanford University Press.

Popenoe, David. 1996. *Life without Father: Compelling New Evidence That Fatherhood and Marriage Are Indispensable for the Good of Children and Society*, Cambridge, MA: Harvard University Press.

Reimers, David M. 1985. *Still the Golden Door: The Third World Comes to America*. New York: Columbia University Press.

Runyan, Anne Sisson. 1996. "Trading Places: Globalization, Regionalization, and Internationalized Feminism." In *Globalization: Theory and Practice*, ed. Gillian Youngs and Eleonore Kofman, 238–52. Cambridge: Polity.

Saldaña-Portillo, María Josefa. 2003. *The Revolutionary Imagination in the Americas and the Age of Development*. Durham, NC: Duke University Press.

Santiago-Valles, Kelvin. 1999. "'Higher Womanhood' among the 'Lower Races': Julia McNair Henry in Puerto Rico and the 'Burdens' of 1898." *Radical History Review* 73 (Winter): 47–73.

Schaeffer-Grabiel, Felicity. 2004. "Cyberbrides and Global Imaginaries: Mexican Women's Turn from the National to the Foreign." *Space and Culture: International Journal of Social Sciences* 7(1):33–48.

Scott, Joan. 1999. "The Evidence of Experience." In *Feminist Approaches to Theory and Methodology: An Interdisciplinary Reader*, ed. Sharlene Hesse-Biber, Christina Gilmartin, and Robin Lyndenberg, 79–99. New York: Oxford University Press.

Tayman, John. 2000. "Bride Hunting in Russia/Project Wife." *Men's Journal*, December, 136–42.

Tolentino, Rolando B. 1999. "Bodies, Letters, Catalogs: Filipinas in Transnational Space." In *Transnational Asia Pacific: Gender, Culture, and the Public Sphere*, ed. Shirley Geok-lin Lim, Larry E. Smith, and Wilmal Dissanayake, 43–68. Urbana: University of Illinois Press.

Truong, Thanh-Dam. 1990. *Sex, Money and Morality: Prostitution and Tourism in Southeast Asia*. London: Zed.

Tyrrell, Ian. 1991. *The Women's Christian Temperance Union in International Perspective, 1880–1930*. Chapel Hill: University of North Carolina Press.

Villipando, Venny. 1989. "The Business of Selling Mail-Order Brides." In *Making Waves: An Anthology of Writings By and About Asian American Women*, ed. Asian Women United of California, 318–326. Boston: Beacon.

GLORIA STEINEM
Sex, Lies, and Advertising

Gloria Steinem is a feminist activist and journalist who was founder and editor for Ms. *Magazine in 1972. She has won numerous awards, and her bestselling books include* Outrageous Acts and Everyday Rebellions *(1983) and* Revolution from Within: A Book of Self Esteem *(1992). This selection, among her most famous essays, was first published in* Ms. *Magazine in 1990.*

> Goodbye to cigarette ads where poems should be.
> Goodbye to celebrity covers and too little space.
> Goodbye to cleaning up language so *Ms.* advertisers won't be
>   boycotted by the Moral Majority.
> In fact, goodbye to advertisers *and* the Moral Majority.
> Goodbye to short articles and short thinking.
> Goodbye to "post-feminism" from people who never say
>   "post-democracy."
> Goodbye to national boundaries and hello to the world.
> Welcome to the magazine of the post-patriarchal age.
> The turn of the century is *our turn!*

That was my celebratory mood in the summer of 1990 when I finished the original version of the exposé you are about to read. I felt as if I'd been released from a personal, portable Bastille. At least I'd put on paper the ad policies that had been punishing *Ms.* for all the years of its nonconforming life and still were turning more conventional media, especially (but not only) those directed at women, into a dumping ground for fluff.

Those goodbyes were part of a letter inviting readers to try a new, ad-free version of *Ms.* and were also a homage to "Goodbye to All That," a witty and lethal essay in which Robin Morgan bade farewell to the pre-feminist male Left of twenty years before. It seemed the right tone for the birth of a brand-new, reader-supported, more international form of *Ms.*, which Robin was heading as editor-in-chief, and I was serving as consulting editor. Besides, I had a very personal kind of mantra running through my head: *I'll never have to sell another ad as long as I live.*

So I sent the letter off, watched the premiere issue containing my exposé go to press, and then began to have second thoughts: Were ad policies too much of an "inside" concern? Did women readers already know that magazines directed at them were filled with editorial extensions of ads — and not care? Had this deceptive system been in place too long for anyone to have faith in changing it? In other words: Would anybody give a damn?

511

After almost four years of listening to responses and watching the ripples spread out from this pebble cast upon the waters, I can tell you that, yes, readers do care; and no, most of them were not aware of advertising's control over the words and images around it. Though most people in the publishing industry think this is a practice too deeply embedded ever to be uprooted, a lot of readers are willing to give it a try—even though that's likely to mean paying more for their publications. In any case, as they point out, understanding the nitty-gritty of ad influence has two immediate uses. It strengthens healthy skepticism about what we read, and it keeps us from assuming that other women must want this glamorous, saccharine, unrealistic stuff.

Perhaps that's the worst punishment ad influence has inflicted upon us. It's made us feel contemptuous of other women. We know we don't need those endless little editorial diagrams of where to put our lipstick or blush—we don't identify with all those airbrushed photos of skeletal women with everything about them credited, *even their perfume* (can you imagine a man's photo airbrushed to perfection, with his shaving lotion credited?)—but we assume there must be women out there somewhere who *do* love it; otherwise, why would it be there?

Well, many don't. Given the sameness of women's magazines resulting from the demands made by makers of women's products that advertise in all of them, we probably don't know yet what a wide variety of women readers want. In any case, we do know it's the advertisers who are determining what women are getting now.

The first wave of response to this exposé came not from readers but from writers and editors for other women's magazines. They phoned to say the pall cast by anticipated or real advertising demands was even more widespread than rebellious *Ms.* had been allowed to know. They told me how brave I was to "burn my bridges" (no critic of advertising would ever be hired as an editor of any of the women's magazines, they said) and generally treated me as if I'd written about organized crime instead of practices that may be unethical but are perfectly legal. After making me promise not to use their names, they offered enough additional horror stories to fill a book, a movie, and maybe a television series. Here is a typical one: when the freelance author of an article on moisturizers observed in print that such products might be less necessary for young women—whose skin tends to be not dry but oily—the article's editor was called on the carpet and denounced by her bosses as "anti-moisturizer." Or how about this: the film critic for a women's magazine asked its top editor, a woman who makes millions for her parent company, whether movies could finally be reviewed critically, since she had so much clout. No, said the editor; if you can't praise a movie, just don't include it; otherwise we'll jeopardize our movie ads. This may sound like surrealism in everyday life, or like our grandmothers advising, "If you can't say something nice, don't say anything," but such are the forces that control much of our information.

I got few negative responses from insiders, but the ones I did get were bitter. Two editors at women's magazines felt I had demeaned them by writing the article. They loved their work, they said, and didn't feel restricted by ads at all. So I would like to make clear in advance that my purpose was and is to change the system, not to blame the people struggling within it. As someone who has written for most women's magazines, I know that many editors work hard to get worthwhile articles into the few pages left over after providing all the "complementary copy" (that is, articles related to and supportive of advertised products). I also know there are editors who sincerely want exactly what the advertisers want, which is why they're so good at their jobs. Nonetheless, criticizing this ad-dominant system is no different from criticizing male-dominant marriage. Both institutions make some people happy, and both seem free as long as your wishes happen to fall within their traditional boundaries. But just as making more equal marital laws alleviates the suffering of many, breaking the link between editorial and advertising will help all media become more honest and diverse.

A second wave of reaction came from advertising executives who were asked to respond by reporters. They attributed all problems to *Ms.* We must have been too controversial or otherwise inappropriate for ads. I saw no stories that asked the next questions: Why had non-women's companies from Johnson & Johnson to IBM found our "controversial" pages fine for their ads? Why did desirable and otherwise unreachable customers read something so "inappropriate"? What were ad policies doing to *other* women's media? To continue my marriage parallel, however, I should note that these executives seemed only mildly annoyed. Just as many women are more dependent than men on the institution of marriage and so are more threatened and angry when it's questioned, editors of women's magazines tended to be more upset than advertisers when questioned about their alliance. . . .

Then came the third wave — reader letters which were smart, thoughtful, innovative, and numbered in the hundreds. Their dominant themes were anger and relief: relief because those vast uncritical oceans of food/fashion/beauty articles in other women's magazines weren't necessarily what women wanted after all, and also relief because *Ms.* wasn't going to take ads anymore, even those that were accompanied by fewer editorial demands; anger because consumer information, diverse articles, essays, fiction, and poetry could have used the space instead of all those oceans of articles about ad categories that had taken up most of women's magazines for years. . . .

Last and most rewarding was the response that started in the fall. Teachers of journalism, advertising, communications, women's studies, and other contemporary courses asked permission to reprint the exposé as a supplementary text. That's another reason why I've restored cuts, updated information, and added new examples — including this introduction. Getting subversive ideas into classrooms could change the next generation running the media.

The following pages are mostly about women's magazines, but that doesn't mean other media are immune.

SEX, LIES, AND ADVERTISING

Toward the end of the 1980s, when glasnost was beginning and *Ms.* magazine seemed to be ending, I was invited to a press lunch for a Soviet official. He entertained us with anecdotes about the new problems of democracy in his country; for instance, local Communist leaders who were being criticized by their own media for the first time, and were angry.

"So I'll have to ask my American friends," he finished pointedly, "how more subtly to control the press."

In the silence that followed, I said: "Advertising."

The reporters laughed, but later one of them took me aside angrily: How dare I suggest that freedom of the press was limited in this country? How dare I imply that *his* newsmagazine could be influenced by ads?

I explained that I wasn't trying to lay blame, but to point out advertising's media-wide influence. We can all recite examples of "soft" cover stories that newsmagazines use to sell ads, and self-censorship in articles that should have taken advertised products to task for, say, safety or pollution. Even television news goes "soft" in ratings wars, and other TV shows don't get on the air without advertiser support. But I really had been thinking about women's magazines. There, it isn't just a little content that's designed to attract ads; it's almost all of it. That's why advertisers—not readers—had always been the problem for *Ms.* As the only women's magazine that didn't offer what the ad world euphemistically describes as "supportive editorial atmosphere" or "complementary copy" (for instance, articles that praise food/fashion/beauty subjects in order to "support" and "complement" food/fashion/beauty ads), *Ms.* could never attract enough ads to break even.

"Oh, *women's* magazines," the journalist said with contempt. "Everybody knows they're catalogs—but who cares? They have nothing to do with journalism."

I can't tell you how many times I've had this argument since I started writing for magazines in the early 1960s, and especially since the current women's movement began. Except as moneymaking machines—"cash cows," as they are so elegantly called in the trade—women's magazines are usually placed beyond the realm of serious consideration. Though societal changes being forged by women have been called more far-reaching than the industrial revolution by such nonfeminist sources as the *Wall Street Journal*—and though women's magazine editors often try hard to reflect these changes in the few pages left after all the ad-related subjects are covered—the magazines serving the female half of this country are still far below the journalistic and ethical standards of news and general-interest counterparts. Most depressing of all, this fact is so taken for granted that it doesn't even rate an exposé.

For instance: If *Time* and *Newsweek*, in order to get automotive and GM ads, had to lavish editorial praise on cars and credit photographs in which newsmakers were driving, say, a Buick from General Motors, there would be a scandal—maybe even a criminal investigation. When women's magazines from *Seventeen* to *Lear's* publish articles lavishing praise on beauty and fashion products, and credit in text, the cover, and other supposedly editorial photographs a particular makeup from Revlon or a dress from Calvin Klein because those companies also advertise, it's just business as usual.

When *Ms.* began, we didn't consider *not* taking ads. The most important reason was to keep the price of a feminist magazine low enough for most women to afford. But the second and almost equal reason was to provide a forum where women and advertisers could talk to each other and experiment with nonstereotyped, informative, imaginative ads. After all, advertising was (and is) as potent a source of information in this country as news or TV or movies. It's where we get not only a big part of our information but also images that shape our dreams.

We decided to proceed in two stages. First, we would convince makers of "people products" that their ads should be placed in a women's magazine: cars, credit cards, insurance, sound equipment, financial services—everything that's used by both men and women but was then advertised only to men. Since those advertisers were accustomed to the division between editorial pages and ads that news and general-interest magazines at least try to maintain, such products would allow our editorial content to be free and diverse. Furthermore, if *Ms.* could prove that women were important purchasers of "people products," just as men were, those advertisers would support other women's magazines, too, and subsidize some pages for articles about something other than the hothouse worlds of food/fashion/beauty. Only in the second phase would we add examples of the best ads for whatever traditional "women's products" (clothes, shampoo, fragrance, food, and so on) that subscriber surveys showed *Ms.* readers actually used. But we would ask those advertisers to come in *without* the usual quid pro quo of editorial features praising their product area; that is, the dreaded "complementary copy."

From the beginning, we knew the second step might be even harder than the first. Clothing advertisers like to be surrounded by editorial fashion spreads (preferably ones that credit their particular labels and designers); food advertisers have always expected women's magazines to publish recipes and articles on entertaining (preferably ones that require their products); and shampoo, fragrance, and beauty products in general insist on positive editorial coverage of beauty aids—a "beauty atmosphere," as they put it—plus photo credits for particular products and nothing too depressing; no bad news. That's why women's magazines look the way they do: saccharine, smiley-faced and product-heavy, with even serious articles presented in a slick and sanitized way.

But if *Ms.* could break this link between ads and editorial content, then we should add "women's products" too. For one thing, publishing ads only for gender-neutral products would give the impression that women have to become "like men" in order to succeed (an impression that *Ms.* ad pages sometimes *did* give when we were still in the first stage). For another, presenting a full circle of products that readers actually need and use would allow us to select the best examples of each category and keep ads from being lost in a sea of similar products. By being part of this realistic but unprecedented mix, products formerly advertised only to men would reach a growth market of women, and good ads for women's products would have a new visibility.

Given the intelligence and leadership of *Ms.* readers, both kinds of products would have unique access to a universe of smart consultants whose response would help them create more effective ads for other media too. Aside from the advertisers themselves, there's nobody who cares as much about the imagery in advertising as those who find themselves stereotyped or rendered invisible by it. And they often have great suggestions for making it better.

As you can see, we had all our energy, optimism, and arguments in good working order.

I thought at the time that our main problem would be getting ads with good "creative," as the imagery and text are collectively known. That was where the women's movement had been focusing its efforts, for instance, the National Organization for Women's awards to the best ads, and its "Barefoot and Pregnant" awards for the worst. Needless to say, there were plenty of candidates for the second group. Carmakers were still draping blondes in evening gowns over the hoods like ornaments that could be bought with the car (thus also making clear that car ads weren't directed at women). Even in ads for products that only women used, the authority figures were almost always male, and voice-overs for women's products on television were usually male too. Sadistic, he-man campaigns were winning industry praise; for example, *Advertising Age* hailed the infamous Silva Thin cigarette theme, "How to Get a Woman's Attention: Ignore Her," as "brilliant." Even in medical journals, ads for tranquilizers showed depressed housewives standing next to piles of dirty dishes and promised to get them back to work. As for women's magazines, they seemed to have few guidelines; at least none that excluded even the ads for the fraudulent breast-enlargement or thigh-thinning products for which their back pages were famous.

Obviously, *Ms.* would have to avoid such offensive imagery and seek out the best ads, but this didn't seem impossible. The *New Yorker* had been screening ads for aesthetic reasons for years, a practice that advertisers accepted at the time. *Ebony* and *Essence* were asking for ads with positive black images, and though their struggle was hard, their requests weren't seen as unreasonable. . . .

Let me take you through some of our experiences—greatly condensed, but just as they happened. In fact, if you poured water on any one of these, it would become a novel:

• Cheered on by early support from Volkswagen and one or two other car companies, we finally scrape together time and money to put on a major reception in Detroit. U.S. carmakers firmly believe that women choose the upholstery color, not the car, but we are armed with statistics and reader mail to prove the contrary: A car is an important purchase for women, one that is such a symbol of mobility and freedom that many women will spend a greater percentage of income for a car than will counterpart men.

But almost nobody comes. We are left with many pounds of shrimp on the table, and quite a lot of egg on our face. Assuming this near-total boycott is partly because there was a baseball pennant play-off the same day, we blame ourselves for not foreseeing the problem. Executives go out of their way to explain that they wouldn't have come anyway. It's a dramatic beginning for ten years of knocking on resistant or hostile doors, presenting endless documentation of women as car buyers, and hiring a full-time saleswoman in Detroit—all necessary before *Ms.* gets any real results.

This long saga has a semi-happy ending: Foreign carmakers understood better than Detroit that women buy cars, and advertised in *Ms.*; also years of research on the women's market plus door-knocking began to pay off. Eventually, cars became one of our top sources of ad revenue. Even Detroit began to take the women's market seriously enough to put car ads in other women's magazines too, thus freeing a few more of their pages from the food/fashion/beauty hothouse.

But long after figures showed that a third, even half, of many car models were being bought by women, U.S. makers continued to be uncomfortable addressing female buyers. Unlike many foreign carmakers, Detroit never quite learned the secret of creating intelligent ads that exclude no one and then placing them in media that overcome past exclusion. Just as an African American reader may feel more invited by a resort that placed an ad in *Ebony* or *Essence*, even though the same ad appeared in *Newsweek*, women of all races may need to see ads for cars, computers, and other historically "masculine" products in media that are clearly directed at them. Once inclusive ads are well placed, however, there's interest and even gratitude from women. *Ms.* readers were so delighted to be addressed as intelligent consumers by a routine Honda ad with text about rack-and-pinion steering, for example, that they sent fan mail. But even now, Detroit continues to ask: "Should we make special ads for women?" That's probably one reason why foreign cars still have a greater share of the women's market in the United States than of the men's.

• In the *Ms.* Gazette, we do a brief report on a congressional hearing into coal tar derivatives used in hair dyes that are absorbed through the skin and may be carcinogenic. This seems like news of importance: Newspapers and newsmagazines are reporting it too. But Clairol, a Bristol-Myers subsidiary that makes dozens of products, a few of which have just come into our pages as ads *without* the usual quid pro quo of articles on hair and beauty, is outraged. Not at newspapers or newsmagazines, just at us. It's bad enough that *Ms.* is the only women's magazine refusing to provide "supportive editorial" praising beauty products, but to criticize one of their product categories on top of it, however generically or even accurately — well, *that* is going too far.

We offer to publish a letter from Clairol telling its side of the story. In an excess of solicitousness, we even put this letter in the Gazette, not in Letters to the Editors, where it belongs. Eventually, Clairol even changes its hair-coloring formula, apparently in response to those same hearings. But in spite of surveys that show *Ms.* readers to be active women who use more of almost everything Clairol makes than do the readers of other women's magazines, *Ms.* gets almost no ads for those dozens of products for the rest of its natural life.

• Women of color read *Ms.* in disproportionate numbers. This is a source of pride to *Ms.* staffers, who are also more racially representative than the editors of other women's magazines (which may include some beautiful black models but almost no black decisionmakers; Pat Carbine hired the first black editor at *McCall's*, but she left when Pat did). Nonetheless, the reality of *Ms.*'s staff and readership is obscured by ads filled with enough white women to make the casual reader assume *Ms.* is directed at only one part of the population, no matter what the editorial content is.

In fact, those few ads we are able to get that feature women of color — for instance, one made by Max Factor for *Essence* and *Ebony* that Linda Wachner gives us while she is president of Max Factor — are greeted with praise and relief by white readers, too, and make us feel that more inclusive ads should win out in the long run. But there are pathetically few such images. Advertising "creative" also excludes women who are not young, not thin, not conventionally pretty, well-to-do, able-bodied, or heterosexual — which is a hell of a lot of women.

• Our intrepid saleswomen set out early to attract ads for the product category known as consumer electronics: sound equipment, computers, calculators, VCRs, and the like. We know that *Ms.* readers are determined to be part of this technological revolution, not to be left out as women have been in the past. We also know from surveys that readers are buying this kind of stuff in numbers as high as those of readers of magazines like *Playboy* and the "male 18 to 34" market, prime targets of the industry. Moreover, unlike traditional women's products that our readers buy but don't want to read articles about, these are subjects they like to see demystified in our pages. There actually *is* a supportive editorial atmosphere.

"But women don't understand technology," say ad and electronics executives at the end of our presentations. "Maybe not," we respond, "but neither do men—and we all buy it."

"If women *do* buy it," counter the decisionmakers, "it's because they're asking their husbands and boyfriends what to buy first." We produce letters from *Ms.* readers saying how turned off they are when salesmen say things like "Let me know when your husband can come in."

Then the argument turns to why there aren't more women's names sent back on warranties (those much-contested certificates promising repair or replacement if anything goes wrong). We explain that the husband's name may be on the warranty, even if the wife made the purchase. But it's also true that women are experienced enough as consumers to know that such promises are valid only if the item is returned in its original box at midnight in Hong Kong. Sure enough, when we check out hair dryers, curling irons, and other stuff women clearly buy, women don't return those warranties very often either. It isn't the women who are the problem, it's the meaningless warranties.

After several years of this, we get a few ads from companies like JVC and Pioneer for compact sound systems—on the grounds that women can understand compacts, but not sophisticated components. Harry Elias, vice president of JVC, is actually trying to convince his Japanese bosses that there is something called a woman's market. At his invitation, I find myself speaking at trade shows in Chicago and Las Vegas trying to persuade JVC dealers that electronics showrooms don't have to be locker rooms. But as becomes apparent, however, the trade shows are part of the problem. In Las Vegas, the only women working at technology displays are seminude models serving champagne. In Chicago, the big attraction is Marilyn Chambers, a porn star who followed Linda Lovelace of *Deep Throat* fame as Chuck Traynor's captive and/or employee, whose pornographic movies are being used to demonstrate VCRs.

In the end, we get ads for a car stereo now and then, but no VCRs; a welcome breakthrough of some IBM personal computers, but no Apple or no Japanese-made ones. Furthermore, we notice that *Working Woman* and *Savvy*, which are focused on office work, don't benefit as much as they should from ads for office equipment either. . . .

• Then there is the great toy train adventure. Because *Ms.* gets letters from little girls who love toy trains and ask our help in changing ads and box-top photos that show only little boys, we try to talk to Lionel and to get their ads. It turns out that Lionel executives *have* been concerned about little girls. They made a pink train and couldn't understand why it didn't sell.

Eventually, Lionel bows to this consumer pressure by switching to a photograph of a boy *and* a girl—but only on some box tops. If trains are associated with little girls, Lionel executives believe, they will be devalued in the eyes of little boys. Needless to say, *Ms.* gets no train ads. If even 20 percent of little girls wanted trains, they would be a huge growth market, but this remains unexplored. In the many toy stores where displays are still gender divided, the "soft" stuff, even modeling clay, stays on the girls' side, while the "hard" stuff, especially rockets and trains, is displayed for boys — thus depriving both. By 1986, Lionel is put up for sale.

We don't have much luck with other kinds of toys either. A *Ms.* department, Stories for Free Children, edited by Letty Cottin Pogrebin, makes us one of the very few magazines with a regular feature for children. A larger proportion of *Ms.* readers have preschool children than do the readers of any other women's magazine. Nonetheless, the industry can't seem to believe that feminists care about children — much less have them.

• When *Ms.* began, the staff decided not to accept ads for feminine hygiene sprays and cigarettes on the same basis: They are damaging to many women's health but carry no appropriate warnings. We don't think we should tell our readers what to do — if marijuana were legal, for instance, we would carry ads for it along with those for beer and wine — but we should provide facts so readers can decide for themselves. Since we've received letters saying that feminine sprays actually kill cockroaches and take the rust off metal, we give up on those. But antismoking groups have been pressuring for health warnings on cigarette ads as well as packages, so we decide we will accept advertising if the tobacco industry complies.

Philip Morris is among the first to do so. One of its brands, Virginia Slims, is also sponsoring women's tennis tournaments and women's public opinion polls that are historic "firsts." On the other hand, the Virginia Slims theme, "You've come a long way, baby," has more than a "baby" problem. It gives the impression that for women, smoking is a sign of progress.

We explain to the Philip Morris people that this slogan won't do well in our pages. They are convinced that its success with *some* women means it will work with *all* women. No amount of saying that we, like men, are a segmented market, that we don't all think alike, does any good. Finally, we agree to publish a small ad for a Virginia Slims calendar as a test, and to abide by the response of our readers.

The letters from readers are both critical and smart. For instance: Would you show a photo of a black man picking cotton next to one of an African American man in a Cardin suit, and symbolize progress from slavery to civil rights by smoking? Of course not. So why do it for women? But instead of honoring test results, the executives seem angry to have been proved wrong. We refuse Virginia Slims ads, thus annoying tennis players like Billie Jean King as well as incurring a new level of wrath: Philip Morris takes away ads for *all* its many products, costing *Ms.* about $250,000 in the first year. After five years, the damage is so great we can no longer keep track.

Occasionally, a new set of Philip Morris executives listens to *Ms.* saleswomen, or laughs when Pat Carbine points out that even Nixon got pardoned. I also appeal directly to the chairman of the board, who agrees it is unfair, sends me to another executive — and *he* says no. Because we won't take Virginia Slims, not one other Philip Morris product returns to our pages for the next sixteen years.

Gradually, we also realize our naïveté in thinking we could refuse all cigarette ads, with or without a health warning. They became a disproportionate source of revenue for print media the moment television banned them, and few magazines can compete or survive without them; certainly not *Ms.*, which lacks the support of so many other categories. Though cigarette ads actually inhibit editorial freedom less than ads for food, fashion, and the like — cigarette companies want only to be distant from coverage on the dangers of smoking, and don't require affirmative praise or photo credits of their product — it is still a growing source of sorrow that they are there at all. By the 1980s, when statistics show that women's rate of lung cancer is approaching men's, the necessity of taking cigarette ads has become a kind of prison.

Though I never manage to feel kindly toward groups that protest our ads and pay no attention to magazines and newspapers that can turn them down and still keep their doors open — and though *Ms.* continues to publish new facts about smoking, such as its dangers during pregnancy — I long for the demise of the whole tobacco-related industry. . . .

• General Mills, Pillsbury, Carnation, Del Monte, Dole, Kraft, Stouffer, Hormel, Nabisco: You name the food giant, we try to get its ads. But no matter how desirable the *Ms.* readership, our lack of editorial recipes and traditional homemaking articles proves lethal.

We explain that women flooding into the paid labor force have changed the way this country eats; certainly, the boom in convenience foods proves that. We also explain that placing food ads *only* next to recipes and how-to-entertain articles is actually a negative for many women. It associates food with work — in a way that says only women have to cook — or with guilt over *not* cooking and entertaining. Why not advertise food in diverse media that don't always include recipes (thus reaching more men, who have become a third of all supermarket shoppers anyway) and add the recipe interest with specialty magazines like *Gourmet* (a third of whose readers are men)?

These arguments elicit intellectual interest but no ads. No advertising executive wants to be the first to say to a powerful client, "Guess what, I *didn't* get you complementary copy." Except for an occasional hard-won ad for instant coffee, diet drinks, yogurt, or such extras as avocados and almonds, the whole category of food, a mainstay of the publishing industry, remains unavailable to us. Period. . . .

• By the end of 1986, magazine production costs have skyrocketed and postal rates have increased 400 percent. Ad income is flat for the whole magazine industry. The result is more competition, with other magazines offering such "extras" as free golf trips for advertisers or programs for "sampling" their products at parties and other events arranged by the magazine for desirable consumers. We try to compete with the latter by "sampling" at what we certainly have enough of: movement benefits. Thus, little fragrance bottles turn up next to the dinner plates of California women lawyers (who are delighted), or wine samples lower the costs at a reception for political women. A good organizing tactic comes out of this. We hold feminist seminars in shopping centers. They may be to the women's movement what churches were to the civil rights movement in the South—that is, *where people are.* Anyway, shopping center seminars are a great success. Too great. We have to stop doing them in Bloomingdale's up and down the East Coast, because meeting space in the stores is too limited, and too many women are left lined up outside stores. We go on giving out fancy little liquor bottles at store openings, which makes the advertisers happy—but not us.

Mostly, however, we can't compete in this game of "value-added" (the code word for giving the advertisers extras in return for their ads). Neither can many of the other independent magazines. Deep-pocketed corporate parents can offer such extras as reduced rates for ad schedules in a group of magazines, free tie-in spots on radio stations they also own, or vacation junkets on corporate planes.

Meanwhile, higher costs and lowered income have caused the *Ms.* 60/40 preponderance of edit over ads—something we promised to readers—to become 50/50: still a lot better than most women's magazines' goals of 30/70, but not good enough. Children's stories, most poetry, and some fiction are casualties of reduced space. In order to get variety into more limited pages, the length (and sometimes the depth) of articles suffers. Though we don't solicit or accept ads that would look like a parody in our pages, we get so worn down that some slip through. Moreover, we always have the problem of working just as hard to get a single ad as another magazine might for a whole year's schedule of ads.

Still, readers keep right on performing miracles. Though we haven't been able to afford a subscription mailing in two years, they maintain our guaranteed circulation of 450,000 by word of mouth. Some of them also help to make up the advertising deficit by giving *Ms.* a birthday present of $15 on its fifteenth anniversary, or contributing $1,000 for a lifetime subscription—even those who can ill afford it.

What's almost as angering as these struggles, however, is the way the media report them. Our financial problems are attributed to lack of reader interest, not an advertising double standard. In the Reagan-Bush era, when "feminism-is-dead" becomes one key on the typewriter, our problems are used to prepare a grave for the whole movement. Clearly, the myth that advertisers go where the readers are—thus, if we had readers, we would have advertisers—is deeply embedded. Even industry reporters rarely mention the editorial demands made by ads for women's products, and if they do, they assume advertisers must be right and *Ms.* must be wrong; we must be too controversial, outrageous, even scatalogical to support. In fact, there's nothing in our pages that couldn't be published in *Time, Esquire,* or *Rolling Stone*—providing those magazines devoted major space to women—but the media myth often wins out. Though comparable magazines our size (say, *Vanity Fair* or the *Atlantic*) are losing more money in a single year than *Ms.* has lost in sixteen years, *Ms.* is held to a different standard. No matter how much never-to-be-recovered cash is poured into starting a magazine or keeping it going, appearances seem to be all that matter. (Which is why we haven't been able to explain our fragile state in public. Nothing causes ad flight like the smell of nonsuccess.)

My healthy response is anger, but my not-so-healthy one is depression, worry, and an obsession with finding one more rescue. There is hardly a night when I don't wake up with sweaty palms and pounding heart, scared that we won't be able to pay the printer or the post office; scared most of all that closing our doors will be blamed on a lack of readers and thus the movement, instead of the real cause. ("Feminism couldn't even support one magazine," I can hear them saying.)

We're all being flattened by a velvet steamroller. The only difference is that at *Ms.*, we keep standing up again.

Do you think, as I once did, that advertisers make decisions based on rational and uniform criteria? Well, think again. There is clearly a double standard. The same food companies that insist on recipes in women's magazines place ads in *People* where there are no recipes. Cosmetics companies support the *New Yorker*, which has no regular beauty columns, and newspaper pages that have no "beauty atmosphere."

Meanwhile, advertisers' control over the editorial content of women's magazines has become so institutionalized that it is sometimes written into "insertion orders" or dictated to ad salespeople as official policy—whether by the agency, the client, or both. The following are orders given to women's magazines effective in 1990. Try to imagine them being applied to *Time* or *Newsweek*.

• Dow's Cleaning Products stipulated that ads for its Vivid and Spray 'n Wash products should be adjacent to "children or fashion editorial"; ads for Bathroom Cleaner should be next to "home furnishing/family" features; with similar requirements for other brands. "If a magazine fails for ½ the brands or more," the Dow order warned, "it will be omitted from further consideration."

• Bristol-Myers, the parent of Clairol, Windex, Drano, Bufferin, and much more, stipulated that ads be placed next to "a full page of compatible editorial."

• S. C. Johnson & Son, makers of Johnson Wax, lawn and laundry products, insect sprays, hair sprays, and so on, insisted that its ads *"should not be opposite extremely controversial features or material antithetical to the nature/copy of the advertised product."* (Italics theirs.)

• Maidenform, manufacturer of bras and other women's apparel, left a blank for the particular product and stated in its instructions: "The creative concept of the _____ campaign, and the very nature of the product itself, appeal to the positive emotions of the reader/consumer. Therefore, it is imperative that all editorial adjacencies reflect that same positive tone. The editorial must not be negative in content or lend itself contrary to the _____ product imagery/message (e.g., *editorial relating to illness, disillusionment, large size fashion, etc.*)."" (Italics mine.)

• The De Beers diamond company, a big seller of engagement rings, prohibited magazines from placing its ads with "adjacencies to hard news or anti-love/romance themed editorial." . . .

• Kraft/General Foods, a giant with many brands, sent this message with an Instant Pudding ad: "urgently request upbeat parent/child activity editorial, mandatory positioning requirements—opposite full page of positive editorial—right hand page essential for creative—minimum 6 page competitive separation (i.e., all sugar based or sugar free gelatins, puddings, mousses, creames [sic] and pie filling)—Do not back with clippable material. Avoid: controversial/negative topics and any narrow targeted subjects."

• An American Tobacco Company order for a Misty Slims ad noted that the U.S. government warning must be included, but also that there must be: "no adjacency to editorial relating to health, medicine, religion, or death."

• Lorillard's Newport cigarette ad came with similar instructions, plus: "Please be aware that the Nicotine Patch products are competitors. The minimum six page separation is required."

Quite apart from anything else, you can imagine the logistical nightmare this creates when putting a women's magazine together, but the greatest casualty is editorial freedom. Though the ratio of advertising to editorial pages in women's magazines is only about 5 percent more than in *Time* or *Newsweek*, that nothing-to-read feeling comes from all the supposedly editorial pages that are extensions of ads. To find out what we're really getting when we pay our money, I picked up a variety of women's magazines for February 1994, and counted the number of pages in each one (even including table of contents, letters to the editors, horoscopes, and the like) that were not ads and/or copy complementary to ads. Then I compared that number to the total pages. Out of 184 pages, *McCall's* had 49 that were nonad or ad-related. Of 202, *Elle* gave readers 48. *Seventeen* provided its young readers with only 51 nonad or ad-related pages out of 226. *Vogue* had 62 out of 292. *Mirabella* offered readers 45 pages out of a total of 158. *Good Housekeeping* came out on top, though only at about a third, with 60 out of 176 pages. *Martha Stewart Living* offered the least. Even counting her letter to readers, a page devoted to her personal calendar, and another one to a turnip, only seven out of 136 pages had no ads, products, or product mentions. . . .

Within the supposedly editorial text itself, praise for advertisers' products has become so ritualized that fields like "beauty writing" have been invented. One of its practitioners explained to me seriously that "It's a difficult art. How many new adjectives can you find? How much greater can you make a lipstick sound? The FDA restricts what companies can say on labels, but we create illusion. And ad agencies are on the phone all the time pushing you to get their product in. A lot of them keep the business based on how many editorial clippings they produce every month. The worst are products [whose manufacturers have] their own name involved. It's all ego."

Often, editorial becomes one giant ad. An issue of *Lear's* featured an elegant woman executive on the cover. On the contents page, we learn she is wearing Guerlain makeup and Samsara, a new fragrance by Guerlain. Inside, there just happen to be full-page ads for Samsara, plus a Guerlain antiwrinkle skin cream. In the article about the cover subject, we discover she is Guerlain's director of public relations and is responsible for launching, you guessed it, the new Samsara. . . .

When the *Columbia Journalism Review* cited this example in one of the few articles to include women's magazines in a critique of ad influence, Frances Lear, editor of *Lear's*, was quoted at first saying this was a mistake, and then shifting to the defense that "this kind of thing is done all the time."

She's right. Here's an example with a few more turns of the screw. Martha Stewart, *Family Circle*'s contributing editor, was also "lifestyle and entertaining consultant" for Kmart, the retail chain, which helped to underwrite the renovation of Stewart's country house, using Kmart products; *Family Circle* covered the process in three articles not marked as ads; Kmart bought $4 million worth of ad pages in *Family Circle*, including "advertorials" to introduce a line of Martha Stewart products to be distributed by Kmart; and finally, the "advertorials," which at least are marked and only *look* like editorial pages, were reproduced and distributed in Kmart stores, thus publicizing *Family Circle* (owned by the New York Times Company, which would be unlikely to do this kind of thing in its own news pages) to Kmart customers. This was so lucrative that Martha Stewart now has her own magazine, *Martha Stewart Living* (owned by Time Warner), complete with a television version. Both offer a happy world of cooking, entertaining, and decorating in which nothing critical or negative ever seems to happen.

I don't mean to be a spoilsport, but there are many articles we're very unlikely to get from that or any other women's magazine dependent on food ads. According to Senator Howard Metzenbaum of Ohio, more than half of the chickens we eat (from ConAgra, Tyson, Perdue, and other companies) are contaminated with dangerous bacteria; yet labels haven't yet begun to tell us to scrub the meat and everything it touches—which is our best chance of not getting sick. Nor are we likely to learn about the frequent working conditions of this mostly female work force, standing in water, cutting chickens apart with such repetitive speed that carpal tunnel syndrome is an occupational hazard. Then there's Dole Food, often cited as a company that keeps women in low-level jobs and a target of a lawsuit by Costa Rican workers who were sterilized by contact with pesticides used by Dole—even though Dole must have known these pesticides had been banned in the United States.

The consumerist reporting we're missing sometimes sounds familiar. Remember the *Ms.* episode with Clairol and the article about potential carcinogens in hair dye? Well, a similar saga took place with L'Oréal and *Mademoiselle* in 1992, according to an editor at Condé Nast. Now, editors there are supposed to warn publishers of any criticism in advance, a requirement that might well have a chilling effect.

Other penalties are increasing. As older readers will remember, women's magazines used to be a place where new young poets and short story writers could be published. Now, that's very rare. It isn't that advertisers of women's products dislike poetry or fiction, it's just that they pay to be adjacent to articles and features more directly compatible with their products.

Sometimes, advertisers invade editorial pages—literally—by plunging odd-shaped ads into the text, no matter how that increases the difficulty of reading. When Ellen Levine was editor of *Woman's Day*, for instance, a magazine originally founded by a supermarket chain, she admitted, "The day the copy had to rag around a chicken leg was not a happy one."

The question of ad positioning is also decided by important advertisers, a rule that's ignored at a magazine's peril. When Revlon wasn't given the place of the first beauty ad in one Hearst magazine, for instance, it pulled its ads from *all* Hearst magazines. In 1990 Ruth Whitney, editor in chief of *Glamour*, attributed some of this pushiness to "ad agencies wanting to prove to a client that they've squeezed the last drop of blood out of a magazine." She was also "sick and tired of hearing that women's magazines are controlled by cigarette ads." Relatively speaking, she was right. To be as controlling as most advertisers of women's products, tobacco companies would have to demand articles in flat-out praise of smoking, and editorial photos of models smoking a credited brand. As it is, they ask only to be forewarned so they don't advertise in the same issue with an article about the dangers of smoking. But for a magazine like *Essence*, the only national magazine for African American women, even taking them out of one issue may be financially difficult, because other advertisers might neglect its readers. In 1993, a group called Women and Girls Against Tobacco, funded by the California Department of Health Services, prepared an ad headlined "Cigarettes Made Them History." It pictured three black singers—Mary Wells, Eddie Kendricks, and Sarah Vaughan—who died of tobacco-related diseases. *Essence* president Clarence Smith didn't turn the ad down, but he didn't accept it either. When I talked with him in 1994, he said with pain, "the black female market just isn't considered at parity with the white female market; there are too many other categories we don't get." That's in spite of the fact that *Essence* does all the traditional food-fashion-beauty editorial expected by advertisers. According to California statistics, African American women are more addicted to smoking than the female population at large, with all the attendant health problems.

Alexandra Penney, editor of *Self* magazine, feels she has been able to include smoking facts in health articles by warning cigarette advertisers in advance (though smoking is still being advertised in this fitness magazine). On the other hand, up to this writing in 1994, no advertiser has been willing to appear opposite a single-page feature called "Outrage," which is reserved for important controversies, and is very popular with readers. Another women's magazine publisher told me that to this day Campbell's Soup refuses to advertise because of an article that unfavorably compared the nutritional value of canned food to that of fresh food—fifteen years ago.

I don't mean to imply that the editors I quote here share my objections to ad demands and/or expectations. Many assume that the women's magazines at which they work have to be the way they are. Others are justifiably proud of getting an independent article in under the advertising radar, for instance, articles on family violence in *Family Circle* or a series on child sexual abuse and the family courts in *McCall's*. A few insist they would publish exactly the same editorial, even if there were no ads. But it's also true that it's hard to be honest while you're still in the job. "Most of the pressure came in the form of direct product mentions," explained Sey Chassler, who was editor in chief of *Redbook* from the sixties to the eighties and is now out of the game. "We got threats from the big guys, the Revlons, blackmail threats. They wouldn't run ads unless we credited them."

What could women's magazines be like if they were as editorially free as good books? as realistic as the best newspaper articles? as creative as poetry and films? as diverse as women's lives? What if we as women—who are psychic immigrants in a public world rarely constructed by or for us—had the same kind of watchful, smart, supportive publications on our side that other immigrant groups have often had?

We'll find out only if we take the media directed at us seriously. If readers were to act in concert in large numbers for a few years to change the traditional practices of *all* women's magazines and the marketing of *all* women's products, we could do it. After all, they depend on our consumer dollars—money we now are more likely to control. If we include all the shopping we do for families and spouses, women make 85 percent of purchases at point of sale. You and I could:

- refuse to buy products whose ads have clearly dictated their surroundings, and write to tell the manufacturers why;

- write to editors and publishers (with copies to advertisers) to tell them that we're willing to pay *more* for magazines with editorial independence, but will *not* continue to pay for those that are editorial extensions of ads;

- write to advertisers (with copies to editors and publishers) to tell them that we want fiction, political reporting, consumer reporting, strong opinion, humor, and health coverage that doesn't pull punches, praising them when their ads support this, and criticizing them when they don't;

- put as much energy and protest into breaking advertising's control over what's around it as we put into changing the images within it or protesting harmful products like cigarettes;

- support only those women's magazines and products that take us seriously as readers and consumers;

- investigate new laws and regulations to support freedom from advertising influence. The Center for the Study of Commercialism, a group founded in 1990 to educate and advocate against "ubiquitous product marketing," recommends whistle-blower laws that protect any members of the media who disclose advertiser and other commercial conflicts of interest, laws that require advertiser influence to be disclosed, Federal Trade Commission involvement, and denial of income tax exemptions for advertising that isn't clearly identified— as well as conferences, citizen watchdog groups, and a national clearinghouse where examples of private censorship can be reported.

Those of us in the magazine world can also use this carrot-and-stick technique. The stick: If magazines were a regulated medium like television, the editorial quid pro quo demanded by advertising would be against the rules of the FCC and payola and extortion would be penalized. As it is, there are potential illegalities to pursue. For example: A magazine's postal rates are determined by the ratio of ad pages to editorial pages, with the ads being charged at a higher rate than the editorial. Counting up all the pages that are *really* ads could make an interesting legal action. There could be consumer fraud cases lurking in subscriptions that are solicited for a magazine but deliver a catalog.

The carrot is just as important. In twenty years, for instance, I've found no independent, nonproprietary research showing that an ad for, say, fragrance is any more effective placed next to an article about fragrance than it would be when placed next to a good piece of fiction or reporting. As we've seen, there are studies showing that the greatest factor in determining an ad's effectiveness is the credibility and independence of its surroundings. An air-tight wall between ads and edit would also shield corporations and agencies from pressures from both ends of the political spectrum and from dozens of pressure groups. Editors would be the only ones responsible for editorial content— which is exactly as it should be.

Unfortunately, few agencies or clients hear such arguments. Editors often maintain the artificial purity of refusing to talk to the people who actually control their lives. Instead, advertisers see salespeople who know little about editorial, are trained in business as usual, and are usually paid on commission. To take on special controversy editors might also band together. That happened once when all the major women's magazines did articles in the same month on the Equal Rights Amendment. It could happen again—and regularly.

Meanwhile, we seem to have a system in which everybody is losing. The reader loses diversity, strong opinion, honest information, access to the arts, and much more. The editor loses pride of work, independence, and freedom from worry about what brand names or other critical words some sincere free-lancer is going to come up with. The advertiser loses credibility right along with the ad's surroundings, and gets more and more lost in a sea of similar ads and interchangeable media.

But that's also the good news. Because where there is mutual interest, there is the beginning of change.

If you need one more motive for making it, consider the impact of U.S. media on the rest of the world. The ad policies we tolerate here are invading the lives of women in other cultures—through both the content of U.S. media and the ad practices of multinational corporations imposed on other countries. Look at our women's magazines. Is this what we want to export?

Should *Ms.* have started out with no advertising in the first place? The odd thing is that, in retrospect, I think the struggle was worth it. For all those years, dozens of feminist organizers disguised as *Ms.* ad saleswomen took their courage, research, slide shows, humor, ingenuity, and fresh point of view into every advertising agency, client office, and lion's den in cities where advertising is sold. Not only were sixteen years of *Ms.* sustained in this way, with all the changeful words on those thousands of pages, but some of the advertising industry was affected in its imagery, its practices, and its understanding of the female half of the country. Those dozens of women themselves were affected, for they learned the art of changing a structure from both within and without, and are now rising in crucial publishing positions where women have never been. *Ms.* also helped to open nontraditional categories of ads for women's magazines, thus giving them a little more freedom—not to mention making their changes look reasonable by comparison.

But the world of advertising has a way of reminding us how far there is to go.

Three years ago, as I was finishing this exposé in its first version, I got a call from a writer for *Elle.* She was doing an article on where women parted their hair: Why, she wanted to know, did I part mine in the middle?

It was all so familiar. I could imagine this writer trying to make something out of a nothing assignment. A long-suffering editor laboring to think of new ways to attract ads for shampoo, conditioner, hairdryers, and the like. Readers assuming that other women must want this stuff.

As I was working on this version, I got a letter from Revlon of the sort we disregarded when we took ads. Now, I could appreciate it as a reminder of how much we had to disregard:

> We are delighted to confirm that Lauren Hutton is now under contract to Revlon.
>
> We are very much in favor of her appearing in as much editorial as possible, but it's important that your publication avoid any mention of competitive color cosmetics, beauty treatment, hair care or sun care products in editorial or editorial credits in which she appears.
>
> We would be very appreciative if all concerned are made aware of this.

I could imagine the whole chain of women — Lauren Hutton, preferring to be in the Africa that is her passion; the ad executive who signed the letter, only doing her job; the millions of women readers who would see the resulting artificial images; all of us missing sources of information, insight, creativity, humor, anger, investigation, poetry, confession, outrage, learning, and perhaps most important, a sense of connection to each other; and a gloriously diverse world being flattened by a velvet steamroller.

I ask you: Can't we do better than this?

NANCY THEBERGE

Reflections on the Body in the Sociology of Sport

Nancy Theberge is Professor of Kinesiology and Sociology at the University of Waterloo in Canada. Her research focuses on sports and work, and her most recent book is about women's ice hockey.

One striking development of contemporary intellectual and popular discourse is a fascination with the body. As an observer recently wrote, "bodies are in, in academia and popular culture" (Frank, 1990, p. 131). Literature on the body comes from various disciplines and addresses a myriad of questions. In this paper, I attempt to draw some connections between an emergent sociology of the body and some key questions and issues in the sociology of sport. The account of the sociology of the body is based on Bryan Turner's 1984 volume entitled *The Body and Society*. To this is added some insights from feminist post-structuralism. These works are significant contributions to social theory. As well, they have particular relevance to the sociology of sport.

THE BODY, SOCIOLOGICAL THEORY, AND THE SOCIOLOGY OF SPORT

Turner (1984, pp. 1–2) began his work from the position that the body has been largely absent from sociological theory. Few social theorists, he said, have taken the embodiment of persons seriously. Moreover, references to the corporal nature of human life raise the specter of social Darwinism, biological reductionism, or social biology. Turner (1984, p. 1) called these traditions analytical cul-de-sacs that have nothing to do with a genuine sociology of the body.

It would be an exaggeration to call the theoretical traditions in the sociology of sport nothing more than analytical cul-de-sacs. Nonetheless, work in this field has been largely devoid of a consideration of the body and of embodiment. Scholarly analysis of sport in the social sciences and humanities has a short history, beginning in the mid 1960s. Perhaps this effort's major success has been to establish the social basis and significance of sport and physical activity. This has been accomplished in numerous ways and in work that reflects the basic theoretical traditions in sociology as well as analyses grounded in political economy, cultural studies, feminism, and other critical perspectives. This work has, for example, examined the political and social bases of sport

531

and physical activity, the ideological implications of sporting practices, and the possibilities for resistance and transformation through these practices.

In its quest to establish the social significance of sport, however, this field has had little to say about the body. It is ironic that in studying sport, where the body is essential to the experience, we have largely missed its meaning and importance. The main exception to this is some work in gender and sport; selections from this work are discussed later in the article. Turner's call for a return of the body to social theory thus has particular relevance to the study of sport and physical activity.

ELEMENTS OF A SOCIOLOGY OF THE BODY

Underlying the call for a turn to the sociology of the body is Turner's argument that the Hobbesian question of social order may be conceptualized as a sociology of the body. Noting that Hobbes' own starting point was the "geometry of bodies," Turner (1984, p. 87) suggested the possibility of a "neo-Hobbesian version of the body," which extends from but significantly transcends Hobbes' formulations. Specifically, Turner (1984, p. 91) proposed that the Hobbesian problem of order as a geometry of bodies has four related dimensions: the reproduction of populations through time and their regulation in space, and the restraint and the representation of the body as a vehicle of the self.

Turner stressed that the saliency of the four dimensions and the institutional forms and processes that are concerned with their resolution are historically conditioned. There is in late capitalism a "representational crisis of self-management" (Turner, 1984, p. 113). Mass consumerism, including mass leisure and entertainment, has masked traditional representational indicators of social class. Social success nonetheless continues to depend on the display of interpersonal skills and self-presentation. Accordingly,

> Successful images require successful bodies, which have been trained, disciplined and orchestrated to enhance our personal value. . . . The new ethic of managerial athleticism is thus the contemporary version of the Protestant ethic, but, fanned by the winds of consumerism, this ethic has become widespread throughout the class system as a life-style to be emulated. The commodified body has become the focus of a keep-fit industry, backed up by fibre diets, leisure centres, slimming manuals and outdoor sports. Capitalism has commodified hedonism. (Turner, 1984, p. 112)

This process of commodification includes a rationalized athleticism: "We jog, slim and sleep not for intrinsic enjoyment, but to improve our chances at sex, work and longevity. The new asceticism of competitive social relations exist to create desire—desire which is subordinated to the rationalization of the body as the final triumph of capitalist development. Obesity has become irrational" (Turner, 1984, p. 112).

An important feature of Turner's analysis is his argument that bringing the body back into social theory allows for a fuller consideration of the social bases of patriarchy. This is so because a material and historical analysis of bodies in Western societies is fundamentally about the control and domination of women under patriarchy. "Any sociology of the body involves a discussion of social control and any discussion of social control must consider the control of women's bodies under patriarchy" (Turner, 1984, pp. 2–3).

Turner (1984) proposed that in modem societies the subordination of women under patriarchy has collapsed and been replaced by a form of domination he called patrism. That is, patriarchy as an "objective social" (Turner, 1984, p. 155) structure of sexual inequality enforced by the exclusion of women from institutional life has been replaced by a system of men's prejudicial beliefs and practices toward women without the systematic backing of law and politics. Some observers will no doubt argue the thesis that structural forms of patriarchy have collapsed. Nonetheless, the power of patristic beliefs and practices that continue the subordination of women is apparent. The problem for a sociology of the body is to develop a historical analysis of the forms and mechanisms of social control and domination of women. This means an analysis of patristic social practices and conditions.

Turner (1984) concluded his volume with a statement of some key features that must guide an emergent sociology of the body. These features have obvious relevance to the sociology of sport. Specifically, a sociology of the body must address some notion of agency, must address the nature–culture dichotomy, and must be social and not individualistic. But to what end do we apply these principles? One answer proposed is that by challenging the dualities of nature and culture the sociology of the body questions the nature of being. "That is, the sociology of the body must ultimately address itself to the nature of social ontology" (Turner, 1984, p. 227).

A summary is perhaps in order. Turner (1984) argued that reclaiming the body in social theory leads to some key issues in the study of society and social order. Under late capitalism the problems of representation have assumed particular significance. Mass consumerism becomes a basis of a new narcissism and hedonism that find expression in the leisure and health industries. These expressions have particular form and meaning for women. For women under the dominant modes of patrism, the "problem" of self-representation is resolved in a variety of practices and forms of embodiment that realize their control. Imagery of emancipation and liberation, fitness and health, veil and mask new forms of domination and exploitation.

POSTSTRUCTURALIST CONTRIBUTIONS

In contrast to the historical absence of considerations of the body in sociology, there is a developing feminist analysis that takes the body as the central focus of interest. Recently, a particularly important turn has been accounts in feminist poststructuralism that take the body as a central locus of the construction of femininity and of gender. Much of this work is an extension or an application of the ground-breaking formulations of Michel Foucault. As critics have noted, Foucault's own work took too little account of gender and the experience and condition of women. Although in developing his thesis Turner has made ample use of Foucault, the taking up of Foucault's project by feminism and its infusion with a specifically feminist agenda has been a significant development.

In the introduction to their edited work titled *Feminism and Foucault*, Diamond and Quinby (1988, p. x) identified four convergences between Foucault and feminism. These common features provide the grounds for an elaboration of the sociology of the body. And as I will show later, they are the basis for contributions to this effort from the sociology of sport. The first is the body as the site of power or the locus of domination. Second is a focus on local and intimate operations of power rather than on larger institutional formulations such as the power of the state. Third is the emphasis on the crucial role of discourse in producing and sustaining power. Fourth is a critique of Western humanism's privileging the experience and accounts of a Western masculine elite.

The appropriation of Foucault for a feminist analysis and the development of feminist poststructuralism are among the most exciting developments on the theoretical landscape. As well, they are developments marked by debate and a myriad of assessments. One point of contention is the possibility for an explicitly feminist politics within poststructuralism. The position adopted here is that the insights of poststructuralism must be grounded in a commitment to feminist praxis. From this position, the discussion in this section attempts to show how some elements of a poststructural feminist account inform an evolving sociology of the body. In the following section, these points are illustrated by examples from the study of sport.

Some clues to the task at hand are provided in a piece by Susan Bordo (1989), titled "The Body and the Reproduction of Femininity: A Feminist Appropriation of Foucault." Bordo (1990, p. 13) described the body as a "text of culture." That is, the body is an account, a rendering of cultural rules, including rules on the construction of gender. At the same time, the body is a locus of social control. A key problem for a feminist analysis is to specify the content of the texts—the meanings and significations of bodies—and the locus and practices of social control that accomplish this account.

Two further points should be stressed. One is that the production of texts is not simply representational—we are talking here of much more than the body as a reflection of particular ideas and interests. Rather, the process is constitutive: The production of bodies is a means to the constitution of social beings and social relations. Second, the conceptualization of bodies as texts has an explicitly political component. A key aspect of Foucault's work is his understanding of power: "When I think of the mechanics of power. I think of its capillary form of existence, of the extent to which power seeps into the very grain of individuals, reaches right into their bodies, permeates their gestures, their posture, what they say, how they learn to live and work with other people" (quoted in Sheridan, 1980, p. 217).

An instance of a feminist appropriation and extension of Foucault is provided in an analysis by Sandra Lee Bartky (1988) on the modernization of patriarchal power. Bartky examined contemporary disciplinary practices that produce a recognizably feminine body. Three categories of practices are identified; each is considered in respect to its forms, means of enforcement, and implications for female identity and subjectivity. One category "aims to produce a body of a certain size and general configuration" (Bartky, 1988, p. 64). The contemporary fashionable female body is "taut" and "slim," and "massiveness, power, or abundance" is met with distaste. Dieting and exercise are the disciplines that impose enforcement. The gendering of exercise is particularly important. Although both men and women exercise, the meaning and aims of these activities may differ, and there is a set of activities (classes, videos, etc.) for women alone that concentrate on form, appearance, and feminization.

A second category of disciplinary practices concentrates on bringing forth from the body "a specific repertoire of gestures, postures and movements" (Bartky, 1988, p. 64). Feminine movement, gesture, and posture "must exhibit not only constriction, but grace and a certain eroticism restrained by modesty" (Bartky, 1988, pp. 67–68).

The third category of feminine disciplinary practices is directed to "the display of the body as an ornamented surface" (Bartky, 1988, p. 64). Bartky suggested that in these practices art and discipline appear to converge; there is, however, less art than generally thought. Skin care, hair care, and hair styling; the proper application of makeup; and the selection of clothes are best understood as disciplinary practices whose outcome is the achievement of a feminine embodiment and feminine subjectivity. These disciplinary practices are important not just as statements of sexual difference. They are part of the process by which the ideal body of femininity, and hence feminine subjectivity, is constructed. Moreover, although the means and products of the project will vary in some particulars, importantly by race and class, Bartky (1988, p. 72) argued that femininity as spectacle is something in which most women are required to participate. Here the emphasis is on institutionalized practice and subjugation; exceptions may occur and be noted, but under current arrangements they are not a means or expression of resistance.

In line with an emphasis on historical and materialist analysis, Bartky attempted to identify the structural sources of disciplinary power. Who, she asked, are the disciplinarians? Her answer was an elaboration of Bryan Turner's notion of patrism. Bartky (1988, p. 74) emphasized that discipline can be institutionally unbound as well as bound. In addition to formal institutional settings of disciplinary authority—the police, the military, the courts, and so on—contemporary practices have an apparently anonymous and dispersed fashion. This creates the impression that "the production of femininity is either entirely voluntary or natural" (Bartky, 1988, p. 75). As Bartky observed, no one is marched off for electrolysis at gun point. The production of femininity, however, is no less the result of the imposition of power and disciplinary authority. And insofar as these operations produce "a 'subjected and practiced,' and inferiorized body, they must be understood as aspects of a far larger discipline, an oppressive and inegalitarian system of sexual subordination" (Bartky, 1988, p. 75).

An additional question that is central to this analysis concerns the possibilities for resistance. Why, Bartky (1988, p. 76) asked, aren't all women feminists? Or, we may ask less ambitiously, Why aren't *more* women feminists? The answer, she proposed, has to do with the importance of disciplinary practices as a means not only of subordination but of embodiment. And from here there are some leads back to the concerns with structure, agency, and ultimately ontology that are central to Bryan Turner's (1984) project to construct a sociology of the body.

Disciplinary practices are a representational means for establishing a "structure of the self" (Bartky, 1988, p. 77). A sense of the self as a distinct and skilled being is critical to the establishment of a secure and stable self-identity. In contemporary societies, categories of masculinity and femininity are "critical elements in an informal social ontology" (Bartky, 1988, p. 77). Feminism, by challenging the basis and legitimacy of these categories, threatens women with a kind of de-skilling. Citing examples relevant to our own discussion, Bartky illustrated her argument with comments on the social significance of homophobia and the "revulsion felt by many at the sight of female bodybuilders"; neither "the homosexual nor the muscular woman can be assimilated easily into the categories that structure everyday life" (Bartky, 1988, p. 78). The significance of these categories as the basis for subjectivity and the construction of the self makes them especially resistant to feminist deconstruction and revision. Reform or liberal feminism that seeks equality in the context of a conventional social ontology is, it is argued, a contradiction in terms and "logically incoherent" (Bartky, 1988, p. 78).

Feminist critiques of Foucault have drawn particular attention to the limitations of his work for a theory of resistance. Following from this, the major contribution of feminist revisions and reappropriations of Foucault perhaps lies in a consideration of the possibility of a feminist praxis. Women's actions in antimilitarist, ecological, and reproductive movements are some examples of these politics. Bartky (1988, p. 82) suggested that one source of resistance is a realization of the "incoherence" and "contradiction" of conventional practices. A key problem in poststructuralist feminism as in the sociology of the body is to identify and theorize practices that question and challenge the incoherence of patriarchal conventions.

THE BODY IN THE SOCIOLOGY OF SPORT

It will be clear to readers familiar with literature in the sociology of sport that research in this field has some clear resonance and connections with the call for a sociology of the body exemplified by Bryan Turner's work and elaborated in feminist poststructuralism. A selection of this work, organized around several major themes, is reviewed next.

The Body, Disciplinary Practices, and Domination

Some of the most important analyses in the sociology of sport are concerned with sport, physical activity, and physical culture as a site of disciplinary practice. Historical analyses (Atkinson, 1978; Lenskyj, 1986) have shown how the exclusion of women from sport was an instance of male control over female bodies that enabled the social as well as physical domination by men of women. The cult of true womanhood was realized in the myth of female frailty that became the basis for the organization and ideology of women's sport early in this century. Support for these beliefs was found in medical pronouncements about women's alleged weaker constitutions and limited capacities for physical exertion. Importantly, these pronouncements were not supported by evidence because little research on these issues had been conducted. Nonetheless, they were the basis for women's exclusion from sport and physical activity except on a limited basis. In turn, this exclusion was taken as evidence of women's frailty.

There is also a growing and increasingly sophisticated analysis of disciplinary practices and subjugation in contemporary sport and physical activity. Again, the targets of these practices and the subjects of domination are women. Catharine MacKinnon (1987, p. 118) spoke to the heart of this issue when she said that "when you ask . . . why has femininity *meant* physical weakness, you notice that someone who is physically weak is more easily available to be raped, available to be molested, open to sexual harassment." Critiques of the feminization of the fitness movement (Birrell & Theberge, 1989; McNeill, 1988; Theberge, 1987) have identified practices and ideologies that sexualize women's physical activity and reproduce their subordination. One account is an analysis of the popular television exercise program "Twenty Minute Workout" (McNeill, 1988). Marketed as a fitness activity, the production is in fact a form of soft pornography that objectifies and fragments women's bodies, framing this in a context of explicit heterosexuality. The possibility of resistance through women's embracing of physical activity has been reworked into a conventional form of bodily oppression and exploitation.

Sport, Gender, and Power

Perhaps the primary social significance of sport is its capacity to offer apparently neutral accounts of the construction of gender. Concerning masculinity, Robert Connell (1987, pp. 84–85) noted that idealized images are "constructed and promoted most systematically through competitive sport." The model of bodily action learned in competitive sport has significance well beyond the athletic encounter. "Prowess of this kind becomes a means of judging one's masculinity" (Connell, 1987, pp. 84–85).

Connell's (1990) own work on the life history of an iron man, one who competes in an event involving swimming, running, and surfing, made this point. The masculine body, constructed and experienced in a particular structural context, is essential to the definition of self, importantly the gendered self, and to social relations.

Mike Messner's (in press) research with retired male athletes also showed how identities are constructed and transformed in part through the physical experience and practice of sport. For men moving through the life course, their experience of their bodies and changes in their locations in and relationship to sport and other social connections are signifiers and constituent features of their evolving personal and social identities.

Consideration of gender and power has also explored the possibilities of transformation so that sport becomes a means of women's empowerment rather than their subjugation. I attempted to explore this theme in a 1987 piece in *Women's Studies International Forum*. That presentation provided a discussion of alternative practices of women's sport that are consistent with a feminist vision of power. These practices included fitness activities pursued in an ideological and social context of empowerment and instances of team sports that are modeled on visions of community and empowerment. For some women, sport has become a means to realize their energy, creativity, and potential. And again, this experience of sport as empowering is tied fundamentally to its physicality, in Nancy Hartsock's (1985) words, its "bodily component" (p. 233). Through the bodily practice of sport some women have come to reclaim and reexperience their selves that have been taken away.

Issues of oppression and resistance in modern forms of women's physical activity are explored further in Laurie Schulze's recent work on women's bodybuilding. Schulze (1990, p. 59) noted the incoherence of the woman bodybuilder, who threatens both conventional constructions of gender and the basis of sexual differentiation. This incoherence provides the potential for a radical displacement and revision of the politics of gender and sexuality. Schulze's research explored this potential through an analysis of both the discourse of bodybuilding and the readings of lesbian subjects.

The discourse of bodybuilding is examined through popular accounts in the media. Here the apparent incoherence and challenge to conventional gender categories is subverted and repositioned into a normative heterosexual regime. Female bodybuilders are marked as unquestionably feminine and heterosexual; muscle is rephrased as "flex appeal." The potential for resistance is subverted, and bodybuilding is repositioned within conventional constructions of masculinity and femininity (Schulze, 1990). Moreover, this presentation is located specifically in the dynamics of consumer capitalism where hard work, asceticism, and success are conjoined. "Under the aegis of body maintenance, the female body-builder can be pulled into the hegemonic system, circulated with the ideas of hard work, self-discipline, competition and success" (Schulze, 1990, p. 65). The new hedonism described by Bryan Turner (1984, p. 112) is realized nicely.

The challenge of women's bodybuilding to constructions of gender is explored further in an analysis of lesbians' readings of the activity. Bodybuild-ing and lesbianism are conjoined by a presentation of both as unconventional, unnatural, and hence "wrong." Indeed, the association of female bodybuilding with lesbianism is one basis of its reworking along normative feminine and hence heterosexual ideals. Schulze (1990) then was interested to learn the rele-vance and significations of women's bodybuilding to lesbians.

Schulze's (1990) effort to examine subjects' readings was exploratory; discussions were limited to a small sample of white, middle- and upper middle-class lesbians. Findings were nonetheless interesting and complex. Some women were distanced by the reworking of the activity into commercialized and nor-matively gendered imagery. For these women, the potential challenge of the activity was lost in its submergence into dominant images and interests. For others, this reworking was incomplete, and the bodybuilders' muscles were viewed as masculine.

Some lesbians read women's bodybuilding as radical in a positive way. One subject observed that "women aren't supposed to look like that" (Schulze, 1990, p. 75); another remarked on the "power," "control," and "pride" of the bodybuilders (Schulze, 1990, p. 76). Both accounts saw the challenge to con-ventional constructions as radical, if not exclusively so.

These challenges, however, are a "slippery sort of purchase" (Schulze, 1990, p. 75) for these women. The confusion of images and meanings— maleness, emphasized femininity, heterosexism, and appeals to conventional notions of fashion—renders the readings problematic. In the end, this prelim-inary work is most enlightening for the questions it raises. These are questions of "gender and sexuality, the formation of subcultures and subjectivity, and the capitalization of cultural forms" (Schulze, 1990, p. 78).

Structural Bases of Disciplinary Power

A third theme is the identification and examination of the structural bases of disciplinary power. Several studies have focused on the educational institution and, specifically, the ideology and practice of physical education. Work by Ali-son Dewar (1987) on the curriculum of a university physical education pro-gram and John Hargreaves (1986) on physical education in the schools have shown how the content and organization of these programs reproduce gender divisions in a way that naturalizes both gender differences in physical perfor-mance and social hierarchies based on gender.

The structural base of the subordination of women has also been explored extensively in studies of media accounts of sport. The analysis of "Twenty

Minute Workout," discussed earlier, showed how visual and auditory signs provide the basis for the construction of cultural meanings of gendered physical activity. The degradation of women is unpacked and located in the techniques and practices employed in filming and presenting the show (McNeill, 1988).

Another analysis of media constructions of women's sport is provided in Messner's 1988 article on the "Female Athlete as Contested Ideological Terrain." Messner (1988) identified a shift in media strategies in portraying female athletes. He suggested that the formerly common strategies of marginalization and trivialization are now apparently too unfair and inappropriate. They have been replaced by another strategy that he described, paraphrasing the media, as "they [female athletes] want to be treated equally with men? Well, let's see what they can do." But given current physiological differences between men and women and the organization of sport around definitions that favor male performance, this strategy is likely once again to reproduce and solidify masculine hegemony. Thus, the ideology of equality becomes a means to explain and justify apparently "natural" differences between men and women.

Support for this thesis can be found in an analysis of the print media in West Germany by Marie-Louise Klein (1988). Her detailed account of sport reports and photographs from national newspapers identified a number of practices that serve to define the anomalous position of women in sport. One such practice is a concentration on unusual achievements and successes. The well-known dictum that in order to succeed a woman must be better than a man is given an intriguing reality in media coverage of sport. Klein's data showed significant differences both in the levels of men's and women's competition reported in the media, where coverage of women concentrates more heavily on higher levels of competition, and in the more frequent references to success and performance in articles on women's sport. In short, women *do* enter into the discourse of sport reports but only when they are world class.

This analysis also showed how print media accounts naturalize gender divisions in sport so that they appear to be the outcome of biological differences. This occurs through the use of male standards and norms to evaluate and interpret women's performances, the presentation of a "psychological modality" (Klein, 1988, p. 143) of the female athlete that is rooted in traditional descriptions of female hysteria (i.e., references to athletes' nerves, dispositions, mettle, emotions, and tears) and, as always, in the sexualization of imagery and accounts of female athletes.

MAKING THE CONNECTIONS

This review suggests some important connections between the sociology of sport and an emergent sociology of the body. A historical sociology of the body focuses on a "representational crisis of self-management" (Turner, 1984, p. 113). Contemporary consumer culture, fueled by a "hedonistic fascination with the body" (Turner, 1984, p. 112) yields a set of dominant disciplinary practices. Work in the sociology of sport, exemplified but by no means confined to the examples reviewed here, offers some key insights into an analysis of these practices. These contributions include the following.

First is the identification and explication of some bases of disciplinary practices. Most notable among institutional bases have been the school system and the media. These analyses have underscored the significance of the bounded *and* unbounded character of disciplinary practices. To be sure, there are some instances in which the agents of authority in the exercise of this power are identifiable, perhaps most notably in the case of the school system and the practice of physical education. But the forms and meanings of disciplinary practices in the contemporary consumer culture are also diffuse. This is one outcome of the expansion in recent decades in the variety, reach, and power of the mass media. The marriage of media technology and logic with patriarchal and commercial interests has surely been one of the major triumphs of hegemonic interests in contemporary culture.

This marriage is evident in some of the works explored here. By exposing the discursive practices underlying the construction of accounts of women's sport, these analyses reveal the underlying ideological interests. The seemingly neutral renderings of media productions of sport mask their part in the reconstitution of dominant meanings and practices.

A particularly significant feature of cultural representations of women's physical activity involved the naturalization of gender differentiation. In his 1982 essay, British sociologist Paul Willis described sport as a "fertile and unsuspecting field" (1982, p. 129) for the legitimation of a certain version of the social reality of gender relations. Willis described the power of sport to offer apparent confirmation of the ideology of female inferiority. The ethic of fairness, presumably paramount in sport, becomes the basis for an ideological interpretation of discrepancy as biological inferiority.

> The fact that no one can deny female difference becomes the fact of female sports inferiority, becomes the fact that females are innately different from men, becomes the fact that women who stray across the defining boundary are in a parlous state. An ideological view comes to be deposited in our culture as a commonsense assumption — of course women are different and inferior. (Willis, 1982, p. 130)

Willis' account, one of the earliest and, still, most astute analyses of the significance of sport to the constitution of gender relations, in many ways set out an agenda for research that has followed. A major problem on this agenda is the analysis of the practices and processes whereby the social reality of women's subordinate status is defined and understood to be the outcome of natural differences. Again, this is evident in the research reviewed here and in other work.

Another theme connecting the literatures in the sociology of the body and the sociology of sport concerns the possibilities for human agency and resistance. Concerning gender and sport, several points are emerging. The first may be described as an increasingly clear understanding of what we are up against. That is, the analysis of the structural bases of disciplinary practices and their locations in wider patriarchal and commercial interests has laid bare some forces of domination. This political and sociological analysis has moved us far from the victim-blaming stage of earlier work on women and sport that was rooted in inappropriate or faulty models based in psychology and social psychology. In this formulation, the "problem" of women in sport was that they are inadequately socialized. Structural problems of access, ideological considerations of meaning and signification were not sufficiently addressed.

Related to this, we now have a better understanding of the implications of varied approaches to change. This has been captured in reviews and debates about the meaning and desirability of liberal, radical, and other models of feminism and feminist change in sport (Birrell, 1984; Boutilier & SanGiovanni, 1983). These accounts were largely discussions of institutional characteristics: integration or separation and the values and ideals incorporated in and enabled by different institutional structures. This work was important in several respects, not least for identifying the need and, in some cases, the basis for a feminist reorientation and reclaiming of sport for women. Again, though, themes from the sociology of the body can push us further. And here the discussion shifts from what has been done to what may follow in the future.

Earlier, borrowing from Sandra Lee Bartky (1988), the question, Why aren't more women feminists? was posed. Bartky (1988, p. 78) suggested that feminist approaches that do not challenge conventional social ontologies of masculinity and femininity are "logically incoherent." This comment provides the basis for a future agenda. An important case in point is attention to and analysis of homophobia and of lesbian identity and experience. For the most part and until recently, the discourse on gender and sport has been silent on this issue. The attention we have seen has been largely devoted to the political and social relations between lesbians and others. These are important issues; homophobia remains a significant problem and the basis for institutional discrimination in sport. There is, however, more to be unraveled; we need to attend to the varieties of experiences and accounts of lesbians in sport and by this, perhaps, contribute to deconstructing the "incoherence" of the lesbian experience.

Criticisms that feminist analyses have failed to speak to the variety of women's experiences are applicable to sport studies. The research discussed previously on lesbianism and women's bodybuilding is an explicit invitation to more developed and detailed analysis of gender, sexuality, and physicality. Research also needs to uncover and explore the meaning and relevance of physical activity among women of color and physically challenged women. Such accounts would expand our understanding and enrich our appreciation of the connections between physicality, embodiment, gender, and ontology. That bodies are "in" is a welcome and important development on the intellectual landscape.

REFERENCES

Atkinson, P. (1978). Fitness, feminism and schooling. In S. Delamont & L. Duffin (Eds.), *The nineteenth century woman: Her physical and cultural world* (pp. 92–133). London, Croom Helm.

Bartky, S. (1988). Foucault, femininity and the modernization of patriarchal power. In I. Diamond & L. Quinby (Eds.), *Feminism and Foucault: Reflections on resistance* (pp. 61–86). Boston: Northeastern University Press.

Birrell, S. (1984). Separatism as an issue in women's sport. *Arena Review*, 8, 49–61.

Birrell, S., & Theberge, N. (1989, June). *The fitness boom and the fragmentation of women's bodies.* Paper presented at meetings of National Women's Studies Association, Towson, MD.

Bordo, S. (1989). The body and the reproduction of femininity: A feminist appropriation of Foucault. In A. Jagger & S. Bordo (Eds.), *Gender/body/knowledge: Feminist reconstructions of being and knowing* (pp. 13–33). New Brunswick, NJ: Rutgers University Press.

Boutilier, M., & SanGiovani, L. (1983). *The sporting woman.* Champaign, IL: Human Kinetics.

Connell, R. W. (1987). *Gender and power.* Stanford, CA: Stanford University Press.

Connell, R. W. (1990). An iron man: The body and some contradictions of hegemonic masculinity. In M. Messner & D. Sabo (Eds.), *Sport, men, and the gender order: Critical feminist perspectives* (pp. 83–95). Champaign, IL: Human Kinetics.

Dewar, A. (1987). The social construction of gender in physical education. *Women's Studies International Forum*, 10, 453–465.

Diamond, I., & Quinby, L. (Eds.) (1988). *Feminism and Foucault: Reflections on resistance.* Boston: Northeastern University Press.

Frank, A.W. (1990). Bringing bodies back in: A decade review. *Theory, Culture & Society*, 7, 131–162.

Hargreaves, J. (1986). Schooling the body. In J. Hargreaves (Ed.), *Sport, power and culture* (pp. 161–181). Cambridge, England: Polity Press.

Hartsock, N. (1985). *Money, sex, and power.* Boston: Northeastern University Press.

Klein, M.-L. (1988). The discourse of women in sports reports. *International Review for the Sociology of Sport*, 23, 139–152.

Lenskyj, H. (1986). *Out of bounds: Women, sport and sexuality.* Toronto: Women's Press.

MacKinnon, C. (1987). Women, self-possession, and sport. In C. MacKinnon, *Feminism unmodified: Discourses on life and law* (pp. 117–124). Cambridge, MA: Harvard University Press.

McNeill, M. (1988). Active women, media representations, and ideology. In J. Harvey & H. Cantelon (Eds.), *Not just a game: Essays in Canadian sport sociology* (pp. 195–211). Ottawa, ON: University of Ottawa Press.

Messner, M. (1988). Sports and male domination: The female athlete as contested ideological terrain. *Sociology of Sport Journal*, 5, 197–211.

Messner, M. (in press). *Power at play: Organized sports and the construction of masculinity.* Boston: Beacon Press.

Schulze, L. (1990). On the muscle. In J. Gaines & C. Herzog (Eds.), *Fabrications: Costume and the female body* (pp. 59–78). New York: Routledge.

Sheridan, A. (1980). *Michel Foucault: The will to truth*. London: Tavistock.

Theberge, N. (1987). Sport and women's empowerment. *Women's Studies International Forum*, 10, 387–393.

Turner, B. (1984). *The body and society*. Oxford, England: Basil Blackwell.

Willis, P. (1982). Women in sport and ideology. In J. Hargreaves (Ed.), *Sport, culture and ideology*, (pp. 117–135). London: Routledge and Kegan Paul.

NAOMI WOLF
The Beauty Myth

Naomi Wolf is a prominent feminist writer and scholar whose book, The Beauty Myth: How Images of Beauty Are Used Against Women *(1992) has been called one of the most significant books of the twentieth century by* The New York Times. *Her other books include* Fire with Fire: The New Female Power and How to Use It *(1994) and* Promiscuities: The Secret Struggle for Womanhood *(1998).*

At last, after a long silence, women took to the streets. In the two decades of radical action that followed the rebirth of feminism in the early 1970s, Western women gained legal and reproductive rights, pursued higher education, entered the trades and the professions, and overturned ancient and revered beliefs about their social role. A generation on, do women feel free?

The affluent, educated, liberated women of the First World, who can enjoy freedoms unavailable to any woman ever before, do not feel as free as they want to. And they can no longer restrict to the subconscious their sense that this lack of freedom has something to do with apparently frivolous issues, things that really should not matter. Many are ashamed to admit that such trivial concerns—to do with physical appearance, bodies, faces, hair, clothes—matter so much. But in spite of shame, guilt, and denial, more and more women are wondering if it isn't that they are entirely neurotic and alone but rather that something important is indeed at stake that has to do with the relationship between female liberation and female beauty.

The more legal and material hindrances women have broken through, the more strictly and heavily and cruelly images of female beauty have come to weigh upon us. Many women sense that women's collective progress has stalled; compared with the heady momentum of earlier days, there is a dispiriting climate of confusion, division, cynicism, and above all, exhaustion. After years of much struggle and little recognition, many older women feel burned out; after years of taking its light for granted, many younger women show little interest in touching new fire to the torch.

During the past decade, women breached the power structure; meanwhile, eating disorders rose exponentially and cosmetic surgery became the fastest-growing medical specialty. During the past five years, consumer spending doubled, pornography became the main media category, ahead of legitimate films and records combined, and thirty-three thousand American women told researchers that they would rather lose ten to fifteen pounds than achieve any other goal. More women have more money and power and scope and legal recognition than we have ever had before; but in terms of how we feel about ourselves *physically*, we may actually be worse off than our unliberated grand-mothers. Recent research consistently shows that inside the majority of the West's controlled, attractive, successful working women, there is a secret "underlife" poisoning our freedom; infused with notions of beauty, it is a dark vein of self-hatred, physical obsessions, terror of aging, and dread of lost control.

It is no accident that so many potentially powerful women feel this way. We are in the midst of a violent backlash against feminism that uses images of female beauty as a political weapon against women's advancement: the beauty myth. It is the modern version of a social reflex that has been in force since the Industrial Revolution. As women released themselves from the feminine mystique of domesticity, the beauty myth took over its lost ground, expanding as it waned to carry on its work of social control.

The contemporary backlash is so violent because the ideology of beauty is the last one remaining of the old feminine ideologies that still has the power to control those women whom second-wave feminism would have otherwise made relatively uncontrollable: It has grown stronger to take over the work of social coercion that myths about motherhood, domesticity, chastity, and passivity no longer can manage. It is seeking right now to undo psychologically and covertly all the good things that feminism did for women materially and overtly.

This counterforce is operating to checkmate the inheritance of feminism on every level in the lives of Western women. Feminism gave us laws against job discrimination based on gender; immediately case law evolved in Britain and the United States that institutionalized job discrimination based on women's appearances. Patriarchal religion declined; new religious dogma, using some of the mind-altering techniques of older cults and sects, arose around age and weight to functionally supplant traditional ritual. Feminists, inspired by Betty Friedan, broke the stranglehold on the women's popular press of advertisers for household products, who were promoting the feminine mystique; at once, the diet and skin care industries became the new cultural censors of women's intellectual space, and because of their pressure, the gaunt, youthful model supplanted the happy housewife as the arbiter of successful womanhood. The sexual revolution promoted the discovery of female sexuality; "beauty pornography"—which for the first time in women's history artificially links a commodified "beauty" directly and explicitly to sexuality—invaded the mainstream to undermine women's new and vulnerable sense of sexual self-worth. Reproductive rights gave Western women control over our own bodies; the weight of fashion models plummeted to 23 percent below that of ordinary women, eating disorders rose exponentially, and a mass neurosis was promoted that used food and weight to strip women of that sense of control. Women insisted on politicizing health; new technologies of invasive, potentially deadly "cosmetic" surgeries developed apace to re-exert old forms of medical control of women.

Every generation since about 1830 has had to fight its version of the beauty myth. "It is very little to me," said the suffragist Lucy Stone in 1855, "to have the right to vote, to own property, etcetera, if I may not keep my body, and its uses, in my absolute right." Eighty years later, after women had won the vote, and the first wave of the organized women's movement had subsided, Virginia Woolf wrote that it would still be decades before women could tell the truth about their bodies. In 1962, Betty Friedan quoted a young woman trapped in the Feminine Mystique: "Lately, I look in the mirror, and I'm so afraid that I'm going to look like my mother." Eight years after that, heralding the cataclysmic second wave of feminism, Germaine Greer described "the Stereotype": "To her belongs all that is beautiful, even the very word beauty itself . . . she is a doll . . . I'm sick of the masquerade." In spite of the great revolution of the second wave, we are not exempt. Now we can look out over ruined barricades: A revolution has come upon us and changed everything in its path, enough time has passed since then for babies to have grown into women, but there still remains a final right not fully claimed.

The beauty myth tells a story: The quality called "beauty" objectively and universally exists. Women must want to embody it and men must want to possess women who embody it. This embodiment is an imperative for women and not for men, which situation is necessary and natural because it is biological, sexual, and evolutionary: Strong men battle for beautiful women, and beautiful women are more reproductively successful. Women's beauty must correlate to their fertility, and since this system is based on sexual selection, it is inevitable and changeless.

None of this is true. "Beauty" is a currency system like the gold standard. Like any economy, it is determined by politics, and in the modern age in the West it is the last, best belief system that keeps male dominance intact. In assigning value to women in a vertical hierarchy according to a culturally imposed physical standard, it is an expression of power relations in which women must unnaturally compete for resources that men have appropriated for themselves.

"Beauty" is not universal or changeless, though the West pretends that all ideals of female beauty stem from one Platonic Ideal Woman; the Maori admire a fat vulva, and the Padung, droopy breasts. Nor is "beauty" a function of evolution: Its ideals change at a pace far more rapid than that of the evolution of species, and Charles Darwin was himself unconvinced by his own explanation that "beauty" resulted from a "sexual selection" that deviated from the rule of natural selection; for women to compete with women through "beauty" is a reversal of the way in which natural selection affects all other mammals. Anthropology has overturned the notion that females must be "beautiful" to be selected to mate: Evelyn Reed, Elaine Morgan, and others have dismissed sociobiological assertions of innate male polygamy and female monogamy. Female higher primates are the sexual initiators; not only do they seek out and enjoy sex with many partners, but "every nonpregnant female takes her turn at being the most desirable of all her troop. And that cycle keeps turning as long as she lives." The inflamed pink sexual organs of primates are often cited by male sociobiologists as analogous to human arrangements relating to female "beauty," when in fact that is a universal, nonhierarchical female primate characteristic.

Nor has the beauty myth always been this way. Though the pairing of the older rich men with young, "beautiful" women is taken to be somehow inevitable, in the matriarchal Goddess religions that dominated the Mediterranean from about 25,000 B.C.E. to about 700 B.C.E., the situation was reversed: "In every culture, the Goddess has many lovers. . . . The clear pattern is of an older woman with a beautiful but expendable youth—Ishtar and Tammuz, Venus and Adonis, Cybele and Attis, Isis and Osiris . . . their only function the service of the divine 'womb.' " Nor is it something only women do and only men watch: among the Nigerian Wodaabes, the women hold economic power and the tribe is obsessed with male beauty; Wodaabe men spend hours together in elaborate makeup sessions, and compete—provocatively painted and dressed, with swaying hips and seductive expressions—in beauty contests judged by women. There is no legitimate historical or biological justification for the beauty myth; what it is doing to women today is a result of nothing more exalted than the need of today's power structure, economy, and culture to mount a counteroffensive against women.

If the beauty myth is not based on evolution, sex, gender, aesthetics, or God, on what is it based? It claims to be about intimacy and sex and life, a celebration of women. It is actually composed of emotional distance, politics, finance, and sexual repression. The beauty myth is not about women at all. It is about men's institutions and institutional power.

The qualities that a given period calls beautiful in women are merely symbols of the female behavior that that period considers desirable: *The beauty myth is always actually prescribing behavior and not appearance.* Competition between women has been made part of the myth so that women will be divided from one another. Youth and (until recently) virginity have been "beautiful" in women since they stand for experiential and sexual ignorance. Aging in women is "unbeautiful" since women grow more powerful with time, and since the links between generations of women must always be newly broken: Older women fear young ones, young women fear old, and the beauty myth truncates for all the female life span. Most urgently, women's identity must be premised upon our "beauty" so that we will remain vulnerable to outside approval, carrying the vital sensitive organ of self-esteem exposed to the air.

Though there has, of course, been a beauty myth in some form for as long as there has been patriarchy, the beauty myth in its modern form is a fairly recent invention. The myth flourishes when material constraints on women are dangerously loosened. Before the Industrial Revolution, the average woman could not have had the same feelings about "beauty" that modern women do who experience the myth as continual comparison to a mass-disseminated physical ideal. Before the development of technologies of mass production — daguerreotypes, photographs, etc. — an ordinary woman was exposed to few such images outside the Church. Since the family was a productive unit and women's work complemented men's, the value of women who were not aristocrats or prostitutes lay in their work skills, economic shrewdness, physical strength, and fertility. Physical attraction, obviously, played its part; but "beauty" as we understand it was not, for ordinary women, a serious issue in the marriage marketplace. The beauty myth in its modern form gained ground after the upheavals of industrialization, as the work unit of the family was destroyed, and urbanization and the emerging factory system demanded what social engineers of the time termed the "separate sphere" of domesticity, which supported the new labor category of the "breadwinner" who left home for the workplace during the day. The middle class expanded, the standards of living and of literacy rose, the size of families shrank; a new class of literate, idle women developed, on whose submission to enforced domesticity the evolving system of industrial capitalism depended. Most of our assumptions about the way women have always thought about "beauty" date from no earlier than the 1830s, when the cult of domesticity was first consolidated and the beauty index invented.

For the first time new technologies could reproduce — in fashion plates, daguerreotypes, tintypes, and rotogravures — images of how women should look. In the 1840s the first nude photographs of prostitutes were taken; advertisements using images of "beautiful" women first appeared in mid-century. Copies of classical artworks, postcards of society beauties and royal mistresses, Currier and Ives prints, and porcelain figurines flooded the separate sphere to which middle-class women were confined.

Since the Industrial Revolution, middle-class Western women have been controlled by ideals and stereotypes as much as by material constraints. This situation, unique to this group, means that analyses that trace "cultural conspiracies" are uniquely plausible in relation to them. The rise of the beauty myth was just one of several emerging social fictions that masqueraded as natural components of the feminine sphere, the better to enclose those women inside it. Other such fictions arose contemporaneously: a version of childhood that required continual maternal supervision; a concept of female biology that required middle-class women to act out the roles of hysterics and hypochondriacs; a conviction that respectable women were sexually anesthetic; and a definition of women's work that occupied them with repetitive, time-consuming, and painstaking tasks such as needlepoint and lacemaking. All such Victorian inventions as these served a double function — that is, though they were encouraged as a means to expend female energy and intelligence in harmless ways, women often used them to express genuine creativity and passion.

But in spite of middle-class women's creativity with fashion and embroidery and child rearing, and, a century later, with the role of the suburban housewife that devolved from these social fictions, the fictions' main purpose was served: During a century and a half of unprecedented feminist agitation, they effectively counteracted middle-class women's dangerous new leisure, literacy, and relative freedom from material constraints.

Though these time- and mind-consuming fictions about women's natural role adapted themselves to resurface in the postwar Feminine Mystique, when the second wave of the women's movement took apart what women's magazines had portrayed as the "romance," "science," and "adventure" of homemaking and suburban family life, they temporarily failed. The cloying domestic fiction of "togetherness" lost its meaning and middle-class women walked out of their front doors in masses.

So the fictions simply transformed themselves once more: Since the women's movement had successfully taken apart most other necessary fictions of femininity, all the work of social control once spread out over the whole network of these fictions had to be reassigned to the only strand left intact, which action consequently strengthened it a hundredfold. This reimposed onto liberated women's faces and bodies all the limitations, taboos, and punishments of the repressive laws, religious injunctions, and reproductive enslavement that no longer carried sufficient force. Inexhaustible but ephemeral beauty work took over from inexhaustible but ephemeral housework. As the economy, law, religion, sexual mores, education, and culture were forcibly opened up to include women more fairly, a private reality colonized female consciousness. By using ideas about "beauty," it reconstructed an alternative female world with its own laws, economy, religion, sexuality, education, and culture, each element as repressive as any that had gone before.

Since middle-class Western women can best be weakened psychologically now that we are stronger materially, the beauty myth, as it has resurfaced in the last generation, has had to draw on more technological sophistication and reactionary fervor than ever before. The modern arsenal of the myth is a dissemination of millions of images of the current ideal; although this barrage is generally seen as a collective sexual fantasy, there is in fact little that is sexual about it. It is summoned out of political fear on the part of male-dominated institutions threatened by women's freedom, and it exploits female guilt and apprehension about our own liberation—latent fears that we might be going too far. This frantic aggregation of imagery is a collective reactionary hallucination willed into being by both men and women stunned and disoriented by the rapidity with which gender relations have been transformed: a bulwark of reassurance against the flood of change. The mass depiction of the modern woman as a "beauty" is a contradiction: Where modern women are growing, moving, and expressing their individuality, as the myth has it, "beauty" is by definition inert, timeless, and generic. That this hallucination is necessary and deliberate is evident in the way "beauty" so directly contradicts women's real situation.

And the unconscious hallucination grows ever more influential and pervasive because of what is now conscious market manipulation: powerful industries — the $33-billion-a-year diet industry, the $20-billion cosmetics industry, the $300-million cosmetic surgery industry, and the $7-billion pornography industry — have arisen from the capital made out of unconscious anxieties, and are in turn able, through their influence on mass culture, to use, stimulate, and reinforce the hallucination in a rising economic spiral.

This is not a conspiracy theory; it doesn't have to be. Societies tell themselves necessary fictions in the same way that individuals and families do. Henrik Ibsen called them "vital lies," and psychologist Daniel Goleman describes them working the same way on the social level that they do within families: "The collusion is maintained by directing attention away from the fearsome fact, or by repackaging its meaning in an acceptable format." The costs of these social blind spots, he writes, are destructive communal illusions. Possibilities for women have become so open-ended that they threaten to destabilize the institutions on which a male-dominated culture has depended, and a collective panic reaction on the part of both sexes has forced a demand for counter-images.

The resulting hallucination materializes, for women, as something all too real. No longer just an idea, it becomes three-dimensional, incorporating within itself how women live and how they do not live: It becomes the Iron Maiden. The original Iron Maiden was a medieval German instrument of torture, a body-shaped casket painted with the limbs and features of a lovely, smiling young woman. The unlucky victim was slowly enclosed inside her; the lid fell shut to immobilize the victim, who died either of starvation or, less cruelly, of the metal spikes embedded in her interior. The modern hallucination in which women are trapped or trap themselves is similarly rigid, cruel, and euphemistically painted. Contemporary culture directs attention to imagery of the Iron Maiden, while censoring real women's faces and bodies.

Why does the social order feel the need to defend itself by evading the fact of real women, our faces and voices and bodies, and reducing the meaning of women to these formulaic and endlessly reproduced "beautiful" images? Though unconscious personal anxieties can be a powerful force in the creation of a vital lie, economic necessity practically guarantees it. An economy that depends on slavery needs to promote images of slaves that "justify" the institution of slavery. Western economics are absolutely dependent now on the continued underpayment of women. An ideology that makes women feel "worth less" was urgently needed to counteract the way feminism had begun to make us feel worth more. This does not require a conspiracy; merely an atmosphere. The contemporary economy depends right now on the representation of women within the beauty myth. Economist John Kenneth Galbraith offers an economic explanation for "the persistence of the view of homemaking as a 'higher calling' ": the concept of women as naturally trapped within the Feminine Mystique, he feels, "has been forced on us by popular sociology, by magazines, and by fiction to disguise the fact that woman in her role of consumer has been essential to the development of our industrial society. . . . Behavior that is essential for economic reasons is transformed into a social virtue." As soon as a woman's primary social value could no longer be defined as the attainment of virtuous domesticity, the beauty myth redefined it as the attainment of virtuous beauty. It did so to substitute both a new consumer imperative and a new justification for economic unfairness in the workplace where the old ones had lost their hold over newly liberated women.

Another hallucination arose to accompany that of the Iron Maiden: The caricature of the Ugly Feminist was resurrected to dog the steps of the women's movement. The caricature is unoriginal; it was coined to ridicule the feminists of the nineteenth century. Lucy Stone herself, whom supporters saw as "a prototype of womanly grace . . . fresh and fair as the morning," was derided by detractors with "the usual report" about Victorian feminists: "a big masculine woman, wearing boots, smoking a cigar, swearing like a trooper." As Betty Friedan put it presciently in 1960, even before the savage revamping of that old caricature: "The unpleasant image of feminists today resembles less the feminists themselves than the image fostered by the interests who so bitterly opposed the vote for women in state after state." Thirty years on, her conclusion is more true than ever: That resurrected caricature, which sought to punish women for their public acts by going after their private sense of self, became the paradigm for new limits placed on aspiring women everywhere. After the success of the women's movement's second wave, the beauty myth was perfected to checkmate power at every level in individual women's lives. The modern neuroses of life in the female body spread to woman after woman at epidemic rates. The myth is undermining—slowly, imperceptibly, without our being aware of the real forces of erosion—the ground women have gained through long, hard, honorable struggle.

The beauty myth of the present is more insidious than any mystique of femininity yet: A century ago, Nora slammed the door of the doll's house; a generation ago, women turned their backs on the consumer heaven of the isolated multi-applianced home; but where women are trapped today, there is no door to slam. The contemporary ravages of the beauty backlash are destroying women physically and depleting us psychologically. If we are to free ourselves from the dead weight that has once again been made out of femaleness, it is not ballots or lobbyists or placards that women will need first; it is a new way to see.